Hardware Security
A Hands-on Learning Approach

T0297771

Hardware Security
A Hands-on Learning Approach

Swarup Bhunia
Mark Tehranipoor

MORGAN KAUFMANN PUBLISHERS
AN IMPRINT OF ELSEVIER

Morgan Kaufmann is an imprint of Elsevier
50 Hampshire Street, 5th Floor, Cambridge, MA 02139, United States

Library of Congress Cataloging-in-Publication Data
A catalog record for this book is available from the Library of Congress

British Library Cataloguing-in-Publication Data
A catalogue record for this book is available from the British Library

ISBN: 978-0-12-812477-2

For information on all Morgan Kaufmann publications
visit our website at https://www.elsevier.com/books-and-journals

 Working together
to grow libraries in
developing countries

www.elsevier.com • www.bookaid.org

Publisher: Katey Birtcher
Acquisition Editor: Steve Merken
Editorial Project Manager: Nathanie McFadden
Production Project Manager: Kiruthika Govindaraju
Designer: Miles Hitchen

Typeset by VTeX

To our beloved family members

Contents

PART 2 HARDWARE ATTACKS: ANALYSIS, EXAMPLES, AND THREAT MODELS

PART 3 COUNTERMEASURES AGAINST HARDWARE ATTACKS

PART 4 EMERGING TRENDS IN HARDWARE ATTACKS AND PROTECTIONS

Preface

Cybersecurity has emerged as a dark side of the digital age, and the scale of the world's cybersecurity problems has become daily news. With the convergence of computing and communications, coupled with exponential increase in data volume in Internet, it remains a rising and critical concern. Hardware plays an increasingly important and integral role in cybersecurity, with many emerging system and application vulnerabilities rooted in hardware, including the recently reported Meltdown and Spectre vulnerabilities in various microprocessors in the market. The emergence of new application space in the internet-of-things (IoT) regime is creating new attack surfaces, and new requirements on hardware to support secure and trusted system operations. Additionally, the design, manufacturing, and distribution of integrated circuits (ICs), printed circuit boards (PCBs), as well as other electronic hardware components (passive or active) are becoming more sophisticated and globally distributed, involving a number of untrusted entities. This horizontal—but very complex—supply chain introduces myriad security issues in hardware, including malicious changes, information leakage, side-channel attacks, counterfeiting, reverse engineering, and piracy activities. The shortened time-to-market for system on chips (SoCs), which serve as the backbone for many modern computing systems, further exacerbates the problem by leaving unintentional vulnerabilities in the design that could be exploited by attackers once the chips are in the field.

The topic of hardware security encompasses wide-ranging security and trust issues, which span the entire lifecycle of electronic hardware, and all its abstraction levels (chips, PCBs, systems, and system of systems). With increasing security vulnerabilities and trust issues, the role of hardware as a trust anchor of a computing system is being challenged. Hence, effective and comprehensive hardware security education is crucial at all levels, including undergraduate and graduate students, and professionals involved in design and deployment of computing systems, to safeguard these systems against diverse hardware security/trust issues. We note that there is an increasing demand of well-trained hardware security professionals in the job market. Existing curriculum at colleges and universities, to our knowledge, do not provide adequate insight into the full spectrum of hardware threats and respective protection approaches. They typically fail to provide: (a) a holistic hardware security education that covers security of all abstraction layers; and (b) a hands-on training approach that we believe is crucial in understanding the security vulnerabilities in a complex system, and the corresponding defense mechanisms. To address this important growing need, we embarked on the project of developing the first-ever textbook dedicated to hardware security and trust.

This book aims to provide holistic hardware security training and education to upper-level undergraduate engineering students. Although targeted primarily towards undergraduate students, it can serve as a useful reference for graduate students, security researchers, and practitioners, and also industry professionals, including design engineers, security engineers, system architects, and chief security officers. This book contains material on the background of modern computing systems, followed by description of security issues and protection mechanism. It also contains a set of well-designed experiments that can be performed in any adequately equipped circuit laboratory to learn different aspects of hardware security, which encompasses security vulnerabilities, attacks, and protection mechanisms. To help students understand the components of modern systems before taking a deeper dive into the specific subject area of security, background chapters cover the basics of computing hardware, circuit theory, active and passive electronic components, chip/PCB design, and test flow.

This book includes description of a unique companion material: a hardware platform, referred to as Hardware Hacking (HaHa) platform, that is easy to model a hardware-software system and ethically 'hack' it to learn diverse hardware security issues and countermeasures. All of the hands-on experiments presented in this book can be implemented on this platform, although alternative hardware modules, for example, the Field Programmable Gate Array (FPGA) development boards, can also be used to perform some of the experiments. The comprehensive coverage of hardware security concepts with relevant background material, and a practical learning approach, are the key distinctive features of this text book, which we believe are essential to prepare students for today's challenging hardware security problems.

Unique features of this text book

- It provides a thorough overview of computer hardware, including the fundamentals of computing systems and implications of security risks therein, studies of known attack methodologies, countermeasures, and case studies. Given this foundation, readers are expected to obtain a thorough understanding of key concepts, which facilitate recognizing and countering hardware security threats in actual products and system designs.
- Each major topic in hardware security (security vulnerabilities, attacks, and appropriate protection mechanisms) is explained in detail, combined with a well-designed hands-on experiment on the topic.
- The book includes the description of a custom electronic hardware platform, called HaHa, which is developed by the book's authors to perform the aforementioned laboratory exercises. This hardware module is specifically designed to illustrate various key concepts using a single platform. The experiment descriptions are provided as companion material, which includes step-by-step descriptions of the experimentation process, observations, reporting format, and advanced options.
- Each chapter is also accompanied by a set of exercises divided into three groups with varying difficulty levels. They are meant to provide readers with questions that help them effectively understand the concepts presented in the chapter.

Organization of the book

The authors have organized the topics based on a decade of experience in teaching hardware security to effectively convey the related concepts. Chapter 1 provides an introduction to the topic of hardware security. It presents preliminary and basic concepts on major topics, for example, hardware attack vectors, attack surfaces, adversary model, causes of hardware attacks and effect on business/economic models, hardware supply chain, and relation between security and trust. This chapter also provides a brief history of hardware security, an overview of the scope of the book, and the lab-based approach.

The remainder of the book is organized in four parts:

1. Part 1: Background on Electronic Hardware
2. Part 2: Hardware Attacks: Analysis, Examples, and Threat Models
3. Part 3: Countermeasures Against Hardware Attacks
4. Part 4: Emerging Trends in Hardware Attacks and Protections

Part 1: Background on Electronic Hardware: Part 1 includes three chapters. Chapter 2 provides a background on digital logic, circuit theory, embedded systems, ICs, application specific integrated circuits (ASICs), FPGAs, PCBs, firmware, hardware-firmware-software interaction, and the role of hardware in system security. Chapter 3 gives an overview of SoC design and test. It describes intellectual property (IP)-based SoC lifecycle, the SoC design process, the verification/test steps, and design-for-test, and design-for-debug infrastructures. The final chapter in this part, Chapter 4, provides an introduction to design and test for PCBs. In particular, this chapter describes PCB lifecycle, PCB design process, and PCB testing methods.

Part 2: Hardware Attacks: Analysis, Examples, and Threat Models: This part of the book covers attacks and vulnerabilities in hardware throughout its lifecycle, and in today's supply chain. Chapter 5 focuses on hardware Trojan attacks in ICs and hardware IPs. It presents different types of Trojans: triggers and payloads, and different threat vectors in the design and fabrication process. Chapter 6 provides a detailed insight into today's electronics supply chain security and integrity issues. Chapter 7 presents security issues in the hardware IP lifecycle, with emphasis on challenges related to hardware IP piracy and IP reverse engineering. This chapter also presents issues related to FPGA IP security issues, as FPGA market and IP supply chain continues to grow. Chapter 8 presents the topic of side-channel attacks (SCA). It covers all forms of side-channel attacks, namely, power side-channel attacks, timing attacks, electromagnetic (EM) side-channel attacks, and fault-injection attacks. Chapter 9 introduces test infrastructure-oriented attacks with focus on scan and JTAG. Different forms of information leakage attacks using on-chip test/debug infrastructure are covered in this chapter. Chapter 10 focuses on physical attacks and microprobing. Chip-level reverse engineering and microprobing attacks at chip level for information leakage, and tampering are also discussed in detail in this chapter. Finally, Chapter 11 presents various attacks on PCB, with emphasis on physical attacks. The physical attacks include snooping of PCB traces for information leakage, PCB reverse-engineering and cloning, and malicious field modification or modchip-type attacks.

Part 3: Countermeasures Against Hardware Attacks: This part of the book focuses on countermeasures against hardware attacks. In particular, countermeasures fundamental to hardware security assurance and building the hardware root of trust are presented. Chapter 12 focuses on design and evaluation of hardware security primitives and their roles in functional security and protection against supply chain issues. It covers common primitives, such as, physical unclonable functions (PUFs) and true random number generators (TRNGs). Chapter 13 presents design-for-security (DFS) and security/trust validation for integrated circuits, security built into a design at different levels, and targeted to prevent different hardware attacks. Chapter 14 discusses hardware obfuscation. It presents a number of obfuscation techniques, including state-space obfuscation, logic locking and camouflaging, and discusses their role in protecting against IP piracy, reverse engineering, and malicious modification. Chapter 15 describes PCB integrity validation and authentication. It presents PCB-level authentication solutions using intrinsic signature of PCBs, and protection of PCB against field attacks.

Part 4: Emerging Trends in Hardware Attacks and Protections: The final chapter in this book (Chapter 16) describes system-level attacks and countermeasures, possibilities of exploiting hardware security vulnerabilities by system/application software, and SoC security architecture for secure systems. Assets in a SoC are major targets of software attacks. Hence, developing secure SoC architecture for protecting these assets is essential. This chapter describes architecture-level solutions for protecting on-chip assets from diverse attacks that rely on access-control or information flow violations, or other vulnerabilities.

We hope that the target readership enjoys the content of this book and greatly benefits from it. We believe that the content of this book will remain highly relevant for many years to come, as the topic of hardware security, as it relates to the broader field of cybersecurity, is consistently growing in scope and relevance.

Companion material

This book has a companion material (available at https://hwsecuritybook.org/) that provides detailed description of the hands-on experiments that use the custom HaHa platform. This modular, flexible, and simple hardware platform is expected to be very effective for hardware security education and training. It is designed to enable students to build a computing system of selected capability by adding various components (for example, sensors or communication units) in a LEGO-like fashion, and connect multiple units wirelessly to create a networked system. It then allows students to implement diverse security attacks ranging from hardware Trojans, side-channel attacks, tampering, reverse engineering, and snooping. We hope the hands-on experiments will serve as an invaluable resource for the students, helping them to thoroughly understand key concepts and stimulating their interest to explore new vulnerabilities, or protection mechanisms.

Book website

Supporting materials and the lab modules for this book are available at the book's own website: www.hwsecuritybook.org. The website will include the following: slides for each chapter, sample homework assignments, sample exams and tests, lab modules for HaHa board, sample projects, videos of a selected number of lab modules, simulation tools, Verilog/VHDL designs, and more. This website will be a hub for any educational materials available to help further students and instructors' understanding of the concepts in hardware and systems security. We will also work with instructors, who teach this course to facilitate widespread sharing of the materials among members of the hardware security community.

For instructors

The "www.hwsecuritybook.org" webpage includes additional materials for instructors only. This part of the site is password protected. If you plan to use it, please contact the webmaster, allow a week to obtain a login username and password via the procedure published on the web. The instructor area will contain original slides, notes supporting each slide, complete set of exams, homework assignments, quizzes, and more. The website also includes answer to selected exercises and exams.

Swarup Bhunia and Mark Tehranipoor

Acknowledgments

Writing the first-ever textbook dedicated to hardware security was harder than we thought, due to many roadblocks we faced, but it was also more rewarding than we ever imagined. It was a long, arduous journey planning the book, preparing the content, and finally putting them in a printable format. The journey, however, was enriched by our friends, colleagues, and students, who contributed to this effort in many ways. This book would not be possible without their valuable inputs that shaped its various elements: from chapter contents, illustrations, and exercises to the hands-on experiments.

First and foremost, we would like to gratefully acknowledge the contributions of our beloved students at the FICS Research, University of Florida, who helped to form and polish the technical content of each chapter. These students, in no particular order, are Adib Nahiyan, Tamzidul Hoque, Abdulrahman Alaql, Dr. Miao He, Huanyu Wang, Prabuddha Chakraborty, Jonathan Cruz, Shubhra Deb Paul, Atul Prasad Deb Nath, Naren Vikram Raj Masna, Sumaiya Shomaji, Sarah Amir, Bicky Shakya, Angela Newsome, Sazadur Rahman, and Moshiur Rahman. We greatly appreciate their devoted efforts in helping us make this book a reality. We are proud to have these excellent students, who, we strongly believe, are in the right trajectory to establish a bright career in the area of hardware and systems security.

Special thanks to Dr. Fahim Rahman, who diligently helped with overall organization and review of the chapters and companion material; Dr. Qihang Shi and Dr. Jungmin Park, who made significant technical contributions to specific chapters; and Shuo Yang, who led the development of the custom hardware platform (the HaHa board), and made major contributions in designing the experiments. All of them belong to FICS Research, University of Florida.

Several prominent hardware security researchers helped us with reviewing the early draft of the chapters. We gratefully recognize their crucial effort in improving the chapter coverage. They are Dr. Sandip Ray (University of Florida), Dr. Seetharam Narasimhan (Intel), Dr. Chester Rebeiro (IIT, Madras), Dr. Abhishek Basak (Intel), Dr. Anirban Sengupta (IIT, Indore), Dr. Xinmu Wang (Northwestern Polytechnical University, China), Dr. Wenjie Che (Enthentica), Dr. Amit Trivedi (University of Illinois, Chicago), Dr. Robert Karam (University of South Florida), and Dr. Wei Hu (Northwestern Polytechnical University, China).

We also sincerely acknowledge the support from National Science Foundation (NSF), which sponsored development of the custom hardware platform. Any opinions, findings, conclusions, or recommendations presented in this book are only those of the authors and contributors, and do not necessarily reflect the views of the National Science Foundation. Finally, we remain grateful to the Elsevier editors and publishing team, in particular, to Nate McFadden, Stephen R. Merken, and Kiruthika Govindaraju, for their continuous support and guidance through the whole process.

INTRODUCTION TO HARDWARE SECURITY

1

CONTENTS

Computer security has become an essential part of the modern electronic world. Hardware security, which deals with the security of electronic hardware, encompassing its architecture, implementation, and validation, has evolved alongside it into an important field of computer security. In the context of this book, "hardware" indicates electronic hardware. Like any field of security, the topic of hardware security focuses on attacks crafted to steal or compromise assets and approaches designed to protect these assets. The assets under consideration are the hardware components themselves, for instance, integrated circuits (ICs) of all types, passive components (such as, resistors, capacitors, inductors), and printed circuit boards (PCBs); as well as the secrets stored inside these components, for instance, cryptographic keys, digital rights management (DRM) keys, programmable fuses, sensitive user data, firmware, and configuration data.

Figure 1.1 illustrates different fields of security related to a modern computing system. Network security focuses on the attacks on a network connecting multiple computer systems, and the mechanisms

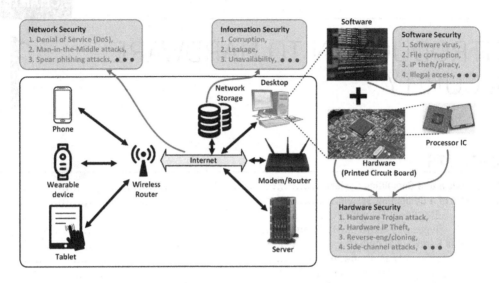

FIGURE 1.1

The landscape of security in modern computing systems.

to ensure its usability and integrity under potential attacks. Software security focuses on malicious attacks on software, often exploiting different implementation bugs, such as inconsistent error handling and buffer overflows, and techniques to ensure reliable software operation in presence of potential security risks. Information security focuses on the general practice of providing confidentiality, integrity, and availability of information through protection against unauthorized access, use, modification, or destruction. Hardware security, on the other hand, focuses on attacks and protection of hardware. It forms the foundation of system security, providing trust anchor for other components of a system that closely interact with it. The remaining chapters of the book illustrate how a variety of attacks on hardware challenge this notion, and how effective countermeasures against these attacks can be employed to ensure the security and trust of hardware.

The book covers all topics related to electronic hardware and systems security encompassing various application domains, including embedded systems, cyber-physical systems (CPS), internet of things (IoT), and biomedical systems (for example, implants and wearables). It describes security and trust issues, threats, attacks, vulnerabilities, protection approaches, including design, validation, and trust monitoring solutions for hardware at all levels of abstraction: from hardware intellectual properties (IPs) to ICs to PCBs and systems. The coverage also includes associated metrics, tools, and benchmarks.

1.1 OVERVIEW OF A COMPUTING SYSTEM

A computing system is a system of interconnected components. The following highlights the major components in such a system and their roles: memory for information storage; processor for information processing, and input/output devices (for example, peripheral devices, such as keyboards, printers, and displays) for interfacing with human users or other systems. These systems are capable of capturing and transforming information; and communicating them with other computing systems. Information storage and processing are often performed on digital data. However, in many applications, there is an analog front-end that acquires analog signals from the physical world, conditions and then digitizes them. A digital processing unit then performs specific operations on the digital form. Optionally, a back-end unit then transforms the processed digital signal into analog to interface with the physical world. Traditionally, computing systems have been broadly classified into two categories: (a) general-purpose systems and (b) embedded systems. The first category included systems, such as desktop, laptop, and servers, which had the following characteristics: (1) complex and optimized architecture, (2) versatile and easily programmable, and (3) suitable for diverse use-case scenarios. On the other hand, the second category included systems, such as digital cameras, home automation devices, wearable health monitors, and biomedical implants, which have the following characteristics: (1) highly customized design, (2) tight hardware-software integration, and (3) unique use-case constraints.

Over the years, the gap between these two categories narrowed with embedded systems becoming more flexible, and having more computing power to handle general-purpose applications. Two new classes of systems have emerged, which borrow features from both categories: (1) cyber-physical systems and (2) internet of things. In the first class, computer-based information processing systems are deeply intertwined with the Internet and its users, and the physical world. Examples of such systems include smart grid, autonomous vehicles, and robotic systems. The second class, on the other hand, includes computing systems that connect to the Internet, the cloud, and other endpoint devices, and interact with the physical world by collecting and exchanging data using embedded sensors and controlling physical devices through actuators. Such devices include smart home automation devices and personal health monitors. Both classes of devices increasingly rely on artificial intelligence to make autonomous decisions, to have situational awareness, and to better respond to different usage patterns through learning. The distinction between these two classes is getting blurred gradually, with CPS having similar characteristics as IoT devices. Devices falling into these classes share many features, which have security implications, such as, (1) long and complex life, during which the security requirements may change; (2) machine-to-machine communication without any human in the loop, which may create an insecure communication link, and need for novel authentication approaches; and (3) mass production in the millions with identical configuration, which can help an attacker identify vulnerabilities of one device, and use that knowledge to break into many.

Moreover, modern computing systems usually do not operate in isolation. They are connected with other computers and/or the cloud, which is a collection of computers that provides shared computing or storage resources to a bunch of other computers. Figure 1.2 shows different components of a modern

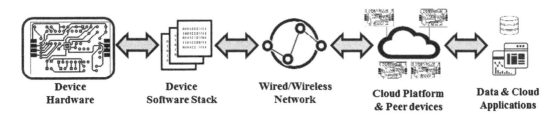

| Device Hardware | Device Software Stack | Wired/Wireless Network | Cloud Platform & Peer devices | Data & Cloud Applications |

FIGURE 1.2

Different layers in the organization of modern computing systems.

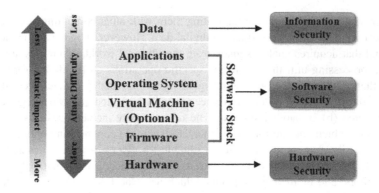

FIGURE 1.3

Attack impact and difficulty at different layers of a computing system.

computing system, for example, a CPS or IoT system, starting from hardware units to cloud and the data/applications in the cloud. Each component in this organization is associated with diverse security issues and corresponding solutions. The weakest link in this complex, often physically distributed system usually determines the security of the whole system. Achieving security of the entire system requires a significant rethinking on how to integrate specific security solutions for each component into a holistic protection approach.

1.2 LAYERS OF A COMPUTING SYSTEM

Modern computing systems can be viewed as an organization consisting of multiple layers of abstraction, as illustrated in Fig. 1.3. The hardware layer lies at the bottom of it, followed by the firmware that interfaces with the physical hardware layer. The firmware layer is followed by the software stack, comprising of an optional virtualization layer, the operating system (OS), and then the application layer. All types of computing systems discussed in the previous sections share this common structure. The data being processed by a computing system is stored in the hardware layer in volatile (for example, static or dynamic random access memory) or non-volatile (such as NAND or NOR flash) memory and accessed by the software layers. A system is connected to another system or to the Internet using networking mechanisms that are realized by a combination of hardware and software components. Computer security issues span all these layers. While hardware security issues are relatively fewer than those at other layers (as shown in Fig. 1.3), they usually have much larger impacts on system security. In particular, they typically affect a much larger number of devices than security issues in software and network, as manifested by the recent discoveries, such as the Spectre and Meltdown bugs [9] in modern processors.

1.2.1 ELECTRONIC HARDWARE

The hardware in a computing system can, itself, be viewed as consisting of three layers, as illustrated in Fig. 1.4. At the top of it, we have a system-level hardware, that is, the integration of all physical

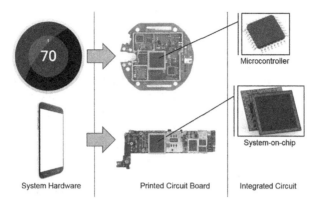

FIGURE 1.4

Three abstraction layers of modern electronic hardware (shown for two example devices).

components (such as PCBs, peripheral devices, and enclosures) that make a system, such as a smart thermostat, or a smartphone. At the next level, we have one or more PCBs, which provide mechanical support and electrical connection to the electronic components that are required to meet the functional and performance requirements of a system. PCBs are typically constructed with multiple layers of an insulating substrate (for example, fiberglass) that allow power and signals to be connected among components using conductive metal (e.g., copper) traces. At the bottom-most layer, we have active components (such as ICs, transistors, and relays), and passive electronic components. Different layers of hardware abstraction bring in diverse security issues, and require commensurate protections. The book covers major security issues and solutions at all levels of hardware abstraction.

1.2.2 TYPES OF ELECTRONIC HARDWARE

The ICs or chips used in a PCB do various tasks, such as signal acquisition, transformation, processing, and transfer. Some of these chips (for example, an encryption or image compression chip) work on digital signals and are called digital ICs, whereas others work on analog or both types of signals, and called analog/mixed-signal (AMS) chips. Examples of the latter type include voltage regulators, power amplifiers, and signal converters. The ICs can also be classified based on their usage model and availability in the market. Application-specific integrated circuits (ASIC) represent a class of ICs, which contain customized functionalities, such as signal processing or security functions, and meet specific performance targets that are not readily available in the market. On the other hand, commercial off-the-shelf (COTS) ICs are the ones, which are already available in the market, often providing flexibility and programmability to support diverse system design needs. These products can be used out-of-the-box, but often needs to be configured for a target application. Examples of COTS components include field programmable gate arrays (FPGA), microcontrollers/processors, and data converters. The distinction between ASIC and COTS is often subtle, and when a chip manufacturer decides to sell its ASICs into the market, they can become "off-the-shelf" to the original equipment manufacturers (OEMs), who build various computing systems using them.

1.3 WHAT IS HARDWARE SECURITY?

Information or data security have remained an issue of paramount concern for system designers and users alike since the beginning of computers and networks. Consequently, protection of systems and networks against various forms of attacks, targeting corruption/leakage of critical information and unauthorized access, have been widely investigated over the years. Information security, primarily based on cryptographic measures, have been analyzed and deployed in a large variety of applications. Software attacks in computer systems have also been extensively analyzed, and a large variety of solutions have been proposed, which include static authentication and dynamic execution monitoring. Study of hardware security, on the other hand, is relatively new, since hardware has been traditionally considered immune to attacks, and hence used as the trust anchor or "root-of-trust" of a system. However, various security vulnerabilities and attacks on hardware have been reported over the last three decades. Earlier, they primarily focused on implementation-dependent vulnerabilities in cryptographic chips leading to information leakage. However, emerging trends in electronic hardware production, such as intellectual-property-based (IP-based) system on chip (SoC) design, and a long and distributed supply chain for manufacturing and distribution of electronic components—leading to reduced control of a chip manufacturer on the design and fabrication steps—have given rise to many growing security concerns. This includes malicious modifications of ICs, also referred to as Hardware Trojan attacks [12], in an untrusted design house or foundry. This is an example of a hardware security issue, which can potentially provide a kill switch to an adversary. Other examples include side-channel attacks, where secret information of a chip can be extracted through measurement and analysis of side-channels, that is, physical signals, such as power, signal propagation delay, and electromagnetic emission; IP piracy and reverse-engineering, counterfeiting, microprobing attacks on ICs, physical tampering of traces or components in PCBs, bus snooping in PCBs, and access to privileged resources through the test/debug infrastructure. They span the entire life-cycle of hardware components, from design to end-of-life, and across all abstraction levels, from chips to PCBs to system. These attacks, associated vulnerabilities and root causes and their countermeasures form the field of hardware security [1,2,10,13,14].

Another important aspect of hardware security relates to the hardware design, implementation, and validation to enable secure and reliable operation of the software stack. It deals with protecting sensitive assets stored in a hardware from malicious software and network, and providing an appropriate level of isolation between secure and insecure data and code, in addition to providing separation between multiple user applications [1]. Two major topics in this area are as follows. (1) Trusted execution environment (TEE), such as ARM's TrustZone, Intel SGX, and Samsung Knox, which protects code and data of an application from other untrusted applications with respect to confidentiality (the ability to observe a data), integrity (the ability to change it), and availability (the ability to access certain data/code by the rightful owner). The confidentiality, integrity, and availability are referred to as CIA requirements. They form three important pillars for secure execution of software on a hardware platform. Establishment of these requirements is enabled by a joint hardware-software mechanism, with hardware providing architectural support for such an isolation, and facilitating effective use of cryptographic functions, and software providing efficient policies and protocols. (2) Protection of security-critical assets in an SoC through appropriate realization of security policies, such as access control and information flow policies, which govern the CIA requirements for these assets. Figure 1.5 depicts these focus areas of the hardware security field.

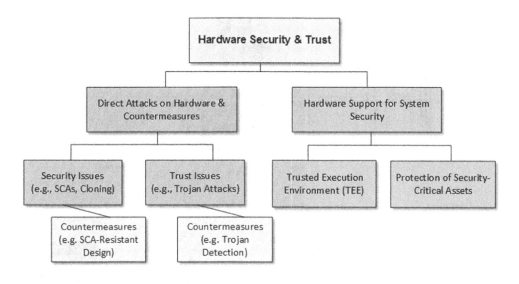

FIGURE 1.5

Scope of hardware security and trust.

1.4 HARDWARE SECURITY VS. HARDWARE TRUST

Hardware security issues arise from its own vulnerability to attacks (e.g., side-channel or Trojan attacks) at different levels (such as, chip or PCB), as well as from lack of robust hardware support for software and system security. On the other hand, hardware trust issues arise from involvement of untrusted entities in the life cycle of a hardware, including untrusted IP or computer-aided design (CAD) tool vendors, and untrusted design, fabrication, test, or distribution facilities. These parties are capable of violating the trustworthiness of a hardware component or system. They can potentially cause deviations from intended functional behavior, performance, or reliability. Trust issues often lead to security concerns, for example, untrusted IP vendor can include malicious implant in a design, which can lead to denial of service (DoS), or information leakage attacks during field operation. However, trust issues can also lead to other incidents, such as poor parametric behavior (for example, reduced performance or energy-efficiency), or degraded reliability, or safety issues. The evolving nature of the global supply chain and the horizontal semiconductor business model are making the hardware trust issues ever more significant. It, in turn, is driving new research and development efforts in trust verification and hardware design for trust assurance.

1.4.1 WHAT CAUSES HARDWARE TRUST ISSUES?

Figure 1.6 shows the major steps in the life cycle of an IC. It starts from a design house creating the functional specifications (e.g., data compression, encryption, or pattern recognition) and parametric specifications (e.g., the operating frequency or standby power) of a design. Next, it goes through a sequence of design and verification steps, where the high-level description of a design (for instance, an architecture level description) is transformed into logic gates, then into a transistor level circuit,

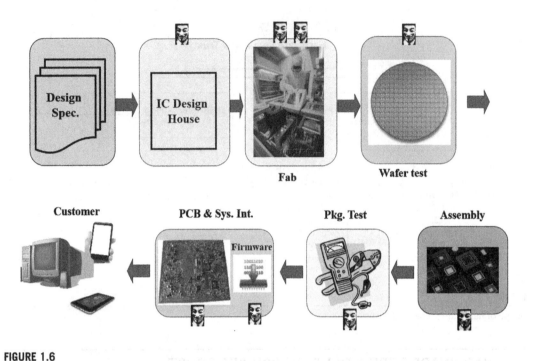

FIGURE 1.6

Major steps in the electronic hardware design and test flow.

and finally, into a physical layout. During this transformation process, a design is verified for correct functional behavior and for performance, power, and other parametric constraints. The layout is then transferred to a fabrication facility, which creates a mask for the layout and then goes through a complex sequence of lithography, etching, and other steps to produce a "wafer", which is typically a circular silicon disk containing a batch of ICs. Each IC in the wafers is then individually tested for certain defects using special test patterns. ICs are referred to as "die" at this stage. These dies are then cut by diamond saw from the wafer and assembled into a package made of ceramic, or other materials. The packaged dies, or ICs, are then tested for compliance with functional and parametric features using another set of test patterns in a manufacturing test facility. This step is vital in the life cycle of an IC, since it ensures that defective chips not meeting functional or parametric specifications are discarded, and do not go into the supply chain. During the early stage of an IC development process, this step is used to identify and debug design bugs (as opposed to manufacturing defects), and information on identified bugs is fed back to the design team in order to incorporate appropriate correction. The testing and debug process for a complex IC is usually facilitated by incorporating specialized structures in a design, which is called design-for-test (DFT) and design-for-debug (DFD) infrastructure, respectively. The primary goal behind inserting these structures is to increase the controllability and observability of internal nodes in a design, which are difficult to access from a fabricated chip. However, as we discuss later, it inherently creates conflict with security goals, which aim to minimize controllability and observability of these nodes, such that an attacker cannot easily access or control internal circuit nodes. For example, direct access to the read/write control for embedded memory in a processor through

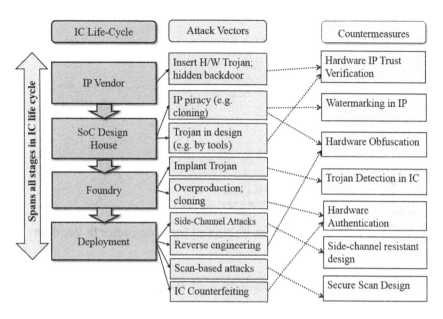

FIGURE 1.7

Attack vectors and countermeasures for each stage in an IC's life span.

the DFT/DFD interface can help an attacker leak, or manipulate sensitive data stored in the protected regions of memory.

The chips that pass manufacturing testing then go into the supply chain for distribution. In current business models, most OEMs acquire these chips from a supply chain, and then integrate them in a PCB, install firmware or configuration bitstream into COTS components, and create a complete system. This long development cycle of hardware involves multiple third-party vendors and facilities. They are often untrusted and globally distributed. In Fig. 1.6, the stages marked by red (medium gray in print version) box are usually untrusted, whereas stages marked with yellow (light gray in print) may or may not be untrusted; the ones marked with green (dark gray in print version) are usually trusted. In the next section, we describe what kind of attacks can be mounted on a hardware in these stages. It is worth noting that, PCB design, fabrication, and test process follow a similar flow, and a horizontal business model—as in the case of IC, where the design and manufacturing companies—is spread around the world to reduce the total production cost. Hence, PCBs are often subject to a similar set of vulnerabilities as ICs.

1.4.2 WHAT SECURITY ISSUES RESULT FROM UNTRUSTED ENTITIES?

Figure 1.7 illustrates some of the key security issues resulting from untrusted design/fabrication/test process for an IC. Connected to the same is our consideration of an SoC life cycle that integrates a number of IPs, typically acquired from third-party IP vendors, into a design that meets functional and performance criteria. These IP vendors are often physically distributed across the globe. Since chip manufacturers do not publish information about their IP sources for business reason, we considered several example SoCs that go into mobile computing platforms (such as cell phones), and created a list

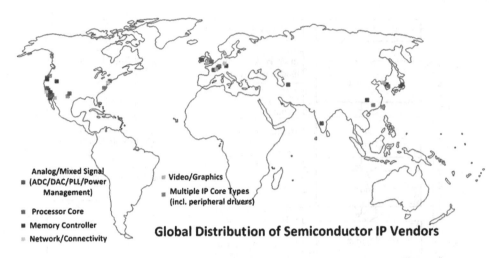

Global Distribution of Semiconductor IP Vendors

FIGURE 1.8

Long and globally distributed supply chain of hardware IPs makes SoC design increasingly vulnerable to diverse trust/integrity issues.

of common IP blocks, which are integrated into these SoCs [1]. Figure 1.8 shows the map of possible sources of these IPs. Usually, an IP design house specializes in a specific class of IP (for example, memory, communication, or crypto-IP). From this map, it is fair to assume that the IPs used in an SoC are very likely to come from different, and physically distributed third-party IP vendors, which would result in these IPs being untrusted from an SoC designer's point of view. Note that a foundry would have access to the entire unencrypted design file for an SoC, consisting of all IP blocks, the interconnect fabric, and the DFT/DFD structures. While a third-party IP vendor can possibly insert a malicious design component or hardware Trojan, untrusted design, fabrication, and test facilities would have several attack options, such as piracy of a design, reverse engineering, and Trojan implantation. As shown in Fig. 1.7, these security issues can be addressed through targeted design or test solutions, which we will describe later in this book.

1.5 ATTACKS, VULNERABILITIES, AND COUNTERMEASURES

In this section, we briefly introduce the main types of hardware attacks, the threat models for these attacks, the known functional and non-functional vulnerabilities, and the countermeasures that can be taken to protect against these attacks.

1.5.1 ATTACK VECTORS

Attack vectors—as they relate to hardware security—are means or paths for bad actors (attackers) to get access to hardware components for malicious purposes, for example, to compromise it or extract secret assets stored in hardware. Example of hardware attack vectors are side-channel attacks, Trojan attacks, IP piracy, and PCB tampering. Attack vectors enable an attacker to exploit implementation

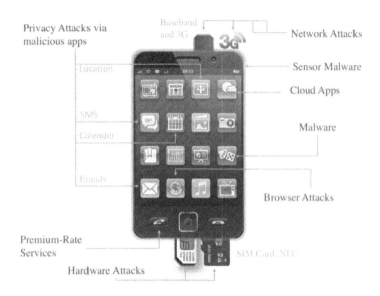

Privacy Attacks via
malicious apps

Baseband
and 3G

Network Attacks

Sensor Malware

Cloud Apps

Malware

Browser Attacks

Location

SMS

Calender

Emails

Premium-Rate
Services

Hardware Attacks

SIM Card, NFC

FIGURE 1.9

Possible attack surfaces in a computing system.

level issues (such as, side-channel attacks and PCB tampering) or take advantage of lack of control on hardware production cycle (such as, Trojan attacks).

1.5.2 ATTACK SURFACE

Attack surface is the sum of all possible security risk exposures. It can also be explained as the aggregate of all known, unknown, and potential vulnerabilities, and controls across all hardware, software, and network components. Tapping into different locations, components, and layers (including hardware/software) of the target system, an attacker can exploit one or more vulnerabilities and mount an attack, for example, extract secret information from a system. Figure 1.9 illustrates major attack surfaces of a smartphone, composed of software, network, data, and hardware components. From the figure, it is evident that the total surface area of a system could be large, and hardware is a critical part of it. In the context of hardware security, attack surfaces define the level of abstraction in which the attacker focuses on launching a hardware attack. Keeping the attack surface as small as possible is a common goal for developing countermeasures. With respect to hardware security, three main attack surfaces are as follows.

Chip Level Attacks: Chips can be targeted for reverse engineering, cloning, malicious insertion, side-channel attacks, and piracy [10,11]. Counterfeit or fake chips can be sold as original units if the attacker can create a copy that has a similar appearance or features as the original. Trojan-infected chips can also find their place in the supply chain, which can pose a threat of unauthorized access, or malfunction. Side-channel attacks can be mounted on a chip with the goal to extract secret information stored inside it. For example, a cryptochip performing encryption with a private key, or a processor running protected code and/or operating on protected data are both vulnerable to leakage of secret information through this attack.

PCB-Level Attacks: PCBs are common targets for attackers, as they are much easier to reverse-engineer and tamper than ICs. Design information of most modern PCBs can be extracted through relatively simple optical inspection (for example, X-Ray tomography) and efficient signal processing. Primary goals for these attacks are to reverse engineer the PCB, and obtain the schematic of the board to redesign it and create fake units. Attackers may also physically tamper a PCB (for instance, cut a trace or replace a component) to make them leak sensitive information, or bypass DRM protection.

System-Level Attacks: Complex attacks involving the interaction of hardware-software components can be mounted on the system. By directly focusing on the most vulnerable parts in a system, such as DFT infrastructure at PCB level (for example, JTAG) and memory modules, attackers may be able to compromise the system's security by gaining unauthorized control and access to sensitive data.

1.5.3 SECURITY MODEL

Attacks on hardware systems can take many forms. An attacker's capabilities, physical or remote access of the system, and assumptions of system design and usage scenarios play essential roles in the techniques that can be used to launch an attack. In order to describe a security issue or solution, it is important to unambiguously describe the corresponding security model. A security model should have two components: (1) Threat Model, which describes the threats including, the purpose and mechanism of an attack; and (2) Trust Model, which describes the trusted parties or components. In order to describe the security issues arising from malicious implants in third-party IPs, the threat model needs to describe the objective of the attackers, for example, to leak secret from an SoC or to disrupt its functional behavior; and the way the attack is mounted, for instance, through the insertion of a Trojan that triggers malicious memory write operation under a rare internal condition. The trust model needs to describe which parties are trusted, for example, the SoC designer and CAD tools are trusted in this case.

1.5.4 VULNERABILITIES

Vulnerabilities refer to weakness in hardware architecture, implementation, or design/test process, which can be exploited by an attacker to mount an attack. These weaknesses can either be functional or nonfunctional, and they vary based on the nature of a system and its usage scenarios. A typical attack consists of an identification of one or more vulnerabilities, followed by exploiting them for a successful attack. Identification of vulnerabilities is usually the hardest step in the attack process. Following is a description of some typical vulnerabilities in hardware systems:

Functional Bug: Most vulnerabilities are caused by functional bugs and poor design/testing practices. They include weak cryptographic hardware implementation and inadequate protection of assets in an SOC. Attackers may find these vulnerabilities by analyzing the functionality of a system for different input conditions to look for any abnormal behaviors. Additionally, vulnerabilities may be discovered accidentally, which makes it easier for an attacker to perform malicious activities using these newly discovered issues in the system.

Side-Channel Bug: These bugs represent implementation-level issues that leak critical information stored inside a hardware component (for example processors or cryptochips) through different forms of side-channels [4]. Attackers may find these vulnerabilities by analyzing the side-channel signals

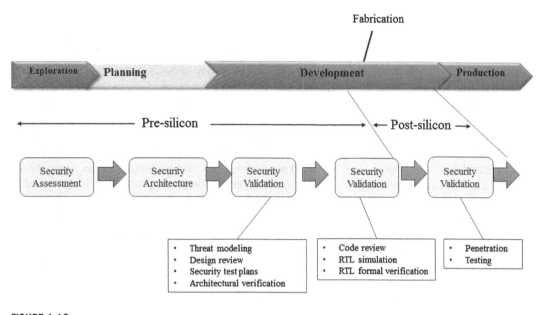

FIGURE 1.10

State of the practice in security design and validation along the life cycle of a system on chip.

during operation of a hardware component. Many powerful attacks based on side-channel bugs rely on statistical methods to analyze the measured traces of a side-channel parameter [2]. Criticality of a side-channel bug depends on the amount of information leakage through a side channel.

Test/Debug infrastructure: Most hardware systems provide a reasonable level of testability and debuggability, which enable designers and test engineers to verify the correctness of operation. They also provide means to study internal operations and processes running in a hardware, which are essential for debugging a hardware. These infrastructures, however, can be misused by attackers, where extraction of sensitive information or unwanted control of a system can be possible using the test/debug features.

Access control or information-flow issues: In some cases, a system may not distinguish between authorized and unauthorized users. This vulnerability may give an attacker access to secret assets and functionality that can be misused or leveraged. Moreover, an intelligent adversary can monitor the information flow during system operation to decipher security-critical information, such as, control flow of a program and memory address of a protected region from a hardware.

1.5.5 COUNTERMEASURES

As hardware attacks have emerged in the past years, countermeasures to mitigate them have also been reported. Countermeasures can either be employed at design or test time. Figure 1.10 shows the current state of the practice in the industry for SoCs in terms of: (a) incorporating security measures in a design (referred to as "security design"), and (b) verifying that these measures protect a system against known attacks (referred to as "security validation"). SoC manufacturing flow can be viewed as consisting of four conceptual stages: (1) exploration, (2) planning, (3) development, and (4) production. The first two stages and part of the development stage form the pre-silicon part of SoC life cycle, which consists of exploring the design space, architecture definition, and then deriving a design that meets design targets. Part of the development stage, followed by the production of SoCs, form the post-silicon part of the SoCs' life, which consists of verifying and fabricating the chips. Security assessment is performed during the exploration stage, which identifies the assets in an SoC, possible attacks on them, and requirements for secure execution of software, when applicable. This step ends up creating a set of security requirements. Next, an architecture is defined (referred to as "security architecture") to address these requirements, which includes protection of test/debug resources against malicious access, and safeguarding cryptographic keys, protected memory regions, and configuration bits. Once the architecture is defined and the design is gradually created, pre-silicon-security validation is performed to make sure the architecture and its implementation adequately fulfill the security requirements. Similar security validation is performed after chips are fabricated (referred to as "post-silicon security validation") to ensure that the manufactured chips do not have security vulnerabilities and, hence, are protected against known attacks. Both pre- and post-silicon security validation come in various forms, which vary in terms of coverage of security vulnerabilities, the resulting confidence, and the scalability of the approach to large designs. These techniques include code review and formal verification during pre-silicon validation, fuzzing, and penetration testing during post-silicon validation [16].

Design solutions: Design-for-security (DfS) practices have emerged as powerful countermeasures. DfS offers effective low-overhead design solutions that can provide active or passive defense against various attacks. DfS techniques, such as obfuscation [6], use of reliable security primitives, side-channel resistance (for example, masking and hiding techniques), and hardening schemes for Trojan insertion, can reliably protect against many major attack vectors. Likewise, SoC security architecture that is resilient against software attacks has been a significant aspect of SoC platform security.

Test and verification solutions: Test and verification techniques have constituted a major category of protection approaches against the diverse security and trust issues. Both pre-silicon verification—functional as well as formal—and post-silicon manufacturing testing have been considered as mechanisms to identify security vulnerabilities and trust issues for chips, PCBs, and systems. The book covers various DfS and test/verification solutions, which are developed to protect hardware against many vulnerabilities.

1.6 CONFLICT BETWEEN SECURITY AND TEST/DEBUG

Security and test/debug of an SoC often impose conflicting design requirements during its design phase. Post-manufacturing testing and debug using DFT, for example, scan chain, and DFD structures constitute some of the important activities in a SoC lifecycle. Effective debug demands internal signals of IP blocks to be observable during execution in silicon. However, security constraints often cause severe restrictions to internal signal observability, thus making debugging a challenge. These constraints arise from the need to protect many critical assets, such as, locks for high-assurance modules, encryption keys, and firmware. While these security assets themselves are difficult to observe during debugging, they also create observability challenge for other signals, for example, signals from an IP containing low-security assets that need to be routed through an IP block with a high-security asset.

Unfortunately, in current industrial practice, this problem is difficult to address. First, it lacks formal centralized control on security assets, since they are determined per-IP basis. Second, debug requirements are usually not considered during the integration of security assets, which often leads to the discovery of the debug issues very late during actual debug with silicon execution. Fixing the problem at that point may require a silicon "respin", that is, design correction followed by re-fabrication, which is expensive and often an unacceptably long process. Hence, there is a growing emphasis to develop hardware architecture, which ensures the security of DFT and DFD infrastructure, while ensuring their desired role in helping with SoC test/debug process.

1.7 EVOLUTION OF HARDWARE SECURITY: A BRIEF HISTORICAL PERSPECTIVE

Over the past three decades, the field of hardware security has been evolving rapidly with the discovery of many vulnerabilities and attacks on hardware. Figure 1.11 provides a brief timeline for the evolution of hardware security. Before 1996, there were only sporadic instances of hardware IP piracy, primarily cloning of ICs, leading to the development of some IP watermarking and other anti-piracy techniques. In 1996, a groundbreaking hardware attack was introduced in the form of timing analysis attack [3], an attack which aims to extract information from a cryptographic hardware on the basis of a systematic analysis of computation time for different operations. In 1997, fault injection analysis was reported as an attack vector that can lead to compromising the security of a system [7]. The attack focuses on applying environmental stress to the system in order to force it to leak sensitive data. The first power analysis based side-channel attack was introduced in 1999 [2]; it focused on analyzing the power dissipations at runtime to retrieve secrets from a cryptochip.

In 2005, there were reports on production and supply of counterfeit ICs, including cloned and re-cycled chips, which created major security and trust concerns. The concept of hardware Trojans was introduced in 2007 [12], which unveiled the possibility of inserting malicious circuits in a hardware design with the aim to disrupt normal functional behavior, leak sensitive information, grant unauthorized control, or degrade the performance of the system. Some recent hardware vulnerabilities that have received significant attention from industry and academic community includes "Meltdown" and "Spectre" [9]; they exploit implementation-dependent side-channel vulnerabilities in modern processors to

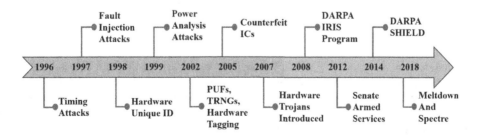

FIGURE 1.11

The evolution of hardware security over the past decades.

access private data from a computer, such as user passwords. These vulnerabilities have been discovered and reported by different processor manufacturers, who have introduced software fixes for them.

Similar to the realm of software security, countermeasures for hardware attacks have been developed in a reactive manner. Over the years, many design and test solutions have evolved to mitigate known attacks. The idea of hardware tagging was introduced in 1998, where every IC instance was assigned with a unique ID. Hardware security primitives, such as physical unclonable functions (PUFs) and true random number generators (TRNGs) were introduced in early 2000 to improve the level of protection against hardware attacks [5,15]. The United States Department of Defense introduced several sponsored research programs to facilitate growth in hardware security solutions. In 2008, DARPA introduced the Integrity and Reliability of Integrated Circuits (IRIS) program to develop techniques for hardware integrity and reliability assurance through destructive and nondestructive analysis. In 2012, a report published by the senate armed services showed that a set of counterfeit devices was discovered in different branches of the US Air Force [8], accentuating the gravity of the problem. The total number of these counterfeits exceeded 1 million, and the investigation concluded with an amendment that enforces counterfeit-avoidance practices. The Supply Chain Hardware Integrity for Electronics Defense (SHIELD) program was introduced by DARPA in 2014 to develop technology to trace and track electronic components—PCB to chip to small passive components—as they move through the supply chain. Over the past decade, many such efforts by both government and industry to enable secure and trusted hardware platform have been observed with more to come in near future.

1.8 BIRD'S EYE VIEW

Table 1.1 provides a bird's-eye view on major hardware security issues and countermeasures, which we have covered in this book. For each attack, it provides information on the adversary, attack surface, and attack objective; whereas for a countermeasure, it lists the stage of hardware lifecycle when it is applied, the goal, and the associated overhead. This table is expected to serve as a quick reference for the readers to some of the key concepts presented in the book.

1.9 HANDS-ON APPROACH

We have included hands-on experiments for several major hardware security topics in this book. We believe a practical learning component is crucial in understanding the diverse security vulnerabilities and the defense mechanisms in a complex system. To do the experiments, we have custom-designed an easy-to-understand, flexible, and ethically "hackable" hardware module, in particular, a printed circuit board (PCB) with basic building blocks that can emulate a computer system and create a network of connected devices. It is called "HaHa", that is Hardware Hacking module. Appendix A provides a detailed description of the HaHa board and associated components. Relevant chapters of the book include a short description of the experiments that can be performed to better understand the topic of the chapters. The experiments, we also hope, would help to stimulate interest in students to further investigate the security issues, and to explore effective countermeasures. In addition to the board, the hands-on experiment platform includes corresponding software modules, and well-written instructions to realize diverse security attacks in this platform, all of which are available as companion materials in the book's own website.

Table 1.1 Bird's-eye view of the hardware attacks & countermeasures

ATTACKS					
Type of Attack	What it is	Adversary	Goal	Life-cycle stages	Chapter #
Hardware Trojan Attacks	Malicious design modification (in chip or PCB)	Untrusted foundry, untrusted IP Vendor, untrusted CAD tool, untrusted design facilities	• Cause malfunction • Degrade reliability • Leak secret info	• Design • Fabrication	Chapter 5
IP Piracy	Piracy of the IP by unauthorized entity	Untrusted SoC Designer, untrusted foundry	• Produce unauthorized copy of the design • Use an IP outside authorized use cases	• Design • Fabrication	Chapter 7
Physical Attacks	Causing physical change to hardware or modifying operating condition to produce various malicious impacts	End user, bad actor with physical access	• Impact functional behavior • Leak information • Cause denial of service	• In field	Chapter 11
Mod-chip Attack	Alteration of PCB to bypass restrictions imposed by system designer	End user	• Bypass security rules imposed through PCB	• In field	Chapter 11
Side-Channel Attacks	Observing parametric behaviors (i.e., power, timing, EM) to leak secret information	End user, bad actor with physical access	• Leak secret information being processed inside the hardware	• In field	Chapter 8
Scan-based Attacks	Leveraging DFT circuits to facilitate side-channel attack	End user, bad actor with physical access	• Leak secret information being processed inside the hardware	• In field • Test-time	Chapter 9
Microprobing	Using microscopic needles to probe internal wires of a chip	End user, bad actor with physical access	• Leak secret information residing inside the chip	• In field	Chapter 10
Reverse Engineering	Process of extracting the hardware design	Design house, foundry, end user	• Extract design details of the hardware	• Fabrication • In field	Chapter 7

(continued on next page)

Table 1.1   (*continued*)

COUNTERMEASURES					
Type of Coun-termeasure	**What it is**	**Parties involved**	**Goal**	**Life-cycle stages**	**Chapter #**
Trust Verification	Verifying the design for potential vulnerabilities to confidentiality, integrity, and availability	• Verification engineer	• Provide assurance against known threats	• Pre-silicon verification • Post-silicon validation	Chapter 5
Hardware Security Primitives (PUFs, TRNGs)	Providing security features to support supply chain protocols	• IP integrator • Value added reseller (for enrollment)	• Authentication • Key generation	• Throughout IC supply chain	Chapter 12
Hardware Obfuscation	Obfuscating the original design to prevent piracy and reverse engineering	• Design house • IP integrator	• Prevent piracy • Reverse engineering • Prevent Trojan insertion	• Design-time	Chapter 14
Masking & Hiding	Design solutions to protect against side-channel attacks	• Design house	To prevent side-channel attacks by reducing leakage or adding noise	• Design-time	Chapter 8
Security Architecture	Enable design-for-security solution to prevent potential and emerging security vulnerabilities	• Design house • IP integrator	Address confidentiality, integrity, and availability issues with design-time solution	• Design-time	Chapter 13
Security Validation	Assessment of security requirements	• Verification and validation engineer	Ensure data integrity, authentication, privacy requirements, access control policies	• Pre-silicon verification • Post-silicon validation	Chapter 16

1.10 EXERCISES

1.10.1 TRUE/FALSE QUESTIONS

1. Hardware is not considered as the "root-of-trust" for system security.
2. Hardware security should not matter if a strong software tool is used to protect user's data.
3. Hardware contains different forms of assets that can be accessed by bad actors.

4. Meltdown and Spectre are two newly discovered vulnerabilities found in most modern processors.
5. Hardware development lifecycle involves a number of untrusted entities.
6. Hardware trust issues do not lead to any security issue.
7. Side-channel attacks are attack vectors that exploit implementation-level weakness.
8. Test and debug features in a hardware often represent a conflict with security objectives.
9. A functional bug can be exploited by an attacker for extracting assets in a SoC.
10. Verification solutions can protect against several hardware security issues.

1.10.2 SHORT-ANSWER TYPE QUESTIONS

1. Describe different levels of abstraction of electronic hardware.
2. State the differences: (1) general-purpose systems vs. embedded systems, (2) ASIC vs. COTS.
3. Describe two major areas of focus for hardware security.
4. What are the hardware trust issues, and how do they impact the security of a computing system?
5. What are the differences between functional and side-channel bugs?
6. Why and how do security and test/debug requirements conflict?
7. Provide examples of some security assets inside SoCs.

1.10.3 LONG-ANSWER TYPE QUESTIONS

1. Describe different aspects of a system's security, and briefly discuss their relative impact.
2. Explain the current state of practice in the security design of and verification process for SoCs.
3. Describe the major steps of the electronic hardware design and test flow, and discuss the security issues in each stage.
4. What are the different attack surfaces for a computing system (say, a smartphone), and for the hardware components inside it?
5. Describe different types of security vulnerabilities in hardware.

REFERENCES

[1] S. Ray, E. Peeters, M.M. Tehranipoor, S. Bhunia, System-on-chip platform security assurance: architecture and validation, Proceedings of the IEEE 106 (1) (2018) 21–37.
[2] P. Kocher, J. Jaffe, B. Jun, Differential power analysis, in: CRYPTO, 1999.
[3] P. Kocher, Timing attacks on implementations of Die–Hellman, RSA, DSS, and other systems, in: CRYPTO, 1996.
[4] F. Koeune, F.X. Standaert, A tutorial on physical security and side-channel attacks, in: Foundations of Security Analysis and Design III, 2005, pp. 78–108.
[5] M. Barbareschi, P. Bagnasco, A. Mazzeo, Authenticating IoT devices with physically unclonable functions models, in: 10th International Conference on P2P, Parallel, Grid, Cloud and Internet Computing, 2015, pp. 563–567.
[6] A. Vijayakumar, V.C. Patil, D.E. Holcomb, C. Paar, S. Kundu, Physical design obfuscation of hardware: a comprehensive investigation of device and logic-level technique, IEEE Transactions on Information Forensics and Security (2017) 64–77.
[7] J. Voas, Fault injection for the masses, Computer 30 (1997) 129–130.
[8] U.S. Senate Committee on Armed Services, Inquiry into counterfeit electronic parts in the Department of Defense supply chain, 2012.
[9] Meltdown and Spectre: Here's what Intel, Apple, Microsoft, others are doing about it. https://arstechnica.com/gadgets/2018/01/meltdown-and-spectre-heres-what-intel-apple-microsoft-others-are-doing-about-it/.
[10] M. Tehranipoor, U. Guin, D. Forte, Counterfeit integrated circuits, Counterfeit Integrated Circuits (2015) 15–36.

[11] R. Torrance, D. James, The State-of-the-Art in Semiconductor Reverse Engineering, ACM/EDAC/IEEE Design Automation Conference (DAC) (2011) 333–338.

[12] M. Tehranipoor, F. Koushanfar, A Survey of Hardware Trojan Taxonomy and Detection, IEEE Design and Test of Computers (2010) 10–25.

[13] Y. Alkabani, F. Koushanfar, Active Hardware Metering for Intellectual Property Protection and Security, Proceedings of 16th USENIX Security Symposium on USENIX Security (2007) 291–306.

[14] G. Qu, F. Koushanfar, Hardware Metering, Proceedings of the 38th annual Design Automation (2001) 490–493.

[15] R. Pappu, B. Recht, J. Taylor, N. Gershenfeld, Physical One-Way Functions, Science (2002) 2026–2030.

[16] F. Wang, Formal Verification of Timed Systems:A Survey and Perspective, Proceedings of the IEEE (2004) 1283–1305.

PART

1

BACKGROUND ON ELECTRONIC HARDWARE

A QUICK OVERVIEW OF ELECTRONIC HARDWARE

2

CONTENTS

Hardware Security. https://doi.org/10.1016/B978-0-12-812477-2.00007-1

2.1 INTRODUCTION

Computing in the 21st century has become pervasive in our daily lives. What was once the domain accessible only to scientists and engineers has now become commonly available in almost every corner of the globe and to every citizen of the world. It is common to see cell phone being used by anyone anywhere in the world even in very remote areas, to see tens of microcontrollers in cars, and that many people carry computers in the form of fitness trackers. In short, computers are everywhere and many people today depend heavily on them for even the most basic tasks in their daily lives, namely shopping, paying bills, checking bank accounts, finding where to eat, etc.

The pervasiveness of modern computing systems is a direct result of constant advancements in integrated circuit (IC) design and fabrication technologies over the past half century. We can trace the history of computing back to inventions such as Charles Babbage's difference engine [1] or the ENIAC of the late 1940s [2]. Modern computer is a direct result of the advent of the transistor, first realized in the form of point-contact transistor fabricated by Bardeen, Shockley, and Brattain at Bell Laboratories in 1947 [3]. The point-contact transistor was relatively bulky and constructed from germanium. Later, other semiconductor materials, notably silicon, were used to realize bipolar transistors and, eventually, field-effect transistors (FETs) in the 1960s [3].

In 1965, Gordon Moore of Intel observed that the number of transistors integrated per square inch doubled every two years [3]. Transistor density, along with switching speeds, indeed continued to double almost every 18–24 months in the next five decades, which made this observation well known in semiconductor industry as "Moore's law". Figure 2.1 illustrates increases in transistor density from the early 1970s to the latest generation of integrated circuits (here, processors) in 2016 [4,5]. Although the continued increase into the early 2000s is quite impressive, it is also worth mentioning that performance increase has already begun to slow down. This is due mainly to the fact that process variations and environmental noises in an integrated circuit making it extremely difficult to achieve the expected performance as a result of technology scaling. Thus, we are now entering an interesting era, where alternative nanoscale technologies are actively pursued for future computing applications as demand continues to remain strong for higher performance and smaller area.

With the slow down of transistor scaling, often pointed to as a sign of the looming end of Moore's law, many researchers have begun to consider "Beyond Moore" or "More than Moore" technology alternatives [5]. One underlying goal of these investigations into new nanoelectronic devices is to find technologies that allow continuation of the performance scaling that has been enjoyed over the past several decades. However, many novel nanotechnologies are often not more robust than today's silicon-based complementary metal-oxide-semiconductor (CMOS) transistors. These emerging devices are often found to offer new opportunities for novel applications or to provide performance improvements through hybrid integration with CMOS [6–8]. Thus, "More than Moore" advocates would argue that nanotechnologies should be considered for the novel applications they are likely to enable, as opposed to simply enhancing the performance of existing computing systems and architectures. Nonetheless, the landscape of integrated circuit design and fabrication technologies are beginning to change right at the time that computing has become commonplace, especially with the advent of Internet of things (IoTs) and smart devices used everywhere.

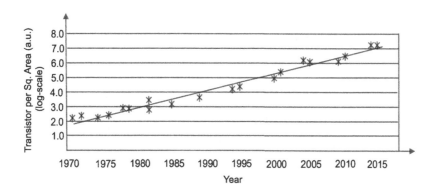

FIGURE 2.1

Illustration of Moore's law, showing a biannual doubling of the number of transistors per unit area.

Nanotechnology is most often defined as the field of study associated with the synthesis and integration of structures with feature sizes less than 100 nm [9]. Considering the fact that gate lengths for silicon CMOS transistors have been below 100 nm (now at 7 nm) for more than a decade now, one would argue that modern electronics has already been dominated by nanotechnology. To differentiate conventional CMOS from non-CMOS nanotechnologies, terms such as "nanoscale CMOS" and "deep submicron" are often used. That being said, several novel forms of semiconductor transistor technology have emerged that are certainly worth considering in the context of "Beyond Moore" nanoelectronics.

2.2 NANOSCALE TECHNOLOGIES
2.2.1 SILICON-ON-INSULATOR

Silicon-on-insulator (SOI) technology has emerged in recent years as a way to improve the performance of semiconductor devices. Specifically, SOI refers to a fabrication technique, where a semiconductor, typically silicon, is layered on top of an insulator, typically silicon dioxide. Since the top semiconductor layer can be very thin, it becomes possible to implement doped diffusion regions that extend all the way through to the insulator underneath. Further, some SOI transistors fall into the category of fully depleted, meaning when the device is on, the entire channel is inverted. In short, the SOI structure leads to a reduced parasitic capacitance and other nonideal effects, such that the performance is drastically improved relative to conventional, non-SOI approaches.

Manufacturing SOI-based devices and circuits can be challenging, depending on how the top semiconductor layer is fabricated on top of the insulator. Ideally, the top semiconductor would be grown via epitaxial techniques, such that the resulting layer is very thin. However, the crystallinity of the oxide/insulator layer typically does not match that of the desired semiconductor, meaning epitaxial growth leads to nonideal behavior. A more common technique for SOI is the use of a thick wafer of the same material as the top semiconductor that is flipped and essentially glued onto the insulator. Since the top semiconductor is manufactured independent of the insulator, it will have the necessary crystallinity required for the desired electronic devices and circuits. However, the process of flipping, glueing, and thinning that top layer tends to be quite expensive.

2.2.2 FinFET TECHNOLOGY

Another approach to yielding nanoscale field effect transistor (FET) is to go vertical. At the device level, going vertical can refer to the advent of FinFET transistors, meaning transistors whose semiconductor channels are fabricated vertically as fin structures. The so-called fin allows a gate to be wrapped around the channel from three sides, leaving only the bottom of the fin/channel open to the underlying bulk substrate. As is the case with SOI, the wrapped gate leads to a more fully depleted channel, hence reduced parasitic effects. The reduction in parasitic capacitance and other nonideal characteristics leads to improved performance. Further, since the fins are fabricated from an existing semiconductor substrate, as opposed to layered on top of an insulator as in the case of SOI, FinFET technology does not suffer from the same manufacturing challenges common to SOI. It is worth mentioning that FinFET technology has become the common approach for sub-32 nm CMOS technology, with companies such as Intel, Samsung, TSMC, and Global Foundries all offering technology nodes at 14 nm and, soon, even at 10 and 7 nm gate lengths [10].

2.2.3 3D INTEGRATED CIRCUITS

As feature sizes shrink to 10 nm and, possibly, even smaller to 7 nm and 5 nm in the near future, it is believed that CMOS transistor technology has been scaled down about as far as possible in terms of lateral dimensions. In order to continue gaining density improvements in modern semiconductor electronics, vertical dimensions must be better utilized. This is the primary objective for development of three-dimensional (3D) integrated circuit technology, known as 3DIC. 3DICs refer to layered approach to manufacturing, where multiple semiconductor substrates (fabricated in same or different foundries) are stacked on top of one another in order to implement circuits vertically as well as laterally. There are several approaches to build a 3DIC, including face-to-face, front-to-back, and SOI-based approaches.

The face-to-face approach to 3DIC is perhaps the simplest because no additional structures need to be implemented in silicon. Instead, the top metal layers of two die or wafers include contact points or landing pads for connecting the two layers together. One layer is then flipped and oriented on top of the other so that connections are made at the predefined contact points. Thus, the resulting 3DIC consists of two semiconductor layers oriented in a face-to-face arrangement. One challenge with the face-to-face approach arises when constructing a 3DIC with more than two layers. In this case, either off-chip connections are needed to connect to other pairs, or a second form of 3DIC is required that utilizes through silicon vias (TSVs) to connect layers oriented in a back-to-back structure.

Many 3D implementations are constructed in some form of a back-to-front arrangement, where each semiconductor layer is oriented with metal layers to the top. In this case, connections across layers require the use of TSVs. Each TSV tends to be larger in the cross-sectional area relative to conventional vias, limiting the number of total TSVs one could integrate onto a single die. However, such 3DIC technologies enable drastic reductions in total wire lengths, thereby reducing delay, improving performance. Further, the ability to stack transistors vertically enables a form of scaling where the number of transistors per unit area continues to rise with an increase in the number of layers. Such integration gives hope to continue meeting Moore's law requirement for both performance and area.

2.2.4 BULK-SILICON TECHNOLOGY

Bulk silicon CMOS continues to be the major workhorse in modern electronics. Although beyond-CMOS nanotechnologies have been emerging, CMOS devices still continue to play a significant role due to technological maturity, cost, performance, and ease of integration. This has led to hybrid CMOS-nanoelectronic approaches, where CMOS is used for functions such as I/O and gain, whereas a nanoscale technology is used for dense memory and/or logic implementations [6]. One major advantage for using nanotechnology is the increased density and ability to squeeze functionality into regular crossbar structures. Further, nanoelectronic materials are continually being explored as extreme low-power alternatives to their CMOS counterparts. This is particularly important for 3D-based architectures, where heat across upper layers becomes a major concern [11,12]. It is believed that CMOS continues to have its place in future ICs and electronic computing systems, emerging systems and application domains such as digital microfluidics, IoT, quantum computers, and neuromorphic computing. Thus, the future for ICs consist of a mixed bag of technologies, including many new devices constructed from emerging nanoscale materials.

2.3 DIGITAL LOGIC

Digital logic is the representation of signals and sequences of a digital circuit using numbers. It is the fundamental concept, underlying behind all modern computing systems, that provides an understanding on how hardware and circuit communicates within a device. This section introduces the basic concept of digital logic. Specifically, we introduce binary logic, combinational circuit, and sequential circuit, such as flip-flops, registers, and memories [13].

2.3.1 BINARY LOGIC

Binary logic or boolean logic is the core concept of boolean algebra that forms "Gates" which all digital electronic circuits and microprocessor based systems are constructed of. Basic digital logic gates perform logical operations of AND, OR, and NOT on binary numbers.

Information is stored in computer systems in binary form. A binary bit represents one of the two possible states, which are generally referred to as logic "1" and logic "0". Specifically, the presence of a positive voltage can be represented as logic "1", high, or true; the absence of a voltage can be represented as logic "0", low, or false. In Boolean Algebra and truth table, these two states are represented as "1" and "0", respectively [14]. Figure 2.2 shows a CMOS circuit, which typically consists of a p-type transistor and an n-type transistor. In digital logic, each transistor is either on or off, which represents a short circuit or an open circuit, respectively. As illustrated in Fig. 2.2, the left side provides logic "true" in binary form, whereas the right side provides logic "false" in binary form.

2.3.2 DIGITAL LOGIC GATES

Digital logic gate is the fundamental building block of digital circuits. There are a number of basic logic gates, which perform logic operations indicated by their names on binary numbers (see Fig. 2.3). As an example, the two-input logic gates have the following features:

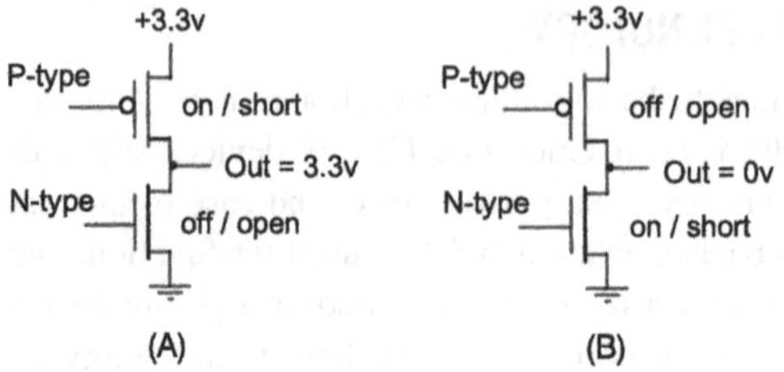

FIGURE 2.2

A binary bit is true (A) vs. false (B).

- AND gate: the output is 1 if all inputs are 1; otherwise, the output is 0.
- OR gate: the output is 1 if at least one input is 1; otherwise, the output is 0.
- XOR gate: the output is 0 if both inputs are same; otherwise, the output is 1.
- NAND gate: the output is 1 if at lease one input is 0; otherwise, the output is 0.
- NOR gate: the output is 1 if both inputs are 0; otherwise, the output is 0.
- NOT gate or inverter: the output is 1 if the input is 0 and the output is 0 if the input is 1.

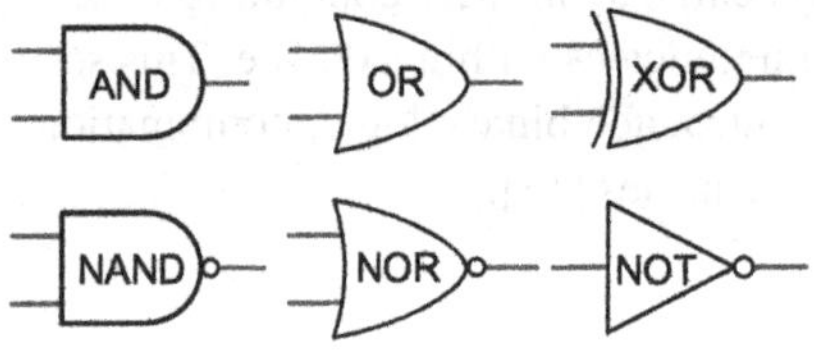

FIGURE 2.3

Basic two-input logic gates.

2.3.3 BOOLEAN ALGEBRA

Boolean Algebra is the mathematical representation for digital logic. The mathematical formats for the above basic logic operations are shown below.

- A AND B is written as AB or $A \cdot B$;
- A OR B is written as $A + B$;
- A XOR B is written as $A \oplus B$;
- NOT A is written as $\sim A$ or A' or $\overline{A}$;
- A NAND B is written as $(AB)'$, $(A \cdot B)'$, or $\overline{(AB)}$;
- A NOR B is written as $(A + B)'$ or $\overline{(A + B)}$.

The laws of Boolean Algebra are listed in Table 2.1, where A, B, and C can be considered as Booleans or individual bits of a logic operation [14].

Table 2.1 Laws of Boolean Algebra [14]

$A\&B = B\&A$	Commutative Law
$A\|B = B\|A$	Commutative Law
$(A\&B)\&C = A\&(B\&C)$	Associative Law
$(A\|B)\|C = A\|(B\|C)$	Associative Law
$(A\|B)\&C = (A\&C)\|(B\&C)$	Distributive Law
$(A\&B)\|C = (A\|C)\&(B\|C)$	Distributive Law
$A\&0 = 0$	Identity of 0
$A\|0 = A$	Identity of 0
$A\&1 = A$	Identity of 1
$A\|1 = 1$	Identity of 1
$A\|A = A$	Property of OR
$A\|(\sim A) = 1$	Property of OR
$A\&A = A$	Property of AND
$A\&(\sim A) = 0$	Property of AND
$\sim(\sim A) = A$	Inverse
$\sim(A\|B) = (\sim A)\&(\sim B)$	De Morgan's Theorem
$\sim(A\&B) = (\sim A)\|(\sim B)$	De Morgan's Theorem

2.3.4 SEQUENTIAL CIRCUIT

Modern digital logic circuits can be divided into two main parts, combinational logic and sequential logic. Combinational logic changes after signal propagation delay when input changes, and its output only relies on its present input. In contrast, sequential logic has at least one clock signal, and consists of blocks of combinational logic divided by memory elements which are driven by clock signals. Therefore, the output of sequential logic depends on both the present and past inputs.

2.3.4.1 Sequential Circuit Elements

Sequential circuit elements (flip-flops and latches) are commonly used for storage of information. To be exact, a flip-flop is used to store a single binary bit and has two states; one of its two states represents "1", the other represents "0". Such data storage is used to store state, and the corresponding circuit is referred to as sequential logic. A flip-flop is clocked, that is, synchronous or edge-triggered, whereas a latch is level-sensitive. We briefly review different types of flip-flops here.

D-Type Flip-Flop

A D flip-flop is widely used as the basic building block of random access memory (RAM) and registers. The D flip-flop captures the D-input value at the specified edge (i.e., rising or falling) of the clock. After the rising/falling clock edge, the captured value is available at Q output. The truth table of D flip-flop is shown in Table 2.2.

Table 2.2 Truth table of D-type flip-flop

Clock	D	Q_{next}
Rising edge	0	0
Rising edge	1	1
Non-rising	X	Q

T-Type Flip-Flop

For a T-Type Flip-Flop, if T-input is high, the output toggles when the clock input is high. If T-input is low, the output remains the same. Hence, T flip-flop can be used for clock division. The truth table of T flip-flop is shown in Table 2.3.

Table 2.3 Truth table of T-type flip-flop

T	Q	Q_{next}	Comment
0	0	0	Hold state (no clk)
0	1	1	Hold state (no clk)
1	0	1	Toggle
1	1	0	Toggle

JK-Type Flip-Flop

The JK flip-flop has two inputs (J and K), and the output can be set as different values based on the inputs. The truth table of JK-type flip-flop is shown in Table 2.4.

Table 2.4 Truth table of JK-type flip-flop

J	K	Q_{next}	Comment
0	0	Q	Hold state
0	1	0	Reset
1	0	1	Set
1	1	$\bar{Q}$	Toggle

2.3.4.2 Timing Parameters

Setup time, hold time, and propagation delay are three important parameters when designing a sequential circuit. These three timing parameters are briefly explained in this section and illustrated in Fig. 2.4.

Setup Time

Setup time (t_{su}) is the minimum amount of time that the data input is required to be stable before the rising/falling edge of the clock, so that the data can be correctly sampled by the clock.

Hold Time

Hold time (t_h) is the minimum amount of time that the data input is required to be stable after the rising/falling edge of the clock, so that the data can be correctly sampled by the clock.

Propagation Delay

Clock-to-output delay (t_{CO})/propagation delay (t_P) is the time that a flip-flop takes to change its output after the rising/falling edge of the clock.

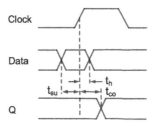

FIGURE 2.4

Timing parameters: setup time, hold time, and clock-to-output delay of a flip-flop.

2.4 CIRCUIT THEORY

A circuit is a network consisting of circuit elements and wires. To be specific, wires are typically designated as straight lines on a schematic, and nodes are locations, where wires connect. All other symbols on a schematic are circuit elements. Resistors, capacitors, and inductors, the three most passive linear circuit elements, which make up electronic circuits, are briefly reviewed in this section.

2.4.1 RESISTORS AND RESISTANCE

As common elements of electronic circuits, resistors are passive two-terminal components that implement electrical resistance. Resistors are typically used in circuits to reduce current flow, adjust signal levels, divide voltages, and bias active elements. There are different types of resistors, including high-power resistors, fixed resistors, and variable resistors, which are used in various applications. The typical schematic diagram of resistors is shown in Fig. 2.5A; the resistor symbol on the right is the International Electrotechnical Commission (IEC) resistor symbol.

Electrical resistance, the quantitative property of a resistor, is defined as

$$\gamma = \frac{\rho L}{A}, \tag{2.1}$$

where ρ is the resistivity of the material, L is the length of the resistor, and A is the cross-section area of the resistor.

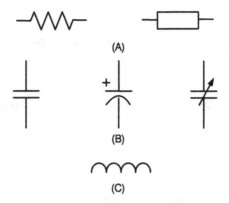

FIGURE 2.5

Typical schematic diagrams of resistor (A), fixed, polarized, and variable capacitors (B), and inductor (C).

2.4.2 CAPACITORS AND CAPACITANCE

Capacitors are passive two-terminal electrical components, which store potential energy in an electric field. They are characterized by capacitance. Capacitors are widely used in different applications. In electronic circuits, they are used to block direct current (DC) while allowing alternating current (AC) to pass. In analog filter networks, they are used to smooth the output of power supplies. In resonant circuits, they are used to tune radios to the specified frequencies. The typical schematic diagram of three types of capacitors is shown in Fig. 2.5B.

Capacitance is defined as the ratio of the electric (positive/negative) charge Q on each conductor to the voltage V between them, which is shown below in Eq. (2.2). The unit of capacitance is the farad (F), defined as one coulomb per volt (1 C/V). Typical values of capacitors in general electronics range from 1 femtofarad (pF = 10^{-15} F) to 1 millifarad (mF = 10^{-3} F).

$$C = \frac{Q}{V}, \tag{2.2}$$

where Q is the positive or negative charge on each conductor, and V is the voltage between them.

In practical uses, charge sometimes affects the capacitor mechanically, hence changing its capacitance. Therefore, capacitance can be calculated as

$$C = \frac{dQ}{dV}. \tag{2.3}$$

2.4.3 INDUCTORS AND INDUCTANCE

Inductors are passive two-terminal electrical components, which store energy in a magnetic field when current flows through it [15]. Typically, an inductor is composed of an insulated wire into a coil around a core. An inductor is characterized by its inductance. Inductors are widely used in AC electronic equipment. In electronic circuits, they are used to block AC while allowing DC to pass. In electronic filters, they are used to separate signals of different frequencies. In addition, along with capacitors, they are used to make tuned circuits for tuning radio and TV receivers. The typical schematic diagram of an inductor is shown in Fig. 2.5C.

Inductance is defined as the ratio of the voltage to the rate of change of current, which is shown below. The unit of inductance is henry (H), and typical values for inductors range from 1 millihenry (mH = 10^{-3} H) to 1 microhenry (μH = 10^{-6} H).

$$L = \frac{\Phi}{I},$$ (2.4)

where Φ is the total amount of magnetic flux through a circuit, which is generated by current I, and depends on the circuit geometric shape.

2.4.4 KIRCHHOFF'S CIRCUIT LAWS

Kirchhoff's circuit laws are linear constraints on the branch voltages and node currents in the lumped element model of electrical circuits. Kirchhoff's circuit laws include Kirchhoff's current law (KCL) and Kirchhoff's voltage law (KVL), which are independent of the nature of the electrical elements [16].

2.4.4.1 Kirchhoff's Current Law

Kirchhoff's current law addresses the conservation of charge entering and leaving a circuit node. As one of the fundamental laws used for circuit analysis, it states that the sum of current flowing into a circuit's node is exactly equal to the sum of current flowing out the same node since it has no other place to go as no charge is lost [15,16].

In other words, the sum of currents meeting at a circuit's node is equal to zero. Also, since current can be seen as a signed quantity, this law is expressed as

$$\sum_{k=1}^{N} I_k = 0.$$ (2.5)

This principle is illustrated in Fig. 2.6. It can be seen that the current entering into the node is equal to the current leaving that node, that is, $i_1 + i_2 = i_3 + i_4$. In other words, the sum of the currents entering and leaving the same node is equal to zero; $i_1 + i_2 - (i_3 + i_4) = 0$.

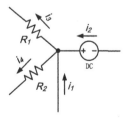

FIGURE 2.6

Kirchhoff's current law.

2.4.4.2 Kirchhoff's Voltage Law

Kirchhoff's voltage law addresses the conservation of energy around a closed circuit loop. It states that the sum of branch voltages around a closed circuit path is equal to zero [15,16].

Since voltage can be seen as a signed (that is, positive or negative) quantity reflecting the polarities and signs of the sources, and voltage drops around the loop, this law can be expressed as

$$\sum_{k=1}^{N} V_k = 0. \tag{2.6}$$

This principle is illustrated in Fig. 2.7. It can be seen that the sum of branch voltages around the loop is equal to zero, that is, $V_1 + V_2 + V_3 + V_4 = 0$.

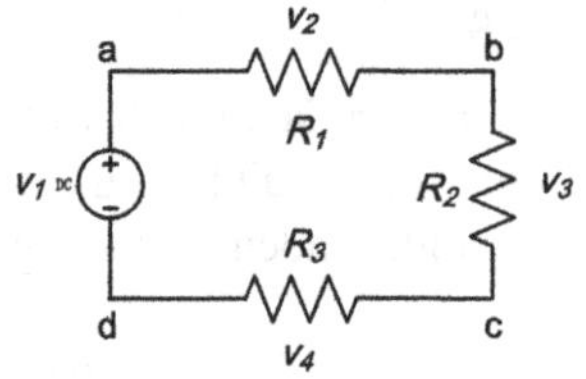

FIGURE 2.7

Kirchhoff's voltage law.

2.5 ASICs AND FPGAs

Application-specific integrated circuits (ASICs) and field programmable gate arrays (FPGAs) are integrated circuits, which serve different ends on the spectrum of applications for modern ICs. Due to their own design philosophy and features, their differences include non-recurring engineering (NRE), cost, flexibility, and performance [17].

2.5.1 ASICs

As the name indicates, an ASIC is an integrated circuit customized and created for a particular purpose rather than for general-purpose use. ASICs are used to implement analog, digital, as well as mixed-signal functionalities in high volume and high performance. Nowadays, the functionality of digital ASICs is generally described using a hardware description language (HDL), for example, Verilog and VHDL. Circuit diagrams were previously used to describe the functionality, but their use has dwindled over the past two decades, as size of the circuit continued to increase.

2.5.2 FPGAs

As the name implies, an FPGA is an integrated circuit, which is designed to be configured by customers after manufacturing; hence, it is field programmable. Similar to an ASIC, customers of an FPGA typically use HDL, such as verilog or VHDL, to specify the configuration of an FPGA.

An FPGA consists of a set of programmable logic blocks and a hierarchy of reconfigurable interconnects. Logic blocks are wired through the reconfigurable interconnects to be configured for different functions. In modern FPGAs, logic blocks include memory elements, such as simple flip-flops or complete memory blocks. Examples of FPGAs are shown in Fig. 2.8, where the left one is a Stratix IV FPGA developed by Altera, and the right one is a Spartan FPGA developed by Xilinx.

FIGURE 2.8

FPGAs from Altera (left) and Xilinx (right).

2.5.3 DIFFERENCE BETWEEN ASICs AND FPGAs

Since ASICs are semi- or full-custom designs, they require higher development costs and often reach into the millions during design and implementation stages. In addition, ASICs are non-reprogrammable once they are produced; hence, changes in the design incur additional cost. Although ASICs have a relatively higher nonrecurring cost, it is justified due to the following facts – (i) ASICs often have higher density and can integrate complex functionalities into a chip, thus providing limited size, low power, as well as low cost designs; (ii) due to its custom feature, the number of transistors is considered very carefully, and minimal resources would be wasted in an ASIC design; (iii) when making large quantities of designs for a specific use, ASICs would be the optimal choice.

FPGAs advantage lies in their flexibility, ability to be reprogrammed in the field, and cost-effectiveness. For example, the reprogrammable nature allows designers and manufacturers to change the design or to send out patches even after products are sold. Customers often utilize this feature to create their prototypes based on FPGAs, so that their designs can be fully debugged, tested, and updated in the real scenario before manufacturing. Although the nonrecurring cost is very limited and, therefore, time to market is fast, some resources on an FPGA are wasted since the package and resources for a specific type of FPGA are standard.

Moreover, when analyzing the production cost in relation to the production volume, using FPGAs becomes costly compared to ASICs as the volume increases. Also, since FPGAs cannot be fully customized, some specific analog blocks have to be added into FPGA platforms. Those functionalities typically require to be implemented by external ICs, thereby further increasing the size and the cost of the final product. The difference between ASICs and FPGAs is summarized in Table 2.5 [17].

Table 2.5 The difference between ASICs and FPGAs

	ASIC	FPGA
Time to market	Slow	Fast
NRE	High	Low
Design flow	Complex	Simple
Power consumption	Low	High
Performance	High	Medium
Unit size	Low	Medium
Unit cost	Low	High

Since modern designs are often cost-constrained, the cost comparison between ASICs and FPGAs is further illustrated in Fig. 2.9. It can be observed that FPGAs are cheaper than ASICs when building low-volume production circuits. However, ASICs become more cost-effective after the volume of 400K units (note that this number is subject to change as technology further scales). In other words, for lower-volume designs, FPGA is capable of reducing costs significantly, whereas ASICs are more efficient and cost-effective on high-volume productions [17].

2.6 PRINTED CIRCUIT BOARD

A printed circuit board (PCB) is a thin board made of laminate materials, such as fiberglass and composite epoxy. Conductive pathways are etched/printed on a board to electrically connect a variety of components on the board, for example, transistors, resistors, and integrated circuits (IC) [18]. In other words, a PCB is developed to mechanically support and electrically connect electronic components through conductive tracks and pads. Components are typically soldered onto the PCB to be mechanically and electrically connected to it. Figure 2.10 shows the picture of a PCB, which was built by the authors of this book with a purpose of hardware hacking. The figure includes conductive traces, vias, and electronic components.

PCBs are widely used in various applications, such as desktop computers, laptop computers, mobile devices, TVs, radios, IoTs, Automotive, digital cameras, and more. They serve as the foundation for many computer components, including graphic card, sound card, adapter card, and expansion card. All these components are further connected to a PCB, that is, the motherboard. While PCBs are universally used in computers, mobile devices, and electrical appliances, it should be noted that PCBs used in mobile devices are typically thinner and contain finer circuits than the ones used in other applications [18].

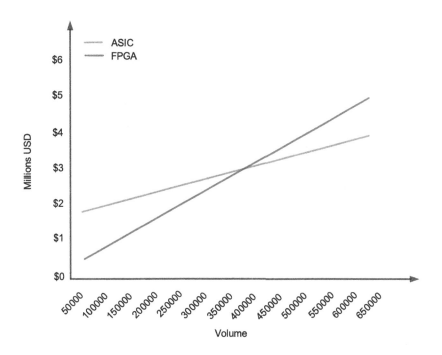

FIGURE 2.9

Total cost of ASIC vs. FPGA for different production volume.

2.6.1 CLASSIFICATION OF PCB

Depending upon requirement, PCBs can be single-sided bond (SSB, that is, one copper layer), double-sided bond (DSB, that is, two copper layers on both sides of one substrate layer), or multi-layer bond (MLB, that is, inner and outer layers of copper, alternating with layers of substrate).

SSB PCB

Single-sided bond PCB has only one side copper layer, the other side is insulated material. Hence, only one-sided copper can be used to manufacture the device as copper is a conductive material.

DSB PCB

Double-sided bond PCB has three layers; two of them are side copper layers. Both ends are coated with copper material, and the middle part is insulating material. Hence, both ends can be used for design, manufacturing, and electronic components placement.

ML PCB

Multi-layer bond PCB has more than two copper layers, where copper is placed in different layers as required. ML PCBs allow for much higher component density, since circuit traces on the inner layers would otherwise take up surface space between components. Nowadays, ML PCBs are mostly used

FIGURE 2.10

A sample printed circuit board.

in different applications. However, ML PCBs make analysis, repair, and circuits in-field modification much more difficult.

2.6.2 PCB DESIGN FLOW

The PCB design flow consists of four stages, that is, part selection, schematic capture and simulation, board layout, and board verification and validation [19]. The PCB design flow is shown in Fig. 2.11.

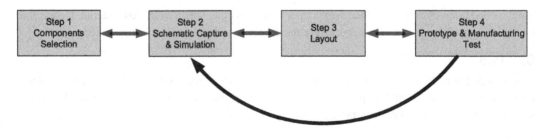

FIGURE 2.11

The PCB design flow.

Part Selection

Components (for example, transistors, resistors, operational amplifiers, and digital components) are the most fundamental part of a design. Part selection stage evaluates and investigates how components coordinate with each other and work as a part of the overall design. Generally, information on physical components is available online, such as datasheets, which provides operating points, switching characteristics, and design considerations.

Schematic Capture and Simulation

As the fundamental stage of PCB design process, capture is a design interface in which graphical symbols of components are placed and connected to build the design topology. Once a schematic is captured, typically SPICE simulation is utilized to predict circuit behavior, to check the integrity of circuit designs, and to analyze the effects of components and signals upon the design. Simulation is able to quickly identify the majority of bugs and errors before the design is physically manufactured, thus greatly reducing both time-to-market and production cost.

Board Layout

Upon capturing the schematic and simulating the design, the physical prototype is built to test the design performance under real workload conditions. Layout is done through EDA tools and in a CAD environment, in which the symbols for components that represented the design in capture stage are seen in the format of the actual component physical dimensions. The final design form in this stage is exported to a Gerber format, which can be used by PCB manufacturers to turn into a physical representation of the board. Although the advanced EDA tools are able to automatically place and route a board, the critical elements and components have to be manually taken care of by experienced engineers with extra scrutiny to ensure the performance and stability of the design.

Prototype Test and Manufacturing Test

Prototype test and manufacturing test are the final steps in the validation of a PCB. Whereas prototype test validates if the design meets the target specifications, manufacturing test at the high-volume production is performed to ensure each device being shipped meets the testing principles and expected responses. If bugs or errors are discovered during the simulation stage are identified at this stage, iterations through the design flow have to be made to address the problem.

2.6.3 CREATING A PCB DESIGN

Typically, a PCB consists of multiple copper layers that are used to conduct electrical signals and various dielectric layers that are used for insulation. The green color found on most PCBs comes from a solder mask. Solder masks also come in other colors, such as blue or red. The fundamental components of a PCB are introduced below [19].

Board Outline

The board outline of a PCB is often cut into a specific shape for a form factor that meets a specific design. When working with devices of small size, the need for a specific shape (for example, round, rectangular, and zig-zag) is important to finalizing a product. Hence, a number of methods used to define the shape of the board outline, such as importing DXF files (a format used by mechanical CAD tools) to define a specific shape for the design.

Creating Copper Routes

Copper routes on a PCB board are used to conduct electrical signals to various components and connectors on the board. The copper pathways are created through layering copper on the board surface(s) and etching away excess copper. Etchings are created by placing a mask over regions of copper pathways and removing all unwanted copper.

Drilling Holes

Drilling holes on a PCB board is required to create signal pathways to different layers on a board, or create areas to attach components on a board. A plated-through hole (PTH) in a board is named as a via that provides electrical connection between a copper route on one layer to a copper route on another layer. Holes for vias are typically created/drilled using a fine drill bit, whereas holes for small micro-vias are created/drilled by way of a laser. There are several types of vias. For instance, a via starting on one outer layer and ending at an inner layer is called a blind via, which does not completely pass through a board. A via connecting copper routes on two inner layers of a board is called a buried via, which does not connect at the surface level of a board.

Components on a PCB

Components on a PCB refer to the semiconductor devices, such as through-hole technology (THT) components and surface-mount devices (SMD). THT parts are often larger with longer pins, which are inserted into drilled holes and soldered one-by-one onto a board. In contrast, SMD parts are often much smaller and allow you to solder much smaller leads to the board surface. Therefore, parts can be attached to the board top/bottom surface instead of having to solder through-hole parts.

Gerber Files

A Gerber file refers to a file format used for PCB manufacturing. Gerber files are utilized by fabrication machines to layout electrical connections, such as trace and pads. The file generally contains necessary information for drilling and milling the circuit board.

2.7 EMBEDDED SYSTEMS

As its name suggests, an embedded system is a microprocessor- or microcontroller-based system, which is designed for a specific function and embedded into a larger mechanical or electrical system. Since embedded systems are developed for some specific task rather than to be a general-purpose system for multiple tasks, they are typically of limited size, low power, and low cost. Embedded systems are widely used in various purposes, such as commercial, industrial, and military applications.

Typically, an embedded system consists of hardware and application software components. Some embedded systems have real-time operating system (RTOS). Some small embedded systems may not have RTOS. Therefore, an embedded system can be defined as a microprocessor- or microcontroller-based, software driven, reliable, and real-time control system. Figure 2.12 shows an embedded system on a plug-in card with multiple components such as processor, memory, power supply, and external interfaces.

FIGURE 2.12

An embedded system on a plug-in card.

2.7.1 EMBEDDED SYSTEM HARDWARE

An embedded system contains a microprocessor or microcontroller that is typically designed to perform computation for real-time operations. Generally, a microprocessor is only a central processing unit (CPU). Hence, other components (for example, memories, communication interfaces) need to be integrated and work with the microprocessor as a whole system. In contrast, a microcontroller is a self-contained system, which includes a CPU, memories (e.g., RAM, flash memory), and peripherals (e.g., serial communication ports).

2.7.2 EMBEDDED SYSTEM SOFTWARE

Microprocessors or microcontrollers used in embedded systems are generally not as advanced when compared to general-purpose processors designed for managing multiple tasks. They often work on a simple, less-memory-intensive program environment [20]. As a result, embedded system software has specific hardware requirements and capabilities. It is tailored to the particular hardware and has time and memory constraints [21]. Programs and operating systems are generally stored in flash memory within embedded systems.

In like manner, the operating systems or language platforms are developed for embedded use, particularly where RTOS is required. Currently, simple versions of Linux operating system or other operating systems, such as Embedded Java and Windows IoT are generally adopted [20].

2.7.3 CHARACTERISTICS OF AN EMBEDDED SYSTEM

The characteristics of an embedded system can be summarized as presented below.

- Specific function: An embedded system is usually designed for a specific function.
- Tightly constrained: An embedded system is tightly resource- and time-constrained. For example, an embedded system has to be fast and tasks-tolerant of slight variations in reaction time (in real-time or near real-time manner), with limited memory and minimum power consumption.
- Real-time and reactive: Real-time or near real-time manner has to be served in many environments. For instance, a global positioning system (GPS) navigator needs to continually provide road and location information, and to send driver alerts to increase situation awareness in a near real-time manner or sometimes real-time manner. Likewise, a car cruise controller is required to continually monitor and react to speed and brake sensors, and also compute the acceleration or deacceleration in a real-time manner. Any delay would make the car out of control, which could give rise to catastrophic results.
- Hardware/Software codesign: An embedded system is typically a computer hardware system with software embedded in it. Hardware is designed for performance and security, while software is designed for more features and flexibility.
- Microprocessor-/Microcontroller-based: A microprocessor or microcontroller is often deployed at the heart of the embedded system and designed to perform operations.
- Memory: A memory is required for an embedded system since programs and operating systems are generally loaded and stored in the memory.
- Connected peripherals: Peripherals are needed to connect input and output devices.

2.8 HARDWARE-FIRMWARE-SOFTWARE INTERACTION

Hardware refers to the physical components of a system, such as the memory, hard disk drive, graphic card, sound card, central processing unit, motherboard, monitor, adapter card, and ethernet cable. Software refers to the instructions or the programs running on hardware, which direct a computer to perform specific tasks or operations, in contrast to hardware upon which the system is built. Computer software is the information processed by systems, for example, data, programs, and libraries. For example, software could be operating systems (OS). OS provides overall control for hardware system and applications, which are programs designed for a specific task. Software is installed and resides on the hard disk and is loaded into memory when it is needed.

Although hardware and software are independent concepts, they require each other to function and neither can be realistically used on its own. Figure 2.13 shows how users interact with application software running on the computer system. It can be observed that the application software interacts with the operating system, which in turn communicates with the hardware. Information flow is indicated by the arrows.

Specifically, most algorithms can be implemented in either hardware or software. Generally, hardware-based algorithm implementation is much faster than software-based, but it can only perform a limited number of instructions, such as additions, comparisons, moves, and copies. Hence, software is utilized to create complex algorithms based on these basic instructions. The software that directly controls hardware is machine language. Software could also be written in low-level assembly language, which is strongly corresponding to machine language instructions, and translated into machine language through the assembler. However, many instructions are required to create even the elementary algorithms since machine languages are too simple. Hence, the majority of software is written

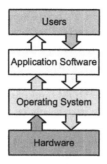

FIGURE 2.13

The diagram of application software, operating system, and hardware.

with high-level programming languages, which are much easier and more efficient for programmers to use, describe, and develop algorithms, since they are much closer than machine languages to natural languages. Then, high-level languages are translated into machine languages using a compiler and an interpreter [22]. The interaction between different software levels and hardware is illustrated in Fig. 2.14.

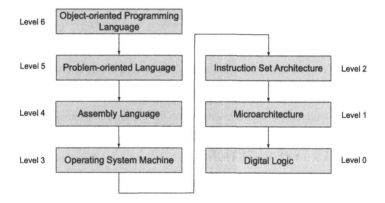

FIGURE 2.14

Multi-level computer systems.

Level 0 is hardware level. Programs in Levels 1, 2, and 3 consist of a series of numbers, which are hard for users to understand and interpret. Level 4 is the assembly language, which is a bit more user-friendly. The instructions at this level become readable and meaningful to users. Level 5 and 6 refer to the majority of software development. For instance, at Level 5, standard programming languages are generally used for development, such as C and C++. At Level 6, object-oriented programming languages become available, such as Java, Python, and .NET.

Firmware refers to a specific class of software that provides the low-level control for the specific hardware in a device. For instance, firmware can provide a standardized operating environment for the device's complex software, or act as the device's operating system that performs control, monitoring, and data manipulation functions. Firmware, such as the basic input-output system (BIOS) of computers, typically contains the basic functions of a device and provides services to higher-level software. Except the simplest, all electronic devices, such as computer systems, computer peripherals, embedded systems, consumer appliances, and Internet-of-thing (IoT) devices, contain firmware. It is stored in nonvolatile memories including ROM, EPROM, and flash memory, and is rarely or never changed after manufacture in contrast to the software. It can only be updated with special installation processes or with administration tools.Therefore, Firmware can be viewed as an intermediate form between hardware and software or a specific class of software embedded in hardware.

Sometimes both software and firmware are needed to be upgraded to correct errors or bugs, add features, or improve the device performance. For example, beta software or beta firmware is an intermediate version, which has not been thoroughly tested. Beta version is far more likely to have bugs than the polished final version since generally bugs or errors can only be manifested by putting the system in the real world.

2.9 EXERCISES

2.9.1 TRUE/FALSE QUESTIONS

1. Hold time is the minimum amount of time that the data input is required to be stable before the rising/falling edge of the clock.
2. Even though ASIC and FPGA have some similar features and are widely used in a variety of applications, they cannot replace each other.
3. Kirchhoff's current law addresses the conservation of charge entering and leaving a circuit node, while Kirchhoff's voltage law addresses the conservation of energy around a closed circuit loop.
4. Firmware can be considered as a specific class of hardware.
5. Resistance can be calculated through the length and the cross-section area of the resistor.

2.9.2 SHORT-ANSWER TYPE QUESTIONS

1. Explain the motivation for developing 3D integrated circuits.
2. Explain the timing constraints in an integrated circuit.
3. Considering a cylindrical resistor of radius 6.0 mm and length 2.0 cm, if the resistivity of the resistor material is 1.8×10^{-6} Ω, calculate the resistance.
4. Explain the similarity between Kirchhoff's Current Law and Kirchhoff's Voltage Law.
5. Explain the difference between ASICs and FPGAs.
6. Explain the interaction between users, application software, and hardware.

2.9.3 LONG-ANSWER TYPE QUESTIONS

1. Find the three currents (I_1, I_2, I_3) and voltages (V_{ab}, V_{bc}, V_{bd}) in the circuit in Fig. 2.15.
2. Describe the typical PCB design flow.
3. Briefly summarize the features of a typical embedded system.
4. Explain the difference and similarity between software and firmware.

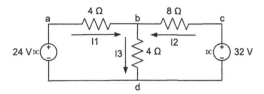

FIGURE 2.15

The circuit for Problem 1.

REFERENCES

[1] D. Harris, S. Harris, Digital Design and Computer Architecture, 2nd edition, Morgan Kaufmann, 2012.

[2] W. Stallings, Computer Organization and Architecture: Designing for Performance, 7th edition, Pearson Education India, 2005.

[3] N.H. Weste, D. Harris, CMOS VLSI Design: A Circuits and Systems Perspective, 4th edition, Pearson Education India, 2010.

[4] G.E. Moore, Cramming more components onto integrated circuits, Electronics Magazine 38 (8) (1965) 114–117.

[5] M.M. Waldrop, More than Moore, Nature 530 (2016) 144–148.

[6] M.M. Ziegler, M.R. Stan, A case for CMOS/nano co-design, in: Proceedings of the 2002 IEEE/ACM International Conference on Computer-Aided Design, ACM, pp. 348–352.

[7] K.K. Likharev, D.B. Strukov, CMOL: devices, circuits, and architectures, in: Introducing Molecular Electronics, Springer, 2006, pp. 447–477.

[8] G.S. Rose, Y. Yao, J.M. Tour, A.C. Cabe, N. Gergel-Hackett, N. Majumdar, J.C. Bean, L.R. Harriott, M.R. Stan, Designing CMOS/molecular memories while considering device parameter variations, ACM Journal on Emerging Technologies in Computing Systems (JETC) 3 (2007) 3.

[9] V. Parihar, R. Singh, K. Poole, Silicon nanoelectronics: 100 nm barriers and potential solutions, in: Advanced Semiconductor Manufacturing Conference and Workshop, 1998. 1998 IEEE/SEMI, IEEE, pp. 427–433.

[10] T. Song, H. Kim, W. Rim, Y. Kim, S. Park, C. Park, M. Hong, G. Yang, J. Do, J. Lim, et al., 12.2 A 7nm FinFET SRAM macro using EUV lithography for peripheral repair analysis, in: Solid-State Circuits Conference (ISSCC), 2017 IEEE International, IEEE, pp. 208–209.

[11] J.H. Lau, T.G. Yue, Thermal management of 3D IC integration with TSV (through silicon via), in: Electronic Components and Technology Conference, 2009. ECTC 2009. 59th, IEEE, pp. 635–640.

[12] K. Tu, Reliability challenges in 3D IC packaging technology, Microelectronics Reliability 51 (2011) 517–523.

[13] M.M. Mano, Digital Logic and Computer Design, Pearson Education India, 2017.

[14] Embedded Systems: Introduction to ARM CORTEX-M Microcontrollers, Volume 1, ISBN 978-1477508992, 2014, http://users.ece.utexas.edu/~valvano/.

[15] C. Alexander, M. Sadiku, Fundamentals of Electric Circuits, 3rd edition, 2006.

[16] J.W. Nilsson, Electric Circuits, Pearson Education India, 2008.

[17] FPGA vs ASIC, what to choose?, anysilicon, https://anysilicon.com/fpga-vs-asic-choose/, Jan. 2016.

[18] R.S. Khandpur, Printed Circuit Boards: Design, Fabrication, Assembly and Testing, Tata McGraw-Hill Education, 2005.

[19] Best practices in printed circuit board design, http://www.ni.com/tutorial/6894/en/#toc6, Aug. 2017.

[20] Embedded system, https://internetofthingsagenda.techtarget.com/definition/embedded-system, Dec. 2016.

[21] E.A. Lee, Embedded Software, Advances in Computers, vol. 56, Elsevier, 2002, pp. 55–95.

[22] A.S. Tanenbaum, Structured Computer Organization, 5th edition, Pearson Prentice Hall, 2006.

SYSTEM ON CHIP (SoC) DESIGN AND TEST

3

CONTENTS

Hardware Security. https://doi.org/10.1016/B978-0-12-812477-2.00008-3

47

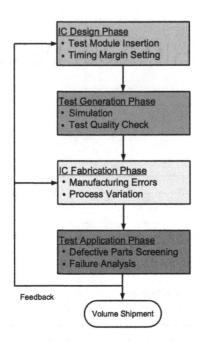

FIGURE 3.1

Simplified IC design, fabrication and test flow.

3.1 INTRODUCTION

As technology feature sizes of devices and interconnects continue to shrink at the rate predicted by Moore's law, gate density and design complexity on integrated circuits (ICs) also continue to increase in recent decades. The nanoscale fabrication process is expected to introduce more manufacturing defects. New failure mechanisms that are not covered by the current fault models are observed in designs fabricated in new technologies with new materials. At the same time, the power and signal integrity issues, which come with scaled supply voltages and higher operating frequencies, increase the number of faults that violate the pre-defined timing margins. As a result, very large scale integration (VLSI) testing has become more and more important and challenging to verify the correctness of design and manufacturing processes. The diagram shown in Fig. 3.1 illustrates a simplified IC production flow. In the design phase, the test modules are inserted in the netlist and synthesized in the layout. Designers set timing margin carefully to account for the difference between simulation and actual operation in the field, such as uncertainties introduced by process variations, temperature variation, power supply noise, and clock jitter. However, due to imperfect design and fabrication processes, there are variations and defects that make the chip violate this timing margin and cause functional failure in the field. Functional bugs, manufacturing errors, and defective packaging process could be the source of these errors. It is thus imperative to screen out the defective chips and prevent shipping them to customers to reduce field returns.

Today, the information collected from testing is used not only to screen defective products from reaching the customers but also to provide feedback to improve the design and manufacturing process (see Fig. 3.1). Therefore, VLSI testing can also improve manufacturing yield level and profitability.

3.1.1 TEST COST AND PRODUCT QUALITY

Although high test quality is preferred, it always comes at the price of high test cost. Trade-offs are necessary to reach the required test quality with minimum cost [1]. In this section, concepts such as test cost, yield, and product quality are introduced. These concepts, when applied to electronic test, lead to economic arguments that justify the need for design-for-testability (DFT) [2].

3.1.1.1 Test Cost

Test cost includes the cost of automatic test equipment (ATE) (initial and running cost), the cost of test development (computer-aided design (CAD) tools, test vector generation, test programming) [3], and the cost of DFT [4]. The scan design techniques can significantly reduce the cost of test generation, and the built-in self-test (BIST) method can lower the complexity and cost of ATE [5].

As shown in Fig. 3.2, the electronic industry tests chips at different levels. Wafer testing is performed during semiconductor device fabrication using ATE. During this step, each device that is present on the wafer is tested for faults—such as stuck-at and transition delay—by applying specifically generated test patterns to it. The wafer is then cut into rectangular blocks, each of which is called a die. Each good die is then packaged, and all packaged devices are tested through final testing again on the same or similar ATE used during wafer testing. After the chips are shipped to the customers, they typically perform PCB testing and system testing (sometime is also called acceptance testing) again because the rule of ten holds according to experience [6]. That is, it is usually ten times more expensive than chip level to repair or replace defective IC at PCB level. After chips are assembled into systems, if a board fault is not caught in PCB testing, it costs ten times as much at the system level than at the board level to find the fault. Since modern systems are much more complex than in 1982 when the empirical rule was first stated in [6], the cost increase is much more than 10 times. For airplanes, a chip fault uncaught in testing can cost thousands or millions times more. Therefore, VLSI testing and use of DFT is essential to reach the goal of high test quality for mission-critical applications, such as automotive, space, and military.

3.1.1.2 Defect, Yield and Defect Level

A manufacturing *defect* is a finite chip area with electrically malfunctioning circuitry caused by errors in the fabrication process. Defect on wafers could be caused by process variations, such as impurities in wafer materials and chemicals, dust particles on masks or in the projection system, mask misalignment, and incorrect temperature control. Typical defects are broken (open) metal wires, missing contacts, bridging between metal lines, missing transistors, incorrect doping levels, void vias, resistive open vias, and many other phenomena that can cause a circuit to fail. In short, a chip with no manufacturing defect is called a good chip. Fraction (or percentage) of good chips produced in a manufacturing process is called *yield*. Yield is commonly denoted by symbol Y in practice. For chip area A, with fault density f, where f is the average number of faults per unit area, fault clustering parameter β, and fault

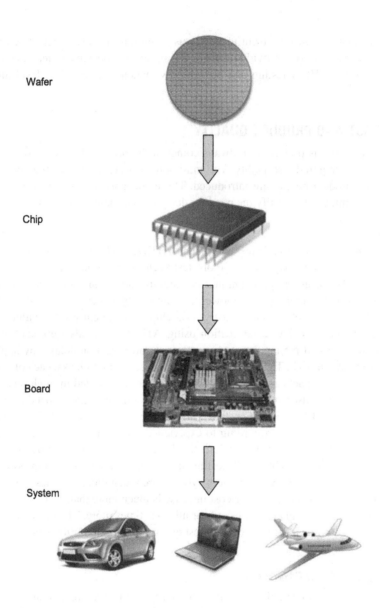

Wafer

Chip

Board

System

FIGURE 3.2

Test levels: wafer, packaged chip, PCB, and system in field.

coverage T, the yield equation [5] is expressed as

$$Y(T) = (1 + \frac{T \cdot A \cdot f}{\beta})^{-\beta}. \tag{3.1}$$

Assuming that tests with 100% fault coverage ($T = 1.0$) remove all faulty chips, the yield $Y(1)$ is

$$Y = Y(1) = (1 + \frac{A \cdot f}{\beta})^{-\beta}. \tag{3.2}$$

Good test process can reject most or all of the defective chips. However, even if it rejects all the faulty chips, it cannot improve the process yield by itself, unless the diagnostic information collected during test is fed back to the design and fabrication process. Briefly, there are two ways of improving the process yield [5]:

- **Diagnosis and repair.** Defective chips are diagnosed and then repaired. Although this will help improve the yield, it increases the cost of manufacturing.
- **Process diagnosis and correction.** By identifying systematic defects and their root cause, the yield can be improved once the cause is eliminated during manufacturing process. Process diagnosis is the preferred method for yield improvement.

A metric used to measure the effectiveness of tests and the manufactured product quality is defect level (DL), which is defined as the ratio of faulty chips among the chips that pass the tests. It is measured as parts per million (ppm). For commercial VLSI chips, a DL greater than 500 ppm is considered unacceptable. For critical applications such as automotive, zero DPPM is sought.

There are two methods for the determination of defect level. One is from the field return data. Chips failing in the field are returned to the manufacturer. The number of returned chips normalized to one million chips shipped is the defect level. The other is using test data. Fault coverage of tests and chip fallout rate are analyzed. A modified yield model is fitted to the fallout data to estimate the defect level, where chip fallout is the fraction of chips failing up to a vector in the test set, which is $1 - Y(T)$.

When chip tests have a fault coverage T, the defect level is given by the following equation [5]:

$$DL(T) = \frac{Y(T) - Y(1)}{Y(T)} = 1 - \frac{Y(1)}{Y(T)} = 1 - (\frac{\beta + T \cdot A \cdot f}{\beta + A \cdot f})^{\beta}, \tag{3.3}$$

where Af is the average number of faults on the chip of area A, and β is the fault clustering parameter; Af and β are determined by test data analysis. This equation represents DL as a fraction that should be multiplied by 10^6 to obtain *ppm*. For zero fault coverage, $DL(0) = 1 - Y(1)$, where $Y(1)$ is the process yield. For a 100% fault coverage, $DL(1) = 0$.

An alternative equation relating defect level, yield, and fault-coverage, in case of unclustered random defects is [7]

$$DL(T) = 1 - Y^{1-T}, \tag{3.4}$$

where T is the fault coverage of tests, and Y is the yield.

3.1.2 TEST GENERATION

3.1.2.1 Structural Test vs. Functional Test

In the past, functional patterns were used to verify if there were any errors at the output of a manufactured IC. A complete functional test will check each entry of the truth table. This may be possible with small input numbers for smaller circuits. However, as the exhaustive testing of all possible input

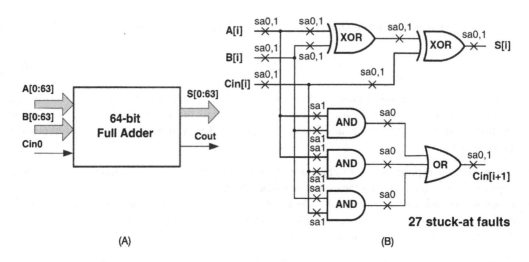

(A)   (B)

FIGURE 3.3

A 64-bit ripple-carry adder: (A) functional test; (B) structural stuck-at fault test.

combinations grows exponentially as the number of inputs and circuit size increase, such a test will be simply too long and impossible for real circuits with several hundred inputs. Eldred derived tests that would observe the state of internal signals at primary outputs of a large digital system in 1959 [8]. Such tests are called structural tests because they depend on the specific structural aspects, such as gate type, interconnect, and netlist of the circuit under test [5]. Structural test has become more attractive over the past two decades because of the controllable testing time and much lowered test cost.

Structural testing is considered a white-box testing because the knowledge of the internal logic of a system is used for test generation. It makes no direct attempt to determine if the overall functionality of the circuit is correct. Instead, it checks whether the circuit has been assembled correctly from low-level circuit elements as specified in the netlist. The stipulation is that, if the circuit elements are confirmed to be assembled correctly, then the circuit should be functioning correctly. Functional test attempts to validate that the circuit under test functions according to its functional specification. Hence, it can be viewed as black-box test. Sequential automatic test pattern generation (ATPG) programs generates complete set of tests for circuit input-output combinations to completely exercise the circuit function. Figure 3.3 shows a 64-bit ripple-carry adder and the logic circuit design for one bit slice of the adder. As can be seen from Fig. 3.3A, the adder has 129 inputs and 65 outputs. Therefore, to exhaustively test it using functional patterns, one needs $2^{129} = 6.80 \times 10^{38}$ input patterns, and to verify $2^{65} = 3.69 \times 10^{19}$ output response. Using an ATE with operating frequency of 1 GHz, it would take 2.15×10^{22} years to apply all these patterns to this adder circuit, assuming that the circuit can operate at 1 GHz too. Today, considering that most circuits size is much larger than this rather simple adder, exhaustive functional test is impractical. It is worth mentioning that small number of functional test patterns are found to be useful to screen timing defects in practice. For some applications, such as microprocessors, functional testing still plays a very important role. However, instead, structural tests are quite fast to apply to this 64-bit adder circuit. There are 27 stuck-at faults in total for one bit adder after we discard the equivalent faults in Fig. 3.3B. For a 64-bit adder, there are $27 \times 64 = 1728$ faults. It needs at most

1728 test patterns. Using 1 GHz ATE it takes only 0.000001728 s to apply these patterns. Since this pattern set covers all possible stuck-at faults in this adder, it achieves same fault coverage as the large functional test pattern set.

3.1.2.2 Fault Models

The following terminologies are commonly used to describe the incorrectness of semiconductor chips:

- **Defect:** A defect in an electronic system is the unintended difference between the implemented hardware and its intended design. Typical defects in VLSI chips are process defects, material defects, aging defects, and package defects.
- **Error:** A wrong output signal produced by a defective system is called an error. An error is an effect whose cause is some "defect."
- **Fault:** A representation of a "defect" at the abstracted function level is called a fault.

Fault model is a mathematical description of how a defect alters design behavior. A fault is said to be detected by a test pattern if, when applying the pattern to the design, any logic value observed at one or more of the circuit's primary outputs differs between the original design and the design with the fault. There are several fault models developed to describe different kinds of physical defects. The most common fault models for modern VLSI test include stuck-at fault, bridging fault, delay faults (transition delay fault and path delay fault), stuck-open faults, and stuck-short faults.

- **Stuck-at faults:** A signal, which is an input or an output of a logic gate or flip-flop is stuck at 0 or 1 value, independent of the inputs to the circuit. Single stuck-at fault is widely used, that is, two faults per line, stuck-at-1 (sa1), and stuck-at-0 (sa0). An example of stuck-at fault in a circuit is shown in Fig. 3.3.
- **Bridging faults:** Two signals are connected together when they should not be. Depending on the logic circuitry employed, this may result in a wired-OR or wired-AND logic function. As there are $O(n^2)$ potential bridging faults, they are normally restricted to signals that are physically adjacent in the design. Sketches of seven typical types of bridging faults are shown in Fig. 3.4. These types are derived from design rule check (DRC), design for manufacturability (DFM) rules, and known bridge between layout features [9]:
  - Type 1: Side-to-Side
  - Type 2: Corner-to-Corner
  - Type 3: Via-to-Via
  - Type 4: End-of-Line
  - Type 5: Side-to-Side Over Wide Metal
  - Type 6: Via Corner to Via Corner
  - Type 7: Side-to-Side with Minimum Width
- **Delay faults:** These faults make the signal propagate slower than normal, and cause the combinational delay of a circuit to exceed clock period. Specific delay faults are: transition delay faults (TDF), path delay faults (PDF), gate delay faults, line delay faults, and segment delay faults. Among them, slow-to-rise and slow-to-fall PDF and TDF are the most commonly used ones. Path delay fault model targets the cumulative delay through the entire list of gates in a path, whereas the transition fault model targets each gate output in the design.

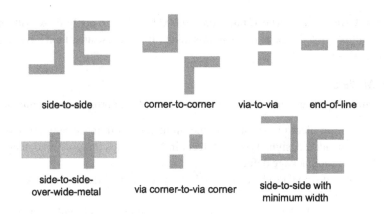

side-to-side   corner-to-corner   via-to-via   end-of-line

side-to-side-
over-wide-metal   via corner-to-via corner   side-to-side with
minimum width

FIGURE 3.4

Seven types of bridging faults.

- **Stuck-open and Stuck-short faults:** A MOS transistor is considered as an ideal switch. Stuck-open and stuck-short faults model the switch being permanently in either the open or the short state. They assume only one transistor is in stuck-open or stuck-short mode. The effect of a stuck-open fault is a floating state at the output of the faulty logic gate. It can be detected in the similar way as detecting a stuck-at fault at the output fault on the gate's output pin. The effect of stuck-short fault is that it short-connects power line and ground line. Measuring quiescent current (IDDQ) can be used to detect such faults and applied as one effective solution.

3.1.2.3 Testability: Controllability and Observability

Testability is represented by *controllability* and *observability* measures that approximately quantify how hard it is to set and observe internal signals of a circuit. Controllability is defined as the difficulty of setting a particular logic signal to a 0 or a 1. Observability is defined as the difficulty of observing the state of a logic signal. Testability analysis can be used for analyzing the difficulty of testing internal circuit parts and—based on it—to redesign or add special test hardware (test point) in the circuit to improve its testability. It can also be used as guidance for algorithms computing test patterns to avoid using hard-to-control lines. Test generation algorithms using heuristics usually apply some kind of testability measures to their heuristic operations, which greatly speed up the test generation process. Through testability analysis, estimation of fault coverage, number of untestable faults and test vector length is also possible.

Testability analysis involves circuit topological analysis without test vectors and search algorithm; it has linear complexity. Sandia controllability observability analysis program (SCOAP) is a systematic, efficient algorithm, proposed by Goldstein [10] and widely used to compute controllability and observability measures. It consists of six numerical measures for each signal (l) in the circuit. Three combinational measures are:

- **CC0(l):** combinational 0-controllability; it represents the difficulty of setting a circuit line to logic 0.
- **CC1(l):** combinational 1-controllability; it represents the difficulty of setting a circuit line to logic 1.
- **CO(l):** combinational observability; it describes the difficulty of observing a circuit line.

Similarly, there are three sequential measures: SC0(l) as sequential 0-controllability, SC1(l) as sequential 1-controllability, and SO(l) as sequential observability. Generally, the three combinational measures are related to the number of signals that may be manipulated to control or observe signal l. The three sequential measures are related to the number of timeframes (or clock cycles) needed to control or observe [5]. The controllability range is between 1 and infinity (∞), and observability range is from 0 to ∞. The higher the measure is, the more difficult it will be to control or observe that line.

According to Goldstein's method in [10], the method to compute combinational and sequential measures is described as below:

- For all primary inputs (PIs) I, set CC0(I) = CC1(I) = 1 and SC0(I) = SC1(I) = 0; for all other nodes N, set CC0(N) = CC1(N) = SC0(N) = SC1(N) = ∞.
- Starting from PIs to primary outputs (POs), use the CC0, CC1, SC0, and SC1 equations, to map logic gate and flip-flop input controllabilities into output controllabilities. Iterate until the controllability numbers stabilize in feedback loops.
- For all POs U, set CO(U) = SO(U) = 0; for all other nodes N, set CO(N) = SO(N) = ∞. Working from POs to PIs, use the CO and SO equations and the pre-computed controllabilities to map output node observabilities of gates and flip-flops into input observabilities. For fanout stems Z with branches Z1, ..., ZN, SO(Z) = min(SO(Z1), ..., SO(ZN)) and CO(Z) = min(CO(Z1), ..., CO(ZN)).
- If any node remains with CC0/SC0 = ∞, then that node is 0-uncontrollable. If any node remains with CC1/SC1 = ∞, then that node is 1-uncontrollable. If any node remains with CO = ∞ or SO = ∞, then that node is unobservable. These are sufficient but not necessary conditions.

When computing controllability for single logic gate, if a logic gate output is produced by setting only one input to a controlling value, then

$$output\ controllability = min(input\ controllabilities) + 1. \tag{3.5}$$

If a logic gate output can only be produced by setting all inputs to non-controlling value, then

$$output\ controllability = \sum(input\ controllabilities) + 1. \tag{3.6}$$

If an output can be controlled by multiple input sets, such as XOR gate, then

$$output\ controllability = min(controllabilities\ of\ input\ sets) + 1. \tag{3.7}$$

For a logic gate with an input signal that needs to be observed,

$$input\ observability = output\ observability$$
$$+ \sum(controllabilities\ of\ setting\ all\ other\ pins\ to\ noncontrolling\ value) + 1. \tag{3.8}$$

Figure 3.5 presents examples of SCOAP controllability and observability calculation using AND, OR, and XOR gates.

Figure 3.6 shows a resettable negative-edge triggered D flip-flop (DFF). The combinational controllabilities CC1 or CC0 measures how many lines in the circuit must be set to make DFF output signal Q

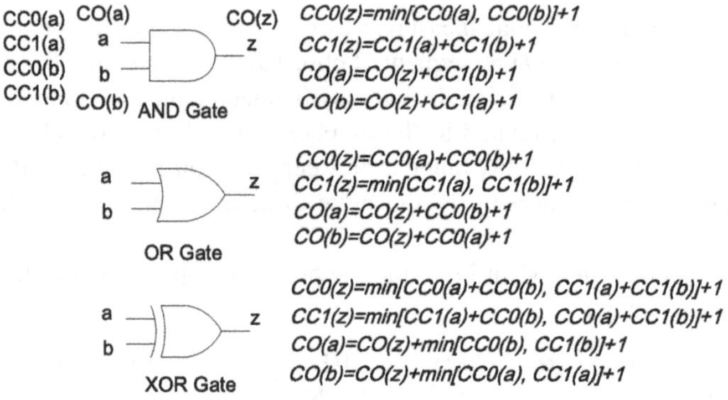

CC0(a) CO(a)
CC1(a) a
CC0(b) b
CC1(b) CO(b)
AND Gate
CO(z) z
CC0(z)=min[CC0(a), CC0(b)]+1
CC1(z)=CC1(a)+CC1(b)+1
CO(a)=CO(z)+CC1(b)+1
CO(b)=CO(z)+CC1(a)+1
a b z
OR Gate
CC0(z)=CC0(a)+CC0(b)+1
CC1(z)=min[CC1(a), CC1(b)]+1
CO(a)=CO(z)+CC0(b)+1
CO(b)=CO(z)+CC0(a)+1
a b z
XOR Gate
CC0(z)=min[CC0(a)+CC0(b), CC1(a)+CC1(b)]+1
CC1(z)=min[CC1(a)+CC0(b), CC0(a)+CC1(b)]+1
CO(a)=CO(z)+min[CC0(b), CC1(b)]+1
CO(b)=CO(z)+min[CC0(a), CC1(a)]+1

FIGURE 3.5

SCOAP controllability and observability calculation.

RS
D
C
DFF
Q
QN

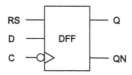

FIGURE 3.6

Resettable, negative-edge-trigged D flip-flop.

as 1 or 0, whereas sequential controllabilities SC1 or SC0 measures how many flip-flops in the circuit must be clocked to set Q to 1 or 0. To control Q line to 1, one must set input D to 1 and force a falling clock edge on C, and the reset signal line RS needs to keep as 0. Note that one needs to add 1 for the sequential measures when signals propagate from flip-flop inputs to output. Thus, CC1(Q) and SC1(Q) are calculated in the following way:

$$\begin{aligned} CC1(Q) &= CC1(D) + CC1(C) + CC0(C) + CC0(RS), \\ SC1(Q) &= SC1(D) + SC1(C) + SC0(C) + SC0(RS) + 1. \end{aligned} \tag{3.9}$$

There are two ways to set Q to 0; either through setting reset signal RS while holding clock C at 0, or clock a 0 through input D. Thus, CC0(Q) and SC0(Q) are calculated using the following equations:

$$\begin{aligned} CC0(Q) &= \min[CC1(RS) + CC0(C), CC0(D) + CC1(C) + CC0(C) + CC0(RS)], \\ SC0(Q) &= \min[SC1(RS) + SC0(C), SC0(D) + SC1(C) + SC0(C) + SC0(RS)] + 1. \end{aligned} \tag{3.10}$$

The input D can be observed at Q by holding RS low and generating a failing edge on the clock line C:

$$\begin{aligned} CO(D) &= CO(Q) + CC1(C) + CC0(C) + CC0(RS), \\ SO(D) &= SO(Q) + SC1(C) + SC0(C) + SC0(RS) + 1. \end{aligned} \tag{3.11}$$

RS can be observed by setting Q to a 1 and using RS:

$$CO(RS) = CO(Q) + CC1(Q) + CC1(C) + CC0(C) + CC1(RS),$$
$$SO(RS) = SO(Q) + SC1(Q) + SC1(C) + SC0(C) + SC1(RS) + 1. \tag{3.12}$$

There are two ways to indirectly observe the clock line C: (1) set Q to a 1 and clock to a 0 from D, or (2) reset the flip-flop and clock to a 1 from D. Thus,

$$CO(C) = \min[CO(Q) + CC0(RS) + CC1(C) + CC0(C) + CC0(D) + CC1(Q),$$
$$CO(Q) + CC1(RS) + CC1(C) + CC0(C) + CC1(D)]$$
$$SO(C) = \min[SO(Q) + SC0(RS) + SC1(C) + SC0(C) + SC0(D) + SC1(Q),$$
$$SO(Q) + SC1(RS) + SC1(C) + SC0(C) + SC1(D)] + 1. \tag{3.13}$$

It is worth noting that if scan design is adopted, scan cells are controllable and observable points for testability analysis. Furthermore, controllability and observability measurement based on SCOAP provides the estimate for the testability of a circuit, which is used to guide test generation and testability improvement [11].

3.1.2.4 Automatic Test Pattern Generation (ATPG)

ATPG is an electronic design automation (EDA) method used to find an input (or test) sequence that, when applied to a digital circuit, enables testers to distinguish between the correct circuit behavior and the faulty circuit behavior caused by defects. These algorithms usually operate with a fault generator program, which creates the minimal collapsed fault list, so that the designer needs not be concerned with fault generation [5]. Controllability and observability measures are used in all major ATPG algorithms. The effectiveness of ATPG is measured by the amount of modeled defects, or fault models, that are detected and the number of generated patterns. These metrics generally indicate test quality (higher with more fault detection) and test application time (higher with more patterns). ATPG efficiency is another important consideration. It is influenced by the fault model under consideration, the type of circuit under test (combinational, synchronous sequential, or asynchronous sequential), the level of abstraction used to represent the circuit under test (register, gate, transistor), and the required test quality [12].

Today, because of the very large circuits' size and shortened time-to-market requirement, all the ATPG algorithms are performed by commercially available EDA tools. Figure 3.7 illustrates the basic ATPG running flow. The tool first reads in the design netlist and library models, then, after building the model, it checks test design rules that are specified in the test protocol file. If any violations occur in this step, the tool reports the violation rule as warning or errors, depending on the severity. Using the ATPG constraints specified by the users, the tool performs ATPG analysis and generates test pattern set. If the test coverage meets the users' needs, test patterns are saved in files with a specific format. Otherwise, the users can modify the ATPG settings and constraints, and rerun ATPG.

It is worth noting that there are two coverage metrics: *test coverage* and *fault coverage*. Test Coverage is the percentage of detected faults among those detectable and gives the most meaningful measure of test pattern quality. Fault Coverage is the percent detected of all faults. It gives no indication of undetectable faults. Usually, test coverage is used in practice as an effectiveness measure of the test patterns generated by the ATPG tool.

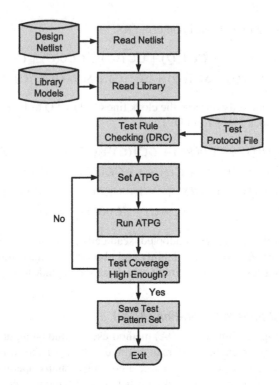

FIGURE 3.7

Basic ATPG flow.

3.2 THE IP-BASED SoC LIFE-CYCLE

SoC is an integrated circuit with all the necessary components for a given system. SoC typically includes analog, digital, and mixed-signal intellectual property (IP) cores. As an evolution of ASIC methodology, it is widely used in various applications due to its high functional density and low power consumption.

Over the past two decades, IP reuse has been extensively studied and developed in industry. IP reuse refers to the inclusion of previously designed and tested components. Since the reused IP has already been designed, verified, and tested, integrators/IP users can reuse the component in a variety of applications. More importantly, IP reuse makes it much cheaper and faster to design and develop a product. Therefore, it becomes a powerful engine to develop modern SoCs in industry to outpace the competition in performance, cost, and time-to-market.

The IP-based SoC life cycle, as shown in Fig. 3.8, refers to the process of design, fabrication, assembly, distribution, usage in the system, and finally end of life. Each step is discussed below in more detail [13]:

Design: Typically, the SoC design cycle involves the following stages. First, design specification is created by a SoC integrator, then the integrator identifies a list of IPs to implement the given specification. Next, all the IP cores, either developed in-house or procured from third party IP vendors, are

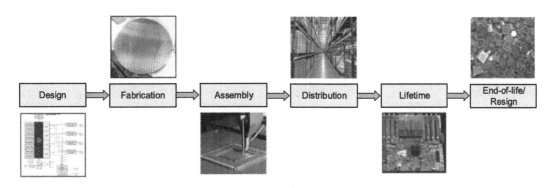

FIGURE 3.8

The IP-based SoC life cycle.

integrated to generate the register transfer level (RTL) SoC design. Following this, the SoC integrator synthesizes the RTL design to a gate-level netlist based on the target technology node. The DFT structures are also inserted to enhance the SoC testability. Then, the netlist is translated into physical layout based on the physical library. Once the timing and power closure is achieved, the final layout in GDSII format is generated. Finally, the chip is sent to foundry for fabrication and test.

The design of today's complex integrated circuits has evolved to a stage, where it is extremely challenging to complete the entire design in-house. In fact, it is common to see the design flow from RTL to GDSII being performed in many different places (even in different countries or continents), mainly to reduce the development cost and time-to-market. Today, design reuse has become an integral part of SoC design. Hard IPs, firm IPs, and soft IPs can be used for this purpose.

Fabrication: Semiconductor device fabrication is the process to make the integrated circuits. The circuits are progressively generated on a wafer made of pure semiconductor materials. The steps for creating the circuits include a sequence of photo lithographic and chemical processing. After that, the manufacturing test is performed to screen out the defective chips and prevent shipping them to next stage.

Today's integrated circuits are manufactured in fabrication facilities (fabs) located all around the world primarily to reduce the manufacturing cost. The design house contracts a foundry to fabricate their designs, discloses the details of their IPs, and also pays for mask-building costs based on their designs. The contract agreement between the foundry and design house is protected by IP rights [14].

Assembly: After fabrication, the foundry sends tested wafers to assembly to cut them into dies. To be specific, here the integrated circuit packaging is called assembly, in which the dies are encapsulated to provide electrical connections, to protect the chip from physical damage and corrosion, and to provide thermal path for dissipating the heat of the chip. Then, assembly performs final tests for those packaged dies before volume shipment.

Distribution: The tested ICs are sent either to the distributors or system integrators (that is, original equipment manufacturers).

System Integration/Lifetime: System integration is the process of assembling together all the components and subsystems into one system to enable them cooperate and act as a whole system.

End-of-life/Resign: When electronics age or become outdated, they are typically retired/resigned and subsequently replaced. Proper disposal techniques are highly advised to extract precious metals and to prevent hazardous materials, such as lead, chromium, and mercury from harming the environment [15].

3.3 SoC DESIGN FLOW

An SoC design flow is illustrated in Fig. 3.9. In Step 1, the design specification is formulated by a SoC integrator, then the integrator identifies a list of IPs to implement the given specification. These IP

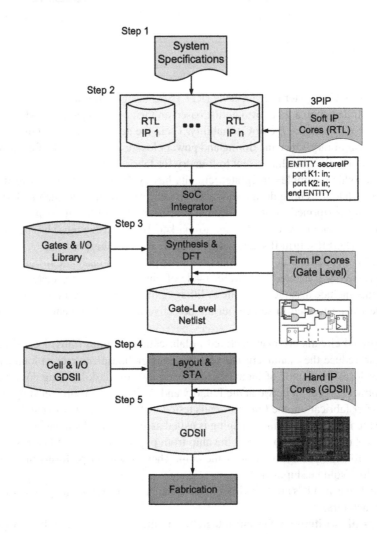

FIGURE 3.9

SoC design flow.

cores are either developed in-house or purchased from third party IP (3PIP) vendors. The 3PIP cores can be procured from the vendors in one of the following three ways [16]:

- Soft IP cores are delivered as synthesizable register transfer level (RTL) hardware description language (HDL);
- Hard IP cores are delivered as GDSII representations of a fully placed and routed core design;
- Firm IP cores are optimized in structure and topology for performance and area, possibly using a generic library.

In Step 2, after developing/procuring all the soft IPs, the SoC design house integrates them to generate the RTL description of the whole system.

In Step 3, the SoC integrator synthesizes the RTL description into a gate-level netlist, based on the logic cells and I/Os of a target technology library. Then, the integrator may integrate gate-level IP cores from a vendor into the netlist. Furthermore, design-for-test (DFT) structures are inserted into the netlist to improve testability.

In Step 4, the gate-level netlist is translated into a physical layout based on logic cells and I/O geometries. It is also possible to import IP cores from vendors in GDSII layout file format at this step.

In Step 5, once static timing analysis (STA) and power closure are complete, developers generate the final layout in GDSII format, and send it out for fabrication.

In Step 6, the chip is fabricated and tested in the foundry/assembly.

3.4 SoC VERIFICATION FLOW

With the increasing complexity and functional density in a single SoC, chip verification becomes more challenging and critical. Verification, also known as pre-silicon validation, mainly refers to the process to ensure the functional correctness and correct transformation from design specifications to the netlist before tape-out, which is shown in Fig. 3.10.

Figure 3.11 outlines the SoC verification flow used in industry. This flow [17] starts with the creation of system specification, which—to some extent—determines and drives the verification strategy. Chip verification planning is concurrently considered with the creation of design specification.

In Step 1, all IPs in the system need to be verified before integration into the system. Specifically, an IP is verified by an IP vendor before sending out to an SoC integrator or an IP user. Since IPs can be delivered in different formats from various IP vendors, the integrator is required to reverify the IP through translating design files and test benches to his/her own application environment [18].

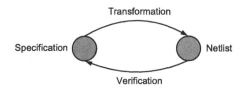

FIGURE 3.10

SoC verification.

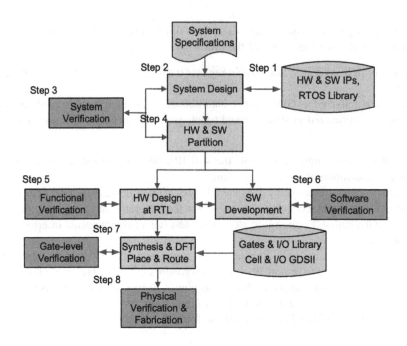

FIGURE 3.11

SoC verification flow.

After individual IP verification, the acquired IP needs to be wrapped with extra logic to communicate with the existing IPs. Then, it is ready to be integrated into the SoC [18].

In Step 2, based on interface protocols, interface verification between blocks in a chip is performed to reduce the final integration efforts, and enable early detection of errors in the system.

In Step 3, SoC level verification is carried out. To be exact, the SoC behavior is modeled based on its specification, and is verified through the behavioral simulation test bench. The test bench could be described using various languages, for example, Verilog/VHDL, C/C++. Furthermore, the test bench is required to be converted to the specified format, which is suitable for both hardware and software verification in the following steps.

In Step 4, once system level verification is complete, the SoC design is partitioned into software and hardware parts based on the software and hardware IP library. Then, the architecture, including software and hardware parts, is verified using the test bench created in the last step.

In Step 5, functional verification is performed on the hardware design at RTL obtained from the last step. Hardware verification uses the test bench created during the process of system behavior verification. Verification at RTL mainly involves line checking, logic simulation, formal verification (that is, equivalence checking and model checking), transaction-based verification, and code coverage analysis.

In Step 6, software verification is carried out based on the system specifications. Software verification and hardware/software (HW/SW) integration can be executed with different methods, including soft prototype, rapid prototype, emulation, and HW/SW co-verification. Take HW/SW co-verification as an example, it is required for SoCs with processor type cores. During this process, HW/SW integration and verification occurs simultaneously. To be specific, co-simulation is performed to couple the current hardware simulators with software emulators/debuggers, which enables the software to be executed on the target hardware design. In turn, the hardware design is provided and stimulated with the actual stimulus. Hence, this co-verification reduces the efforts to create the hardware test bench, and allows earlier hardware and software integration. In addition, it provides a significant performance improvement for system verification.

In Step 7, RTL design is synthesized with the target technology library to generate the gate-level netlist. The netlist is typically verified through formal equivalence checking tool to ensure the RTL design is logically equivalent with the netlist. Since the netlist is usually inserted with DFT components (for example, scan chains) and clock tree in order to meet the testability and the timing requirements, the updated netlist has to be reverified using formal equivalence checking tool to ensure the functional correctness of the updated design. Timing verification is then performed from the gate-level stage to the physical layout stage to avoid any timing violations, thereby to meet timing budget/requirements.

In Step 8, verification is carried out on the integrated circuit physical layout to ensure the design meets certain criteria. It involves design rule check (DRC), layout versus schematic (LVS), electrical rule check (ERC), antenna effect analysis, and signal integrity (SI) analysis, including high current, IR-drop, crosstalk noise, and electromigration. Any violations must be resolved before the chip is manufactured. Once the physical layout verification is complete, the design is ready for sign-off and tape-out.

3.5 SoC TEST FLOW

Compared with SoC verification, SoC test, also known as manufacturing test or production test, is the process to verify whether the design was manufactured correctly. This is mainly due to the fact that the fabrication process is unfortunately imperfect, thus giving rise to defects in chips. It involves different levels of test [19]. The concept comparison between verification and test is shown in Fig. 3.12.

SoC test is the process for screening the manufactured chips; it involves wafer sort, burn-in test, structural test, characterization, and functional test.

The first step during manufacturing test is wafer test. During this step, all dies on the wafer are tested to detect faults through applying test patterns to dies while they are on the wafer. Typically, wafer test employs a wafer prober to supply the necessary electrical excitation to dies on the wafer. It

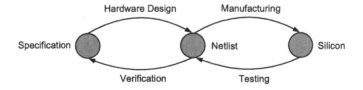

FIGURE 3.12

SoC verification vs. SoC test.

is performed through the application of evaluation methods, including wafer final test (WFT), circuit probe (CP), and electronic die sort (EDS). Once wafer test is complete, it is ready for packaging.

The second step is performed to identify manufacturing defects or faults. This process uses automatic test pattern generation (ATPG) tool to generate test patterns, which enables the test engineer to distinguish between the correct circuit behavior and the faulty circuit behavior. Test equipment such as automatic test equipment (ATE) is utilized to apply test patterns and check responses automatically.

The third step is targeted to characterize and screen chips before shipping to customers. Characterization is the process to find the ideal operating parameters of the chip, such as frequency and voltage. In modern SoCs, high speed I/Os, for example, PCI express, DDR, and Ethernet are also required for characterization through applying various electrical parameters in order to achieve the optimal transmission and error rates.

The fourth step is functional test used to identify functional defects in a chip through applying functional test patterns. Functional test patterns, which run at actual speeds, are utilized to exercise the different parts of the chip to achieve the specified coverage.

The last step is burn-in stress test for the packaged die. It is a temperature/bias reliability stress test used to detect and screen out early life failures.

3.6 DESIGN-FOR-DEBUG

As technology continued to scale further in the last few decades, functional density in a system, either on a single die (as in SoC) or on a single package (system in package (SiP)), has also increased significantly. The number of programmable cores in a system will continue to increase in the foreseeable future [20,21]. Moreover, each core can execute various functions, such as embedded software, hardware accelerators, and dedicated peripheral functions [22], or is integrated with different types of sensors [23].

For a large and complex system, techniques, such as verification, static timing analysis, simulation, and emulation methods cannot guarantee that all errors in hardware and software parts are detected and cleared before the first tape-out [22]. The challenge design and debug engineers face is that some system errors remain undetected until the first silicon is available. These errors typically include—but not limited to—functional errors, timing violations, and design rule check violations.

The reason some errors remain undetected before the first tape-out is that system verification methods in use today can only be applied to the chip model, not to the actual silicon. With the increased complexity of the model, most verification methods are hard to be applied exhaustively due to their computational cost. Therefore, in order to reduce time-to-market and cost, those errors have to be detected as early as possible once the first silicon is available [24]. Hence, design-for-debug (DFD) techniques are required to reduce the time and development cost for locating and fixing those errors, thereby improving the overall system development process.

SoC debug, also referred to as post-silicon validation, happens after the first silicon is available. It is a process to validate all test cases of the silicon/chip for practical deployment and to qualify the design for those test models. During this process, the manufactured design is tested for the functional correctness in a lab setup similar to the deployment in the real application. SoC debug typically involves validating the chip in a system-level environment with software/applications running on the hardware to test all the features and interfaces of the design [19].

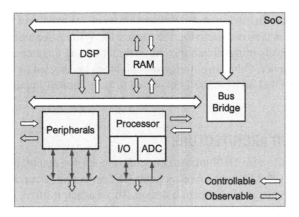

FIGURE 3.13

Debug support for SoC.

Debug support is composed of on-chip DFD architecture and software. As shown in Fig. 3.13, the strategy of implementing debug support is to place access points within a system, hence the controllability and observability of internal signals are available from outside during silicon execution. As chip complexity increases, much attention has been paid to application software besides on-chip debug architecture. The infrastructure provided by debug support forms the basis of development tools and activities such as debuggers, profilers and calibration [25].

3.6.1 DEBUG REQUIREMENTS

System debugging necessitates observing the internal behavior of the chip from outside by applying the appropriate stimuli. Through controlling the system state and repeatedly applying stimuli, a design and debug engineer is able to identify and locate the errors that remained in the system. Following is a list of the fundamental requirements for an effective and efficient debugging system [24,25]:

- External access to the internal system state and critical signals;
- External access to control system operation and facilities, including various peripherals;
- Limited impact on system behavior and overhead in terms of area and number of pins.

External access to the internal system state and critical signals: Debugging an IC requires tracing critical signals of the chip, and extracting the contents of registers and embedded memories, hence, facilitating debug engineers to diagnose and derive the root cause of the chip failure. Due to the large amount of data modern SoCs produce in a few clock cycles, it is unrealistic and unnecessary to trace and collect all that information, especially by a real-time debugging system. Therefore, only the critical signals and the contents of relevant registers and memory arrays are required to be extracted.

External access to control system operation and facilities, including various peripherals: In order to debug the system, an engineer has to control the system operation to create customized triggers and interrupts, and to perform a sequence of operations such as reset, configuration, activation, stop, dumping, single-step, and resume.

Limited impact on system behavior and overhead in terms of area and number of pins: Since debugging infrastructure is aimed at deriving the causes for system execution failure, on-chip DFD architecture needs to be easily plugged into the chip without having a noticeable impact on the chip's external and internal behavior. Otherwise, the errors might go undetected or be manifested in an improper way. In addition, DFD architecture is expected to have limited impact on area overhead and number of pins.

3.6.2 ON-CHIP DEBUG ARCHITECTURE

It is a common practice to reuse DFT infrastructure developed for manufacturing test in integrated circuits for silicon debug [26,27]. As the most popular DFT technique, scan design enables read/write access to all or subset of storage elements in a design. To be exact, it offers direct control of storage elements to a specified value and direct observation of storage elements and, hence the internal states of a circuit. Scan design is realized by replacing flip-flops by scan flip-flops and connecting them to form one or more shift registers in the test mode.

There are three primary advantages to reuse DFT infrastructure for debugging system. First, DFT structure is easily adaptable to various system architectures. Second, since DFT techniques have been well developed and widely practiced over the past few decades, there is limited impact on a design in terms of testability, area overhead, and power consumption, and, hence manufacturing and debug cost. Third, design reuse is essential and critical for modern SoC designs to maintain low cost and reduce time-to-market.

Apart from placing scan chains through critical control paths and data paths to facilitate chip controllability and observability, it is necessary for debug software to interact with on-chip DFD architecture to make debug features available from a workstation. In a nutshell, scan-based on-chip debug architecture, software-based debug support, and run-control features form the foundation of a debugging system.

3.6.3 EXAMPLES OF ON-CHIP DEBUG ARCHITECTURES

A scan design only uses a single scan path to reduce routing overhead, which limits its performance. A generic implementation for on-chip DFD architecture is to multiplex multiple scan chains onto the limited digital pins available for debugging in the application. Thereafter, the critical internal signals can be observed through these pins [24,25].

In [28], besides the scan chains, DFD modules are added into the system to provide silicon debug functionality. Furthermore, debug software is developed and used in design validation phase and silicon validation phase, and interacts with on-chip DFD structure to enable the simulator to communicate with the actual silicon execution.

In [29], the authors developed a debugger tool by leveraging the JTAG boundary scan architecture, which is typically used for testing purpose. They also designed a hardware module for more critical real-time debugging. The boundary scan architecture is responsible for controlling scan chains through JTAG interface and embedded hardware module.

The debugging system [27] developed based on IEEE Standard 1149.1 was successfully used in system debug, test, and manufacturing of Ultra-SPARC-III system. The characteristics for debug and testability were achieved through introducing a few user-defined instructions (example, Shadow and Mask) and extra logic to the chip core, and I/Os (such as, core shadow chain and I/O shadow chain). Based on these features, the critical internal states of the Ultra-SPARC-III can be accessed and controlled during system operation. Furthermore, extra logic was inserted into boundary-scan structure to maintain support for test and debug features. With the combination of shadow chains and on-chip trigger circuits, the captured data can be extracted without interrupting chip operation, thereby addressing the latency and runtime problem caused by pure scan-based control architecture.

At present, besides the infrastructures for tracing signals, dumping storage elements, and triggering customized interrupts, the complexity of SoCs requires standardizing on-chip DFD architecture to enable EDA vendors to create software APIs for accessing and controlling hardware architecture for system-level debug [31]. For example, the facilities provided by ARM Coresight^{TM} architecture [30] is used for tracing, synchronization, time-stamping hardware and software events, the trigger logic, and standardized DFD access and trace transport [31].

3.7 STRUCTURED DFT TECHNIQUES OVERVIEW
3.7.1 DESIGN-FOR-TESTABILITY

DFT techniques are widely used in modern integrated circuits. DFT is a general term applied to design methods that lead to more thorough and less costly testing. In general, DFT is achieved by employing extra hardware circuits for test purpose. The extra test circuits provide improved access to internal circuit elements. Through these test circuits, the local internal state can be controlled and/or observed more easily. It adds more controllability and observability to the internal circuits. DFT plays an important role in the development of test programs and as an interface for test application and diagnostics. With appropriate DFT rules implemented, many system design benefits ensue giving rise to easy detection and location of failures. Generally, integrating DFT in the development cycle can help:

- Improve fault coverage
- Reduce test generation time
- Potentially shorten test length and reduce test memory
- Reduce test application time
- Support hierarchical test
- Realize concurrent engineering
- Reduce life cycle costs

These benefits come at the price of extra cost from pin overhead, more area, and thus low yield, performance degradation, and longer design time. However, DFT reduces the overall costs of the chip, as it is a cost-effective methodology and, hence widely used in IC industry.

Three types of components need test in electronic systems: digital logic, memory blocks, and analog or mix-signal circuits. There are specific DFT methods for each type of components. DFT methods for digital circuits include ad hoc methods and structured methods. Ad hoc DFT method relies on good design experience and experienced designers to find the problem area, such as low coverage area. Sometimes circuit modification or test-point insertion may be required to improve the testability for these areas. The ad hoc DFT techniques are usually too labor-intensive and do not guarantee good results from ATPG. For these reasons, for large circuits it is discouraged to use ad hoc DFT. The common structured methods include: scan, partial scan, BIST, and boundary scan; from among them, BIST is commonly used for memory block testing. The following provides a short introduction to each of these structured DFT techniques.

3.7.2 SCAN DESIGN: SCAN FLIP-FLOP, SCAN CHAIN AND SCAN TEST COMPRESSION

Scan is the most popular DFT technique. Scan design offers simple read/write access to all or subset of storage elements in a design. It also enables direct control of storage elements to an arbitrary value (0 or 1) and direct observation of the states of storage elements and, hence, the internal states of the circuit. In short, it gives the circuit enhanced controllability and observability.

3.7.2.1 Scan Flip-Flop

Scan design is realized by replacing flip-flops by scan flip-flops (SFFs) and connecting them to form one or more shift registers in the test mode. Figure 3.14 illustrates an SFF design based on D-type flip-flop (DFF). A multiplexer is added in front of the DFF to construct a scan D-type flip-flop (SDFF). The test enable (TE) signal controls the working mode of the SDFF. When it is high, it selects the test mode and the scan-in (SI) bits are taken as the input of the DFF. When the TE signal is low, the SDFF works as in functional mode. It acts as a normal DFF and takes value D from the combination circuits as the input to the DFF.

SFF is generally used for clock edge-trigged scan design, whereas level-sensitive scan design (LSSD) cell is used for level-sensitive, latch-based designs. Figure 3.15 shows a polarity-hold shift register latch design that can be used as an LSSD scan cell. The scan cell consists of two latches, a master two-port D-latch L1 and a slave D-latch L2. D is the normal data line and CK is the normal clock line. Line +L1 is the normal output. Lines SI, A, B, and L2 form the shift portion of the latch. SI is the shift data in and +L2 is the shift data out. A and B are the two phase, nonoverlapping shift clocks. The major advantage of using an LSSD scan cell is that it can be used for latch-based design. In addition, it avoids performance degradation introduced by the MUX in shift-register modification. As LSSD scan cells are level-sensitive, designs using LSSD are guaranteed to be race-free. However, this technique requires routing for the additional clocks, which increases routing complexity. It can only be used for slow test application; normal speed testing is impossible.

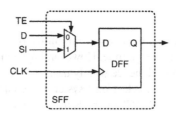

FIGURE 3.14

A scan flip-flop (SFF) constructed with D-type flip-flop and multiplexer.

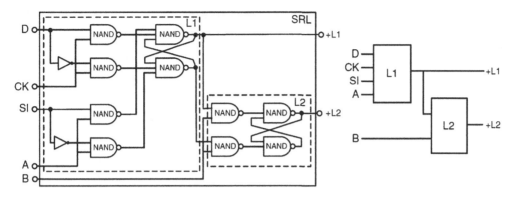

FIGURE 3.15

Level-sensitive scan design (LSSD) cell.

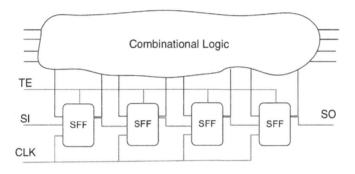

FIGURE 3.16

Scan chain in a design.

3.7.2.2 Scan Chain

Figure 3.16 shows a scan chain in a sequential circuit design. The SFFs are stitched together to form a scan chain. When test enable signal TE is high, the circuit works in test (shift) mode. The inputs from scan-in (SI) are shifted through the scan chain; the scan chain states can be shifted out through scan chain and observed at the scan-out (SO) pin. The test program compares the SO values with expected values to verify the chips performance.

Multiple scan chains are often used to reduce the time to load and observe. SFFs can be distributed among any number of scan chains, each having a separate scan-in (SI) and scan-out (SO) pin. The integrity of scan chains must be tested prior to application of scan test sequences. A shift sequence $00110011\ldots$ of length $n + 4$ in scan mode ($TC = 0$) produces 00, 01, 11, and 10 transitions in all flip-flops and observes the result at scan chain output SO, where n is the number of SFFs in the longest scan chain.

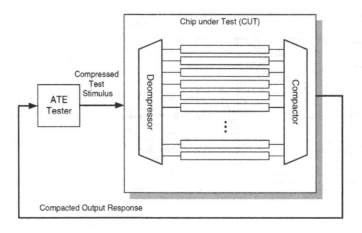

FIGURE 3.17

Scan test compression.

3.7.2.3 Scan Test Compression

As chips become larger and more complex, the growing test-data volume causes a significant increase in test cost because of much longer test time and large tester memory requirements. For a scan-based test, the test data volume is proportional to the number of test cycles, whereas the number of test cycles and test time are related to the number of scan cells, scan chains, and scan patterns as shown in Eq. (3.14). Shift frequency is at a fraction of functional clock frequency (because of high percentage of switching activity). Although, theoretically, increasing shift frequency reduces test time, in practice shift frequency cannot be increased too much due to power dissipation and design constraints.

$$Test\ Cycles \approx \frac{Scan\ Cells \times Scan\ Patterns}{Scan\ Chains},$$

$$Test\ Time \approx \frac{Scan\ Cells \times Scan\ Patterns}{Scan\ Chains \times Shift\ Frequency}. \tag{3.14}$$

As manufacturing test cost depends very strongly on the volume of test data and test time, one of the key requirements is to reduce them dramatically. Test Compression was developed to help address this problem. There are large portion of don't-care bits left when an ATPG tool generates a test for a set of faults. Test compression takes advantage of the small number of significant values to reduce test data and test time. Generally, the idea is to modify the design to increase the number of internal scan chains and shorten maximum scan-chain lengths. As illustrated in Fig. 3.17, these chains are then driven by an on-chip decompressor, usually designed to allow continuous flow decompression, where the internal scan chains are loaded as data are delivered to the decompressor. Many different decompression methods can be used [33]. One common choice is a linear finite state machine, where the compressed stimuli are computed by solving linear equations. For industrial circuits with test vectors' care-bits ratio ranging from 3% to 0.2%, the test compression based on this method often results in compression ratios of 30–500 times [32].

A compactor is required to compact all the internal scan-chain outputs to the output pins. As can be seen from Fig. 3.17, it is inserted between the internal scan-chain outputs and the tester scan channel

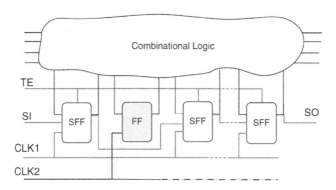

FIGURE 3.18

Partial scan design.

outputs. The compactor must be synchronized with the data decompressor, and must be capable of handling unknown (X) states, which may come from false and multicycle paths, or other unexpected reasons.

3.7.3 PARTIAL SCAN DESIGN

Whereas full scan design replaces all flip-flops with SFFs, partial scan design only selects a subset of flip-flops to be scanned, which provides a wide spectrum of design solutions that tradeoff testability for the overheads (that is, area and power overheads) incurred by the scan design.

Figure 3.18 illustrates the concept of partial scan. Being different from the full scan design shown in Fig. 3.16, not all the flip-flops are SFFs. Two separate clocks are used for scan operation and functional operation.

Selection of flip-flops that can provide the best improvements in testability is a critical part of the partial scan design process. Most SFF selection methods are based on one or several of the following techniques: testability analysis, structural analysis, and test generation [34]. Testability-based methods analyze the testability of the circuit using SCOAP measures and improve the testability by partial scan. However, for circuits with complex structure, the fault coverage achieved may not be adequate using these techniques. Partial scan selection by structural analysis aims to remove all feedback loops from a circuit, and thus simplify the circuit structure for the test generation algorithm. The problem for such techniques is that, for many circuits, it may be infeasible or unnecessary to break all feedback loops to achieve desirable fault coverage. Test generation-based methods exploit information from the test generator to drive the scan selection process. The main advantage of using test generation-based techniques is that it is possible to target specific fault detection objectives rather than simplify the circuit or improve testability of specific regions in the circuit. However, the procedure typically results in expensive computational and storage requirements [34].

As a separate clock is used for the scan operation, the states of the non-SFFs can be frozen during the scan operation and any state can be scanned into the scan register without affecting the states of the non-SFFs. In this way, test vectors can be efficiently generated by a sequential circuit test generator. However, it poses problem in the need for multiple clock trees and tight constraint on clock skew when routing of clock signals.

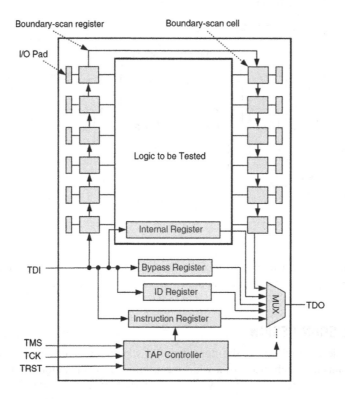

FIGURE 3.19

Boundary scan architecture.

3.7.4 BOUNDARY SCAN

The boundary-scan technique uses a shift-register stage to test factors such as interconnects and clusters of logic and memories. The boundary-scan register consists of boundary scan cells, which are inserted adjacent to each component pin, so that signals at component boundaries can be controlled and observed using scan testing principles. The boundary scan controller has also emerged as the standard mechanism on SoC designs for initiating and controlling the multiple internal memory BIST controllers. Boundary scan is now a well-known and documented IEEE standard, and some test software vendors offer automated solutions. IEEE 1149.1, also known as JTAG or boundary scan, was introduced in 1990 [35]. This standard endeavors to solve test and diagnostic problems arising from loss of physical access caused by the increasing use of high pin count and BGA devices, multi-layer PCBs, and densely packed circuit board assemblies. The standard outlines predefined protocols for testing and diagnosing manufacturing faults. It also provides a means for onboard programming of nonvolatile memory devices such as Flash, or in-system programming of devices like PLDs and CPLDs.

Figure 3.19 illustrates the essential boundary-scan architecture. The block of logic circuits to be tested is connected to multiple boundary-scan cells. The cells are created along with the IC circuitry when the chip is fabricated. Each cell can monitor or stimulate one point in the circuitry. The cells are then connected serially to form a long shift register, whose serial input, designated Test Data Input

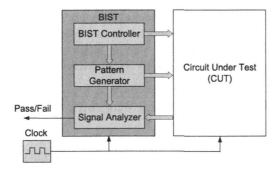

FIGURE 3.20

Built-in self-test architecture.

(TDI), and serial output ports, and designated Test Data Output (TDO) become the basic I/O of a JTAG interface. The shift register is clocked through external clock signal (TCK). In addition to the serial in, serial-out, and clock signals, a Test Mode Select (TMS) input is provided, as well as an optional Test Reset pin (TRST). The TMS, TCK, and TRST signals are applied to a finite state machine called the test access port (TAP) controller. Along with external binary instructions, it controls all of the possible boundary-scan functions. To stimulate the circuit, test bits are shifted in; this is called a test vector.

The primary advantage of boundary-scan technology is the ability to observe and control data independently of the application logic. It also reduces the number of overall test points required for device access, which can help lower board fabrication costs and increase package density. Simple tests using boundary scan on testers can find manufacturing defects, such as unconnected pins, a missing device, and even a failed or dead device. In addition, boundary scan provides better diagnostics. With boundary scan, the boundary-scan cells observe device responses by monitoring the input pins of the device. This enables easy isolation of various classes of test failures. Boundary scan can be used for functional testing and debugging at various levels, from IC tests to board-level tests. The technology is also useful for hardware/software integration testing and provides system-level debug capability [36].

3.7.5 BIST METHODS

Built-in self-test, or BIST, is a DFT methodology involving the insertion of additional hardware and software features into integrated circuits to allow them to perform self-testing, thereby reducing dependence on an external ATE and, thus, reducing testing cost. The BIST concept is applicable to about any kind of circuit. BIST is also a solution to the testing of circuits that have no direct connections to external pins, such as embedded memories used internally by the devices. Figure 3.20 shows BIST architecture. In BIST, a test pattern generator generates test patterns and a signature analyzer (SA) compares test responses. The entire process is controlled by BIST controller.

The two most common categories of BIST are the Logic BIST (LBIST) and the Memory BIST (MBIST). LBIST, which is designed for testing random logic, typically employs a pseudorandom pattern generator to generate input patterns that are applied to the device's internal scan chain, and a multiple input signature register (MISR) for obtaining the response of the device to these input test patterns. An incorrect MISR output indicates a defect in the device. MBIST is used specifically for testing memories. It typically consists of test circuits that apply a collection of write-read-write se-quences for memories. Complex write-read sequences are called algorithms, such as MarchC, Walking 1/0, GalPat, and Butterfly. The cost and benefit models for MBIST and LBIST are presented in [37]. It analyzes the economic effects of built-in self-test for logic and memory cores.

Advantages of implementing BIST include:

- low test cost, since it reduces or eliminates the need for external electrical testing using an ATE
- improved testability and fault coverage
- support of concurrent testing
- shorter test time if the BIST can be designed to test more structures in parallel
- at-speed testing

Disadvantages of implementing BIST include:

- silicon area, pin counts, and power overhead for the BIST circuit
- performance degradation, timing issues
- possible issues with the correctness of BIST results, since the on-chip testing hardware itself can fail

3.8 AT-SPEED DELAY TEST

At-speed delay test is widely used to test timing-related failures. It has become a common practice for modern semiconductor industry to include at-speed test in its test flow. This section briefly introduces the basics of at-speed delay test, including its application, fault models used, test clock configuration, and some challenging issues when applying delay test on nanometer designs.

3.8.1 WHY AT-SPEED DELAY TEST?

As technology scales, feature size of devices and interconnects shrink and silicon chip behavior be-comes more sensitive to on-chip noise, process and environmental variations, and uncertainties. The spectrum of defects now includes more problems, such as high-impedance shorts, in-line resistance, power supply noises, and crosstalk between signals, which are not always detected with the traditional stuck-at fault model. The number of defects that cause timing failure (setup/hold time violation) is on the rise. This leads to increased yield loss and escape, and reduced reliability. Thus, structured delay test, using transition delay fault model and path delay fault model, are widely adopted because of their low implementation cost and high test coverage. Transition fault testing models delay defects, such as large gate delay faults, for detecting timing-related defects. These faults can affect the circuit's per-formance through any sensitized path passing through the fault site. However, there are many paths passing through the fault site, and TDFs are usually detected through the short paths. Small delay defects can only be detected through long paths. Therefore, path delay fault testing for a number of selected critical (long) paths has become a necessity. In addition, small delay defects may escape when testing speed is slower than functional speed. Therefore, at-speed test is preferred to increase the realis-tic delay fault coverage. In [38], it is reported that the defects per million rates are reduced by 30–70% when at-speed testing is added to the traditional stuck-at tests.

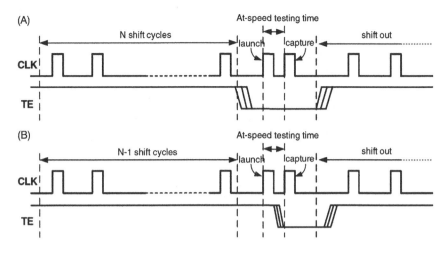

FIGURE 3.21

Clock and Test Enable waveforms for LOC and LOS tests.

3.8.2 BASICS ON AT-SPEED TEST: LAUNCH-OFF-CAPTURE (LOC) AND LAUNCH-OFF-SHIFT (LOS)

The transition fault and path delay fault are the two most widely used fault models for at-speed delay test. Path delay model targets the cumulative delay through the entire list of gates in a predefined path, whereas the transition fault model targets each gate output in the design for a slow-to-rise and slow-to-fall delay fault [5]. The transition fault model is more widely used than path delay because it tests for at-speed failures at all nets in the design, and the total fault list is equal to twice the number of nets. On the other hand, there are billions of paths in a modern design to be tested for path delay fault, leading to high analysis effort. This makes path delay fault model very cost-intensive compared to transition fault model.

Compared to static testing with the stuck-at fault model, testing logic at-speed requires a test pattern with two vectors. The first vector launches a logic transition value along a path, and the second part captures the response at a specified time, determined by the system clock speed. If the captured response indicates that the logic involved did not transition as expected during the cycle time, the path fails the test and is considered to contain a defect.

Scan based at-speed delay testing is implemented using launch-off-capture (LOC) (also referred to as broadside [39]) and Launch-off-shift (LOS) delay tests. LOS tests are generally more effective, achieving higher fault coverage with significantly fewer test vectors, but require a fast scan enable, which is not supported by most designs. For this reason, LOC-based delay test is more attractive and used by more industry designs. Figure 3.21 shows the clock and test enable waveforms for LOC and LOS at-speed delay tests. From this figure, one can see that LOS has a high requirement of TE signal timing. An at-speed test clock is required to deliver timing for at-speed tests. There are two main sources for the at-speed test clocks; one is the external ATE and the other is on-chip clocks. As the clocking speed and accuracy requirements rise, since the complexity and cost of the tester increase, more and more designs include a phase-locked loop or other on-chip clock generating circuitry to

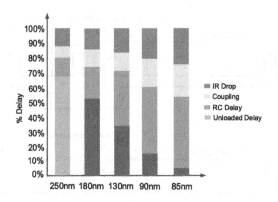

FIGURE 3.22

Parasitic effects with respect to process node.

supply internal clock source. Using these functional clocks for test purposes can provide several advantages over using the ATE clocks. First, test timing is more accurate when the test clocks exactly match the functional clocks. Secondly, the high-speed on-chip clocks reduce the ATE requirements, enabling use of a less expensive tester [38].

3.8.3 AT-SPEED DELAY TEST CHALLENGES

As circuit complexity and functional frequency increase, power integrity and timing integrity are becoming more and more important to circuit design and test. The test power consumption, supply voltage noise, and crosstalk noise caused by signal coupling effect, and hot spots caused by nonuniform on-chip temperature will significantly impact yield and reliability. As shown in Fig. 3.22, with technology node shrinking, the percentage of delay caused by coupling effect between signal lines (crosstalk noise), and IR-drop on power and ground lines (power supply noise), is responsible for a larger portion. Power supply noise and crosstalk noise are becoming two important noises that impact circuit's timing integrity. The lower supply rails in today's ICs mean much less immunity from signal integrity problems that tie directly into power integrity [40]. Supply voltages on many high-end ICs are now down to 1 V and below, leading to decreasing margins for voltage fluctuation. Simultaneous switching noise can cause ground to fluctuate, leading to difficult-to-isolate signal-integrity problems and timing issues. What makes it more challenging is that power, timing, and signal integrity (SI) effects are all interdependent at 90-nm and below.

Timing failures are often the result of a combination of weak points in a design and silicon abnormalities, which reduce the noise immunity of the design and expose it to SI issues. For example, a poor power planning or missing power vias can incur on-chip power droop for some test vectors. The power droop can impact a gate(s) on a critical path and it may cause timing failure. This failure may only be recreated with certain test vectors as inputs. If the corresponding test vector is not included in the test pattern set, the failure becomes an escape and cannot be reproduced during diagnosis with the current test pattern set. Current automatic test pattern generation tools are not aware of the switching distribution on the layout and the pattern-induced noises. There are escapes and "No Problem Found" parts returned by customers, which have passed the tests using the layout-unaware test patterns generated by ATPG tools. Thus, high-quality test patterns are imperative to capture noise-induced delay problems during production test and identify noise-related failures during diagnosis [41,42].

3.9 **EXERCISES**

3.9.1 **TRUE/FALSE QUESTIONS**

1. Full scan design is the only option in terms of scan chain insertion.
2. In terms of controllability and observability provided by test point insertion, control points have no impact on observability, and observation points have no impact on controllability.
3. SoC debug can be considered as pre-silicon validation, while SoC verification can be considered as post-silicon validation.
4. Small delay defects may escape when testing speed is higher than functional speed.
5. LBIST and MBIST are the most two common classifications of BIST.

3.9.2 **SHORT-ANSWER TYPE QUESTIONS**

1. The yield of a manufacturing process is defined as the fraction of acceptable parts among all parts fabricated [5]. If the number of acceptable parts is 5000, and the number of total parts that are fabricated is 7000; calculate the yield.
2. Defect level, also known as reject rate, is defined as the fraction of faulty chips among all chips passing the test, which can be expressed as parts per million (PPM) [5]. If the number of faulty chips passing final test is 10, the total number of chips passing final test is 50,000; calculate the defect level.
3. If each chip has 92% fault coverage and 70% yield, calculate the defect level.
4. List the types of common fault models.
5. What are delay faults? What are the differences between transition delay faults (TDF) and path delay faults (PDF)?
6. Explain ATPG. How can one measure the effectiveness of ATPG?
7. How do you consider that your SoC verification has a good coverage? Explain.
8. Considering an IP core, the first silicon success rate for unverified IP core is 90 percent, whereas the first silicon success rate for verified IP core is 98 percent.
   (a) If a SoC consists of 10 such unverified IP cores, what is the first silicon success rate for the SoC?
   (b) If a SoC consists of 8 such verified IP cores and 2 unverified IP cores, what is the first silicon success rate for the SoC?
   (c) If a SoC consists of 10 such verified IP cores, what should be the success rate for each verified IP core in order to achieve 90 percent of the first silicon success rate for the SoC?
   Note: You do not need to consider the interconnection issues and other IPs within the chip.
9. (a) If a scan-based design has 6400 scan flip-flops that can be constructed as 100 scan chains each with equal length, the number of test patterns is 5000, and testing clock cycle is 10 ns; what would be the test cycle and test time?

(b) What are the main factors impacting manufacturing cost? How can one reduce the manufacturing cost?

10. What are the differences between full scan design and partial scan design?

3.9.3 LONG-ANSWER TYPE QUESTIONS

1. What are the differences between functional test and structural test?

2. (a) When doing manufacturing test for a design, consider the number of detected faults in the design is 81,506, the number of detectable faults in the design is 87,122, and the number of undetectable faults in the design is 103. What are the test coverage and fault coverage, respectively? Round your answer to 2 decimal places.

(b) What types of faults are contained in – detected faults, possibly detected faults, undetectable faults, ATPG untestable faults, and not detected faults?

3. What are the differences between verification, debug, and test for a SoC?

REFERENCES

[1] H.B. Druckerman, M.P. Kusko, S. Pateras, P. Shephard, Cost trade-offs of various design for test techniques, in: Economics of Design, Test, and Manufacturing, 1994. Proceedings, Third International Conference on the IEEE, p. 45.
[2] V.D. Agrawal, A tale of two designs: the cheapest and the most economic, Journal of Electronic Testing 5 (1994) 131–135.
[3] I. Dear, C. Dislis, A.P. Ambler, J. Dick, Economic effects in design and test, IEEE Design & Test of Computers 8 (1991) 64–77.
[4] J. Pittman, W. Bruce, Test logic economic considerations in a commercial VLSI chip environment, in: Proceedings of the 1984 International Test Conference on the Three Faces of Test: Design, Characterization, Production, IEEE Computer Society, pp. 31–39.
[5] M. Bushnell, V. Agrawal, Essentials of Electronic Testing for Digital, Memory and Mixed-Signal VLSI Circuits, vol. 17, Springer Science & Business Media, 2004.
[6] B. Davis, The Economics of Automatic Testing, BookBaby, 2013.
[7] T.W. Williams, N. Brown, Defect level as a function of fault coverage, IEEE Transactions on Computers 30 (1981) 987–988.
[8] R.D. Eldred, Test routines based on symbolic logical statements, Journal of the ACM (JACM) 6 (1959) 33–37.
[9] M. Keim, N. Tamarapalli, H. Tang, M. Sharma, J. Rajski, C. Schuermyer, B. Benware, A rapid yield learning flow based on production integrated layout-aware diagnosis, in: Test Conference, 2006. ITC'06. IEEE International, IEEE, pp. 1–10.
[10] L. Goldstein, Controllability/observability analysis of digital circuits, IEEE Transactions on Circuits and Systems 26 (1979) 685–693.
[11] L.-T. Wang, C.-W. Wu, X. Wen, VLSI Test Principles and Architectures: Design for Testability, Academic Press, 2006.
[12] L. Lavagno, G. Martin, L. Scheffer, Electronic Design Automation for Integrated Circuits Handbook-2 Volume Set, CRC Press, Inc., 2006.
[13] U. Guin, D. Forte, M. Tehranipoor, Anti-counterfeit techniques: from design to resign, in: Microprocessor Test and Verification (MTV), 2013 14th International Workshop on, IEEE, pp. 89–94.
[14] T. Force, High performance microchip supply, Annual Report, Defense Technical Information Center (DTIC), USA, 2005.
[15] H. Levin, Electronic waste (e-waste) recycling and disposal-facts, statistics & solutions, Money Crashers (2011), https://www.moneycrashers.com/electronic-e-waste-recycling-disposal-facts/.
[16] V. Alliance, VSI alliance architecture document: Version 1.0, VSI Alliance, vol. 1, 1997.
[17] P. Rashinkar, P. Paterson, L. Singh, System-on-a-Chip Verification: Methodology and Techniques, Springer Science & Business Media, 2007.
[18] F. Nekoogar, From ASICs to SOCs: A Practical Approach, Prentice Hall Professional, 2003.
[19] Verification, validation, testing of asic/soc designs – what are the differences, anysilicon, http://anysilicon.com/verification-validation-testing-asicsoc-designs-differences/, 2016.

[20] D. Patterson, et al., The parallel computing landscape: a Berkeley view, in: International Symposium on Low Power Electronics and Design: Proceedings of the 2007 International Symposium on Low Power Electronics and Design, vol. 27, pp. 231.

[21] D. Yeh, L.-S. Peh, S. Borkar, J. Darringer, A. Agarwal, W.-M. Hwu, Roundtable-thousand-core chips, IEEE Design & Test of Computers 25 (2008) 272.

[22] B. Vermeulen, Design-for-debug to address next-generation SoC debug concerns, in: Test Conference, 2007. ITC 2007. IEEE International, IEEE, pp. 1.

[23] M.T. He, M. Tehranipoor, Sam: A comprehensive mechanism for accessing embedded sensors in modern SoCs, in: Defect and Fault Tolerance in VLSI and Nanotechnology Systems (DFT), 2014 IEEE International Symposium on, IEEE, pp. 240–245.

[24] B. Vermeulen, S.K. Goel, Design for debug: catching design errors in digital chips, IEEE Design & Test 19 (2002) 37–45.

[25] A.B. Hopkins, K.D. McDonald-Maier, Debug support for complex systems on-chip: a review, IEE Proceedings, Computers and Digital Techniques 153 (2006) 197–207.

[26] Y. Zorian, E.J. Marinissen, S. Dey, Testing embedded-core based system chips, in: Test Conference, 1998. Proceedings. International, IEEE, pp. 130–143.

[27] F. Golshan, Test and on-line debug capabilities of IEEE Standard 1149.1 in UltraSPARC/sup TM/-III microprocessor, in: Test Conference, 2000. Proceedings. International, IEEE, pp. 141–150.

[28] G.-J. Van Rootselaar, B. Vermeulen, Silicon debug: scan chains alone are not enough, in: Test Conference, 1999. Proceedings. International, IEEE, pp. 892–902.

[29] D.-Y. Jung, S.-H. Kwak, M.-K. Lee, Reusable embedded debugger for 32-bit RISC processor using the JTAG boundary scan architecture, in: ASIC, 2002. Proceedings. 2002 IEEE Asia-Pacific Conference on, IEEE, pp. 209–212.

[30] Coresight on-chip trace and debug architecture, http://infocenter.arm.com/help/index.jsp?topic=/com.arm.doc.set.coresight/index.html, 2010.

[31] A. Basak, S. Bhunia, S. Ray, Exploiting design-for-debug for flexible SoC security architecture, in: Design Automation Conference (DAC), 2016 53nd ACM/EDAC/IEEE, IEEE, pp. 1–6.

[32] J. Rajski, J. Tyszer, M. Kassab, N. Mukherjee, Embedded deterministic test, IEEE Transactions on Computer-Aided Design of Integrated Circuits and Systems 23 (2004) 776–792.

[33] N.A. Touba, Survey of test vector compression techniques, IEEE Design & Test of Computers 23 (2006) 294–303.

[34] V. Boppana, W.K. Fuchs, Partial scan design based on state transition modeling, in: Test Conference, 1996. Proceedings. International, IEEE, pp. 538–547.

[35] C. Maunder, Standard test access port and boundary-scan architecture, IEEE Std 1149.1-1993a, 1993.

[36] R. Oshana, Introduction to JTAG, Embedded Systems Programming, 2002.

[37] J.-M. Lu, C.-W. Wu, Cost and benefit models for logic and memory BIST, in: Design, Automation and Test in Europe Conference and Exhibition 2000. Proceedings, IEEE, pp. 710–714.

[38] B. Swanson, M. Lange, At-speed testing made easy, EE Times 3 (2004), http://www.eedesign.com/article/showArticle.jhtml?articleId=21401421.

[39] J. Savir, S. Patil, Broad-side delay test, IEEE Transactions on Computer-Aided Design of Integrated Circuits and Systems 13 (1994) 1057–1064.

[40] D. Maliniak, Power integrity comes home to roost at 90 nm, EE Times 3 (2005).

[41] J. Ma, J. Lee, M. Tehranipoor, Layout-aware pattern generation for maximizing supply noise effects on critical paths, in: VLSI Test Symposium, 2009. VTS'09. 27th IEEE, IEEE, pp. 221–226.

[42] J. Ma, N. Ahmed, M. Tehranipoor, Low-cost diagnostic pattern generation and evaluation procedures for noise-related failures, in: VLSI Test Symposium (VTS), 2011 IEEE 29th, IEEE, pp. 309–314.

PRINTED CIRCUIT BOARD (PCB): DESIGN AND TEST

4

CONTENTS

Hardware Security. https://doi.org/10.1016/B978-0-12-812477-2.00009-5

4.1 INTRODUCTION

Printed Circuit Boards (PCBs) can be defined as rugged nonconductive boards built on substrate-based structure as shown in Fig. 4.1. The PCBs are mainly used to provide electrical connection and mechanical support to the electrical components of a circuit. They are prevalent in electronic devices and can be easily identified as the green-colored board in most cases. Based on the design specifications and requirements, many active (for example, operational amplifiers and batteries) and passive components (such as inductors, resistors, and capacitors) are mounted on the PCBs to match the form factor of the final design. Form factor can be defined as a feature of any hardware design that specifies the size, shape, and other relevant physical properties of the PCB in its entirety. While determining a form factor of a PCB design, aspects such as chassis, mounting schemes, and board configurations are taken into consideration. The connection among the components on a PCB are established with copper interconnects (routes), which act as the pathway for the electrical signals.

An Austrian engineer named Paul Eisler was the first to develop PCBs during the time of World War II. His patented methodologies for PCB etching process, various mechanisms of interconnect routing, and employment of electrical conduit in the boards are put to practice for decades [6]. Since its first development, PCB designs have significantly evolved over time. Modern-day PCBs largely vary in complexity, starting from single layer PCBs to complex designs with as many as 20 to 30 layers with hidden vias and embedded components [18]. PCB vias can be defined as vertical interconnect accesses for establishing the electrical connection through one or more adjacent layers of the circuit board.

PCBs play a vital role in area, power, performance, reliability, and security of a computing system. The PCB design and test process should consider these parameters. This chapter provides an overview of the PCBs with a highlight on current practices of design and test. It discusses the electrical com-

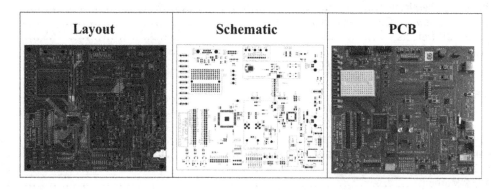

FIGURE 4.1

Modern PCBs are very complex with multiple layers and several components arranged in a compact manner to minimize the overall size. A modern PCB in different forms, such as layout, schematic, and its final output is shown in this figure.

ponents used in a PCB and different types of boards available. It also presents a brief history of PCB evolution highlighting the changes in PCB design with technological progress. The complete life cycle of modern PCB design is also depicted in the chapter with an illustrative description of the steps and parties involved in these steps.

4.2 EVOLUTION OF PCB AND COMPONENTS

The first patent for PCB was documented under the title "Printed Wire", and it can be traced back to early 1900s. In 1925, Charles Ducas filed the patent for printed wire technique to develop an electrical path on the surface of an insulated material. The concept was revolutionary as it demonstrated an efficient way of designing electric circuits without the complexity of vigorous wiring. Consequently, the design tremendously improved the overhead and performance results of conventional circuits. However, it was in 1943, when the first PCB came into production. Dr. Paul Eisler from Austria pioneered the development of the first operational PCB after World War II [6,24]. A short timeline of PCB evolution is given in the following subsections.

4.2.1 TIMELINE OF PCBs

Before the full-fledged production of PCBs in the electronics industry, the common norm was to implement point-to-point connections. The major drawbacks of this practice involved developing large sockets that required regular maintenance and replacement. Moreover, these components made the designs bulky and often led to design flaws. However, it was possible to address these issues by integrating the components on a PCB that could drastically improve the area, power, and performance. The major milestones for PCB design are described below (Fig. 4.2).

1920s: In the 1920s, commonly referred to as the roaring twenties, the material for PCBs varied significantly, ranging from Bakelite and Masonite to pieces of plain and thin wood. The practice was to drill holes in the board material and insert flat brass wires in the holes for completing the path of the circuit. Despite the lack of efficiency or craftsmanship in building PCBs at the earlier stages, the designs were able to meet the electrical requirements. The significant number of these boards were used in radios and gramophones. The invention by Charles Ducas, that is, exploiting conductive ink on an insulating material for electrical connectivity, was the highlight of this decade. This period introduced the idea of flat conductors, multilayer PCBs, and through-hole application in two layers, which was patented by a German Inventor Albert Hanson in 1903 [6,8].

1930s to 1940s: The application of proximity fuse in precision weapons of World War II accelerated the development and application of PCB in the late 30s and early to mid-40s. The purpose of employing a proximity fuse in the weapons was to acquire greater distance with higher accuracy. In 1943, Dr. Paul Eisler patented this method of developing PCBs. He proposed the use of copper foil on a nonconductive base, reinforced by glass. The initial application scope of the patent was radios and communication equipment. However, the application range grew over time in the later years. The production of double-sided PCBs with plated through holes in 1947 also extended the application range. This design addressed many limitations of previous designs by providing an efficient way of developing electronic circuits [1,3,6].

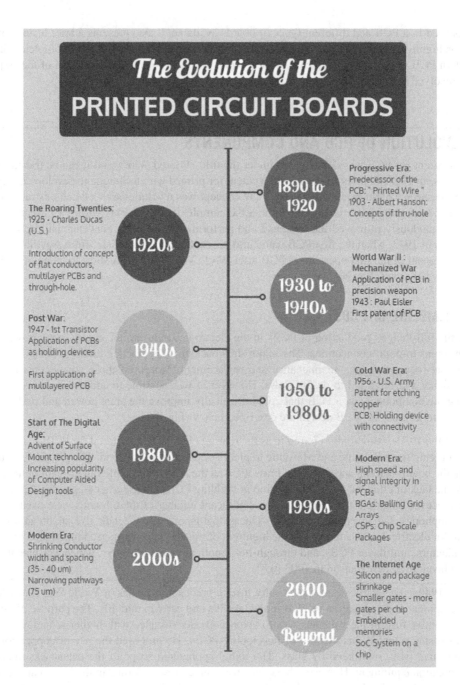

FIGURE 4.2

The evolution of printed circuit boards over time.

1950s to 1960s: Between the 1950s to 1960s, different variations of board materials were employed in PCB designs, including various kinds of resins and other compatible materials. At that time, the wiring was installed on one side of the boards, whereas the electrical components were inserted on the other side. PCBs at this time were adopted in many applications as it helped to eliminate the rigorous process of installing bulky wiring and greatly improved the performance of the circuit. A major stepping stone in the development of PCB was a patent titled "Process of Assembling Electrical Circuits". It was filed to the U.S. Patent Office in 1956 by a small group of scientists from the U.S. Army. They introduced a technique for drawing the wiring pattern and photographing the pattern on a zinc plate. The zinc plate is used as a printing plate for circuit boards in offset printing press. The wires were printed on the copper foil using an acid-resistant ink and, later, they were etched by acid solutions. In 1957, The Institute of Printed Circuits (IPC) decided to form a coalition. The first general meeting of the organization took place in Chicago, Illinois in the same year [6,9].

1960s to 1970s: The concept of multi-layer PCBs came into production in 1960. The maximum number of layers in the manufactured board varied over a range from 2 to 5. The first batch of boards was manufactured with 4:1, red-and-blue line vellum method. This process helped with the hand taping of components and tracks. Afterwards, a precision method was employed to produce the 1:1 negative manufacturing film. The process enhanced the pipelining of the design cycle and helped with speedy production. It took about 2 hours of effort for an experienced designer to produce the layout of a PCB with an equivalent of 14-pin ICs mounted on the board. By the 70s, the circuitry and overall size of PCBs started getting significantly smaller than the previous versions. The hot air soldering methods came into regular practice in this period. Moreover, a Japanese practice of developing liquid photo imageable masks (LPIs), using a wide variety of aqueous material, was adopted by many PCB manufacturers. Eventually, this practice became the industry standard in the later years. RS-274-D, a machine-based formatting method for vector photoplotters was introduced by Gerber Scientific Inc. in this decade [6].

1980s: In the 1980s, the PCB producers started choosing the surface mounting technique for integrating components on a board over the through-hole method. The preference led to the subsequent reduction in the size of a PCB without posing any obstacle for PCB functionality. An improvement on the data formatting of RS-274-D was released in 1986. The new release, RS-274X, provided support for embedded aperture information and eliminated the necessity of external aperture definitions files [10].

1990s: The size and price of PCB boards started decreasing in the 90s, while the complexity of the boards was increasing due to multi-layer designs. The multi-layer construction, however, helped the progress by facilitating the incorporation of rigid and flexible PCBs in the design. The era of high density interconnect (HDI) began in 1995 through the use of micro-via technology in PCB production [6,7].

2000 to Present: The highlight of this decade involves a peak market value of 10 billion USD for the first time in United States. PCB fabrication industry and the ELIC (Every Layer Interconnect) process flow started from 2010. ELIC provides smaller pitches and eliminates the mechanical holes inside the board, which consumes space, thus increasing interconnect density. In ELIC process, a PCB supports HDI using several layers of copper-filled stacked in-pad microvias. During this period, enhanced usage

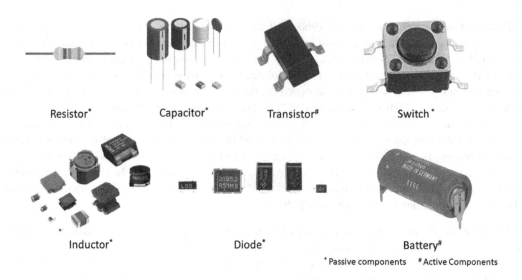

Resistor*   Capacitor*   Transistor#   Switch*

Inductor*   Diode*   Battery#

* Passive components   # Active Components

FIGURE 4.3

Various active and passive components used in PCBs.

of 3-D modeled boards and System on Chips aid the process of developing compact PCBs with greater performance. Consequently, these technology enablers keep the PCB design industry dynamic and rapidly adaptable in the future [5,6].

4.2.2 MODERN PCB COMPONENTS

Every PCB is comprised of various electronic components (Fig. 4.3). These components are typically industrial products manufactured individually in bulk with a wide range of values. They are provided with electronic terminals to build electronic circuits. Electronic components are packaged based on their type, functionality, and application. Common classification of electronic components is done depending on the energy source. The components, which act as energy sources, are called active components, whereas the components that need external sources of energy for working are called passive components [15].

In DC circuits, active components rely on energy sources like batteries. In some cases, they can introduce power into the circuits. In AC circuits, active components comprise of transistors and tunnel diodes. Passive components cannot introduce energy in the circuit. They are completely dependent on power from the AC circuit to which they are connected. These components have two electronic terminals. Some of the passive devices include resistors, inductors, and capacitors.

Some of the active components are described next:

• Battery: Batteries provide required voltage to the circuit; these are primarily used in DC circuits.
• Transistor: A transistor is used to amplify the charge; they are also used to switch electronic signals.

Some of the passive components are described next:

- Resistors: Resistors control the flow of current through them; they are also color-coded to facilitate recognizing their resistance.
- Capacitors: Capacitors store potential energy in the form of an electric field.
- Inductors: Inductors store electrical energy in the form of a magnetic field when a current passes through it.
- Diode: Diode conducts current only in one direction; they have very low resistance in the forward current path and large resistance to restrict it in opposite direction.
- Switches: Switches are used to block or change the direction of the current.

4.3 PCB LIFE CYCLE

Modern PCBs are built through a complex process consisting of number of stages. Multiple entities get involved in the PCB design and manufacturing process. A brief overview of the PCB life cycle is described in this section (Fig. 4.4).

4.3.1 PCB DESIGNER

The first entity in the PCB life cycle is the design engineer. The PCB designer goes through the basic steps of design flow, that is, part research and selection, schematic capture and simulation, board

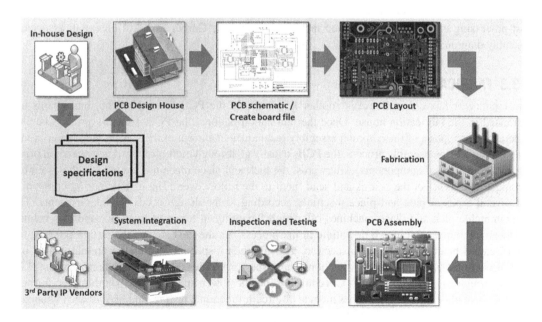

FIGURE 4.4

Detailed illustration of PCB life cycle.

layout, and verification and validation to finalize the complete process. Once the designer is satisfied with the final version of the design, the design is forwarded to the design house with exact design specifications.

4.3.2 DESIGN HOUSE

The design house of PCB obtains required design specifications and necessary design files from the design engineer. The design files can come from third-party vendors or in-house design engineers. Once the design files are acquired, the engineer at the design house starts creating the board files by analyzing the netlist. A netlist is a list of components that describe the connection among components in any specific design.

Once the netlist is finalized, the engineers in the design house create libraries for the components of the design. In this stage, the design engineers review and analyze the data sheet for each of the components. The key information retrieved from the datasheet include mechanical dimensions, package types, symbols, footprints, and pad stacks. As a good design practice, the components with mechanical constraints are placed first on the board in the component placement phase. Then, the placement of performance-critical components, such as microprocessors, video graphic arrays (VGAs), memory, and FPGA is performed, followed by the placement of other components, such as decoupling capacitors, passive elements, and test points [6].

After the placement of components, the nets or interconnect wires are routed on the board. The critical nets are given higher priority in the routing process. Afterward, the non-critical nets are either hand-routed or automatically routed using a design tool. Finally, the design is verified by performing a design rule check and eliminating the errors. The final step of PCB design in the design house is post-processing of the design. This step includes creating the Gerber and drill files with associated assembly diagrams.

4.3.3 FABRICATION HOUSE

The foundry or fabrication house is another key entity in the PCB life cycle. The final boards are fabricated in the fabrication house. Once the fabrication is done, the PCB assembly process begins. A detailed description of the common assembly techniques in current practice is provided later in this chapter. During the assembly process, the PCBs usually go through multiple steps, such as stencil printing and placement of components. Afterwards, the pick and place machines are used in the assembly technique line to select the boards and send them to the reflow oven. The manufacturing companies use several types of pick and place machines according to the design needs and requirements. The programmable pick and place machines offer high flexibility in terms of high-mix and low-volume products without causing much downtime in the process. As the next step of the design process, the manufactured boards proceed for inspection. The common inspection techniques are automated optical inspection (AOI) and X-ray inspection. The inspector verifies the physical integrity of the PCB design through automated machines. Once this is done, the power-up tests of the boards are performed. Commonly applied testing approaches include in-circuit, functional testing, and JTAG-based boundary scan testing. Each of the PCBs is tested rigorously to verify and validate the functionality of the circuit operation. Different simulation environments are generated to evaluate the performance of a PCB in the real-life scenario. In case of faulty boards, repairs are performed followed by testing that checks if

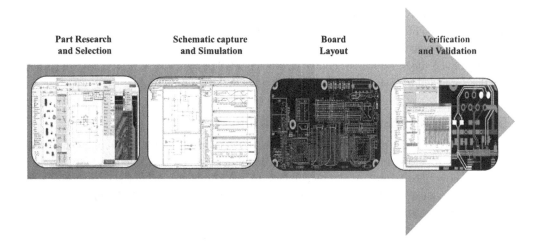

| Part Research and Selection | Schematic capture and Simulation | Board Layout | Verification and Validation |

FIGURE 4.5

Basic steps of PCB design process.

they meet the performance targets. Furthermore, feedback is provided to the design engineers based on the analyzed faults in order to take necessary measures to prevent further disruptions [1].

4.3.4 CURRENT BUSINESS MODEL

Due to the global economic trend, current business models of PCB design and fabrication increasingly rely on extensive outsourcing. The manufacturers are more prone to integrating untrusted third-party vendors in the PCB design and fabrication steps for cost minimization. The cost benefit of outsourcing the PCB design/fabrication to a foreign country with economical labor is primary driving factor of PCB business model. Other factors behind adopting a global business model include time-to-market requirements, resource constraints, rapid growth, and collaboration. However, the security implications of such a global business model can be severe if necessary measures are not taken to ensure the trust and reliability of the product obtained from third-party entities. It is important for any PCB manufacturer to make judicious tradeoff between cost and efficiency benefits through outsourcing and associated security concerns [1,12,30]. Major steps of PCB design process are delineated next in this section. These steps are generally applicable to all PCBs designed across the world.

- Component Research and Selection
- Schematic Capture and Simulation
- Board Layout
- Verification and Validation

Figure 4.5 illustrates the steps of PCB design flow. In the current practice of PCB design flow, the schematic capture and simulation phase is well integrated with the board layout phase. The integration is usually made convenient by the usage of a single corporate toolchain. However, the starting point for any PCB design is performing part research and selection, and finalizing the design with prototype validation. Unfortunately, these two steps of the design flow are isolated and separated from the core stages. The separation often leads to major challenge, as every PCB design goes through a large number of iterations before reaching the final stage. Lack of integration in the iterative design process leads to improper use of task times. Hence, the goal of an efficient PCB design process is to remove the isolation between the initial and final stages, and integrate them with the entire flow.

4.3.5 COMPONENT RESEARCH AND SELECTION

The very first step of PCB design is the research and selection of the physical components. Components such as resistors, transistors, operational amplifiers, processors, memory, etc. act as the building blocks of the design. A significant task in the part research and selection phase is to investigate and evaluate each of the components and determine their role in the design topology. The design specifications and device performance information for each of these components can be found at numerous online repositories of datasheets. Datasheets usually contain important information, such as design considerations, operating points, and switching characteristics [11, 12].

Most manufacturers have the component datasheets available on their websites as well as web repositories, such as DatasheetCatalog.com. Obtaining different components and physically developing a breadboard prototype is often the most time-consuming step of the design process. This process involves purchasing different components and breadboarding those at the preliminary phase of design. Physical breadboarding is preferred by engineers who want to obtain a better understanding of the functionality of the components instead of simply going over the product datasheets.

However, the usage of a schematic capture and simulation tool can help designers avoid the initial expenses of purchasing the components and developing a physical breadboard. There are many off-the-shelf commercial tools that can generate the simulation environment and overall behavior of the circuit. For instance, a designer can select any of the open-source PCB design software (for example, TinyCAD, KiCAD, ExpressPCB, EasyEDA, and DesignSpark PCB) and select the required components from the database to design the circuit. Furthermore, the operation of the components can be visualized with the associated simulation models. Thus, the capture and simulation environment can help in creating the design and simulating the operation of the circuitry quickly. The omission of the physical implementation of a breadboard prototype reduces the design expenses, and time required for the selection procedure [28].

4.3.6 SCHEMATIC CAPTURE

The design process starts with the selection and placement of right components in the circuit. All the schematic generation tools provide a database of components from which the engineer chooses the desired component. Due to the enormity of the number of components, the tools offer categorized groups of each class. The classes are designed according to component type and functionality. The initial schematic design process can be summarized in the following steps: navigating the component database, selecting the desired part, and placing the part in the circuit with proper wiring. Some tools provide a wireless working environment to reduce the efforts of continuous switching between the placement of parts and wiring modes [29]. The circuit schematic is usually represented in the form of symbols in ASCII and DIN standard and connected to each other by wires.

4.3.7 SIMULATION

Once the schematic is prepared, a PCB designer typically utilizes a simulation environment, for example, SPICE or XSPICE, to simulate the behavior of the design and evaluate the effects of different circuit components and signals. Simulation is a critical part of the design as it captures the behavior and performance of the circuit without building it physically. By definition, simulation is a mathematical representation that depicts the functionality of a real circuit component under varying conditions, including specific operating voltages and temperatures. Through simulation, it is possible to test the design topology and find out if any modification is required before building the prototype. Thus, simulation saves time, effort, and money by providing the opportunity to quickly fix the flaws of any PCB design before reaching the prototype stage.

The depiction of the real-life behavior of components in a simulation environment depends on the accuracy of device models. Thus, it is important to develop device models as accurate as possible as it has great impact on the designer's analysis of the PCB design. Many models of devices, such as BJTs, FETs, and operational amplifiers are designed with high accuracy to demonstrate the real-world behavior via simulation. The precision percentage of the results is finely tuned with advanced features, for instance, parasitic effects and complex behaviors of the devices. For effective simulation of circuits, PCB design engineers are expected to have good knowledge of SPICE or any of its variants. It is basically a text-based language used to simulate circuits effectively.

4.3.8 BOARD LAYOUT

The third step of any PCB design flow is building a robust prototype. The robustness of the design, however, will depend on the efficacy of schematic capturing and validity testing via proper simulation. The prototype development is required to evaluate the design for real-life performance. The development process requires a CAD environment that supports the format of an exact physical dimension of components used in the design. The CAD tool for generating layout outputs the final design in the form of Gerber files. The Gerber files are later utilized by the manufacturers in the industry to produce the actual physical boards. The ICs and other components are placed on the PCB during the layout design phase. Furthermore, the components are connected to each other via current conducting conduits, i.e., copper traces (routes). As a final step of this phase, the form factor of the respective PCB is calculated. Determining the right form factor of the board is crucial as it ensures that the design will fit inside the physical environment in which the PCB will be used.

Many advanced CAD tools are available for automated placement and routing. However, it is important to use these tools judiciously. For instance, designs operating at critical conditions or under tight energy or performance constraint, require a high level of scrutiny. Generally use of manual methods is the best approach for performance-critical parts of a PCB design. For lesser critical parts of the design, however, the application of automated tools, such as auto-router, is an accepted norm.

4.3.9 PROTOTYPE TEST

The final steps of PCB design flow are prototype development, followed by manufacturing test. The purpose of prototype testing is to verify if the design meets the intended or desired specifications. On the other hand, the manufacturing tests evaluate the appropriate standards of the final product being deployed in field. Any design flaw discovered at a later stage leads to additional expenses in terms of time and money. Therefore, iterative approaches in the schematic capture and simulation phase greatly help to produce a flawless product up to the final stages.

While performing the prototype tests, the real-life operation of the PCB is analyzed and the results are compared with original design specification. Through these tests, a test engineer verifies the final product with the design specs obtained from the design engineer and evaluates the performance of the end product. Finally, based on the results, the engineers conclude on whether to forward the product to market or re-evaluate for further performance improvement.

4.3.10 BEST PRACTICES IN OVERALL DESIGN FLOW

As an engineer moves through the design flow, from part selection to layout, integration becomes paramount in streamlining the creation of PCBs, reduce iterations, correct common errors, and have a faster transition to market. This integration, as discussed in this chapter, breaks down the walls that generally disrupts the traditional design flow, and is a best practice in board-level design.

It merges the part selection, schematic capture, simulation, board layout, and design validation in a single thread. Existing schematic capture tools can be exploited to test and validate the PCB designs for any topology. Moreover, features like a large repository of components and wiring can expedite the design process. An interactive simulation environment and tools for advanced analysis and virtual prototyping are the key components that allow a designer to reduce the design errors and develop an improved simulation model for board level designs. Finally, a designer can exploit the manual and automatic layout tools and effectively produce Gerber data for creating PCB prototypes [13,14,29].

4.4 PCB ASSEMBLY PROCESS

The primary steps of PCB assembly are the placement of electrical components on the board and soldering the components to the substrate. Whereas these steps are typically followed for hand soldering components into the through holes, the assembly process of modern PCBs is fairly complex. It is a multi-step process that offers the flexibility to incorporate various package types and a diverse range of substrates and materials. The current practice also facilitates adaptability of PCB designs in terms of reliability and defect level threshold with varying amount of production quantities. In general, the steps listed below describe the PCB assembly process with more accuracy:

- Preparing the component and substrate material on the board
- Applying flux and solder
- Melting the solder to complete the connections
- Cleaning the soldering as a part of post-processing
- Inspecting and testing the final product

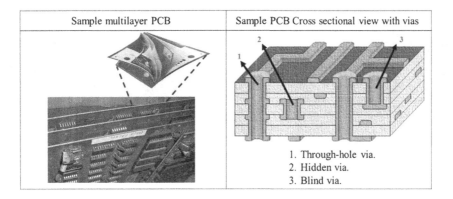

Sample multilayer PCB	Sample PCB Cross sectional view with vias
	1. Through-hole via. 2. Hidden via. 3. Blind via.

FIGURE 4.6

A sample multilayer PCB and its cross-sectional view with different kinds of vias.

In many instances, some of these steps are merged together or omitted, based on the product requirements. It is the responsibility of the manufacturer to adopt an assembly process that encompasses all the crucial steps. The assembly process of the PCB can be broadly categorized into through-hole technology and Surface Mount Technology (SMT). Each of these technologies offers various levels of automation in the assembly process, based on the equipment resources. The degree of automation usually depends on the design of the boards, expenditure of the equipment, bill of materials, and the manufacturing costs.

4.4.1 THROUGH-HOLE TECHNOLOGY

Through-hole technology can be defined as the assembly process in which the lead of electrical components are inserted into the holes on the boards and mounted through soldering process (Fig. 4.6). This technology was automated by the application of wave soldering. A major disadvantage of this technique is the low density of assembly. It poses a great obstacle to the miniaturization of the design and flexibility of functionality, due to the requirement of additional board space for large components and big holes. An advantage of this technology is lower assembly cost compared to alternative approaches. Even in case of fully automated assembly process that incorporates wave soldering, selective soldering, or past-in-hole/reflow, the overall equipment and setup cost of through-hole techniques is usually lower than surface-mount techniques.

4.4.2 SURFACE MOUNT TECHNOLOGY

The components can be placed on one side or both sides of a board. The initial motivation for developing SMT was facilitating the assembling of hybrid microcircuits (HMCs) into ceramic substrates. Later, SMTs were developed for laminate substrates as well. The major advantage of SMT lies in increased board density with a higher number of small components. In SMT, small vias are employed to connect sides and internal layers as the replacement of conventional large holes. SMT also helps with miniaturization of PCBs and improvement of performance by aiding finer traces and shortened

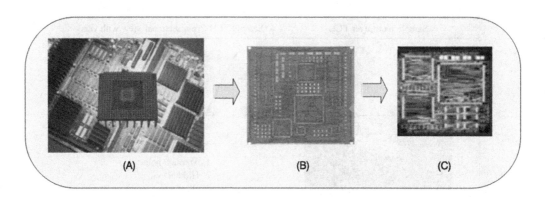

FIGURE 4.7

An illustrative example of a CPU with a different component, assembly, and PCB technologies over time. (A) First RISC processor developed in 1986: 14-layer through-hole board with a surface area of 128 square inches. (B) The same processor in 1991: 10-layer board on a surface area of 16 square inches (built with SMT). (C) The processor in 1995: HDI board with a surface area of 4 square inches (includes buried and blind vias and sequential build-up microvias).

components in the circuit. The common practice in SMT is to use smaller devices, such as resistor, capacitors, and inductors. SMT also facilitates the usage of embedded passive devices like resistors and capacitors placed inside the board laminate. Consequently, the embedded passive devices provide a larger surface area for the active components of a design.

4.4.3 PCB COMPLEXITY TREND AND SECURITY IMPLICATIONS

Shrinking size of the components, increasing complexity of a design that requires large number of components to be integrated into a PCB, and the advent of efficient packaging techniques, for instance, the ball grid array (BGA), system on chip (SoC), chip-scale packaging (CSP), and chip-on-board (COB) guided the progression of conventional PCB technologies to HDI era. Figure 4.7 shows an example of the changes in interconnect technology over time. The figure shows the evolution of a computer central processing unit (CPU) due to the changing trends in component technology, PCB technology, and assembly technology. It also shows the direction and rate of the changes of technologies that drive the PCB design trends over time [19–21].

The current drivers in packaging and interconnect technology selection are mainly the speed of operation, power consumption, thermal management, electronic interference, and system operating environment. The shift towards the miniaturization and portability of electronic devices is another factor that determines the PCB design and technology trend. However, with the rapid increase in PCB design complexity, there are rising concerns about the security aspects of modern PCBs in the design community. It is possible for any rogue entity to take advantage of today's complex and highly integrated PCB designs with 20 to 30 layers, hidden vias, and embedded passive components to tamper or insert additional malicious circuitry in the form of hardware Trojan. Current industry practices do not employ adequate security measures to deter such threats. There is a critical need to design PCBs that are resilient against these security threats while meeting the performance and other constraints. A detailed description of the security vulnerabilities and potential attack scenarios on modern-day PCB designs is provided in Chapter 11 of this book.

4.5 PCB DESIGN VERIFICATION

Despite the diversity of application areas, the requirements for unimpaired operation and high performance are common in every system built upon the PCBs. There are many instances of performance critical systems in which human lives are at stake. Consequently, it is of utmost importance that the PCBs should perform flawlessly. The inspection and testing process constitutes a significant part of any PCB life cycle. The challenges of PCB testing mostly arise from the complexity of dealing with PCBs containing hundreds of components and thousands of soldering connections. To overcome such obstacles, the PCB manufacturing companies incorporate a variety of inspections and testing methodologies to produce high-quality end products.

A taxonomy of PCB verification approaches is shown in Fig. 4.8. During the inspection and testing phases, the faulty boards are identified and considered for repair. The cyclic process of getting feedback on the manufactured board helps engineers to continuously improve the design through multiple iterations. Each PCB is inspected and tested by the manufacturer according to the design and performance specifications to ensure the maximum yield and reliability from the final product. Hence, inspection and testing are key stages in the PCB life cycle. In this section, a brief description of different PCB inspection and testing methods will be provided to help the reader get a better insight on inspection and testing processes suitable for any PCB.

4.5.1 OVERVIEW OF PCB INSPECTION AND TESTING

For a reasonably simple PCB consisting of few components and solder connections, manual visual inspection (MVI) might suffice for detecting the placement errors on the board or solder problems. However, the process of MVI is inherently limited to the flaws of human inspectors performing repetitive tasks. It is very likely that a human inspector may overlook defects in a design. Any unidentified defect in the manual inspection stage may cause serious flaws during system operation. To mitigate the errors introduced by human involvement in the inspection process, the inspection process has been

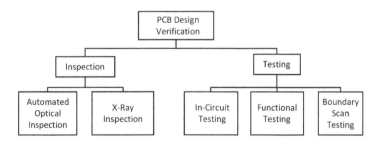

FIGURE 4.8

A taxonomy of PCB verification methodologies.

automated. Automated optical inspection (AOI) processes are integrated with pre-reflow, post-reflow, or both, to detect and pinpoint potential faults in a board. Pick-and-place machines with AOI capability are usually employed to check for misalignment and faulty components [26].

A major obstacle in the AOI process was posed by the advent of SMT. It enabled the integration of smaller components, novel microchip packages, and aided the development of complex multi-layered boards. Due to the increased density of PCBs, it is difficult to analyze the solder joints and chip packages with ball grid arrays (BGAs) that have connections inside the packages. The issues caused by the difficulty to view the layered contents of the complex PCBs is addressed by X-ray based inspection methodologies. The Automated X-ray inspection (AXI) helps the PCB inspectors analyze the multi-layered and double-sided dense PCBs with components and interconnect fabric.

The inspection process is followed by testing of PCBs. Whereas inspection techniques, such as AOI, checks for overall PCB construction quality and major flaws (e.g., missing component), detailed PCB testing is essential for high-level quality assurance. The commonly employed testing mechanisms are in-circuit tests (ICTs), functional tests (FCTs), and JTAG-based boundary scan tests. ICTs help to verify if a board and each of its components are performing according to the specifications. FCTs, on the other hand, are applied to conclude with a pass/fail decision on a PCB. Boundary scan tests are inspired by the limitations of conventional tests (that is, functional and in-circuit tests), such as failure to employ bed-of-nails fixtures on modern PCBs with double sided components and reduced spacing of interconnects. Boundary scan tests facilitate built-in test delivery system and provide standardized test ports and buses.

4.5.2 PCB DEFECTS

PCB boards can have a variety of defects due to improper design practices. The commonly found defects in the PCBs include misaligned components, incomplete solder connections, and short circuit caused by excess solders. A summary of the common defects of PCBs is presented in Table 4.1. The table also provides a classification of the defects based on the type, rate of occurrence, and relevance to soldering issues [16,17,25].

Table 4.1 An illustrative summary of defects commonly found in PCBs

Defect	Rate (%)	Type	Solder related
Open	25	Structural	Yes
Insufficient solder	18	Structural	Yes
Short	13	Structural	Yes
Missing electrical component	12	Structural	No
Misaligned component	8	Structural	Yes
Defective electrical component	8	Electrical	No
Wrong component	5	Electrical	No
Excess solder	3	Structural	Yes
Missing nonelectrical component	2	Structural	Yes
Wrong orientation	2	Electrical	No
Defective nonelectrical component	2	Structural	No

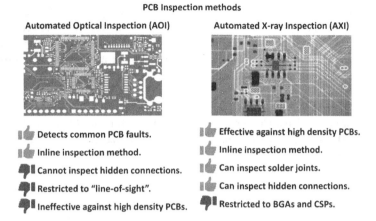

FIGURE 4.9

Comparison of PCB inspection methods.

4.5.3 PCB INSPECTION

The early detection of any fault in the PCB significantly reduces the repairing cost. Hence, a manufacturer incorporates inspection of the PCBs at various stages of the life cycle. In the subsequent sections, two PCB inspection methods, that is, automated optical inspection and automated X-ray inspection, which are commonly practiced in the industry (Fig. 4.9), are described in detail.

4.5.3.1 Automated Optical Inspection (AOI)

AOI is a process of visually inspecting the PCBs. The process involves the use of multiple high-definition cameras to capture images and videos of the board under test from multiple angles. The high-quality images are stitched together to form a large image file. Then, the resultant image is compared with the golden board (ideal board with exact design specifications) to figure out the discrepancies. AOI systems are employed to primarily find out physical defects. The type of defects can be scratches, strains, or nodules on the boards. Moreover, AOI can help detect issues, such as open and short circuits and thinning of soldering due to manufacturing flaws. Other defects commonly identified by the AOI systems include missing components and wrongful or skewed alignments. In every case, the performance of AOIs surpasses the ability of human inspectors through greater accuracy in a shorter time period [27].

The current practice in the industry involves the application of 3-D AOI equipment that can determine the component height as well. Previously, it was not feasible to measure the height of several components through the conventional 2-D AOI machines. Further, the 3-D AOI machines deliver superior performance in terms of capturing height-sensitive devices, for example, leaded components. The 2-D AOI machines use colored lighting from multiple angles and also incorporates side-angle cameras for inspecting these devices. However, the process does not produce accurate results. 3-D AOI machines, on the other hand, facilitate the detection of coplanarity for height-sensitive devices. The contemporary AOI technologies are well-reputed in the industry and compatible with various commercial standards. However, these techniques are capable of detecting many common errors in the PCBs;

can be well-integrated with the existing steps of PCB manufacturing; and deployed in-line. The major disadvantage of the AOI techniques includes failure to inspect hidden interconnects inside the BGAs and component packages. AOI machines inherently suffer from a limited visibility when it comes to complex PCBs. Furthermore, AOI machines might produce erroneous results when inspecting densely loaded PCBs due to hidden or shadowed components.

4.5.3.2 X-Ray Inspection

With the advent of SMT, the density of the components on a PCB is steadily increasing. Modern PCBs typically contain 20,000 or more solder joints. Moreover, SMT has helped the development of novel chip packages, such as, BGAs and CSPs, where the solder connections are not visible and, hence, cannot be inspected by conventional AOI equipment. To address the issues of limited visibility in modern PCBs, the X-ray inspection equipment is developed to scan solder joints inside the components and check for potential defects in a design. The X-ray inspection can be either manual or automatic. The rate of X-ray absorption by different materials vary according to their atomic weight. Any material with heavier weight is inclined to a higher amount of X-ray absorption. Consequently, materials with lighter elements provide comparatively better transparency in X-ray inspection. The solder joints of the PCBs are usually made of heavier elements, such as bismuth, tin, indium, silver, and lead. The PCBs, on the other hand, are made of lighter elements, for example, carbon, copper, aluminum, and silicon. X-ray inspections are efficient for analyzing solders as these joints show up very well when exposed to X-ray. However, most packages, including board substrate, component leads, and ICs are not properly visible through X-ray inspection.

The working principle of AOI and X-ray inspection is different as the X-rays are not reflected from the design under test (DUT). The X-rays pass through the design and help the extraction of an image on the other side of the board. Thus, X-ray inspection can aid the process of inspecting BGAs, where the interconnects are inside the components. As the shadow of components is not an issue in X-ray inspection, it is possible to inspect complex and highly dense boards with this mechanism. For instance, X-ray based inspection methods provide an internal view of solder joints of PCBs and help to determine any existing bubbles in the joints. These methods also help with the visibility of solder joint heels. The major advantage of X-ray-based inspection is the transparency in case of chip packages with connections underneath the components. These techniques also help with thorough inspection of a densely loaded board including the solder joints. The disadvantages of the X-ray-based inspection method are as follows. It is not well understood since the technology is newer and the investment in the technology is only effective for specific packages, e.g. BGAs and CSPs.

4.5.4 PCB TESTING

Once the inspection is completed, the manufactured boards become ready for testing. In this section, the in-circuit testing, functional testing, and JTAG-based boundary scan testing methods, which are most commonly employed in the industry (Fig. 4.10), are explained in detail [22,24].

4.5.4.1 In-Circuit Test (ICT)

The purpose of the ICT is to verify the design specifications through the exact list and placement of components. The common approach of performing ICTs include testing a loaded PCB with electrical probes and determining any discrepancy in the functionality caused by open or short circuit scenario.

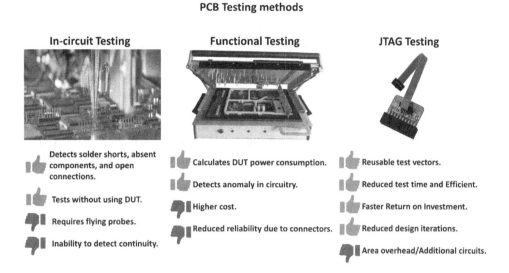

PCB Testing methods

In-circuit Testing	Functional Testing	JTAG Testing
Detects solder shorts, absent components, and open connections.	Calculates DUT power consumption.	Reusable test vectors.
Tests without using DUT.	Detects anomaly in circuitry.	Reduced test time and Efficient.
Requires flying probes.	Higher cost.	Faster Return on Investment.
Inability to detect continuity.	Reduced reliability due to connectors.	Reduced design iterations.
		Area overhead/Additional circuits.

FIGURE 4.10

Comparison of PCB testing methods.

These probes also help to find out if the resistance, capacitance, or inductance of a design is correct according to the design specs. To perform the ICT, a set of flying probes or a fixture of bed-of-nails is required. A bed-of-nails tester is basically a test fixture made of arrays of small, spring-loaded pogo pins. The pins are connected to every node of the circuitry of the DUT. A successful connection between the nodes and pins establishes contact between the tester and the numerous testing points of the circuitry. However, the bed-of-nails fixtures are usually expensive to set up and not very compliant with changes based on design types. Further, these testers do not work very well with densely loaded PCBs.

A solution to the obstacles faced by the bed-of-nails tester is the usage of roving or flying probes. The deployment of flying probe involves using a fixture to hold the board steadily, and roving the tester probes constant over the required points of contact. As the movement of the probes can be programmed as per requirement, the flying probe facilitates testing of large number of boards with various design specifications. ICT tests, however, do not verify the operational validity of the boards as it assumes that the circuit is fully operational and delivers error-free performance.

The ICTs are efficient at finding physical defects, such as short or open circuit situation due to soldering, detecting missing or wrong components, and open connection between components. Testing the circuit without the power supply is another key aspect of ICT as the process of power input is associated with the risk of potential circuit damage. The ICT requires expensive test fixtures for the bed-of-nails or elaborate programming for roving probe set up. Moreover, these tests do not check the continuity of the design through the connectors of the circuit. Thus, there is a possibility that ICT might overlook existing connector faults in the circuit.

4.5.4.2 Functional Test (FCT)

FCTs are performed on PCBs to determine the functionality of a design. FCT is usually the final step of the manufacturing process. A manufacturer seeks to detect faults in the final hardware through functional testing. Any unmitigated fault in the final product might adversely affect the operation of the target system. Hence, a suite of functional tests is used to determine the quality of a board. The requirements of typical functional tests vary, based on the systems and designs under test. The development and testing procedures for functional testing also vary accordingly. The edge connectors and test probe pins of a PCB are utilized to interface the design with the functional testing tools. The testing also includes generating the proper electrical environment to simulate the operating conditions for the design. Hot Mock-up is a form of functional test prevalent in the industry. Other forms of testing include cycling the design with a comprehensive range of operational tests.

Primarily, functional tests help to identify defects in the PCB. These tests also help in determining the power consumption of the design under test. Functional testing can be applied to both analog and digital circuitry. However, the programming associated with functional testing is expensive as it requires a comprehensive understanding of the DUT and the working environment. The process typically requires costly high-speed instrumentation for the characterization of signals under consideration. Another drawback is that functional testing is performed through the connectors, which might result in further reliability issues due to regular wear and tear.

4.5.4.3 JTAG Boundary Scan Tests

In today's PCB industry, Joint Test Action Group (JTAG) boundary scan test is considered as an industry standard post-assembly verification and testing. The boundary scan technology of JTAG facilitates accessibility to numerous signals and device pins of complex modern ICs. Boundary scan cells are exploited to access the required signals via Test Access Port (TAP). The TAP can consist of two, four, or five signals based on the version of the JTAG being used. The four or five pin interface helps to establish a daisy-chained connection to test multiple chips located on the board. It is possible to test and control the states of the signals through the TAP interface. Hence, TAP helps with monitoring and detection of PCB faults via run-time operations. The operational modes of boundary scan cells can be classified into two categories, that is, functional and test mode. In functional mode, the scan cells do not have any effect on device operation. In test mode, the functional cores of the devices are isolated from the pins and boundary scan cells are employed to control and monitor values from devices under test. Figure 4.11A shows the system-level block diagram of JTAG-based boundary scan test signals and connection. Figure 4.11B shows the JTAG interface on real-life PCB.

JTAG-based boundary scan testing is easier to perform in comparison to traditional functional testing as the control pins are disconnected from enabled devices, and there is no requirement of additional pin configuration or booting to use the pins for testing purposes. The TAP interface significantly minimizes the physical access required for testing the PCB board by providing the opportunity to control and monitor the enabled signals of the device. The boundary scan capability of JTAG can be utilized mainly in two ways: a) To obtain good coverage in testing, connection testing is applied on the PCB boards that relies on the device capabilities of JTAG and the connections and nets on the board; b) One can use the JTAG enabled devices on a PCB to enhance test coverage and to communicate with peripheral devices that lack JTAG support. Figure 4.12 shows the cross-sectional view of an IC with JTAG boundary scan integrated into its periphery [23].

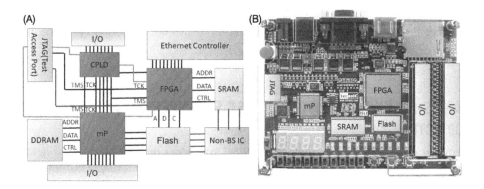

FIGURE 4.11

(A) System level block diagram of JTAG-based boundary scan test access. (B) Illustrative depiction of JTAG interface on PCB.

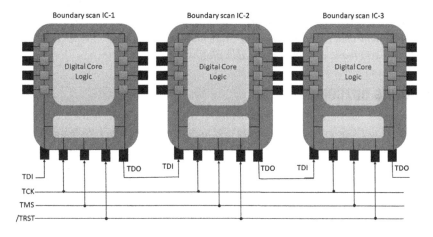

FIGURE 4.12

Integrated circuits with JTAG boundary scan.

JTAG reduces the cost of test generation by reducing the expenses and complexities associated with bed-of-nails fixture of ICT. Moreover, JTAG addresses the issues raised by the limitations of physical access for testing the interconnects placed between devices on a multi-layer PCB. The reusable test vectors of JTAG minimizes the expenses significantly. Conventional ICT techniques poses serious challenges in the diagnostic process of structural failures. On the contrary, JTAG provides an efficient way to testing these failures with reduced test pins and lesser testing time. Consequently, JTAG technique is cost-effective compared to ICT approaches. However, JTAG suffers from the drawback of area overhead for additional circuitry. Further, in many cases, it might be a challenging task to evaluate the effect of JTAG boundary cell capabilities on the circuit size as it depends on implementation details. In terms of design constraints, JTAG technique requires higher design effort to integrate the boundary scan into the periphery of the functional core.

4.6 HANDS-ON EXPERIMENT: REVERSE ENGINEERING ATTACKS

4.6.1 OBJECTIVE

This experiment is designed to give students practical experience on reverse engineering attacks on electronic hardware. In particular, it allows students to reverse-engineer a simple two-layer PCB.

4.6.2 METHOD

By setting the HaHa platform as the target of the attack, the students will apply a design-capturing technique to retrieve all the necessary design details for a PCB needed to re-create the design from the actual hardware. The experiment focuses on design information retrieval using visual inspection for the two-layered example PCB. The information includes both the type of components and the routing structure of the system under attack. Next, the students need to compile the obtained information to recreate a detailed schematic design of the HaHa platform.

4.6.3 LEARNING OUTCOME

Through carrying out the steps of the experiment, the students will experience the ease and the challenges with respect to PCB reverse engineering and understand the vulnerability associated with PCB piracy. They will also learn how to track components, capture their connectivity, and identify their functionality as it relates analyzing and debugging a PCB. Finally, this experiment is expected to help students understand the countermeasures to PCB reverse engineering and motivate them in developing new solutions.

4.6.4 ADVANCED OPTIONS

Additional exploration on this topic can be done through the application of this attack on more complex PCBs having complex circuitry with basic obfuscation.

More details about the experiment are available in the supplementary document. Please visit: http://hwsecuritybook.org.

4.7 EXERCISES

4.7.1 TRUE/FALSE QUESTIONS

1. The primary purpose of Printed Circuit Boards is to provide mechanical support and electrical connectivity.
2. Battery is a passive component found on PCBs.

3. Conductive substrate material is the base of any PCB board.
4. Part research and selection is a vital step of PCB design.
5. The manufacturers in the PCB industry have their own fabrication labs.
6. Automation in PCB inspection can produce worse results compared to manual inspection.
7. Functional testing verifies the circuit operation of the design.
8. Power-up testing can damage the PCB.
9. X-ray-based inspection is detrimental to PCB base material.
10. Surface Mount Technology facilitates the production of densely loaded complex PCBs.

4.7.2 SHORT-ANSWER TYPE QUESTIONS

1. What are some major events in the history and evolution of PCB design and development?
2. Briefly describe two automated PCB inspection techniques commonly used in the industry.
3. State the differences between in-circuit testing and functional testing.
4. Label the PCB components in the following figure.

5. What is JTAG-based boundary scan testing? How does it address the limitations of in-circuit testing?
6. What are the two common PCB assembly techniques? Briefly describe them.

4.7.3 LONG-ANSWER TYPE QUESTIONS

1. Briefly describe the common PCB components in terms of active and passive electrical elements.
2. Describe the life cycle of a modern PCB with a brief description about the steps and parties involved.
3. Describe the PCB design process with brief descriptions about the major steps.
4. Briefly discuss the contemporary PCB testing techniques with their advantages and disadvantages.
5. Briefly discuss the PCB assembly techniques currently practiced with their pros and cons.
6. Discuss the taxonomy of PCB design verification.
7. Briefly discuss the JTAG testing.

REFERENCES

[1] J. Li, P. Shrivastava, Z. Gao, H.-C. Zhang, Printed circuit board recycling: a state-of-the-art survey, IEEE Transactions on Electronics Packaging Manufacturing 27 (1) (2004) 33–42.

[2] J. Howard, Printed circuit board, Metal Finishing 11 (95) (1997) 117.

[3] Y. Crama, J. van de Klundert, F.C. Spieksma, Production planning problems in printed circuit board assembly, Discrete Applied Mathematics 123 (1–3) (2002) 339–361.

[4] J. LaDou, Printed circuit board industry, International Journal of Hygiene and Environmental Health 209 (3) (2006) 211–219.

[5] H.-H. Loh, M.-S. Lu, Printed circuit board inspection using image analysis, IEEE Transactions on Industry Applications 35 (2) (1999) 426–432.

[6] M.W. Jawitz, Printed Circuit Board Materials Handbook, McGraw Hill Professional, 1997.

[7] A. Kusiak, C. Kurasek, Data mining of printed-circuit board defects, IEEE Transactions on Robotics and Automation 17 (2) (2001) 191–196.

[8] I.E. Sutherland, D. Oestreicher, How big should a printed circuit board be? IEEE Transactions on Computers 100 (5) (1973) 537–542.

[9] T.F. Carmon, O.Z. Maimon, E.M. Dar-El, Group set-up for printed circuit board assembly, The International Journal of Production Research 27 (10) (1989) 1795–1810.

[10] J. Vanfleteren, M. Gonzalez, F. Bossuyt, Y.-Y. Hsu, T. Vervust, I. De Wolf, M. Jablonski, Printed circuit board technology inspired stretchable circuits, MRS Bulletin 37 (3) (2012) 254–260.

[11] P.-C. Chang, Y.-W. Wang, C.-Y. Tsai, Evolving neural network for printed circuit board sales forecasting, Expert Systems with Applications 29 (1) (2005) 83–92.

[12] O. Maimon, A. Shtub, Grouping methods for printed circuit board assembly, The International Journal of Production Research 29 (7) (1991) 1379–1390.

[13] M. Gong, C.-J. Kim, Two-dimensional digital microfluidic system by multilayer printed circuit board, in: Micro Electro Mechanical Systems, 2005. MEMS 2005. 18th IEEE International Conference on, IEEE, 2005, pp. 726–729.

[14] P. Hadi, M. Xu, C.S. Lin, C.-W. Hui, G. McKay, Waste printed circuit board recycling techniques and product utilization, Journal of Hazardous Materials 283 (2015) 234–243.

[15] P.T. Vianco, An overview of surface finishes and their role in printed circuit board solderability and solder joint performance, Circuit World 25 (1) (1999) 6–24.

[16] E. Duman, I. Or, The quadratic assignment problem in the context of the printed circuit board assembly process, Computers & Operations Research 34 (1) (2007) 163–179.

[17] P. Johnston, Printed circuit board design guidelines for ball grid array packages, Journal of Surface Mount Technology 9 (1996) 12–18.

[18] S. Ghosh, A. Basak, S. Bhunia, How secure are printed circuit boards against Trojan attacks? IEEE Design & Test 32 (2015) 7–16.

[19] W. Jillek, W. Yung, Embedded components in printed circuit boards: a processing technology review, The International Journal of Advanced Manufacturing Technology 25 (2005) 350–360.

[20] S. Paley, T. Hoque, S. Bhunia, Active protection against PCB physical tampering, in: Quality Electronic Design (ISQED), 2016 17th International Symposium on, IEEE, pp. 356–361.

[21] J. Carlsson, Crosstalk on printed circuit boards, SP Rapport, 1994, p. 14.

[22] B. Sood, M. Pecht, Controlling moisture in printed circuit boards, IPC Apex EXPO Proceedings (2010).

[23] O. Solsjö, Secure key management in a trusted domain on mobile devices, 2015.

[24] S.H. Hwang, M.H. Cho, S.-K. Kang, H.-H. Park, H.S. Cho, S.-H. Kim, K.-U. Shin, S.-W. Ha, Passively assembled optical interconnection system based on an optical printed-circuit board, IEEE Photonics Technology Letters 18 (5) (2006) 652–654.

[25] B. Archambeault, C. Brench, S. Connor, Review of printed-circuit-board level EMI/EMC issues and tools, IEEE Transactions on Electromagnetic Compatibility 52 (2) (2010) 455–461.

[26] T. Hubing, T. Van Doren, F. Sha, J. Drewniak, M. Wilhelm, An experimental investigation of 4-layer printed circuit board decoupling, in: Electromagnetic Compatibility, 1995. Symposium Record., 1995 IEEE International Symposium on, IEEE, 1995, pp. 308–312.

[27] H. Rau, C.-H. Wu, Automatic optical inspection for detecting defects on printed circuit board inner layers, The International Journal of Advanced Manufacturing Technology 25 (9–10) (2005) 940–946.

[28] R.G. Askin, Printed circuit board family grouping and component, Naval Research Logistics 41 (1994) 587–608.

[29] V.J. Leon, B.A. Peters, A comparison of setup strategies for printed circuit board assembly, Computers & Industrial Engineering 34 (1) (1998) 219–234.

[30] G. Reinelt, A case study: TSPs in printed circuit board production, in: The Traveling Salesman: Computational Solutions for TSP Applications, 1994, pp. 187–199.

HARDWARE ATTACKS: ANALYSIS, EXAMPLES, AND THREAT MODELS

HARDWARE TROJANS

5

CONTENTS

Hardware Security. https://doi.org/10.1016/B978-0-12-812477-2.00010-1

5.1 INTRODUCTION

The complexity of modern system on chip (SoCs), amplified by time-to-market pressure, makes it infeasible for a single design house to complete an entire SoC without outside support. Also, the cost to build and maintain a fabrication unit (or foundry) for modern technology nodes makes it infeasible for the majority of SoC design houses to afford their own fabs. Given these factors, and added pressure for lowering time-to-market, the semiconductor industry has shifted to a horizontal business model over the past two decades, where time-to-market and manufacturing costs are lowered through outsourcing and design reuse. In this model, SoC designers often obtain licenses for third party intellectual property (3PIP) cores, design an SoC by integrating the various 3PIPs with their own IPs, and outsource the SoC design to contract foundries and assemblies for fabrication, testing, and packaging.

Due to the emerging trend of outsourcing the design and fabrication services to external facilities and increasing reliance on third-party Intellectual Property (IP) cores, SoCs are becoming increasingly vulnerable to malicious activities and alterations referred to as hardware Trojans (HT). Hardware Trojans are malicious modifications to original circuitry inserted by adversaries to exploit hardware or to use hardware mechanisms to create backdoors in the design. These backdoors can leak sensitive (or private) information as well as enable launching other possible attacks, for example, denial of service and reduction in reliability. They have raised serious concerns regarding possible threats to military systems, financial infrastructures, transportation security, and household appliances. Hardware Trojans have reportedly been used as 'kill switches' and backdoors in foreign military weapon systems [1]. Current and former U.S. military and intelligence executives agree that the dangers of hardware Trojans hidden in a chip are among the most severe threats the nation faces in the event of a war [2].

Detection of hardware Trojans is extremely difficult, for several reasons. First, given the large number of soft, firm, and hard IP cores used in SoCs, and the high complexity of today's IP blocks, detecting a small malicious alteration is extremely difficult. Second, nanometer SoC feature sizes make detection by physical inspection and destructive reverse engineering very difficult, time consuming, and costly. Moreover, destructive reverse engineering does not guarantee that the remaining SoCs will be Trojan-free, especially when Trojans are selectively inserted into a portion of the chip population. Third, Trojan circuits, by design, are typically activated under very specific conditions (for example, connected to low-transition probability nets or sensing a specific design signal, such as power or temperature), which makes them unlikely to be activated and detected using random or functional stimuli. Fourth, tests used to detect manufacturing faults, such as stuck-at and delay faults cannot guarantee detection of Trojans. Such tests operate on the netlist of a Trojan-free circuit and, therefore, cannot activate and detect Trojans. Even when 100% fault coverage for all types of manufacturing faults is possible, there are no guarantees as far as Trojans are concerned. Finally, as physical feature sizes decrease because of improvements in lithography, process and environmental variations have an increasingly greater impact on the integrity of the circuit parametric behavior. Thus, detection of Trojans using simple analysis of these parametric signals would be ineffective. All these factors make the detection of Trojan in an SoC a very challenging task.

The following section discusses the modern SoC design flow and how the rogue entities in this flow can insert hardware Trojans. Thereafter, a comprehensive Trojan taxonomy is presented. This taxonomy systematically categorizes hardware Trojans, which facilitate the development of Trojan mitigation, detection, and protection techniques. Further, a detailed description of the state-of-the-art countermeasures for Trojan threat both in terms of detection and prevention is presented.

5.2 SoC DESIGN FLOW

A typical SoC design flow is shown in Fig. 5.1. Design specification by the SoC integrator is generally the first step. For example, the SoC integrator first identifies what functionalities need to be incorporated in the SoC, and what will be the targeted performance. The integrator then identifies a list of functional blocks to implement the SoC. These functional blocks have intellectual property values and are commonly referred to as IPs. These IP cores are either developed in-house or purchased from 3PIP developers. These 3PIP cores can be procured either as soft IP (register-transfer level (RTL)), firm IP (gate level), and hard IP (layout) [3].

After developing/procuring all the necessary soft IPs, the SoC design house integrates them to generate RTL specification of the whole SoC. The RTL design goes through extensive functional testing to verify the functional correctness of the SoC and also to find any design bugs. SoC integrator synthesizes the RTL description into a gate-level netlist based on a target technology library. Synthesis is a process by which an RTL code is transformed into a hardware implementation consisting of logic gates with the help of a computer aided design (CAD) tool, for example, Design Compiler of Synop-

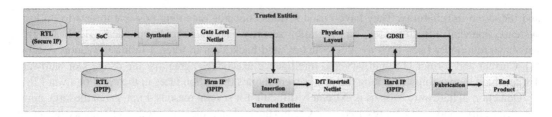

FIGURE 5.1

System on chip (SoC) design flow.

sys. The CAD tools also optimize the design with the target to minimize area, timing or power. The gate-level netlist then goes through formal equivalence checking to verify that the netlist is equivalent to the RTL representation. The SoC designer may also integrate a firm IP core from a vendor into the SoC netlist at this stage. The SoC integrator then integrates design-for-test (DFT) structures to improve the design's testability. However, in many cases, the DFT insertion is outsourced to third party vendors who specialize in designing test and debug structures, such as built-in self-test (BIST) and compression structures. In the next step, the gate-level netlist is translated into a physical layout design. It is also possible to import hard IP cores from vendors and integrate them at this stage. After performing static timing analysis (STA) and power closure, the SoC integrator generates the final layout in GDSII format and sends it out to a foundry for fabrication. The generated GDSII file contains layer-by-layer information needed to fabricate the SoC on a silicon wafer. The foundry fabricates the SoC and performs structural tests on the die and wafer to find manufacturing defects. After fabrication, the foundry sends tested wafers to the assembly line to cut the wafers into die, and package the die to produce chips [4].

5.2.1 HARDWARE TROJAN INSERTION: POTENTIAL ADVERSARIES

In the hardware supply chain, there are potential adversaries who have the capability and access to insert Hardware Trojans into the IC design. A brief discussion about these adversaries follows.

3PIP Vendor: Due to short time-to-market constraints, design houses are increasingly becoming dependent on third party vendors to procure IPs. These IPs are designed by hundreds of IP vendors distributed across the world. Such IPs cannot be assumed trusted as hardware Trojans can be maliciously inserted into them. The 3PIP vendors have full control over their IP and can insert stealthy Trojans, which would be extremely difficult, if not impossible, to detect using traditional test and verification techniques.

Detection of Trojans in 3PIPs is challenging as there is no golden reference against which to compare a given IP core during verification. Also, the system integrator only has the black-box knowledge of the IP, that is, the system integrator only knows high-level functionality of the design. However, he/she does not know the low-level implementation design of the Trojan. A large industrial-scale IP core can include thousands of lines of code. It is an extremely challenging task to identify the few lines of RTL code that represents a Trojan in the IP core [5].

DFT Vendor: In the current hardware design flow, the DFT insertion process is generally outsourced to third party vendors who specialize in designing test and debug structures. These vendors have access to the whole design and have the capability to incorporate stealthy malicious circuitry in the design.

Also, DFT vendors incorporate additional test and debug hardware into the original design to improve test coverage of the design. These additional hardware can also include hardware Trojans.

Fabrication: Due to the complexity and cost of semiconductor chip fabrication, most design houses have become fabless, that is, they fabricate their products in third party foundries offshore to lower cost. In this process, the foundry has access to the whole SoC design and can maliciously tamper with the design. Therefore, a rogue foundry has a unique opportunity to insert hardware Trojan in the SoC. It can exploit the empty spaces in the SoC to introduce malicious functionality in addition to the actual functionality. Trojan inserted by rogue foundry is extremely difficult, if not impossible to detect. The reason is that unlike the pre-silicon design stage, a fabricated SoC offers very limited verification and validation options.

5.3 HARDWARE TROJANS

A hardware Trojan (HT) is defined as a malicious, intentional modification of a circuit design that results in undesired behavior when the circuit is deployed [6]. SoCs that are 'infected' by a hardware Trojan may experience changes in their functionality or specification, may leak sensitive information, or may experience degraded or unreliable performance. Hardware Trojan poses a serious threat to any hardware design being deployed in a critical operation.

As the hardware Trojans are inserted at the hardware level, software-level countermeasures may be inadequate to address the threat posed by HT. Also, detection of Trojans in a hardware design is challenging as there is no golden version against which to compare a given design during verification. In theory, an effective way to detect a Trojan is to activate the Trojan and observe its effects, but a Trojan's type, size, and location are unknown, and its activation is, most likely, a rare event. A Trojan can be, therefore, well hidden during the normal functional operation of the chip and activated only when the triggering condition is applied.

5.3.1 HARDWARE TROJAN STRUCTURE

The basic structure of a Trojan in a 3PIP can include two main parts, trigger and payload [3]. A Trojan trigger is an optional part that monitors various signals and/or a series of events in the circuit. The payload usually taps signals from the original (Trojan-free) circuit and the output of the trigger. Once the trigger detects an expected event or condition, the payload is activated to perform malicious behavior. Typically, the trigger is expected to be activated under extremely rare conditions, so the payload remains inactive most of the time. When the payload is inactive, the IC acts like a Trojan-free circuit, making it difficult to detect the Trojan.

Figure 5.2 shows the basic structure of the Trojan at gate level. The trigger inputs $(T_1, T_2, ..., T_k)$ come from various nets in the circuit. The payload taps the original signal Net_i from the original (Trojan-free) circuit and the output of the Trigger. Since the trigger is expected to be activated under rare condition, the payload output stays at the same value most of the time, Net_i. However, when the trigger is active, that is, *TriggerEnable* is "0", the payload output will be different from Net_i; this could result in injecting an erroneous value into the circuit and causing error at the output. Note that Trojans at RTL would have similar functionality to the one shown in Fig. 5.2.

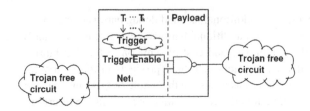

FIGURE 5.2

Trojan structure.

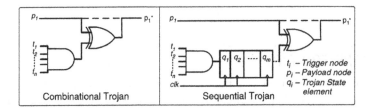

FIGURE 5.3

Example of combinational and sequential Trojan models.

5.3.2 TROJAN MODELING

Many different Trojans have been developed over the years by researchers using different Trojan models to demonstrate the capability and efficacy of their proposed Trojan countermeasure approaches. This section discusses the digitally triggered and a digital payload Trojan model that has been most commonly used. In this model, it is assumed that a Trojan will be activated by rare circuit node conditions and will have its payload as a critical node in terms of functionality, but low observable node in terms of testing, to evade detection during normal functional testing. If the Trojan includes sequential elements, such as rare-event triggered counters, then the Trojan may be even harder to detect.

Figure 5.3 shows generic models for combinational and sequential Trojans [7]. The trigger condition is an n-bit value at internal nodes, which is assumed to be rare enough to evade normal functional testing. The payload is defined as a node that is inverted when the Trojan is activated. To make it more difficult to detect, one might consider a sequential Trojan, which requires the rare event to repeat 2^m times before the Trojan gets activated and inverts the payload node. The sequential state machine is considered in its simplest form to be a counter, and the effect of the output on the payload is considered to be an XOR function to have maximal impact. In more generic models, the counter can be replaced by any Finite State Machine (FSM) and the circuit can be modified as a function of Trojan output and the payload node. In like manner, the Trojan trigger condition is modeled as an AND function of several rare nodes in order to make the combined event highly rare. However, the attacker may choose to reuse existing logic within the circuit to implement the trigger condition, without adding too many extra gates.

It is worth noting—when choosing rare values at internal nodes as inputs for the Trojan—that the combined rare event must be excitable; otherwise, the Trojan will never be triggered in real life.

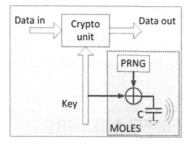

FIGURE 5.4

An example Trojan design with capability of leaking secret information from inside a cryptochip through power side-channels.

5.3.3 HARDWARE TROJAN EXAMPLES

This section provides some examples of hardware Trojans. It describes what will be the potential Trojans in a cryptomodule and in a general purpose processor.

5.3.3.1 Trojans in Cryptographic Engines

A possible Trojan attack in a cryptoengine can try to subvert the security mechanisms. The payload could range from a mechanism that presents dummy keys, predefined by the attacker, instead of the actual cryptographic keys used for sensitive encryption or signature verification operations, to leaking the secret hardware keys via covert side-channels, for example, information leaked through a power trace. Figure 5.4 provides an example of such a Trojan, which attempts to leak a secret key from inside a cryptographic module through power side-channels using a technique called malicious off-chip leakage, enabled by side-channels (MOLES) [8]. Other targets could be a random number generator used for deriving random session keys for a particular operation, or the debug passwords used for unlocking test mode access to security-sensitive signals. Researchers have also proposed leaking such secret information over wireless channels [9] by using low-bandwidth modulation of the transmitted signal.

5.3.3.2 Trojans in General-Purpose Processors

In general-purpose processors, an attacker at the fabrication facility can implement a backdoor, which can be exploited in the field by a software adversary [10–13]. For example, modern processors implement a hardware chain of trust to ensure that malware cannot compromise the hardware assets, such as secret keys and memory range protections. By using different stages of firmware and boot code authentication, one can ensure that the operating system (OS) kernel and lower levels, such as hypervisor, are not corrupted. However, in such systems, the attacker at an untrusted fabrication facility could implement a backdoor, which disables the secure booting mechanism under certain rare conditions or when presented with a unique rare input condition in the hands of an end-user adversary [10]. Likewise, other objectives that could be realized with the help of hardware Trojans would be able to bypass memory range protections using buffer overflow attacks, or gain access to privileged assets by evading the access control protection mechanisms implemented in the hardware.

This section discusses the Trojan threat from application-specific integrated circuit (ASIC) perspective. The next section will discuss the Trojan threat for FPGA design flow and supply chain.

5.4 HARDWARE TROJANS IN FPGA DESIGNS

FPGAs are widely used today in an array of embedded applications, ranging from telecommunications and data centers to missile guidance systems. Unfortunately, the outsourcing of FPGA production and the use of untrusted third party IPs has also given rise to the threat of Trojan insertion in them. FPGA-based Trojans can be in the form of IP blocks (hard, soft or firm), which get loaded onto a generic FPGA fabric and cause malicious activity (such as denial-of-service and leakage) on the system in which the FPGA is deployed. Such FPGA IP-based Trojans are more or less similar to their counterparts in an ASIC design flow, with the exception of layout-based Trojans, which are not applicable to FPGAs. However, Trojans that 'pre-exist' in an FPGA fabric and could potentially be inserted by an untrusted foundry or vendor pose unique threats and challenges of their own. FPGAs contain a large volume of reconfigurable logic in the form of lookup tables, block RAM, and programmable interconnects, which can be used to realize any arbitrary sequential or combinational design. However, there might be a significant amount of reconfigurable logic open to a malicious party (for example, the FPGA foundry or even the FPGA vendor) who can load a hardware Trojan and affect the FPGA-integrated system or compromise the IP loaded onto the FPGA. These FPGA device-specific hardware Trojans and their effects are explained in [14] and summarized below.

5.4.1 ACTIVATION CHARACTERISTIC

Hardware Trojans in FPGAs can have activation characteristics similar to the ones described in Section 5.3.1 and 5.3.2, such as always-on or triggered. However, a unique characteristic of FPGA device-based hardware Trojans is that they can either be IP-dependent or IP-independent.

5.4.1.1 IP-Dependent Trojans

A malicious foundry or FPGA vendor may implement a hardware Trojan that can monitor the logic values of several lookup tables (LUTs) in the FPGA fabric. Once triggered, such Trojans can corrupt other LUT values, load incorrect values into block RAMs (BRAMs), or sabotage configuration cells. Since any arbitrary IP may be loaded onto the FPGA, the malicious foundry or vendor could distribute trigger LUTs throughout the FPGA so that the probability of the Trojan triggering and causing malfunction may increase.

5.4.1.2 IP-Independent Trojans

A malicious foundry or vendor may also implement a Trojan into an FPGA chip that is completely independent of the IP loaded onto it. Such Trojans can occupy a small portion of FPGA resources and malfunction IP-independent but critical FPGA resources, such as digital clock managers (DCM). One potential mode of attack would be a Trojan increasing or decreasing the design clock frequency by manipulating the configuring SRAM cells of the DCM unit, which can cause failure in sequential circuits.

5.4.2 PAYLOAD CHARACTERISTICS

FPGA device-based Trojans can also bring about unique malicious effects, such as causing malfunction of FPGA resources or leakage of the IP loaded onto the FPGA.

5.4.2.1 Malfunction

Hardware Trojans in FPGA devices can either cause logical malfunction by corrupting LUT(s) or SRAM values, thereby affecting the functionality of the implemented IP, or by causing physical damage to the FPGA device. For example, a triggered hardware Trojan could reprogram an I/O port set as an input to become an output I/O port, while suppressing the configuration cells that prevent it from being programmed as such. This would cause a high short-circuit current to flow between the FPGA and the system it is connected to, thereby leading to physical device failure.

5.4.2.2 IP Leakage

FPGAs today offer bitstream encryption capabilities in order to protect the IP loaded onto an FPGA device. However, such encryption only prevents a direct or unauthorized readback by software. A hardware Trojan may circumvent such protection by either leaking the decryption key, or even the entire IP. The Trojan may tap the decryption key as it comes out of non-volatile memory, or the actual decrypted IP, which could then be exfiltrated either via covert side-channels (for example, power traces) or through JTAG, USB or I/O ports.

5.5 HARDWARE TROJANS TAXONOMY

Developing a better understanding of hardware Trojans and creating effective defenses require a framework that groups similar Trojans together to enable a systematic study of their characteristics. Detection, mitigation, and protection techniques can then be developed for each Trojan class along with benchmarks to serve as the basis for comparing countermeasures. In addition, experimental implementations can be created for Trojan classes yet to be observed, thereby fostering proactive defense.

Taxonomy is developed based on hardware Trojans' physical, activation, and functional characteristics. In this regard, hardware Trojans are classified based on five attributes: (1) insertion phase, (2) abstraction level, (3) activation mechanism, (4) payload, and (5) location (shown in Fig. 5.5) [15].

5.5.1 INSERTION PHASE

Hardware Trojans can be inserted throughout SoC design flow. As the abovementioned Trojan's attribute suggests, Trojans can also be classified based on the phases in which they are inserted.

5.5.1.1 Specification Phase

In this phase, chip designers define the system's characteristics: the target environment, expected function, size, power, and delay. While the SoC development is in this phase, functional specifications or

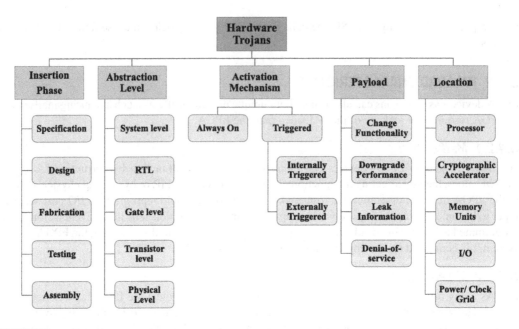

FIGURE 5.5

Taxonomy of hardware Trojans.

other design constraints can be altered. For example, a Trojan at the specification phase might change the hardware's timing requirements.

5.5.1.2 Design Phase

Developers consider functional, logical, timing, and physical constraints as they map the design onto the target technology. At this point, they can use third-party IP blocks and standard cells. Trojans might be in any of the components that aid the design. For example, a standard cell library can be tampered with Trojans.

5.5.1.3 Fabrication Phase

During this phase, developers create a mask set and use wafers to produce the masks. Subtle mask changes can have serious effects. In an extreme case, an adversary can substitute a different mask set. Alternatively, chemical compositions might be altered during fabrication to increase the electromigration in critical circuitry, such as power supplies and clock grids, which would accelerate failures.

5.5.1.4 Testing Phase

The IC testing phase is important for hardware trust, not only because it is a likely phase for Trojan insertion, but also because it provides an opportunity for Trojan detection. Testing is only useful for detection when done in a trustworthy manner. For example, an adversary who inserted a Trojan in the fabrication phase would want to have control over the test vectors to ensure that the Trojan is not detected during test. Trustworthy testing ensures that the test vectors will be kept secret and faithfully applied, and that the specified actions accept/reject, and binning will be faithfully followed. An attacker can take advantage of not-detected (ND) faults by automatic test pattern generation (ATGP) tools. By doing so, a Trojan that uses these ND faults will never be activated.

5.5.1.5 Assembly Phase

Developers assemble the tested chip and other hardware components on a printed circuit board (PCB). Every interface in a system, where two or more components interact is a potential Trojan insertion site. Even if all the ICs in a system are trustworthy, malicious assembly can introduce security flaws in the system. For example, an unshielded wire connected to a node on the PCB can introduce unintended electromagnetic coupling between the signal on the board and its electromagnetic surroundings. An adversary can exploit this for information leakage and fault injection.

5.5.2 ABSTRACTION LEVEL

Trojan circuits can be inserted at various hardware abstraction levels. Their functionality and the structure are dependent on the abstraction level at which they are inserted.

5.5.2.1 System Level

At the system level, the different hardware modules, interconnections, and communication protocols used are defined. At this level, the Trojans may be triggered by the modules in the target hardware. For example, the ASCII values of the inputs from the keyboard can be interchanged.

5.5.2.2 Register-Transfer Level

At the RTL, chip designers describe each functional module in terms of registers, signals, and Boolean functions. A Trojan can be easily designed and inserted at the RTL because the attacker has full control over the design's functionality. For example, a Trojan implemented at this level might halve the rounds of a cryptographic algorithm by making a round counter to advance in two steps instead of one.

5.5.2.3 Gate Level

At this level, an SoC is represented as an interconnection of logic gates. An attacker can carefully control all aspects of the inserted Trojan, including its size and location. For example, a Trojan might be a simple comparator consisting of basic gates (AND, OR, XOR gates) that monitor the chip's internal signals.

5.5.2.4 Transistor Level

Chip designers use transistors to build logic gates. This level gives the Trojan designer control over circuit characteristics, such as power and timing. The attacker can insert or remove individual transistors, altering the circuit functionality, or modify transistor sizes to alter circuit parameters. For example, a transistor-level Trojan might be a transistor with low gate width that can cause more delay in the critical path.

5.5.2.5 Physical Level

This level describes all circuit components and their dimensions and locations, and is the design's physical level, where a Trojan can be inserted. An attacker can insert Trojans by modifying the size of the wires and distances between circuit elements and reassigning metal layers. For example, changing the width of the clock wires, timing critical nets or metal wires in the chip can cause clock skew.

5.5.3 ACTIVATION MECHANISM

Some Trojans are designed to be always on, whereas others remain dormant until triggered. A triggered Trojan needs an internal or external event to be activated. Once the trigger activates a Trojan, it can remain active forever or return to a dormant state after a specified time.

5.5.3.1 Internally Triggered

An internally triggered Trojan is activated by an event within the target device. The event might be either time-based or physical-condition-based. A counter in the design can trigger a Trojan at a predetermined time, resulting in a silicon timebomb. Similarly, a Trojan can trigger when the chip temperature exceeds a certain threshold.

5.5.3.2 Externally Triggered

An externally-triggered Trojan requires external input to the target module to activate. The external trigger can be user input or component output. User-input triggers include push buttons, switches, keyboards, or keywords and phrases in the input data stream in a system. Component-output triggers might be from any of the components that interact with the target device. For example, a Trojan in a cryptomodule can derive its trigger condition from the applied plaintext input and triggers when it observes a specific plaintext, or a combination of plaintext and operating conditions.

One can also classify the triggered Trojans into two categories: (1) Analog triggered and (2) Digital triggered. Analog-triggered Trojans are triggered analog signals, such as temperature and voltage. Digitally triggered Trojans are triggered by logic-conditions, such as state of the flip-flops, state of a logic net, counter, clock signal, data, instruction, and/or interrupts.

5.5.4 PAYLOAD

Trojans can also be characterized by their payload, that is, the malicious effects caused by them when they become activated. The severity of these effects on target hardware or systems can range from subtle disturbances to catastrophic system failures.

5.5.4.1 Change Functionality

Trojan can change the functionality of the target device, and cause subtle errors that might be difficult to detect during manufacturing test. For example, a Trojan might cause an error detection module to accept inputs that should be rejected.

5.5.4.2 Downgrade Performance

A Trojan can downgrade performance by intentionally changing device parameters. These include functional, interface, or parametric characteristics, such as power and delay. For example, a Trojan might insert more buffers in the chip's interconnections and, hence, consume more power, which in turn could drain the battery quickly.

5.5.4.3 Leak Information

A Trojan can also leak information through both covert and overt channels. Sensitive data can be leaked via radio frequency, optical or thermal power, timing side-channels, and interfaces, such as RS-232 and JTAG (Joint Test Action Group). For example, a Trojan might leak a cryptographic algorithm's secret key through unused RS-232 ports.

5.5.4.4 Denial-of-Service

A denial-of-service (DoS) Trojan can cause the target module to exhaust scarce resources, such as bandwidth, computation, and battery power. It could also physically destroy, disable, or alter the device's configuration, for example, causing the processor to ignore the interrupt from a specific peripheral. DoS can be either temporary or permanent.

5.5.5 LOCATION

A hardware Trojan can be inserted in a single component or spread across multiple component, for example, processor, memory, input/output, power supply, or clock grid. Trojans distributed across multiple components can act independently of one another or together as a group to accomplish their attack objectives.

5.5.5.1 Random Logic

A Trojan can be inserted into the random logic portion of an SoC. Detection of such Trojans are extremely challenging since understanding functionality of random logic is difficult, hence making it limited to generate effective test stimuli. Size of such logic in an SoC can be quite large.

5.5.5.2 Processing Unit

Any Trojan embedded into the logic units that are part of the processor can be grouped under this category. A Trojan in the processor might, for example, change the instructions' execution order.

5.5.5.3 Cryptographic Accelerator

Cryptomodules are likely target for Trojan insertion as these modules work with assets, such as private keys and sensitive plaintext. A Trojan in a cryptomodule can leak the secret key (attack on confidentiality) or replace the key (attack on integrity), and compromise the security of the overall system.

5.5.5.4 Memory Units

Trojans in the memory blocks and their interface units fall in this category. These Trojans might alter the value stored in the memory and also blockread or blockwrite access to certain memory locations, for example, change the contents of a programmable read-only memory in an SoC.

5.5.5.5 Input/Output Port

Trojans can reside in a chip's peripherals or within the PCB. These peripherals interface with the external components and can give the Trojan control over data communication between the processor and the system's external components. For example, a Trojan might alter the data coming through a JTAG port.

5.5.5.6 Power Supply

Modern SoCs include many voltage islands, a large number of locally distributed voltage regulators, and dynamic voltage/frequency systems, where the chip frequency is adjusted in the field by changing VDD as the chip ages in the field. Trojans could be inserted by an adversary to alter the voltage and current supplied to the chip, causing failures.

5.5.5.7 Clock Grid

Trojans in the clock grid can change the clock's frequency, insert glitches in the clock supplied to the chip, and launch fault attacks. These Trojans can also freeze the clock signal supplied to the rest of the chip's functional modules. For example, a Trojan might increase the clock signal skew supplied to specific parts of a chip, causing hold-time violation on short paths.

5.6 TRUST BENCHMARKS

A "trust benchmark" is a benchmark circuit (generic circuits at the RTL, gate or layout level), which has Trojan(s) deliberately added to it at hard-to-detect, impactful, and/or opportunistic locations (for example, rare nodes and layout white-space), for the purpose of comparing impacts of Trojans and the effectiveness of different Trojan detection techniques [16]. The current trust benchmarks are available at http://www.trust-hub.org/benchmarks.php.

Each benchmark comes ready with documentation, that provides important features of the trust benchmark, such as trigger probability (for gate/layout level Trojans), exact effect of the Trojan, input combination required to trigger Trojan (for RTL/gate-level), Trojan-induced delay or capacitance, and size of Trojan/overall circuit. Additionally, for some benchmarks, a "golden model" is provided, that is, a version of the same circuit without Trojans, which is essential for analyzing trust benchmarks against different attack models. Finally, for most of the trust benchmarks, two test benches are included, one of which can be used with the golden model (for debugging and test purposes), and the other can be used to trigger the Trojan. For RTL trust benchmarks, the test bench is in the form of Verilog/VHDL format that have the Trojan trigger specified. For netlist/gate-level benchmarks, exact test patterns to trigger the Trojan are provided. Finally, the documentation for each trust benchmark contains the exact form and location of the inserted Trojan. For example, for RTL Trojans, the part of the RTL code that implements the Trojan has been documented. For gate-level circuits, a snippet of the Trojan netlist has also been provided. The exact location and implementation of the Trojan have also been provided to make it easier for researchers to present results in terms of detection accuracy. However, it should be noted that such information must only be used a posteriori, as taking into account the Trojan implementation and location beforehand might unfairly bias detection techniques. Lastly, it is relevant to note that, generally, Trojan benchmarking is an ongoing effort, and more trust benchmarks are being developed to cover the Trojan taxonomy and improve on existing ones.

The following are some of the representative benchmarks from approximately a hundred benchmarks developed so far:

5.6.1 BENCHMARK NAMING CONVENTION

Trust benchmark follows the following naming convention to assign a unique name to each Trojan benchmark in a trust benchmark circuit: **DesignName-Tn#$**, where,

- **DesignName:** The name of the main design without a Trojan.
- **Tn (Trojan number):** It is of a maximum two digits. The same Trojan number in different designs does not represent the same Trojan.
- **# (Placement number):** The second to last digit indicates the different placement of the same Trojan in a circuit and ranges from 0 to 9.
- **$ (Version number):** The last digit in a benchmark name indicates the version of the Trojan and ranges from 0 to 9. This was added as a feature in case a new version of the same Trojan with the same placement would have been developed. The version number would differentiate the older version from the new one.

For example, MC8051-T1000 indicates that Trojan number 10 (T10) was inserted in the microcontroller 8051 (MC 8051) at the location number 0, and its version is 0. As another example, dma-T1020 means that Trojan number 10 (T10) was inserted in the DMA circuit at the location number 2 and its version is 0. As aforementioned, Trojan T10 in DMA is not necessarily the same as Trojan T10 in MC8051.

5.6.2 SAMPLE TRUST BENCHMARKS

Following are some benchmarks with a brief description of their enclosed Trojan:

- **Insertion Phase – Fabrication:** Trojans can also be realized by adding/removing gates or changing the circuit layout during GDSII development, and the mask during fabrication.
  Sample Benchmark: EthernetMAC10GE-T710 contains a Trojan triggered by a combinational comparator circuit, which seeks a specific 16-bit vector. The probability of Trojan activation in this case is 6.4271e-23. When the Trojan is triggered, its payload gains control over an internal signal in the circuit.
- **Abstraction Level – Layout:** Trojans can be realized by varying circuit mask, adding/removing gates, or changing gate and interconnect geometry to impact circuit reliability.
  Sample Benchmark: EthernetMAC10GE-T100 contains a Trojan on a critical path. A particular net is widened to increase coupling capacitance, thereby enabling crosstalk.
- **Activation Mechanism – Triggered Externally:** Trojans become activated under certain external conditions, such as by an externally enabled input.
  Sample Benchmark: RS232-T1700 contains a Trojan triggered by a combinational comparator. The trigger input probability is $1.59e^{-7}$ and it is externally controlled. Whenever the Trojan is triggered, its payload gains control over a particular output port.
- **Effect – Change Functionality:** After activation, a Trojan will change the functionality of a circuit.
  Sample Benchmark: RS232-T1200 contains a Trojan triggered by a sequential comparator with probability $8.47e^{-11}$. Whenever the Trojan is triggered, its payload gains control over a particular output port.
- **Location – Power Supply:** A Trojan can be placed in the chip power network.

Sample Benchmark: EthernetMAC10GE-T400 is modified with narrow power lines in one part of the circuit layout.

- **Physical Characteristic – Parametric:** A Trojan can be realized by changing circuit parameters, such as wire thickness.

    Sample Benchmark: EthernetMAC10GE-T100 contains a Trojan on the critical path. This Trojan widens a particular internal wire to cause timing violation.

Table 5.1 Trust benchmark characteristics

Category	Trojan Type	No.	Main Circuits
Insertion Phase	Specification	0	–
	Design	80	AES, BasicRSA, MC8051, PIC16F84, RS232, s15850, s35932, s38417, s38584
	Testing	0	–
	Assembly	0	–
Abstraction Level	RTL	51	AES-T100, b19, BasicRSA, MC8051, PIC16F84, RS232
	Gate	25	b19, EthernetMAC10GE, RS232, s15850, s35932, s38417, s38584, VGA LCD
	Layout	12	EthernetMAC10GE, MultPyramid, RS232
Activation Mechanism	Always On	11	AES-T100, MultPyramid, EthernetMAC10GE
	Triggered	79	AES, b19, BasicRSA, MultPyramid, PIC16F84l, RS232, s15850
Payload	Change Functionality	35	b19, Ethernet MAC10GE, MC8051, RS232, s15850, s35932, s38417, s38584
	Degrade Performance	3	EthernetMAC10GE, MultPyramid, s35932
	Leak Information	24	AES, BasicRSA, PIC16F84, s35932, s38584
	DoS	34	AES, BasicRSA, EthernetMAC10GE, MC8051, MultPyramid, PIC16F84, RS232
Location	Processor	26	b19, b19, BasicRSA, MC8051, MultPyramid, PIC16F84, s15850, s35932, s38417, s38584
	Crypto Modules	25	AES-T100 to T2100, BasicRSA-T100
	Memory	0	–
	I/O	4	MC8051, wb_conmax
	Power Supply	2	MC8051-T300, wb_conmax
	Clock Grid	2	EthernetMAC10GE

Table 5.1 presents a complete list of trust benchmarks that have been developed so far. They are categorized based on the Trojan taxonomy, including the number of trust benchmarks available for each type and the names of the main circuits/benchmarks into which the Trojans have been inserted. For instance, Table 5.1 shows that 25 Trojans are inserted at the gate-level, 51 at the RTL, and 12 at the

layout level, under the row "Abstraction Level". As another example, the "Payload" row shows that 35 Trojans change circuit functionality, 3 degrade circuit performance, 24 leak information to the outside of a chip, and 34 perform a denial-of-service attack when activated. Note that some benchmarks fall under more than one category. Currently, there are a total of 91 trust benchmarks on the Trust-Hub website.

5.7 COUNTERMEASURES AGAINST HARDWARE TROJANS

Several Trojan detection approaches have been developed over the years. Without loss of generality, these approaches are classified into two broad categories, Trojan Detection and Trojan Prevention, each of which can further be classified into several subcategories, as shown in Fig. 5.6.

5.7.1 TROJAN DETECTION

Trojan detection is the most straightforward and commonly used approach to deal with hardware Trojans. It aims to verify the existing designs and fabricated SoCs without any supplementary circuitry. They are performed either at the design stage (that is, pre-silicon) to validate SoC designs or after the manufacturing stage (that is, post-silicon) to verify fabricated SoCs.

5.7.1.1 Post-silicon Trojan Detection

These techniques are employed after the chip is fabricated; they can be classified into destructive and nondestructive methods, as illustrated in Fig. 5.6.

Destructive methods: These techniques typically use destructive reverse-engineering to depackage an IC, and obtain images of each layer in order to reconstruct the design-for-trust validation of the end product. Destructive reverse engineering has the potential of giving very high assurance that any malicious modification in the IC can be detected, but it comes with high cost and could take several weeks and months for an IC of reasonable complexity. Additionally, at the end of this invasive process, the IC cannot be used, and one can only obtain the information for a single IC sample. Note that reverse engineering of modern complex SoCs is a tedious and error-prone process. Hence, in order to obtain the entire chip structure reverse engineered, one may use tens of ICs as deprocessing and depackaging could cause unintentional errors in the reverse engineering process. Therefore, in general, destructive approaches do not seem viable for Trojan detection. However, destructive reverse engineering on a limited number of samples can be attractive to obtain the characteristics of a golden batch of SoCs. Bao et al. [17] presented a machine learning method which adapts one-class support vector machine (SVM) to identify Trojan-free ICs for the golden model.

Functional tests: These techniques attempt to activate Trojans by applying test vectors and comparing the responses with the correct results. To be effective, such techniques require availability of a golden response. While at first glance this is similar in spirit to manufacturing tests for detecting manufacturing defects, conventional manufacturing tests using functional/structural/random patterns perform poorly in detecting hardware Trojans [12]. Intelligent adversaries can design Trojans that are activated under very rare conditions, so they can go undetected under structural and functional tests during the manufacturing test process. Banga and Hsiao [18] and Chakraborty et al. [19] developed test pattern generation methods to trigger such rarely activated nets, and improved the possibility of observing

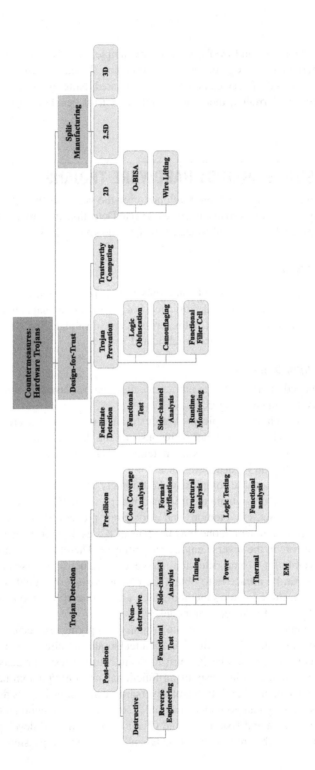

FIGURE 5.6

Taxonomy of hardware Trojan countermeasures.

Trojan's effects from primary outputs. However, due to the numerous logical states in a circuit, it is impractical to enumerate all states of a real design. Additionally, instead of changing the functionality of the original circuit [20], a Trojan that transmits information via nonfunctional means, for example, with an antenna or by modifying the specification, leads to functional tests failure to detect these kinds of Trojans.

Side-channel signal analysis: These approaches detect hardware Trojans by measuring circuit parameters, such as delay [21,22], power (transient [23] and leakage power [24]), temperature [25], and radiation [26,27]. They take advantage of side effects (that is, extra path delay, power, heat, or electromagnetic radiation) caused by additional circuits and/or activity from Trojan trigger/payload activation. However, the majority of the detection techniques assume that "golden ICs" (Trojan-free ICs) are available for comparison in order to identify Trojan-infected ICs. For example, Agrawal et al. [23] first demonstrated the use of side-channel profiles, such as power consumption and electromagnetic emanation for Trojan circuit detection. The process went as follows: The authors first generated the power signature profiles of a small number of ICs randomly selected from a batch of manufactured ICs. These ICs served as golden masters (Trojan-free ICs). Once profiled the golden masters underwent a rigorous destructive reverse-engineering phase, where they were compared piece by piece against the original design. If Trojan free, the ICs were then accepted as genuine ICs and their profiles served as power templates. The remaining ICs could then be tested efficiently and in a nondestructive manner by simply applying the same stimuli and building their power profiles. The profiles were compared using statistical techniques, such as principal component analysis against the templates obtained from the golden masters.

Side-channel analysis methods may succeed in detecting Trojans to some degree. However, their difficulty lies in achieving high coverage of every gate or net, and in extracting the tiny, abnormal side-channel signals of hardware Trojans in the presence of process and environmental variations. As the feature size of ICs shrinks and the number of transistors continue to increase, the increasing levels of process variations can easily mask the small side-channel signals induced by low-overhead and rarely triggered Trojans. Since they observed that filler cells are more reflective than other functional cells, recently, Zhou et al. [27] presented a backside imaging method to produce a pattern based on filler cells placed in the IC layout. Although this technique does not require golden chip, the comparison between the simulated image and measured optical image still suffers from the variations in the manufacturing process. Additional challenges include taking clear images at higher resolution that takes enormous amount of time.

5.7.1.2 Pre-silicon Trojan Detection

These techniques are used to help SoC developers and design engineers to validate third-party IP (3PIP) cores and their final designs. Existing pre-silicon detection techniques can be broadly classified into code coverage analysis, formal verification, structural analysis, logic testing, and functional analysis.

Code Coverage Analysis: Code coverage is defined as the percentage of lines of code that has been executed during functional verification of the design. This metric gives a quantitative measure of the completeness of the functional simulation of the design. Code coverage analysis can also be applied to identify suspicious signals that may be a part of a Trojan, and validate the trustworthiness of an 3PIP. Hicks et al. [13] presented a technique named unused circuit identification (UCI) to find the lines of RTL code that have not been executed during simulation. These unused lines of codes can be considered to be part of a malicious circuit. Here, the authors proposed to remove these suspicious lines of RTL

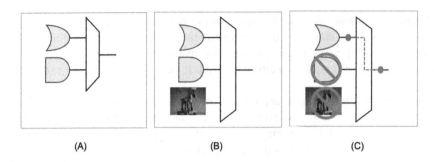

(A)   (B)   (C)

FIGURE 5.7

High-level overview of the unused circuit identification (UCI) technique. (A) designers develop hardware designs, (B) a rogue entity inserts hardware Trojan into the design, and (C) UCI technique identifies and removes suspicious circuits.

code from the hardware design and emulate it in the software level. Figure 5.7 illustrates the high-level flow of the UCI technique. This technique, however, does not guarantee the trustworthiness of a 3PIP. Authors in [28] have demonstrated that hardware Trojans can be designed to defeat UCI technique. This type of Trojans derive their triggering circuits from less likely events to evade detection from code coverage analysis.

Formal Verification: Formal methods, such as symbolic execution [29], model checking [30], and information flow [31] have been traditionally applied to software systems for finding security bugs and improving test coverage. Formal verification has also been shown to be effective in verifying the trustworthiness of 3PIP [32,33]. These approaches are based on the concept of proof-carrying code (PCC) to formally validate the security-related properties of an IP. In these approaches, an SoC integrator provides a set of security properties in addition to the standard functional specification to the IP vendor. A formal proof of these properties, alongside the hardware IP, is then provided by the third party vendor. SoC integrator then validates the proof by using the PCC. Any malicious modification of the IP would violate this proof, thereby indicating the presence of hardware Trojan. Figure 5.8 shows the overview of the PCC-based Trojan detection technique

Rajendran et al. [34] presented a technique to formally verify malicious modification of critical data in 3PIP by hardware Trojans. The proposed technique is based on bounded model checking (BMC). Here, the BMC checks for the property, "does critical information get corrupted?", and outputs if the property is being violated in the given IP. Also BMC reports the sequence of input patterns, which violates this property. It is possible to extract the triggering condition of the Trojan from the reported input patterns. Another similar approach has been shown in [35], which formally verifies unauthorized information leakage in 3PIPs. This technique checks for the property, "does the design leak any sensitive information?". Due to the problem of space explosion, the limitation of these approaches is that the processing ability of the model checking is relatively limited. Although, these techniques present a promising approach for Trojan detection, each has certain challenges and limitations [36].

Structural Analysis: Structural analysis employs quantitative metrics to mark signals or gates with low activation probability as suspicious. Salmani et al. [37] presented a metric named 'Statement Hardness'

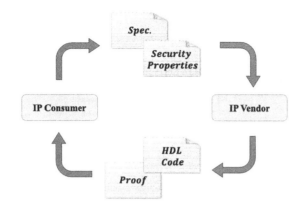

FIGURE 5.8

Overview of proof-carrying code (PCC) based Trojan detection technique.

to evaluate the difficulty of executing a statement in the RTL code. Areas in a circuit with large value of 'Statement Hardness' are more vulnerable to Trojan insertion. At gate level, an attacker would most likely target *hard-to-detect* areas of the gate level netlist to insert Trojan. *Hard-to-detect* nets are defined as nets that have low transition probability and are not testable through well-known fault testing techniques, such as stuck-at, transition delay, path delay, and bridging faults [38]. Inserting a Trojan in *hard-to-detect* areas would reduce the probability to trigger the Trojan and, thereby, reduce the probability of being detected during verification and validation testing. Tehranipoor et al. [5] proposed metrics to evaluate *hard-to-detect* areas in the gate-level netlist. The limitations of code/structural analysis techniques are that they do not guarantee Trojan detection, and manual postprocessing is required to analyze suspicious signals or gates, and determine if they are a part of a Trojan.

Logic Testing: The principal idea of logic testing is the same as the functional tests described earlier in the post-silicon Trojan detection section. The logic testing is conducted with simulation, whereas functional tests have to be performed on a tester for applying input patterns and collecting output responses. Therefore, existing techniques for functional tests are also applicable to logic testing. Of course, logic testing also inherits functional tests' pros and cons.

Functional Analysis: Functional analysis applies random input patterns and performs functional simulation of the IP to find suspicious regions of the IP that have similar characteristics of a hardware Trojan. The basic difference between functional analysis and logic testing is that logic testing aims to apply specific patterns to activate a Trojan, whereas functional analysis applies random patterns, and these patterns are not directed to trigger the Trojan. Waksman et al. [39] presented a technique named Functional Analysis for Nearly-unused Circuit Identification (FANCI), which flags nets having weak input-to-output dependency as suspicious. This approach is based on the observation that a hardware Trojan is triggered under very rare condition. Therefore, the logic implementing the trigger circuit of a Trojan is nearly-unused or dormant during normal functional operation. Here, the authors have proposed a metric called 'Control value' to find 'nearly-unused logic' by quantifying the degree of controllability of each input net has on its output function. 'Control value' is computed by applying random input patterns and measuring the number of output transitions. If the control value of a

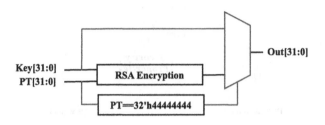

FIGURE 5.9

RSA-T100 Trojan. This Trojan leaks the private key when the plaintext (PT) data is *32'h44444444*.

net is lower than a predefined threshold, then the net is flagged as suspicious. For example, for the RSA-T100 [16] Trojan, the triggering condition is *32'h44444444* (shown in Fig. 5.9). The "Control value" for the triggering net is 2^{-32}, which is expected to be lower than the predefined threshold. The major limitations of FANCI are that this approach produces a large number of false-positive results and does not specify any method to verify if the suspicious signals are performing any malicious operation. Also, Zhang et al. [40] have shown how to design Trojans to defeat FANCI. Here, they design Trojan circuits, whose trigger vector arrives over multiple clock cycles. For example, for the RSA-T100 Trojan, the triggering sequence can be derived over 4 cycles, making the 'Control value' of the triggering net 2^{-8}. Furthermore, FANCI cannot identify 'Always On' Trojans, which remain active during their lifetime and do not have any triggering circuitry.

Authors in [41] presented a technique called VeriTrust to identify potential triggering inputs of a hardware Trojan. The proposed technique is based on the observation that input ports of the triggering circuit of a hardware Trojan keeps dormant during normal operation and, therefore, are redundant to the normal logic function of the circuit. VeriTrust works as follows: first it performs functional simulation of the IP with random input patterns and traces the activation history of the inputs ports in the form of sums-of-product (SOP) and product-of-sum (POS). VeriTrust then identifies redundant inputs by analyzing the SOPs and POSs, which are unactivated during functional simulation. These redundant input signals are potential triggering inputs of a hardware Trojan. VeriTrust technique aims to be independent of the implementation style of hardware Trojan. However, this technique also produces a large number of false-positive results because of incomplete functional simulation and unactivated entries belonging to normal function. Also, authors in [40] designed Trojans that can defeat VeriTrust by ensuring that the Trojan-triggering circuit is driven by a subset of functional inputs, in addition to triggering inputs. VeriTrust also shares the same limitation of FANCI, that is, not being able to identify "Always On" Trojans.

5.7.2 DESIGN-FOR-TRUST

As described in the previous section, detecting a quiet, low-overhead hardware Trojan is still very challenging with existing techniques. A potentially more effective way is to plan for the Trojan problem in the design phase through design-for-trust. These methodologies are classified into four classes according to their objectives.

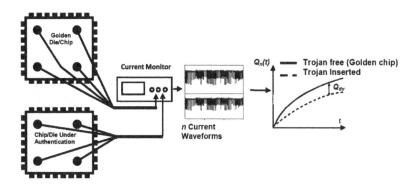

FIGURE 5.10

Current integration (charge) method.

5.7.2.1 Facilitate Detection

Functional Test: Triggering a Trojan from inputs and observing the Trojan effect from outputs are difficult due to the stealthy nature of Trojans. A large number of low-controllable and low-observable nets in a design significantly hinder the possibility of activating a Trojan. Salmani et al. [42] and Zhou et al. [43] attempted to increase controllability and observability of nodes by inserting test points into the circuit. Another approach proposed to multiplex two outputs of a DFF, Q and $\overline{Q}$, through a 2-to-1 multiplexer, and select either of them. This extends the state space of the design and increases the possibility of exciting/propagating the Trojan effects to circuit outputs, making them detectable [18]. These approaches are beneficial not only to functional-test-based detection techniques but also to side-channel-based methods that need partial activation of Trojan circuitry.

Side-channel Signal Analysis: A number of design methods have been developed to increase the sensitivity of side-channel-based detection approaches. The amount of current a Trojan can draw could be so small that it can be submerged into an envelope of noise and process variations effects; therefore, it may be undetectable by conventional measurement equipments. However, Trojan-detection capability can be greatly enhanced by measuring currents locally, and from multiple power ports/pads. Figure 5.10 shows the current (charge) integration methodology for detecting hardware Trojans presented in [44]. Salmani and Tehranipoor [45] proposed to minimize background side-channel signals by localizing switching activities within one region, while minimizing them in other regions through a scan-cell reordering technique. Additionally, some newly developed structures or sensors are implemented in the circuit to provide a higher detection sensitivity compared to conventional measurements. Ring oscillator (RO) structures [46], shadow registers [47], and delay elements [48] on a set of selected short paths are inserted for path delay measurements. RO sensors [49] and transient current sensors [50,51] are able to improve sensitivity to voltage and current fluctuations caused by Trojans, respectively. Besides, integration of process variation sensors [52,53] can calibrate the model or measurement, and minimize the noise induced by manufacturing variations.

Runtime Monitoring: As triggering all types and sizes of Trojans during pre-silicon and post-silicon tests is very difficult, runtime monitoring of critical computations can significantly increase the level of trust with respect to hardware Trojan attacks. These runtime monitoring approaches can utilize existing or supplemental on-chip structures to monitor chips behaviors [10,54] or operating conditions,

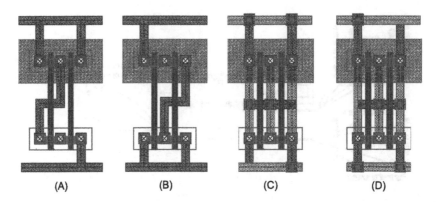

(A) (B) (C) (D)

FIGURE 5.11

(A) and (B) show standard cell layout of traditional 2-input NAND and NOR gates, respectively. Here, the metal layers are different and, therefore, easy to differentiate. (C) and (D) show camouflaged standard cell layouts of 2-input NAND and NOR gates, respectively. Note that, the metal layers are identical and, therefore, difficult to distinguish.

such as transient power [50,55] and temperature [25]. They can disable the chip upon detection of any abnormalities or bypass it to allow reliable operation, albeit with some performance overhead. Jin et al. [56] present a design of an on-chip analog neural network that can be trained to distinguish trusted from untrusted circuit functionality based on measurements obtained via on-chip measurement acquisition sensors.

5.7.2.2 Prevent Trojan Insertion

These techniques consist of preventive mechanisms that attempt to thwart hardware Trojan insertion by attackers. To insert targeted Trojans, typically attackers need to understand the function of the design first. Attackers who are not in the design house usually identify circuit functionality by reverse engineering.

Logic Obfuscation: Logic obfuscation attempts to hide the genuine functionality and implementation of a design by inserting built-in locking mechanisms into the original design. The locking circuits become transparent, and the right function appears only when a right key is applied. The increased complexity of identifying the genuine functionality without knowing the right input vectors can lower the ability of inserting a targeted Trojan by attackers. For combinational logic obfuscation, XOR/XNOR gates could be introduced at certain locations in a design [57]. In sequential logic obfuscation, additional states are introduced in a finite state machine to conceal its functional states [19]. In addition, some techniques proposed to insert reconfigurable logics for logic obfuscation [58,59]. The design is functional when the reconfigurable circuits are correctly programmed by the design house or end-user.

Camouflaging: Camouflaging is a layout-level obfuscation technique to create indistinguishable layouts for different gates by adding dummy contacts, and faking connections between the layers within a camouflaged logic gate [60,61] (shown in Fig. 5.11). The camouflaging technique can hinder attackers from extracting a correct gate-level netlist of a circuit from the layout through imaging different layers; in that way, the original design is protected from insertion of targeted Trojans. Additionally, Bi et al.

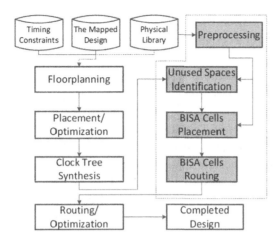

FIGURE 5.12

The BISA insertion flow.

[62] utilized a similar dummy contact approach and developed a set of camouflaging cells based on polarity-controllable SiNW FETs.

Functional Filler Cell: Since layout design tools are typically conservative in placement, they cannot fill 100% of the area with regular standard cells in a design. The unused spaces are usually filled with filler cells or decap cells that do not have any functionality. Filler cells are usually used during engineering change order (ECO) for improving debug and yield, whereas decaps are used to manage peak current in the chip, especially in areas where instantaneous power is quite significant. Thus, the most covert way for attackers to insert Trojans in a circuit layout is replacing filler cells, and to some degree decaps, because removing these nonfunctional cells has the smallest impact on electrical parameters. The built-in self-authentication (BISA) approach fills all white spaces with functional filler cells during layout design [63]. The inserted cells are then connected automatically to form a combinational circuitry that could be tested. A failure during later testing denotes that a functional filler has been replaced by a Trojan. Figure 5.12 shows the general BISA insertion flow. The white rectangles in Fig. 5.12 are conventional ASIC design flow, whereas the dark rectangles represent the additional steps required for BISA. These steps are as follows: (i) preprocessing (gather detailed information about the standard cell library), (ii) unused space identification, (iii) BISA cell placement, and (iv) BISA cell routing.

5.7.2.3 Trustworthy Computing

The third class of design for trust is trustworthy computing on untrusted components. The difference between runtime monitoring and trustworthy computing is that trustworthy computing is tolerant to Trojan attacks by design. Trojan detection and recovery at runtime—acting as the last line of defense—is necessary, especially for mission-critical applications. Some approaches employ a distributed software scheduling protocol to achieve a Trojan-activation-tolerant trustworthy computing system in a multicore processor [64,65]. Concurrent Error Detection (CED) techniques can be adapted to detect malicious outputs generated by Trojans [66,67]. In addition, Reece et al. [68] and Rajendran et al. [67] proposed to use a diverse set of 3PIP vendors to prevent Trojan's effects. The technique in [68] verifies the integrity of a design via comparison of multiple 3PIPs with another untrusted design performing a similar function. Rajendran et al. [67] utilize operation-to-3PIP-to-vendor allocation constraints to prevent collusions between 3PIPs from the same vendor.

For the design for trust (DFT) techniques that require circuitry added during the front-end design phase, the potential area and performance overheads are the chief concerns to designers. As the size of a circuit increases, the number of quiet (low controllability/observability) nets/gates will increase the complexity of processing and produce a large time/area overhead. Thus, the DFT techniques for facilitating detection are still difficult to apply to a large design that contains millions of gates. In addition, the preventive DFT techniques need to insert additional gates (logic obfuscation) or modify the original standard cells (camouflaging), which could degrade the chip performance significantly, and affect their acceptability in high-end circuits. The functional filler cells also increase power leakage.

5.7.2.4 Split-Manufacturing for Hardware Trust

Split-manufacturing has been proposed recently as an approach to enable use of state-of-the-art semiconductor foundries while minimizing the risks to an IC design [69]. Split manufacturing divides a design into Front End of Line (FEOL) and Back End of Line (BEOL) portions for fabrication by different foundries. An untrusted foundry performs FEOL manufacturing (higher-cost), then ships wafers to a trusted foundry for BEOL fabrication (lower-cost; shown in Fig. 5.13). The untrusted foundry does not have access to the layers in BEOL and, thus, cannot identify the "safe" places within a circuit to insert Trojans.

Existing split manufacturing processes rely on either 2D integration [70–72], 2.5D integration [73], or 3D integration [74]. The 2.5D integration first splits a design into two chips fabricated by the untrusted foundry and then inserts a silicon interposer containing interchip connections between the chip and package substrate [73]. Therefore, a portion of interconnections could be hidden in the interposer that is fabricated in the trusted foundry. In essence, it is a variant of 2D integration for split manufacturing. During the 3D integration, a design is split into two tiers fabricated by different foundries. One tier is stacked on top the other, and the upper tiers are connected with vertical interconnects called TSVs. Given the manufacturing barriers to 3D in industry, 2D- and 2.5D-based split manufacturing techniques are more realistic today. Vaidyanathan et al. [75] demonstrate the feasibility of split fabrication after metal 1 (M1) on test chips and evaluated the chip performance. Although the split after M1 attempts to hide all intercell interconnections and can obfuscate the design effectively, it leads to high manufacturing costs. Additionally, several design techniques have been proposed to enhance a design's security with split manufacturing. Imeson et al. [76] present a k-security metric to select necessary wires to be lifted to a trusted tier (BEOL) to ensure the security when split at a higher layer. However, lifting a large number of wires in the original design introduces large timing and power overhead and significantly impact chip performance. An obfuscated BISA (OBISA) technique can insert dummy circuits into the original design to further obfuscate the design with split manufacturing [77].

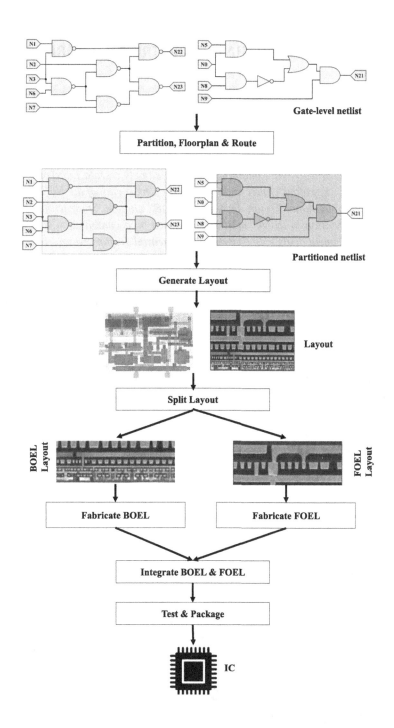

FIGURE 5.13

Split-manufacturing based IC design flow.

5.8 HANDS-ON EXPERIMENT: HARDWARE TROJAN ATTACKS

5.8.1 OBJECTIVE

This experiment is designed to give students an exposure to various forms of hardware Trojan attacks.

5.8.2 METHOD

The experiment is composed of several parts, all of which are designed on the HaHa platform. The first part of the experiment deals with mapping a design, namely a Data Encryption Standard (DES) module, i.e., a symmetric-key block cipher module, into the FPGA chip of the HaHa board. The second part illustrates the combinational Trojan design in the DES module. Students have to incorporate a malicious design modification to trigger malfunction based on a combination trigger condition. The second part of the experiment deals with designing a sequential Trojan instance in the same module.

5.8.3 LEARNING OUTCOME

By performing the specific steps of the experiments, students will learn different types of Trojan design, how they activate, and how they cause malicious impacts. They will also experience the challenges with respect to protecting a design against Trojan attacks.

5.8.4 ADVANCED OPTIONS

Additional exploration on this topic can be done through design of more complex Trojans, e.g., ones that can be triggered by temperature and ones that leak information (protection mechanisms were not included in the experiment).

More details about the experiment are available in the supplementary document. Please visit: http://hwsecuritybook.org.

5.9 EXERCISES

5.9.1 TRUE/FALSE QUESTIONS

1. 100% fault coverage ensures Trojan detection.
2. Trojan triggers are derived from low transition probability nets.
3. All hardware Trojans have a trigger.
4. Foundry is a trusted entity in the SoC design flow.
5. In general, sequential Trojans are more difficult to trigger compared to the combinational Trojans.
6. Trojans cannot be inserted after chip fabrication.

5.9.2 LONG-ANSWER TYPE QUESTIONS

1. Describe the motives of the semiconductor industry to shift to a horizontal business model. How does the horizontal business model introduce the risk of hardware Trojan insertion?

2. Who are the potential adversaries to implant a hardware Trojan? Provide a brief description on each of them. In your opinion, which one is the most difficult to defend?

3. Provide a brief description of a generic Trojan structure.

4. Describe the difference between a combinational and a sequential Trojan.

5. Provide an example of hardware Trojan in a cryptomodule.

6. Give a comparison of hardware Trojans in ASIC and FPGA designs.

7. Illustrate the Trojan taxonomy.

8. Describe the classification of Trojans based on the "Activation Mechanism".

9. Describe the classification of Trojans based on the "Payload".

10. Illustrate the taxonomy of Trojan countermeasures.

11. Briefly describe the built-in self-authentication (BISA) technique. Consider the following scenario: A rogue foundry wants to insert Trojan in BISA-protected design. The foundry wants to replace higher driving strength gates with the same functionality lower driving strength gates, for example, replace 8x buffer with 1x buffer, to make room for Trojan cell insertion. Give your opinion if such attacks can be initiated.

5.9.3 MATHEMATICAL PROBLEMS

1. The RSA-T100 Trojan is triggered when a 32-bit specific plaintext is applied. Calculate the probability of triggering this Trojan if one uses random patterns as plaintext.

2. The AES-T1000 Trojan is triggered when a 128-bit specific plaintext is applied. Calculate the probability of triggering this Trojan if one uses random patterns as plaintext.

3. The AES-T1100 Trojan is triggered when four specific 128-bit plaintext is applied in a specific order. Calculate the probability of triggering this Trojan if one uses random patterns as plaintext.

REFERENCES

[1] S. Adee, The hunt for the kill switch, IEEE Spectrum 45 (2008) 34–39.

[2] J. Markoff, Old trick threatens the newest weapons, The New York Times (2009), https://www.nytimes.com/2009/10/27/science/27trojan.html.

[3] A. Nahiyan, M. Tehranipoor, Code coverage analysis for IP trust verification, in: Hardware IP Security and Trust, Springer, 2017, pp. 53–72.

[4] M. Tehranipoor, F. Koushanfar, A survey of hardware Trojan taxonomy and detection, IEEE Design & Test of Computers 27 (2010).

[5] M. Tehranipoor, H. Salmani, X. Zhang, Integrated Circuit Authentication: Hardware Trojans and Counterfeit Detection, Springer Science & Business Media, 2013.

[6] K. Xiao, D. Forte, Y. Jin, R. Karri, S. Bhunia, M. Tehranipoor, Hardware Trojans: lessons learned after one decade of research, ACM Transactions on Design Automation of Electronic Systems 22 (2016) 6.

[7] R.S. Chakraborty, F.G. Wolff, S. Paul, C.A. Papachristou, S. Bhunia, MERO: a statistical approach for hardware Trojan detection, in: CHES, vol. 5747, Springer, 2009, pp. 396–410.

[8] L. Lin, W. Burleson, C. Paar, MOLES: malicious off-chip leakage enabled by side-channels, in: Proceedings of the 2009 International Conference on Computer-Aided Design, ACM, pp. 117–122.

[9] Y. Liu, Y. Jin, Y. Makris, Hardware Trojans in wireless cryptographic ICs: silicon demonstration & detection method evaluation, in: Proceedings of the International Conference on Computer-Aided Design, IEEE Press, pp. 399–404.

[10] G. Bloom, B. Narahari, R. Simha, OS support for detecting Trojan circuit attacks, in: Hardware-Oriented Security and Trust, 2009. HOST'09. IEEE International Workshop on, IEEE, pp. 100–103.

[11] S.T. King, J. Tucek, A. Cozzie, C. Grier, W. Jiang, Y. Zhou, Designing and implementing malicious hardware, in: LEET'08, 2008, pp. 1–8.

[12] S. Bhunia, M.S. Hsiao, M. Banga, S. Narasimhan, Hardware Trojan attacks: threat analysis and countermeasures, Proceedings of the IEEE 102 (2014) 1229–1247.

[13] M. Hicks, M. Finnicum, S.T. King, M.M. Martin, J.M. Smith, Overcoming an untrusted computing base: detecting and removing malicious hardware automatically, in: Security and Privacy (SP), 2010 IEEE Symposium on, IEEE, pp. 159–172.

[14] S. Mal-Sarkar, A. Krishna, A. Ghosh, S. Bhunia, Hardware Trojan attacks in FPGA devices: threat analysis and effective counter measures, in: Proceedings of the 24th edition of the Great Lakes Symposium on VLSI, ACM, pp. 287–292.

[15] R. Karri, J. Rajendran, K. Rosenfeld, M. Tehranipoor, Trustworthy hardware: identifying and classifying hardware trojans, Computer 43 (10) (2010) 39–46.

[16] B. Shakya, T. He, H. Salmani, D. Forte, S. Bhunia, M. Tehranipoor, Benchmarking of hardware Trojans and maliciously affected circuits, Journal of Hardware and Systems Security (2017) 1–18.

[17] C. Bao, D. Forte, A. Srivastava, On application of one-class SVM to reverse engineering-based hardware Trojan detection, in: Quality Electronic Design (ISQED), 2014 15th International Symposium on, IEEE, pp. 47–54.

[18] M. Banga, M.S. Hsiao, A novel sustained vector technique for the detection of hardware Trojans, in: VLSI Design, 2009 22nd International Conference on, IEEE, pp. 327–332.

[19] R.S. Chakraborty, S. Bhunia, Security against hardware Trojan through a novel application of design obfuscation, in: Proceedings of the 2009 International Conference on Computer-Aided Design, ACM, pp. 113–116.

[20] X. Wang, M. Tehranipoor, J. Plusquellic, Detecting malicious inclusions in secure hardware: challenges and solutions, in: Hardware-Oriented Security and Trust, 2008. HOST 2008. IEEE International Workshop on, IEEE, pp. 15–19.

[21] Y. Jin, Y. Makris, Hardware Trojan detection using path delay fingerprint, in: Hardware-Oriented Security and Trust, 2008. HOST 2008. IEEE International Workshop on, IEEE, pp. 51–57.

[22] K. Xiao, X. Zhang, M. Tehranipoor, A clock sweeping technique for detecting hardware Trojans impacting circuits delay, IEEE Design & Test 30 (2013) 26–34.

[23] D. Agrawal, S. Baktir, D. Karakoyunlu, P. Rohatgi, B. Sunar, Trojan detection using IC fingerprinting, in: Security and Privacy, 2007. SP'07, IEEE Symposium on, IEEE, pp. 296–310.

[24] J. Aarestad, D. Acharyya, R. Rad, J. Plusquellic, Detecting Trojans through leakage current analysis using multiple supply pads, IEEE Transactions on Information Forensics and Security 5 (2010) 893–904.

[25] D. Forte, C. Bao, A. Srivastava, Temperature tracking: an innovative run-time approach for hardware Trojan detection, in: Computer-Aided Design (ICCAD), 2013 IEEE/ACM International Conference on, IEEE, pp. 532–539.

[26] F. Stellari, P. Song, A.J. Weger, J. Culp, A. Herbert, D. Pfeiffer, Verification of untrusted chips using trusted layout and emission measurements, in: Hardware-Oriented Security and Trust (HOST), 2014 IEEE International Symposium on, IEEE, pp. 19–24.

[27] B. Zhou, R. Adato, M. Zangeneh, T. Yang, A. Uyar, B. Goldberg, S. Unlu, A. Joshi, Detecting hardware Trojans using backside optical imaging of embedded watermarks, in: Design Automation Conference (DAC), 2015 52nd ACM/EDAC/IEEE, IEEE, pp. 1–6.

[28] C. Sturton, M. Hicks, D. Wagner, S.T. King, Defeating UCI: building stealthy and malicious hardware, in: Security and Privacy (SP), 2011 IEEE Symposium on, IEEE, pp. 64–77.

[29] C. Cadar, D. Dunbar, D.R. Engler, et al., KLEE: Unassisted and automatic generation of high-coverage tests for complex systems programs, in: OSDI, vol. 8, pp. 209–224.

[30] A. Biere, A. Cimatti, E.M. Clarke, M. Fujita, Y. Zhu, Symbolic model checking using SAT procedures instead of BDDs, in: Proceedings of the 36th Annual ACM/IEEE Design Automation Conference, ACM, pp. 317–320.

[31] A.C. Myers, B. Liskov, A Decentralized Model for Information Flow Control, vol. 31, ACM, 1997.

[32] Y. Jin, B. Yang, Y. Makris, Cycle-accurate information assurance by proof-carrying based signal sensitivity tracing, in: Hardware-Oriented Security and Trust (HOST), 2013 IEEE International Symposium on, IEEE, pp. 99–106.

[33] X. Guo, R.G. Dutta, Y. Jin, F. Farahmandi, P. Mishra, Pre-silicon security verification and validation: a formal perspective, in: Proceedings of the 52nd Annual Design Automation Conference, ACM, p. 145.

[34] J. Rajendran, V. Vedula, R. Karri, Detecting malicious modifications of data in third-party intellectual property cores, in: Proceedings of the 52nd Annual Design Automation Conference, ACM, p. 112.

[35] J. Rajendran, A.M. Dhandayuthapany, V. Vedula, R. Karri, Formal security verification of third party intellectual property cores for information leakage, in: VLSI Design and 2016 15th International Conference on Embedded Systems (VLSID), 2016 29th International Conference on, IEEE, pp. 547–552.

[36] A. Nahiyan, M. Sadi, R. Vittal, G. Contreras, D. Forte, M. Tehranipoor, Hardware Trojan detection through information flow security verification, in: International Test Conference (DAC), 2017, IEEE, pp. 1–6.

[37] H. Salmani, M. Tehranipoor, Analyzing circuit vulnerability to hardware Trojan insertion at the behavioral level, in: Defect and Fault Tolerance in VLSI and Nanotechnology Systems (DFT), 2013 IEEE International Symposium on, IEEE, pp. 190–195.

[38] H. Salmani, M. Tehranipoor, R. Karri, On design vulnerability analysis and trust benchmarks development, in: Computer Design (ICCD), 2013 IEEE 31st International Conference on, IEEE, pp. 471–474.

[39] A. Waksman, M. Suozzo, S. Sethumadhavan, FANCI: identification of stealthy malicious logic using boolean functional analysis, in: Proceedings of the 2013 ACM SIGSAC Conference on Computer & Communications Security, ACM, pp. 697–708.

[40] J. Zhang, F. Yuan, Q. Xu, DeTrust: Defeating hardware trust verification with stealthy implicitly-triggered hardware Trojans, in: Proceedings of the 2014 ACM SIGSAC Conference on Computer and Communications Security, ACM, pp. 153–166.

[41] J. Zhang, F. Yuan, L. Wei, Y. Liu, Q. Xu, VeriTrust: verification for hardware trust, IEEE Transactions on Computer-Aided Design of Integrated Circuits and Systems 34 (2015) 1148–1161.

[42] H. Salmani, M. Tehranipoor, J. Plusquellic, A novel technique for improving hardware Trojan detection and reducing Trojan activation time, IEEE Transactions on Very Large Scale Integration (VLSI) Systems 20 (2012) 112–125.

[43] B. Zhou, W. Zhang, S. Thambipillai, J. Teo, A low cost acceleration method for hardware Trojan detection based on fan-out cone analysis, in: Hardware/Software Codesign and System Synthesis (CODES+ ISSS), 2014 International Conference on, IEEE, pp. 1–10.

[44] X. Wang, H. Salmani, M. Tehranipoor, J. Plusquellic, Hardware Trojan detection and isolation using current integration and localized current analysis, in: Defect and Fault Tolerance of VLSI Systems, 2008. DFTVS'08, IEEE International Symposium on, IEEE, pp. 87–95.

[45] H. Salmani, M. Tehranipoor, Layout-aware switching activity localization to enhance hardware Trojan detection, IEEE Transactions on Information Forensics and Security 7 (2012) 76–87.

[46] J. Rajendran, V. Jyothi, O. Sinanoglu, R. Karri, Design and analysis of ring oscillator based design-for-trust technique, in: VLSI Test Symposium (VTS), 2011 IEEE 29th, IEEE, pp. 105–110.

[47] J. Li, J. Lach, At-speed delay characterization for IC authentication and Trojan Horse detection, in: Hardware-Oriented Security and Trust, 2008. HOST 2008, IEEE International Workshop on, IEEE, pp. 8–14.

[48] A. Ramdas, S.M. Saeed, O. Sinanoglu, Slack removal for enhanced reliability and trust, in: Design & Technology of Integrated Systems in Nanoscale Era (DTIS), 2014 9th IEEE International Conference on, IEEE, pp. 1–4.

[49] X. Zhang, M. Tehranipoor, RON: an on-chip ring oscillator network for hardware Trojan detection, in: Design, Automation & Test in Europe Conference & Exhibition (DATE), 2011, IEEE, pp. 1–6.

[50] S. Narasimhan, W. Yueh, X. Wang, S. Mukhopadhyay, S. Bhunia, Improving IC security against Trojan attacks through integration of security monitors, IEEE Design & Test of Computers 29 (2012) 37–46.

[51] Y. Cao, C.-H. Chang, S. Chen, Cluster-based distributed active current timer for hardware Trojan detection, in: Circuits and Systems (ISCAS), 2013 IEEE International Symposium on, IEEE, pp. 1010–1013.

[52] B. Cha, S.K. Gupta, Efficient Trojan detection via calibration of process variations, in: Test Symposium (ATS), 2012 IEEE 21st Asian, IEEE, pp. 355–361.

[53] Y. Liu, K. Huang, Y. Makris, Hardware Trojan detection through golden chip-free statistical side-channel fingerprinting, in: Proceedings of the 51st Annual Design Automation Conference, ACM, pp. 1–6.

[54] J. Dubeuf, D. Hély, R. Karri, Run-time detection of hardware Trojans: the processor protection unit, in: Test Symposium (ETS), 2013 18th IEEE European, IEEE, pp. 1–6.

[55] Y. Jin, D. Sullivan, Real-time trust evaluation in integrated circuits, in: Proceedings of the Conference on Design, Automation & Test in Europe, European Design and Automation Association, p. 91.

[56] Y. Jin, D. Maliuk, Y. Makris, Post-deployment trust evaluation in wireless cryptographic ICs, in: Design, Automation & Test in Europe Conference & Exhibition (DATE), 2012, IEEE, pp. 965–970.

[57] J.A. Roy, F. Koushanfar, I.L. Markov, Ending piracy of integrated circuits, Computer 43 (2010) 30–38.

[58] A. Baumgarten, A. Tyagi, J. Zambreno, Preventing IC piracy using reconfigurable logic barriers, IEEE Design & Test of Computers 27 (2010).

[59] J.B. Wendt, M. Potkonjak, Hardware obfuscation using PUF-based logic, in: Proceedings of the 2014 IEEE/ACM International Conference on Computer-Aided Design, IEEE Press, pp. 270–277.

[60] J. Rajendran, M. Sam, O. Sinanoglu, R. Karri, Security analysis of integrated circuit camouflaging, in: Proceedings of the 2013 ACM SIGSAC Conference on Computer & Communications Security, ACM, pp. 709–720.

[61] R.P. Cocchi, J.P. Baukus, L.W. Chow, B.J. Wang, Circuit camouflage integration for hardware IP protection, in: Proceedings of the 51st Annual Design Automation Conference, ACM, pp. 1–5.

[62] Y. Bi, P.-E. Gaillardon, X.S. Hu, M. Niemier, J.-S. Yuan, Y. Jin, Leveraging emerging technology for hardware security-case study on silicon nanowire FETs and graphene SymFETs, in: Test Symposium (ATS), 2014 IEEE 23rd Asian, IEEE, pp. 342–347.

[63] K. Xiao, M. Tehranipoor, BISA: Built-in self-authentication for preventing hardware Trojan insertion, in: Hardware-Oriented Security and Trust (HOST), 2013 IEEE International Symposium on, IEEE, pp. 45–50.

[64] D. McIntyre, F. Wolff, C. Papachristou, S. Bhunia, Trustworthy computing in a multi-core system using distributed scheduling, in: On-Line Testing Symposium (IOLTS), 2010 IEEE 16th International, IEEE, pp. 211–213.

[65] C. Liu, J. Rajendran, C. Yang, R. Karri, Shielding heterogeneous MPSoCs from untrustworthy 3PIPs through security-driven task scheduling, IEEE Transactions on Emerging Topics in Computing 2 (2014) 461–472.

[66] O. Keren, I. Levin, M. Karpovsky, Duplication based one-to-many coding for Trojan HW detection, in: Defect and Fault Tolerance in VLSI Systems (DFT), 2010 IEEE 25th International Symposium on, IEEE, pp. 160–166.

[67] J. Rajendran, H. Zhang, O. Sinanoglu, R. Karri, High-level synthesis for security and trust, in: On-Line Testing Symposium (IOLTS), 2013 IEEE 19th International, IEEE, pp. 232–233.

[68] T. Reece, D.B. Limbrick, W.H. Robinson, Design comparison to identify malicious hardware in external intellectual property, in: Trust, Security and Privacy in Computing and Communications (TrustCom), 2011 IEEE 10th International Conference on, IEEE, pp. 639–646.

[69] Trusted integrated circuits (TIC) program announcement, http://www.iarpa.gov/solicitations_tic.html, 2011, [Online].

[70] K. Vaidyanathan, B.P. Das, L. Pileggi, Detecting reliability attacks during split fabrication using test-only BEOL stack, in: Proceedings of the 51st Annual Design Automation Conference, ACM, pp. 1–6.

[71] M. Jagasivamani, P. Gadfort, M. Sika, M. Bajura, M. Fritze, Split-fabrication obfuscation: metrics and techniques, in: Hardware-Oriented Security and Trust (HOST), 2014 IEEE International Symposium on, IEEE, pp. 7–12.

[72] B. Hill, R. Karmazin, C.T.O. Otero, J. Tse, R. Manohar, A split-foundry asynchronous FPGA, in: Custom Integrated Circuits Conference (CICC), 2013 IEEE, IEEE, pp. 1–4.

[73] Y. Xie, C. Bao, A. Srivastava, Security-aware design flow for 2.5D IC technology, in: Proceedings of the 5th International Workshop on Trustworthy Embedded Devices, ACM, pp. 31–38.

[74] J. Valamehr, T. Sherwood, R. Kastner, D. Marangoni-Simonsen, T. Huffmire, C. Irvine, T. Levin, A 3-D split manufacturing approach to trustworthy system development, IEEE Transactions on Computer-Aided Design of Integrated Circuits and Systems 32 (2013) 611–615.

[75] K. Vaidyanathan, B.P. Das, E. Sumbul, R. Liu, L. Pileggi, Building trusted ICs using split fabrication, in: 2014 IEEE International Symposium on Hardware-Oriented Security and Trust (HOST), pp. 1–6.

[76] F. Imeson, A. Emtenan, S. Garg, M.V. Tripunitara, Securing computer hardware using 3D integrated circuit (IC) technology and split manufacturing for obfuscation, in: USENIX Security Symposium, pp. 495–510.

[77] K. Xiao, D. Forte, M.M. Tehranipoor, Efficient and secure split manufacturing via obfuscated built-in self-authentication, in: Hardware Oriented Security and Trust (HOST), 2015 IEEE International Symposium on, IEEE, pp. 14–19.

ELECTRONICS SUPPLY CHAIN

CONTENTS

Hardware Security. https://doi.org/10.1016/B978-0-12-812477-2.00011-3

6.1 INTRODUCTION

The trend of transistor scaling has enabled designers to fit an increasing amount of functionality on a single chip. Integrating the overall functionality of a system into a single chip improves the performance (for example, speed and power) while reducing the cost by minimizing the required silicon area. Such a chip is referred to as a system on chip (SoC), and the vast majority of modern mobile and handheld devices contain SoCs, as do many embedded devices. In general, an SoC contains analog components (for example, radio-frequency receiver, analog-to-digital converter, network interfaces), digital components (such as a digital signal processing unit, graphics processing unit, central processing units, and cryptographic engine), and memory elements (for instance, RAM, ROM, and flash) [1,2].

The complexity of designing modern SoCs is amplified by time-to-market pressure, making it infeasible for a single design house to complete an entire SoC without outside support. Additionally, the cost to build and maintain a fabrication facility (commonly known as a foundry or fab) for modern technology nodes is now in the multi-billion dollar range. As a result, the majority of SoC design houses can no longer afford their own fab. Impacted by these factors, the semiconductor industry has shifted to a horizontal business model over the past two decades. In this model, time-to-market and manufacturing costs are lowered through outsourcing and design reuse. To be more specific, SoC design houses obtain licenses for third party intellectual property (3PIPs), design an SoC by integrating the various 3PIPs with their own IP, and outsource the SoC design to contract foundries and assemblies for fabrication and packaging. Although this model has lowered time-to-market and manufacturing costs through outsourcing and design reuse, it has also introduced security and trust issues in the final product. This chapter discusses the composition of modern electronic hardware supply chain, the security and trust issues associated with it, and the potential countermeasures to address these concerns [3].

6.2 MODERN ELECTRONIC SUPPLY CHAIN

Figure 6.1 shows the modern system on chip (SoC) design flow and its corresponding supply chain. The following subsections discuss the flow and supply chain in details.

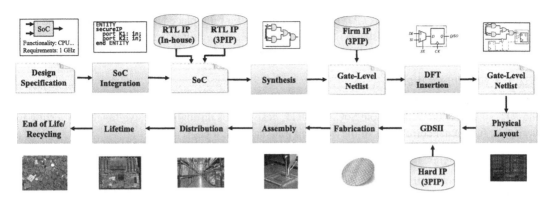

FIGURE 6.1

Supply chain of system on chip (SoC) design.

6.2.1 DESIGN

The design of an SoC includes multiple steps, for example, design specifications, SoC integration, synthesis, insertion of test and debug structures, physical layout generation, and functional and performance verification.

6.2.1.1 Design Specification

In the first step, the SoC integrator (commonly called design house) specifies the high-level requirements and blocks of the SoC. For example, the SoC integrator first identifies what functionalities need to be incorporated in the SoC and what the targeted performance will be. It then identifies a list of functional blocks to implement the SoC. These functional blocks have intellectual property (IP) values and are commonly referred to as IPs. These IP cores are either developed in-house or purchased from 3PIP developers. This decision is mainly driven by economic factors. For example, if an SoC integrator decides to incorporate a GPU unit in the SoC, then he/she could direct his/her hardware designers to develop the GPU unit. However, often it is more economically feasible to procure this IP from third-party vendors who specialize in designing GPUs.

6.2.1.2 3PIP Acquisition

The third party intellectual property cores can be procured in the following three forms:

- Soft IP cores are delivered as synthesizable register transfer level (RTL) code written in hardware description language (HDL), for example, Verilog or VHDL. The soft IP cores are similar to a high-level programming code, such as C, with the difference being they are developed for hardware implementation. Most IPs are procured as soft IPs as they offer more flexibility.
- Firm IP cores are delivered as gate-level implementation of the IP, possibly using a generic library. The firm IP cores are synthesized from the RTL code, and represented as a netlist consisting of logic gates and wires. Unlike soft IP cores, a firm IP does not possess the behavioral information of the IP. Therefore, firm IPs offer less flexibility as compared with soft IPs.

- Hard IP cores are delivered as GDSII representations of a fully placed and routed design. The hard IPs are integrated at the last stages of the design process. They offer least flexibility, but at a lower cost. For example, most memory IPs are procured as hard IPs.

6.2.1.3 SoC Integration

After developing/procuring all the necessary soft IPs, the SoC design house integrates them to generate the RTL specification of the whole SoC. The RTL design goes through extensive functional testing to verify the functional correctness of the SoC and find any design bugs.

6.2.1.4 Synthesis

The SoC integrator synthesizes the RTL description into a gate-level netlist based on a target technology library. Synthesis is a process by which an RTL code is transformed into a hardware implementation consisting of logic gates. Synthesis process is performed by computer-aided design (CAD) tools, for example, Design Compiler from Synopsys. The CAD tools also optimize the design with the objective of minimizing area, timing, or power. The gate-level netlist then goes through formal equivalence checking to verify that the netlist is equivalent to the RTL representation. The SoC designers may also integrate a firm IP core from a vendor into the SoC netlist at this stage.

6.2.1.5 DFT Insertion

Design-for-test (DFT) refers to the addition of test infrastructure together with the use of test algorithms to generate effective tests to improve testability of an SoC. Higher testability leads to improved test coverage, test quality, and lower test costs. DFT enables the IC to be thoroughly tested during fabrication, package assembly, and in the field to ensure its correct functionality. To achieve these objectives, the SoC integrator integrates the DFT structure into the SoC. However, in many cases, the DFT insertion is outsourced to third party vendors who specialize in designing test and debug structures (e.g., scan, built-in self-test (BIST), and compression structures).

6.2.1.6 Physical Layout

In this step, the gate-level netlist is translated into a physical layout design. Here, each gate is translated into its transistor level layout. Physical layout also performs transistor placement and wire routing as well as clock tree and power grid placement. It is also possible to import hard IP cores from vendors and integrate them into the SoC at this stage. After performing static timing analysis (STA) and power closure, SoC integrator generates the final layout in GDSII format and sends it out to a foundry for fabrication. The generated GDSII file contains layer-by-layer information needed to fabricate the SoC on a silicon wafer.

6.2.2 FABRICATION

As the technology for integrated circuits and SoCs shrinks to very deep sub-micron levels, the complexity and cost of chip fabrication increase significantly. Therefore, only a few companies can afford to maintain state-of-the-art fabrication facilities. Most design houses have become fabless, that is, they fabricate their products by third-party offshore foundries. In this process, the SoC designers enjoy reduced cost and state-of-art fabrication technologies, however, at the cost of reduced control over product integrity and, therefore, reduced trust in the manufacturing process. The foundry also performs

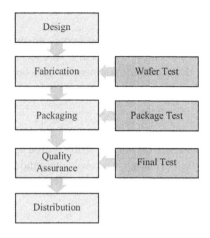

FIGURE 6.2

SoC design and test flow.

structural/functional tests on the die to find manufacturing defects. These defects are caused by imperfections in the fabrication processes. The fraction of defect-free chips produced in a manufacturing process is called *yield*. The faulty chips are discarded, and the good chips are sent to assembly to be packaged.

6.2.3 ASSEMBLY

After fabrication, the foundry sends tested wafers to the assembly line to cut the wafers into several die, and package the good ones to produce chips. Advanced assembly operation also includes wafer/die bumping, die placement, solder reflow, underfill, encapsulation and substrate ball attach. After these processes are done, Assembly performs structural tests to find defects in the chip that could be introduced during the assembly process. Figure 6.2 shows the test process, where the package test is performed at the assembly, followed by the final test for the quality assurance. After performing these tests, the chips without defects are shipped to the distributors, or to the system integrators.

Note that the Wafer Test and the Package Test performed by the foundry and the assembly, respectively, are mostly structural tests, for example, automatic-test-pattern-generation-based (ATPG-based) tests. These tests are performed to find defects in the chip introduced during the fabrication and assembly process. These tests do not necessarily test chip functionality, which ensures the proper functionality of the chips. On the contrary, the Final Test performed during the Quality Assurance process mostly focuses on testing chip functionality.

6.2.4 DISTRIBUTION

The tested ICs are sent either to the distributors or to system integrators. The distributors sell these ICs in the market. These distributors are of several types, including OCM authorized distributors, independent distributors, internet-exclusive suppliers, and brokers.

6.2.5 LIFETIME

The lifetime process starts by combining all the components and subsystems together to produce the final product, for example, a printed circuit board (PCB). This job is typically outsourced to a third-party company, which mounts all the necessary components into one or more PCB to make the final product. Once the final product is assembled, it is sent to the consumer.

6.2.6 END-OF-LIFE

When electronics age or become outdated, they are typically retired and, subsequently, replaced. Proper disposal techniques are highly advised to extract precious metals and prevent hazardous materials, such as lead, chromium, and mercury from harming the environment.

6.3 ELECTRONIC COMPONENTS SUPPLY CHAIN ISSUES

Due to the globalization of the electronics supply chain, many security vulnerabilities can be intentionally or unintentionally introduced by entities involved in the supply chain. Also, with most of these entities involved in the design, manufacturing, integration, and distribution located across the globe, original IP owners and the SoC integrators no longer have the ability to control and monitor the entire process. In other words, trust becomes a major concern in the modern design flow. The IP owners cannot have complete trust in the SoC designers, whereas the SoC designers may not trust IP owners, the foundries, or assemblies [1].

Here, security and trust vulnerabilities in the supply chain are classified into two different classes (shown in Fig. 6.3). Some design issues may cause security vulnerabilities in the integrated circuits and systems, whereas trust issues are mostly associated with factors, such as counterfeiters gaining illegal profit and attackers gaining control of the chip by malicious inclusions.

6.4 SECURITY CONCERNS

This section discusses vulnerabilities maliciously introduced by insertion of hardware Trojans and unintentionally introduced by CAD tools, design mistakes, and test/debug structures.

6.4.1 HARDWARE TROJANS

A hardware Trojan is defined as a malicious modification of a circuit design that results in undesired behavior when the circuit is deployed in the field [4]. Details of hardware Trojan, its structure and potential adversaries who are capable of inserting Trojan are discussed in Chapter 5.

6.4.2 CAD TOOLS

Computer-aided design (CAD) software used to design, test, and validate SOCs can unintentionally introduce vulnerabilities into SoCs [9], because they were not designed with security in mind; instead, their design is driven primarily by conventional metrics such as area, timing, power, yield, and testa-

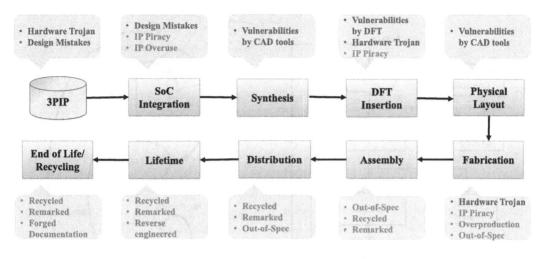

FIGURE 6.3

Vulnerabilities in the hardware supply chain. The red (dark gray in print version) and blue (light gray in print version) colored text represent security and trust issues, respectively.

bility. Designers who overly rely on these tools can, therefore, fall victim to "lazy engineering" [10], where the design is optimized without being aware of impacts on security. This can result in backdoors through which sensitive information can be leaked (that is, violation of a confidentiality policy), or an attacker can gain control of a secured system (violation of integrity policy). For example, finite state machines (FSMs) often contains don't-care conditions in which a transition, next state, or output is not specified. A synthesis tool will optimize the design by replacing don't-care conditions with deterministic states and transitions. A vulnerability will be introduced if a protected state (for example, kernel mode) becomes illegally accessible by the new states/transitions [11].

The controller circuit of an AES encryption module is used as another case study to demonstrate the vulnerability introduced by the CAD tools. The state transition diagram of the FSM shown in Fig. 6.4B implements the AES encryption algorithm on the data path shown in Fig. 6.4A. The FSM is composed of 5 states, and each of these states controls specific modules during the ten rounds of AES encryption. After ten rounds, the "Final Round" state is reached, and the FSM generates the control signal *finished* $= 1$, which stores the result of the "Add Key" module (that is, the ciphertext) in the "Result Register". For this FSM, the Final Round is a protected state, because, if an attacker can gain access to the Final Round without going through the "Do Round" state, then premature results will be stored in Result Register, potentially leaking the secret key. Now, during the synthesis process if a don't-care state is introduced that has direct access to a protected state, then it can create vulnerability in the FSM by allowing the attacker to utilize this don't-care state to access the protected state. Let us consider that the "Don't-care_1" state, shown in Fig. 6.4B, is introduced by the synthesis tool and this state has direct access to the protected state Final Round. Introduction of the Don't-care_1 state represents a vulnerability introduced by the CAD tool because this don't-care state can facilitate fault, and Trojan-based attack. For example, an attacker can inject a fault to go to the Don't-care_1 state, and access the protected state Final Round from this state. The attacker can also utilize the Don't-care_1 to

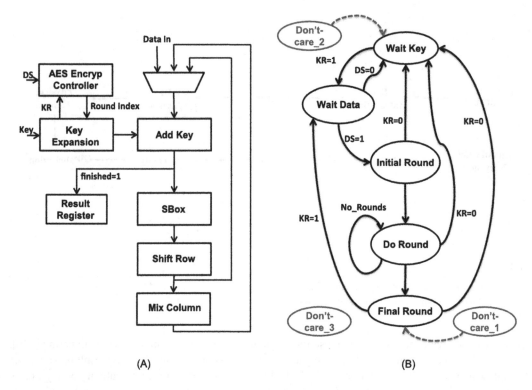

(A)   (B)

FIGURE 6.4

Unintentional vulnerabilities created by CAD tools. (A) and (B) show data path and finite state machine (FSM) of AES encryption module. KR and DS stand for Key Ready and Data Stable signals, respectively; the red (gray in print version) marked states and transitions represent the don't-care states, and transitions introduced by the CAD tool.

implant a Trojan. The presence of this don't-care state gives the attacker a unique advantage because this state is not taken into consideration during validation and testing; therefore, it is easier for the Trojan to evade detection.

Additionally, during the synthesis process, CAD tools flatten all the modules of the design together and try to optimize the design for power, timing, and/or area. If a secure module, such as encryption module is present in an SoC, design flattening and the multiple optimization processes can lead to merging trusted blocks with those untrusted. These design steps, which the designer has little control of, can introduce vulnerabilities and cause information leakage [12].

6.4.3 DESIGN MISTAKES

Traditionally the design objectives are driven by cost, performance, and time-to-market constraints; whereas, security is generally neglected during the design phase. Additionally, security-aware design practices do not yet exist. Thus, many security vulnerabilities can be created unintentionally by de-

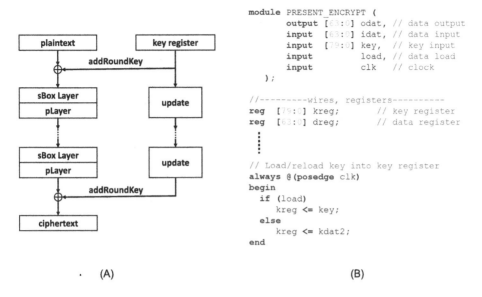

```
module PRESENT_ENCRYPT (
    output [63:0] odat, // data output
    input  [63:0] idat, // data input
    input  [79:0] key,  // key input
    input         load, // data load
    input         clk   // clock
);

//---------wires, registers----------
reg [79:0] kreg;        // key register
reg [63:0] dreg;        // data register

// Load/reload key into key register
always @(posedge clk)
begin
    if (load)
        kreg <= key;
    else
        kreg <= kdat2;
end
```

(A)   (B)

FIGURE 6.5

Unintentional vulnerabilities created by design mistakes. (A) Top-level description of PRESENT, (B) Verilog implementation of PRESENT.

sign mistakes or a designer's lack of understanding of security problems [15]. Design engineers may not have sufficient knowledge in hardware and information security due to the high complexity of the designs and diversity of security problems. For instance, security is often in direct conflict with the intuition that engineers have developed for IC testing. Design-for-test and design-for-debug infrastructures can, themselves, provide backdoors if not properly designed.

This is illustrated further with a case study [15]. Figure 6.5A shows the top-level description of PRESENT encryption algorithm [13]. A segment of its Verilog implementation is shown in Fig. 6.5B. One can see that the key is directly being assigned to the register, defined as "kreg" in the module. Although the encryption algorithm itself is secure, a vulnerability is unintentionally created in its hardware implementation. When this design is implemented, the "kreg" register will be included in the scan chain, and an attacker can gain access to key through scan-chain-based attack [16].

Also, different implementation style of a same algorithm can have different levels of security. In a recent study [17], two AES SBox architectures, PPRM1 [18] and Boyar and Peralta [19], were analyzed to evaluate which design is more susceptible to fault-injection attack. The analysis showed that P-AES is more vulnerable to fault-injection attack than the B-AES architecture.

6.4.4 TEST/DEBUG STRUCTURE

High testability is important for critical systems to ensure proper functionality and reliability throughout their lifetime. Testability is a measure of controllability and observability of signals (that is, nets) in a circuit. Controllability is defined as the difficulty of setting a particular logic signal to "1" or "0", and

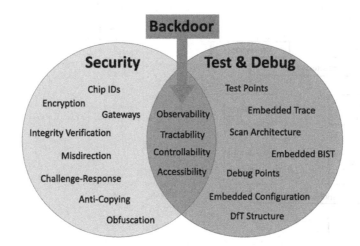

FIGURE 6.6

Requirement for high-quality test and debug contradicts security.

observability is defined as the difficulty of observing the state of a logic signal. To increase testability and debug, it is very common to integrate design-for-test (DFT) and design-for-debug (DFD) structures in a complex design. However, the increased controllability and observability added by DFT and DFD structures can create numerous vulnerabilities by allowing attackers to control or observe internal states of an IC [20].

In general, test and debug can be viewed as the opposite of security when it comes to accessing circuit internals, as shown in Fig. 6.6. Unfortunately, the DFT and DFD structures cannot be simply avoided in modern designs, because of large amount of unexpected defects and errors that occur during the fabrication deep sub-micron devices. Additionally, National Institute of Standards and Technology (NIST) requires that any design used in critical applications needs to be properly testable, both in pre- and post-manufacturing. Therefore, the DFT and DFD structures must be incorporated in ICs, though these structures may create vulnerability. Thus, it is necessary to verify whether any security vulnerability is introduced by the DFT and DFD.

6.5 TRUST ISSUES

The counterfeiting and IC/IP overuse issues in the hardware supply chain is discussed in this section. The US Department of Commerce defines a counterfeit component as one that

- is an unauthorized copy
- does not conform to original chip manufacturer (OCM) design, model, and/or performance standards
- is not produced by the OCM or is produced by unauthorized contractors
- is an off-specification, defective, or used OCM product sold as new or working; or

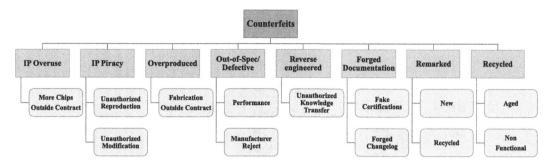

FIGURE 6.7

Taxonomy of counterfeit IPs and ICs.

- has incorrect or false markings and/or documentation

The above definition does not include all possible scenarios, where an entity in the component supply chain sources electronic components that are authentic and certified by the OCMs. For example, one may copy the entire design of a component by reverse engineering [21,22], manufacture them, and then sell them in the market under the OCM's identity. An untrusted foundry or assembly may source extra components without disclosing it to the OCM [23,24]. All these scenarios impact the security and reliability of a system utilizing such components. Thus, the above definition of counterfeiting was expanded using a comprehensive taxonomy of counterfeit types [25]. Figure 6.7 shows this taxonomy of counterfeit types. Descriptions of each type are given in the subsections below.

6.5.1 IP OVERUSE

The IP author/owner is the producer and legal owner of the IP. His/her interest includes providing a valuable product and preventing loss through disclosure of the IP to either competition or IP users [26]. The IP user/SoC integrator is the receiving party that seeks possession and rights to use the IP in their product. In general, the IP owner gives license to the SoC designer to integrate their IPs to a specific number of chips. A rogue SoC designer may produce more chips and report a lesser number to the IP owner in order to reduce licensing costs. Put simply, the problem is that the IP owners have little, if any, means to verify how many chips have been fabricated with their IPs. Profit is lost if the IP is used in more chips than the licensed number.

6.5.2 IP PIRACY

A dishonest SoC designer may legally purchase a 3PIP core from an IP vendor, but make clones (that is, illegitimate copies of the original IP) to sell to other SoC designers. Also, the SoC designer can make certain modification and sell the modified IP as a new IP. For example, an SoC integrator may purchase a crypto-accelerator IP from an IP owner. He/she then develops an cryptographic hash engine to calculate the digest. Then, the rogue SoC designer can sell the crypto-accelerator with a hash engine as a new IP to other SoC designers.

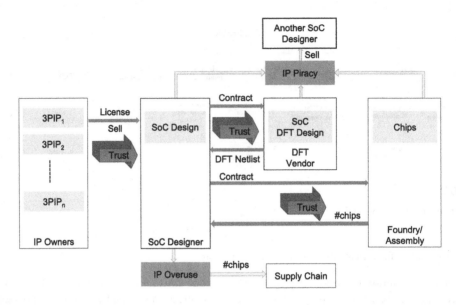

FIGURE 6.8

Lack of trust between 3PIP vendors and SoC designers, SoC designers and DFT vendor, and SoC designers and foundries in modern design/fabrication flow.

The SoC designer can also be potential victim of IP piracy. When the SoC design is outsourced to a third party vendor for synthesis or DFT insertion, that vendor has access to the entire design. As an example, a rogue DFT vendor working on the netlist version of the SoC can sell parts of the SoC design as firm IP to other SoC designers. Similarly, untrusted foundries may sell illegal copies of the GDSII files that they receive from SoC designers for fabrication.

Figure 6.8 shows the lack of trust between 3PIP vendors and SoC designers, SoC designers and DFT vendors, and SoC designers and foundries in modern design/fabrication flow; and how the lack of trust has led to IP overuse and piracy.

Note that the current semiconductor IP market is valued at $3.306 billion, and is estimated to reach $6.45 billion by 2022 [27] with the emergence of IoT devices. Thus, IP owners have a clear economic incentive to protect their products and, therefore, IP overuse and IP piracy pose a significant threat to them.

6.5.3 OVERPRODUCTION OF INTEGRATED CIRCUITS

Untrusted foundries and assemblies can produce more than the number of chips they are contracted to manufacture [28,29]. As no R&D cost are incurred for these chips, they as a result will receive larger profits by selling these chips under the SoC designer's name. In addition, they can overbuild chips practically at no cost by reporting a lower yield (that is, a higher percentage of defect-free chips to the total number of chips) to the SoC designer or IP owner.

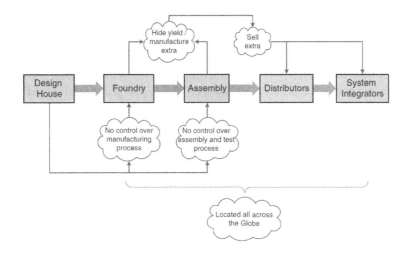

FIGURE 6.9

Overproduction by untrusted foundry/assembly due to lack of control over fabrication and assembly of integrated circuits.

This process of manufacturing and selling outside the agreement with the design house (that is, the components' intellectual property (IP) owner) is known as "overproduction". This issue occurs because the design houses cannot monitor the fabrication and assembly process, nor obtain the actual yield information (shown in Fig. 6.9). A well understood concern with overproduction is the inevitable loss in profit for the design houses. Design companies usually invest a large amount of time and effort in the research and development (R&D) of their products. When an untrusted foundry or assembly overproduces and sells these components, the design house loses possible revenue that could have been gained from selling those components. A bigger concern with overproduced components is that of reliability. Overproduced components may simply end up in the market with minimal or no testing for reliability and functionality. These components may find their way back into the supply chain for many critical applications such as military equipment and consumer products, which raises concern for safety and reliability. Further, since these components bear the same name of the design houses, failure of these components would then tarnish the reputation of the original component manufacturer.

6.5.4 SHIPPING OUT-OF-SPEC/DEFECTIVE PARTS

A part is considered defective if it produces an incorrect response in post-manufacturing tests. As discussed in Section 6.2.2 and 6.2.3, an SoC goes through wafer test, package test, and final functional test to find if the chips are functioning according to the target specification, as indicated by Fig. 6.2. The chips rejected from these test processes should be destroyed (if they are nonfunctional), downgraded (if they are found not to satisfy the specification), or otherwise be properly disposed of. However, if they are sold on the open market instead, either knowingly by an untrusted entity or by a third-party who has stolen them, there will be an inevitable increase in their risk of failure.

6.5.5 REVERSE ENGINEERING OF INTEGRATED CIRCUITS

Reverse engineering (RE) [21,22] is the process of examining an original component in order to fully understand its structure and functionality. It can be achieved by extracting the physical interconnection information layer-by-layer destructively or non-destructively, followed by image processing analysis to reconstruct the complete structure for a component [21,30]. The prime motivation for reverse engineering a component is to make an existing copy of it, often by the competitors of the OCM. An entity involved in reverse engineering often possesses expensive and sophisticated instruments. Scanning electron microscope (SEM) or transmission electron microscope (TEM) are commonly used to take images of each layer of a component after delayering. An automated software can be used to stitch the images together to form a complete structure. For example, ICWorks Extractor from Chipworks Inc. (Ottawa, Canada) has the capability to form a 3D structure by combining all the images from the internal layers of a chip [21]. Reverse engineering can also occur by unauthorized knowledge transfer from a person with access to the part's design, which causes loss of profit for the OCM.

6.5.6 FORGED DOCUMENTATION

The documentation shipped with any component contains information regarding its specifications, testing, certificates of conformance (CoC), and statement of work (SoW). By modifying or forging these documents, a component can be misrepresented and sold, even if it is nonconforming or defective. It is often difficult to verify the authenticity of such documents, because the archived information for older designs and older parts may not be available at the OCM anymore. Legitimate documentation can also be copied and associated with parts from a lot that do not correspond with the legitimate documentation. The incentive for counterfeiters and risks associated with parts linked with forged documentation are similar to those discussed above for remarking.

6.5.7 REMARKING OF INTEGRATED CIRCUITS

Electronic components contain markings on their packages to uniquely identify them and their functionality. The marking contains information, such as part identifying number (PIN), lot identification code or date code, device manufacturer's identification, country of manufacture, electrostatic discharge (ESD) sensitivity identifier, certification mark, and so forth.

Clearly, components' markings are very important. They identify component's origin and, most importantly, determine how the component should be handled and used. For example, a space-grade component can withstand conditions (such as a wide range of temperatures and radiation levels) that would cause instant failure for a commercial-grade component. Factors such as the component manufacturer and grade also determine how much the component is worth. The price of space and military-grade components can be significantly higher than commercial grade components. For example, a BAE radiation-hardened processor, such as the RAD750, could cost in the range of tens of thousands of dollars compared to a commercial processor, which could be in the range of a few hundred dollars [32]. These space-grade processors are used in satellites, rovers, and space shuttles, and are designed to withstand a wide range of temperatures and radiation levels typically found in space. Herein lies the incentive for remarking a component (that is, changing its original markings). A counterfeiter can drive up a component's price on the open market by changing its markings to that of a higher grade or better manufacturer. However, such remarked components will not be able to withstand the

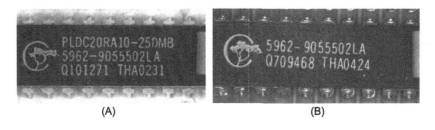

(A)   (B)

FIGURE 6.10

(A) Remarked chip, (B) original chip.

harsh conditions of their more durable, higher-grade counterparts. This can create substantial issues if such components end up in critical systems. A notable example of this is the P-8A Poseidon Aircraft incident, which was brought to light during a hearing held by the US Senate Committee on Armed Services in 2011 [33]. It was found that the ice-detection module aboard the P-8A Poseidon aircrafts, which transports anti-submarine and anti-surface warfare missiles, was found with counterfeit FPGA units. The ice-detection module is a critical component, which warns a pilot of ice that has developed on the surface of the aircraft. In this case, it was found that the FPGA units controlling the module were used and falsely remarked as being produced by Xilinx. On further analysis of the supply chain, the components were actually traced back to a manufacturer in Shenzhen, China.

It is fairly easy to remark a component that is indistinguishable from the original markings to the naked eye. A component is first prepared for remarking by either chemically or physically removing the original marking, and then blacktopping (resurfacing) the surface to hide any physical marks or imperfections that have been left from the marking-removal process. False markings are then printed either by laser marking or ink marking onto the components to appear as though produced by the OCMs. Figure 6.10 shows a remarked, and the original chip [31]. The original chip has two lines of marking. Notice that the remarking quality is good enough to make it look almost similar to the original chip.

6.5.8 RECYCLING OF INTEGRATED CIRCUITS

The term "recycled" refers to an electronic component that is reclaimed or recovered from a system, and is then modified to be misrepresented as a new component of an OCM. Recycled parts may exhibit lower performance and have a shorter lifetime due to aging, because of their prior usage. Further, the reclaiming process (removal under a very high temperature, aggressive physical removal from boards, washing, sanding, repackaging, and so on) could damage the part(s), introduce latent defects that pass initial testing but are prone to failure in later stages in the field, or make them completely nonfunctional, due to exposure to extreme conditions in an uncontrolled environment. Such parts will, of course, be unreliable and render the systems that unknowingly incorporate them equally unreliable.

The United States Senate Committee on Armed Services held a hearing regarding an investigation of counterfeit electronic parts in the defense supply chain, and the investigation revealed that e-waste from discarded electronic components are being used for these recycled counterfeit parts [34,35]. In the United States, only 25% of electronic waste was properly recycled in 2009 [36]. These figures might be comparable, or even worse, for many other developing or developed countries. This huge resource of

| Collect Discarded PCBs | Retrieve ICs from PCBs | Remove Original Marking | Apply Counterfeit Marking | Clean to Appear as New |

FIGURE 6.11

A typical IC recycling process.

e-waste allows counterfeiters to pile up an extremely large supply of components. These components are then recycled from the stockpile of e-waste using a crude process. A typical recycling process is as follows:

1. The recycler collects discarded printed circuit boards (PCBs) from which used components (such as digital ICs, analog ICs, capacitors, and resistors) can be harvested.
2. The PCBs are heated over an oven flame. When the soldering material starts to melt, the recycler smashes the PCB over a bucket to detach and collect the components.
3. The original marking of the components are removed by microblasting, where blasting agents are bombarded on a component's surface. Compressed air is generally used to accelerate the blasting particles. Some popular blasting agents include aluminum oxide powder, sodium bicarbonate powder, and glass bead. The choice of blasting agent depends on the components package type, such as dual in-line package (DIP) and plastic leaded chip carrier (PLCC).
4. A new coating material is applied to the component by using blacktopping and resurfacing.
5. New markings, same as the original grade-level marking, containing identification data, such as PIN number, date/lot code, manufacturer logo, and country of manufacture, are then printed either by ink printing or laser printing on the new blacktopped surface.
6. The component leads, balls, and/or columns are reworked (cleaning and straightening of leads, replating leads with new materials, forming new solder balls, and so forth) to make them appear new.

Figure 6.11 shows a recycling process documented by NASA [37]. Clearly, the recycling process impacts the reliability of recycled components, as they are subjected to harsh handling practices and impacts, such as the following:

1. The components are not protected against electrostatic discharge (ESD) and electrical overstress (EOS).
2. Moisture sensitive components are not properly baked and dry-packed.
3. The components may be damaged due to (a) high recycling temperature, (b) mechanical shock due to smashing and other handling, (c) humidity levels from cleaning with water and storage in damp conditions, and (d) other mechanical and environmental stress resulting from the recycling process.

In effect, the recycled components are degraded even further by such processes. This only exacerbates the prior effects of aging due to usage of the component in a system.

6.6 **POTENTIAL COUNTERMEASURES**

This section presents a brief discussion on the countermeasures that have been proposed to address the hardware supply-chain issues. Some of these techniques are based on academic research, and some are adopted by the industry. Further, this section presents the challenges associated with these techniques.

6.6.1 **HARDWARE TROJAN DETECTION AND PREVENTION**

Several Trojan detection and prevention approaches have been developed over the years. The readers are referred to Chapter 5 of this book for more details.

6.6.2 **SECURITY RULE CHECK**

To identify security vulnerabilities, unintentionally introduced by design mistake or by CAD tools, the Design Security Rule Check (DSeRC) concept was developed in [15,64]. This framework is intended to be integrated in the conventional chip design flow to analyze vulnerabilities of a design and assess its security at various stages of the design process, including the register transfer level (RTL), gate-level netlist, design-for-test (DFT) insertion, and physical design. The DSeRC framework reads the design files, constraints, and user input data, and check for vulnerabilities at all levels of abstraction (RTL, gate level, and physical layout level). Each of the vulnerabilities is tied with a set of rules and metrics, so that each design's security can be quantitatively measured. To successfully implement this framework, one needs wide-ranging access, such as to information-flow security verification, signal leakage analysis, and access control, all during the chip design flow [3,11,65]. The readers are referred to Chapter 13 of this book for more details on DSeRC framework.

6.6.3 **IP ENCRYPTION**

In order to protect confidentiality of IPs, and provide a common markup syntax for IP design that is interoperable across different electronic design and automation (EDA) tools and hardware flows, the IEEE SA-Standards Board developed the P1735 standard [26]. This standard has been adopted by EDA and semiconductor companies and IP vendors. The P1735 standard provides recommended practices for using encryption in order to ensure confidentiality of IP. To support interoperability and broad adoption, it also specifies a common markup format to represent an encrypted IP. The markup format uses standard-specific variables, or pragmas, to identify and encapsulate different portions of the protected IP. It also uses these pragmas to conduct functions, such as specifying the encryption and digest algorithms.

The standard also provides mechanisms to support rights management and licensing. Together these regulatory guides enable IP authors to assert fine-grained access control. With the rights management functionality, an IP author can assert which output signals are accessible to the IP user when the EDA tool simulates the IP. The licensing functionality allows access to authorized users only, for example, companies that have paid for the rights to use the IP.

The basic workflow of the standard is shown in Fig. 6.12. The standard mandates AES–CBC (but allows for other blockciphers) and RSA (≥ 2048) for symmetric and asymmetric encryption, respectively. For AES it recommends a keysize of 128 or 256. Note that while the tool may perform

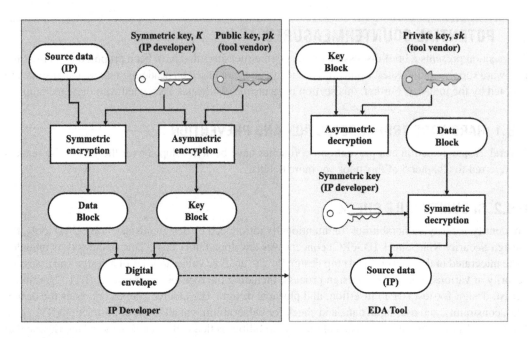

FIGURE 6.12

Workflow of the P1735 standard.

simulation, synthesis, and other processes on the IP, it never reveals the IP in its plaintext format to the IP user [26].

The current standard has unfortunately some cryptographic mistakes that have been exploited to recover the entire underlying plaintext of the encrypted IP without the knowledge of the key. The authors in [2] provide recommendation to address the limitations of the standard. Even if the limitations of IEEE-P1735 standards are addressed, the IP encryption scheme alone cannot address supply-chain issues like overproduction.

6.6.4 LOGIC OBFUSCATION

Another possible approach for preventing IP piracy and IC overproduction is through logic obfuscation. This technique places additional gates (defined as key gates) in a design to functionally lock a design, which can only be unlocked by applying the correct key [29,66,67]. For example, in Fig. 6.13B, a XOR key gate is placed to functionally lock the design shown in Fig. 6.13A. Depending on the chip unlock key $CUK[i]$ value, the D or $\overline{D}$ will appear at the output of the key gate. The correct value of the $CUK[i]$ generates the correct value of D, which is only known to the designer, who has original netlist. Ideally logic obfuscation has the potential to provide protection against both IP piracy and IC overproduction. However, different attacks, that is, SAT attack [68], key sensitization attack [69],

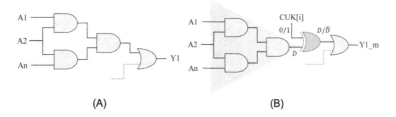

FIGURE 6.13

(A) Original netlist; (B) Obfuscated netlist with key gates shown in orange (dark gray in print version). CUK[i] represents the ith bit of the key.

removal attack have been proposed to break the logic obfuscation. These attacks utilize the locked netlist and the input-output response on the unlocked chip to extract the key.

6.6.5 HARDWARE WATERMARKING

Watermarking can be utilized to validate the authorship of an IP. Watermarking techniques uniquely identify an IP by creating a unique fingerprint in it [70–73]. As the watermarking technique is passive, one cannot use it to prevent IP overuse, IP piracy, and IC overproduction. Rather, it can only be used to verify proof of IP use.

6.6.6 IC METERING

The metering approaches have been designed to prevent IC overproduction by attempting to giving an SoC designer control over the number of ICs manufactured. These approaches can be either passive or active. Passive approaches uniquely identify each IC, and register the ICs using challenge-response pairs. Later, suspect ICs taken from the market are checked for proper registration [70,74–77]. For passive metering techniques, one major limitation is that they cannot actively prevent overproduction. For example, the SoC designers have to count on the foundries/assemblies to send them all defect-free chips, and trust them blindly on yield information. An untrusted foundry/assembly can hide actual yield information, and practically build huge amount of defect-free chips.

Active metering approaches lock each IC until it is unlocked by the SoC designer [1,24,29,78,79]. For example, Secure Split-Test (SST) [24,79] has been proposed to secure the manufacturing and testing process of SoC, and give control back to the SoC designers to prevent counterfeit, defective and/or out-of-spec SoC from entering supply chain. In SST, each chip is locked during the testing process. The SoC designer is the only entity who can interpret the locked test results and can unlock the passing chips. In this way, SST can prevent overproduction, and also prevent chips from reaching the supply chain. SST also establishes unique key for every chip, which drastically improves security against supply chain attacks. Guin et al. [1] presented an active metering approach named FORTIS, which combines the concept of IP encryption, logic obfuscation, and SST to ensure trust among all entities in the hardware supply chain. The FORTIS technique can effectively address supply-chain issues, including IP piracy, IC overproduction, out-of-spec ICs, remarked, and cloned ICs.

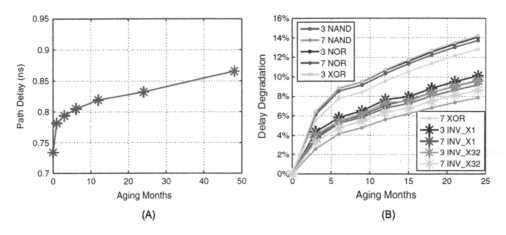

FIGURE 6.14

Path delay degradation due to aging. (A) Delay of an arbitrary path and (B) Delay degradation of different gate chains.

6.6.7 ECID AND PUF-BASED AUTHENTICATION

ECID and PUF-based authentication approaches have been proposed to identify remarked and cloned ICs. The main idea here is to tag ICs with unique IDs, and track them throughout the supply chain. The electronic-chip-ID-based (ECID-based) approaches rely on writing the unique ID into a nonprogrammable memory, such as One-Time-Programmable [OTP] and ROM. This requires post-fabrication external programming, such as laser fuses [80] or electrical fuses (eFuses) [81]. The eFuse is gaining popularity over the laser fuse because of its small area and scalability [81].

Alongside ECID, silicon physically unclonable functions (PUFs) have received much attention as a new approach for IC identification and authentication [82,83]. Silicon PUFs exploit inherent physical variations (process variations) that exist in modern integrated circuits. These variations are uncontrollable and unpredictable, making PUFs suitable for IC identification and authentication [28,84]. The variations can help generate a unique signature for each IC in a challenge-response form, which allows later identification of genuine ICs.

6.6.8 PATH-DELAY FINGERPRINTING

Path delay fingerprinting [85] was proposed to screen recycled ICs without adding extra hardware in the design. Since these recycled ICs have been used in the field, the performance of such ICs must have been degraded due to the impact of aging. Due to negative/positive bias temperature instability (NBTI/PBTI) and hot carrier injection (HCI), the path delays in recycled ICs will become larger. The larger path delays indicate higher probability of an IC being used for a long period of time in the field. Figure 6.14 shows the path delay degradation due to aging. The path was aged for 4 years, using simulation, with NBTI and HCI effects at room temperature. One can observe from Fig. 6.14A that the degradation of the path used for 1 year is around 10%, whereas if the circuit is used for 4 years, the degradation is about 17%, indicating that most aging occurred at the early usage phase of the circuit.

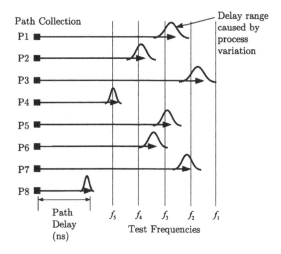

FIGURE 6.15

Clock sweeping.

Figure 6.14B presents the delay degradation of different chains, consisting of INVX1, INVX32, AND, NOR, and XOR gates, after 2 years of aging. It can be seen that different chains age at slightly different rates, which depends on the structure of the gates. The XOR gate chain has the highest aging rate, which helps to select the paths for fingerprinting.

In the path-delay fingerprinting approach, statistical data analysis is used to classify recycled (aging causes the delay variation) and new ICs (process variation causes the delay variation). Since the path delay information is measured during the manufacturing test process, no extra hardware circuitry is required for this technique.

6.6.9 CLOCK SWEEPING

The Clock sweeping technique was introduced in [86] for identifying recycled ICs. This technique applies patterns to a path multiple times with different frequencies to find a frequency at which the path cannot propagate its signal. By observing the frequencies at which the path can and cannot propagate its signal, one can measure the delay of the path with some degree of precision. The path-delay information can be used to create unique binary identifiers to differentiate between recycled and new ICs. The Clock sweeping technique has the following advantages: First, this technique can be applied to ICs already in the supply chain, including legacy designs. Second, it uses data that can be obtained through use of existing pattern sets and testing hardware capabilities. Finally, no additional hardware is necessary, as there is no area, power, or timing overhead to the technique.

Figure 6.15 shows a visual example of clock sweeping being performed on several paths. Assume that paths P1 through P8 are paths in the circuit, which end with a capturing flip-flop, and have some delay in nanoseconds. Each of the eight paths can be swept (tested) at the frequencies f_1 through f_5. All paths will be able to propagate their signal at f_1, as this is the rated frequency of the IC design. However, at f_2, the path P3 will usually fail to propagate its signal. At frequency f_3, path P3 will always

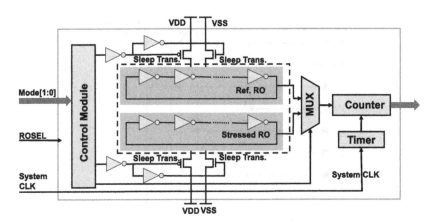

FIGURE 6.16

CDIR sensor.

fail to propagate its signal. Path P8 will succeed in propagating its signal at all five clock frequencies in this example, because it is too short to test with clock sweeping. All of the paths have some number of frequencies they will pass at, some they may fail at, and some they are guaranteed to fail at. Process variations change which frequency each path will fail at between different ICs.

6.6.10 COMBATING DIE AND IC-RECYCLING (CDIR) STRUCTURES

CDIR structures utilize IC aging phenomenon to authenticate if ICs are counterfeit or not. RO-Based CDIR sensor has been proposed in [87,88], where two ring oscillators (ROs) are embedded within the chip. The first RO is called the reference RO and is designed to age at a slow rate. The second RO is referred to as the stressed RO, and it is designed to age at a much faster rate than the reference RO. As the IC is used in the field, the stressed RO's rapid aging reduces its oscillation frequency, whereas the reference RO's oscillation frequency remains largely static over the chip's lifetime. Thus, a large disparity between the two ROs' frequencies implies that the chip has been used. To overcome global and local process variations, the two ROs are placed physically very close together so that the process and environmental variations between them are negligible.

Figure 6.16 shows the structure of this simple RO-CDIR, which is composed of a control module, a reference RO, a stressed RO, a MUX, a timer, and a counter. The counter measures the cycle count of the two ROs during a time period controlled by the timer. The system clock is used in the timer to minimize the measurement period variations due to circuit aging. The MUX selects which RO is going to be measured, and is controlled by the ROSEL signal. The inverters in the ROs can only be replaced by gates that can construct a RO, such as NAND and NOR. It will not change the effectiveness of the RO-CDIR significantly, according to prior analysis in [87]. In 90 nm technology, a 16-bit counter can operate at a frequency of up to 1 GHz, which means that an inverter-based RO must be composed of at least 21 stages [87]. The readers are referred to Chapter 12 of this book for more details on CDIR sensor.

6.6.11 ELECTRICAL TESTS

Electrical tests are efficient and nondestructive ways of detecting counterfeit ICs. The majority of defects due to counterfeiting can be detected by electrical tests. In addition, die- and bondwire-related defects may also be detected by these tests. The major advantage of introducing electrical tests in to a test plan is that they can identify cloned, out-of-spec/defective, and overproduced components along with the recycled and remarked components, as most of the electrical defects may be present in those components.

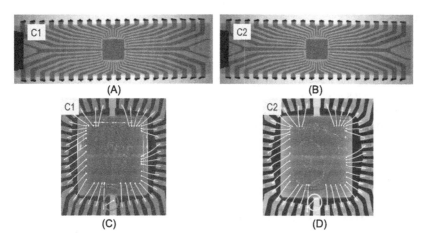

FIGURE 6.17

Counterfeit defects detected by X-ray imaging. (A) and (B) show the X-ray images of 2D lead frame view of counterfeit chips C1 and C2, respectively. (C) and (D) show the X-ray images of 3D die view of counterfeit chips C1 and C2, respectively. The red (medium gray in print version) and yellow (light gray in print version) circles represent that the bond wire connection is different between C1 and C2.

6.6.12 PHYSICAL INSPECTION

Physical inspection is the first set of tests conducted, to identify for possible evidence of counterfeiting. As part of the physical inspection procedure, the ICs are thoroughly inspected using imaging techniques of the exterior and interior. The exterior part of the package and leads of the component are analyzed using exterior tests. For example, the physical dimensions of the components are measured either by handheld or automated test equipment. Any abnormal deviation of measurement from the specification sheet indicates that the component may be counterfeit.

The chemical composition of the component is verified using material analysis. Defects such as wrong materials, contamination, oxidation of leads, and packages can be detected. There are several tests that can perform material analysis, for example XRF, EDS, and FTIR. The internal structures, such as die and bondwires of the components, may be inspected by delid/decapsulation or X-ray imaging. Figure 6.17 shows the counterfeit defects detected by X-ray imaging. There are three mainstream methods commercially available for decapsulation: chemical-, mechanical-, or laser-based solutions. Chemical decapsulation involves etching away the package with an acid solution.

Mechanical decapsulation involves grinding the part until the die is exposed. Once the part has been decapsulated and the required structures exposed, the interior tests need to be performed. These may include observation of the presence of an authentic die, gross cracks on the die, delamination, any damage on the die, die marking, missing or broken bond wires, reworked bonds, and bond-pull strength.

6.7 EXERCISES

6.7.1 TRUE/FALSE QUESTIONS

1. DFT structures are inserted only by the SoC designers.
2. Apart from fabrication, Foundries also perform tests to find defective ICs.
3. All hardware Trojans have a trigger.
4. The foundry is a trusted entity in the SoC design flow.
5. All security vulnerabilities are intentionally introduced.
6. DFT does not create security issues.
7. SoC developers are potential victims of IP piracy.
8. Out-of-spec. parts have reliability issues.

6.7.2 LONG-ANSWER TYPE QUESTIONS

1. Describe the motives of the semiconductor industry to shift to a horizontal business model.
2. How does horizontal business model reduce cost and time-to-market?
3. Why are most companies becoming fabless?
4. Describe the different types of IPs that can be procured from third-party vendors.
5. What types of tests are performed on a fabricated chip by the Foundry and the Assembly?
6. Who are the potential adversaries to implant a hardware Trojan? Provide a brief description on each of them. In your opinion, which one is most difficult to defend?
7. How can CAD tools introduce vulnerabilities? Explain with examples.
8. Why cannot test and debug structures simply be removed when they are creating unintentional security vulnerabilities?
9. Describe the taxonomy of different types of counterfeits.
10. Explain how IP overuse and IP piracy may take place. Provide respective examples.
11. Why do overproduced ICs cost less than their original counterpart?
12. Why does using out-of-spec chips pose a threat?
13. Why are Trojans inserted by the foundry difficult to detect?
14. What are the fundamental limitations of using IP encryption alone to address counterfeit issues?

6.7.3 MATHEMATICAL PROBLEMS

Let us consider the following data for a semiconductor design company "X":

- Actual yield, $Y = 0.9$
- Die area $A = 1.5 \text{ cm} \times 1.5 \text{ cm}$

- Dies are processed on an $R = 200$ mm diameter wafer at \$1500/wafer
- Each mask cost \$100,000 (Total 10 masks)
- 5-man development team at \$200,000 per designer
- CAD tool costs are \$1,000,000
- Market for this part is 2,000,000 units

1. If the company wants to make 10% profit on each chip, what would be the cost of the chip in the market, calculate the cost of each chip for the semiconductor design company X?
2. Calculate the number of out-of-spec (due to yield) chips per wafer. Assume that a rogue Assembly want to sell these out-of-spec chips in the marker. How much profit will he/she make per each wafer?
3. Assume that the foundry reported a lower yield of $Y = 0.8$ instead of the actual yield ($Y = 0.9$). How would it affect the cost of each chip for the semiconductor design company X? How much profit will the foundry make per each wafer by reporting a lower yield?
4. Assume that the semiconductor design company X have placed a watermark in metal 5 layer to proof the ownership of its chip. The rogue foundry wants to eliminate the given watermark, and sell the chip as its own. To do this, the foundry recurs a cost of \$10,000 for reverse engineering and redoing metal 5 layout. Also, the foundry needs to produce a new mask for metal 5. Compare the production cost of each chip of the foundry and company X. Assume that the volume is the same for both.
5. Assume that the semiconductor design company X introduces an active metering technique to address the counterfeit issue. The active metering technique introduces 10% area overhead. Calculate the new cost of each chip with countermeasure. If the company wants to make 10% profit on each chip, what would be the new cost of the chip in the market?

REFERENCES

[1] U. Guin, Q. Shi, D. Forte, M.M. Tehranipoor, FORTIS: a comprehensive solution for establishing forward trust for protecting IPs and ICs, ACM Transactions on Design Automation of Electronic Systems (TODAES) 21 (2016) 63.
[2] A. Chhotaray, A. Nahiyan, T. Shrimpton, D. Forte, M. Tehranipoor, Standardizing bad cryptographic practice, in: Proceedings of the 2017 ACM SIGSAC Conference on Computer and Communications Security (CCS), 2017, ACM, pp. 1533–1546.
[3] A. Nahiyan, M. Sadi, R. Vittal, G. Contreras, D. Forte, M. Tehranipoor, Hardware Trojan detection through information flow security verification, in: International Test Conference (DAC), 2017, IEEE, pp. 1–6.
[4] K. Xiao, D. Forte, Y. Jin, R. Karri, S. Bhunia, M. Tehranipoor, Hardware Trojans: lessons learned after one decade of research, ACM Transactions on Design Automation of Electronic Systems 22 (2016) 6.
[5] M. Tehranipoor, F. Koushanfar, A survey of hardware Trojan taxonomy and detection, IEEE Design & Test of Computers 27 (2010).
[6] J. Markoff, Old trick threatens the newest weapons, The New York Times (2009), https://www.nytimes.com/2009/10/27/science/27trojan.html.
[7] A. Nahiyan, M. Tehranipoor, Code coverage analysis for IP trust verification, in: Hardware IP Security and Trust, Springer, 2017, pp. 53–72.
[8] M. Tehranipoor, H. Salmani, X. Zhang, Integrated Circuit Authentication: Hardware Trojans and Counterfeit Detection, Springer Science & Business Media, 2013.
[9] C. Dunbar, G. Qu, Designing trusted embedded systems from finite state machines, ACM Transactions on Embedded Computing Systems (TECS) 13 (2014) 153.

[10] D.B. Roy, S. Bhasin, S. Guilley, J.-L. Danger, D. Mukhopadhyay, From theory to practice of private circuit: a cautionary note, in: Computer Design (ICCD), 2015 33rd IEEE International Conference on, IEEE, pp. 296–303.

[11] A. Nahiyan, K. Xiao, K. Yang, Y. Jin, D. Forte, M. Tehranipoor, AVFSM: a framework for identifying and mitigating vulnerabilities in FSMfs, in: Design Automation Conference (DAC), 2016 53nd ACM/EDAC/IEEE, IEEE, pp. 1–6.

[12] T. Huffmire, B. Brotherton, G. Wang, T. Sherwood, R. Kastner, T. Levin, T. Nguyen, C. Irvine, Moats and drawbridges: an isolation primitive for reconfigurable hardware based systems, in: Security and Privacy, 2007. SP'07. IEEE Symposium on, IEEE, pp. 281–295.

[13] A. Bogdanov, L.R. Knudsen, G. Leander, C. Paar, A. Poschmann, M.J. Robshaw, Y. Seurin, C. Vikkelsoe, Present: An Ultra-Lightweight Block Cipher, in: CHES, vol. 4727, Springer, 2007, pp. 450–466.

[14] OpenCores, http://opencores.org, Accessed August 2018.

[15] K. Xiao, A. Nahiyan, M. Tehranipoor, Security rule checking in IC design, Computer 49 (2016) 54–61.

[16] J. Lee, M. Tehranipoor, C. Patel, J. Plusquellic, Securing scan design using lock and key technique, in: Defect and Fault Tolerance in VLSI Systems, 2005. DFT 2005. 20th IEEE International Symposium on, IEEE, pp. 51–62.

[17] B. Yuce, N.F. Ghalaty, P. Schaumont, TVVF: estimating the vulnerability of hardware cryptosystems against timing violation attacks, in: Hardware Oriented Security and Trust (HOST), 2015 IEEE International Symposium on, IEEE, pp. 72–77.

[18] S. Morioka, A. Satoh, An optimized S-Box circuit architecture for low power AES design, in: International Workshop on Cryptographic Hardware and Embedded Systems, Springer, 2002, pp. 172–186.

[19] J. Boyar, R. Peralta, A small depth-16 circuit for the AES S-box, in: IFIP International Information Security Conference, Springer, 2012, pp. 287–298.

[20] J. Da Rolt, A. Das, G. Di Natale, M.-L. Flottes, B. Rouzeyre, I. Verbauwhede, Test versus security: past and present, IEEE Transactions on Emerging topics in Computing 2 (2014) 50–62.

[21] R. Torrance, D. James, The state-of-the-art in IC reverse engineering, in: CHES, vol. 5747, Springer, 2009, pp. 363–381.

[22] I. McLoughlin, Secure embedded systems: the threat of reverse engineering, in: Parallel and Distributed Systems, 2008. ICPADS'08. 14th IEEE International Conference on, IEEE, pp. 729–736.

[23] F. Koushanfar, G. Qu, Hardware metering, in: Proceedings of the 38th Annual Design Automation Conference, ACM, pp. 490–493.

[24] G.K. Contreras, M.T. Rahman, M. Tehranipoor, Secure split-test for preventing IC piracy by untrusted foundry and assembly, in: Defect and Fault Tolerance in VLSI and Nanotechnology Systems (DFT), 2013 IEEE International Symposium on, IEEE, pp. 196–203.

[25] U. Guin, D. DiMase, M. Tehranipoor, A comprehensive framework for counterfeit defect coverage analysis and detection assessment, Journal of Electronic Testing 30 (2014) 25–40.

[26] IEEE, 1735–2014 – IEEE recommended practice for encryption and management of electronic design intellectual property (IP), 2014.

[27] Markets Research, Global Semiconductor IP Market – Global forecast to 2022, Technical Report, https://www.marketsandmarkets.com/PressReleases/semiconductor-ip.asp. (Accessed August 2018), [Online].

[28] Y. Alkabani, F. Koushanfar, Active hardware metering for intellectual property protection and security, in: USENIX Security Symposium, pp. 291–306.

[29] R.S. Chakraborty, S. Bhunia, HARPOON: an obfuscation-based SoC design methodology for hardware protection, IEEE Transactions on Computer-Aided Design of Integrated Circuits and Systems 28 (2009) 1493–1502.

[30] R.J. Abella, J.M. Daschbach, R.J. McNichols, Reverse engineering industrial applications, Computers & Industrial Engineering 26 (1994) 381–385.

[31] S.C.I. Tester, Sentry counterfeit IC detector is your very own electronic sentry, guarding the entrance to your production facility from the attack of counterfeit components, https://www.abielectronics.co.uk/News/News8.php. (Accessed August 2018), [Online].

[32] J. Rhea, BAE systems moves into third generation rad-hard processors, Military & Aerospace Electronics 13 (2002).

[33] Senate Hearing 112–340, The committee's investigation into counterfeit electronic parts in the department of defense supply chain, https://www.hsdl.org/?view&did=725638. (Accessed August 2018), [Online].

[34] United States Senate Armed Services Committee, Inquiry Into Counterfeit Electronic Parts in the Department of Defense Supply Chain, https://www.hsdl.org/?view&did=709240. (Accessed August 2018), [Online].

[35] United States Senate Armed Services Committee, Suspect counterfeit electronic parts can be found on internet purchasing platforms, https://www.hsdl.org/?view&did=703697. (Accessed August 2018), [Online].

[36] United States Environmental Protection Agency, Electronic waste management in the United States through 2009, https://nepis.epa.gov/Exe/ZyPURL.cgi?Dockey=P100BKKL.TXT. (Accessed August 2018), [Online].

[37] B. Hughitt, Counterfeit electronic parts, NEPP Electron. Technol. Work, NASA Headquarters, Office of Safety and Mission Assurance, 2010.

[38] H. Salmani, M. Tehranipoor, Analyzing circuit vulnerability to hardware Trojan insertion at the behavioral level, in: Defect and Fault Tolerance in VLSI and Nanotechnology Systems (DFT), 2013 IEEE International Symposium on, IEEE, pp. 190–195.

[39] H. Salmani, M. Tehranipoor, R. Karri, On design vulnerability analysis and trust benchmarks development, in: Computer Design (ICCD), 2013 IEEE 31st International Conference on, IEEE, pp. 471–474.

[40] A. Waksman, M. Suozzo, S. Sethumadhavan, FANCI: identification of stealthy malicious logic using Boolean functional analysis, in: Proceedings of the 2013 ACM SIGSAC Conference on Computer & Communications Security, ACM, pp. 697–708.

[41] J. Zhang, F. Yuan, L. Wei, Y. Liu, Q. Xu, VeriTrust: verification for hardware trust, IEEE Transactions on Computer-Aided Design of Integrated Circuits and Systems 34 (2015) 1148–1161.

[42] X. Zhang, M. Tehranipoor, Case study: detecting hardware Trojans in third-party digital IP cores, in: Hardware-Oriented Security and Trust (HOST), 2011 IEEE International Symposium on, IEEE, pp. 67–70.

[43] J. Rajendran, V. Vedula, R. Karri, Detecting malicious modifications of data in third-party intellectual property cores, in: Proceedings of the 52nd Annual Design Automation Conference, ACM, p. 112.

[44] J. Rajendran, A.M. Dhandayuthapany, V. Vedula, R. Karri, Formal security verification of third party intellectual property cores for information leakage, in: VLSI Design and 2016 15th International Conference on Embedded Systems (VLSID), 2016 29th International Conference on, IEEE, pp. 547–552.

[45] Y. Jin, B. Yang, Y. Makris, Cycle-accurate information assurance by proof-carrying based signal sensitivity tracing, in: Hardware-Oriented Security and Trust (HOST), 2013 IEEE International Symposium on, IEEE, pp. 99–106.

[46] W. Hu, B. Mao, J. Oberg, R. Kastner, Detecting hardware Trojans with gate-level information-flow tracking, Computer 49 (2016) 44–52.

[47] J.J. Rajendran, O. Sinanoglu, R. Karri, Building trustworthy systems using untrusted components: a high-level synthesis approach, IEEE Transactions on Very Large Scale Integration (VLSI) Systems 24 (2016) 2946–2959.

[48] M. Hicks, M. Finnicum, S.T. King, M.M. Martin, J.M. Smith, Overcoming an untrusted computing base: detecting and removing malicious hardware automatically, in: Security and Privacy (SP), 2010 IEEE Symposium on, IEEE, pp. 159–172.

[49] C. Sturton, M. Hicks, D. Wagner, S.T. King, Defeating UCI: building stealthy and malicious hardware, in: Security and Privacy (SP), 2011 IEEE Symposium on, IEEE, pp. 64–77.

[50] J. Zhang, F. Yuan, Q. Xu, DeTrust: defeating hardware trust verification with stealthy implicitly-triggered hardware Trojans, in: Proceedings of the 2014 ACM SIGSAC Conference on Computer and Communications Security, ACM, pp. 153–166.

[51] C. Bao, D. Forte, A. Srivastava, On application of one-class SVM to reverse engineering-based hardware Trojan detection, in: Quality Electronic Design (ISQED), 2014 15th International Symposium on, IEEE, pp. 47–54.

[52] S. Bhunia, M.S. Hsiao, M. Banga, S. Narasimhan, Hardware Trojan attacks: threat analysis and countermeasures, Proceedings of the IEEE 102 (2014) 1229–1247.

[53] M. Banga, M.S. Hsiao, A novel sustained vector technique for the detection of hardware Trojans, in: VLSI Design, 2009 22nd International Conference on, IEEE, pp. 327–332.

[54] R.S. Chakraborty, S. Bhunia, Security against hardware Trojan through a novel application of design obfuscation, in: Proceedings of the 2009 International Conference on Computer-Aided Design, ACM, pp. 113–116.

[55] X. Wang, M. Tehranipoor, J. Plusquellic, Detecting malicious inclusions in secure hardware: challenges and solutions, in: Hardware-Oriented Security and Trust, 2008. HOST 2008. IEEE International Workshop on, IEEE, pp. 15–19.

[56] Y. Jin, Y. Makris, Hardware Trojan detection using path delay fingerprint, in: Hardware-Oriented Security and Trust, 2008. HOST 2008, IEEE International Workshop on, IEEE, pp. 51–57.

[57] K. Xiao, X. Zhang, M. Tehranipoor, A clock sweeping technique for detecting hardware Trojans impacting circuits delay, IEEE Design & Test 30 (2013) 26–34.

[58] D. Agrawal, S. Baktir, D. Karakoyunlu, P. Rohatgi, B. Sunar, Trojan detection using fingerprinting, in: Security and Privacy, 2007. SP'07. IEEE Symposium on, IEEE, pp. 296–310.

[59] J. Aarestad, D. Acharyya, R. Rad, J. Plusquellic, Detecting Trojans through leakage current analysis using multiple supply pads, IEEE Transactions on Information Forensics and Security 5 (2010) 893–904.

[60] D. Forte, C. Bao, A. Srivastava, Temperature tracking: an innovative run-time approach for hardware Trojan detection, in: Computer-Aided Design (ICCAD), 2013 IEEE/ACM International Conference on, IEEE, pp. 532–539.

[61] F. Stellari, P. Song, A.J. Weger, J. Culp, A. Herbert, D. Pfeiffer, Verification of untrusted chips using trusted layout and emission measurements, in: Hardware-Oriented Security and Trust (HOST), 2014 IEEE International Symposium on, IEEE, pp. 19–24.

[62] B. Zhou, R. Adato, M. Zangeneh, T. Yang, A. Uyar, B. Goldberg, S. Unlu, A. Joshi, Detecting hardware Trojans using back-side optical imaging of embedded watermarks, in: Design Automation Conference (DAC), 2015 52nd ACM/EDAC/IEEE, IEEE, pp. 1–6.

[63] K. Xiao, M. Tehranipoor, BISA: built-in self-authentication for preventing hardware Trojan insertion, in: Hardware-Oriented Security and Trust (HOST), 2013 IEEE International Symposium on, IEEE, pp. 45–50.

[64] A. Nahiyan, K. Xiao, D. Forte, M. Tehranipoor, Security rule check, in: Hardware IP Security and Trust, Springer, 2017, pp. 17–36.

[65] G.K. Contreras, A. Nahiyan, S. Bhunia, D. Forte, M. Tehranipoor, Security vulnerability analysis of design-for-test exploits for asset protection in SoCs, in: Design Automation Conference (ASP-DAC), 2017 22nd Asia and South Pacific, IEEE, pp. 617–622.

[66] X. Zhuang, T. Zhang, H.-H.S. Lee, S. Pande, Hardware assisted control flow obfuscation for embedded processors, in: Proceedings of the 2004 International Conference on Compilers, Architecture, and Synthesis for Embedded Systems, ACM, pp. 292–302.

[67] J.A. Roy, F. Koushanfar, I.L. Markov, Ending piracy of integrated circuits, Computer 43 (2010) 30–38.

[68] P. Subramanyan, S. Ray, S. Malik, Evaluating the security of logic encryption algorithms, in: Hardware Oriented Security and Trust (HOST), 2015 IEEE International Symposium on, IEEE, pp. 137–143.

[69] M. Yasin, J.J. Rajendran, O. Sinanoglu, R. Karri, On improving the security of logic locking, IEEE Transactions on Computer-Aided Design of Integrated Circuits and Systems 35 (2016) 1411–1424.

[70] F. Koushanfar, G. Qu, M. Potkonjak, Intellectual property metering, in: Information Hiding, Springer, 2001, pp. 81–95.

[71] E. Castillo, U. Meyer-Baese, A. García, L. Parrilla, A. Lloris, IPP@HDL: efficient intellectual property protection scheme for IP cores, IEEE Transactions on Very Large Scale Integration (VLSI) Systems 15 (2007) 578–591.

[72] J. Huang, J. Lach, IC activation and user authentication for security-sensitive systems, in: Hardware-Oriented Security and Trust, 2008. HOST 2008. IEEE International Workshop on, IEEE, pp. 76–80.

[73] D. Kirovski, Y.-Y. Hwang, M. Potkonjak, J. Cong, Protecting combinational logic synthesis solutions, IEEE Transactions on Computer-Aided Design of Integrated Circuits and Systems 25 (2006) 2687–2696.

[74] K. Lofstrom, W.R. Daasch, D. Taylor, IC identification circuit using device mismatch, in: Solid-State Circuits Conference, 2000. Digest of Technical Papers. ISSCC. 2000 IEEE International, IEEE, pp. 372–373.

[75] J.W. Lee, D. Lim, B. Gassend, G.E. Suh, M. Van Dijk, S. Devadas, A technique to build a secret key in integrated circuits for identification and authentication applications, in: VLSI Circuits, 2004. Digest of Technical Papers. 2004 Symposium on, IEEE, pp. 176–179.

[76] S.S. Kumar, J. Guajardo, R. Maes, G.-J. Schrijen, P. Tuyls, The butterfly PUF protecting IP on every FPGA, in: Hardware-Oriented Security and Trust, 2008. HOST 2008. IEEE International Workshop on, IEEE, pp. 67–70.

[77] G.E. Suh, S. Devadas, Physical unclonable functions for device authentication and secret key generation, in: Proceedings of the 44th Annual Design Automation Conference, ACM, pp. 9–14.

[78] Y. Alkabani, F. Koushanfar, M. Potkonjak, Remote activation of ICs for piracy prevention and digital right management, in: Proceedings of the 2007 IEEE/ACM International Conference on Computer-Aided Design, IEEE Press, pp. 674–677.

[79] M.T. Rahman, D. Forte, Q. Shi, G.K. Contreras, M. Tehranipoor, CSST: preventing distribution of unlicensed and rejected ICs by untrusted foundry and assembly, in: Defect and Fault Tolerance in VLSI and Nanotechnology Systems (DFT), 2014 IEEE International Symposium on, IEEE, pp. 46–51.

[80] K. Arndt, C. Narayan, A. Brintzinger, W. Guthrie, D. Lachtrupp, J. Mauger, D. Glimmer, S. Lawn, B. Dinkel, A. Mitwalsky, Reliability of laser activated metal fuses in drams, in: Electronics Manufacturing Technology Symposium, 1999. Twenty-Fourth IEEE/CPMT, IEEE, pp. 389–394.

[81] N. Robson, J. Safran, C. Kothandaraman, A. Cestero, X. Chen, R. Rajeevakumar, A. Leslie, D. Moy, T. Kirihata, S. Iyer, Electrically programmable fuse (EFUSE): from memory redundancy to autonomic chips, in: Custom Integrated Circuits Conference, 2007. CICC'07, IEEE, IEEE, pp. 799–804.

[82] R. Pappu, B. Recht, J. Taylor, N. Gershenfeld, Physical one-way functions, Science 297 (2002) 2026–2030.

[83] L. Bolotnyy, G. Robins, Physically unclonable function-based security and privacy in RFID systems, in: Pervasive Computing and Communications, 2007. PerCom'07. Fifth Annual IEEE International Conference on, IEEE, pp. 211–220.

[84] X. Wang, M. Tehranipoor, Novel physical unclonable function with process and environmental variations, in: Proceedings of the Conference on Design, Automation and Test in Europe, European Design and Automation Association, pp. 1065–1070.

[85] X. Zhang, K. Xiao, M. Tehranipoor, Path-delay fingerprinting for identification of recovered ICs, in: Defect and Fault Tolerance in VLSI and Nanotechnology Systems (DFT), 2012 IEEE International Symposium on, IEEE, pp. 13–18.

[86] N. Tuzzio, K. Xiao, X. Zhang, M. Tehranipoor, A zero-overhead IC identification technique using clock sweeping and path delay analysis, in: Proceedings of the Great Lakes Symposium on VLSI, ACM, pp. 95–98.

[87] X. Zhang, N. Tuzzio, M. Tehranipoor, Identification of recovered ICs using fingerprints from a light-weight on-chip sensor, in: Proceedings of the 49th Annual Design Automation Conference, ACM, pp. 703–708.

[88] U. Guin, X. Zhang, D. Forte, M. Tehranipoor, Low-cost on-chip structures for combating die and IC recycling, in: Proceedings of the 51st Annual Design Automation Conference, ACM, pp. 1–6.

HARDWARE IP PIRACY AND REVERSE ENGINEERING

7

CONTENTS

7.1 INTRODUCTION

Semiconductor industry is increasingly relying on a hardware IP based design flow, where reusable, pre-verified hardware modules are integrated to create a complex SoC design of intended functionality. Due to increasing design/verification cost and faster time-to-market demands, it has been difficult for a single manufacturing company to design, develop, and fabricate a complete SoC. Consequently, IP-based hardware design process has become a global trend, where IP vendors design, characterize, and verify hardware IP blocks of specific functionality. Most SoC design houses purchase these IP blocks from third-party IP vendors—often distributed across the globe—which are then integrated into an SoC. Such an approach can significantly reduce the design/verification cost (due to reuse of IPs), while drastically lowering the time to market (by alleviating the design/verification time of SoC building blocks).

Hardware IP blocks can be classified into three broad categories based on their use cases and types of signal they process: (1) Digital IPs, where an IP receives digital inputs and process them to produce digital outputs, for example, processor core, graphics processing units (GPUs), digital signal processing blocks, encryption/decryption block, and embedded memory; (2) Analog and mixed-signal IPs, where some or all of the inputs/outputs of an IP are analog signals, and information processing is done on analog or mixed (digital and analog) signals, such as analog-to-digital or digital-to-analog-converter, amplifier, and integrator; and (3) infrastructure IPs, which are nonfunctional IPs integrated into an SoC to facilitate various operations, such as test, debug, verification, and security. Due to evergrowing computing demands, modern SoCs tend to include many heterogeneous processing cores, for example, multiprocessor SoC (MPSoC), together with reconfigurable cores, in order to incorporate logic that is likely to change as standards and requirements evolve. These IP blocks are integrated with an interconnect fabric (for instance, a bus, or network-on-chip interconnect) to meet target functionality and performance of a system.

The pervasive practice of integrating hardware IPs into an SoC design, however, severely affects the security and trustworthiness of SoC computing platforms. Statistics show that the global market for third-party semiconductor IPs is growing at a steady rate over the years, and it is predicted that it will grow by about 10% between 2018–2022 [1]. Due to growing complexity of the IPs and the SoC integration process, SoC designers increasingly tend to treat these IPs as a black-box and rely on the IP vendors on the structural/functional integrity of these IPs. However, such design practices greatly increase the number of untrusted components in an SoC design and make the overall system security a pressing concern. Hardware IPs acquired from untrusted third-party vendors can have diverse security and integrity issues. An adversary inside an IP design house can deliberately insert a malicious implant or design modification to incorporate hidden/undesired functionality. Such additional functionalities can serve broadly two purposes for an adversary: (1) it can cause malfunction in the SoC that integrates the IP; and (2) it can facilitate information leakage through a hardware backdoor that enables unauthorized access or by directly leaking secret information (e.g. cryptographic key, or internal design details of an SoC) from inside a chip.

In addition to deliberate malicious changes in a design, IP vendors can also unintentionally incorporate design features, e.g., hidden test/debug interfaces that can create critical security loopholes. In 2012, a breakthrough study by a group of researchers in Cambridge revealed an undocumented hardware-level backdoor in a highly secure military-grade ProAsic3 FPGA device from MicroSemi (formerly Actel) [2]. Similarly, IPs can have uncharacterized parametric behavior (e.g. power/thermal), which can be exploited by an attacker to cause irrecoverable damage to an electronic system. In a recent report, researchers have demonstrated such an attack where a malicious update of a firmware destroys the processor it is controlling by affecting the power management system. It manifests a new attack mode for IPs, where firmware/software update can maliciously affect the power/performance/temperature profile of a chip to either damage a system or reveal secret information using an appropriate side-channel attack, e.g. a fault or timing attack [3].

SoC designers require solutions to verify the integrity of an IP acquired from an untrusted vendor. On the other hand, the IPs themselves become vulnerable to piracy and reverse engineering attacks. Bad actors in a design house with access to an IP can steal and claim ownership of it. They can make pirated copies of the design, overproduce, and sell them illegally [4,5]. They can also reverse engineer an IP to understand the design intent and/or to make modifications to it for altering its functionality. The modified IPs can then be used in a SoC design or sold illegally without paying revenue to the original IP vendor. Hence, IP vendors need solutions to protect these IPs from piracy and RE attacks.

In this chapter, we describe possible attacks on hardware IPs in the life cycle of modern electronic products. We focus on two major classes of attacks: (1) tampering attacks resulting in IP trust issues, and (2) IP piracy and reverse engineering attacks. We consider both ASIC and FPGA design flows and describe the corresponding IP security issues.

7.2 HARDWARE INTELLECTUAL PROPERTY (IP)

An IP core is commonly defined as a reusable and modular unit of logic, cell, block, or IC layout designed and owned by an IP vendor. Whether targeted for ASIC or FPGA design flow, the IP blocks act as the basic building blocks of any hardware design. Due to the reusable and portable nature of IP cores, they play a major role in the current trend of the semiconductor industry towards globalization [6]. A single SoC typically contains IPs from multiple vendors. For example, the power management circuitry may come from an analog IP vendor in USA, whereas the cryptographic IP core might come from a separate vendor in Europe. These IPs can generally be classified as (i) soft IP, (ii) firm IP, and (iii) hard IP (illustrated in Fig. 7.1). A brief description of each class is provided below:

Soft IP: An IP developed in synthesizable register transfer level (RTL) format is known as a *soft IP*. RTL is basically a representation of the digital circuitry through flow of data between registers and logical operations on those signals carrying the data. Soft IPs are designed using hardware description languages, such as Verilog, SystemVerilog, or VHSIC hardware description language (VHDL), using control/data flow constructs supported by them. The application of HDL to create hardware IPs is analogous to the way software IPs are developed through computer programming languages, such

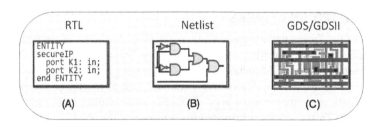

(A)   (B)   (C)

FIGURE 7.1

Different types of hardware IP cores. (A) Soft IPs, i.e. register transfer level (RTL) representation of hardware designs. (B) Firm IPs, i.e. gate-level netlists. (C) Hard IPs, layout of an IP usually represented as graphic database system (GDS/GDSII) files.

as C, C++, Java, and Python. Generally, chip designers have limited accessibility and capability of function-level modification if the soft IPs are obtained from third-party vendors.

Firm IP: An IP represented as a gate-level netlist is known as a *firm IP*. The netlist is basically a Boolean-algebra-based abstraction that shows how the logical functions of the IP are implemented through generic gates and standard cells. The firm IP cores also have high portability; they can be mapped to any process technology. Firm IPs are comparatively difficult to reverse engineer than soft IPs.

Hard IP: A hardware IP represented in a layout format, such as GDS (graphic database system), is known as a *hard IP* or a *hard macro*. These IPs are already mapped to a particular process technology. Hard IPs are the final form of IPs before the layout of the whole chip (e.g., an SoC) is created. Consequently, it is not possible to customize these IP cores for different process technologies by the manufacturers. However, due to the low-level representation, hard IPs are useful in the precise determination of area, timing, and performance profile of a chip. Analog and mixed-signal IPs often come in the form of hard IPs, as these are usually defined in the low-level physical description.

7.3 SECURITY ISSUES IN IP-BASED SoC DESIGN

An illustration of different attack types on Hardware IPs in terms of attackers and intent of the attacks is provided in Fig. 7.2 [7]. The following are the common security threats on hardware IPs.

Hardware Trojans: An adversary present in the design house or in the foundry can incorporate malicious circuitry in a design.

IP piracy and IC overbuilding: It is possible for an IP user or a rogue actor in untrusted foundry to pirate the IP and deliver it to unauthorized entities or market competitors. The foundry can produce pirated copies of the IC without the knowledge and permission of the parent company. The overproduced ICs can be sold in the black market at a cheaper price.

Reverse Engineering (RE): Reverse engineering refers to the process, where an adversary tries to reveal the functionality of the original design to reuse the IP illegally. The level of abstraction in RE may vary, based on the IP or IC, and the attacker's intent.

7.3.1 HARDWARE TROJAN ATTACKS

The functionalities of the Trojan include controlling, modifying, disabling, or snooping the contents of the design under attack [4,8,9]. Detecting a stealthy hardware Trojan can be extremely difficult in any hardware IP. The current practice of functional and formal testing methods fails to verify the circuits exhaustively due to scalability issues. Alternative solutions, such as reverse engineering and machine learning based methods, are either infeasible or ineffective in providing high confidence. A detailed discussion on hardware Trojan attacks is provided in Chapter 5 of the book.

7.3.1.1 Attack Model

Two different attack instances are considered in the hardware Trojan attack model [7]. Both attack scenarios are illustrated in Fig. 7.3. In the first scenario, an attacker in the foundry maliciously manipulates the lithographic masks of the IC to insert a Trojan. The insertion procedure might include

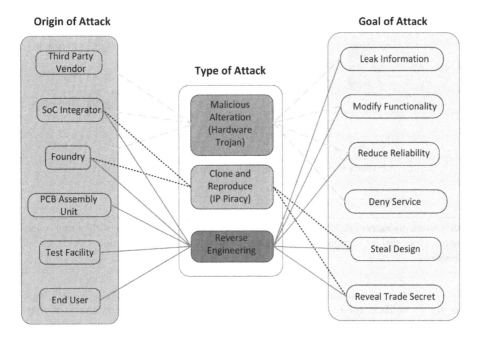

FIGURE 7.2

A classification of attacks on hardware IPs. It shows origin, type, and goal of each attack. The primary attack types are malicious alteration (i.e., hardware Trojan), cloning and reproduction, and reverse engineering.

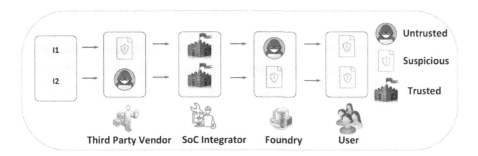

FIGURE 7.3

Two hardware Trojan attack scenarios: (I1) by an attacker in the foundry; (I2) by a rogue third-party vendor. Three types of entities are considered in every attack: an untrusted entity or the attacker, the trusted entity or the defender, and the suspicious entity, which can be an attacker or an accomplice to the attacker.

addition, deletion, or modification of functional gates from the original design [5,10]. The user and third-party vendor are considered suspicious and untrusted, respectively. In the second attack instance, the presence of a rogue entity is considered in a third-party design house, or an in-house chip design

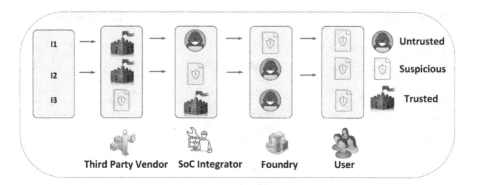

FIGURE 7.4

Three possible attack instances of IC/IP piracy and overproduction are considered here. IC/IP piracy concerns mostly arise from untrusted SoC design house and foundry, whereas the IC overproduction issues come solely from untrusted foundries.

team. It is highly unlikely for the verification team to detect such an inside attack, if they are not informed about the vulnerability beforehand [11,12]. All other entities are assumed untrusted in this attack instance.

7.3.2 IP PIRACY AND OVERPRODUCTION

An attacker with access to an IP (for example, a chip design house that buys an IP core from the IP vendor) can steal and claim ownership of the design. The attacker can make an illegal copy or "clone" of the IP. If the IC design house is the adversary, then it can sell it to another chip design house (after minor modification) claiming the IP to be its own [13]. Likewise, an untrusted fabrication house can make an illegal copy of the GDS-II database supplied by a chip design house and, then, illegally sell them as hard IP. An untrusted foundry can manufacture and sell counterfeit copies of the IC under a different brand-name [14].

7.3.2.1 Attack Model

Three different attack instances are illustrated in Fig. 7.4 [7]. Instance 1 shows that an attacker situated in IC integration house can pirate the 3PIP (third-party IP) and overproduce the IC illegally. The user and IC foundry is untrusted in this scenario, whereas 3PIP vendor is trusted. It is possible for the attacker to make pirated copies more than the licensed number allowed by the parent company. Instance 2 depicts how an attacker located in the foundry can extract the layout of a design and make pirated copies of the 3PIP. The trustworthiness of the SoC integrator and user is not guaranteed in this attack. The vendors are a trusted entity in this scenario. In the case of instance 3, the adversary is located in the foundry and is capable of pirating the IC design for illegal overproduction and subsequent selling to untrusted users. Third-party IP sellers are deemed suspicious in this instance. However, the SoC integrator is assumed to be trusted [15].

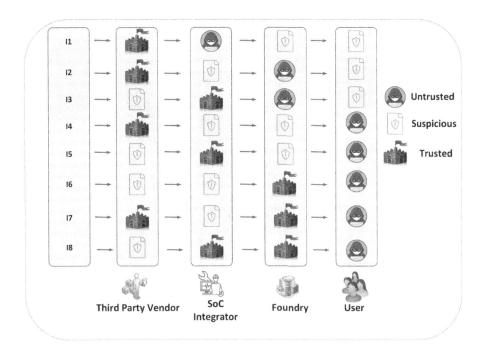

FIGURE 7.5

Reverse engineering attacks in IP. Eight (8) individual attack scenarios have been considered with varying degrees of threats originating from multiple sources. Third-party vendors, SoC integrators, chip foundry, and end-users are deemed to be the key entities of the attack instances.

7.3.3 REVERSE ENGINEERING

Reverse engineering is a complex process involving steps, such as attempts to infer the functionality of the design, extraction of the gate-level netlist, and identification of the device technology [16]. Several techniques and tools have been analyzed by researchers for reverse engineering IPs and ICs [17]. Reverse engineering knowledge can be illegally employed to steal or pirate a design, identify device technology, and illegally fabricate target IC. The primary objective of reverse engineering is to successfully procure an expected level of abstraction of the design. Once the abstraction level is reached, an adversary can exploit the primary input/output to figure out the functionality of the design. An adversary can also employ the knowledge obtained via reverse engineering to extract a gate level netlist of a competitor's IP. Thus, it is feasible for a malicious entity to misuse stolen IP as their own invention, sell it, or fabricate illegal ICs [16]. The target level of abstraction that any adversary wants to acquire depends on the purpose for the reverse engineering.

Figure 7.5 illustrates several attack instances of reverse engineering [7]. Instance 1 illustrates the possibility of an attacker reverse engineering the third-party IP in the SoC integration house. In this case, the foundry and users are assumed untrustworthy. The third-party vendor, however, is assumed to be trustworthy. A solution to this security issue is obfuscating the design (as described in Chapter 14) to prevent the access of the attacker to the original or golden design in the design house.

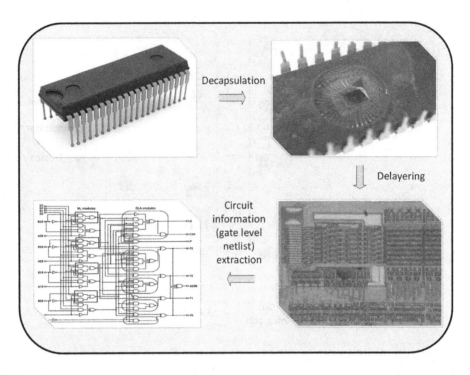

Decapsulation

Delayering

Circuit information (gate level netlist) extraction

FIGURE 7.6

The basic steps of IC reverse engineering include removing the die from package, decapsulation of the IC, multiple stages of delayering, followed by scanning electron microscope (SEM) imaging of each layer, and finally, the gate-level netlist extraction to retrieve design functionality.

Instance 2 portrays an attack scenario, where the adversary can retrieve the third-party IP from the layout of an IC in the foundry. Similar to instance 1, the 3PIP vendor is assumed trusted, but the SoC integrator and user are assumed to be suspicious. Delivering an obfuscated design to the untrusted SoC integrator and the associated foundry would be an appropriate solution against such attack.

Instance 3 depicts an attack scenario, where an adversary launches a reverse engineering attack on the IC in the foundry. The attacker can retrieve the transistor-level layout from the reverse engineered design and, eventually, obtain the gate-level netlist. In this scenario, the SoC integrator is trusted, but the 3PIP provider and user are untrusted. Obfuscation of the target design is an effective solution in this attack scenario [17–19]. In instances 4 to 8, the attack scenarios depict user as someone, who does the reverse engineering. The reverse engineering process for an IC typically includes steps, such as, depackaging the IC, delayering it, obtaining layer images, and extracting the design netlist. Whereas design obfuscation by the third-party vendor is a solution applicable to scenario 4, scenario 5 requires an obfuscation of the layout by the SoC integrator. In case of attack instances 6 to 8, camouflaging the design by a trusted foundry would prevent the security breaches. Camouflaging provides an additional layer of security beyond design obfuscation.

Several approaches have been studied in the literature to explore the vulnerabilities of reverse engineering and develop countermeasures. Researchers have proposed algorithms for extracting gate-level netlists from the layout [19]. It has been shown that an exploitation of structural isomorphism can help to reveal the functionality of data path modules [18]. Attacks based on the behavioral matching of unknown units against known library components, such as adders, counters, and registers are also investigated [20]. In some cases, Boolean satisfiability theorem is applied to reveal the functionality of unknown modules through comparison with known library modules [21].

7.3.3.1 An Illustrative Example of IC Reverse Engineering

Figure 7.6 illustrates the key steps of reverse engineering an IC. The first step is removing the die from the package without causing any damage to its physical structure and functionality. Once the die is removed, it is cleaned and planarized for scanning electron microscope (SEM) imaging. The process of SEM imaging is performed in an iterative manner through decapsulation and multiple stages of delayering. SEM images of isolated regions are taken at first, and the group of images are stitched together later for extracting design information after each of the delayering steps. The final goal of the process is to extract the gate-level netlist (a list of connections among the components of the design) from the images and retrieve the circuit functionality from the netlist. Commercially available CAD tools can be used to obtain the circuit functionality from gate-level netlists.

7.4 SECURITY ISSUES IN FPGA

FPGAs are *reprogrammable* devices that have long been used as a prototyping platform for hardware designs. Over time, FPGAs have found applications in various domains, including automotive, networking, defense, and consumer appliances. Designs mapped onto the FPGA could potentially perform better in terms of power consumption and execution speed compared to software implementation in general-purpose processors. When a given task is implemented in a processor, it has to be executed within the architectural restrictions inherent to its general-purpose design. However, for FPGAs, the hardware design itself can be transformed appropriately and optimized for the target application (for example, data encryption or digital signal processing) through re-wiring configurable hardware resources. Hence, FPGAs typically provide higher performance and energy-efficiency in many applications than their processor counterparts. The combination of improved performance and reconfigurability opens the door for applications that require both, such as artificial intelligence and signal processing. FPGAs are being increasingly used in many security-critical systems. Therefore, designs mapped onto FPGAs have become an attractive target for adversaries who try to compromise a system. Furthermore, designs mapped to FPGAs are often considered as valuable IPs, which are vulnerable to theft and piracy. In this section, we describe these security issues in detail. The following subsections contain a brief description of the internals of FPGAs, design mapping process, and production lifecycle of FPGA-based systems. We also discuss the vulnerable points within this development cycle, and describe the attack models in detail.

7.4.1 FPGA PRELIMINARIES

To make a hardware IP or design functional, FPGAs use various reconfigurable resources. The design (that is, the RTL code or gate-level netlist) has to be transformed to a specific format that can use those resources inside the FPGA. If programmed correctly, the configured FPGA hardware provides the same functionality as the intended design. Most importantly, this design could be updated at any time by reprogramming the FPGA with a different configuration file. The process of generating the configuration file (also known as the bitstream) from the actual hardware design is shown in Fig. 7.7A.

FPGAs could be viewed as an array of programmable modules, where each module can efficiently serve a different purpose. The design and definition of internal resources vary across different FPGA vendors, such as Xilinx, Altera (currently Intel), and MicroSemi. However, in this section, we follow the naming conventions used by one of the major FPGA vendors, Xilinx. In Xilinx FPGAs, some of the common programmable modules are lookup tables (LUTs), Configurable Logic Blocks (CLBs), Connection Boxes (CBs), Switch Boxes (SBs), Block RAM (BRAM), Digital Signal Processing (DSP) blocks, and Input-Output Blocks (IOBs). Figure 7.7B shows a simplified architecture of the programmable fabric of an FPGA containing these diverse resources.

During the bitstream generation process, the design is first broken down to small segments of Boolean functions, each suitable for specific programmable hardware component inside the FPGA. This is referred to as *synthesis*, and the output is an FPGA-mapped netlist. Figure 7.8 shows a Full Adder design represented in gate-level format and its corresponding FPGA-synthesized version. Several gates are merged to one LUT that contains the Boolean function as the configuration bit (shown in hexadecimal). This netlist is then placed and routed, which defines the configuration of the connection boxes and switch boxes. Finally, the configuration bits are concatenated into a single file, called the *bitstream*, which is used to configure the FPGA. This process of bitstream generation and programming is done using a software tool provided by the FPGA vendor, such as the Vivado Design Suite for

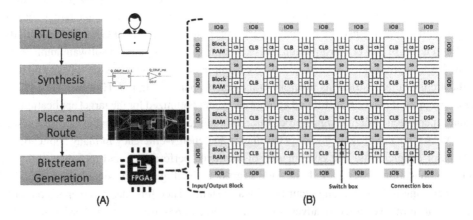

(A)   (B)

FIGURE 7.7

(A) FPGA bitstream generation flow, where an RTL design is converted to a stream of configuration bits that is used to program a FPGA. (B) Simplified architecture of an FPGA fabric containing CLBs, Block RAMs, DSP blocks, routing resources, and IO Blocks. Whereas the idea of having programmable resources is common across the FPGAs of all vendors, the available resources and their organization differ.

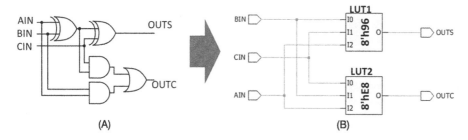

FIGURE 7.8

Example of FPGA synthesis: (A) A gate-level design of full-adder, (B) FPGA mapped netlist consisting of LUTs with 8-bit configuration contents $8'h86$ and $8'hE8$ after synthesizing the design using a vendor tool.

Xilinx FPGAs. More details regarding the fundamentals of FPGA architecture and its application are available in [22].

7.4.2 LIFECYCLE OF FPGA-BASED SYSTEM

An FPGA bitstream is vulnerable to different threats throughout the development and operational life-cycle of the system. Therefore, the vulnerabilities should be addressed at appropriate stages of its development. Depending on the application, the entities involved in each step and the corresponding lifecycle could differ. We discuss various possible entities, followed by an example lifecycle for FPGA that illustrates major vulnerabilities.

7.4.2.1 Entities

We consider the possible individuals, manufacturers, and hardware/software vendors that could directly or indirectly affect the security of the FPGA-mapped IP. These entities are briefly introduced below:

FPGA Vendor: Vendors offer the FPGA devices or FPGA-based solutions to the end users or developers, who integrate FPGAs into their products. Altera and Xilinx are the lead vendors in the programmable logic market. In 2014, Xilinx held almost 45%–50% of the market share, whereas Altera accounted for 40%–45% [23]. Just like the IC design houses, most of the FPGA vendors are fabless, and they depend on off-shore foundries and other third-party manufacturers.

Off-Shore Foundry: FPGAs consist of a base array integrated with different peripherals, and other components. The design and manufacturing process of the base array is similar to the ones for standard IC. As shown in Fig. 7.9, an FPGA vendor sends the layout of the base array in the form of GDSII (mask files) for fabrication.

Off-Shore Facility: The fabricated base array is forwarded to another facility for packaging, and assembly of the FPGA device. This facility could also be off-shore to reduce the manufacturing cost [24].

FPGA-based System Developer: FPGAs are widely integrated into systems, including automotive, defense, network processing, and consumer electronics. The companies developing such products buy FPGAs directly from a vendor, or through a third-party distributor as standalone FPGA ICs or ICs mounted on PCBs. They also buy or develop soft IPs, firmware, software, and various hardware com-

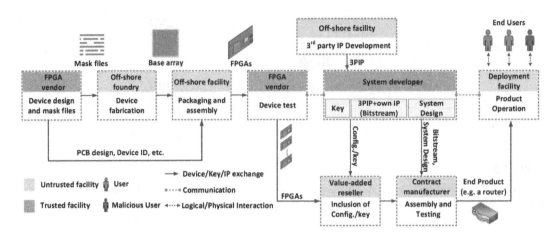

FIGURE 7.9

Figure illustrates the development lifecycle of an FPGA-based system. The base array of the FPGA is typically fabricated in an off-shore foundry. If the FPGA is sold as a board-level solution, the subsequent assembly process is performed at another third-party facility. These FPGAs (standalone ICs or boards) are bought through distributors assigned by the actual FPGA vendor. Based on the system developer's requirement, a contract manufacturer assembles a complete FPGA-based product.

ponents as needed. The integration of all the hardware and software components are often done through third parties. The developers often embed security features within the system to prevent cloning, reverse engineering, and tampering. When designing future devices, the FPGA vendors often discuss with their major consumers what security features they would like to see in future FPGA hardware.

Value-Added Reseller: A value-added reseller (VAR) usually programs features or configurations (modes of operation) to an existing product on behalf of the system developer. Though the presence of a VAR—in addition to the primary manufacturer—may appear redundant, it could become a necessity for the integration of confidential features that could not be shared with the primary manufacturer. For instance, storing cryptographic keys in an FPGA [25] may require a VAR, since providing both the decryption key and the encrypted bitstream to the same third-party could facilitate IP theft. Besides, FPGA vendors may only certify certain third-parties to sell or distribute devices on their behalf [26]. Therefore, a VAR could be present in many supply chains.

Contract Manufacturer: Development and deployment of the complete product may require assembling, repairing, and testing of large volumes of PCBs, and shipping them to the product buyer. Therefore, a system developer could hire one or more capable third-party manufacturers. The system design and components are sent to the contract manufacturer (CM) for production and testing. The CM may also buy the required components (hardware or software) on behalf of the system designer.

End User: Once purchased, the system is deployed by the owner to serve the customer. The owner could be a government entity, private corporation, or an individual buying the product. In addition to an authorized customer, the product could interact with someone having illegal access. Both the owner and the users are considered end-users having a certain level of knowledge of the system, privilege, and physical access. While most end-users would interact with the system only to receive the intended service, certain users may have malicious intent, such as compromising the system or stealing critical information.

7.4.2.2 Lifecycle

Figure 7.9 provides an overview of the development lifecycle of an FPGA-based product. The flow could be realized differently with another set of entities, based on the application, end-product, or the company developing the system. However, we attempted to construct a flow that covers all possible vulnerabilities relevant to the hardware design implemented on the FPGA in form of a bitstream.

Since various forms of bitstream vulnerabilities could stem from the underlying FPGA hardware itself, we begin with the FPGA device production phase initiated by the FPGA vendor. The vendor defines the architecture of the base array, consisting of various programmable units (that is, CLB, CB, BRAM) that performs as the reconfigurable platform. The vendor develops the base-array layout to generate the corresponding masks for fabrication. Since most of the design houses (and the FPGA vendors) are fabless, the masks are sent to a third-party fabrication facility. This leads to vulnerabilities, including malicious modification of the base-array layout, and various forms of IP theft issues. Furthermore, due to its known regular structure, insertion of malicious logic into the base-array design could be easier [24]. For instance, an attacker could insert a Trojan logic within the base array that observes the configuration bits of a switch box inside FPGA, and triggers only when a certain bit pattern is found. Once triggered, the malicious logic can modify the configuration of other resources, leading to a denial-of-service attack, or leakage of secret information. A list of possible triggers and payloads is presented in [24].

As mentioned earlier, an FPGA could either be purchased as standalone IC, or as a board-level solution. For developing board-level solutions, a board-level design containing the base array is specified by the vendor. Similar to the base-array fabrication, the board-level assembly process could also be exported to the same, or a different third-party, where the fabricated base array is placed on a PCB and, then, assembled with other peripheral components according to the design. It is possible that an adversary in the untrusted facility could make a malicious modification to the board-level design that either leaks the bitstream, causes logical (design functionality), or physical (device functionality) malfunction. Though the FPGAs are tested by the vendor, insertion of board and chip-level hardware Trojans, which circumvent the testing procedure is a viable threat since only a small segment of the test cases can be covered [24,27].

System developers who require FPGAs for building their products usually buy them through third-party distributors, who are certified by the FPGA vendor. If a contract manufacturer is involved in the development process, the devices are sent to the CM facility, where FPGAs are assembled with other hardware and software components. Various forms of attacks on bitstream such as cloning, reverse engineering, and tampering could take place at this stage. However, as mentioned earlier, the system developer would introduce security features to protect against such attacks.

7.4.2.3 Attacks on FPGA Bitstream

A wide range of attacks on FPGA bitstream have been reported over time. Major classes of attacks on bitstream are shown in Fig. 7.10. The proliferation of FPGA devices in mission-critical applications has involved resourceful entities, such as nation states and funded organizations in the list of possible adversaries interested to break opponent's system. Furthermore, the distributed lifecycle of the FPGA-based system is involving more and more untrusted entities that present new adversaries. Below, we

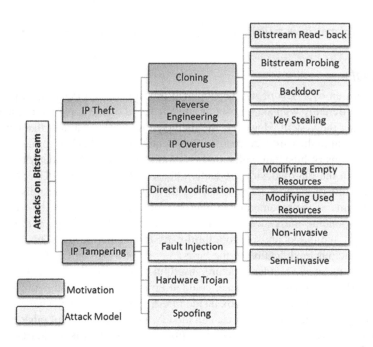

FIGURE 7.10

Various forms of attacks on FPGA bitstream with diverse motivation.

present various malicious motives to attack FPGA bitstream, along with corresponding attack models to accomplish them.

1. IP Theft: A design mapped onto the FPGA usually requires significant time and effort to develop, which makes the configuration bitstream of the design a valuable IP. Theft of an IP includes cloning, i.e., illegally using, or distributing the bitstream. The theft could also take place in the form of reverse engineering, where the design and functionality are extracted by analyzing the bitstream.

1(a) Cloning: The very nature of the FPGA device makes it vulnerable to cloning, since the same bitstream can be used in similar devices if found unencrypted, or even encrypted (if the encryption key is available). Throughout the development and deployment lifecycle of an FPGA-based system, the underlying bitstream could be prone to cloning attacks in a number of ways discussed below.

- *Bitstream Readback*
  Recall from Chapter 4, that JTAG is a common standard for in-circuit test. It is also used as a programming interface in majority of FPGAs. Programming and testing operations are initiated by sending different commands into the interface. Commands even exist for the retrieval of the configuration bits from the FPGA for bitstream integrity verification [28]. Therefore, unless deactivated, this could facilitate easy access to the unencrypted version of the bitstream.

- *Bitstream Probing*
  The volatile nature of SRAM FPGAs requires the bitstream to be loaded onto the reprogrammable fabric via the programming channel (for example, JTAG) from an external memory (i.e. flash) when

the system powers up. Therefore, intercepting this bitstream transfer using an electrical probe is one possible attack vector that facilitates cloning [29,30]. This attack is not applicable to nonvolatile (such as flash-based) FPGAs, since the configuration bits are always stored inside the reconfigurable fabric. Therefore, only invasive attacks on the non-volatile reconfigurable fabric are possible. Since physical access to a device with bitstream is required for mounting a probing attack, either an adversary at the contract manufacturer, or a malicious end user with physical access, could be the one attempting this.

- *Stealing of Decryption Key*
Many modern FPGAs come with a built-in authentication block, e.g., based on keyed-hash message authentication codes (HMAC), which produces a fixed length message authentication code from an arbitrary length bitstream. Many FPGAs today also include a bitstream decryption (e.g., AES) block to support encrypted bitstream. An encrypted form of bitstream typically resides in the configuration flash. If authentication is used, the authentication key, and the hash digest, are encrypted along with the bitstream. As shown in Fig. 7.11, during power-up, the encrypted bitstream, authentication key, and hash are decrypted using the key stored inside the nonvolatile memory. Using the built-in authentication block inside the FPGA, a digest of the decrypted bitstream is generated, which is compared with the previously decrypted digest. If the bitstream has not been tampered prior configuration, the two digests must match. Hence, the symmetric encryption key is an essential secret in providing confidentiality and integrity to the bitstream. In the presence of a successful attack on the key, the bitstream not only becomes vulnerable to IP theft, but also could be tampered, because the authentication key is encrypted along with the bitstream. Side-channel attacks, such as differential power analysis (DPA), described in detail in Chapter 8, have been proven effective in retrieving the key [31–33]. Such attacks involve measuring and analyzing the power at power-up, when the key is used to decrypt the bitstream. The key could also be leaked through an adversary at VAR facility responsible for storing the key. If the key is stored inside the eFUSEs, the physical changes caused by the eFUSE programming could be seen through the metal layers in a decapped chip, using an SEM. Such an attack could only be mounted by a resourceful attacker, capable of performing destructive reverse engineering. Finally, during a remote upgrade, an attacker could try to obtain both the encrypted bitstream and the encryption key by intercepting the communication between the authorized person and the device.

1(b) Reverse Engineering: Bitstream reverse engineering (BRE) can allow an attacker to extract information on how a design was implemented. This facilitates intelligent modification of the IP, potentially for malicious reasons. An adversary may buy an existing FPGA-based product from the market; extract the IP through BRE; improve the functionality of the IP; and then use or resell it. Furthermore, bitstream tampering efforts to bypass certain restrictions may require the knowledge of the high-level design obtainable only through BRE. Successful plain-text BRE has been demonstrated for certain series of FPGA devices [34–36]. However, due to the absence of a standardized bitstream format, newer, potentially more sophisticated approaches, may be required for FPGAs of different series and vendors. The bitstream reversal process is further complicated by the presence of encryption. Unless an attacker has access to the key, the only way to understand the functionality of an encrypted bitstream (to a limited extent), is to treat the mapped design like a black-box, and observe the functional outputs for various inputs.

1(c) IP Overuse: IP overuse is one of the few instances in the lifecycle of an FPGA-based system, where the entity developing the system itself could be the adversary. At present, the system developer

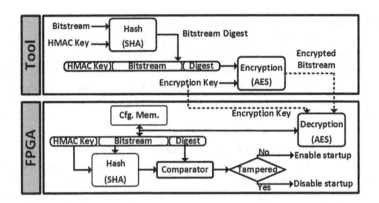

FIGURE 7.11

Typical flow for FPGA bitstream encryption and authentication.

buying third-party IPs in the form of RTL or bitstream could use them in any number of FPGAs. However, the IP developer may want her/his/its designs to be used in a fixed number of devices, or may want to charge per instance of use. To facilitate this, an active metering scheme that enables a pay-per-use licensing model was proposed in [37]. In current FPGA devices, if a unique unchangeable identifier is in place, the third-party IP provider could use that identifier to compile individual IPs for different devices to restrict the use of their IPs to a fixed number of devices. Node-locking of FPGA bitstream, similar to node-locked licensing approach in software, has been examined through low-overhead architectural modifications to the base array [38], and through a bitstream obfuscation technique [39].

2. Tampering: Malicious modification of bitstreams is a major concern for FPGA-based systems. An attacker could modify the bitstream to bypass certain restrictions, or to evade a security feature executed by the bitstream. Bitstream tampering could also be used to trigger a logical or physical malfunction at a specific time during the operation of the device. Several attack models exist for bitstream tampering, as discussed below.

- *Fault Injection*
  At run-time, individual bits of the mapped configuration could be altered by injecting faults in both a non-invasive and semi-invasive manner. While non-invasive attacks require no physical change to the target hardware, a semi-invasive attack requires a limited amount of hardware change to facilitate the attack. Non-invasive fault injection approaches include focused radiation and power adjustment [40]. A semi-invasive attack in the form of optical fault injection has been demonstrated with flashgun and laser pointer to change individual bits of SRAM in a microcontroller [41]. These equipments are readily available and are relatively inexpensive. Therefore, a similar attack model is a viable threat for SRAM FPGAs.
- *Direct Modification*
  Direct modification of unencrypted bitstream to implement hardware Trojans has been demonstrated in [42]. However, the attack focuses on modifying unused resources, which appears to be a string of zeros in the configuration bits. This facilitates easy modification without rendering the bitstream

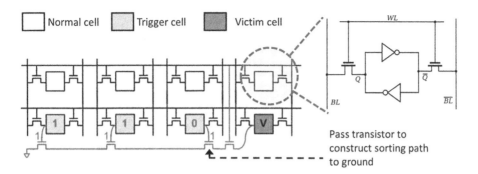

FIGURE 7.12

Hardware Trojan implemented in SRAM to compromise the value stored onto the victim cell (marked in red; dark gray in print version), when a specific pattern (1-1-0) is stored on the trigger cells (marked in gray).

nonfunctional, as may happen if used regions of the bitstream were modified instead. In [43], a cryptographic implementation of AES and 3DES on an FPGA was tampered by reverse engineering of the bitstream mapping format. This was done by iteratively mapping known functions, observing the changes in the bitstream, and repeating until the critical portion of the bitstream was identified. The ultimate goal of tampering was to leak a secret information that is processed within the design. In [44], a technique to extract the secret key of an FPGA implementation of an AES cryptomodule was demonstrated by performing a fixed set of bitstream manipulations. These rules are independent of the FPGA family and do not require an in-depth knowledge of the mapped design.

- *Hardware Trojan*
  During the manufacturing of FPGA devices in an untrusted foundry, hardware Trojans could be inserted into the base array layout, which, once triggered, can modify the configuration bits of a specific FPGA resource to induce a logical, or physical, malfunction. One motivation of the attacker at the foundry could be to create a bad reputation for the vendor, while providing a competitive edge to others [24]. The feasibility of implementing such Trojans in an SRAM array has been verified in [45]. As shown in Fig. 7.12, several trigger cells in the SRAM could be used to enable a path constructed using pass transistors that are maliciously inserted in the layout. If a particular pattern is stored onto those trigger cells, the path activates and shorts the victim cell to ground. The payload compromises the ability of the victim cell to store a specific value (0 or 1). Such Trojans could be used for forcing a desired value to specific configurable components (that is, LUTs) at a specific instance, as intended by the attacker.

- *Unauthorized Reprogramming*
  An FPGA could be reprogrammed with a completely different bitstream by an adversary. This could happen when the attacker has physical access to the FPGA, or can intercept the communication of bitstream during a remote upgrade. Such an attack could be mounted with the goal to infect other modules of the system using the compromised FPGA. Also, attackers may try to resell an FPGA-based product under a different vendor's name by replacing the original proprietary software with

Threats	ASIC Flow	FPGA Flow
IP reverse engineering	Possible through IC reverse engineering	Possible through bitstream reverse engineering
Trojan insertion pre-deployment	Possible in netlist and layout	Possible in netlist, layout, and bitstream
Trojan insertion Infield	Generally considered infeasible	Possible through bitstream manipulation
IP cloning	Possible by untrusted foundry or IP integrator	Possible by IP integrator and end user

FIGURE 7.13

Comparison of IP-oriented threats between ASIC and FPGA.

their own. If the original bitstream only allows proprietary software, such malicious reprogramming would be necessary.

The security issues pertaining to hardware IPs, including piracy and reverse engineering, have received significant attention in recent years. In this chapter, we focused on the major security issues for hardware IP (in both ASIC and FPGA design flow) during its life cycle. We analyzed that threat models for these flows, and pinpointed several open issues related to piracy, reverse engineering, and tampering. For a better understanding of these vulnerabilities, attacks are classified according to adversary's location, intention, and the surface of attack. Various forms of threats applicable to ASIC and FPGA are summarized in Fig. 7.13. Any modern electronic system relies on the trusted and secure operation of the underlying hardware IPs. Security issues in all hardware IPs used in a system need to be adequately addressed in order to build a secure and trusted system.

7.5 HANDS-ON EXPERIMENT: REVERSE ENGINEERING AND TAMPERING
7.5.1 OBJECTIVE

This experiment is designed to give students the opportunity to perform FPGA bitstream reverse engineering attacks. The experiment consists of several parts. These parts are designed on the HaHa platform, which utilizes an Altera MAX10 series FPGA chip. The experiment illustrates a method of reverse engineering an unencrypted bitstream with the goal of piracy or understanding the design intent, or its malicious modification.

7.5.2 METHOD

Students have to first map an example design into the FPGA module inside HaHa platform and generate the bitstream. Next, the students use a matching tool to compare the generated bitstream with an existing one; the goal of this tool is to identify known functions in the bitstream using a bitstream template. The students will also create various designs with minimal differences and compare the generated bitstreams.

7.5.3 LEARNING OUTCOME

By performing the specific steps of the experiments, the students will learn how bitstreams are generated and what format they use. They will use that knowledge to reverse engineer the bitstreams and retrieve the gate-level netlist of the design. They will also explore the challenges with respect to protecting an FPGA design against bitstream reverse engineering attacks.

7.5.4 ADVANCED OPTIONS

Additional exploration on this topic can be done through tampering the bitstream to obtain a hamming distance of 50% from the original output.

More details about the experiment is available in the supplementary document. Please visit: http:// hwsecuritybook.org.

7.6 EXERCISES
7.6.1 TRUE/FALSE QUESTIONS

1. Modern-day ASIC design flow involves third-party vendors.
2. In-house designs are always trustworthy.
3. The primary goals of cloning an IP are piracy and overproduction.
4. Hardware Trojans could help in cloning ICs.
5. Foundries are considered trustworthy entities throughout the IC design flow.
6. Encrypted FPGA bitstreams cannot be tampered for bypassing a logic implemented within the design.
7. If encryption and authentication are used together, the threat of bitstream tampering can be completely mitigated.
8. The side-channel analysis is an invasive attack for stealing the decryption key.
9. Without knowing the bitstream to be mapped in the FPGA, a Trojan cannot be included in the FPGA hardware by the foundry.
10. FPGA-based implementations typically consume more power and area compared to their ASIC counterpart.

7.6.2 SHORT-ANSWER TYPE QUESTIONS

1. Which phases of the ASIC lifecycle are vulnerable to hardware attacks?
2. List the entities capable of launching attacks on hardware in different phases of the design flow.
3. What are the different methods of FPGA bitstream tampering?
4. Describe how built-in authentication and encryption features operate in an FPGA.
5. What is the motivation behind bitstream reverse engineering from an attacker's perspective?

7.6.3 LONG-ANSWER TYPE QUESTIONS

1. Describe the lifecycle of a modern electronic hardware / ASIC design.

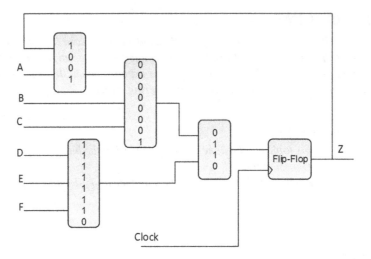

FIGURE 7.14

Figure for long-answer type question 6 and question 7.

2. Classify the attacks on hardware IPs in terms of the attacker's origin and intent. Briefly describe possible attack instances of hardware Trojan and IC overproduction.
3. How can an IP be exploited via reverse engineering? Briefly explain potential attack instances of reverse engineering.
4. Describe the typical development lifecycle of an FPGA-based product.
5. Describe the different attacks on an FPGA bitstream, which could occur during field operation.
6. Consider the FPGA synthesized netlist with four LUTs and one flip-flop (Fig. 7.14). The corresponding configuration bits are provided in binary (consider the top bit as MSB). Reverse the design to its gate-level version.
7. Consider the FPGA-synthesized netlist referred to in Question 6. With the minimum possible modification of LUT contents, mount a bitstream tampering attack that permanently inverts the output from the original one, and draw the tampered netlist.

REFERENCES

[1] Global Semiconductor IP Market Report 2018–2022.
[2] S. Skorobogatov, C. Woods, Breakthrough Silicon Scanning Discovers Backdoor in Military Chip, in: International Workshop on Cryptographic Hardware and Embedded Systems, Springer, pp. 23–40.
[3] E. Messmer, RSA Security Attack Demo Deep-Fries Apple Mac Components, 2014.
[4] R.S. Chakraborty, S. Narasimhan, S. Bhunia, Hardware Trojan: Threats and Emerging Solutions, in: High Level Design Validation and Test Workshop, 2009. HLDVT 2009. IEEE International, IEEE, pp. 166–171.
[5] S. Bhunia, M. Abramovici, D. Agrawal, P. Bradley, M.S. Hsiao, J. Plusquellic, M. Tehranipoor, Protection against Hardware Trojan Attacks: Towards a Comprehensive Solution, IEEE Design & Test 30 (2013) 6–17.
[6] D. Forte, S. Bhunia, M.M. Tehranipoor, Hardware Protection Through Obfuscation, Springer, 2017.

[7] M. Rostami, F. Koushanfar, R. Karri, A Primer on Hardware Security: Models, Methods, and Metrics, Proceedings of the IEEE 102 (2014) 1283–1295.

[8] K. Xiao, D. Forte, Y. Jin, R. Karri, S. Bhunia, M. Tehranipoor, Hardware Trojans: Lessons Learned after One Decade of Research, ACM Transactions on Design Automation of Electronic Systems (TODAES) 22 (2016) 6.

[9] S. Bhunia, M.S. Hsiao, M. Banga, S. Narasimhan, Hardware Trojan Attacks: Threat Analysis and Countermeasures, Proceedings of the IEEE 102 (2014) 1229–1247.

[10] F. Wolff, C. Papachristou, S. Bhunia, R.S. Chakraborty, Towards Trojan-Free Trusted ICs: Problem Analysis and Detection Scheme, in: Proceedings of the Conference on Design, Automation and Test in Europe, ACM, pp. 1362–1365.

[11] R.S. Chakraborty, S. Paul, S. Bhunia, On-demand Transparency for Improving Hardware Trojan Detectability, in: Hardware-Oriented Security and Trust, 2008. HOST 2008, IEEE International Workshop on, IEEE, pp. 48–50.

[12] S. Narasimhan, S. Bhunia, Hardware Trojan detection, in: Introduction to Hardware Security and Trust, Springer, 2012, pp. 339–364.

[13] E. Castillo, U. Meyer-Baese, A. García, L. Parrilla, A. Lloris, IPP@HDL: Efficient Intellectual Property Protection Scheme for IP Cores, IEEE Transactions on Very Large Scale Integration (VLSI) Systems 15 (2007) 578–591.

[14] A.B. Kahng, J. Lach, W.H. Mangione-Smith, S. Mantik, I.L. Markov, M. Potkonjak, P. Tucker, H. Wang, G. Wolfe, Constraint-Based Watermarking Techniques for Design IP Protection, IEEE Transactions on Computer-Aided Design of Integrated Circuits and Systems 20 (2001) 1236–1252.

[15] R.S. Chakraborty, S. Bhunia, HARPOON: an Obfuscation-based SoC Design Methodology for Hardware Protection, IEEE Transactions on Computer-Aided Design of Integrated Circuits and Systems 28 (2009) 1493–1502.

[16] S.E. Quadir, J. Chen, D. Forte, N. Asadizanjani, S. Shahbazmohamadi, L. Wang, J. Chandy, M. Tehranipoor, A survey on chip to system reverse engineering, ACM Journal on Emerging Technologies in Computing Systems (JETC) 13 (2016) 6.

[17] N. Asadizanjani, S. Shahbazmohamadi, M. Tehranipoor, D. Forte, Non-destructive PCB Reverse Engineering using X-ray Micro Computed Tomography, in: 41st International Symposium for Testing and Failure Analysis, ASM, pp. 1–5.

[18] M.C. Hansen, H. Yalcin, J.P. Hayes, Unveiling the ISCAS-85 Benchmarks: a Case Study in Reverse Engineering, IEEE Design & Test of Computers 16 (1999) 72–80.

[19] W.M. Van Fleet, M.R. Dransfield, Method of Recovering a Gate-Level Netlist from a Transistor-Level, 2001, US Patent 6,190,433.

[20] W. Li, Z. Wasson, S.A. Seshia, Reverse Engineering Circuits using Behavioral Pattern Mining, in: Hardware-Oriented Security and Trust (HOST), 2012 IEEE International Symposium on, IEEE, pp. 83–88.

[21] P. Subramanyan, N. Tsiskaridze, K. Pasricha, D. Reisman, A. Susnea, S. Malik, Reverse Engineering Digital Circuits using Functional Analysis, in: Proceedings of the Conference on Design, Automation and Test in Europe, EDA Consortium, pp. 1277–1280.

[22] I. Kuon, R. Tessier, J. Rose, FPGA Architecture: Survey and Challenges, Foundations and Trends in Electronic Design Automation 2 (2008) 135–253.

[23] K. Morris, Xilinx vs. Altera, calling the action in the greatest semiconductor rivalry, EE Journal (February 25, 2014).

[24] S. Mal-Sarkar, A. Krishna, A. Ghosh, S. Bhunia, Hardware Trojan Attacks in FPGA Devices: Threat Analysis and Effective Countermeasures, in: Proceedings of the 24th Edition of the Great Lakes Symposium on VLSI, ACM, pp. 287–292.

[25] K. Wilkinson, Using Encryption to Secure a 7 Series FPGA Bitstream, Xilinx, 2015.

[26] Xilinx, Authorized Distributors, https://www.xilinx.com/about/contact/authorized-distributors.html, 2017. (Accessed 3 December 2017), [Online].

[27] S. Ghosh, A. Basak, S. Bhunia, How Secure are Printed Circuit boards Against Trojan Attacks? IEEE Design & Test 32 (2015) 7–16.

[28] Xilinx, Readback Options, 2009.

[29] R. Druyer, L. Torres, P. Benoit, P.-V. Bonzom, P. Le-Quere, A Survey on Security Features in Modern FPGAs, in: Reconfigurable Communication-Centric Systems-on-Chip (ReCoSoC), 2015 10th International Symposium on, IEEE, pp. 1–8.

[30] S.M. Trimberger, J.J. Moore, FPGA Security: Motivations, Features, and Applications, Proceedings of the IEEE 102 (2014) 1248–1265.

[31] A. Moradi, A. Barenghi, T. Kasper, C. Paar, On the Vulnerability of FPGA Bitstream Encryption against Power Analysis Attacks: Extracting Keys from Xilinx Virtex-II FPGAs, in: Proceedings of the 18th ACM Conference on Computer and Communications Security, ACM, pp. 111–124.

[32] A. Moradi, M. Kasper, C. Paar, Black-Box Side-Channel Attacks Highlight the Importance of Countermeasures, in: Topics in Cryptology–CT-RSA 2012, 2012, pp. 1–18.

[33] A. Moradi, D. Oswald, C. Paar, P. Swierczynski, Side-Channel Attacks on the Bitstream Encryption Mechanism of Altera Stratix II: facilitating black-box analysis using software reverse-engineering, in: Proceedings of the ACM/SIGDA International Symposium on Field Programmable Gate Arrays, ACM, pp. 91–100.

[34] J.-B. Note, É. Rannaud, From the bitstream to the netlist, in: FPGA, vol. 8, p. 264.

[35] Z. Ding, Q. Wu, Y. Zhang, L. Zhu, Deriving an NCD file from an FPGA bitstream: Methodology, Architecture and Evaluation, Microprocessors and Microsystems 37 (2013) 299–312.

[36] F. Benz, A. Seffrin, S.A. Huss, Bil: a Tool-Chain for Bitstream Reverse-Engineering, in: Field Programmable Logic and Applications (FPL), 2012 22nd International Conference on, IEEE, pp. 735–738.

[37] R. Maes, D. Schellekens, I. Verbauwhede, A Pay-Per-Use Licensing Scheme for Hardware IP Cores in Recent SRAM-based FPGAs, IEEE Transactions on Information Forensics and Security 7 (2012) 98–108.

[38] R. Karam, T. Hoque, S. Ray, M. Tehranipoor, S. Bhunia, MUTARCH: Architectural Diversity for FPGA Device and IP Security, in: Design Automation Conference (ASP-DAC), 2017 22nd Asia and South Pacific, IEEE, pp. 611–616.

[39] R. Karam, T. Hoque, S. Ray, M. Tehranipoor, S. Bhunia, Robust Bitstream Protection in FPGA-based Systems through Low-Overhead Obfuscation, in: ReConFigurable Computing and FPGAs (ReConFig), 2016 International Conference on, IEEE, pp. 1–8.

[40] S. Trimberger, J. Moore, FPGA Security: from Features to Capabilities to Trusted Systems, in: Proceedings of the 51st Annual Design Automation Conference, ACM, pp. 1–4.

[41] S.P. Skorobogatov, R.J. Anderson, et al., Optical Fault Induction Attacks, in: CHES, vol. 2523, Springer, 2002, pp. 2–12.

[42] R.S. Chakraborty, I. Saha, A. Palchaudhuri, G.K. Naik, Hardware Trojan Insertion by Direct Modification of FPGA Configuration Bitstream, IEEE Design & Test 30 (2013) 45–54.

[43] P. Swierczynski, M. Fyrbiak, P. Koppe, C. Paar, FPGA Trojans through Detecting and Weakening of Cryptographic Primitives, IEEE Transactions on Computer-Aided Design of Integrated Circuits and Systems 34 (2015) 1236–1249.

[44] P. Swierczynski, G.T. Becker, A. Moradi, C. Paar, Bitstream Fault Injections (BiFI)–Automated Fault Attacks against SRAM-based FPGAs, IEEE Transactions on Computers (2017).

[45] T. Hoque, X. Wang, A. Basak, R. Karam, S. Bhunia, Hardware Trojan attack in Embedded Memory, in: IEEE VLSI Test Symposium (VTS), IEEE, 2018.

SIDE-CHANNEL ATTACKS

CONTENTS

Hardware Security. https://doi.org/10.1016/B978-0-12-812477-2.00013-7
Copyright © 2019 Elsevier Inc. All rights reserved.

8.1 INTRODUCTION

Side-channel attacks (SCA) is a noninvasive attack that is based on targeting the implementation of a cryptographic algorithm rather than analyzing its statistical or mathematical weakness. These attacks exploit physical information leaking from various indirect sources or channels, such as, the target device's power consumption, electromagnetic (EM) radiation, or the time taken for a computation. These channels are referred to as "side channels". The information embedded in side-channel parameters depend on the intermediate values computed during the execution of a crypto-algorithm, and are correlated with the inputs and the secret key of the cipher [1]. An adversary can effectively extract the secret key by observing and analyzing side-channel parameters with relatively cheap equipment, and within a very short time span, ranging from a few minutes to a few hours. Due to these reasons, SCA poses a major threat to cryptographic devices, especially smart cards and IoT devices, for which an attacker can have easy access to these physical parameters.

Figure 8.1 illustrates how a device leaks side-channel information while operating. Common side-channel attacks, such as power attacks, monitor the device's power consumption. Typically, this is done by incorporating a current path at V_{dd} or Gnd pin of a chip, which is performing the cryptographic operation, to record power dissipation for such an operation. The device's power consumption captures switching activity of the relevant transistors, which depends on inputs to a cryptographic function, such as the plaintext and the key. While the device is in operation, the power consumption can be measured using an oscilloscope, and the relation between the power consumption and the secret key is analyzed in various ways. Simple power analysis (SPA) is a technique to directly interpret the collected traces of power consumption for a set of inputs. It requires relatively detailed knowledge about the implementation of a cryptographic algorithm and a skilled adversary to interpret secret key information by visually examining the power consumption. Figure 8.2 provides the overview of the process of SCA. In contrast, differential power analysis (DPA) is a statistical analysis approach that does not require detailed knowledge of the target hardware implementation, which may be considered as a black box. DPA has been shown to be effective in finding a correlation between power consumption and processed data related to the secret key by statistical methods. In order to perform DPA successfully, however, often large number of power measurements are required.

8.2 BACKGROUND ON SIDE-CHANNEL ATTACKS

The first reported instance of SCA was an attack on a government agency in 1965. The attack was applied to a cryptographic machine that produced ciphertexts using a key that was reset every day [6].

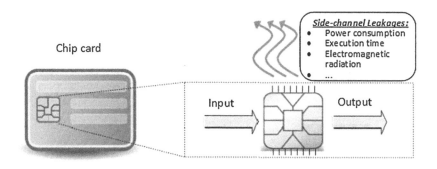

FIGURE 8.1

Side-channel leakages while a cryptographic hardware is in operation.

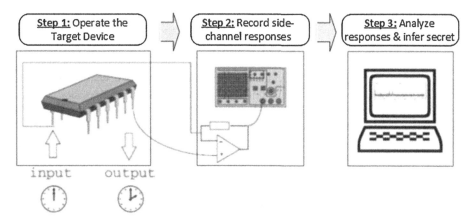

FIGURE 8.2

The data collection process of side-channel attacks, where a controlled attack scheme is enforced, and the measurements are provided back to the processing unit in order to perform the side-channel analysis. The process is usually iterative to ensure a wider functional coverage and optimized results.

By recording the sound of the module, attackers were able to derive the secret key. They related the number of click sounds, which were produced by the machine, to the value of the key. Since then SCAs have greatly evolved and relied on several other parameters, e.g., power, timing, and EM. The timeline in Fig. 8.3 shows the evolution of SCAs over past five decades.

8.2.1 TAXONOMY OF SIDE-CHANNEL ATTACKS

Based on the level of control that an attacker may have on a device prior to performing SCAs, they can be classified into passive and active attacks. Passive attacks (such as power, timing, or EM SCAs) do not require an attacker to interfere with the functionality or the operation of the device under attack [10]. The attack is usually launched in a manner that allows the system to behave normally as if the

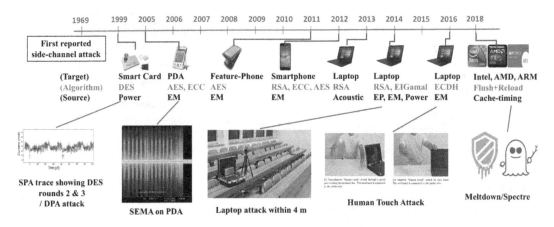

FIGURE 8.3

Evolution of side-channel attacks.

attack is not in effect. On the other hand, active attacks aim to interfere with the operation of the device under attack, where an attacker tends to influence how the device behaves, and what operation it performs. By actively controlling the behavior of the device, an attacker gains the advantage of selectively extracting side-channel information that can help break a cryptographic module, or extract the secret key.

Each side-channel attack can be done in many ways. Typically, a simple nonexhaustive approach has been introduced first, and then a refined and more complex approach is developed to enhance the amount and quality of extracted side-channel information. In case of power analysis attacks, as mentioned earlier, an adversary can perform a simple analysis, where a power signal is simply visually inspected. In a more sophisticated version of the attack, namely, DPA, multiple power traces are statistically analyzed to derive more robust information about the secret key.

Figure 8.4 shows the taxonomy of SCAs. Depending on the general source of side-channel information, there are several forms of SCA. They are: power SCA, EM SCA, fault injection attack, and timing SCA. Each SCA can be classified according to specific attack method: applied analysis methods, such as simple observation and statistical methods; side-channel signal generation methods, such as voltages and clocks; or analysis granularity, such as microarchitecture and system level analysis. [11].

8.2.2 UNCOMMON SIDE-CHANNEL ATTACKS

Besides the common ones described earlier, there are several other side-channel signals that can leak information about stored secrets in a hardware. These signals include emitted sound, temperature, and vibration. The analysis of these signals to extract secret information is not widely researched. One example of these uncommon SCAs is acoustic side-channel analysis [22]. It resembles the first reported SCA in 1965 in terms of the side-channel signal used in the attack [6]. The attack focuses on systems that produce sounds while being operated (such as, 3D printers), where program information can be extracted from the leaked acoustic signals. The captured sound signal is run through a series

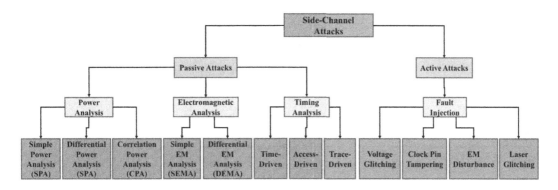

FIGURE 8.4

Taxonomy of general side-channel attacks.

of signal processing and machine-learning stages that can accomplish reconstructing the operation and producing an output similar to that of the device under attack. Other uncommon side-channels, such as, temperature and vibration, can also leak a significant amount of critical information about the device under attack. In order to build secure systems, all forms of side-channels need to be considered as a valid threat to information leakage, and adequate countermeasures need to be incorporated.

8.3 POWER ANALYSIS ATTACKS

The basic idea of power analysis attacks is to reveal secret information from a device by analyzing its power consumption [12]. The attack is non-invasive, and it requires physical access to the device, due to the need to capture current signatures that are produced while the device is undergoing an operation. Power analysis attacks are mainly used to extract the secret key of cryptographic systems, as it has been used to successfully break the Advanced Encryption Standard (AES) in a few minutes.

Power analysis attacks have been studied extensively by academic and industrial researchers as a dominant form of SCA. Various power analysis attacks, such as, SPA, DPA, and correlation power analysis (CPA) have been developed to reveal critical information about the device under attack. A set of power measurements is required for each side-channel analysis to be applied; these sets vary in scope and form, depending on the type of attack, the complexity of the design, and the accuracy of the data collection process. Each power signal captured during the analysis is called a power trace. An attacker usually needs to use a large number of power traces in all attack modes before applying the power analysis attack.

In this section, we explore what causes power signals to exist, and what factors would affect the shape of these signals. We also discuss the types of power signals that are generated during the device's operation, and how to capture them accurately. We explain the types of attacks that can be applied, and what information is extracted from a successful attack. Finally, we discuss the countermeasures, and what can be done to prevent attackers from performing SCAs.

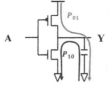

A	Y	Power
$0 \to 0$	$1 \to 1$	P_{11}
$0 \to 1$	$1 \to 0$	P_{10}
$1 \to 0$	$0 \to 1$	P_{01}
$1 \to 1$	$0 \to 0$	P_{00}

$P_{01}, P_{10} \gg P_{00}, P_{11} \approx 0$

FIGURE 8.5

Dynamic power of an inverter.

8.3.1 ORIGINS OF SIDE-CHANNEL LEAKAGE IN POWER CONSUMPTION

Two factors affect the power consumption of a device; the first factor is the dynamic power, which is caused by the switching activities of transistors within the device. The second factor is the leakage power, which is an unwanted behavior of a transistor, associated with the leakage current generated in its off state. An adversary is usually interested in capturing the dynamic power signals as they are directly related to the functional behavior of the device, i.e., specific operations going inside a device. For example, the dynamic power of an inverter is related to the switching activities of the input and the output, as shown in Fig. 8.5. Let P_{ij} be the power consumption, where the output value of the inverter is changed from i to j, for $i, j \in \{0, 1\}$. P_{01} and P_{10} are much greater than P_{00} and P_{11}, since the capacitor connected to the output is charged or discharged when the output value is switched; P_{00} and P_{11} are almost zero since there is no charging or discharging activity. Based on this characteristic, an adversary can estimate the status of the output or input by measuring the power of an inverter. If the input of an inverter originates from a secret key, the power side-channel leakage gives an adversary a clue about the secret key.

8.3.2 ACQUISITION OF POWER SIGNALS

The process of capturing power signals is straightforward and easily accomplished by a capturing equipment with high sampling rates, for example, an oscilloscope, which can be obtained at reasonably small cost. The process of power acquisition requires basic knowledge about the functionality of a device, where an input pattern is applied, and the power traces are captured during the processing of those patterns.

The power signals are captured by measuring the change in current levels in the voltage supply transmission lines. Usually, an oscilloscope measures the voltage drop across a precision sense resistor connected between the power rail (e.g., output of a voltage regulator that delivers power to a PCB) and V_{dd} or Gnd pin of the target device. Figure 8.6 presents an overview of a power analysis setup, where a cryptographic system is being controlled by a computer that applies input patterns, observes the outputs, measures the power consumption, and performs necessary analysis to extract the secret key.

Collected power traces include noise, which consists of algorithmic and natural electrical noise. The algorithmic noise is caused by the switching activity of other modules, and the natural electrical noise results from various environmental effects, e.g., electromagnetic inference. To eliminate noise, an adversary can pass the acquired power traces through a filtering phase. This filter removes the natural

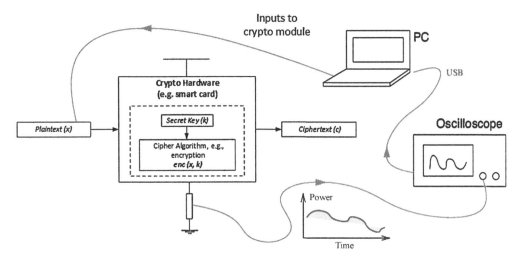

FIGURE 8.6

Typical setup for a power analysis attack on a crypto hardware.

noises that are caused by the device and other surroundings. A process of identifying noise levels and frequency bands can be applied to design the noise reduction filter, and accurately capture the power trace. A number of power traces can be averaged to remove noise and smoothen the signal. Depending on the device, the implementation of the algorithm, and type of attack, the number of power traces can vary from a single trace to millions of traces.

8.3.3 TYPES OF POWER ANALYSIS

We introduce three types of power side-channel analysis: simple power analysis (SPA), differential power analysis (DPA), and correlation power analysis (CPA).

8.3.3.1 Simple Power Analysis (SPA)

SPA is a technique that aims to observe power measurements obtained while the device under attack is in operation mode. This type of analysis does not require any advanced or statistical processing stages. SPA attacks are usually applied to devices with limited accessibility, where one or few power traces are available. SPA can be applied to a single power trace, where the attacker attempts to observe critical information or secret keys from that trace. When SPA is applied to multiple power traces captured from numerous occurrences, these traces are averaged to remove noise. In both cases, the attacker can only apply a successful attack if the recorded power consumption can lead to critical information about the device being revealed [15].

Visual inspection of power traces is considered the primary form of SPA attack, where a power trace shows a sequence of patterns that can lead to identifying key bits, instructions, or functions. Each instruction in a processor causes a specific pattern that can be visually identified in the power trace. Hence, visual inspection can prove useful when looking for clear patterns in the device under attack.

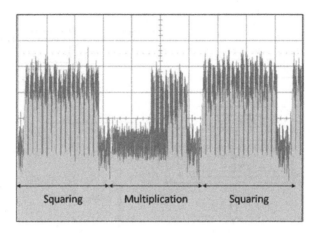

FIGURE 8.7

Part of a modular exponentiation power traces in RSA decryption [18].

Figure 8.7 shows a sequence of patterns corresponding to squaring and multiplication operations for a modular exponentiation in the RSA decryption.

Template attacks are a more advanced form of SPA, where known and recognized patterns in the power trace are characterized and stored as templates. Power traces collected from the target device are matched to the templates, and then corresponding operations are recognized. SPA can also be used as the first step to a more advanced approach, where power traces are used to identify the length of pipelines, processor load, microarchitectural events (such as, cache misses and hits), and the different functions that may trigger when changing the input patterns.

8.3.3.2 Differential Power Analysis (DPA)

DPA attacks are the most common type of side-channel attacks, due to the fact that attackers are not required to have prior knowledge about the hardware architecture of the device under attack to perform the analysis. Additionally, DPA has been proven very effective in obtaining high-quality signals in a noisy environment. Compared to SPA, DPA typically requires larger number of traces; more data collection makes DPA more powerful. DPA is widely used to reveal secret keys of cryptographic systems by obtaining power traces while the system is encrypting or decrypting data blocks [8].

In DPA, an adversary can successfully exploit data dependency of the power consumption, which gives them the ability to observe internal transitions, and extract secret keys and critical information. Implementation of DPA attack requires two phases: data collection and data analysis. In the data collection phase, different input patterns are applied to the device while recording the power traces in a high sampling rate. Averaging the measured traces, and applying a bandpass filter that is tuned to remove noise, can help improve the quality of traces. In the data analysis phase, statistical analysis, such as the difference of means is applied. Figure 8.8 shows an example of DPA being applied to an AES block. Based on the decision function, for example, the MSB of the substitution box (SBOX) [11] operation in Fig. 8.8, power traces are classified into two sets, and then the difference between means

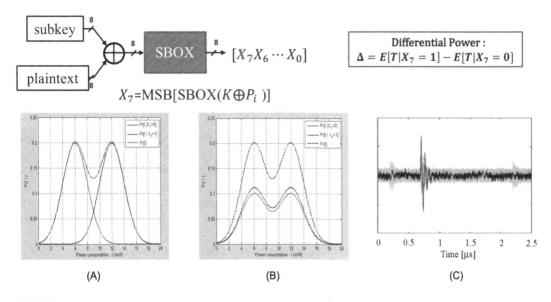

FIGURE 8.8

DPA attack to reveal a secret key. The probability density function for a correct key guess is shown in (A), the probability density function for a wrong key guess is shown in (B), the difference of means is shown in (C).

of the two sets is calculated as follows:

$$\Delta = \frac{\sum_{i=1}^{m} D(K, P_i) T_i}{\sum_{i=1}^{m} D(K, P_i)} - \frac{\sum_{i=1}^{m} (1 - D(K, P_i)) T_i}{\sum_{i=1}^{m} (1 - D(K, P_i))}.$$

In the equation above, $D(K, P_i) = MSB(SBOX(K \oplus P_i))$, K is the guessed key of an adversary, P_i is the plaintext, and T_i is a collected power trace, when the device is performing SBOX operation. If the guessed key is correct, then the conditional probability density functions given by $D = X_7 = 0$ and $D = X_7 = 1$, are completely different as shown in Fig. 8.8A. Otherwise, the conditional probability density functions are similar, as shown in Fig. 8.8B. Therefore, in case of the correct guessed key, the difference of means is the largest and in other cases, the difference of means is almost zero, as shown in Fig. 8.8C [9].

High-order DPA is a technique that utilizes multiple points in the entire power trace, or high-order statistics of a point, such as the second, third, and higher moments (i.e., variance, skewness, and kurtosis). This technique can successfully exploit the device's vulnerabilities, and bypass the traditional power analysis countermeasures.

DPA targets the correlated regions of the device's power consumption, which gives an adversary the ability to automate the analysis, and even train it to adapt to a device and environmental variations. The amount of information, the low cost, and the noninvasive nature of the attack make it one of the most powerful side-channel analysis attacks. It is worth emphasizing that DPA has been used to successfully attack many devices [24].

8.3.3.3 Correlation Power Analysis (CPA)

CPA is an advanced form of SCA that exploits the correlation between the power consumption, and the Hamming distance or Hamming weight of the target function, for example, the output of the SBOX operation. The first step of the CPA attack is to determine the intermediate value of the cryptographic algorithm executed by the device under attack, that is, the target function, which is denoted by $v_i = f(d_i, k^*)$, where d_i is the ith plaintext or ciphertext, and k^* is the hypothesis of a component of the secret key [16].

The second step is to measure the power consumption of the cryptographic device while it encrypts or decrypts D, different data inputs, including the target function at the first step. We denote the power trace as $\vec{t}_i = (t_{i,1}, t_{i,2}, \ldots, t_{i,t^*}, \ldots, t_{i,L})^T$, corresponding to input d_i, where L denotes the length of the trace, and t_{i,t^*} is the power consumption when the target function at the first step is performed. An adversary measures a trace for each of the D data inputs, and hence, the traces can be written as matrix $\mathbf{T}$ of size $D \times L$: $\mathbf{T} = (\vec{t}_1, \vec{t}_2, \ldots, \vec{t}_{t^*}, \ldots, \vec{t}_L)$, where $\vec{t}_j$ for $j = 1, \ldots, L$ is a column vector of size $D \times 1$.

The third step is to calculate a hypothetical intermediate value for all possible k : $v_{i,j} = f(d_i, k_j)$ for $i = 1, \ldots, D$ and $j = 1, \ldots, K$.

The fourth step is to map the hypothetical intermediate values to the hypothetical power consumption values: $h_{i,j} = g(v_{i,j}) = g(f(d_i, k_j))$ for $i = 1, \ldots, D$ and $j = 1, \ldots, K$. The most commonly used power consumption models are the Hamming-distance and the Hamming-weight models. The $D \times K$ matrix $\mathbf{H}$ is made at this step: $\mathbf{H} = (\vec{h}_1, \ldots, \vec{h}_K)$, where $\vec{h}_i$ for $i = 1, \ldots, K$ is a vector of size $D \times 1$.

The fifth step is to compare the hypothetical power consumption model with the measured power traces. In order to measure the linear relationships between the two vectors $\vec{h}_i$ and $\vec{t}_j$ for $i = 1, \ldots, K$ and $j = 1, \ldots, T$, the correlation coefficient is calculated:

$$r_{i,j} = \frac{\sum_{d=1}^{D}(h_{d,i} - \overline{h_i})(t_{d,j} - \overline{t_j})}{\sqrt{\sum_{i=1}^{D}(h_{d,i} - \overline{h_i})^2 \sum_{i=1}^{D}(t_{d,j} - \overline{t_j})^2}}$$

where $\overline{h_i}$ and $\overline{t_j}$ denote the mean values of the vector $\vec{h}_i$ and $\vec{t}_j$, respectively. If r_{k^*, t^*} of the correct key k^* and the specific time t^* has the distinct peak value, then the CPA attack is successful.

8.3.4 POWER SIDE-CHANNEL ATTACK COUNTERMEASURES

In order to remove dependency between power consumption and intermediate values of the executed cryptographic algorithm, the cryptographic hardware can be implemented with secure primitive logic cells (such as sense-amplified-based logic (SABL) [19], wave dynamic differential logic (WDDL) [20], and t-private logic circuit [21]) at the design stage. These secure logic styles use different methods to make the power consumption of the performed operation independent of the processed data values, thus preventing leakage of secret information (i.e., key) in power traces. SABL and WDDL consume equal amounts of power in each clock cycle, but t-private logic circuit randomizes amounts of power consumption in each clock cycle by masking each bit with t random bits. In other words, SABL and WDDL implement the *hiding countermeasure*, and t-private logic circuit implements the *masking countermeasure*.

Table 8.1 Secure logic style

	SABL	WDDL	t-private logic
SCA resistance	✓	✓	✓
Probing resistance	✗	✗	✓
Method	Hiding	Hiding	Random masking
Design	Full custom	Semicustom	Semicustom
Area	Medium	Low	High
Power	Medium	High	Low

Whereas all these secure cells have varying level of robustness against SCAs, only t-private logic circuit prevents the probing attack, which allows an adversary to observe only t-limited number of internal nodes per each clock cycle. In terms of their implementation, t-private logic circuit and WDDL are implemented with the general CMOS digital cell library, but each SABL cell should be full-customized. Of these secure logic design styles, t-private has the largest circuit area, but the power consumption of t-private logic circuit is the smallest. Since SABL and WDDL have two-phase (the pre-charge phase and the evaluation phase), during each clock cycle in which phase signals are switched, the power consumptions of SABL and WDDL are larger than that of t-private logic circuit. Table 8.1 shows the summary of these secure logic styles.

8.3.5 HIGHER-ORDER SIDE-CHANNEL ATTACKS

Higher-order side-channel attacks exploit multiple leakages, corresponding to several intermediate values during execution of a cryptographic algorithm [26]. The $(n + 1)$st-order SCA is effective in the nth-order masking countermeasures, in which an intermediate value is masked with n random values. When an intermediate value is masked with a random value in the cryptographic device, second-order DPA or CPA attacks can be performed in order to reveal the secret key. For example, we assume that the input and output of AES SBOX operations are concealed with the same mask r as follows: $v = (p \oplus k) \oplus r, u = \text{SBOX}(p \oplus k) \oplus r$, and two intermediate values are stored in a register. The SBOX input and output are targeted in the second-order CPA attack. For the attack, adversary's hypothetical function h is defined as the Hamming distance between two intermediated values: $h_{k_i} = HW(v \oplus u) = HW((p \oplus k_i) \oplus \text{SBOX}(p \oplus k_i))$, and two points l_1 and l_2 of collected power traces when two intermediate values are stored in a register are combined as the absolute-difference function: $t = |l_1 - l_2|$. The reason to use the absolute-difference function among other functions, such as summation, subtraction, or square of summation to combine two points, is that the absolute-difference function has a higher correlation to the hypothetical function [26].

If the guessed key is equal to the correct key, the correlation between the hypothetical function and the combined function has the maximum value: $k^* = \arg\max_{k_i \in \mathcal{K}} \rho(h_{k_i}, t)$, where k^* is the correct key. Consequently, the correct key can be revealed by comparing the hypothetical power consumption with the combined power trace.

8.3.6 POWER SCA SECURITY METRIC

A device's security against SCAs needs to be evaluated using appropriate metric. There are different methods to measure the level of protection of the device under attack. These methods assess the difficulty of performing a successful SCA, and the time required to successfully extract the critical information from the device.

The test vector leakage assessment (TVLA) is a common assessment approach to measure how easy it is to detect any data leakages in a device. This assessment is done by applying a predefined set of test inputs, detecting leakage, and evaluating the ability to extract significant information from the traces. The leakage assessment is based on Welch's t-test, which is used to test the hypothesis that two populations have equal means when two samples have unequal variance and unequal sample size. In the side-channel evaluation process, n side-channel measurements are collected while the device under the test operates with a secret key. The n measurements $\bar{\mathbf{p}}^i = [p_0^i, \ldots, p_{m-1}^i]$ for $i = 1, \ldots, n$, where m is the number of the sampling points, are classified into two sets by the determinant function D: $S_0 = \{\bar{\mathbf{p}}^i | D = 0\}$, and $S_1 = \{\bar{\mathbf{p}}^i | D = 1\}$. If the t-test statistic

$$t = \frac{\mu_0 - \mu_1}{\sqrt{\frac{\sigma_0^2}{N_0} + \frac{\sigma_1^2}{N_1}}}$$

is out of the confidence interval, $|t| > C$, then the null hypothesis, $H_o : \mu_0 = \mu_1$ is rejected. This means that two groups are distinguishable and the implementation has high probability to leak information. Thus, it does not pass the leakage assessment test. Let us assume that the threshold value C is chosen as 4.5, which leads to a confidence of > 0.99999 to reject the null hypothesis, and the determinant function D is defined as

$$D = \begin{cases} 0 & \text{if plaintext is random,} \\ 1 & \text{if plaintext is fixed,} \end{cases}$$

which is referred to as *nonspecific fixed-vs-random* test.

Another method used to measure side-channel vulnerability is to apply the attack success rate analysis. This success rate is defined as the number of successful attacks (i.e., the key is derived through the attack) divided by the total number of performed attacks, where the maximum rate of 100% means the device is attacked successfully every time a side-channel analysis is applied, and the minimum of 0%, which means the device is protected against all attacks. This assessment can also reflect the time needed for the attacker to extract critical information from the device.

8.4 ELECTROMAGNETIC (EM) SIDE-CHANNEL ATTACKS

EM SCA focuses on measuring electromagnetic waves that are emitted from ICs in operation. These EM waves are defined as synchronized oscillations of electric and magnetic fields that propagate at the speed of light through a vacuum [14].

In this section, we discuss the origin of different EM signals, and the equipment needed to capture them. We differentiate between intentional and unintentional EM signals. We also address the amount and type of information that could be leaked through EM side-channel. We describe a data acquisition process that can capture low energy, yet critical, EM signals. We explain various types of EM based side-channel attacks that could be applied using side-channel analysis, such as simple electromagnetic attacks (SEMA), and differential electromagnetic attacks (DEMA). Finally, we outline possible countermeasures to protect devices against EM side-channel attacks.

8.4.1 ORIGIN OF EM SIGNALS

The EM waves are produced as current flows across a device, where transistor and interconnect switching activities occur with changing input patterns. This current flow results in the EM signals. EM signals of specific current flow may not only be affected by the physical or functional structure of the device, but can also be affected by the EM waves of other components, and their current flows.

An adversary usually aims to capture EM signals that are produced by current flows of data processing stages, where most waves occur, due to the switching activity of a device while performing a data processing operation. These waves are usually considered unintentional, and they allow critical information to be leaked naturally during operation. When applying EM side-channel analysis, switching activities can be easily captured and translated into a series of events and instances that occur in each clock cycle. This type of attack is similar to the power side-channel analysis, where a one-dimensional view of current activity is used to extract critical secret from a device. Power analysis attacks, such as DPA, however, cannot extract any spatial information, e.g., the location of a specific current activity. On the other hand, an EM side-channel attack can also identify the location of an EM signal, which makes it a powerful attack vector.

8.4.2 EM EMANATIONS

EM emanation is defined as the process that causes the target device to generate EM signals. There are two types of EM emanations: intentional and unintentional emanations. Next, we describe these two broad types.

8.4.2.1 Intentional Emanations

Intentional EM emanation results from current flows that are applied to cause the device to emit an electromagnetic response [17]. These current flows are usually in the form of short bursts and sharp rising edges, which cause a high-power emanation that would be readily observable across a full frequency band. Often, the applied current flow targets a higher frequency band to quickly capture the response due to noise and other interfering emissions in a lower frequency band. The objective of an attacker in this type of emanation is to isolate the EM response of the targeted critical data path. In order to do this, a tiny and sensitive EM probe is needed. Delayering of the device may also help improve the captured signal quality.

8.4.2.2 Unintentional Emanations

When an adversary applies EM side-channel analysis, focusing on unintentional emanation can help identify critical paths and acquire their data values. The increased complexity and reduced size of modern ICs result in electric and electromagnetic coupling between components, which is an uncontrolled phenomenon that can generate a compromising signal. These components may act as modulators; they generate a carrier signal that can be intercepted and post-processed to acquire the carried data.

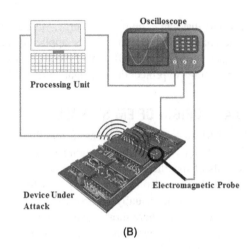

(A) (B)

FIGURE 8.9

(A) A picture of an EM probe being placed on an FPGA; (B) EM Side-channel analysis setup.

Modulation of the signals can be either an amplitude modulation (AM), or a frequency modulation (FM). In AM, the coupling between the carrier signal and the data signal result in an AM emanation; the data signal can be extracted by demodulating the AM signal using a tuned receiver. In FM, the coupling results in a frequency shifted signal; this signal can be demodulated by using an FM receiver.

8.4.3 ACQUISITION OF EM SIGNALS

EM signals often propagate through conduction and radiation; these signals can be intercepted using sensors, such as a near-field probe or an antenna. Using these sensors allows the EM signal to be transferred into a current signal, which is post-processed to remove noise, and limit the frequency band in order to apply the EM analysis. The quality of the received signal is usually improved if the used sensor is shielded from unwanted frequency bands, or other EM interferences.

Post-processing of the signal may include filtering frequency bands that are not related to the targeted critical data path, which requires prior knowledge of the frequency band that holds the information. In order to obtain that knowledge, a spectrum analyzer is commonly used to identify carriers and noise; then a post-processing filter can be tuned only to allow critical information to pass. Figure 8.9 shows an illustration of a measurement setup for the EM attack.

8.4.4 TYPES OF EM ANALYSIS

There are two main types of EM analysis: Simple and differential electromagnetic analysis, SEMA and DEMA, respectively.

8.4.4.1 Simple Electromagnetic Analysis (SEMA)

In SEMA, an attacker obtains a single time domain trace to observe, and gain knowledge about the device directly. The attack is only valid when there is prior knowledge about the device's architecture, or the security policy, applied. The primary objective in SEMA is to obtain critical information via visual inspection of the EM signal trace, where a sequence of transitions at the startup of the system may include information about the secret key used to encrypt/decrypt data. The use of SEMA is usually the first step of EM SCA, where the necessary information can be observed to carry on a more detailed analysis using DEMA.

8.4.4.2 Differential Electromagnetic Analysis (DEMA)

The attacker applies DEMA to the device to exploit information that cannot be visually observable. DEMA generally utilizes a self-referencing approach, which compares the analyzed signal with an equivalent one in a different area of the device (spatial referencing), or in a different time (temporal referencing). DEMA does not require much knowledge about the device under attack; most information can be exploited when obtaining different forms of EM signals in different places and times. The analysis in DEMA can help identify functional and structural details of the target device. It can also track a process flow and determine how a signal propagates inside the device. These details obtained by DEMA can help reverse engineer the device, or give the attacker the ability to disable the security policy of the system physically.

8.4.5 EM SCA COUNTERMEASURES

To protect against EM SCAs, many countermeasures can help add a layer of protection, while maintaining the device's performance and quality of service. Redesigning the circuit to reduce the coupling issue is one of the primary countermeasures. Additionally, adding a layer of shielding to the device to prevent EM signals from propagating is another significant measure. Introducing nonfunctional modules that produce EM noise can also prevent critical information from being easily intercepted due to the high amount of noise being applied in the same frequency band.

Other functional countermeasures may hide critical processes from being detected, such as introducing a crucial nonlinear processing sequence when using a cryptographic system. By injecting dummy instructions or operations between the stages of a cryptographic process, the adversary can be prevented from differentiating between key-bits and dummy-bits, even when performing successful EM side-channel attacks. Due to the existence of several methods to intercept uncontrolled EM signals, many attacks have been successful in extracting critical information, even when encryption is applied. Hence, countermeasures should be introduced as early as possible in the design phase for the device to be adequately protected against EM SCAs.

8.5 FAULT INJECTION ATTACKS

Unlike power analysis attacks, fault injection attacks are active attacks, where a crypto-device is intentionally injected with a fault that leads to a leakage of the secret key [1,7]. The injected fault is designed to introduce a temporary malfunction during the device operation. This malfunction is typically a disturbance of a few memory or register bits. As the execution continues, the disturbance, i.e.,

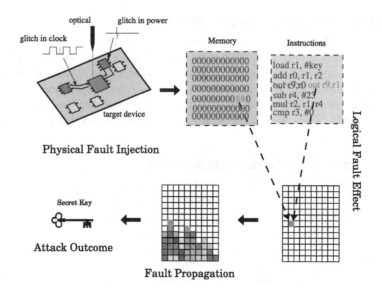

FIGURE 8.10

In a fault injection attack, or fault attack, a physical fault is deliberately injected in a device during its operation with the objective of leaking critical information. Such a fault can be injected by disturbing the clock or voltage source, or by using a laser beam, in order to modify memory or register locations, or to induce other fault effects (e.g., skip an instruction). In a crypto device, such a disturbance often gets propagated to other locations during the execution, and eventually results in a faulty ciphertext. The faulty ciphertext can then be evaluated to retrieve the secret key.

single/multiple memory bit-flip, propagates to other memory locations and eventually results in a corrupted output. We call this corrupted output a faulty ciphertext. If the fault is injected precisely and has specific properties, an attacker can use the faulty ciphertext to derive the secret key. Figure 8.10 shows the entire process involved in a fault attack. Several encryption schemes, such as AES, RSA, and ECC have been demonstrated to be vulnerable to this attack.

A typical attack starts with injecting a fault to an operational device, which can either be a voltage or a clock source glitch [4,5]. Other techniques, such as electromagnetic radiation, or physical probing, or passing a laser beam through the device can also be used for the fault injection. The device is then analyzed by observing the faulty outputs; these outputs can potentially help extract the secret key. The attack is considered semi-invasive, as the physical modification is sometimes needed for the fault to be properly injected.

The attack requires prior knowledge about the design in order for it to be successful. Choosing the type of fault, the location and time of the injection process, is not possible when the device is treated as a black box. An example of a simple fault injection attack on AES is shown in Fig. 8.11. Let k_0 represent the bit 0 of the AES key. Now, consider that a stuck-at-zero fault is injected in k_0 during the initial Key Addition operation, which forces the value of k_0 to be zero. There are two possible outcomes. First, if $k_0 = 0$ prior to fault injection, then the fault induced has no effect on the output. On the other hand, if $k_0 = 1$, then the fault toggles the value of $p_0 \oplus k_0$. This is a disturbance, which

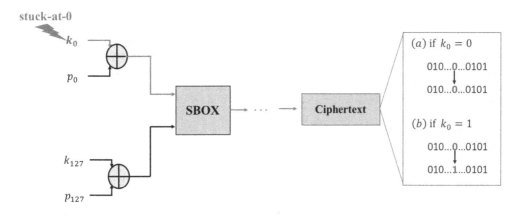

stuck-at-0

k_0

p_0

SBOX → ... → Ciphertext

k_{127}

p_{127}

(a) if $k_0 = 0$

010...0...0101
↓
010...0...0101

(b) if $k_0 = 1$

010...0...0101
↓
010...1...0101

FIGURE 8.11

A simple fault injection attack on AES; the target bit is k_0.

then gets propagated as execution progresses, resulting in a faulty ciphertext. In this case, the faulty ciphertext will be different from that of the fault-free ciphertext, generated from the same plaintext. The attacker, thus, identifies the value of k_0.

In a similar way, by independently injecting faults in key bits k_1 to k_{127}, the attacker can retrieve the entire AES key. This attack—though easy to understand—is very difficult to perform in practice. This is due to the fact that 128 precisely placed and timed faults are required to be generated by an attacker. Each fault should exactly force one bit of the key to zero. Since this simple attack, many stronger and powerful fault attacks have been proposed. The strongest attack can recover the entire secret key with just a single fault injection. This attack requires a fault to be injected at the 8th round of AES. The attack also relaxes the fault injection requirements; the fault only needs to randomly modify a single byte in the 8th round.

8.5.1 FAULT INJECTION TECHNIQUES

Fault injection techniques can vary based on the type of device, and the amount of information available to the attacker. The following subsections explain the main types of fault injection techniques.

8.5.1.1 Voltage Glitching

Voltage glitching is considered the basic fault injection technique, where a device is supplied with a lower than normal voltage level. By running the device in this state, faults would start to appear at the output of the device. The precision and type of fault are controlled by the level of the supplied voltage; a more faulty behavior is obtained as the voltage supply is lowered further. This technique is not invasive and it does not require specific timing patterns. When applying this attack, faults will propagate uniformly across the device, which can give an advantage to the attacker in terms of accessibility to rarely-activated nodes and registers in the device.

8.5.1.2 Tampering With Clock Pin

Another basic fault injection technique involves an attacker subjecting the device with a faulty clock signal. The fault can either be a glitch in the clock, or the voltage level of the signal. This noninvasive attack forces the device to generate faulty outputs across all clocked operations. The attacker needs to have access to the clock signal of the device in order to precisely control the fault, which is a relatively easy task.

8.5.1.3 EM Disturbances

EM Disturbances can be applied to a device to inject faults. Generating EM signals and directing them to a device can cause the operation of the system to be compromised. By controlling the EM signal, different types of behavioral changes in functionality can be observed, and with the right input patterns and enough iterations, the device can leak the secret key of the cryptographic module. Since EM signals are applied to the entire device, the attack affects the system uniformly, as the faults can be injected at any location in the device.

8.5.1.4 Laser Glitching

Applying a laser beam to a specific area of a device can cause a fault to be injected [3]. Data in registers and states can be modified when intentionally applying a strong laser beam. Beams can be controlled in terms of strength and polarization, which allows the attacker to either inject faults to a specific area, or to the entire device. Injected errors can propagate to the output of the design, and successfully leak the secret key of the cryptographic module.

8.5.2 FAULT INJECTION COUNTERMEASURES

Countermeasures for fault injection attacks are limited, as tools and equipment used to inject errors are easy to obtain. The level of accessibility to main ports of the design (such as, the power and clock lines) make these attacks very difficult to combat. Nevertheless, there are some measures that can be taken to avoid leaking critical information when faults are introduced.

One of the most common fault injection attack countermeasures is based on replication of critical operations, which is a popular solution for fault-tolerant computing [2]. Here, the crypto operations are repeated, and the two outputs are compared. If found different, the system assumes that a fault has been injected, and appropriate actions are taken. The replication can be done spatially or temporally. Spatial replication, especially applicable in hardware crypto accelerators, has redundant circuit blocks to recompute specific crypto operations. Temporal replication reuses the same circuit blocks to perform the recomputation at different time. Whereas the spatial countermeasure does not affect the execution time for crypto operation (but adds area overhead), the temporal countermeasure does not affect the area requirements (but adds delay overhead). The former is, therefore, suited for high-speed applications, whereas the latter is suited for small devices.

An alternate protection approach is based on error-detection schemes, such as parity checks. The scheme adds a detection mechanism that disables the critical functionality of the device when it is operating in a faulty environment. Compared to replication, they have typically less overheads. However, they are not very efficient in detecting multiple fault injections. Overhead goes up significantly with the need to detect and/or correct multiple faults. These protection methods are also inspired by similar techniques used in building fault-tolerant systems. Anti-tamper protection modules are also an option.

These can be used to reduce the impact of fault injection attacks. Anti-tamper protection modules can act as scanning tools that look for and report any physical modification attempts. These modules are limited to physical and semi-invasive attacks.

8.6 TIMING ATTACKS

Timing analysis is an SCA that is used to extract critical information about the device under attack by analyzing the execution time of each operation under different setups and input patterns [13]. Every operation performed in a silicon-based device takes a certain amount of time to complete. This time can vary due to the type of operation, the input data, the technology used to build the device, and the properties of the environment, in which the device is operating.

In this section, we show how timing attack is applied, methods used to increase the accuracy of the analysis, what information can be obtained, and countermeasures that could prevent the attack from being successful.

8.6.1 TIMING ATTACKS ON CRYPTOGRAPHIC HARDWARE

An adversary often applies timing analysis on cryptographic systems to extract the secret key, where timing analysis can help the attacker determine which subsets of the key are correct, and which subsets are not. The way an adversary measures the delay of a signal is by applying a change in the input, and recording the delay that occurs before the output is updated. Other techniques include focusing on power or EM signals to analyze the delay; this is mainly used when the device under attack has a sequential circuit, or uses pipelines. Environmental conditions may help an adversary perform effective timing analysis, where different operating temperatures may affect the speed of data flow. For example, higher temperature typically causes a slower data flow, which can help differentiate between parallel or high-speed operations.

Figure 8.12A shows an overview of a naive modular exponentiation algorithm, and Fig. 8.12B shows the total time of 10,000 executions of 3 different modular-exponentiation software implementations: (1) straightforward, (2) square-and-multiply, and (3) Montgomery with square-and-multiply implementations. As shown in this figure, the execution time depends on the exponent. In the case of straightforward implementation, as the exponent increases, the execution time also increases linearly. In other cases, the execution time is related to the number of 1's in the binary exponent number, that is, the Hamming weight of the exponent.

Timing attacks are usually applied along with other side-channel attacks, since more information can be extracted when different analysis methods are employed. Power analysis is one example that works well with timing attacks; the power trace does not only show the pattern in which the operation performed is correlated to, but also how long it took before the operation is completed. The order of operation is also revealed when applying timing analysis to power signals; this order can help identify the type of process the device is running, and may even allow the adversary to reverse engineer the device.

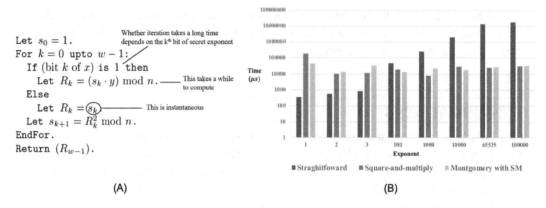

(A)   (B)

FIGURE 8.12

(A) Square and multiply algorithms used for a modular exponentiation operation, and (B) the total time of 10,000 executions of 3 different modular-exponentiation software implementations.

8.6.2 CACHE-TIMING ATTACK IN PROCESSOR

Another powerful timing analysis attack, called cache-timing attack, is applied to the cache memory of a processor. The main objective of the cache-timing attack is to measure the time for cache access and then to relate the timing values to the information being processed. The cache access time is different for the following two cases: (1) when the requested data by the processor is available in the cache (i.e., cache hit), and (2) when the cache does not have the data available and requests it from the main memory (i.e., cache miss). Retrieving data from the main memory, or from cache levels closer to the main memory in the memory hierarchy of a processor, takes longer time than that from cache levels closer to the processor core. These timing differences have been exploited in SCAs. To measure the time, an attacker can flush the monitored memory line from the cache hierarchy (FLUSH phase), and then wait to allow the victim program to access the memory line (WAIT phase). An attacker then reloads the memory line, measuring the time to load it (RELOAD phase). If the victim accesses the memory line during the wait phase, the reload operation takes a shorter time. Otherwise, the requested line needs to be brought from the memory, and the reload takes significantly longer time. Figure 8.13 shows the timing of the attack phases with and without the victim access. This attack is called `Flush+Reload` attack [23].

8.6.3 TIMING ATTACKS COUNTERMEASURES

To protect devices against timing attacks, designers can do the following: (1) randomize the delay of different operations, or (2) make all operations take the same time, thus preventing information leakage through timing channel. While constant-time implementations can guarantee security against timing attacks, they are not easily achievable in practice. Randomization on the other hand, for instance, by adding random delays to the execution of a task, is easier to accomplish. While it makes the attack more difficult, it cannot, however, guarantee the security of an implementation against timing attacks. Randomization is done by creating various execution paths and adding different delays to different

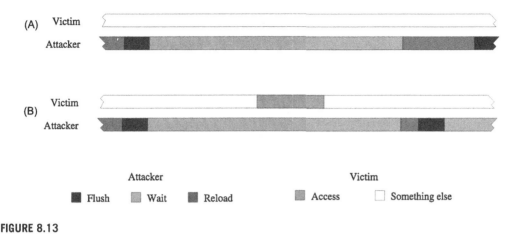

FIGURE 8.13

Timing of `Flush+Reload` attack: (A) without victim access; (B) with victim access [23].

paths. One way to apply delay to a path is to place a series of buffers in the path during circuit design, where the number of buffers can be controlled by the designer to maintain the desired delay.

8.6.4 TIMING LEAKAGE METRICS

In order to evaluate key-dependent timing leakage in a crypto module, test vector leakage assessment methodology can be used. We define timing leakage assessment based on Welch's t-test. Here, it is relevant to repeat that the latter evaluation method is used to test the hypothesis that two populations have equal means when two samples have unequal variance and unequal sample size. For example, two sets of RSA decryptions are defined as the following:

Set 1: n timing measurements during decrypting the same n random ciphertexts with a fixed key: $X_1 = \{t_i | t_i = \#cycle(C_i^{K^*} \mod N), i = 1, \ldots, n\}$.

Set 2: n timing measurements during decrypting the same n random ciphertexts with n random keys: $X_2 = \{t_i | t_i = \#cycle(C_i^{K_i} \mod N), i = 1, \ldots, n\}$. Let the means and variances of X_1 and X_2 be $\bar{X}_1, \bar{X}_2, S_1^2$, and S_2^2. If the t-test statistic

$$t = \frac{\bar{X}_1 - \bar{X}_2}{\sqrt{\frac{S_1^2}{n} + \frac{S_2^2}{n}}} \tag{8.1}$$

is out of the confidence interval, $|t| > T$, then the null hypothesis, $H_0 : \bar{X}_1 = \bar{X}_2$ is rejected. This means that two sets are distinguishable and the implementation has high probability to leak timing information. Thus, it does not pass the leakage assessment test. This is referred to as *nonspecific fixed-vs-random* test. There are other timing leakage tests available in the literature.

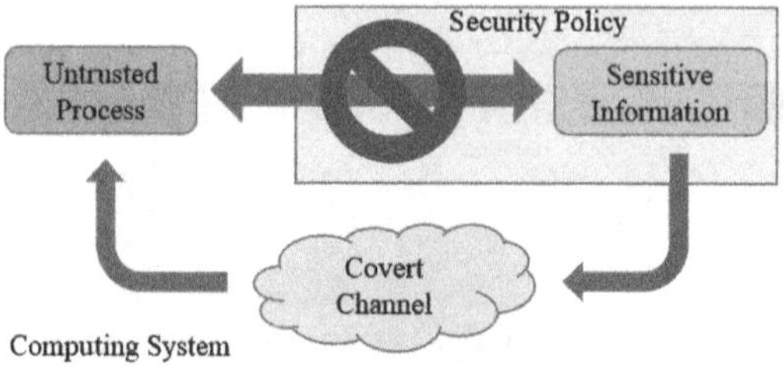

FIGURE 8.14

An overview of a covert channel that bypasses the system security policy and forms an unauthorized communication channel with an untrusted process.

8.7 COVERT CHANNELS

Similar to side channels, covert channels are information leakage channels. However, there are significant differences between their information leakage mechanisms. A covert channel is one that allows communication between software processes that are not authorized to communicate within a system [25]. These communication channels are often not monitored, as security policies may not be able to recognize them. Figure 8.14 illustrates the formation of covert channels. Different types of covert channels have been discovered in modern computing systems. The most common type of covert channels is the storage covert channel, which utilizes the headers of data packets to transfer data. Another type is the timing covert channel, where the communication occurs by modulating allocated resources.

Covert channels can also exist in hardware implementation, where a stealthy malicious circuit with a very rare triggering condition is injected into the system during design phase. When triggered, this circuit can leak sensitive information to the primary outputs of the system, and only the attacker would know how to trigger this circuit.

Compared to SCAs, the exploitation of covert channels is usually more difficult, as an attacker needs to have knowledge about the type and location of sensitive information to leak. This can be accomplished through an attacker's access to the detailed knowledge about the implementation or ability to modify a design at development stage in order to create a covert channel. On the other hand, SCAs typically do not require access to such knowledge. Further, they do not require any design modification, since side-channel signals are naturally generated. Although covert channels are harder to implement, they can typically leak much more sensitive information than side channel analysis.

The detection process of covert channels is very challenging as the number of possible methods for communication can be very large. However, there are mitigation methods that can reduce the number of covert channels. The commonly used method is a validation process that detects and eliminates all malicious functions in the system. The other method is to limit the access to stored data to one process at a time so that other processes cannot form a channel and receive the leaked data.

Side-channel attacks pose a significant threat to the semiconductor industry. Many side-channel analysis attacks cannot be prevented since the origin of these side-channel signals are natural. Many techniques have been evolving in the past decade as the attacker's capabilities have dramatically increased. Table 8.2 shows a summary of the side-channel attacks discussed in this chapter.

Table 8.2 Summary of side-channel attacks

Side-Channel Attack	Measured Parameters	Analysis Methods	Countermeasures
Power Analysis	Current signature and power consumption patterns	Simple power analysis (SPA) Differential power analysis (DPA) Correlation power analysis (CPA)	Power consumption masking Power consumption hiding
EM Analysis	Intentional and non-Intentional electromagnetic emission	Simple EM analysis (SEMA) Differential EM analysis (DEMA)	EM emission shielding EM noise generation modules
Fault Analysis	Invalid outputs, underpowered behavior, and Laser/UV Glitching Responses	Comparative approach to analyze responses before and after fault insertion	Error detection schemes Anti-tamper protection modules
Timing Analysis	Operation delays, time elapsed when different input patterns are applied	Analysis to relate operation delay to the nature of the function	Randomized operational delay Fixed operational delay

The decreasing effort to perform these attacks, and diminishing cost of the measurement instruments, make it easy to exploit side-channel vulnerabilities and help break traditional cryptographic systems. Many countermeasures have been proposed to prevent SCAs. These countermeasures have also evolved over time in their effectiveness and cost, and are being increasingly deployed in new devices to protect against diverse forms of SCAs.

8.8 HANDS-ON EXPERIMENT: SIDE-CHANNEL ATTACK
8.8.1 OBJECTIVE
This experiment is designed to help students explore different types of side-channel attacks for a cryptomodule. The experiment allows students to perform noninvasive side-channel attacks using the HaHa platform.

8.8.2 METHOD
First part of the experiment illustrates the power side-channel attacks, where simple and differential power analysis (SPA and DPA) are applied to an AES design (simplified version) mapped to the FPGA. Students will apply the power analysis while the encryption process is running. Next, the students will capture enough power traces to extract the encryption key of the AES. The second part of the experiment focuses on the fault injection attack, where students will deliberately inject faults into the module in order to leak the encryption key.

8.8.3 LEARNING OUTCOME
By performing the specific steps of the experiments, the students will understand how secret information can leak from inside a chip through different modes of side-channel attacks. They will understand the

side-channel signal measurement and analysis steps, and the physical mechanisms for fault injection. They will also explore the level of information that can be extracted through side-channel analysis.

8.8.4 ADVANCED OPTIONS

Additional exploration on this topic can be done through investigation on how different countermeasures (for example, power balancing or masking) can help mitigate these attacks.

More details about the experiment are available in the supplementary document. Please visit: http://hwsecuritybook.org.

8.9 EXERCISES

8.9.1 TRUE/FALSE QUESTIONS

1. The device under attack does not need to be physically available to the attacker in order to apply the side-channel analysis.
2. Attackers are not often able to perform side-channel attacks due to the high cost of analysis equipment.
3. No prior knowledge of the device's functionality is required to perform power analysis attacks.
4. SPA will always give more information about the device than DPA.
5. Post processing is a step that aims to take out noise and unwanted parts of the power signal.
6. EM emanation is always intentionally done to perform EM analysis attacks.
7. When done properly, EM analysis can provide more information about the device than power analysis.
8. Fault analysis are invasive attacks that usually destroy the device when performed.
9. Timing analysis is only applicable to designs that are purely sequential.
10. Side-channel countermeasures can be applied to the device at any part of its lifetime.

8.9.2 SHORT-ANSWER TYPE QUESTIONS

1. Describe the main idea of side-channel analysis.
2. What information can be gained when successfully applying a side-channel attack?
3. Explain an invasive and noninvasive attack.
4. Explain SPA and DPA. What are the differences between them?
5. Describe what tools and equipment are required to perform power analysis attacks.
6. Describe approaches of protecting a chip against power analysis attacks.
7. What is EM emanation, and how is it used to apply EM analysis attacks?
8. Explain the main objective of fault analysis attacks and how they are performed.
9. Describe the main idea of timing attacks and what tools are required to perform it.
10. How can side-channel attack countermeasures protect the device, and how would these countermeasures affect the performance of the system?

8.9.3 LONG-ANSWER TYPE QUESTIONS

1. Side-channel attacks are applied to any silicon-based system, where a variety of system architectures may be used in the device under attack. How can an attacker perform side-channel analysis on a system that performs parallel-based operations compared to sequentially-based operations?

2. Suppose an attacker is attempting to reverse engineer a device using a side-channel attack. What process should the attacker take to accurately obtain internal information about the device, and what side-channel analysis techniques should be used?

3. Applying EM analysis to capture critical information can be tricky, many factors can affect the quality of the signal. What measures should the attacker take to successfully perform the attack in a noisy environment, and what are the pros and cons of applying EM analysis over power analysis in this case?

4. Attackers can force a device to change a specific internal value using advanced techniques, such as laser injection processes. When applying these techniques to large and complex designs, what measures should the attacker take before applying fault attacks? Where in the design should the attacker start injecting faults, and what information can the attacker leak using this type of attacks?

5. Analyzing the delay of the output of a device can be used to gain knowledge about the design; one countermeasure used is to randomize the delays every time an operation is performed. How can this random delay be implemented? What are the challenges that the designer may face when applying this countermeasure?

REFERENCES

[1] A. Barenghi, L. Breveglieri, I. Koren, D. Naccache, Fault Injection Attacks on Cryptographic Devices: Theory, Practice, and Countermeasures, Proceedings of the IEEE 100 (11) (2012) 3056–3076.
[2] C. Giraud, DFA on AES, in: International Conference on Advanced Encryption Standard, Springer Berlin Heidelberg, 2004.
[3] S. Skorobogatov, R. Anderson, Optical Fault Induction Attacks, in: International Workshop on Cryptographic Hardware and Embedded Systems, Springer Berlin Heidelberg, 2002.
[4] A. Barenghi, G. Bertonit, L. Breveglieri, M. Pellicioli, G. Pelosi, Fault Attack on AES with Single-Bit Induced Faults, in: Information Assurance and Security (IAS), 2010 Sixth International Conference on, IEEE, 2010.
[5] M. Agoyan, J. Dutertre, D. Naccache, B. Robisson, A. Tria, When Clocks Fail: On Critical Paths and Clock Faults, in: International Conference on Smart Card Research and Advanced Applications, Springer Berlin Heidelberg, 2010.
[6] F. Standaert, Introduction to Side-Channel Attacks, in: Secure Integrated Circuits and Systems, Springer, Boston, MA, 2010, pp. 27–42.
[7] Y. Zhou, D. Feng, Side-Channel Attacks: Ten Years After Its Publication and the Impacts on Cryptographic Module Security Testing, IACR Cryptology ePrint Archive 2005 (2005) 388.
[8] P. Kocher, J. Jaffe, B. Jun, Differential Power Analysis, in: Annual International Cryptology Conference, Springer Berlin Heidelberg, 1999.
[9] E. Prouff, DPA Attacks and S-Boxes, in: International Workshop on Fast Software Encryption, Springer Berlin Heidelberg, 2005.
[10] S. Guilley, L. Sauvage, J. Danger, D. Selmane, R. Pacalet, Silicon-level Solutions to Counteract Passive and Active Attacks, in: Fault Diagnosis and Tolerance in Cryptography, 2008. FDTC'08. 5th Workshop on, IEEE, 2008.
[11] S. Guilley, P. Hoogvorst, R. Pacalet, J. Schmidt, Improving Side-Channel Attacks by Exploiting Substitution Boxes Properties, in: International Conference on Boolean Functions: Cryptography and Applications (BFCA), 2007.
[12] W. Hnath, Differential Power Analysis Side-Channel Attacks in Cryptography, Diss., Worcester Polytechnic Institute, 2010.
[13] P. Kocher, Timing Attacks on Implementations of Diffie–Hellman, RSA, DSS, and Other Systems, in: Advances in Cryptology CRYPTO96, Springer, 1996, pp. 104–113.
[14] J. Quisquater, D. Samyde, ElectroMagnetic Analysis (EMA): Measures and Counter-measures for Smart Cards, in: Smart Card Programming and Security, 2001, pp. 200–210.

[15] C. Clavier, D. Marion, A. Wurcker, Simple Power Analysis on AES Key Expansion Revisited, in: International Workshop on Cryptographic Hardware and Embedded Systems, Springer, 2014, pp. 279–297.

[16] E. Brier, C. Clavier, F. Olivier, Correlation Power Analysis with a Leakage Model, in: International Workshop on Cryptographic Hardware and Embedded Systems, Springer, 2004, pp. 16–29.

[17] D. Strobel, F. Bache, D. Oswald, F. Schellenberg, C. Paar, SCANDALee: A Side-ChANnel-based DisAssembLer using Local Electromagnetic Emanations, in: Proc. Design, Automation, and Test in Europe Conf. and Exhibition (DATE), Mar. 2015, pp. 139–144.

[18] J. Courrege, B. Feix, M. Roussellet, Simple Power Analysis on Exponentiation Revisited, in: CARDIS, 2010.

[19] K. Tiri, M. Akmal, I. Verbauwhede, A Dynamic and Differential CMOS Logic with Signal Independent Power Consumption to Withstand Differential Power Analysis on Smart Cards, in: Solid-State Circuits Conference, 2002. ESSCIRC 2002. Proceedings of the 28th European, 2002, pp. 403–406.

[20] K. Tiri, I. Verbauwhede, A VLSI Design Flow for Secure Side-Channel Attack Resistant ICs, in: Proceedings of the Conference on Design, Automation and Test in Europe – Volume 3, DATE '05, IEEE Computer Society, Washington, DC, USA, 2005, pp. 58–63.

[21] Y. Ishai, A. Sahai, D. Wagner, Private Circuits: Securing Hardware against Probing Attacks, in: Advances in Cryptology – CRYPTO 2003, 23rd Annual International Cryptology Conference, Santa Barbara, California, USA, August 17–21, 2003, Proceedings, in: Lecture Notes in Computer Science, vol. 2729, Springer, 2003, pp. 463–481.

[22] M. Faruque, S. Chhetri, A. Canedo, J. Wan, Acoustic Side-Channel Attacks on Additive Manufacturing Systems, in: Cyber-Physical Systems (ICCPS), 2016 ACM/IEEE 7th International Conference, Vienna, Austria, 2016, 2016.

[23] Y. Yarom, K. Falkner, FLUSH+RELOAD: A High Resolution, Low Noise, L3 Cache Side, in: Proceedings of the 23rd USENIX Conference on Security Symposium (SEC'14), USENIX Association, Berkeley, CA, USA, 2014, pp. 719–732.

[24] S. Mangard, E. Oswald, T. Popp, Power Analysis Attacks: Revealing the Secrets of Smart Cards, 1st ed., Springer Publishing Company, Incorporated, 2010.

[25] B. Lampson, A Note on the Confinement Problem, Communications of the ACM (1973) 613–615.

[26] M. Rivain, E. Prouff, Provably Secure Higher-Order Masking of AES, in: Cryptographic Hardware and Embedded Systems, CHES 2010, Springer Berlin Heidelberg, 2010, pp. 413–427.

TEST-ORIENTED ATTACKS

CONTENTS

Hardware Security. https://doi.org/10.1016/B978-0-12-812477-2.00014-9

9.1 INTRODUCTION

Testability and security inherently contradict each other [1]. The testability of a chip can be defined by the amount of controllability and observability that the test engineer is granted. The higher degree of controllability and observability allowed, the easier it is to test the circuit under test (CUT). The test is not only easier to perform, but the result of the test becomes more reliable due to the higher fault coverage.

On the other hand, security ensures that anything in a circuit is safely stored within itself. The most common manner of providing security is to hide the information behind some form of recognition that would be able to tell an authorized user from an attacker. Modern-day security in all realms uses this method to protect vital assets, whether it is a security code for a home, retinal scanner for a lab, or encryption key for information. Simply put, security relies on making information obscure, and difficult, to figure out.

When trying to relate testability and security together in a chip, security is clearly contradicted by testability. By designing for testability, a designer is essentially revealing vital information about the chip through the use of scan test. If the aim of designing a chip is security, it is very difficult to justify the amount of controllability and observability that testability aims to provide because of test-related leaks. It is also necessary, however, to ensure that the chip will function properly through testing in a fast and reliable manner. The only system secure from any leaks is one without any controllable inputs and observable outputs, but this is absurd from both a testability and usability standpoint.

Chip security has grown concern mostly to protect IP from malicious users and hackers. There are many hackers in the world with many different motivations. They range from the noble (attempting to make their fellow developers aware of their pitfalls), to the malicious (stealing information), and to simply the curious [2]. The skill-set of hackers vary as much as their intentions.

Testability and security have what appears to be a mutually exclusive relationship. It is very difficult to satisfactorily meet the needs of both specifications. A middle ground must be met between the fully controllable and observable CUT and a black box. If one considers the hacker during design, a clearer relationship between testability and security can more easily be concluded. If the designer can target specifically, which features he/she would like to prevent access to, it may be easier to make design compromises between testability and security.

9.2 SCAN-BASED ATTACKS

Controllability and observability of a circuit under test have significantly reduced as chip design complexity continues to increase. This problem greatly affects test engineers' ability to perform fast and reliable tests using the primary input and primary output alone, which negatively affect time to market and the number of defective parts delivered to the customer. Design-for-testability (DFT) addresses this issue by considering manufacturing test during design.

Scan-based DFT is one commonly practiced technique that greatly improves controllability and observability by modifying flip-flops into a long chain, essentially creating a shift register. This allows test engineers the ability to treat each flip-flop in the scan chain as a controllable input and observable output.

Unfortunately, the same properties that scan improves upon for testing also creates a severe security hazard. Scan chains become an easily exploitable side channel for cryptanalysis [3,4] due to the possibility of placing the CUT into any state (controllability), and stop the chip in any intermediate state for analysis (observability). Because of the widespread use of scan-based testing, this side channel has become a major concern in the industry [5].

These concerns add to an already mounting problem of hardware security. Other side-channel attacks, such as differential power analysis [6], timing analysis [7], and fault-injection [8,9] attacks have also been shown to be potentially serious sources of security failures. Tamper-resistant designs [10,11] propose to mend these leaks. However, scan chains are necessary to expose any defects in the chip that may exist. Whereas disabling the scan chains after manufacturing test (for example, by blowing fuses) has become a common practice for applications, such as smartcards [12], there are also applications that require in-field testing, which make it impossible to deliberately destroy access to the test ports.

As scan-based attacks require minimally invasive techniques to perform the attack [12], this exploit becomes accessible to attackers with a wide-variety of knowledge and resources [1]. A security measure that prevents scan-based attacks requires the ability to scale the desired level of security on the application. Such a measure must also minimally affect the ability of a test engineer to efficiently test the chip after fabrication.

The latter point must be keenly considered, as the entire purpose of using scan is for testing. Although the goals of security and testing appear to be contradictory, the security of the chip can easily fail if it is not properly tested.

9.2.1 SCAN-BASED ATTACK CATEGORIZATION

Developing a secure scan design is dependent on targeting both the type of attacker [1], and how they can potentially make the attack. The authors categorize the scan-based attacks into two types: scan-based observability and scan-based controllability/observability attacks. Each requires that a hacker has access to the test control (TC) pin. The type of attack depends on how a hacker decides to apply stimuli. The proposed low-cost secure scan design removes the hacker's ability to correlate test response data by creating a random response when an unauthorized user attempts access, which prevents hackers from exploiting the two attacks described in the remainder of this section.

9.2.1.1 Scan-Based Observability Attack

A scan-based observability attack relies on a hacker's ability to use the scan chain to take snapshots of the system at any time, which is a result of the observability from scan-based testing. Figure 9.1A shows the necessary steps to perform a scan-based observability attack.

The hacker begins this attack by observing the position of critical registers in the scan chain. First, a known vector is placed on the primary input (PI) of the chip, and the chip is allowed to run in functional mode until the targeted register is supposed to have data in it. At this point, the chip is placed into test mode using TC, and the response in the scan chain is scanned-out. The chip is reset, and a new vector that will cause a new response only in the targeted register is placed on the PI. The chip again is run in functional mode for the specific number of cycles, and then set into test mode. The new response is scanned-out and analyzed with the previous response. This process continues until there are enough responses to analyze where in the scan chain the targeted register is positioned.

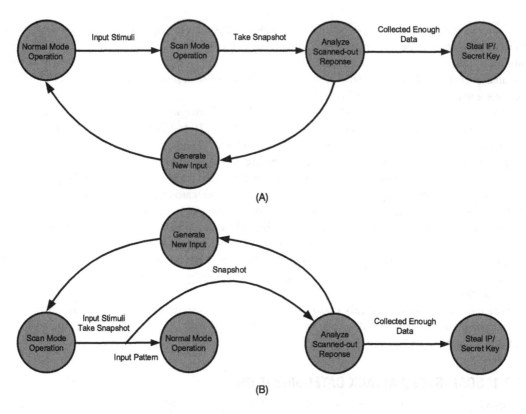

FIGURE 9.1

Summary of the steps necessary to perform successful scan-based attacks: (A) scan-based observability attack and (B) scan-based controllability/observability attack.

Once the targeted register is determined, a similar process can be used to either determine a secret key in the case of cryptochips, or determine design secrets (or IP) for a particularly innovative chip.

9.2.1.2 Scan-Based Controllability/Observability Attack

Scan-based controllability/observability attacks take a different approach to applying stimuli to the CUT, which is shown in Fig. 9.1B. Scan-based controllability/observability attacks begin by applying the stimuli directly into the scan chain as opposed to the PI. In order to mount an effective attack, the hacker must first determine the position of any critical registers, as was done for the scan-based observability attack. Once located, the hacker can load the registers with any desired data during test mode. Next, the chip can be switched to functional mode using the vector the hacker scanned-in, potentially bypassing any information security measures. Finally, the chip can be switched back to test mode to allow the hacker a level of observability, which the system's primary output (PO) would not provide otherwise.

As opposed to using a known vector to scan-in to the chain, hackers also have the opportunity to choose a random vector to induce a fault in the system. Based on the fault-injection side-channel attack

[8,9], by inducing a fault, the chip may malfunction, potentially revealing critical data. The scan chain becomes an easily accessible entry point for inducing a fault, and makes the attack easily repeatable. In order to protect from such side-channel attacks, additional hardware security measures must be included in the design.

9.2.2 THREAT MODELS

An attacker in the supply chain tries to use the scan chain (sometimes through JTAG [13]) to [14]:

- Steal critical information from an SoC (for example, crypto IP) [15,16].
- Violate confidentiality and integrity policies [17].
- Pirate IP design by unlocking an obfuscated IP [9,18].
- Illegally take control of the chip [19].

The scan-based noninvasive attack methods making such malicious acts possible are [14]:

Scan-facilitated differential attack: Differential attack has been proposed in [9,20]. By applying challenge pairs, running the crypto-algorithm, and comparing the responses, the key can be obtained. This attack has been facilitated by scan, due to added controllability and observability. Through switching from functional mode to test mode, the attacker can identify key flip-flops from the scan chain; then the key can be recovered through the already constructed correlation among input pairs, key flip-flops, and key [21]. Although some test mode protection techniques attempt to reset data registers when the chip is switched to test mode, test-mode-only differential attacks have recently been discussed in [22]. Furthermore, differential attacks are reported even in the presence of advanced DFT structures, that is, on-chip compression, Xmasking, and X-tolerance [22,23].

Attacks designed for specific countermeasures: In addition to the on-chip compression used in DFT structures, scan chain reordering and obfuscation have been developed as countermeasures, which can be defeated by the following attacks:

- Resetting and flushing attacks: By resetting the scan cells or flushing the scan chain with the known patterns, the fixed inverted bits [24], and modified bits [25] in the obfuscated scan chain, can be identified so that the plain text can be deciphered.
- Bit-role identification attack: For countermeasures using the key & lock scheme [1,26–29], the scanned-out responses are determined by the test authentication status. The authentication key bit-flipping would make scan out vectors differ, whereas a nonkey bit would not. This would significantly reduce the difficulty of identifying the key bits (especially for malicious users in fab or assembly).
- Combinational function recovery attack: Since the scan chains unfold the sequential logic as combinational, and directly reveal the internal state of the circuit, extracting design information from them has become easier. Thus, the device's functionality can be reverse engineered [18].

9.2.3 TEST-ORIENTED THREAT MODELS APPLICABLE TO DIFFERENT STAGES OF SUPPLY CHAIN

In the supply chain, a design goes through SoC integrator (or SoC design house), foundry, assembly/test facilities, original equipment manufacturer (OEM), electronics manufacturing service (EMS) provider, distributor, and end customer [30]. Thus, it is worthy to analyze the security risks due to scan-based attacks at each stage [31].

- IC Integrator: Here, the IC or SoC integrator refers to the members belonging to IC design house (or IP owner), who integrates custom logic, 3PIPs, and peripherals macros to form the whole IC. In other words, an IC integrator can be either a design, verification, DFT, or even a firmware engineer within the IC design house. Hence, the threat model is that, during integration, the confidentiality and integrity policies can be violated by a malicious IC integrator. For example, a malicious frontend RTL Designer, who is eligible to access the RTL code, can leak function of IP cores.
- Foundry: Before wafer slicing, all individual dies are tested on wafer by applying scan-based test patterns, and scanning out test responses to ATE. Likewise, a malicious foundry can pirate IP design utilizing the unobfuscated full-scan. Furthermore, some of the existing secure scan solutions have been proven to be insecure. Thus, sensitive information (such as keys and seeds) for the secure scan can be the target of a malicious foundry.
- Assembly/Test Facilities: As described in [32], for many cases, the structural test carried by foundry on wafer is enough for quality assurance. However, for some IC design houses making chip for industrial (that is, automotive) and military applications, the packaged ICs are required to be thoroughly tested after packaging, which extends the scan accessibility to assembly/test, and even OEM/EMS. Hence, the risks for scan-based attacks at assembly/test facilities are similar to those at foundry.
- OEM/EMS: At OEM or EMS, the printed circuit board (PCB) (equipment carrying IC) is developed; at the same time, the IC is programmed/configured to work with the system. To keep in-field failure analysis ability, usually scan chains are accessed through JTAG interface [3]. The keys and seeds for crypto IP (such as AES, DES, or RSA) loaded into IC in these stages can be leaked. Moreover, programs illegally utilizing scan chain to control the IC can also be loaded into the device at this stage.
- Distributor: The distributor loads customized programs into IC for different customers, as required. The risks in this stage are similar to OEM/EMS.
- End Customer: Malicious end customers (or hackers) may be interested in the sensitive information stored in the IC (that is, device configuration bits). The scan chain accessibility makes crypto IP (such as AES, DES, or RSA) vulnerable. Scan chains can also be used by attackers to illegally control the IC.

In summary, there are many opportunities for malicious entities within the supply chain to exploit the scan chains. Figure 9.2 shows the attacks each malicious entity in the supply chain can potentially carry out. Therefore, protecting IPs against scan-based attacks throughout the supply chain is necessary.

9.2.4 DYNAMICALLY OBFUSCATED SCAN (DOS)

The authors in [31] propose a design and test methodology against scan-based attacks throughout the supply chain, which includes a dynamically obfuscated scan for protecting IP/ICs. By perturbing test patterns/responses, and protecting the obfuscation key, the proposed architecture is proven to be robust

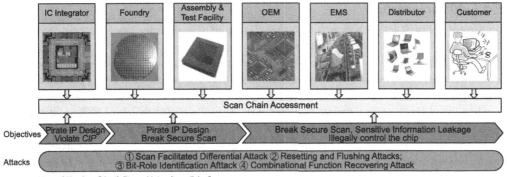

FIGURE 9.2

Attacker's objectives throughout IC supply chain.

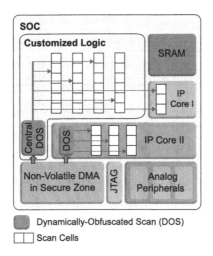

FIGURE 9.3

Overview of an SoC protected by DOS architecture.

against existing noninvasive scan-based attacks, and can protect all scan data from attackers in foundry, assembly, and system development, without compromising the testability.

An overview of the proposed secure scan in a SoC is shown in Fig. 9.3. The DOS architecture reads Control Vector from nonvolatile direct memory access (DMA) in secure zone, and provides protection to scan chains. The DOS architecture has capacity and flexibility to provide protection for IP owner, and IC integrator. According to Fig. 9.3, IP owner can either integrate one DOS into IP, as IP core II, or share the central DOS belonging to the customized logic, as IP core I.

9.2.4.1 DOS Architecture

As illustrated in Fig. 9.4, the DOS architecture is composed of a linear feedback shift register (LFSR), a Shadow chain with XOR gates, and a Control Unit.

LFSR: The LFSR is adopted to generate a λ-bit obfuscation key (λ is the length of scan chains), which is used to scramble scan in/out vectors as shown in Fig. 9.4. The obfuscation key is protected through the AND gates of the Shadow chain. The LFSR is driven by the control unit, and changes its output only when the obfuscation key update is required. It should be noted that for LFSR, a seed with all zeros is illegal when using an XOR feedback; the LFSR would remain in locked-up state and continue providing all zero obfuscation Key. Therefore, the scan chains cannot be obfuscated. To avoid the above scenario, it is suggested that some of XOR gates in LFSR would be replaced with XNOR gates.

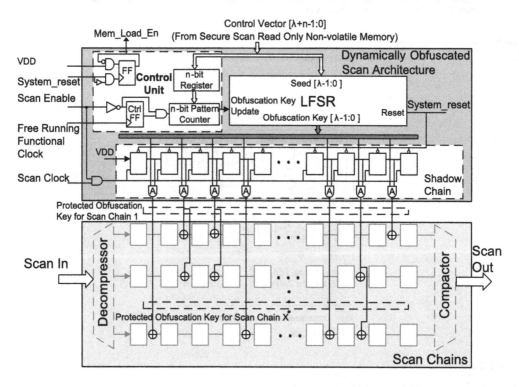

FIGURE 9.4

Detailed architecture of the DOS.

Shadow chain and XOR gates: As shown in Fig. 9.4, the input of the Shadow chain is the λ-bit obfuscation key generated by the LFSR, whereas the outputs are $k[\lambda \times \alpha]$ bit protected obfuscation keys, where α is the permutation rate (the percentage of bits permuted inside each DFT scan chain), and k is the number of scan chains [31]. The Shadow chain is designed for propagating the obfuscation key at the i_{th} scan cell along the scan chain, when the i_{th} scan clock comes. Therefore, the Shadow chain is able to – (i) protect the obfuscation key from being leaked through resetting attack, (ii) prevent any unscrambled data from being scanned out, and (iii) prevent adversaries from scanning in values intentionally, and at the same time, make no impact on structural and chain tests.

It can be seen that the Shadow chain is designed as a cascade of λ flip-flops, which is driven by the scan clock gated by scan enable signal. As shown in Fig. 9.4, the data input of its first flip-flop is connected to Vdd. The XOR gate inserted after the i_{th} scan cell of scan chain X is controlled by the output of the i_{th} flip-flop of the Shadow chain through a type A AND gate. As shown in Fig. 9.4, the type A AND gates of DOS are the AND gates connecting the scan cells within Shadow chain, the obfuscation key bits generated by the LFSR, and the XOR gates inserted into the scan chain, which actually are used to gate the individual obfuscation key bits by the scan cells of Shadow chain.

After reset, as the scan clock forces the flip-flop along the Shadow chain to logic "1", one by one, only when the last flip-flop in the Shadow chain becomes logic "1" at the λ_{th} scan clock, the scrambled response starts to show up at the scan output. At the same time, the Shadow chain's i_{th} flip-flop starts to obfuscate the i_{th} flip-flop of Scan chain X at the i_{th} scan clock, which prevents the attacker from scanning in any intended values. Therefore, if the attacker keeps flushing the scan chain, an original or inverted scan in sequence shows up at the scan output after λ bits of zeros. Furthermore, as the protected obfuscation key has settled down after the whole chain is scanned, the Shadow chain does not impact the DFT launching or capturing process, such as when applying stuck-at or transition delay faults. The scrambled test responses are then scanned out. The Shadow chain should be synchronously reset with the LFSR at any reset event. As all of the DFT scan chains are scanned synchronously, and the length of the scan chain is usually short with on-chip compression, the architecture only needs a single short Shadow chain, which has low area penalty. Furthermore, as the Shadow chain is plugged into the scan chains, it is not bypassable.

Control unit: The control unit, as shown in Fig. 9.4, is designed to control memory loading and LFSR activities. It is composed of a small n-bit register, a n-bit pattern counter, and a control flip-flop. During system initialization, a control vector is loaded from the secure scan read-only nonvolatile DMA, which includes a λ-bit seed for the LFSR, an n-bit value p (determining the obfuscation key update frequency), and the maximum obfuscation key update count. The control unit of DOS generates the Mem_Load_En signal. This signal allows the control vector of DOS to be loaded from DMA, once the system resets. The control vector is determined by the IC designer. As a part of system firmware, the control vector is stored into read only nonvolatile memory located in secure zone with DMA, which satisfies: 1) immediate control vector accessing: the control vector is automatically loaded into DOS at powering up, which can be guaranteed by hard coding the control vector address in DMA; 2) limited readability: the control vector can only be read by DOS, which can be satisfied by using the handshaking signal Mem_Load_En (in Fig. 9.4) generated by DOS, as an input of the DMA address accessing authorization. Additionally, as shown in Fig. 9.4, during scan, Mem_Load_En also ensures that the control vector can only be read after the reset event. Furthermore, the memory encryption technique such as [45], which allows the control vector to be stored into the nonvolatile memory in an encrypted manner, is recommended, but not required. When the pattern counter value reaches p, the obfuscation key is updated. Otherwise, the obfuscation key is locked. As sometimes the set of test patterns cannot be delivered at once, this feature offers the IP owner flexibility to dynamically add new patterns with updated obfuscation key.

9.2.4.2 The Obfuscation Flow of DOS Architecture

Based on the three major components discussed above, the obfuscation flow of the proposed design is summarized below. In Step 1, during system initialization, a control vector is loaded into the LFSR and the control unit, which is composed of a seed for the LFSR and a vector to determine the obfuscation key update frequency. In Step 2, the obfuscation key is generated at the output of the LFSR, which is driven by the control unit. In Step 3, during the first λ scan clocks after reset, the protected obfuscation key is generated bit by bit based on the Shadow chain and the obfuscation key. In Step 4, at the λ_{th} scan clock, the protected obfuscation key settles down. Then, all the test patterns and responses scrambles as a result of the protected obfuscation key.

Figure 9.5 shows the timing diagram of DOS architecture. It can be seen that the obfuscation key is generated at the output of the LFSR in waveform (C), and is dynamically changed every p pattern (p is configurable by the IP owner), when the obfuscation key update is enabled and generated by the control unit (waveforms (C) and (F)). As presented before, after reset, the protected obfuscation key for scan chain X, generated by the Shadow chain, is updated bit by bit with the scan clock, and settles down at the λ_{th} scan clock (waveform (G)). During the period of the first λ scan clocks, the scan out is locked to "0". Once the λ_{th} scan clock comes, the scan out starts to output obfuscated responses (waveform (H)).

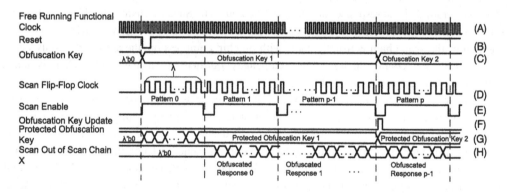

FIGURE 9.5

The timing diagrams for DOS architecture.

9.2.5 LOW-COST SECURE SCAN (LCSS)

Figure 9.6 presents the LCSS solution. LCSS is implemented by inserting dummy flip-flops into the scan chains; it inserts the key into the test patterns with respect to the position of the dummy flip-flops in the chains. By doing so, it verifies that all vectors scanned-in come from an authorized user, and the correct response can be safely scanned-out after functional mode operation. If the correct key is not integrated into the vector, an unpredictable response is scanned-out, making analysis very difficult for an attacker. By using an unpredictable response, a hacker would not be able to immediately realize that their intrusion has been detected, as could be discerned if the CUT were to immediately reset [33].

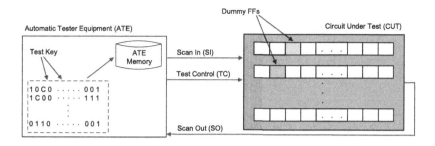

FIGURE 9.6

Sample test pattern stored in ATE with test key bits located in pattern with respect to the location of the dummy flip-flops in the CUT.

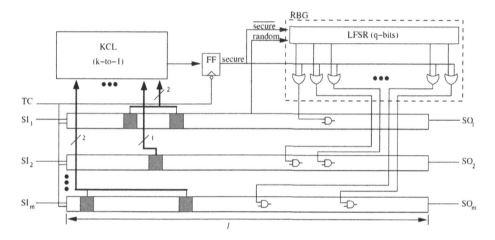

FIGURE 9.7

LCSS architecture.

9.2.5.1 LCSS Architecture

The state of the scan chain is dependent on the test key that is integrated into all test vectors. There are two possible states for the chain: secure and insecure. By integrating the key, all vectors scanned-in can be verified to be from a trustworthy source (secure). Without a correct key integrated into the test vector, when scanning in a new vector and scanning out the response, the response will be randomly altered to prevent reverse engineering of sensitive data that is being stored in registers (insecure). By altering the response scanned-out of the chain, both the scan-based observability and scan-based controllability/observability attacks are prevented, as any attempt to correlate the responses from various inputs will prove unsuccessful due to the random altering of the data.

The LCSS architecture is shown in Fig. 9.7, and a more detailed look at a secure scan chain is provided in Fig. 9.8. In order to use the same key for every test vector, dummy flip-flops (dFFs) are inserted and used as test key registers. Each dFF is designed similar to a scan cell, except that there

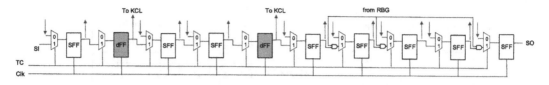

FIGURE 9.8

An example of the LCSS with integrated dummy flip-flops and random response network.

is no connection to a combinational block. The number of dFFs included in the scan chain depends on the level of security the designer would like to include, since the number of dFFs determines the size of the test key. When implementing LCSS for multiple-scan design, the test key is inserted into the scan chain before it is broken into multiple scan chains. This ensures that the key can be randomly distributed throughout the many scan chains without needing to have a constant number of key registers in each chain.

All dFFs are concurrently checked by the Key Checking Logic (KCL), which is made of a block of combinational logic. The k-input block, where k is the total number of dFFs in the scan design (length of the test key), has a fan-out of a single FF (KCL-FF), which is negative edge-sensitive to test control (TC). TC is sometime called test enable (TE); it enables test mode (TC $= 1$ enables test mode, whereas TC $= 0$ switches scan flip-flops to functional mode). As the CUT switches from test mode to functional mode (TC falls), the FF clocks in the output of the key checking logic. The KCL-FF is then used to inform the remainder of the secure design of the current secure or insecure state of the vector in the scan chain.

There is potential for the KCL to be implemented using a variety of more secure options, since the KCL will, essentially, be the same for all chips fabricated using the same design. One such option would be to implement a post-fabrication configurable KCL. This KCL implementation would allow different test keys from chip to chip, and would prevent the possibility of determining a single key to compromise all chips of the same design. However, as each of the devices has a different test key, essentially a new test pattern set would need to be generated for each individual chip. This would either create a significant increase in test time, or require a new secure test protocol that would need the tester to insert the test key into the pattern dynamically.

The third component of the LCSS architecture ensures the random response in the scan chain, when the test key fails to be verified by the KCL. The output of the KCL-FF fans out to an array of q 2-input OR gates. The second input of each OR gate comes from a q-bit LFSR that has been randomly seeded using one of a variety of options including, but not limited to, the value already present at reset, a random signal from an FF in the scan chain as shown in Fig. 9.7, or a random signal from the output of a separate random number generator [34]. The former option provides the least amount of overhead, but potentially the least secure, whereas the latter has the most security, but also the most overhead. By also using a secure signal to the LFSR, the LFSR seed can continually be changed by an additional random source. Together, the LFSR and OR gate array make up the random bit generator (RBG). The RBG output is used as input to the random response network (RRN) that has also been inserted into the scan chain. The RRN can be made of both AND and OR gates to equalize the random transitions, and prevent the random response from being all zeros, or all ones. The optimal choice for randomness would be to use XOR gates, but as XORs add more delay, the design choice was to use AND, and OR gates. As the dFFs are used to check the test key, dFFs must be placed before any gates of the RRN in the scan chain, as shown in Fig. 9.8. If this principle is not applied, any key information that is trying to pass a gate of the RRN in the scan chain may potentially get altered, either preventing the test key from ever being verified, or even randomly changing a value to the correct key.

Normal mode operation of the CUT is unaffected by the addition of the LCSS design, since the dFFs are only used for testing, and security purposes and are not connected to the original design.

9.2.5.2 LCSS Test Flow

The low-cost secure scan design deviates very little from current scan test flow. As the security of the scan chain is ensured by integrating a test key into the test vectors themselves, no additional pins are necessary to use LCSS.

After a system reset, and TC has been enabled for the first time, the secure scan design begins in an insecure state, causing any data in the scan chain to be modified as it passes through each RRN gate in the chain. In order to begin the testing process, the secure scan chain(s) must be initialized with the test key in order to set the output of the KCL-FF to 1. Only the test key is required to be in this initialization vector, since any other data beyond the first RRN gate will most likely be modified. During this time the KCL will constantly check the dFFs for a correct key. After the initialization vector has been scanned-in, the CUT must be switched to functional mode for one clock in order to allow the KCL-FF to capture the result from the KCL. If the KCL verifies the key stored in the dFFs, the KCL-FF is set to 1 and propagates the signal to the RRN, which becomes transparent for the next round of testing, allowing the new vector to be scanned-in without alteration.

Testing can continue as normal, once the initialization process has been finished. However, the chain can return to insecure mode at any time during scan testing, if the correct test key is not present in all subsequent test vectors, requiring the k-bit key to be in all test patterns. Should that occur, the RRN will again affect the response in the scan chain, and the initialization process must again be performed in order to resume a predictable testing process.

9.2.6 LOCK & KEY

Lock & Key solution was developed to neutralize the potential for scan-based side-channel attacks [1]. The Lock & Key technique provides a flexible security strategy to modern designs, without significant changes to scan structure used in practice. Using this technique, the scan chains in a system on chip (SoC) are divided into smaller subchains. With the inclusion of a test security controller, access to subchains are randomized when being accessed by an unauthorized user. Random access reduces repeatability and predictability, making reverse engineering more difficult. Without proper authorization, an attacker would need to unveil several layers of security before gaining proper access to the scan chain in order to exploit it. The proposed Lock & Key technique is design-independent, while maintaining a relatively low area overhead.

9.2.6.1 Lock & Key Architecture

The Lock & Key technique can be used to secure both single- and multiple-scan designs. For either case, the scan chain is divided into smaller subchains of equal length. Test vectors are not sequentially shifted into each subchain, but rather an LFSR performs a pseudorandom selection of a subchain to be filled. Figure 9.9 shows the architecture for the Lock & Key technique for a single-scan design. This technique provides a trade-off between testability and security, since the LFSR, during insecure mode, will protect the scan chain but also requires a nonsequential scan chain access when the user has been verified.

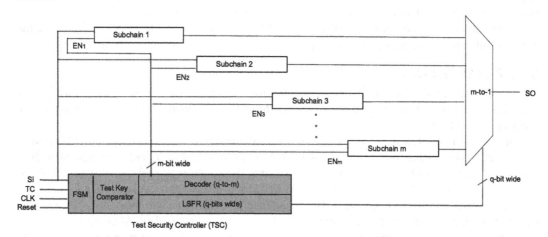

FIGURE 9.9

Architecture of Lock & Key security measure.

This method prevents scan chain manipulation without the presence of a valid test key. This is ensured by the test security controller (TSC), which consists of four main components: a finite state machine (FSM), test key comparator, LFSR, and decoder. There are two states the TSC can be in, namely, secure and insecure modes. The secure mode signifies that a trusted user is accessing the scan chain, so the TSC will select subchains in a predictable nonsequential order. The insecure mode signifies a state, where the user attempting to access the scan chain is considered untrustworthy until deemed otherwise with a correct test key. Unless the test key is entered and confirmed to be correct, the TSC will unpredictably select subchains using the LFSR to scan in (SI) and scan out (SO), presenting the user with false information about the scan chain.

A test engineer must perform two steps before sending in a test vector into the scan chain for the first time. After enabling test control for the first time after a system reset occurs, the TSC controls all functions of the subchains until an authorized or unauthorized party is detected. A test key must be the first pattern fed into the TSC. During the first k cycles after TC has been enabled, the first k-bits applied to the SI will be serially passed to the test key comparator, and checked. After the k cycles, the FSM will receive the result. If the key matches the test key stored in a tamper proof nonvolatile memory, the secure signal will be raised, allowing the TSC to begin operation in a secure mode, in which it will remain until the CUT is reset. If the secure signal remains low, operation in the insecure mode will resume. If the test key passes and the TSC enters secure mode, the test engineer then has the ability to seed the LFSR with a known seed in order to predict the order of the LFSR's selection of subchains. Otherwise, the LFSR will work with the unpredictable random seed created in the LFSR right after a system reset.

With the LFSR seeded, formation of the scan chain can begin. Using a decoder to interface between the LFSR and the subchains, the TSC uses a one-hot output method to enable one subchain at a time to read from SI. The output of the LFSR is also directly connected to the multiplexer selector bits' allowance of the data from the subchain to pass to SO. Assuming the length of each subchain is l-bit long, after l clock cycle, the LFSR will shift to a new value, and the decoder will disable the currently active subchain, and select a new subchain to read from SI. After $n_{dff} = l \times m$ cycles, where m is the number of subchains, l is the length of subchain, and n_{dff} is the length of the scan chain, the full length of the scan chain is initialized with the first test vector. TC can again be set to zero to place the CUT into normal mode for one cycle to allow the pattern to propagate and capture the response back into the scan chain. When the CUT has returned to test mode, a new test vector is scanned into the subchains, while scanning out the response.

Since test key verification is a one time startup check, a failed test key causes the TSC to remain in an insecure mode until the CUT is reset. This essentially locks the scan chain from being used correctly for the duration of the testing process. This locking mechanism is also fairly transparent to a hacker, since without prior knowledge of the security scheme, the chip would appear to be working as it should, while still giving the hacker false data.

9.2.6.2 Design of Lock & Key

The Lock & Key technique depends on the design of the TSC, which is composed of four components. A finite state machine (FSM) controls the current mode of the TSC; the test key comparator is only used when TC is enabled for the first time, returning a secure or insecure result; the LFSR selects a single subchain during scan operation, and controls the output multiplexer; and the decoder translates the output of the LFSR into a one-hot enable scheme. Figure 9.10 shows the signals passed between each of the components of the TSC. Communication between each of the components is kept to a minimum to reduce routing, and the overall size of the TSC.

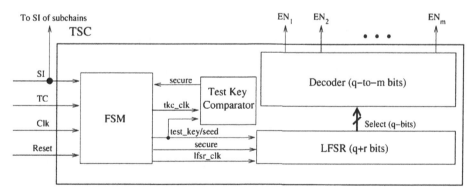

FIGURE 9.10

TSC design scheme.

The FSM block consists of simple state logic and two counters. The state logic controls the test key comparator and LFSR. The FSM also determines, according to the response of the test key comparator, whether to seed the LFSR with a vector from SI, or to use the random seed created in the LFSR by the system reset. The random seed can be created many different ways, including using a true random number generator (TRNG). The first counter used in FSM block was a $\log_2(q)$ counter, which is used only for seeding the LFSR, where q is the length of the LFSR. The second counter is a $\log_2(l)$ counter used for clocking the LFSR after l cycles, shifting the contents of the LFSR to enable a new subchain.

The test key comparator is used once, only after the system has been reset and put into test mode for the first time. In order to keep the comparator small, and since the test key from SI is read serially, each bit is serially checked against the key being stored on the chip in a secure memory. As each bit is compared, an FF stores the running result, which is eventually read by the FSM. After k cycles, the final result is read by the FSM determining whether the TSC will run in a secure mode, or continue in an insecure mode.

When designing the Lock & Key technique, the goal is to have the ability to ensure security of the scan chains, while maintaining simplicity and design independence. To prevent the decoder from becoming too complex, an LFSR with a primitive polynomial configuration allows the selection of $m = 2^q - 1$ subchains, where q is the size of the LFSR in secure mode. Using a primitive polynomial allows the selection of all subchains once, and only once, during a test round. If a nonprimitive polynomial configuration is used, unless additional logic is included, some subchains may be selected more than once, or never selected at all. Using the q bits from the LFSR, the decoder enables one of m outputs leaving the others at zero. Since there is at least one primitive polynomial for all values of q, the LFSR is guaranteed to choose each subchain once, before repeating for any length of the LFSR [35].

The number of FFs in the design before scan insertion does not necessarily need to be evenly divisible by m. There are two possibilities to resolve this issue. The first is the inclusion of dummy FFs (in form of test points: control test point and observe test point), which has become a common practice when dealing with delay testing [35]. The total number of FFs, n, and the total number of dummy FFs, n_{dFF}, needed is noted as follows:

$$n_{dFF} = \begin{cases} 0 & \text{when } (n \mod m) = 0, \\ m - (n \mod m) & \text{otherwise.} \end{cases} \tag{9.1}$$

The second option would be to pad portions of the test pattern that are related to the shorter subchains. This would immediately shift out any dummy values at the beginning of the pattern, and would have no effect on the functional operation of the CUT. This option requires less design effort, since it does not use additional logic, but does add overhead to the test pattern. However, due to test compression techniques, the overhead would be minimal, since the dummy values can be set to values that maximize compression.

The choice of a primitive polynomial significantly simplifies the design of the decoder. The decoder can directly translate the output of the LFSR into a run of zeros, and choose one to directly control each subchain. This method not only shortens design time, but also reduces the area overhead of the TSC as a whole, since additional logic is not needed to ensure all subchains are selected once during a test round.

The problem with using a primitive polynomial configured LFSR is the predictability of its behavior. If the LFSR were to remain unchanged for insecure mode operation, determining the order would not take long, since the order is always the same, only the start and end points would differ. To avoid this predictability, the LFSR configuration must be altered when set to insecure mode. By modifying the LFSR to incorporate an additional r-bits for insecure mode operation, the primitive polynomial LFSR becomes a nonprimitive polynomial LFSR. As can be seen in Fig. 9.11, the additional bits are hidden behind a multiplexer, and only become active for insecure mode operation. The interface between the LFSR and the decoder is not affected. Since the original LFSR only makes up a smaller part

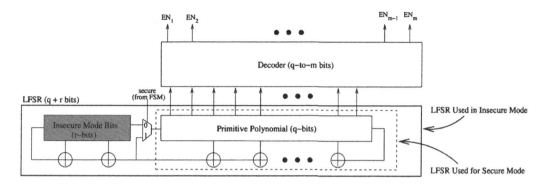

FIGURE 9.11

Modifiable LFSR determined by security mode of TSC.

of the insecure mode LFSR, repetitively selecting the same subchain during one test cycle becomes possible, which results in a more complex output. A shorter periodicity is not a concern, as it was in secure mode, since all subchains do not need to be accessed, but the facade of a fully functional scan chain still exists.

9.2.7 SCAN INTERFACE ENCRYPTION

A countermeasure against scan-based side channel attacks could be done through the encryption of the scan chain content [36]. These attacks use an efficient and secure block cipher placed at each scan port to decrypt/encrypt scan patterns/responses at each scan input/output, respectively.

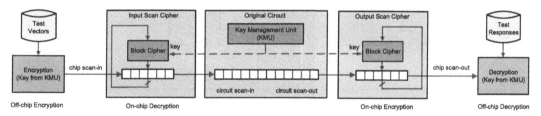

FIGURE 9.12

Scan interface encryption structure.

As illustrated in Fig. 9.12, two block ciphers are inserted into the circuit. Whereas the input scan cipher decrypts test patterns provided by ATE, the output scan cipher encrypts test response before sending back to ATE. Based on this scheme, the test flow is as follows [36]:

- Generate test patterns for CUT and calculate expected test responses;
- Off-chip encryption of the test patterns based on pre-selected (e.g., AES) encryption algorithm and secret key;
- On-the-fly decryption of the test patterns with input block cipher, then scan in patterns for CUT;

- On-the-fly encryption of the test responses with output block cipher before response extraction;
- Off-chip decryption of test responses to get the original responses and compare them with the expected ones.

9.2.8 OBFUSCATED SCAN

Secure scan architecture using test key randomization (SSTKR) was developed to address security and testability issues [37]. Specifically, SSTKR is a key-based technique to prevent an attacker from illegally obtaining critical information while using scan infrastructure. The authentication keys are generated through linear feedback shift register and inserted into test vectors.

Furthermore, test keys are embedded into test vectors in two different ways, that is, with dummy flip-flops and without dummy flip-flops. In the first case, dummy flip-flops holding the key are inserted into the scan chain to randomize scan outputs. It should be noted that all dummy flip-flops should not be connected to the combinational logic. In the second case, authentication keys are inserted into the positions of don't-care bits, generated by ATPG to reduce area overhead and test time. The structure of SSTKR for the above two cases are illustrated in Fig. 9.13 and Fig. 9.14, respectively.

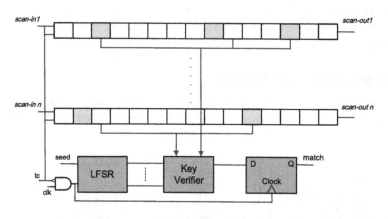

FIGURE 9.13

SSTKR architecture.

9.2.9 SCAN-CHAIN REORDERING

A secure scan tree architecture was developed to protect cryptosystem against scan-based attacks [38]. This architecture offers low area overhead compared with the traditional scan tree architecture followed by a compactor, locking, and test access port (TAP) architecture. In contrast to the normal scan tree architecture, as shown in Fig. 9.15, this architecture is based on the flipped scan tree (F-scan tree). To be exact, they adopt special flip-flops (that is, flipped FFs), in which inverter gates are added at the scan-in pin of scan flip-flop. The flipped scan tree architecture is built through normal SDFFs and flipped FFs. Since the attacker cannot identify the position of inverters, he/she is neither able to control the inputs, nor observe the outputs of the flip-flops.

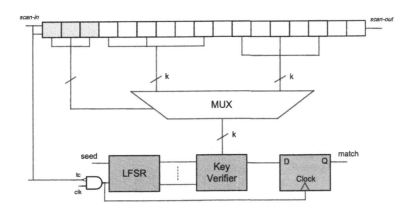

FIGURE 9.14

SSTKR architecture without using dummy FFs.

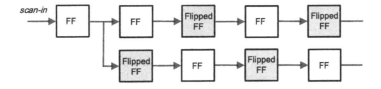

FIGURE 9.15

Flipped scan tree.

9.3 JTAG-BASED ATTACKS

Initially, the IEEE Standard 1149.1, also known as JTAG or boundary scan, was introduced in 1990 [39] to address the need for a standardized interconnect test that could be performed on a printed circuit board (PCB), or other substrate. In recent years, the accessibility of the 1149.1 standard has been extended from the chip periphery to on-chip debugging [40,41]. Based on JTAG protocol, test signals include test clock input (TCK), test mode select input (TMS), test data input (TDI), test data output (TDO), and test reset input (TRST).

The JTAG architecture, shown in Fig. 9.16, consists of the following parts: (a) the TAP controller, a 16-state finite state machine driven by TCK, TMS, and TRST signals, which generates the internal clock and control signals for the instruction register (IR); (b) the user-defined registers (UDRs), and (c) the obligatory registers (e.g., bypass register (BR), boundary scan register (BSR), and IDCODE Register). The IR is used to load and update the instructions shifted from the TDI terminal, which determines the action to be performed, and the TDR to be accessed. The instruction decoder (IDEC) is responsible for decoding the instructions as the selection signal to enable TDR between TDI and TDO. User-defined registers are introduced to access internal logic of the chip.

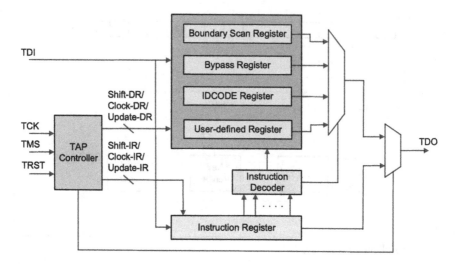

FIGURE 9.16

The JTAG architecture.

Several user defined instructions corresponding to the UDRs are introduced in the private instruction set. Each time only one public or private instruction is loaded into the IR, the corresponding data register is enabled and placed between TDI and TDO.

As can be seen from the state diagram, shown in Fig. 9.17, there are two similar branches: the instruction register (IR) scan and the data register (DR) scan. The IR branch is used to operate on the IR, whereas the DR branch is used for operations on the current TDR.

9.3.1 JTAG HACKS

IEEE 1149.1 standard was initially developed without considering security. Specifically, JTAG is designed to use scan-based testing to access internal logic of the chip and inter-chip wiring. Since JTAG is not aware of the chip's reaction to external commands, hacking a device using JTAG is technically possible. As a result, over the past decade, JTAG-based attacks have become feasible. For example, when a debugging software, such as open on-chip debugger (OpenOCD) is given control over JTAG interface, it can manipulate JTAG on the target device, and send vectors to it, which the chip interprets as valid commands [43]. Also, JTAG has been used to hack Xbox 360 to bypass DRM policies of the device [44]. In addition, JTAG is initially used in ARM11 processor to provide extensive test and debug capabilities. However, JTAG has been exploited to unlock services of cell phones (for example, to hack iphones [45]).

In [13], the authors analyze various attacks based on JTAG. The vulnerabilities are coming from the daisy-chaining topology of JTAG wiring, as shown in Fig. 9.18. They examine the potential threats in the following scenarios: 1) acquire secret data through overhearing JTAG data path; 2) acquire an embedded asset through placing test patterns to JTAG lines; 3) acquire test patterns and test responses in the daisy-chain; 4) intercept test patterns sent to other chips, and send bogus responses to the tester.

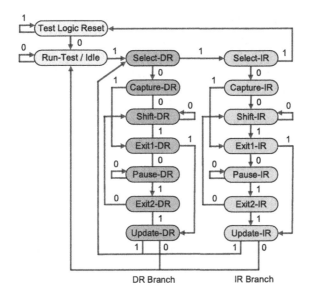

FIGURE 9.17

JTAG TAP controller state diagram.

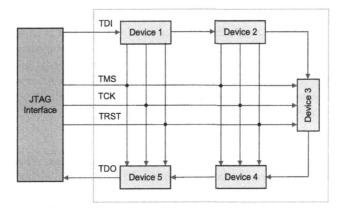

FIGURE 9.18

A JTAG system with daisy-chain topology.

9.3.2 JTAG DEFENSES

Over the past two decades, researchers in industry and academia have focused on developing countermeasures against JTAG hacks. The methodologies developed include destruction of JTAG after use, password protection of JTAG, hiding JTAG behind a system controller, and crypto JTAG with embedded keys. These methods are explained in detail in the following.

9.3.2.1 Destruction of JTAG After Use

In some cases, JTAG is only needed during debug process and manufacturing test. Once the chip is manufactured, tested and shipped to the customers, the JTAG component becomes a source of vulnerabilities. Thus, in these circumstances, engineers can disable the JTAG component before volume shipment. Typically, the JTAG fuses can be blown for security consideration. However, since the process of blowing the physical fuse is not reversible, some techniques [46] are developed to achieve finer control over the test infrastructure; hence, some test capabilities can be secured. Such designs are usually developed with more than one fuse.

9.3.2.2 Password Protection of JTAG

In [47], the authors proposed a methodology, named as "Protected JTAG", to prevent unauthenticated and unauthorized users from accessing private and confidential information. However, it still allows debugging, and testing functions to be performed by authorised users. To be specific, this scheme provides different protection levels and access modes. Protection levels define the actual protection of device, whereas access modes are the configured attributes defining default protection level, and availability of protection feature. This method uses a secure server that utilizes an ephemeral elliptic curve key pair to authenticate and authorize the user's JTAG access request. Once the authentication and authorization are successful, the device holds the authenticated and authorized state during the debugging and testing process.

9.3.2.3 Hiding JTAG Behind a System Controller

Another approach to address JTAG security issue is to hide JTAG behind a system controller [48]. To be exact, the system controller is usually implemented on a PCB, and acts as an agent to communicate with the chip to be tested. This method improves system security without modifying design. Security protocol implemented through the system controller authenticates all accesses. In addition, the authenticated users can only access the authorized parts. Not only can the system controller act as an agent between the tester and chips, it can also store test patterns, and automatically test chips when a test routine is invoked [48].

9.3.2.4 Crypto JTAG With Embedded Keys

An approach to protect JTAG relies on embedding keys with cryptoengine. There are three security components included in this approach, namely a hash function, a stream cipher, and a message authentication code [13]. They are used to authenticate the devices to be tested, encrypt test vectors and responses, and prevent unauthentic JTAG messages. Furthermore, protocols are constructed based on these security components to address the potential security threat introduced by JTAG.

9.4 HANDS-ON EXPERIMENT: JTAG ATTACK
9.4.1 OBJECTIVE

This experiment is designed to introduce the JTAG attack to the students. The experiment is designed on the HaHa platform and utilizes the JTAG infrastructure (that is, the ports and connection of the FPGA and microcontroller chip in a JTAG chain), which connects the JTAG-compliant chips in a PCB in a chain for the purpose of test, debug, and probing after manufacture. Since there is a growing trend of using JTAG for programming FPGA and CPLD devices, their security is of utmost importance.

9.4.2 METHOD

The first part of the experiment will allow the students to build a hacking tool that acts as a JTAG programmer. Students need to first learn how to locate the chip's ID, using instructions sent by the hacked JTAG programmer. Next, the students will use the hacked module to attack other modules in the HaHa platform.

9.4.3 LEARNING OUTCOME

By performing the specific steps of the experiments, the students will learn the level of accessibility that a hacked JTAG can provide, and the best techniques to modify a target chip and maliciously control it. They will also gain experience about the challenges and opportunities with respect to protecting hardware against JTAG attacks.

9.4.4 ADVANCED OPTIONS

Additional exploration on this topic can be done through configuring the JTAG to get the delay of the JTAG paths to create a signature.

More details about the experiment is available in the supplementary document. Please visit http:// hwsecuritybook.org.

9.5 EXERCISES
9.5.1 TRUE/FALSE QUESTIONS

1. Malicious entities within the whole supply chain can perform attacks through exploiting the scan chains.
2. Testability and security do not contradict each other.
3. Scan-based DFT used by test engineer have no impact on security.
4. Destruction of JTAG after use is developed to improve security and has no impact on testability.
5. The TAP controller is a finite state machine driven by TCK, TMS, and TRST signals.

9.5.2 SHORT-ANSWER TYPE QUESTIONS

1. List the potential threats when an attacker in the supply chain performs scan-based attacks.
2. List three scan-based noninvasive attacks.
3. Explain the purpose of placing the Shadow chain into the dynamically obfuscated scan (DOS) architecture.
4. How to choose the number of dFFs inserted in the scan chain? Explain.
5. Introduce a few more scan-based attacks countermeasures besides which are discussed in this chapter.

9.5.3 LONG-ANSWER TYPE QUESTIONS

1. Explain the relationship between testability and security.
2. List several countermeasures against JTAG hacks and explain any one of them in detail.

REFERENCES

[1] J. Lee, M. Tehranipoor, C. Patel, J. Plusquellic, Securing scan design using lock and key technique, in: Defect and Fault Tolerance in VLSI Systems, 2005. DFT 2005. 20th IEEE International Symposium on, IEEE, pp. 51–62.

[2] P. Ludlow, High Noon on the Electronic Frontier: Conceptual Issues in Cyberspace, MIT Press, 1996.

[3] B. Yang, K. Wu, R. Karri, Scan-based side channel attack on dedicated hardware implementations of data encryption standard, in: Test Conference, 2004. Proceedings. ITC 2004, International, IEEE, pp. 339–344.

[4] B. Yang, K. Wu, R. Karri, Secure scan: a design-for-test architecture for crypto chips, IEEE Transactions on Computer-Aided Design of Integrated Circuits and Systems 25 (2006) 2287–2293.

[5] R. Goering, Scan design called portal for hackers, EE Times (Oct 2004), https://www.eetimes.com/document.asp?doc_id=1151658.

[6] P. Kocher, J. Jaffe, B. Jun, Differential power analysis, in: Annual International Cryptology Conference, Springer, 1999, pp. 388–397.

[7] P.C. Kocher, Timing attacks on implementations of Diffie–Hellman, RSA, DSS, and other systems, in: Annual International Cryptology Conference, Springer, 1996, pp. 104–113.

[8] D. Boneh, R.A. DeMillo, R.J. Lipton, On the importance of checking cryptographic protocols for faults, in: International Conference on the Theory and Applications of Cryptographic Techniques, Springer, 1997, pp. 37–51.

[9] E. Biham, A. Shamir, Differential fault analysis of secret key cryptosystems, in: Annual International Cryptology Conference, Springer, 1997, pp. 513–525.

[10] O. Kömmerling, M.G. Kuhn, Design principles for tamper-resistant smartcard processors, Smartcard 99 (1999) 9–20.

[11] M. Renaudin, F. Bouesse, P. Proust, J. Tual, L. Sourgen, F. Germain, High security smartcards, in: Design, Automation and Test in Europe Conference and Exhibition, 2004. Proceedings, vol. 1, IEEE, pp. 228–232.

[12] S.P. Skorobogatov, Semi-invasive attacks: a new approach to hardware security analysis, Technical Report UCAM-CL-TR-630, University of Cambridge Computer Laboratory, 2005.

[13] K. Rosenfeld, R. Karri, Attacks and defenses for JTAG, IEEE Design & Test of Computers 27 (2010).

[14] D. Zhang, M. He, X. Wang, M. Tehranipoor, Dynamically obfuscated scan for protecting IPs against scan-based attacks throughout supply chain, in: VLSI Test Symposium (VTS), 2017 IEEE 35th, IEEE, pp. 1–6.

[15] D. Mukhopadhyay, S. Banerjee, D. RoyChowdhury, B.B. Bhattacharya, Cryptoscan: a secured scan chain architecture, in: Test Symposium, 2005. Proceedings. 14th Asian, IEEE, pp. 348–353.

[16] R. Nara, K. Satoh, M. Yanagisawa, T. Ohtsuki, N. Togawa, Scan-based side-channel attack against RSA cryptosystems using scan signatures, IEICE Transactions on Fundamentals of Electronics Communications and Computer Sciences 93 (2010) 2481–2489.

[17] G.K. Contreras, A. Nahiyan, S. Bhunia, D. Forte, M. Tehranipoor, Security vulnerability analysis of design-for-test exploits for asset protection in SoCs, in: Design Automation Conference (ASP-DAC), 2017 22nd Asia and South Pacific, IEEE, pp. 617–622.

[18] L. Azriel, R. Ginosar, A. Mendelson, Exploiting the scan side channel for reverse engineering of a VLSI device, Technion, Israel Institute of Technology, 2016, Tech. Rep. CCIT Report 897.

[19] D. Hely, M.-L. Flottes, F. Bancel, B. Rouzeyre, N. Berard, M. Renovell, Scan design and secure chip, in: IOLTS, vol. 4, pp. 219–224.

[20] S.P. Skorobogatov, R.J. Anderson, Optical fault induction attacks, in: International Workshop on Cryptographic Hardware and Embedded Systems, Springer, 2002, pp. 2–12.

[21] J.D. Rolt, G.D. Natale, M.-L. Flottes, B. Rouzeyre, A novel differential scan attack on advanced DFT structures, ACM Transactions on Design Automation of Electronic Systems (TODAES) 18 (2013) 58.

[22] S.M. Saeed, S.S. Ali, O. Sinanoglu, R. Karri, Test-mode-only scan attack and countermeasure for contemporary scan architectures, in: Test Conference (ITC), 2014 IEEE International, IEEE, pp. 1–8.

[23] A. Das, B. Ege, S. Ghosh, L. Batina, I. Verbauwhede, Security analysis of industrial test compression schemes, IEEE Transactions on Computer-Aided Design of Integrated Circuits and Systems 32 (2013) 1966–1977.

[24] G. Sengar, D. Mukhopadhyay, D.R. Chowdhury, Secured flipped scan-chain model for crypto-architecture, IEEE Transactions on Computer-Aided Design of Integrated Circuits and Systems 26 (11) (2007) 2080–2084.

[25] Y. Atobe, Y. Shi, M. Yanagisawa, N. Togawa, Dynamically changeable secure scan architecture against scan-based side channel attack, in: SoC Des. Conf. ISOCC Int., 2012, pp. 155–158.

[26] J. Lee, M. Tebranipoor, J. Plusquellic, A low-cost solution for protecting IPs against scan-based side-channel attacks, in: Proc. VLSI Test Symposium (VTS), 2006, pp. 42–47.

[27] M.A. Razzaq, V. Singh, A. Singh, SSTKR: secure and testable scan design through test key randomization, in: Proc. of Asian Test Symposium (ATS), 2011, pp. 60–65.

[28] S. Paul, R.S. Chakraborty, S. Bhunia, Vim-scan: a low overhead scan design approach for protection of secret key in scan-based secure chips, in: Proc. VLSI Test Symposium (VTS), 2007.

[29] J. Lee, M. Tehranipoor, C. Patel, J. Plusquellic, Securing designs against scan-based side-channel attacks, IEEE transactions on dependable and secure computing 4 (4) (2007) 325–336.

[30] J.P. Skudlarek, T. Katsioulas, M. Chen, A platform solution for secure supply-chain and chip life-cycle management, Computer 49 (2016) 28–34.

[31] X. Wang, D. Zhang, M. He, D. Su, M. Tehranipoor, Secure scan and test using obfuscation throughout supply chain, IEEE Transactions on Computer-Aided Design of Integrated Circuits and Systems 37 (9) (2017) 1867–1880.

[32] M. Tehranipoor, C. Wang, Introduction to Hardware Security and Trust, Springer Science & Business Media, 2011.

[33] D. Hely, F. Bancel, M.-L. Flottes, B. Rouzeyre, Test control for secure scan designs, in: Test Symposium, 2005. European, IEEE, pp. 190–195.

[34] B. Jun, P. Kocher, The Intel random number generator, Cryptography Research Inc., 1999, white paper.

[35] M. Bushnell, V. Agrawal, Essentials of Electronic Testing for Digital, Memory and Mixed-Signal VLSI Circuits, vol. 17, Springer Science & Business Media, 2004.

[36] M. Da Silva, M.-l. Flottes, G. Di Natale, B. Rouzeyre, P. Prinetto, M. Restifo, Scan chain encryption for the test, diagnosis and debug of secure circuits, in: Test Symposium (ETS), 2017 22nd IEEE, IEEE, pp. 1–6.

[37] M.A. Razzaq, V. Singh, A. Singh, SSTKR: secure and testable scan design through test key randomization, in: Test Symposium (ATS), 2011 20th Asian, IEEE, pp. 60–65.

[38] G. Sengar, D. Mukhopadhyay, D.R. Chowdhury, An efficient approach to develop secure scan tree for crypto-hardware, in: Advanced Computing and Communications, 2007. ADCOM 2007. International Conference on, IEEE, pp. 21–26.

[39] C. Maunder, Standard test access port and boundary-scan architecture, IEEE Std 1149.1-1993a, 1993.

[40] J. Rearick, B. Eklow, K. Posse, A. Crouch, B. Bennetts, IJTAG (Internal JTAG): A step toward a DFT standard, in: Test Conference, 2005. Proceedings. ITC 2005, IEEE International, IEEE, 8 pp.

[41] M.T. He, M. Tehranipoor, An access mechanism for embedded sensors in modern SoCs, Journal of Electronic Testing 33 (2017) 397–413.

[42] IEEE standard test access port and boundary-scan architecture: Approved February 15, 1990, IEEE Standards Board; Approved June 17, 1990, American National Standards Institute, IEEE, 1990.

[43] JTAG explained (finally!): Why "IoT", software security engineers, and manufacturers should care, http://blog.senr.io/blog/jtag-explained, Sept. 2016.

[44] Free60 SMC Hack, http://www.free60.org/SMC_Hack, Jan. 2014.

[45] L. Greenemeier, iPhone hacks annoy AT&T but are unlikely to bruise apple, Scientific American (2007).

[46] L. Sourgen, Security locks for integrated circuit, US Patent 5,101,121, 1992.

[47] R.F. Buskey, B.B. Frosik, Protected JTAG, in: Parallel Processing Workshops, 2006. ICPP 2006 Workshops. 2006 International Conference on, IEEE, 8 pp.

[48] C. Clark, M. Ricchetti, A code-less BIST processor for embedded test and in-system configuration of boards and systems, in: Test Conference, 2004. Proceedings. ITC 2004. International, IEEE, pp. 857–866.

[49] D. Hely, F. Bancel, M.-L. Flottes, B. Rouzeyre, Secure scan techniques: a comparison, in: On-Line Testing Symposium, 2006. IOLTS 2006. 12th IEEE International, IEEE, 6 pp.

[50] J. Da Rolt, G. Di Natale, M.-L. Flottes, B. Rouzeyre, A smart test controller for scan chains in secure circuits, in: On-Line Testing Symposium (IOLTS), 2013 IEEE 19th International, IEEE, pp. 228–229.

PHYSICAL ATTACKS AND COUNTERMEASURES

CONTENTS

Hardware Security. https://doi.org/10.1016/B978-0-12-812477-2.00015-0
245

10.1 INTRODUCTION

Physical attacks are divided into three categories: noninvasive, semi-invasive, and invasive attacks. A noninvasive attack does not require any initial preparations of the device under test, and will not physically harm the device during the attack. The attacker can either tap the wires to the device, or plug it into a test circuit for the analysis. Invasive attacks require direct access to the internal components of the device, which normally requires a well-equipped and knowledgeable attacker to succeed. Meanwhile, invasive attacks are becoming constantly more demanding and expensive, as feature sizes shrink, and device complexity increases. There is a large gap between noninvasive and invasive attacks. Many attacks fall into this gap, called semi-invasive attacks. They are not very expensive as classical penetrative invasive attacks, but are as easily repeatable as noninvasive attacks. Like invasive attacks, they require depackaging the chip in order to get access to its surface. However, the passivation layer of the chip remains intact, as semi-invasive methods do not require creating contacts to the internal wires. This chapter mainly focuses on invasive physical attacks. Reverse engineering, microprobing attack, and invasive fault injection attack are the most common physical attacks, and will be introduced, respectively, in the rest of this chapter.

10.2 REVERSE ENGINEERING

Reverse engineering (RE) is the process involving the thorough examination of an object to achieve a full understanding of its construction and/or functionality; a method used by attackers as part of mounting their attack. RE is now widely used to clone, duplicate, or reproduce systems and devices in various security-critical applications, such as smartcards, smartphone, military, financial, and medical systems [1]. In this section, the RE of electronic systems, which can be achieved by extracting the system's underlying physical information through destructive or nondestructive methods, is discussed [2,3].

The motivation for RE could be "honest" or "dishonest," as shown in Table 10.1 [4–6]. Those with honest motivations tend to perform RE for verification, fault analysis, research, and education of an existing product. In many countries, RE is legal, as long as patents and design copyrights are not violated [7]. However, RE could be used to clone, pirate, or counterfeit a design, to develop an attack, or to insert a hardware Trojan. Such actions are considered dishonest. If the functionality of a cloned system is close enough to the original one, then the dishonest entity, or individuals, could sell large amounts of counterfeit products without prohibitive research and development costs required by the IP owner [8]. One example of dishonest RE took place during World War II. An American B-29 bomber was captured, reverse engineered, and cloned by the former Soviet Union (Tupolev Tu-4 bomber) [9]. The original and the cloned bombers are shown in Fig. 10.1. The configuration of the two bombers are almost the same, except for the engines and cannons.

Aside from RE of large systems, sensitive data, such as critical design parameters and personal secret information can also be extracted, or cloned, from electronic chips and printed circuit boards (PCBs). For example, it is quite easy to reverse engineer a PCB, because of its simple architecture and

Table 10.1 Motivation for reverse engineering

"Honest" motivations	"Dishonest" motivations
Failure analysis and defect identification	Fault injection attacks
Detection of counterfeit products [5,8]	Counterfeiting
Circuit analysis to recover manufacturing defects	Tampering
Confirmation of IP	IP piracy and theft
Hardware Trojan detection [6]	Hardware Trojan insertion
Analysis of a competitor's/obsolete product	Illegal cloning of a product
Education and research	Development of attacks

(A)   (B)

FIGURE 10.1

An example of RE from World War II: (A) a U.S. Air Force B-29 bomber, and (B) a Soviet Union Tupolev Tu-4 bomber, a reverse-engineered copy of the B-29.

increasing reliance on commercial off-the-shelf components. RE of PCBs and ICs could also provide opportunities for the future attacks against them. For example, many smartcards today contain ICs that store personal information and perform transactions. Dishonest parties could reverse engineer these ICs to access the confidential information of the card holder, commit financial crimes, and so forth.

Another concern in electronics industry is IC piracy through RE [10]. In 2010, Semiconductor Equipment and Materials International (SEMI) published a survey about IP infringement. The survey revealed that 90% of semiconductor companies experienced IP infringement, and 54% of them faced serious infringement on their products [11]. Many dishonest companies can illegally clone the circuits and techniques to mass produce, and sell those pirated copies in open market without authorization. The latter results in unrecoverable losses to the IP owner. Counterfeit ICs and systems may also be tampered, leading to vulnerabilities and life-threatening issues.

To summarize, RE is a long-standing problem that is of great concern to today's governments, militaries, various industries, and individuals due to: (1) the attacks and security breaches that could occur through the RE of classified systems, such as those of the military and financial institutions; (2) the safety issues and costs resulting from unintended use of counterfeit products in critical systems and infrastructures; (3) the loss in profits and reputation for IP owners; and (4) the negative impact that RE has on new product innovations, and incentives for research and development.

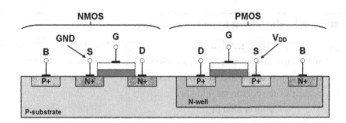

FIGURE 10.2

Simplified cross-sectional view of CMOS transistors.

As a result of these concerns, researchers, companies, and the defense departments of many nations are persistently seeking anti-RE techniques to prevent adversaries from accessing their protected products and systems. For example, the U.S. DoD is currently conducting research on anti-RE technologies that may prevent classified data, weapons, and IP from being compromised by foreign adversaries [12]. The objective of the DoD's antitamper program is to obstruct unapproved technology transfer, maximize the costs of RE, enhance U.S.'s coalition military capacities, train the DoD community, and educate the DoD community on antitampering technologies [13]. Unfortunately, most of this task is classified, and therefore is not available to the industrial sector or the wider research community.

Anti-RE techniques should have the ability to monitor, detect, resist, and react to invasive and non-invasive attacks. Several techniques could be used as anti-RE. For example, tamper-resistant materials and sensors have been used to resist theft or RE [14]. Hard barriers like ceramics, steel, and bricks have been used to separate the top layer of the electronic devices, so that tampering or RE attempts might be foiled by the destruction of the protective devices. To protect against microprobing attempts, single chip coatings have also been applied. Many different packaging techniques could also be used to protect a device: brittle packages, aluminum packages, polished packages, and bleeding paint, and holographic and other tamper-responding tapes, and labels [14]. Sensors of interest include voltage sensors, probe sensors, wire sensors, PCB sensors, motion sensors, radiation sensors, and top-layer sensor meshes. Materials like epoxy with potting, coating, and insulation have been used to block x-ray imaging attempts.

In addition, obfuscation software and hardware security primitives have been used for the protection of systems and software. These anti-RE techniques can be helpful for protecting confidential information from different types of RE attempts. Some other methods for protecting these systems are as follows: bus encryption, secure key storage, side-channel attack (SCA) protection, and tamper-responding technology [14,15].

Following is a presentation on the RE of electronic devices from chip to system levels:

(1) Chip-level RE: A chip is an IC comprised of electronic devices that are fabricated using semiconductor material. A chip has package material, bond wires, a lead frame, and die. Each die has several metal layers, vias, interconnections, passivation, and active layers [16]. In Fig. 10.2, a simplified cross-sectional view of NMOS and PMOS is shown respectively. As shown in this figure, polysilicon gates (G) of NMOS and PMOS transistors are connected together somewhere off the page to form the input of the inverter. The source (S) of the PMOS of the inverter is connected to a metal Vdd line, and the source of the NMOS is connected to a metal ground (GND) line. The drains (D) of the PMOS

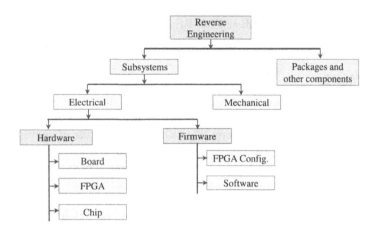

FIGURE 10.3

Taxonomy of RE.

and NMOS are connected together with a metal line for the output of the CMOS inverter. The chip could be analog, digital, or mixed signal. Digital chips include application-specific integrated circuits (ASICs), field-programmable gate arrays (FPGAs), and memories. RE of chips can be nondestructive or destructive. X-ray tomography is a nondestructive method of RE that can provide layer-by-layer images of chips, and is often used for the analysis of internal vias, traces, wire bonding, capacitors, contacts, or resistors. Destructive analysis, on the other hand, might consist of etching and grinding every layer for analysis. During the delayering process, pictures are taken by either a scanning electron microscope (SEM), or a transmission electron microscope (TEM).

(2) PCB-level RE: Electronic chips and components are mounted on a laminated nonconductive PCB [17] and electrically interconnected using conductive copper traces and vias. The board might be single or multilayered, depending on the complexity of the electronic system. RE of PCBs begins with the identification of the components mounted on the board, its traces on the top and bottom (visible) layers, its ports, and so forth. After that, delayering or x-ray imaging could be used to identify the connections, traces, and vias of the internal PCB layers.

(3) System-level RE: Electronic systems are comprised of chips, PCBs, and firmware. A system's firmware includes the information about the system's operation and timing, and is typically embedded within nonvolatile memories (NVMs), such as ROM, EEPROM, and Flash. For more advanced designs with FPGAs (for example, Xilinx FPGAs), the firmware-like netlists are also stored within the NVM memories (also called bitstream). By reading out and analyzing the contents in the memory, RE can provide a deeper insight into the system under attack.

Based on the preceding discussions, a comprehensive taxonomy of RE is shown in Fig. 10.3. First, RE is performed to tear down the product or system to identify the subsystems, packages, and other components. The subsystems could be electrical or mechanical. In this chapter, only electrical subsystems are focused. The electrical subsystems under analysis consist of hardware and firmware. A reverse engineer could analyze the FPGA, board, chip, memory, and software to extract all information. This effort is concerned with RE when it is done with malicious intentions, and with anti-RE as a remedy against this form of RE. This type of RE and anti-RE for each level, including equipment, techniques, and materials, is examined.

10.2.1 EQUIPMENT

Advanced RE requires a set of specialized equipment. Below, a short summary of some of the equipment commonly used in RE is presented as shown in Figs. 10.4, 10.5, and 10.6.

Optical high/super-resolution microscopy (digital). The limitations of conventional digital microscopy include limited depth of field, a very thin focus field, and keeping all parts on an object simultaneously in focus [18]. To overcome these limitations, optical high-resolution microscopes are now being used. Optical super-resolution microscopes take a series of images and put them together to create a 3D image that reflects different heights. However, optical microscopes can only be used to analyze PCB and chip exteriors, as the resolution is too low for current chip feature sizes ($\ll$ 100 nm).

Scanning electron microscopes. In a SEM, focused beams of electrons are used to produce images [22]. For a sample, the electrons interact with atoms, a process that produces signals for detection. It is expected that reverse engineers would start with a cross section of an unknown chip. SEM could be used for analyzing the cross section, and the composition and thickness of each layer of the die. The object could be magnified by 10 times, to approximately 30,000 times. SEM provides the following advantages over traditional microscopes:

– *Higher resolution*: SEM has higher resolution, and with high magnification, it can resolve the features on the submicron level.

– *Large depth of field*: When a specimen (for example, the internal elements of a chip) is focused on for an image, the height of the specimen is called the depth of field. The SEM has a depth of field that is more than 300 times greater than that of a light microscope, which means that a specimen's otherwise unobtainable details can be obtained with a SEM.

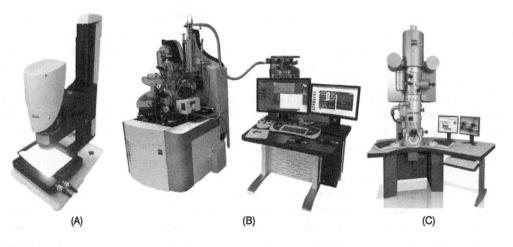

(A)　　　　(B)　　　　(C)

FIGURE 10.4

(A) Optical microscopy. (B) Scanning electron microscope (SEM). (C) Transmission electron microscope (TEM).

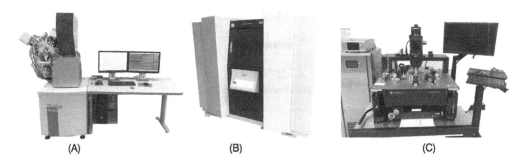

FIGURE 10.5

(A) Focused ion beam (FIB). (B) High-resolution x-ray microscopy. (C) Probe station.

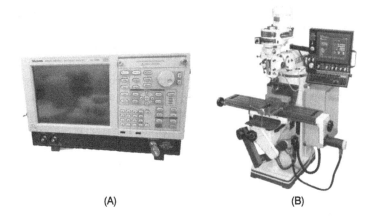

FIGURE 10.6

(A) Logic analyzer. (B) Computer numerical control (CNC) [30].

Transmission electron microscopes. With TEMs, a beam of electrons is transmitted through and interacts with a sample [21,23]. Like SEMs, TEMs have a very high spatial resolution, which can provide detailed information about the internal structures of a sample [24]. In addition, a TEM can be used to view a chip's cross-section and its internal layers.

Focused ion beam. The working principle of a focused ion beam (FIB) is the same as a SEM, but instead of using an electron beam, an ion beam is used. The ion beam enables one to perform material deposition and removal with nanometer resolution, which can be used for TEM sample preparation, and circuit editing. There are different types of ion sources for the ion beam, but the most popular one is gallium (Ga) liquid metal. The new generation of these tools is called *plasma* FIB (PFIB), which works at a higher power, and results in shorter material processing time.

Scanning capacitance microscopy. For the illustration of dopant profiles on the 10 nm scale of semiconductor devices, scanning capacitance microscopy (SCM) is used because of its high spatial resolution [3]. A probe electrode is applied at the top of the sample surface, and this electrode then

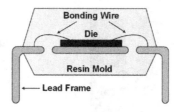

FIGURE 10.7

Cross-sectional view of IC parts.

scans across the sample. The change in electrostatic capacitance between the surface and the probe is used for obtaining information about the sample [28].

High-resolution x-ray microscopy. X-ray microscopy is used to nondestructively test a sample, such as a chip or a PCB board. With this method, x-rays are used to produce a radiograph of the sample, which shows its thickness, assembly details, holes, vias, connectors, traces, and any defects that might be present [28].

Probe stations. Probe station supports a wide variety of electrical measuring, device and wafer characterization, failure analysis, submicron probing, optoelectronic engineering tests, and more. There are up to 16 positioners in these kinds of systems located on a vibration isolated frame, which stabilizes the platen. These features enable a highly reliable and repeatable testing process down to the submicron level. A pull-out vacuum chuck stage holds the testing samples and the motorized platen, whereas the chuck and positioners provide enough flexibility to perform tests on many different samples.

Logic analyzers. A logic analyzer is an electronic instrument that can observe and record multiple signals on a digital system or digital circuits simultaneously. The use of a logic analyzer can facilitate RE at the chip, board, and system levels. In the case of FPGA bitstream RE, the logic analyzer can be adopted to measure the JTAG communication signals between the FPGA and external memory.

Computer numerical control. The need for automating machining tools, which are typically controlled manually, led to the creation of the computer numerical control (CNC), where computers control the process [30]. CNCs can run mills, lathes, grinds, plasma cutters, laser cuts, and so forth. The motion is controlled along all three main axes, which enables a 3D process.

10.2.2 CHIP-LEVEL RE

An IC typically consists of a die, a lead frame, wire bonding, and molding encapsulant, as shown in Fig. 10.7. The package of a chip can be classified in different ways. The materials that are used can be ceramic or plastic [31]. Considering that ceramics are costly, plastics are commonly used as the package material. Packaging can also be wire bond or flip chip [32]. In wire bond packaging, wires are connected to the lead frame. There are several types of wire bonding: concentric bond rings, double bonds, and ball bonding. In contrast, flip-chip packaging is a technique that allows for a direct electrical connection between face-down ("flipped" so that its top side faces down) electronic components, and substrates, circuit boards, or carriers. This electrical connection is formed from conductive solder bumps instead of wires. Flip chips have several advantages over wire bond packaging: superior electrical and thermal performance, higher input-output capability, and substrate flexibility. However, flip-chips are often considered more costly than wire bonds [32].

At the chip level, the goal of the RE process is to find package materials, wire bonding, different metal layers, contacts, vias and active layers, and interconnections between metal layers. The RE process has several different steps:

– *Decapsulation:* Decapsulation exposes the internal components of the chip, which allows for the inspection of the die, interconnections, and other features.

– *Delayering:* The die is analyzed layer by layer, destructively, to see each metal, passivation, poly, and active layer.

– *Imaging:* An image is taken of each layer in the delayering process by using SEM, TEM, or SCM.

– *Post-processing:* In this process, the images from the previous step are analyzed, schematic and high-level netlists are created for functional analyses, and the chip is identified. Each of these steps is discussed in greater detail in the following sections.

10.2.2.1 Decapsulation

First, reverse engineers identify the package materials and remove the chip's packaging. Depot is the traditional method by which an acid solution is used for removing the package [3]. A package may be made from different kinds of materials, so one has to be precise when choosing the acid. These acid solutions are used to etch off the packaging material without damaging the die and interconnections. Mechanical and thermal methods are used to remove a die from ceramic packages. These methods are applied to both polish the ceramic materials and remove the lids [3].

To remove the die package, one can use selective or nonselective methods. Wet chemical etching and plasma etching can be used as selective techniques, whereas nonselective techniques would be thermal shock, grinding, cutting, and laser ablation. Different kinds of decapsulation methods and their pros and cons are shown in Table 10.2.

After decapsulation, the die needs to be cleaned before delayering and/or imaging can be performed, because dust may be present, resulting in artifacts [33]. Different methods for cleaning the dust are outlined next:

– *Spray cleaning:* A syringe filled with acetone is attached to a very fine blunt-tip needle. The syringe is then used to spray particles off of the die.

– *Acid cleaning:* To remove organic residues, fresh acid can be used after decapsulation.

– *Ultrasonic cleaning:* Water, detergent (lab grade), or solvents can be used for ultrasonic cleaning after bare die decapsulation.

– *Mechanical swabbing:* The die should be gently brushed with an acetone-soaked lab wipe, which should be lint-free to avoid contaminating the die. The sample is scratched carefully to avoid loosening the bond wires.

10.2.2.2 Delayering

Modern chips are made up of several metal layers, passivation layers, vias, contact, poly, and active layers. Reverse engineers must perform cross-section imaging of a chip, using SEM or TEM to identify the number of layers, metal material, layer thickness, vias, and contacts. The knowledge from cross-sectional imaging is critical (that is, thickness of the layers), as it determines how the delayering must be performed.

Table 10.2 Decapsulation of a die using different methods and their pros and cons

Decapsulation Methods		Pros	Cons
Chemical	Wet	Using sulfuric or nitric acid, it has a high etch rate Works well when die size is small compared to package	Does not work with ceramic packages Acid can damage lead frame, and bond wires Isotropic etch
	Dry	Removes material with good selectivity Can remove any material	Slow for ceramic packages Contamination of etcher may result in uneven removal of material
Mechanical	Grinding and polishing	Even removal of material Easy to use More suitable for flip chips	Works when lead frame is higher than back side of the die Does not work on certain areas
	Milling	Removes material in a specific area Three-axis material removal	Needs professional skills to work with CNC Accuracy of material removal is limited with the tool accuracy
	Thermal shock	Fast and inexpensive process Easy to perform	High risk of damaging die Not controllable in specific areas
Nanoscale fabrication techniques	High-current FIB	High accuracy in material removal (nm) Can be performed on controlled area	Expensive, Requires, high operation skills Slow milling rate ($30 \ nm^3/s$)
	Plasma FIB	High accuracy in material removal (nm) Can be performed on controlled area Faster milling rate ($2000 \ nm^3/s$)	Expensive Requires high operation skills
	Laser ablation	Accurate in material removal (μm) Can be performed on controlled area Faster milling rate ($10^6 \ \mu m^3/s$)	Expensive Requires high operation skills

Table 10.3 Wet etching recipes for different types of metals and etching process [34]

Material to Be Etched	Chemicals	Ratio	Etching Process and Comments
Aluminum (Al)	H_3PO_4 : Water : Acetic Acid : HNO_3	16:2:1:1	PAN Etch; 200 nm/min @ 25 °C; 600 nm/min @ 40 °C
Aluminum (Al)	NaOH : Water	1:1	May be used @ 25 °C but etches faster at a higher temperature
Silicon (Si)	HF : HNO_3 : Water	2:2:1	–
Copper (Cu)	HNO_3 : Water	5:1	–
Tungsten (W)	HF : HNO_3	1:1	–
Polysilicon (Si)	HNO_3 : Water : HF	50:20:1	Remove oxide first; 540 nm/min @ 25 °C
Polysilicon (Si)	HNO_3 : HF	3:1	Remove oxide first; High etch rate: 4.2 µm/min
Silicon, dioxide, (SiO_2)—thermally grown	HF : Water	1:100	Very slow etch; 1.8 nm/min @ 25 °C
Silicon dioxide, (SiO_2)—thermally grown	HF	–	Very rapid etch; 1.8 nm/min @ 25 °C
Silicon nitride (Si_3N_4)	Refluxing phosphoric acid	–	Use at 180 °C; 6.5 nm/min @ 25 °C; Plasma etching is preferred for removing Si_3N_4

Several methods can be used simultaneously when a chip is delayered, such as wet/plasma etching, grinding, and polishing. A reverse engineer should determine the etchants needed, and the time required to remove each layer, because the layout could depend on the specific technology, which could be either CMOS, or bipolar. For example, memory device vias are much higher than others, so etching is challenging, because one has to remove a large amount of material. Several types of metals and required wet etchants are shown in Table 10.3 [34].

Once the etchants are determined for delayering a specific layer and metal, a reverse engineer will begin by etching the passivation layer; then, the reverse engineer will take an image of the highest metal layer; after that, the reverse engineer will etch the metal layer. This same process is repeated for each layer, including the poly and active layers. When delayering a chip, the layer surface has to be maintained as planar, and one at a time, each layer should be etched carefully and accurately [3,4]. In addition, the layer thickness of a chip could vary because of manufacturing process variations. The best approach is to have one die for every level of delayering. For example, when delayering is done for a four-layer chip, a reverse engineer could use four dies for each metal layer of the chip.

To delayer a chip accurately, an advanced laboratory should have one or more of the following pieces of mechanical equipment [4]: a semi-automated polishing machine, a semi-automated milling machine, a laser, a gel etch, a CNC milling machine, and an ion beam milling machine. When the chip has been delayered, one could face the following challenges [4]:

– *Planarity of the layer:* The planarity of the layer could be conformal or planarized. In a conformal layer, some portion of the different layers and vias could appear on the same plane. However, in a planarized layer, only one layer appears at a time. Conformal layers are more challenging.

– *Material removal rate:* The equipment could be slow or fast and could underetch or overetch.

– *Die size:* Thickness, length, and width can vary.

– *Number of samples:* There may not be enough parts to image each layer separately (that is, information on a layer could be missing if delayering is not done accurately).

– *Selectivity of the material:* One must be careful to remove one material but not another (for example, removing a metal layer without affecting the vias).

10.2.2.3 Imaging

During the delayering process, thousands of high-resolution images are taken to capture all of the information contained in each layer. Later, these images can be stitched together, and then studied to recreate the chip. For the purposes of imaging, many high-resolution microscopes and x-ray machines could be used as discussed in Section 10.2.1.

10.2.2.4 Post-Processing

The post-processing or circuit extraction after delayering consists of the following steps: (1) image processing, (2) annotation, (3) gate-level schematic extraction, (4) schematic analysis and organization, and (5) high-level netlist extraction from the gate-level schematic. Each of these steps is described in greater detail as follows:

Image Processing. Taking images manually is becoming increasingly difficult, because the size of the ICs is shrinking, along with many of their features [3]. Advanced electrical labs now use automated instruments (x-rays, SEMs, digital microscopes) that are equipped to take images of entire layers of ICs and PCBs. Then, the automated software can be used to stitch the images together with minimal error, and synchronize the multiple layers without misalignment. In addition, it is important to establish the lineup of the layers' contacts and vias before the extraction.

Annotation. After the completion of the aligned layers and stitched images, the extraction of the circuit starts. This stage in the process includes making note of transistors, inductors, capacitors, resistors, diodes, other components, the interconnection of the layers, vias, and contacts. The circuit extraction could be an automated or a manual process. For example, Chipworks has an ICWorks extractor tool that can look at all of the imaged layers of the chip and align them for extraction [3]. The tool can be used to view several layers of a chip in multiple windows, simultaneously. The ICWorks extractor tool might also be used for the annotation of wires and devices. Image recognition software (2D or 3D) is used for the recognition of standard cells in digital logic. Automated image recognition software helps to facilitate the extraction of large blocks of digital cells quickly.

Gate-level schematic extraction. Sometimes the images are imperfect, as the images may be taken manually. Additionally, the annotation process and image recognition for digital cells could be erroneous. Therefore, verification is needed before the creation of a schematic. Design rule checks could be used to detect any issues related to minimum-sized features or spaces, wire bonding, vias, and connections [3]. After this stage, tools such as ICWorks can extract an interconnection netlist from which a flat schematic could be created. The schematic could be checked for any floating nodes, shorted input or output, or supplies and nets that have no input or output. The annotations, netlist, and schematic depend on each other, so changing one could affect the others.

Schematic analysis and organization. The schematic analysis should be done thoughtfully and carefully with proper hierarchy and design coherence. For the analysis and organization of a schematic, the reverse engineer could use public information on the device, such as its datasheet, technical report, marketing information, and patents. This could help to facilitate an analysis of the architecture and circuit design. Some structures, such as differential pairs and bandgap references, could be easily recognizable.

High-level netlist extraction from gate-level schematic. After circuit extraction is performed on the stripped IC (derivation of circuit schematic diagram), several techniques [35–37] could be applied to get the high-level description for analysis and validation of the functionality of the chip, using simulation. [35] proposed RE from a gate-level schematic of ISCAS-85 combinational circuits to get the circuit functionality by computing truth tables of small blocks, looking for common library components, looking for structures with repetition, and identifying bus and control signals. [38] presents RE of gate-level netlists to derive the high-level function of circuit components based on behavioral pattern mining. The approach is based on a combination of pattern mining from the simulation traces of the gate-level netlist, and interpreting them for the pattern graph. [38] proposed an automatic way to derive word-level structures that could specify operations from the gate-level netlist of a digital circuit. The functionality of logic blocks is isolated by extracting the word-level information flow of the netlist, while considering the effect of gate sharing. A variety of algorithms are used by [37] to identify the high-level netlist with module boundaries. The algorithms are applied for verification to determine the functionality of components, such as register files, counters, adders, and subtractors.

10.2.3 CHIP-LEVEL ANTI-RE

There are several approaches for the anti-RE of ICs, which include camouflage, obfuscation, and other techniques. Following is a description of these methods:

10.2.3.1 Camouflage

Layout-level techniques such as cell camouflage [39,40] and dummy contacts could be used to hinder adversaries who want to perform RE on a chip. In the camouflage technique, the layout of standard cells with different functionalities is made to appear identical. One can introduce camouflage to a standard gate by using real and dummy contacts, which can enable different functionalities, as shown in Fig. 10.8. In Figs. 10.8A and 10.8B, the layouts of two-input, NAND and NOR gates, are shown. These gates functionalities can be easily identified by their layouts. In contrast, Figs. 10.8C and 10.8D show camouflaged two-input NAND and NOR gates with layouts that appear identical. If regular layouts are used for standard gates, automated image processing techniques can easily identify the functionality of the gates (see Figs. 10.8A and 10.8B). Camouflaging (see Figs. 10.8C and 10.8D) can make it more difficult to perform RE with automated tools. If the functionality of the camouflage gates of the design is not correctly extracted, the adversary will end up with the wrong netlist.

10.2.3.2 Obfuscation

Obfuscation techniques entail making a design or system more complicated to prevent RE, while also allowing the design or system to have the same functionality as the original. There are several different obfuscation approaches in the literature [41,42]. The hardware protection through obfuscation of netlist could be used against piracy and tampering, and the technique could provide protection at every level of the hardware design and manufacturing process [42]. The approach is achieved by obfuscating the functionality by systematically modifying the state-transition function and internal logic structure of the gate-level IP core. The circuit will traverse the obfuscated mode to reach the normal mode only for specific input vectors, which are known as the "key" for the circuit.

[41] proposed a technique of interlocking obfuscation in the register transfer level (RTL) design, which could be unlocked for a specific dynamic path traversal. The circuit has two modes: entry mode

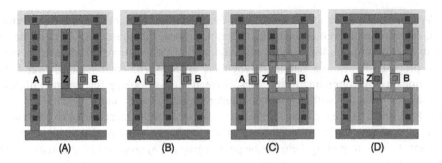

FIGURE 10.8

(A) Standard NAND gate and (B) NOR gate. These gates could be easily differentiable by looking at the top metal layers. (C) Camouflaged NAND gate and (D) NOR gate. These gates have identical top metal layers and are, therefore, harder to identify.

(obfuscated) and functional mode. The functional mode is operational when there is a formation of a specific interlocked code word. The code word is encoded from input to the circuit, which is applied in entry mode to reach the functional mode. This code word is interlocked into the transition functions, and is protected from RE by increasing the interaction with the state machine. The additional benefit is that any minor change or alteration to the circuit made by an adversary will be magnified due to the interlocking obfuscation. The technique has a large area overhead, so there is a trade-off between the area overhead and the level of protection. Higher protection levels require larger overheads.

10.2.3.3 Other Techniques

Today, most companies are fabless, meaning that the fabrication of chips is outsourced. A semiconductor foundry is given the design [43] to fabricate the chips. To accomplish post-fabrication control of the ICs that are produced in such plants, IC hardware metering protocols have been put in place to prevent IC piracy [10,44]. ICs can be identified by active metering, which is a process by which parts of the chip can be used for locking and unlocking by the design house. Physical unclonable functions (PUFs) can be used to generate secret keys to protect from cloning [44,45]. PUF is difficult to duplicate. Therefore, RE and cloning of the whole chip could be possible, but the reverse engineer would not be able to activate the cloned chip.

[11] proposed a reconfigurable logic barrier scheme that separates information flow from the inputs to the outputs. This technique is used in the IC pre-fabrication stage for protection against IC piracy. The information could flow with the correct key, but the barrier would interrupt flow for the incorrect key. The main difference between the logic barrier scheme and the obfuscation techniques, described in Section 10.2.3.2, is that the logic barrier scheme is based on the proper locking locations of the barrier in the design instead of randomized ones. This technique is used for effectively maximizing the barrier with minimum overhead by utilizing better-defined metrics, node positioning, and enhancing the granularity from XOR gates to look-up tables (LUTs).

An external key could be placed in every chip for protection against IC piracy. This method is called end piracy of integrated circuits (EPIC) [15]. This key is produced by the IP holder, and is

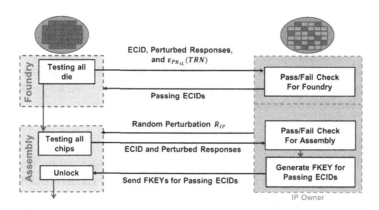

FIGURE 10.9

Overview of the secure split-test (SST).

unique. Manufacturers must send the ID to the IP holder for the chip to become functional, and the IP holder must then send the activation key to enable the activation of the chip with the ID. The random ID is generated by several techniques. This ID is generated before the testing of the IC. This key prevents cloning of the IC from RE, and controls how many chips should be made. The EPIC technique's limitations include complex communication with the IP holder, which could impact test time and time to market. Additionally, this technique requires higher levels of power consumption.

[46] proposed a bus-based IC locking and activation scheme for preventing unauthorized manufacturing. The technique involves the scrambling of the central bus, so that the design can be locked at the manufacturing site as a means of guaranteeing the chip's uniqueness. The central bus is controlled by both reversible bit permutations and substitutions. A true number generator is applied to establish the code for the chip, and the Diffie–Hellman key exchange protocol is employed during activation.

[47] proposed a method called secure split-test (SST) for securing the manufacturing and testing process of SoC, and give control back to the SoC designers to prevent counterfeit, defective and/or out-of-spec SoC from entering the supply chain. In SST, each chip is locked during the testing process. The SoC designer is the only entity who can interpret the locked test results, and unlock the passing chips. In this way, SST can prevent overproduction, and also prevent chips from reaching the supply chain. SST, in addition, establishes unique key for every chip, which drastically improves security against supply chain attacks.

SST consists of the following components: (1) true random number generator (TRNG); (2) fuse-based storage for true random numbers (TRNs); (3) public key encryption/decryption unit; (4) scan-locking module; and (5) functional-locking block. An overview of SST is shown in Fig. 10.9. One can assume that an ECID has been securely generated before starting tests using the mod-EaaS approach developed in Task 1. The test process at the foundry begins with an initialization step, where the TRNG generates a TRN (similar to the protocol in Task 1) and stores it in a nonvolatile memory. This TRN is used to both uniquely perturb test responses, and lock each IC. TRN is shared with the IP owner by encrypting it with a public key PK_IC, hardcoded into the IC design. By knowing TRN, the IP owner can determine if the IC passes tests, and how to generate the key (referred to as FKEY) to unlock the IC. The IP owner will identify which die pass, and send the corresponding ECIDs to the foundry. The foundry sends only the passing die to the assembly for packaging. The IP owner sends a random number $R_I P$ to the assembly for each IC. The $R_I P$ adds randomness to the process, in case the foundry/assembly collude during the test process. A similar round of communication occurs between assembly and IP owner. The IP owner generates FKEYs and sends them with the associated ECIDs to the assembly only for the ICs that pass testing. The FKEY is burnt into nonvolatile memory of the corresponding IC, thereby unlocking it.

10.2.4 BOARD-LEVEL RE

The goal of board-level RE is to identify all components on the board and the connections between them. All of the components used in a design are called the bill of materials (BOM) [1]. The components and parts of a PCB could be any of the following: microprocessors, microcontrollers, decoupling capacitors, differential pairs, DRAMs, NAND flashes, serial EEPROMs, serial NOR flashes, and crystals/oscillators. There could be silkscreen markings, high-speed serial/parallel ports, program/debug ports, JTAGs, DVIs, HDMIs, SATAs, PCIs, Ethernets, program/debug ports, and display ports [3,48]. To identify the components, test points, and parts of the PCB, silkscreen markings are often used [1]. For example, D101 may be a diode, and Z12 might be a zener diode.

IC identification via chip and die markings. Some electronic components mounted on the PCB can be identified easily through the use of IC markings, but fully custom and semicustom ICs are difficult to identify. Using standard off-the-shelf parts with silkscreen annotations will assist the RE process. If the ICs have no markings, then the manufacturer's logo can give an idea of the functionality of the chip. Custom devices, which are developed in-house, are difficult to identify [1], because a custom device could be undocumented, or documentation could be provided only under a nondisclosure agreement.

IC markings can be divided into the following four parts [49]:

- The first is the prefix, which is the code that is used to identify the manufacturer. It could be a one- to a three-letter code, although a manufacturer might have several prefixes.
- The second part is the device code, which is used to identify a specific IC type.
- The next part is the suffix, which is used to identify the package type and temperature range. Manufacturers modify their suffixes frequently.
- A four-digit code is used for the date, where the first two digits identify the year and the last two identify the number of the week. In addition, manufacturers could cipher the date into a form only known by them.

The marking conventions of a Texas Instruments (TI) chip for the first and second line is shown in Fig. 10.10. The TI chips could have an optional third and fourth line with information related to the trademark and copyright. After identifying the manufacturer and IC markings, the reverse engineer could find the detailed functionality of the chip from the datasheets, which are available on the Internet [50,51].

If the IC marking is not readable, because it has faded away due to prior usage in the field or the manufacturer did not place a marking for security purposes, the reverse engineer could strip off the package, and read the die markings to identify the manufacturer and the chip's functionality [49]. The die marking could help to identify the mask number, part number, date of the die mask completion or copyright registration, company logo, and the trademark symbol. A die marking could match the

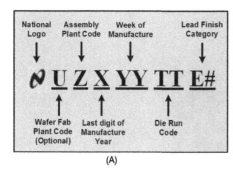
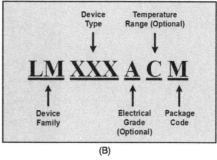

FIGURE 10.10

Marking convention on the TI chips for (A) the first line and (B) the second line.

package marking depending on the manufacturer. Then the datasheet information could be used to assess the die. Die markings are similar within families of chips made by the same manufacturer [52]. So, if someone can find the functionality of one chip, then that person can also identify the functionality of the chip family, because of the almost similar die markings that are shared by the chips in that family. For example, the Qualcomm MSM8255 processor is identical to the MSM7230 in both functionality and design, and both chips are from the Snapdragon family of ICs [52]. The only difference between these two chips is their clock speed. After identifying the components of the PCB, the reverse engineer would want to identify the PCB-type, which could be any of the following: single sided (one copper layer), double sided (two copper layers), or multi-layered. In multi-layered PCBs, chips are connected to each other on the front and the back, and through the internal layers. Some of the internal layers are used as power and ground layers. Conductors of different layers are connected with vias, and delayering is needed to identify these connections.

Destructive analysis of PCBs. Before PCB delayering, images of the placement and orientation of all outer layers' components are captured [1]. Then the components could be removed, drilled hole positions could be observed, and it could be determined whether there are any buried or blind vias. The PCB delayering process is similar to the one described for chips, and therefore will not be discussed further. After the PCB is delayered, images of each layer can be taken [48]. Then the composition and the thickness of the layers should be noted. It is important to track the impedance control of high-speed signals and the characteristics of the PCB. The dielectric constant, prepreg weave thickness, and resin-type should also be determined [1].

Nondestructive 3D imaging of PCBs using x-ray tomography. X-ray tomography is a noninvasive imaging technique that makes it possible to visualize the internal structure of an object without the interference of over-and underlayer structures. The principle of this method is to acquire a stack of 2D images, and then use mathematical algorithms such as the direct Fourier transform and center slice theory [53] to reconstruct the 3D image. These 2D projections are collected from many different angles, depending on the quality needed for the final image. The object properties, such as dimension and material density, source/detector distance to object, source power, detector objective, filter, exposure time, number of projections, center shift, and beam hardening are important to consider in the selection of the tomography process parameters. Internal and external structures will be ready to analyze when

FIGURE 10.11

PCB mounted on a sample holder.

the 3D image is reconstructed [48]. A discussion of how to select the right values for any of these parameters is outside the scope of this article. More information on tomography parameters is available in [54].

As an example, the traces and via holes of a four-layer custom PCB using a Zeiss Versa 510 x-ray machine are analyzed [55]. To make sure that features on the board can be observed, they selected a fine pixel size, which gives us high enough image quality. After several rounds of optimization, the tomography parameters for obtaining the best quality images are selected. The process is completely automated after setting the parameters, can be performed without the need for oversight, and should be widely applicable to most PCBs.

For the four-layer custom board in Fig. 10.11, all traces, connections, and via holes are clearly captured. To validate the effectiveness of the tomography approach, the results are compared to the board design files previously used to produce the PCB. The board includes a front side, back side, and two internal layers. The internal layers correspond to power and ground. The via holes connect the traces on two sides of the board, and are also connected to either power or ground layers. The internal power layer is presented in the design layout in Fig. 10.12.

The 3D image of the board is reconstructed using a combination of thousands of virtual 2D slices. These slices can be viewed and analyzed separately. The thickness of each of these is same as the pixel size (that is, 50 μm). In Fig. 10.13, one slice is provided, which shows the information of the internal power layer.

By comparing the tomography results and the design layout of the board, one can see a clear difference between the via holes that are connected, and those that are not connected to the internal layer. Soldered joints constitute a highly x-ray absorbing material, and result in white contrast for the associated pixels. However, plastic has a lower density and is more x-ray transparent, which results in a dark contrast. Thus, one can easily determine which via holes are connected to an internal layer. The same principle will let us detect the traces on the side layers of the board due to the presence of copper on the traces, as shown in Fig. 10.14.

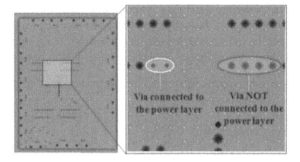

FIGURE 10.12

Layout design of the internal power layer.

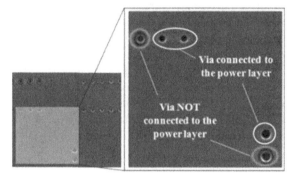

FIGURE 10.13

Virtual slicing presents power layer.

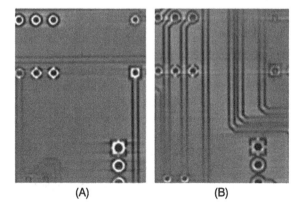

(A)   (B)

FIGURE 10.14

Reconstructed (A) top and (B) bottom layers of a PCB.

Netlist extraction after imaging. After capturing images of the PCB via delayering or x-ray tomography, connections between all of the components could be discovered, which would yield a PCB layout netlist. Then commercial tools could be used for converting the layout back into schematic [56]. To create the netlist from the collected images, one should verify the following:

- connection between the components of original board (a datasheet could be helpful to find the connection for original functionality),
- unexpected shorts and hanging Vdd,
- pin connections between components.

Several techniques have been used for analyzing x-ray images in prior work [57,60]. Wu et al. [57] uses a visual inspection system for PCBs. The elimination subtraction method is used, which subtracts the perfect PCB image (the template) from the inspected image, and locates the defects in the PCB. Mat et al. [58] applied structuring technique to a raw PCB image (input) using a morphological operation. After that, a dilation and erosion function is applied, so that a fine-segmented image of the PCB tracks can be achieved. Koutsougeras et al. [59] applied an automatic Verilog HDL model generator, which includes the image-processing technique that is used to identify the components and their connections. After that, a circuit graph is obtained, which corresponds to a primitive schematic circuit of the board. Finally, Verilog HDL is generated from the circuit graph. A Verilog XL simulator is used for testing the performance. The layers of the circuit card assemblies/PCBs are separated using x-ray stereo imaging in [60]. The focus is to identify the solder joints and traces on the different layers of a multi-layered PCB. In the automated process technique, photos are taken from one- or two-layer PCBs. Then, a C++ program is used to automatically reverse engineer the netlist.

10.2.5 BOARD-LEVEL ANTI-RE

Ensuring complete protection from PCB-level RE is a difficult task, and thus the goal of anti-RE methods is to simply make RE prohibitively expensive and time consuming. A summary of PCB-level anti-RE techniques follows [1]:

1. Tamper-proof fittings (such as torx), custom screw shapes, adhesively bonded enclosures, and fully potting the space around a PCB could be used for protection against physical attacks.
2. Custom silicon, unmarked ICs, missing silkscreens with minimum passive components, and a lack of information from the Internet could complicate RE. Additionally, the elimination of JTAG and debug ports from silicon can make the RE process harder.
3. Ball grid array (BGA) devices are better, because such devices do not have exposed pins. Back-to-back BGA placement in a PCB board could be most secure, because of the inaccessibility of the unrouted JTAG pins with controlled depth drilling on any side of the PCB. For back-to-back BGA placement, the PCB needs to be multilayered, which will increase the RE cost for layer-by-layer analysis. The problem is that back-to-back BGA packaging is complex and expensive.
4. If the devices are operating in an unusual fashion (for example, if there are jumbled addresses and data buses), then, it would be hard to find the functionality of the device. Obfuscation (that is, wiring connections between used pins to unused pins, having spare inputs and outputs from processors to route signals, dynamically jumbling buses, and jumbling the PCB silkscreen annotations) could

Table 10.4 Implementation challenges of anti-RE techniques for board level

Anti-RE Techniques	Design Cost	Manufacturing Impact	RE Cost
Tamper-proof fittings such as torx and custom screws shapes	Moderate	Low	Very low
Fully potting the space around a PCB	Low	Moderate	Low
Missing silkscreen with minimum passive components	Low	Low	Low
Custom silicon and unmarked IC	Low	Moderate	Low
BGA devices	Low	High	High
Routing, signals for inner, layers only	Moderate	High	Moderate
Multilayer PCB	High	Moderate	Very high
Using blind and buried vias	Moderate	Very high	Moderate
Dynamically jumbled buses	Low	Very low	Low
Route through ASIC	Very High	Moderate	High
Route through FPGA	Moderate	Moderate	Moderate
Elimination of JTAG and debug ports	Low	Moderate	Low

complicate the RE process. However, such techniques also require the use of more complex chips, and complicated design methods.

Many of the preceding methods are difficult to implement and could significantly increase design and manufacturing costs. Table 10.4 shows the effectiveness of anti-RE techniques at the board level [1]. A total of five levels are used for scaling, based on identifying design cost, manufacturing impact, and RE cost.

10.2.6 SYSTEM-LEVEL RE

With chip- and PCB-level RE processes, the purpose is to obtain the netlist of the chip and board in the embedded system, which represents the function and interconnections of the design. To make the design fully functional, the system operation codes and control instructions, which are defined by firmware, should be retrieved as well. This is referred as system-level RE.

Parallel to the embedded system design, involving ASICs and MCU/DSPs, there are designs based on FPGAs, whose share of market has been increasing in modern product design. Considering the fact that the hardware functionality and interconnection (referred to as the netlist) are enclosed in the binary configuration file (called the bitstream), the RE process of FPGA is completely different from the ASIC chip-level RE, which is mainly based on geometrical characteristics of the chip layout (see Section 10.2.2). Here, FPGA RE is categorized into the system-level RE as well, as both the firmware in MCUs, DSPs, and so forth, and netlist information, are stored in the NVM devices.

In this section, first various NVM storage devices are introduced, and then the RE methods used to extract the firmware/netlist accordingly are discussed.

10.2.6.1 Firmware/Netlist Information Representation

Firmware and netlist information can be stored via read-only memory (ROM), electrically erasable programmable ROM (EEPROM), or Flash memory. ROM is a type of memory, whose binary bits are programmed during the manufacturing process. Currently, ROM is still among the most popular

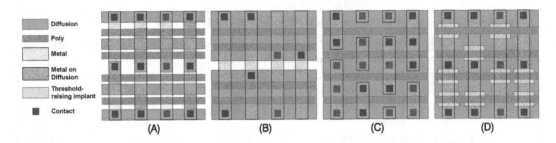

FIGURE 10.15

Illustrations of (A) active-layer programming ROM, (B) contact-layer programming ROM, (C) metal-layer programming ROM, and (D) implant programming ROM.

storage media due to its low cost per cell, high density, and fast access speed. From the perspective of ROM physical implementation, ROM devices can be typically classified into four types [61], as shown in Fig. 10.15:

- Active-layer programming ROM: The logic state is represented by the presence or absence of a transistor. As shown in Fig. 10.15A, a transistor is fabricated by simply bridging polysilicon over the diffusion area.
- Contact-layer programming ROM: A bit is encoded by the presence or absence of a via, which connects the vertical metal bitline with the diffusion area as illustrated in Fig. 10.15B.
- Metal-layer programming ROM: The binary information is encoded by short circuiting the transistor, or not as shown in Fig. 10.15C.
- Implant programming ROM: The different logic state is achieved by different doping levels in the diffusion area (see Fig. 10.15D). Generally, higher doping levels will raise the on/off voltage threshold, which will disable the transistor.

Compared to ROM, EEPROM provides users with the capability to reprogram its content. As shown in Fig. 10.16A, one bit cell of EEPROM is composed of two transistors: floating gate transistor (FGT) and select transistor (ST). The FGT is feathered with two stacked gates: a control gate (CG) and a floating gate (FG). The logic state of the bit cell is encoded in the FGT by the presence or absence of electrons stored in the FG. Being isolated electrically, the FG can retain the electrons when powered off. Flash memory (see Fig. 10.16B) has almost the same structure as EEPROM, except for the absence of ST, which is irrelevant to the logic state, and only allows EEPROM to be byte addressable.

An FPGA bitstream is essentially a vector of bits encoding the netlist information in FPGA, which defines hardware resources usage, interconnection, and initial states at the lowest level of abstraction. The logic blocks are configured to represent the basic digital circuit primitives, such as combinational logic gates and registers. The connection blocks and switch blocks are configured to be the interconnections between different logic blocks. Other hardware resources, such as I/O buffers, embedded RAM, and multipliers, can be programmed according to different requirements. Therefore, all information about the netlist can be obtained from the bitstream file.

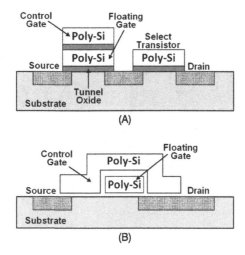

FIGURE 10.16

Illustrations of (A) EEPROM and (B) Flash.

10.2.6.2 ROM RE

To reverse engineer the ROM content, one can take advantage of modern optical and electron microscopy to observe the binary states of each cell, as indicated below:

- Active-layer programming ROM: The metal layer and poly layer need to be removed using the delayering approaches discussed in Section 10.4, for they will obscure the active layer underneath.
- Contact-layer programming ROM: It is much easier to reverse engineer this kind of ROM, as there is often no need to delayer the metal layer and the poly layer. In the relatively old ROM technology, the contact layer is clearly visible, but in more modern technologies, some delaying is still needed to expose the contact layer before observation.
- Metal-layer programming ROM: This type of ROM can be directly observed under a microscope without having to perform any delayering process.
- Implant programming ROM: This type of ROM is inherently resistant to optical microscopy, as different logic states appear identical. To observe the impact of different doping levels, additional dopant-selective crystallographic etch techniques [62] should be utilized to separate the two logic states.

Generally, ROM only provides limited protection against RE. Among all types of ROM, the metal-layer programming ROM offers the worst security, because the metal layer is easy to obtain with little effort, whereas the implant programming ROM provides the highest level of protection available.

10.2.6.3 EEPROM/Flash RE

Since EEPROM and Flash memory have similar structures and the same logic storage mechanism (as discussed earlier), they often can be reverse engineered by the same procedures. Considering that EEPROM/Flash represent different states by electrons, not by the geometric difference, x-ray technology

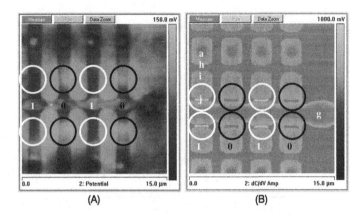

FIGURE 10.17

(A) SKPM scan and (B) SCM scan from the backside of Flash memory [64].

cannot be used to detect the contents. Further, any attempt to delayer and measure the electrons in the FG, such as SEM and TEM, will change the electron distribution, thereby disturbing the content inside.

For quite long time, the EEPROM/Flash technology has been regarded as the most robust memory defense against RE. Recently, several methods [63–65], although very expensive and requiring specialized equipment, were proposed to extract the contents in EEPROM/Flash correctly. Note that both of the following methods are applied from the backside of the memory, as traditional front-side delaying and imaging will cause the charges in the FG to vanish [63].

Scanning Kelvin probe microscopy procedure. The scanning Kelvin probe microscopy (SKPM) procedure [66] directly probes the FG potential through the tunnel oxide layer with a thickness of 10 nm, which isolates the FG with the transistor channel as illustrated in Fig. 10.16A. Thus, the first step is to remove the silicon from the back side of the memory, and leave the tunnel oxide layer undamaged to avoid charging/discharging of the FG. Then, the bit value can be read under the SKPM scan by applying a DC voltage to the probe tip. As shown in Fig. 10.17A, the scanning data from SKPM shows the 2D distributions of potential difference between the tip and the memory cell. The potential difference between the charged FG (associated with "0") and the tip is much higher than that between the uncharged FG (associated with "1") and the tip, which leads to a brighter area for the bit "0" (circled in black in Fig. 10.17A).

Scanning capacitance microscopy (SCM) procedure. Unlike the SKPM procedure, the SCM procedure measures the capacitance variations between the tip (with the sample in the contact mode) and the high-sensitivity capacitance SCM's sensor [67]. Given the fact that the holes will be coupled in the transistor channel with the existing electrons in the FG, the SCM sensor will detect the logic states via probing the carrier (hole) concentration. Thus, the back-side delayering should keep a silicon thickness of 50 to 300 nm to leave the transistor channel undamaged. Then, the bit information can be read as depicted in Fig. 10.17B. The SCM signal shows that the charged FG (associated with "0") has a darker signal (circled in black), which is consistent with high density of holes.

Comparisons between the SKPM procedure and the SCM procedure are summarized in Table 10.5. Note that with technology scaling, the electrons stored in the FG have been reduced to fewer than 1000

Table 10.5 Comparison between SKPM and SCM procedures

Property	SKPM Procedure	SCM Procedure
Delayering position	Back side	Back side
Delayering depth	Entire silicon	50–300 nm thickness
Sensitivity	Low	High
Measured carriers	Electrons	Holes
Measured parameter	Potential	Capacitance
Operation mode	Noncontact	Contact
Application	All EEPROM and some Flash	All EEPROM and Flash

electrons for 90nm-node NAND Flash [64]. In this case, the SKPM procedure can no longer recognize two logic states accurately, whereas the SCM still performs well.

10.2.6.4 RE of FPGAs

FPGA RE involves analyzing the configuration bitstream file and transforming the bitstream file into the hardware netlist, which consists of all components and interconnections at the RTL. To fulfill this goal, hackers need to go through the following steps: get access to the bitstream file from the Flash memory, decrypt the bitstream (if encrypted), and finally build the mapping relationship between the bitstream file and the netlist.

Bitstream Access. SRAM-based FPGA stores the logic cells states in the SRAM, which cannot retain the data after power loss. Therefore, an external NVM device (typically Flash) is adopted to hold the configuration bitstream file and transfer the bitstream file at system boot-up to initiate the SRAM in FPGA. The separation between the bitstream file and FPGA makes it easy to dump the contents of the bitstream file. By using a logic analyzer, one can easily wiretap the JTAG data and command lines to capture the communication between the FPGA and Flash memory during startup.

Bitstream Decryption. To increase the security level of FPGA, most FPGA manufacturers encrypts the bitstream file before storing it in the Flash memory with the encryption standards, such as triple data encryption standard (DES) and advanced encryption standard (AES) [68]. Now the wiretapped encrypted bitstreams will not yield any information for RE, as long as the cryptographic key remains hidden inside the FPGA.

The bitstream decryption process in FPGA RE depends entirely on the attacker's ability to discover the key. Typically, the keys are stored in the embedded NVM by programming the FPGA before loading the encrypted bitstream into FPGA. The invasive and destructive attacks to find out the cryptographic key are usually infeasible, as they will trigger tamper detection in the FPGA to zeroize the secret keys. Thus far, no public report exists on a successful invasive attack toward SRAM-based FPGA.

Recently, it has been reported that the bitstream encryption of several mainstream FPGA series [69–71] is vulnerable to the side channel attacks (SCAs) [72]. Basically, an SCA is a noninvasive attack to exploit the relationship between physical information (power, timing, and electromagnetic emanation) and certain hardware operations in the FPGA implementation. The triple DES encrypted bitstream file from the Xilinx VirtexII Pro FPGA was successfully cracked by the SCA the first time in [69]. The leaked timing and power consumption information is collected when the encrypted bitstream is decrypted by the dedicated hardware engine within the FPGA. By analyzing the collected power consumption and timing behavior, the hypothetical structure of the internal triple DES module can be verified. Finally, the divide-and-conquer approach is applied to guess and verify a small portion of the key (for example, six bits for triple DES), which reduces the computation's complexity. This process is repeated until the entire key is obtained. The more recent Xilinx FPGAs (Virtex-4 and Virtex-5), which employ a more advanced encryption module (AES-256), have been cracked in [70] by a more sophisticated type of correlation power analysis [73].

In a similar way, the FPGA power consumption or electromagnetic radiation is measured, while the decryption block is operating in the FPGA. More recently, the cryptographic keys in the Altera's Stratix II and Stratix III FPGA families have also been revealed by the same SCA [71]. The fact that all of the preceding attacks can be conducted within several hours reveals the vulnerability of the bitstream encryption.

Bitstream Reversal. Prior to converting the bitstream file into the corresponding hardware netlist, one needs to understand the bitstream structure, which is usually documented by FPGA vendors, and is accessible online. Typically, a bitstream file consists of four parts [74]: command header, configuration payload, command footer, and startup sequence. In the case of the Xilinx FPGA, the configuration payload determines the configuration points (such as LUT, memory, register, and multiplexer) and the programmable interconnection points (switch box). The goal of the bitstream reversal is to find out the mapping relationship between the configuration payload with the configuration points, and the programmable interconnection points. However, this mapping relationship is proprietary and undocumented, which makes the bitstream file itself serve as an obfuscated design to protect the hardware netlist. In the past decade, there have been several attempts to achieve a bitstream reversal.

- *Partial bitstream reversal.* This kind of bitstream reversal only focuses on extracting some specific configurable blocks in FPGA, such as the LUT, configurable logic block, and multiplier from the bitstream file. [75] shows the possibility to identify the embedded IP cores by extracting the contents of the LUT in the Xilinx Virtex-II FPGA.
- *Full bitstream reversal.* [76] makes the first public attempt to convert the bitstream file into the netlist. The set-theoretic algorithm and cross-correlation algorithm [76] were used to build a database linking the bitstream bits to the associated resources (configuration points and programmable interconnect points) in the FPGA. Then, the database is utilized to produce the desired netlist based on any given bitstream file in Xilinx Virtex-II, Virtex-4 LXT, and Virtex-5 LXT FPGAs. This method, however, cannot fully create the netlist, as it only relies on the information from the accessible Xilinx design language (XDL) file, generated from the Xilinx EDA tool, which only provides information on the active configurable resources. The missing information on the static, unused configurable resources in the FPGA, places it some distance away from full bitstream reversal. In [77], XDLRC (Xilinx design language report), a more detailed file generated from Xilinx EDA tool, is used to enhance the creation of the mapping database. Unlike XDL, the XDLRC file can offer all of the information available about active and static configurable resources. However, the test results in [77] indicate new issues that the cross-correlation algorithm cannot perfectly relate all resources in the FPGA with the bits in the bitstream file. Therefore, due to the absence of well-developed bitstream reversal technique, the FPGA embedded system is more robust against RE, compared to ASIC designs and microcontroller designs.

10.2.7 SYSTEM-LEVEL ANTI-RE

In this section, the solutions to increase the cost of RE on firmware and FPGA bitstreams are analyzed and discussed.

10.2.7.1 Anti-RE for ROMs

The most effective solution for increasing the complexity and difficulty of RE against ROM is to use the camouflage method. Simply speaking, the designer makes all of the memory cells identical under optical inspection, no matter what the contents. This type of solution, although increases the costs of manufacture, will force the attacker to spend considerably more time, money, and effort to get access to the ROM contents. Recall that for the implant programming ROM in Section 10.2.6.1, the use of different doping levels to encode information constitutes one kind of camouflage technique. Several other camouflage techniques are provided next.

Camouflage Contacts. Different from the contact-layer programming ROM (see Fig. 10.15B), where the absence or presence of contact will expose the logic states, the camouflage contacts act as false connections between the metal layer and active layer to make the true contacts and the false contacts indistinguishable under optical microscopy [78]. To decode the contents, careful chemical etching has to be applied to find the real contacts, and this is time consuming. From the viewpoint of time/cost, this technique will also increase production periods, and lower the manufacturing yield.

Camouflage Transistors. To improve the security of active-layer programming ROM (see Fig. 10.15A), false transistors are made to confuse the RE attempts, instead of using the absence of transistors [79]. The false transistors, essentially with no electrical functions, have the same top-down view as the true transistors under an optical microscope. To crack the information, the attackers have to use more advanced electrical microscopes to analyze the top view and even the cross-sectional view of the ROM, which is usually economically prohibitive. This kind of design will definitely increase the difficulty of RE on the large scale, whereas it only requires minimal effort during manufacturing.

Camouflage Nanowires. Through the use of nano material, ROM cells are fabricated within the vertical connections between the bit lines and the word lines of a ROM array [80]. The real connections between bit lines and word lines act as transistors, whereas the nonelectrical dummy connections only play the role of design camouflage. Due to the small dimensions of the nanowires, the tiny differences between the dummy connections and real connections are indiscernible, even under advanced electrical microscopy. The major challenge with camouflage nanowires, however, is to manufacture the ROM at high enough volume and yield.

Practically all of the preceding camouflage techniques only need to be adopted on a portion of the whole ROM. To develop a stronger anti-RE ROM, more than one anti-RE technique can be used at once.

Antifuse one-time programming. Admittedly, traditional ROMs are inherently vulnerable to RE procedures. Even ROMs equipped with auxiliary anti-RE designs can only offer limited protection against destructive and invasive RE, though they make the design and fabrication process much more complicated. Currently, ROM replacements (example, antifuse one-time programming (AF-OTP) memory devices) are gaining considerable interest.

The AF-OTP memory exploits, whether the gate oxide is in breakdown or is intact to indicate two logic states. Gate oxide breakdown is achieved after fabrication by applying high voltage to the gate of the transistor. Among several proposed structures [81–83], the split channel 1T transistor antifuse [83] exhibits many advantages over the conventional ROM, with respect to cell area, access speed, and

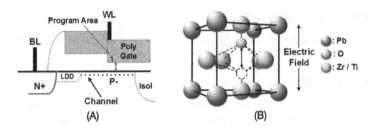

FIGURE 10.18

Illustrations of one memory cell antifuse-OTP (A) and ferroelectric RAM (FeRAM) (B).

immunity to RE. As shown in Fig. 10.18A, the antifuse transistor acts like a capacitor when unprogrammed, but a conductive path will be formed once the oxide is ruptured following the programming operation. Due to the angstrom-level difference between the programmed and unprogrammed antifuse, existing RE techniques (for example, delayering from either the front side or back side, FIB-based voltage contrast [84], and top-down view or cross-sectional view from electrical microscopy) will not expose any information contained, not to mention the fact that it is difficult to locate the oxide breakdown. Additionally, the antifuse memory is compatible with the standard CMOS technology, and thus no additional masks or processing steps are required for fabrication. Considering the security, performance, and cost, the antifuse memory may eventually replace current ROM devices with the feature size continuously scaling down [82].

10.2.7.2 Anti-RE for EEPROMs/Flashs

To reverse engineer the EEPROM/Flash memory, attackers prefer to delayer from the back side to avoid disturbing the floating charges. Thus, the most effective countermeasure would be to prevent back-side attacks. Here, some back-side attack detection methods are briefly introduced, and then one alternative to EEPROM/Flash is reviewed, which can inherently tolerate the back-side attacks.

Circuit parameter sensing. Performing the delayering process from the back side will thin the bulk silicon. By burying two parallel plates in the bulk silicon to form a capacitor, the capacitance sensing [85] can detect the capacitance reduction when the attacker polishes from the back side. When the capacitance reaches below a certain threshold, it will trigger the EEPROM/Flash memory to activate an erase operation. The capacitor, perpendicular to the bulk silicon, was previously a challenge to achieve. Fortunately, the emergence of the through-silicon via technique [86] makes it much easier to fabricate. Similarly, other parameters, such as resistance [87], can be measured and compared to the predefined reference resistance threshold.

Light Sensing. By optically monitoring the back side of the chip, the light-sensing method will equip at least one pair of light-emitting and light-sensing devices in the front side of chip, and light reflection module at the bottom of the silicon bulk [88]. The light-emitting device is configured to emit light, which can penetrate the bulk, be reflected by the light reflection module, and then be collected by the light-sensing device. Once the delayering is applied, the changes in light distribution at the light-sensing device can trigger the self-destruction of the data contained in the memory. This method can certainly make the RE process more time consuming. However, the costs associated with manufacturing and the power consumption from continuous light emitting, and sensing, make it less attractive in practice.

It is worth mentioning that once the detection signal generated from the preceding sensing methods is activated, the memory will automatically erase all or part of its contents. This policy, however, will not cause too much trouble for the RE attackers. For example, the attack can either isolate the charge pump, which provides the power to erase, or ground the detection signal by using a FIB to eventually render all detection-erasure methods useless. In addition, even if the memory successfully erases all of the contents, the attackers still have the chance to determine the actual values according to the residual electrons on the FG due to data remanence [89].

Ferroelectric RAM memory. As mentioned previously, the use of electrons on FGs to represent the logic states makes the EEPROM/Flash memory vulnerable to RE. Recently, ferroelectric RAM (FeRAM) has been shown to be a promising candidate for replacing EEPROM/Flash memory. The motive for FeRAM development is to substantially shorten write time, and lower write power consumption. Recently, it was reported that FeRAM can still possess very strong protections for the contained state [90].

Distinct from the EEPROM/Flash storage mechanism, FeRAM stores data by the polarization states of molecules. These kinds of molecules, located at the middle layer of an FeRAM cell, are capacitors filled with a ferroelectric crystalline material, usually a lead-zirconium-titanate (PZT or $Pb(ZrTi)O_3$) compound. As shown in Fig. 10.18B, the two polarization states, simply the shift up/down of Zr/Ti atom in PZT, represent two different logic states. Due to the high dielectric constant of PZT, the states remain, and only flip under the external electric field.

Due to the special state representations, the difference between two states under optical and electrical inspection is invisible. This is because the distance of the shift up/down (see Fig. 10.18B) is in the scale of nanometer, thereby exposing nothing to the top-down view. One possible attack to reveal the contents, although economically prohibitive, is to carefully slice and analyze the cross-sectional view under SKPM/SCM cell by cell to inspect the difference between the two states.

10.2.7.3 Anti-RE for FPGAs

The fact that the encrypted SRAM FPGA can provide enough RE resilience leaves less space for the research and development of anti-RE techniques compared to the ASIC design. Nevertheless, the existing FPGA anti-RE techniques are categorized into three groups according to the FPGA RE procedure (bitstream hiding, side-channel resistance, and bitstream antireversal). Following is a description of each of these groups:

Bitstream hiding. By integrating the bitstream storage memory with FPGA, the Flash FPGA and antifuse FPGA [91] do not require external configuration memory, leaving the direct wiretapping useless. Unlike the SRAM FPGA, the Flash FPGA does not need bitstream download during powerup, due to the Flash memory nonvolatility. The antifuse FPGA has been widely used in military applications because of its higher RE resilience. As discussed in Sections 10.2.6.3 and 10.2.7.1, an attempt to delayer the Flash memory and antifuse memory, let alone the Flash FPGA and antifuse FPGA, to read out the memory contents, is quite challenging and requires specialized equipment. Although these FPGAs require more fabrication steps than SRAM FPGA, and lack enough programmability due to limited writing times of the Flash/antifuse memories, they are becoming the dominant choice in critical applications.

Side-channel resistance. The recent success of SCAs on the FPGA proves that the leakage of information poses a large threat to FPGA security. Thus, it is necessary to develop the side-channel resistance designs to protect the cryptographic keys. Intuitively, the most effective side-channel resis-

Table 10.6 Costs of anti-RE techniques and RE for system level

Anti-RE Techniques		Anti-RE Cost	RE Cost	Yield Loss
ROM	Camouflage contacts	High	Moderate	Low
	Camouflage transistors	Low	High	Moderate
	Camouflage nanowires	High	High	High
	AF-OTP	Low	Very high	Very low
EEPROM/Flash	Circuit parameter sensing	Moderate	Low	Moderate
	Light sensing	High	Low	Moderate
	FeRAM memory	Moderate	Very high	Very low
FPGA	Bitstream hiding	Very low	High	–
	Side-channel resistance	Moderate	High	–
	Bitstream antireversal	Low	High	–

tance design is to remove the dependency between deciphering operations and power consumption. Tiris et al. [92] presented a dynamic and differential CMOS logic implementation. This technique utilizes a constant power consumption and circuit delay, irrespective of different circuit operations. Wu et al. [93] proposed to adopt the asynchronous logic design to obtain power consumption independent of computations and data. These methods, although effective against SCA, lead to much larger area and power consumptions compared to the standard CMOS logic.

Another group of side-channel resistance designs can be found in the noise addition group. By introducing random power noise to make the power consumption of decryption nondeterministic, it is quite difficult for the attacker to determine which part of the power consumption is from the decryption. Again, this kind of method will introduce new power consumption. In [94], the power reduction technique is proposed to lower the power consumption overhead from noise generation.

Bitstream antireversal. Until now, full bitstream reversal has only been theoretically possible. As one can imagine, the invasive attacks in the future may successfully find out the entire mapping between the encoding bits from the bitstream file and the hardware resources in the FPGA. FPGA vendors should study potential countermeasures to impede bitstream reversal under noninvasive attacks. Currently, bitstream reversal strongly depends on the amount of publicly available information (for example, user guides) and undocumented information (for instance, files generated by EDA tools). It would do well for FPGA vendors to take the possibility of RE attacks into account when releasing new information to hinder potential bitstream reversal attempts.

Another consideration is partial configuration. The critical configuration bits in the bitstream file (such as the IP core) are stored in the Flash memory within the FPGA, whereas other noncritical parts are still loaded from the external memory. This partial configuration only leaves the wiretapper partial information about the whole FPGA mapping information, thereby fundamentally eliminating the potential of bitstream reversal.

10.2.7.4 Summary of Anti-RE Techniques for System Level

Table 10.6 illustrates the cost and the associated yield loss of the system-level anti-RE techniques discussed next. To assess the feasibility of the anti-RE techniques, the costs of RE/anti-RE are classified into five levels based on the previous discussions: very low, low, moderate, high, and very high. It is worth mentioning that the costs of anti-RE techniques mainly consist of the design and manufacturing costs, whereas the yield loss is estimated from the manufacturing perspective. Other factors, such as power, area, and reliability are not included for lack of open literature. Note also that Table 10.6 only reflects present RE/anti-RE costs. With more effective RE/anti-RE techniques emerging in the future, both RE and anti-RE costs will vary accordingly. In practice, the techniques with lower costs for anti-RE, but higher costs for RE, in Table 10.6 will be more preferably accepted. For ROM, the best choice is clearly antifuse OTP, which has low anti-RE costs, but makes RE very challenging. For EEPROM/Flash, the options are limited, but FeRAM appears to be the most promising. Finally, for FPGAs, bitstream hiding stands out as the best candidate.

10.3 PROBING ATTACK

Physical attacks are capable of bypassing the confidentiality and integrity provided by modern cryptography through observation of a chip's silicon implementation. Such attacks are especially threatening to the integrated circuits (ICs) in smartcards, smartphones, military systems, and financial systems, which process sensitive information. Unlike noninvasive side channel analysis (for example, power or timing analysis), probing directly accesses the internal wires of a security-critical module and extracts sensitive information in electronic format. Probing, in unison with reverse engineering and circuit edit, poses a serious threat to mission-critical applications, and thus demands development of effective countermeasures from the research community [95].

Probing attacks are already a part of the current reality. The most recent example of it emerged when FBI requested help in defeating the passcode retry counter of the Apple iPhone 5c owned by a terrorist suspect. Researchers reverse engineered the proprietary protocol used by the phone's NAND flash, mirrored (copied) the contents, and then brute-forced the passcode in less than a day [96]. While in this case the attack was conducted by researchers, compromise of military technologies through probing could have catastrophic consequences that cost lives. In such instances, advanced IC failure analysis and debug tools are used to internally probe the ICs. Among such tools, focused ion beam (FIB) is the most dangerous.

FIBs use ions at high beam currents for site-specific milling and material removal. The same ions can also be injected close to a surface for material deposition. These capabilities allow FIBs to cut or add traces to the substrate within a chip, thereby enabling them to redirect signals, modify trace paths, and add/remove circuits. Though FIB was initially designed for failure analysis, a skilled attacker can use it to obtain on-chip keys, establish privileged access to memory, obtain device configuration, and/or inject faults. This can be accomplished by rerouting them to an existing output pin, creating a new contact for probing, or reenabling IC test mode. Most of these techniques would not be possible without a FIB. While countermeasures against probing, such as active meshes, optical sensors, and analog sensors have been proposed, they are clumsy, expensive, and ad-hoc. It has been shown time and again that an experienced FIB operator can easily bypass them via circuit edit. In [97], well-known hacker Christopher Tarnovsky probed the firmware of the Infineon SLE 66CX680P/PE security/smart chip from the frontside (that is, top metal layer) by rewiring its active mesh, and making contact with its buses using FIB.

FIB-assisted probing attacks are expected to increase for a variety of reasons. FIBs are becoming cheaper and easier to access than ever before (for example, FIB time can be purchased for a couple hundred dollars per hour). Further, as FIB capabilities continue to improve for failure analysis, more powerful attacks will be enabled. In contrast, non-invasive and semi-invasive attacks either do not scale to modern semiconductors with Moore's law, or can be mitigated by inexpensive countermeasures. As non-invasive and semi-invasive attacks continue to become less effective, one can expect attackers to migrate to FIB. For these reasons, it is of the utmost importance to stay ahead of attackers and develop more effective countermeasures against FIB-based probing. Since FIB capabilities are almost limitless, the best approaches should make probing as costly, time consuming, and frustrating as possible. A significant challenge in doing so lies in the fact that the time, effort, and cost to design a FIB-resistant chip must remain reasonable, especially to design engineers who are generally not security experts. This could be especially important in the upcoming internet-of-things (IoT) era, which will likely consist of an abundance of low-end chips that are easily physically accessed.

In this section, the state-of-the-art research in the field of circuit edit and anti-probing is presented, the challenges are highlighted, and future research directions for CAD and test communities are offered. The rest of the chapter is organized as follows: Section 10.3.1 reviews technical background related to probing attacks and Section 10.3.2 introduces existing countermeasures against probing attacks and their limitations.

10.3.1 PROBING ATTACK FUNDAMENTALS

Comprehension of the adversary's goal and the techniques he/she uses to successfully carry out probing is the first step in overcoming this significant threat. In this section, technical details of the probing process are reviewed, and associations between technical requirements, decisions, and perceived limitations of state-of-the-art techniques are made.

10.3.1.1 Probing Attack Targets

It is essential for both attackers and countermeasure designers to determine which signals are more likely to be targeted in a probing attack. Such signals are termed as *assets*. An asset is a resource of value, which is worth protecting from an adversary [98]. Unfortunately, a more palpable definition of asset has not been proposed or agreed upon. To help illustrate the wide range of possible information that could be assets, here a few quintessential examples that are the most likely targets for probing attacks are enumerated.

Keys: Keys of an encryption module (for example, private key of a public key algorithm) are archetypal assets. They are usually stored in nonvolatile memory on the chip. If the key is leaked, the root of trust it provides will become compromised, and could serve as a gateway to more serious attacks. An example is original equipment manufacturer (OEM) keys that are used to grant legitimate access to a product, or chip. Leakage of such keys will result in tremendous loss of revenue for the product owner, denial of service, or information leakage.

Firmware and configuration bitstream: Electronic intellectual properties (IPs), such as low-level program instruction sets, manufacturer firmware, and FPGA configuration bitstreams are often sensitive, mission critical, and/or contain trade secrets of the IP owner. Once compromised, counterfeiting, cloning, or exploits of system vulnerabilities could be facilitated.

On-device protected data: Sensitive data, such as health and personal identifiable information, should be kept private. Leakage of such information could result in fraud, embarrassment, or property/brand damage for the data owner.

Device configuration: Device configuration data control the access permissions to the device. They specify which services or resources can be accessed by each individual user. If the configurations are tampered with, an attacker could illegally gain access to resources to which, otherwise, he/she had no access.

Cryptographic random number: Hardware generated random numbers, such as keys, nonces, one-time pads, and initialization vectors for cryptographic primitives also require protection. Compromising this type of asset will weaken the cryptographic strength of the digital services on the device.

10.3.1.2 Essential Technologies for a Probing Attack

A successful probing attack entails a time-consuming and sophisticated process. Countermeasure designers are often interested in ways to make this process go astray. For this purpose, the central approaches and technologies used in published attacks in the following sections are examined.

Front-side vs. back-side: Probing attack targets are those metal wires that carry assets, henceforth called target wires. The most common approach to reach target wires is to expose them from the back end of line (BEOL), that is, from the top metal layer towards silicon substrate (illustrated in Fig. 10.19A). This is called a front-side probing attack. Exposure of target wires is first facilitated with FIB milling. Then, an electric connection to the target wire can be established, for example, by conductor deposition capability of the FIB. Finally, extraction of sensitive information ensues.

A back-side probing attack, that is, probing that occurs through the silicon substrate, was proposed in [99]. Back-side attack targets are not limited to wires. By exploiting a phenomenon during transistor activity, known as photon emission, transistors can also be probed to extract information.

Electrical probing vs. optical probing: The method to access assets shown in Fig. 10.19A is typical for electrical probing, that is, accessing an asset carrying signal via electrical connection. A different approach is optical probing, as shown in Fig. 10.19B. Optical probing techniques are often used in back-side probing to capture photon-emission phenomena during transistor switching. When transistors are switching, they spontaneously emit photons without external stimuli. By passively receiving and analyzing the photons emitted from a specific transistor, the signal processed by that transistor can be inferred. Compared to electrical probing, the optical approach has the advantage of being a purely passive observation, which makes it very difficult to detect. In addition to photon emission analysis, laser voltage technique (LVX), or electro-optical frequency modulation (EOFM), are also used during back-side attacks. These techniques actively illuminate the switching transistors, and then infer asset signal values by observing the reflected light.

The primary deficiency of optical probing lies in the fact that photons emitted in these techniques are infrared, due to silicon energy band gap, which has a wavelength of 900 nm or higher [99]. Therefore, the optical resolution between transistors is limited to within one order of magnitude of the wavelength, due to Rayleigh criterion.

10.3.1.3 Essential Steps of a Probing Attack

In this subsection, the examination of probing attack fundamentals are continued by outlining its essential steps.

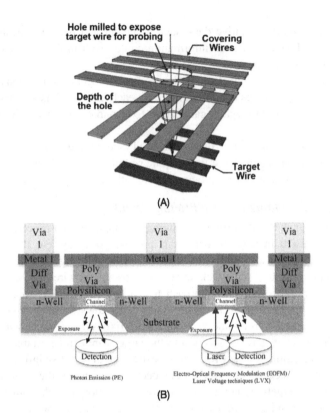

FIGURE 10.19

(A) Milling from BEOL through covering wires (purple and green [medium and light gray in print version, respectively]) to reach target wires (blue [dark gray in print version]); (B) Optical probing: photon emission (PE) and electro-optical frequency modulation (EOFM), or laser voltage techniques (LVX) are used for passive and active measurements, respectively.

Decapsulation: The first stage of most invasive physical attacks is to either partially or fully remove the chip package in order to expose the silicon die. This requires adequate practice and expertise in handling harmful chemicals. Acid solutions, such as fuming nitric acid combined with acetone at 60 °C, are often used to remove plastic packages [100]. Decapsulation can also be done from the back-side of the chip by removing the copper plate mechanically, without chemical etching.

Reverse Engineering: Reverse engineering [55] is the process of extracting design information from something, typically to reproduce it. In the case of probing, reverse engineering is used to understand how the chip works, which requires that the layout and netlist be extracted. By studying the netlist, the attacker can identify the assets. One-to-one correspondence between the netlist and layout can then determine the locations of target wires and buses; and in the event where cutting off a wire is unavoidable, determining whether the cut would impact asset extraction. State-of-the-art tools, such as ICWorks from Chipworks, can perform automatic extraction of netlists from images of each layer

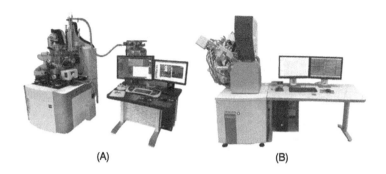

FIGURE 10.20

(A) Scanning electron microscope (SEM); (B) Focused ion beam (FIB). Note that attacker does not need to purchase all these instruments since rent by time is quite low-cost.

taken with optical or scanning electron microscopes (SEM in Fig. 10.20A), which greatly reduces the attacker's effort.

Locating target wires: Once the probing wire targets have been identified by reverse engineering, the next stage is locating the wires associated with the target on the IC under attack. The crux of the problem here is that while the attacker has located target wires on sacrificial devices during reverse engineering process, he/she now has to find the absolute coordinates of the point to mill blindly. This requires a precise-enough kinematic mount, and fiducial markers (that is, visual points of reference on the device) to base these absolute coordinates.

Reaching target wire and extracting information: With the help of modern circuit editing tools like FIB (see Fig. 10.20B), a hole can be milled to expose the target wire. State-of-the-art FIBs can remove and deposit material with nanometer resolution, which allows an attacker with a FIB to edit out obstructing circuitry, or deposit conducting paths that may serve as electrical probe contacts. This feature indicates that many countermeasures can be disabled by simply disconnecting a few wires, and that a FIB-equipped attacker could field as many concurrent probes as logic analyzer allows. Once a target wire is exposed—assuming it is contacted without triggering any probing alarm signals from active or analog shields—the asset signals need to be extracted, for example, with a probe station. The difficulty of this step depends on a few factors. First, software and hardware processes might need to be completed before the asset is available. Further, the sensitive information may not be in the same clock cycle. If the chip has an internal clock source to prevent external manipulation, the attacker will need to either disable it, or synchronize his own clock with it.

10.3.2 EXISTING COUNTERMEASURES AND LIMITATIONS

In the past decade, researchers have proposed various technologies to protect security-critical circuits against probing attacks. In this section, a few representative countermeasures are reviewed and their limitations are highlighted. Unfortunately, to date, none of them offer a satisfactory solution. Further, no method has been proposed to adequately address back-side probing attacks.

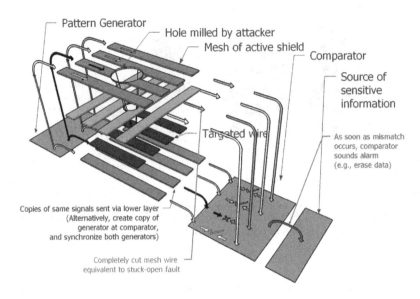

Pattern Generator

Hole milled by attacker

Mesh of active shield

Comparator

Source of sensitive information

As soon as mismatch occurs, comparator sounds alarm (e.g., erase data)

Targeted wire

Copies of same signals sent via lower layer (Alternatively, create copy of generator at comparator, and synchronize both generators)

Completely cut mesh wire equivalent to stuck-open fault

FIGURE 10.21

Basic working principle of active shields.

10.3.2.1 Active Shields

Active shield is, so far, the most investigated probing countermeasure. In this approach, a shield which carries signals is placed on the top-most metal layer to detect holes milled by FIB. The shield is referred to as "active" because signals on these top layer wires are constantly monitored to detect if milling has cut them [101]. Figure 10.21 shows one illustrative example. As shown in the figure, a digital pattern is generated from a pattern generator, transmitted through the shield wires on top-most metal layer, and then compared with a copy of itself transmitted from lower layer. If an attacker mills through the shield wires on top layer to reach target wire, the hole is expected to cut open one or more shield wires, thereby leading to a mismatch at the comparator and triggering an alarm signal to erase or stop generating sensitive information. Despite its popularity, active shields are not without shortcomings. Their biggest problems are that they impose large overheads on the design, but at the same time are very vulnerable to attacks with advanced FIBs, for example, circuit editing attacks.

10.3.2.2 Analog Shields and Sensors

An alternative approach to active shield is to construct an analog shield. Instead of generating, transmitting, and comparing digital patterns, analog shields monitor parametric disturbances with its mesh wires.

In addition to shield designs, the probe attempt detector (PAD) [102] (shown in Fig. 10.22) also uses capacitance measurement on selected security critical wires to detect additional capacitance introduced by a metal probe. Compared to active shields, analog shields detect probing without test patterns and require less area overhead. The PAD technique is also unique in remaining effective against electrical

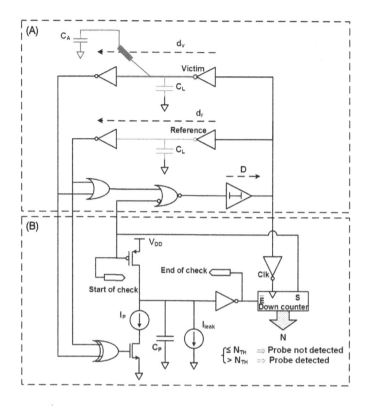

FIGURE 10.22

Probing attempt detector (PAD).

probing from the back-side. The problem with analog sensors or shields is that analog measurements are less reliable due to process variations, a problem further exacerbated by feature scaling.

10.3.2.3 t-Private Circuits

The t-private circuit technique is proposed in [103] based on the assumption that the number of concurrent probe channels that an attacker could use is limited, and exhausting this resource deters an attack. In this technique, the circuit of a security-critical block is transformed so that at least $t + 1$ probes are required within one clock cycle to extract one bit of information. First, masking is applied to split computation into multiple separate variables, where an important binary signal x is encoded into $t + 1$ binary signals by XORing it with t independently generated random signals ($r_{t+1} = x \oplus r_1 \oplus \cdots \oplus r_t$) as shown in Fig. 10.23. Then, computations on x are performed in its encoded form in the transformed circuit. x can be recovered (decoded) by computing $x = r_1 \oplus \cdots \oplus r_t \oplus r_{t+1}$. The major issue with t-private circuit is that the area overhead involved for the transformation is prohibitively expensive.

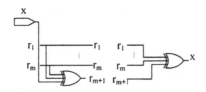

FIGURE 10.23

Input encoder (left) and output decoder (right) for masking in t-private circuits.

10.3.2.4 Other Countermeasure Designs

Some other countermeasures are implemented in real ICs, but less reported as novel designs because they are more or less dated. One known countermeasure that deters decapsulation stage of probing attacks is a light sensor that is sometimes included in a tamper-resistant design. Some other techniques include scrambling wires and avoiding repetitive patterns in shield mesh to impede the locating-target-wire stage of probing attacks. They are not particularly effective as exploits against them have been detailed in [97].

10.4 INVASIVE FAULT INJECTION ATTACK

Another type of physical attack that proved to be very effective to compromise cryptographic devices and processor's control flow is the invasive fault injection attack, which is realized through injecting faults by laser or focused ion beam (FIB) into a cryptographic device, and observing the corresponding outputs [104–106]. Using differential fault analysis (DFA) [107] methods, the secret key can be extracted. The fault injection techniques involved in this type of attack relies on having direct access to the silicon die, and the ability to target individual transistors in a very precise manner. These techniques are very powerful and have been demonstrated to be highly successful attack methods [108,109].

One example of optical fault injection techniques is a strong and precisely focused light beam that affects the behavior of one or more logic gates in a circuit. A strong radiation of a transistor may form a temporary conductive channel in the dielectric, which, in turn, may cause the switch of a state. For example, by targeting one of the transistors in a static random-access memory (SRAM) cell, the value stored in this cell could be flipped up or down at will [61,110].

A standard SRAM cell consists of six transistors, as shown in Fig. 10.24. Two pairs of p- and n-channel transistors create a flip-flop, while two other n-channel transistors are used for read and write. If the transistor VT1 could be opened for a very short time, then the state of the flip-flop could be changed. By exposing the transistor VT4 to light, the state of the cell would be switched to the opposite value. The main anticipated difficulties are: focusing the ionizing radiation down to several micrometers spot and choosing the proper intensity. The Microchip PIC16F84 microcontroller with 68 bytes of on-chip SRAM memory was used [110]. The light from a photo flash lamp was focused using the microscope optics. By shielding the light from the flash with an aperture made from aluminum foil, the state of only one cell can be changed. Focusing the light spot from the lamp on the area shown by

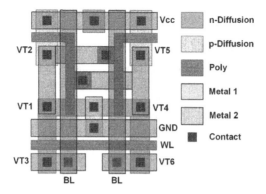

FIGURE 10.24

Layout of SRAM cell.

the white circle caused the cell to change its state from "1" to "0". By focusing the spot on the area shown by the black circle, the cell changed its state from "0" to "1", or remained in state "1".

Since the currents flowing inside a floating gate cell are much smaller than inside a SRAM cell, EPROM, EEPROM, and Flash memory cells are more vulnerable to fault injection attacks. EEPROM and Flash memory devices can be attacked by local heating technique [111], which use lasers to achieve modification. This was implemented with inexpensive laser diode module mounted on a microscope. The contents of the memory can be altered by locally heating up a memory cell inside a memory array, which can compromise the security of a semiconductor chip.

Nowadays, common optical fault injection facilities consist of a laser emitter, focusing lens, and a placement surface with stepper motors to achieve an accurate focusing of the beam. However, for this, or similar fault injection techniques, it is almost impossible to achieve subwavelength precision, which means the number of gates hit by the radiation is limited by the etching technology and the laser wavelength.

Focused ion beam (FIB) is one of the most accurate and powerful fault injection technique that enables an attacker to edit the circuit, reconstruct missing buses, cut existing wires, and mill through layers by depositing or removing material on the circuit die. For instance, Torrance and James [112] reported a successful reconstruction of an entire read bus of a memory containing a cryptographic key without damaging the contents of the memory. State-of-the-art FIBs can operate at a precision of 1 nm, that is, less than a tenth of the gate width of the smallest etchable transistor. FIB workstations require very expensive consumables, and a strong technical background to fully exploit their capabilities.

The countermeasures to prevent FIB-based fault injection attacks are almost the same with probing attacks as illustrated in Section 10.3.2. The basic strategies to prevent against fault injection attacks are intrusion detection, algorithmic resistance, and error detection. Common countermeasures against fault injection attacks have been illustrated in previous chapters. Most of these countermeasures can also be used to prevent against invasive fault injection attacks.

10.5 EXERCISES

10.5.1 TRUE/FALSE QUESTIONS

1. Optical microscopy can be used to produce transistor images in latest technology node.
2. If each metal layer has the same wire width and space, internal layer is better than top layer to build active shield to prevent bypass attack.
3. Different doping profiles of a transistor are not easily detectable via optical microscopy.
4. Flash memory can be reverse engineered using x-ray technology.
5. If there is no specific mechanism to protect a chip against probing attacks, it is recommended to hide sensitive nets on lower metal layers, such as Metal 1 or Metal 2, to achieve more coverage from higher metal layers.

10.5.2 SHORT-ANSWER TYPE QUESTIONS

1. What are the differences between reverse engineering with honest and dishonest motivations?
2. List three categories of reverse engineering and their differences.
3. Identifying components on a PCB is an important step in PCB-level RE. However, would only reading the label and marks on the package be sufficient to identify the real component?
4. If KEY bits are the only asset in an encryption module and these KEY bits have been properly protected against probing attack, would it be fair to assume that this crypto hardware is probing-resistant design? Explain.
5. Assume that an asset wire is on Metal 2, and a shield is planned to be built on either Metal 7 or Metal 8 to prevent probing attack. In your opinion, which layer is better to use? Explain why. Also assume that a cone-shaped hole will be milled during the probing attack, and the metal on layers 7 and 8 has the same width and space. Hint: Only consider the geometric relation of asset and shield wires.
6. Illustrate the basic steps to perform a front-side electrical probing attack.
7. Compared to clock glitch-based fault injection attack, what are the pros and cons of a laser-based optical fault injection attack?
8. Can an attacker utilize modern optical or electron microscopy to reverse engineering EEPROM?

10.5.3 MATHEMATICAL PROBLEMS

1. Considering Fig. 10.25, at least how many images are needed to figure out the interconnections of this chip?
2. Assuming that a shield is placed on the top layer of the chip, the shield width is 150 nm, the shield space is 500 nm, the shield wire thickness is 200 nm, a target wire is on metal 2 and the shield to target layer depth is 5000 nm, what is the maximum FIB aspect ratio that this shield can protect against? [Hint: Considering that a complete cut of shield wires can be detected and only consider perpendicular milling.]
3. Assuming that a shield is placed horizontally on the top layer of the chip, the shield width is 150 nm, the shield wire thickness is 200 nm, a vertical target wire is on metal 2, the length of this target wire is 3000 nm, and the shield to target layer depth is 5000 nm, what is the maximum shield space to protect against FIB-based probing attack whose maximum aspect ratio is 6? How

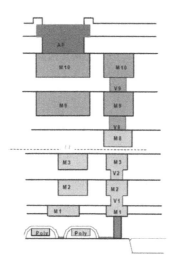

FIGURE 10.25

Interconnects of a chip.

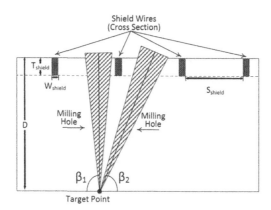

FIGURE 10.26

Probing attack scenarios.

many shield wires are needed to protect the target wire at least? Hint: Consider that a complete cut of shield wires can be detected and only consider perpendicular milling.

4. For Fig. 10.26, assume that a shield is placed vertically on the top layer of the chip, the shield width is 150 nm, the shield thickness is 200 nm, the shield spacing is 1 μm, a target probing point is located on M2 (in the quarter of two shield wires), the depth from shield layer to target point is 5 μm, a complete cut of shield wires can be detected, and a partial cut of shield wires is allowed. Answer the following questions:

(a) If only perpendicular milling is allowed ($\beta = 90°$), can a FIB with 5 aspect ratio probe the target point without a complete cut of any shield wire?

(b) If angled milling is allowed ($\beta \leq 90°$), can a FIB with 5 aspect ratio probe the target point without a complete cut of any shield wire?

REFERENCES

[1] I. McLoughlin, Secure embedded systems: the threat of reverse engineering, in: 2008 14th IEEE International Conference on Parallel and Distributed Systems, pp. 729–736.

[2] R.J. Abella, J.M. Daschbach, R.J. McNichols, Reverse engineering industrial applications, Computers and Industrial Engineering 26 (1994) 381–385.

[3] R. Torrance, D. James, The state-of-the-art in IC reverse engineering, in: C. Clavier, K. Gaj (Eds.), Cryptographic Hardware and Embedded Systems – CHES 2009, Springer Berlin Heidelberg, Berlin, Heidelberg, 2009, pp. 363–381.

[4] INSA, Interconnect design rules, Available at https://moodle.insa-toulouse.fr/pluginfile.php/2632/mod_resource/content/0/content/interconnect_design_rules.html.

[5] U. Guin, D. DiMase, M. Tehranipoor, Counterfeit integrated circuits: detection, avoidance, and the challenges ahead, Journal of Electronic Testing 30 (2014) 9–23.

[6] C. Bao, D. Forte, A. Srivastava, On application of one-class SVM to reverse engineering-based hardware Trojan detection, in: Fifteenth International Symposium on Quality Electronic Design, pp. 47–54.

[7] T.J. Biggerstaff, Design recovery for maintenance and reuse, Computer 22 (1989) 36–49.

[8] U. Guin, D. DiMase, M. Tehranipoor, A comprehensive framework for counterfeit defect coverage analysis and detection assessment, Journal of Electronic Testing 30 (2014) 25–40.

[9] S.K. Curtis, S.P. Harston, C.A. Mattson, The fundamentals of barriers to reverse engineering and their implementation into mechanical components, Research in Engineering Design 22 (2011) 245–261.

[10] M.T. Rahman, D. Forte, Q. Shi, G.K. Contreras, M. Tehranipoor, CSST: preventing distribution of unlicensed and rejected ICs by untrusted foundry and assembly, in: 2014 IEEE International Symposium on Defect and Fault Tolerance in VLSI and Nanotechnology Systems (DFT), pp. 46–51.

[11] A. Baumgarten, A. Tyagi, J. Zambreno, Preventing IC piracy using reconfigurable logic barriers, IEEE Design Test of Computers 27 (2010) 66–75.

[12] SpacePhotonics, Anti-tamper technology, Available at http://www.spacephotonics.com/Anti_Tamper_Systems_Materials.php, 2013.

[13] DoD, Anti-tamper executive agent, Available at https://at.dod.mil/content/short-course, 2014.

[14] S.H. Weingart, Physical security devices for computer subsystems: a survey of attacks and defenses, in: Ç.K. Koç, C. Paar (Eds.), Cryptographic Hardware and Embedded Systems — CHES 2000, Springer Berlin Heidelberg, Berlin, Heidelberg, 2000, pp. 302–317.

[15] J.A. Roy, F. Koushanfar, I.L. Markov, EPIC: ending piracy of integrated circuits, in: 2008 Design, Automation and Test in Europe, pp. 1069–1074.

[16] Britannica.com, Integrated circuit (IC), Available at http://www.britannica.com/EBchecked/topic/289645/integrated-circuit-IC, 2014.

[17] MaximIntegrated, Glossary term: printed-circuit-board, Available at http://www.maximintegrated.com/en/glossary/definitions.mvp/term/Printed-Circuit-Board/gpk/973, 2014.

[18] Nikon, Microscopy, Available at http://www.microscopyu.com/, 2013.

[19] Nikon, Optical microscopy, Available at https://www.microscopyu.com/museum/model-smz1500-stereomicroscope.

[20] JEOL, Scanning electron microscope (SEM), Available at https://www.jeol.co.jp/en/products/list_sem.html.

[21] ZEISS, Transmission electron microscope (TEM), Available at http://jiam.utk.edu/facilities/microscopy/tem/index.php.

[22] Purdue.edu, Scanning electron microscope, Available at http://www.purdue.edu/ehps/rem/rs/sem.htm, 2014.

[23] SharedResources, Transmission electron microscope (TEM), Available at http://sharedresources.fhcrc.org/services/transmission-electron-microscopy-tem, 2014.

[24] Stanford.edu, Stanford microscopy facility, Available at https://microscopy.stanford.edu/, 2014.

[25] ThermoFisher, Focused ion beam (FIB), Available at https://www.fei.com/products/fib/.

[26] ZEISS, X-ray microscope, Available at https://www.zeiss.com/microscopy/int/products/x-ray-microscopy.html.

[27] FormFactor, Probe station, Available at https://www.formfactor.com/products/probe-systems/.

[28] GE, Inspection and NDT, Available at https://www.gemeasurement.com/inspection-and-nondestructive-testing, 2014.

[29] Tektronix, Logic analyzer, Available at https://www.tek.com/logic-analyzer.

[30] Grizzly, Computer numerical control (CNC), Available at http://users.dsic.upv.es/~jsilva/cnc/index.htm.

[31] R. Joshi, B.J. Shanker, Plastic chip carrier package, in: 1996 Proceedings 46th Electronic Components and Technology Conference, pp. 772–776.

[32] G. Phipps, Wire bond vs. flip chip packaging, Advanced Packaging Magazine 14, 7, 28, 2005.

[33] C. Tarnovsky, Deconstructing a 'secure' processor, in: Black hat federal, Available at http://www.blackhat.com/presentations/bh-dc-10/Tarnovsky_Chris/BlackHat-DC-2010-Tarnovsky-DASP-slides.pdf, 2010.

[34] SharedResources, Wet etching recipes, Available at http://www.eesemi.com/etch_recipes.htm, 2013.

[35] M.C. Hansen, H. Yalcin, J.P. Hayes, Unveiling the ISCAS-85 benchmarks: a case study in reverse engineering, IEEE Design Test of Computers 16 (1999) 72–80.

[36] W. Li, Z. Wasson, S.A. Seshia, Reverse engineering circuits using behavioral pattern mining, in: 2012 IEEE International Symposium on Hardware-Oriented Security and Trust, pp. 83–88.

[37] P. Subramanyan, N. Tsiskaridze, K. Pasricha, D. Reisman, A. Susnea, S. Malik, Reverse engineering digital circuits using functional analysis, in: 2013 Design, Automation Test in Europe Conference Exhibition (DATE), pp. 1277–1280.

[38] W. Li, A. Gascón, P. Subramanyan, W. Yang Tan, A. Tiwari, S. Malik, N. Shankar, S.A. Seshia, WordRev: finding word-level structures in a sea of bit-level gates, 2013, pp. 67–74.

[39] J. Rajendran, M. Sam, O. Sinanoglu, R. Karri, Security analysis of integrated circuit camouflaging, in: Proceedings of the 2013 ACM SIGSAC Conference on Computer & Communications Security, CCS '13, ACM, New York, NY, USA, 2013, pp. 709–720.

[40] SypherMedia, Circuit camouflage technology, Available at http://www.smi.tv/SMI_SypherMedia_Library_Intro.pdf, 2012.

[41] A.R. Desai, M.S. Hsiao, C. Wang, L. Nazhandali, S. Hall, Interlocking obfuscation for anti-tamper hardware, in: Proceedings of the Eighth Annual Cyber Security and Information Intelligence Research Workshop, CSIIRW '13, ACM, New York, NY, USA, 2013, 8.

[42] R.S. Chakraborty, S. Bhunia, Harpoon: an obfuscation-based SoC design methodology for hardware protection, IEEE Transactions on Computer-Aided Design of Integrated Circuits and Systems 28 (2009) 1493–1502.

[43] R. Maes, D. Schellekens, P. Tuyls, I. Verbauwhede, Analysis and design of active IC metering schemes, in: 2009 IEEE International Workshop on Hardware-Oriented Security and Trust, pp. 74–81.

[44] F. Koushanfar, Integrated circuits metering for piracy protection and digital rights management: an overview, in: Proceedings of the 21st Edition of the Great Lakes Symposium on Great Lakes Symposium on VLSI, GLSVLSI '11, ACM, New York, NY, USA, 2011, pp. 449–454.

[45] B. Gassend, D. Clarke, M. van Dijk, S. Devadas, Silicon physical random functions, in: Proceedings of the 9th ACM Conference on Computer and Communications Security, CCS '02, ACM, New York, NY, USA, 2002, pp. 148–160.

[46] J.A. Roy, F. Koushanfar, I.L. Markov, Protecting bus-based hardware IP by secret sharing, in: 2008 45th ACM/IEEE Design Automation Conference, pp. 846–851.

[47] G.K. Contreras, M.T. Rahman, M. Tehranipoor, Secure split-test for preventing IC piracy by untrusted foundry and assembly, in: 2013 IEEE International Symposium on Defect and Fault Tolerance in VLSI and Nanotechnology Systems (DFTS), pp. 196–203.

[48] J. Grand, Printed circuit board deconstruction techniques, in: 8th USENIX Workshop on Offensive Technologies (WOOT 14), USENIX Association, San Diego, CA, 2014.

[49] CTI, Counterfeit components avoidance program, Available at http://www.cti-us.com/CCAP.htm, 2013.

[50] DatasheetCatalog2013, Datasheet, Available at http://www.datasheetcatalog.com/, 2013.

[51] Alldatasheet, Electronic components datasheet search, Available at http://www.alldatasheet.com/, 2014.

[52] TechInsights, Sony Xperia play teardown and analysis, Available at http://www.techinsights.com/teardowns/sony-xperia-play-teardown/, 2014.

[53] X. Pan, Unified reconstruction theory for diffraction tomography, with consideration of noise control, Journal of the Optical Society of America A 15 (1998) 2312–2326.

[54] N. Asadizanjani, S. Shahbazmohamadi, E. Jordan, Investigation of Surface Geometry Thermal Barrier Coatings Using Computed X-Ray Tomography, vol. 35, 2015, pp. 175–187.

[55] S.E. Quadir, J. Chen, D. Forte, N. Asadizanjani, S. Shahbazmohamadi, L. Wang, J. Chandy, M. Tehranipoor, A survey on chip to system reverse engineering, ACM Journal on Emerging Technologies in Computing Systems 13 (2016) 6.

[56] B. Naveen, K.S. Raghunathan, An automatic netlist-to-schematic generator, IEEE Design Test of Computers 10 (1993) 36–41.

[57] W.-Y. Wu, M.-J.J. Wang, C.-M. Liu, Automated inspection of printed circuit boards through machine vision, Computers in Industry 28 (1996) 103–111.

[58] Ruzinoor Che Mat, Shahrul Azmi, Ruslizam Daud, Abdul Nasir Zulkifli, Farzana Kabir Ahmad, Morphological operation on printed circuit board (PCB) reverse engineering using MATLAB, Proc. Knowl. Manage. Int. Conf. Exhibit. (KMICE) (2006) 529–533.

[59] C. Koutsougeras, N. Bourbakis, V. Gallardo, Reverse engineering of real PCB level design using VERILOG HDL, International Journal of Engineering Intelligent Systems for Electrical Engineering and Communications 10 (2) (2002) 63–68.

[60] H.G. Longbotham, P. Yan, H.N. Kothari, J. Zhou, Nondestructive reverse engineering of trace maps in multilayered PCBs, in: AUTOTESTCON '95. Systems Readiness: Test Technology for the 21st Century. Conference Record, pp. 390–397.

[61] S.P. Skorobogatov, Semi-invasive attacks – a new approach to hardware security analysis, Technical Report UCAM–CL–TR–630, University of Cambridge Computer Laboratory, April 2005.

[62] F. Beck, Integrated Circuit Failure Analysis: A Guide to Preparation Techniques, John Wiley & Sons, 1998.

[63] C.D. Nardi, R. Desplats, P. Perdu, F. Beaudoin, J.-L. Gauffier, Oxide charge measurements in EEPROM devices, in: Proceedings of the 16th European Symposium on Reliability of Electron Devices, Failure Physics and Analysis, Microelectronics Reliability 45 (2005) 1514–1519.

[64] C. DeNardi, R. Desplats, P. Perdu, J.-L. Gauffier, C. Guérin, Descrambling and data reading techniques for flash-EEPROM memories. Application to smart cards, in: Proceedings of the 17th European Symposium on Reliability of Electron Devices, Failure Physics and Analysis. Wuppertal, Germany 3rd–6th October 2006, Microelectronics Reliability 46 (2006) 1569–1574.

[65] C. De Nardi, R. Desplats, P. Perdu, C. Guérin, J. Luc Gauffier, T.B. Amundsen, Direct measurements of charge in floating gate transistor channels of flash memories using scanning capacitance microscopy 2006, 2006.

[66] NREL, Scanning Kelvin probe microscopy, Available at http://www.nrel.gov/pv/measurements/scanning_kelvin.html, 2014.

[67] B. Bhushan, H. Fuchs, M. Tomitori, Applied Scanning Probe Methods X: Biomimetics and Industrial Applications, vol. 9, Springer, 2008.

[68] T. Wollinger, J. Guajardo, C. Paar, Security on FPGAs: state-of-the-art implementations and attacks, ACM Transactions on Embedded Computing Systems (TECS) 3 (2004) 534–574.

[69] A. Moradi, A. Barenghi, T. Kasper, C. Paar, On the vulnerability of FPGA bitstream encryption against power analysis attacks: extracting keys from Xilinx Virtex-II FPGAs, in: Proceedings of the 18th ACM Conference on Computer and Communications Security, CCS '11, ACM, New York, NY, USA, 2011, pp. 111–124.

[70] A. Moradi, M. Kasper, C. Paar, Black-box side-channel attacks highlight the importance of countermeasures: an analysis of the Xilinx Virtex-4 and Virtex-5 bitstream encryption mechanism, in: Proceedings of the 12th Conference on Topics in Cryptology, CT-RSA'12, Springer-Verlag, Berlin, Heidelberg, 2012, pp. 1–18.

[71] P. Swierczynski, A. Moradi, D. Oswald, C. Paar, Physical security evaluation of the bitstream encryption mechanism of Altera Stratix II and Stratix III FPGAs, ACM Transactions on Reconfigurable Technology and Systems 7 (2014) 34.

[72] S. Drimer, Volatile FPGA design security – a survey, in: IEEE Computer Society Annual Volume, IEEE, Los Alamitos, CA, 2008, pp. 292–297.

[73] E. Brier, C. Clavier, F. Olivier, Correlation power analysis with a leakage model, in: M. Joye, J.-J. Quisquater (Eds.), Cryptographic Hardware and Embedded Systems – CHES 2004, Springer Berlin Heidelberg, Berlin, Heidelberg, 2004, pp. 16–29.

[74] S. Drimer, Security for volatile FPGAs, Technical report UCAM-CL-TR-763, University of Cambridge, Computer Laboratory, 2009.

[75] D. Ziener, S. Assmus, J. Teich, Identifying FPGA IP-cores based on lookup table content analysis, in: 2006 International Conference on Field Programmable Logic and Applications, pp. 1–6.

[76] J.-B. Note, E. Rannaud, From the bitstream to the netlist, in: Proceedings of the 16th International ACM/SIGDA Symposium on Field Programmable Gate Arrays, FPGA '08, ACM, New York, NY, USA, 2008, pp. 264–271.

[77] F. Benz, A. Seffrin, S.A. Huss, Bil: a tool-chain for bitstream reverse-engineering, in: 22nd International Conference on Field Programmable Logic and Applications (FPL), pp. 735–738.

[78] B. Vajana, M. Patelmo, Mask programmed ROM inviolable by reverse engineering inspections and method of fabrication, 2002, US Patent App. 10/056,564.

[79] L. Chow, W. Clark, G. Harbison, J. Baukus, Use of silicon block process step to camouflage a false transistor, 2007, US Patent App. 11/208,470.

[80] H. Mio, F. Kreupl, IC chip with nanowires, 2008, US Patent 7,339,186.

[81] H.K. Cha, I. Yun, J. Kim, B.C. So, K. Chun, I. Nam, K. Lee, A 32-KB standard CMOS antifuse one-time programmable ROM embedded in a 16-bit microcontroller, IEEE Journal of Solid-State Circuits 41 (2006) 2115–2124.

[82] B. Stamme, Anti-fuse memory provides robust, secure NVM option, Available at http://www.eetimes.com/document.asp?doc_id=1279746, 2014.

[83] J. Lipman, Why replacing ROM with 1T-OTP makes sense, Available at http://www.chipestimate.com/tech-talks/2008/03/11/Sidense-Why-Replacing-ROM-with-1T-OTP-Makes-Sense, 2014.

[84] VirageLogic, Design security in nonvolatile Flash and antifuse FPGAs (NVM), Available at http://www.flashmemorysummit.com/English/Collaterals/Proceedings/2009/20090811_F1A_Zajac.pdf, 2014.

[85] G. Bartley, T. Christensen, P. Dahlen, E. John, Implementing tamper evident and resistant detection through modulation of capacitance, 2010, US Patent App. 12/359,484.

[86] D.H. Kim, K. Athikulwongse, S.K. Lim, A study of through-silicon-via impact on the 3d stacked IC layout, in: 2009 IEEE/ACM International Conference on Computer-Aided Design – Digest of Technical Papers, pp. 674–680.

[87] J. Van Geloven, P. Tuyls, R. Wolters, N. Verhaegh, Tamper-resistant semiconductor device and methods of manufacturing thereof, 2012, US Patent 8,143,705.

[88] F. Zachariasse, Semiconductor device with backside tamper protection, 2012, US Patent 8,198,641.

[89] S. Skorobogatov, Data remanence in flash memory devices, in: J.R. Rao, B. Sunar (Eds.), Cryptographic Hardware and Embedded Systems – CHES 2005, Springer Berlin Heidelberg, Berlin, Heidelberg, 2005, pp. 339–353.

[90] P. Thanigai, Introducing advanced security to low-power applications with FRAM-based MCUs, Available at http://www.ecnmag.com/articles/2014/03/introducing-advancedsecurity-low-power-applications-fram-mcus, 2014.

[91] Actel, Design security in nonvolatile Flash and antifuse FPGAs, Available at http://www.actel.com/documents/DesignSecurity_WP.pdf, 2002.

[92] K. Tiri, I. Verbauwhede, A dynamic and differential CMOS logic style to resist power and timing attacks on security IC's, Cryptology ePrint Archive, Report 2004/066, 2004.

[93] J. Wu, Y.-B. Kim, M. Choi, Low-power side-channel attack-resistant asynchronous S-box design for AES cryptosystems, in: Proceedings of the 20th Symposium on Great Lakes Symposium on VLSI, GLSVLSI '10, ACM, New York, NY, USA, 2010, pp. 459–464.

[94] L. Benini, E. Omerbegovic, A. Macii, M. Poncino, E. Macii, F. Pro, Energy-aware design techniques for differential power analysis protection, in: Proceedings 2003. Design Automation Conference (IEEE Cat. No. 03CH37451), pp. 36–41.

[95] H. Wang, D. Forte, M.M. Tehranipoor, Q. Shi, Probing attacks on integrated circuits: challenges and research opportunities, IEEE Design Test 34 (2017) 63–71.

[96] S. Skorobogatov, The bumpy road toward iPhone 5c NAND mirroring, ArXiv preprint arXiv:1609.04327, 2016, Available at https://arxiv.org/ftp/arxiv/papers/1609/1609.04327.pdf.

[97] C. Tarnovsky, Security failures in secure devices, in: Proc. Black Hat DC Presentation, 74, Feb. 2008, Available at http://www.blackhat.com/presentations/bh-dc-08/Tarnovsky/Presentation/bh-dc-08-tarnovsky.pdf, 2008.

[98] ARMInc., Building a secure system using TrustZone technology, Available at http://infocenter.arm.com/help/topic/com.arm.doc.prd29-genc-009492c/PRD29-GENC-009492C_trustzone_security_whitepaper.pdf, 2017.

[99] C. Boit, C. Helfmeier, U. Kerst, Security risks posed by modern IC debug and diagnosis tools, in: 2013 Workshop on Fault Diagnosis and Tolerance in Cryptography, pp. 3–11.

[100] S. Skorobogatov, Physical attacks on tamper resistance: progress and lessons, in: Proc. 2nd ARO Special Workshop Hardware Assurance, Washington, DC, USA, 2011, Available at http://www.cl.cam.ac.uk/sps32/ARO_2011.pdf.

[101] J.M. Cioranesco, J.L. Danger, T. Graba, S. Guilley, Y. Mathieu, D. Naccache, X.T. Ngo, Cryptographically secure shields, in: 2014 IEEE International Symposium on Hardware-Oriented Security and Trust (HOST), pp. 25–31.

[102] S. Manich, M.S. Wamser, G. Sigl, Detection of probing attempts in secure ICs, in: 2012 IEEE International Symposium on Hardware-Oriented Security and Trust, pp. 134–139.

[103] Y. Ishai, A. Sahai, D. Wagner, Private circuits: securing hardware against probing attacks, in: D. Boneh (Ed.), Advances in Cryptology – CRYPTO 2003, Springer Berlin Heidelberg, Berlin, Heidelberg, 2003, pp. 463–481.

[104] A. Barenghi, L. Breveglieri, I. Koren, D. Naccache, Fault injection attacks on cryptographic devices: theory, practice, and countermeasures, Proceedings of the IEEE 100 (2012) 3056–3076.

[105] R. Anderson, M. Kuhn, Low cost attacks on tamper resistant devices, in: B. Christianson, B. Crispo, M. Lomas, M. Roe (Eds.), Security Protocols, Springer Berlin Heidelberg, Berlin, Heidelberg, 1998, pp. 125–136.

[106] D. Boneh, R.A. DeMillo, R.J. Lipton, On the importance of eliminating errors in cryptographic computations, Journal of Cryptology 14 (2001) 101–119.

[107] E. Biham, A. Shamir, Differential fault analysis of secret key cryptosystems, in: B.S. Kaliski (Ed.), Advances in Cryptology — CRYPTO '97, Springer Berlin Heidelberg, Berlin, Heidelberg, 1997, pp. 513–525.

[108] D. Boneh, R.A. DeMillo, R.J. Lipton, On the importance of checking cryptographic protocols for faults, in: W. Fumy (Ed.), Advances in Cryptology — EUROCRYPT '97, Springer Berlin Heidelberg, Berlin, Heidelberg, 1997, pp. 37–51.

[109] F. Bao, R.H. Deng, Y. Han, A. Jeng, A.D. Narasimhalu, T. Ngair, Breaking public key cryptosystems on tamper resistant devices in the presence of transient faults, in: B. Christianson, B. Crispo, M. Lomas, M. Roe (Eds.), Security Protocols, Springer Berlin Heidelberg, Berlin, Heidelberg, 1998, pp. 115–124.

[110] S.P. Skorobogatov, R.J. Anderson, Optical fault induction attacks, in: B.S. Kaliski, ç.K. Koç, C. Paar (Eds.), Cryptographic Hardware and Embedded Systems – CHES 2002, Springer Berlin Heidelberg, Berlin, Heidelberg, 2003, pp. 2–12.

[111] S. Skorobogatov, Local heating attacks on flash memory devices, in: 2009 IEEE International Workshop on Hardware-Oriented Security and Trust, July 2009, pp. 1–6.

[112] R. Torrance, D. James, The state-of-the-art in IC reverse engineering, in: Proceedings of the 11th International Workshop on Cryptographic Hardware and Embedded Systems, CHES '09, Springer-Verlag, Berlin, Heidelberg, 2009, pp. 363–381.

ATTACKS ON PCB: SECURITY CHALLENGES AND VULNERABILITIES

CONTENTS

11.1 INTRODUCTION

Modern PCBs typically integrate a number of ICs with high pin complexity and large number of passive components into a miniature layout [1]. Survey results show that 14% of today's PCBs are currently operating in the 1–10 GHz frequency range to support high-speed data communication [2].

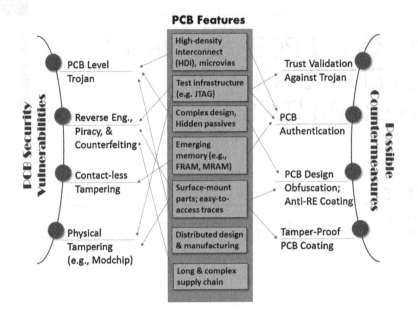

FIGURE 11.1

An illustration showing how the features of modern PCBs create new vulnerabilities. It also shows possible counter-measures, some of which benefit from these features.

The complexity and cost of PCB design are also rising rapidly. With increasing complexity of PCBs—including high-density interconnects, hidden vias, passive components in internal layers, and multiple layers (6–20 layers)—system integrators are increasingly relying on third-party PCB manufacturers. Moreover, the long and distributed supply chain of PCBs is becoming highly vulnerable to diverse attacks that compromise PCB integrity and trustworthiness. A PCB can be deliberately tampered by an adversary through insertion of malicious components, or targeted design changes, that can trigger a malfunction or leak secret information after deployment. Otherwise, these compromised PCBs may suffer from significant performance and reliability issues [3]. On the other hand, counterfeiting has become a major concern in the PCB industry. Counterfeit PCBs pose a major threat in mission-critical systems with serious potential consequences during field operation. Figure 11.1 shows some salient features of modern PCB, arising from the current trend in PCB design, manufacturing, and distribution, and the corresponding security vulnerabilities. It also shows a set of countermeasures at different stages of PCB life cycle (design and test) that one can employ to address these threats. Some of these PCB features can be leveraged to built the countermeasures, e.g., the JTAG infrastructure can be used in trust validation and PCB authentication, as shown in the figure.

Hardware Trojan attacks at the IC level have been extensively studied in recent times. Researchers have analyzed the impact of these attacks and explored possible countermeasures. However, vulnerability with respect to hardware Trojan attacks at higher levels, in particular at PCB level, have not been widely explored. Previous studies have covered security of PCBs against piracy and various post-fabrication tampering attacks. JTAG and other field programmability features in a PCB, for example, probe pins, unused sockets, and USB have been extensively exploited by hackers to gain access to internal features of the designs, snoop secret key, collect test responses, and manipulate JTAG test pins. One instance of such attack demonstrated that a Xbox gaming console can be hacked by using JTAG to disable the DRM protection. Modern PCBs are becoming increasingly vulnerable to malicious modification of PCBs during design or fabrication in untrusted design or fabrication facilities. Such a vulnerability creates a new class of threat for PCBs. The emerging business model of PCB design and fabrication, which favors extensive outsourcing and integration of untrusted components/entities in the PCB lifecycle to lower manufacturing cost [4–6], makes hardware Trojan attacks in PCBs highly feasible.

A closer look at several major electronic products and their PCB manufacturers reveals that PCBs are often designed in various countries. Moreover, reliance on third-party manufacturing facilities makes the PCB fabrication process untrustworthy and, hence, vulnerable to malicious modifications. Furthermore, an adversary can be present inside the design house and can implant a Trojan into a PCB design. PCBs in today's complex and highly integrated designs contain as many as 20 to 30 layers with hidden vias and embedded passive components [7] to minimize the form factor. This presents a great opportunity for an attacker to deliberately modify a PCB design by tampering the interconnect lines at the internal layers, or altering the components.

Due to the highly distributed nature of PCB design flow, maintaining high levels of security standard across the entire supply chain system has become a challenging task. Consequently, the weak links of the PCB life cycle are more vulnerable to security breaches and malicious attacks by rogue entities. Incorporation of untrusted vendors across the globe is exacerbating the situation by introducing novel threats in PCB life cycle and supply chain system. Despite the associated risks, the manufacturing companies are being compelled to adopt the existing horizontal business model for PCB production to cope up with changing landscapes of the semiconductor industry and reduce design, and manufacturing cost.

The relative ease of reverse engineering a PCB (compared to IC) using home-based solutions has also been reported in the literature. An adversary can steal a PCB design or reverse engineer a fabricated PCB to obtain the design information. Next, he/she can make pirated and counterfeit copies, or resell reverse-engineered PCB designs. Moreover, it is possible to extract the vulnerable points and launch cleverly crafted attacks on PCBs. A broad classification of the attacks on PCBs is illustrated in Fig. 11.2. The primary categories in the taxonomy include piracy and counterfeiting issues, hardware Trojan attacks, and in-field alteration. In this chapter, each attack category is discussed in detail. We present relevant case studies to further illustrate the attacks and vulnerabilities. The limitations of traditional PCB testing in verifying the security and trustworthiness of a PCB are also discussed. Finally, an in-field alteration attack, referred to as Modchip attack, is explained with an example attack launched on commercial Xbox gaming console [10–12].

11.2 PCB SECURITY CHALLENGES: ATTACKS ON PCB
In this section, we describe some of the attacks on PCB in detail.

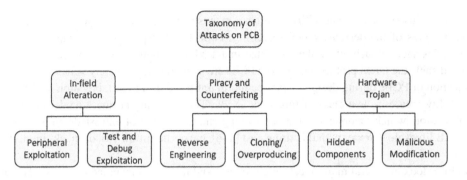

FIGURE 11.2

A taxonomy of attacks on PCBs.

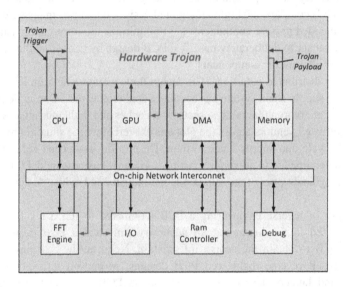

FIGURE 11.3

A generic overview of hardware Trojan at PCB level.

11.2.1 HARDWARE TROJANS IN PCB

A generic model of hardware Trojan attack on a PCB is illustrated in Fig. 11.3. At PCB level, hardware Trojans may have two types of payload. First, Trojans can interrupt or maliciously change the functionality of a PCB, making it fail during field operation. For example, addition of a capacitor on PCB signal lines can cause disruption in the regular circuit operation and communication among the components in the board. Such alteration can lead to in-field failure. Second, a Trojan can leak sensitive information from a PCB design. An example of such attack would be inserting a capacitor-based leakage circuitry to extract critical system information, such as keys of cryptographic modules.

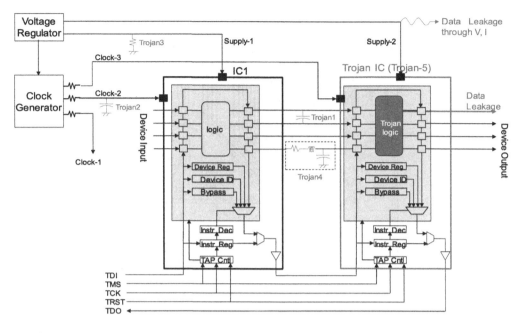

FIGURE 11.4

An illustration of hardware Trojan insertion into a PCB as a hidden component.

11.2.1.1 Hidden Components

In a multilayer PCB board, an adversary can insert additional electrical components in one of the layers to obtain secret information by leaking it through various means. Similarly, an attacker can cause malfunctioning or operate the PCB beyond its regular specifications by inserting malicious components in the original design. One instance of such attack would be, replacing the original IC with a tampered, counterfeit, or custom-designed IC containing hardware Trojans. The new IC may have nearly equivalent functional and performance specifications, making the Trojan hard to detect using conventional PCB testing. An illustrative example of such Trojan in PCB-level design is provided in Fig. 11.4.

11.2.1.2 Malicious Modifications

An adversary may also modify the resistance, inductance, or capacitance values of signal traces of a PCB. An example of such modification is reduction of the width of an internal layer trace to increase its resistance. Consequently, this alteration may lead to design failure over a longer period of operation due to overheating. Similar attacks could be employed to change the coupling capacitance of the traces leading to delay failure. Introducing additional coupling voltage in the circuitry requires modifications, such as altering inter-trace distance through re-routing, and selectively changing dimensions of traces and dielectric properties. Attacks can be mounted to degrade operating voltage in a PCB by incorporating high-resistance paths in the internal layers. The interconnection between two components can also be corrupted to disrupt the design functionality by introducing impedance mismatch. To evade

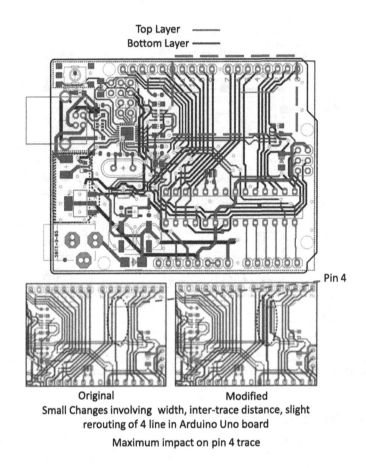

Top Layer ———
Bottom Layer ———

Pin 4

Original   Modified
Small Changes involving width, inter-trace distance, slight
rerouting of 4 line in Arduino Uno board

Maximum impact on pin 4 trace

FIGURE 11.5

Minor modifications in an Arduino UNO PCB layout to insert a hardware Trojan without addition of any new component.

conventional PCB testing, these Trojans need to be triggered by rare internal conditions in a PCB or through external trigger mechanisms, which are difficult to exercise during test.

An illustrative example of malicious trace modification attack on PCB is demonstrated on a commercial Arduino Uno board (Fig. 11.5). The attack shows a possible approach for tampering trace lines in PCBs. The major impacts of such tampering are: degradation of the output voltage and circuit failure caused by delay, or additional coupling voltage. It involves altering the trace thickness and inter-trace distance by 2X of the original design, and rerouting a single trace. Note that the modification is difficult to trace via traditional testing approaches, though it is incorporated on a relatively simple two-layer PCB. An increase in the design complexity with additional layers would enhance the chances of the alteration to evade visual-inspection-based testing, such as optical or X-ray imaging. Moreover, it is generally hard to detect these modifications via functional and parametric testing of PCB, as these tests are applied for verifying the limited functionality of the board. It is not a feasible option to adopt exhaustive testing methodology due to time and resource constraints. Figure 11.5 depicts the modified trace lines and the impact of the modification. Note that the voltage degradation at Pin 4 is expected to lead to board malfunction during field operation.

11.2.2 IN-FIELD ALTERATION

11.2.2.1 Peripheral Exploitation

Peripheral exploitation can be defined as an attempt made by an attacker to exploit on-board ICs and other electrical components (active and passive) to launch an attack. Common instances of peripheral exploitation include mounting rogue ICs on the original design, changing the connection of wires via soldering, rerouting the circuit data path to evade or substitute a security block, or access restricted block on the PCB. An example of such attack is Modchip attack [11]. Modchips represent a unique class of components capable of maliciously changing the function of a PCB. They are also used to limit access to restricted part of a design. Modchips are often mounted on set-top boxes and gaming consoles for manipulating the built-in protection in these devices [13].

11.2.2.2 Test and Debug Exploitation

PCB design features, such as JTAGs, USBs, test pins, and test/debug structures can be exploited as attack surfaces by an adversary. An attacker can exploit these features to understand the intent of a design, and mount attacks more efficiently with minimal alterations.

- **JTAG interface:** As discusses in Chapter 4, JTAG is an industry standard developed to test and debug PCBs after fabrication. JTAG integrates several test features of the board for the ease of testing and debugging. For example, JTAG has access to data and address bus of onboard chips for testing functionality and performance. Such accessibility, however, can be exploited by an attacker to retrieve sensitive design information or stored secrets in a PCB. An attacker can attempt to gain control over chip data and address buses of the board to mount an attack on the data bus by exploiting JTAG. The attack requires acquiring information about the instruction registers, such as the size and functionality of the registers through a trial-and-error method. Once the relevant information is obtained, specific instructions can be executed to get access to the system data, and feed the bus with corrupted data. Another example of JTAG attack would be reverse engineering the design via connectivity inspections of components onboard.
- **Test pins or probe pads.** Most ICs are designed with probe pads and test pins to observe and control important signals for test and debug purposes. An adversary can tap these pins and monitor the critical signals to gain information about the functionality of the design, or feed malicious data into the design. Test pins can also be exploited for reverse engineering, where a test input can trigger certain data, address and control signals that can help identify the board functionality. A list of additional vulnerabilities originating from common PCB design features is provided in Table 11.1.

11.2.3 PIRACY AND COUNTERFEITING

11.2.3.1 Reverse Engineering

PCBs are highly vulnerable to reverse engineering. An adversary can purchase a PCB, or a system containing a PCB, from the market, and attempt to reverse engineer it. It has been demonstrated in prior work that even a complex multilayer PCB can be completely reverse engineered in a relatively

Table 11.1 Various attack surfaces created by PCB design features	
Security vulnerability in PCB	Possible exploitation for hardware / physical attacks
JTAG	Control of scan chain/data bus for illegal access to memory/logic
RS232, USB, Firmware, Ethernet	Access to internal memory of an IC, leaking secret data
Test Pins	Access to internal scan chain to leak data from ICs
Unused pins, multiple layers, hidden vias	Alteration of connections using internal layers/hidden vias

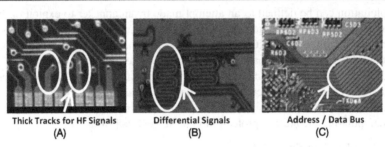

Thick Tracks for HF Signals   Differential Signals   Address / Data Bus
(A)   (B)   (C)

FIGURE 11.6

Visual inspection of PCB can reveal critical design information: (A) Thicker traces for high-frequency signals; (B) Pair of signals for differential signaling; (C) Group of traces indicating bus.

simple manner with low-cost home-based solutions. A reverse engineered PCB can then be cloned to produce unauthorized copies. PCB reverse engineering may also help an adversary to better understand the design and then tamper it effectively. An adversary can create counterfeit copies of a PCB after reverse engineering the design. It is generally easy to assemble counterfeit PCBs since most PCBs use active/passive components that are readily available in the market. These PCBs can simply be low-quality fakes or can include malicious circuits, i.e., hardware Trojan, as discussed before [8]. Finally, the process of reverse engineering, may enable an attacker to extract critical security information of a design; identify any vulnerability therein; and then develop powerful attacks on the system [9].

11.2.3.2 Cloning

Attackers can clone original PCBs with malicious intents. Visual inspection of the PCB boards can reveal critical information about the design and facilitate the PCB cloning process. Illustrative examples of such scenarios are depicted in Fig. 11.6. The description of each type of vulnerability is as follows:

- **Distinct properties of special signals:** An adversary can guess the functionalities of different signals by their distinct properties. For instance, the thickness of the trace and the group of traces of a data bus provide clues about the functionality. Similarly, pins tied with identical pull-up/down resistors indicate that they belong to a bus.
- **Remnant signatures from test or debug:** When the test and debug pins are accessed through ports, the remnant of soldering provides intuitive clues about the functionality of these pins. An empty socket on the PCB can also be exploited by an adversary for mounting an attack.
- **Miscellaneous hints:** Apart from the attack surfaces provided by component-level hooks, a PCB design itself reveals lots of information to an adversary in fabrication house that can facilitate pow-

erful Trojan attacks. Figure 11.6 depicts how traditional design features and miscellaneous hints can be exploited by attackers to comprehend design functionality.

11.3 ATTACK MODELS

Trojan attacks in PCB can be divided into two broad classes as described below.

Case 1: PCB design is trusted. In this attack scenario, it is assumed that the designs are obtained from trusted parties. The fabrication facility is deemed untrustworthy and flagged as possible source of an attack. Moreover, it is assumed that an intelligent attacker is capable of evading conventional post-manufacturing tests. The goal of the attacker is to trigger the attack in a rare situation (that is, involving a rare combination of inputs) that is difficult to check via regular functional or parametric testing.

Case 2: PCB design is not trusted. The threat model for this instance considers both the board design and fabrication facility to be untrusted. Only the functional and parametric specifications of the board are trusted. In this instance, an attacker has a higher flexibility of maliciously altering the design and/or choosing fake or untrustworthy (and potentially malicious) components. Again, an attacker would try to hide the modifications to avoid detection during functional and parametric testing process.

Note that in both cases, there are two possible objectives of the attacker: 1) malfunction, and/or 2) information leakage. The possible Trojan attacks of different forms on a PCB are described in the following sections.

11.3.1 ATTACK INSTANCES

11.3.1.1 Design House is Trusted

This attack arises when the PCB is designed by a trusted designer and outsourced for fabrication. During the manufacturing process, it is possible for the adversary to insert malicious modifications intelligently, such that the final design structurally matches the original one. In such case, no additional components—such as logic and traces—are integrated but the design will produce undesired functionality under certain conditions. The goals for altering the existing traces can be: increasing the mutual coupling capacitance, characteristic impedance, or loop inductance by changing internal layer routing and inserting small leakage paths. Additional components with an ultra-low area and power requirements can also be inserted in the internal layers. The small alterations can be confined to the internal layers of a multilayer PCB. Hence, chances of detection with visual inspection, optical imaging, and x-ray based imaging techniques are low. Also, it is infeasible to perform exhaustive functional testing with a large number of test nodes. Consequently, the malicious functions are very unlikely to get triggered during the in-circuit and boundary-scan-based functional testing. Additional components with ultra-low area and power requirements can also be inserted in the internal layers.

In this section, two Trojan examples are presented as attack instances. In the first case, a multilayer PCB (10 cm length) is considered with possible application in a high-speed communication and video streaming systems. In this board, there are two high-frequency (HF) PCB traces in an internal layer running parallel to each other. Usually, HF traces are routed in the internal layer, shielded by power and ground planes to avoid interference (Fig. 11.7A). However, the procedure significantly complicates

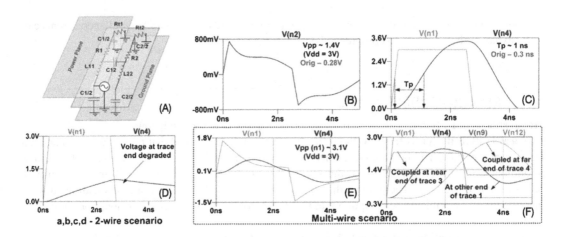

FIGURE 11.7

This set of figures illustrates the results of PCB level Trojan attacks. In this attack scenario, specific traces and properties of the PCBs are altered without introducing any new component into the original design. The figures are depicted as follows: (A) A lumped two-trace PCB system with associated components, that is, resistors, capacitor, and inductors; (B) The near and far-end voltages of trace-2; (C) The propagation delay in trace 1 (at node n1 and n4) at 220 MHz with an input voltage of 3 V peak-to-peak; (D) Insertion of a leakage resistance path from trace 1 to ground changes the far-end voltage of the respective trace; (E) and (F) illustrate how the trace property changes in a 4-wire scenario. In particular, it depicts the effect of coupled voltages in the near and far-end of victim traces, while all aggressors are switching in phase with a frequency of 220 MHz and a peak-to-peak voltage of 3 V; (F) shows the voltage profile at node 9, that is, the near-end of trace 3 and node 12, that is, the far-end of trace 4.

the internal layer testing and debugging, and creates an attack surface for the attacker. The dimensions of the traces are chosen carefully to carry normal HF signals, that is, 1 ounce copper trace with width and thickness of 6 mils and 1.4 mils, respectively. The dielectric is FR-4 with a relative permittivity of 4.5. The inter-trace distance is chosen to be 30 to 40 mils to avoid the negative effects of mutual inductive and capacitive coupling. These HF traces are modeled by lumped parametric form. Functional simulation results show a maximum coupled near- and far-end voltage of ~300 mVpp on one of the traces. The other trace is swept with pulse voltages of 3 Vpp at 10–500 MHz, with a 50% duty cycle. The maximum propagation delay for the pulse across the active trace is ~0.4 ns.

Following are the effects of various trace level modifications we observed during fabrication with the aforementioned setup: the inter-trace distance in the internal layers reduced by 2x; widths of both wires increased by 2x, and the thickness increased by 1.5x. Due to the minimal nature of the changes in a small target region of an internal layer, these manipulations are mostly undetectable during structural testing. The dielectric permittivity of the insulator between the traces increased to 5.5 to model moisture retention in certain insulating areas, add impurity to epoxy base and hence, facilitate the aging effect. As the permittivity is selectively altered by an adversary in a small area, the accelerated aging tests have a low probability of detecting the change. However, the impact of these changes on associated circuit parameters can be significant. At 220 MHz, the near-end peak-to-peak voltage in trace(2) is ~1.4 V for an input pulse voltage of 3 Vpp in trace(1) (Fig. 11.7B). This is an extraneous interference and may cause unexpected behavior in terms of erroneous circuit activation or feedback. The propagation delay increases by 2x, beyond 1 ns (Fig. 11.7C), which can induce functional failures for higher switching frequencies and greater trace lengths. An attacker can insert and exploit a leakage path to drain the target signals via ground. As a result, there is voltage degradation, which is demonstrated in Fig. 11.7D by plotting the distorted waveforms at the far end of trace(1). The ultimate goal of the attacker is to cause circuit malfunction through severe voltage degradation. This attack can easily evade detection by conventional PCB testing, as these are not exhaustive, due to prohibitive cost and time-to-market requirements.

One strategy to enhance mutual coupling is intentional rerouting of multiple HF traces. If the process is adapted for different planes, the effect of coupling becomes even more prominent. This phenomenon can be observed by minimizing the distance between traces located in the same plane, and increasing the thickness and widths of trace lines. It is highly unlikely that these minute changes will get noticed during the structural and functional tests. The consequence of these alterations, however, can be quite significant on circuit performance, as demonstrated in Fig. 11.7E–F. The resultant coupling voltages measured at the near- and far-end of the target trace were 3.1 V and 1.3 V, respectively. It should be noted that these were peak-to-peak voltage values with in-phase rising/falling transition on the three adjacent traces (one in-plane, one above, and one below) (Fig. 11.7E). This is 3 to 4 times greater than the scenario when active traces were switching in opposite directions. Such interference could certainly lead to failure situations, such as erroneous activation, feedback, and degraded circuit performance. The voltage profile at the far end of trace demonstrated some distortions along with an average propagation delay of 1 ns, while other traces were inactive (Fig. 11.7F). The propagation delay increased with the increasing number of neighboring traces and lengths of the traces. This could lead to delay failures at operations with high switching speed. Extraneous coupled voltages for traces three and four are delineated in Fig. 11.7F. The primary observation from the results is that these Trojan attacks via alteration of traces are extremely hard to detect, as they are sensitized in a very rare set of conditions. In case of multi-wire scenario, the degraded performance was significant only in two out of eight possible combinations of transition polarity (that is, all rising/falling pulses) in three neighboring PCB traces. The frequency of operation of the system and the input vector patterns delivered by selective trace properties and routing alterations made during PCB fabrication were exploited as the triggering condition of the Trojan.

11.3.1.2 Design House is Untrusted

The combination of the untrusted design house and foundry manifoldly increases the vulnerability of Trojan attack. For this instance, the system designer is assumed to be a trusted entity. The primary task of the system designer is to verify the functionality and performance of the design through post-manufacturing PCB testing. In this attack scenario, the capability of the attacker is not limited to trace-level modifications. Access to untrusted foundry opens the opportunity for an attacker to modify the design structurally, and integrating additional malicious components that can get triggered by a predetermined set of conditions. Intelligently designed Trojan can be made stealthy by making it difficult to detect through optical inspection and setting the trigger condition to rare internal signal states. To further illustrate the attack scenario, a Trojan attack is demonstrated through a microcontrolled fan-speed controller. The controller works with a 12-V brushless DC fan that relies on the inputs of a temperature sensor. Based on the temperature reading, the sensors deliver an output voltage varying over 0 to 5 V. The voltage values are digitized by an ADC (analog-to-digital converter) and sent to the

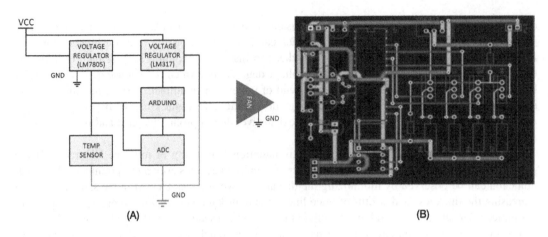

FIGURE 11.8

Example attack scenario when design house is untrusted: (A) Trojan inserted fan controller circuit; (B) A 2-layer PCB layout of the original circuit.

microcontroller to adjust the fan speed accordingly. The adjustment is done via linear regulation of fan input voltage.

Hardware Trojan attacks aiming at deliberate changes in the system functionality can be mounted via subtle structural modification of the PCBs. In this instance, it is possible to hamper the correct functionality of a microcontroller by launching a Trojan attack. Figures 11.8A and 11.9 refer to such an attack instance. In this attack scenario, the microcontroller contains three electrical components, that is, a PMOS transistor, a resistor, and a capacitor. The system is designed in a manner that the capacitor gets charged through the output of a specific voltage regulator, that is, LM317 connected to the fan circuitry. The attacker aims at triggering the Trojan by specific sets of values obtained from the resistor and the capacitor. The timing of the Trojan activation can also be fine-tuned via manipulation of the capacitive and resistive values. Once the Trojan is triggered, it nullifies the functionality of the PMOS transistor located in between the ADC and the temperature sensor. Consequently, the micro-controller will deem the null input as a temperature value of very low range, and reduce the fan speed significantly. Such failure, inaccurate temperature detection in mission-critical devices, may lead to catastrophic consequences. Moreover, the aforementioned Trojan can easily evade the functional test-ing phases by applying a large value of a time constant. The target design, a 2-layer PCB designed for microcontroller fan system, is illustrated in Fig. 11.8B. The figure depicts the design in pre-fabrication stage. Figure 11.9 demonstrates the Trojan in the fabricated PCB, the triggering of the attack, and the payload deliverance.

11.3.2 IN-FIELD ALTERATION

It is possible for an adversary to launch an attack on a PCB irrespective of its origin; a trusted or untrusted design house, through in-field physical alterations, if the system allows unauthorized access.

FIGURE 11.9

A fabricated PCB board, demonstrating triggering and payload of a Trojan.

11.3.2.1 Modchip Attack

A dominant, yet, least discussed security threat to the PCB is in-field alteration. The alteration can be caused by mounting ICs, soldering wires, rerouting paths to avoid or substitute existing blocks, adding or replacing components, exploiting traces, ports or test interfaces, and in many other ingenious ways. Circumventing DRM protection by tampering the PCB of a gaming console is a prominent example of PCB tampering. Physical alteration to disable built-in restrictions allows the user to play pirated, burnt, or unauthorized versions of a game on the hacked console. Modchips are devices that are used to alter the functionality or disable restrictions within a system, such as a computer or a video game system. Modchips usually contain a microcontroller, FPGA, or CPLD (complex programmable logic device) in order to attack the host system. They are soldered into the host system on top of the security-critical traces, as can be seen in Fig. 11.10. An industry-standard interface designed by Intel functions through the low-pin-count data bus, as shown in Fig. 11.10. The LPC bus is used for testing and debugging the Xbox during the production phase. Once these devices are installed they are often used for illegal purposes, such as playing illegally copied games and other forms of digital rights violations. For instance, Xbox Modchips can modify or disable the built-in restrictions integrated into Xbox consoles, allowing the users to play pirated games on the tampered consoles. Piracy leads to loss of revenue for game developers, and a reduced budget for future games.

An adversary can perform such tampering on a PCB to bypass DRM key-based protections in various systems. An illustration of such PCB-tampering attack is given in Fig. 11.11. The figure shows an attack instance, where the channel access grant signal of a TV set-top box is reliant on the DRM keys stored in a nonvolatile memory. A standard comparator is employed to grant the access signal in accordance to the channel number and corresponding DRM key. The comparator delivers a high signal in case of key match, and vice versa. However, it is possible to get access to the channels irrespective of the DRM keys by tampering the access grant signal wire. An attacker can tamper the wire by connecting it to the Vdd signal originating from a voltage regulator. Consequently, the access grant wire will always send a high signal to the channel-control circuitry, and the attacker will be given access to protected channels without the right keys. The tampered PCB trace is highlighted in red (dark gray in print version) to depict the attack mechanism. A protection scheme against such attacks would be integration of additional tamper-detection and protection circuitry for the critical

(A)   (B)

FIGURE 11.10

An illustration of Modchip attack. Physical tampering of the PCB of an Xbox gaming console is depicted in the figures: (A) Modchip wired to PCB of Xbox via low-pin-count (LPC) bus; (B) An illustration of LPC bus with associated pins of Modchip.

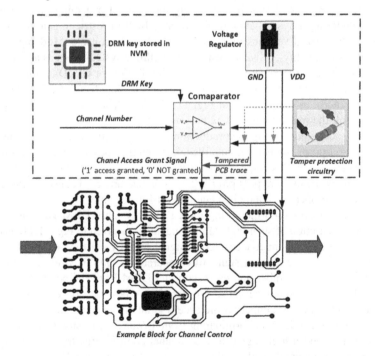

FIGURE 11.11

An illustrative example of Digital Rights Management (DRM) protection bypass through in-field PCB tampering.

traces on a PCB. The green (medium gray in print version) block in the PCB diagram (Fig. 11.11) shows a high-level representation of a resistance-sensing circuitry for the critical traces in the PCB. The physical tamper-detection and protection circuitry consists of a microcontroller and an e-fuse that trips the circuit in case of anomalies detected in resistance of the critical traces. Hardware attacks like Modchip alterations may jeopardize a company's profit margin. Video game piracy through tampered consoles caused around 1.45 billion pound sterling loss in sales in the UK in 2010. This led to around 1000 fewer jobs in the video game industry during that period [11,14]. These attacks also victimize the consumers when the gaming consoles or computing systems are resold in the market after tampering. These counterfeits cannot be trusted for a secure and safe operation. Mobile devices, embedded system, and the IoT devices are also vulnerable to the threats of Modchip attacks. Example of such attacks would be interfering with the data between DRAM, NAND flash, and SoCs via Modchips. Modchips can also be exploited to retrieve and alter data and system codes written from memory to SoC.

11.4 HANDS-ON EXPERIMENT: BUS SNOOPING ATTACK
11.4.1 OBJECTIVE

This experiment is designed to give students exposure to noninvasive bus-snooping attacks in a system. The attack is applied on the HaHa platform. The objective of this experiment is to give students practical experience to snooping through physical PCB-probing techniques.

11.4.2 METHOD

Students have to first map an example design into the microcontroller and the accelerometer on the HaHa platform. Next, the students will place testing probes in different wires between the microcontroller and the accelerometer to capture and observe the data flow. The example design allows the students to control the type of the mapped operation, while analyzing the behavior of each operation.

11.4.3 LEARNING OUTCOME

By performing the specific steps of the experiments, the students will learn how a bus-snooping attack is done, the associated challenges, and tools and techniques that can be used by an attacker to extract critical information from the PCB under attack. They will also experience the opportunities and explore possible solutions with respect to protecting hardware against snooping attacks.

11.4.4 ADVANCED OPTIONS

Additional exploration on this topic can be done through locating and applying the snooping attack to other components and interfaces (for example, processor-memory bus, Bluetooth communication, and interface).

More details about the experiment are available in the supplementary document. Please visit: http://hwsecuritybook.org.

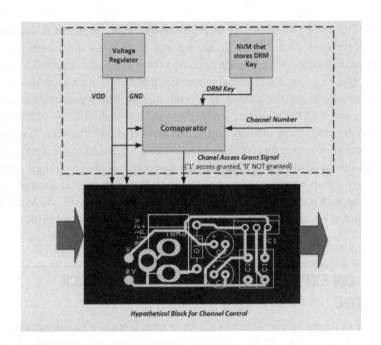

FIGURE 11.12

High-level block diagram of a PCB used in a TV set-top box.

11.5 EXERCISES

11.5.1 TRUE/FALSE QUESTIONS

1. Hardware Trojans in PCB could help cloning the design.
2. Modern-day PCBs are designed with a single layer.
3. JTAGs can be exploited to hack scan-chains.
4. It is not possible to leak information via PCB test pins.
5. Modchip attack is an example of in-field alteration.
6. Only untrusted design houses are vulnerable to PCB attacks.
7. Trusted design houses are not susceptible to malicious attacks.
8. Modchip attacks are prevalent in gaming consoles.
9. PCB reverse engineering requires industry-grade equipment and expertise.
10. It is comparatively easier to find a Trojan in multilayer PCBs.

11.5.2 SHORT-ANSWER TYPE QUESTIONS

1. Define hardware Trojans.
2. What is the definition of a Modchip?

3. What is JTAG?

4. What primary purpose a PCB serves in any electronic hardware system?

5. Describe possible attacks on a PCB.

6. In the high level block diagram of a PCB used in a TV set top box (Fig. 11.12), the Digital Right Management (DRM) key is stored in a non-volatile memory (NVM) which goes to a comparator that generates the channel grant access signal. Describe a possible tampering attack that can bypass this protection. You can update the drawing to illustrate your attack. You need to incorporate your attack within the dotted box.

7. What would be a possible solution to protect against the aforementioned tampering attacks?

8. What is PCB reverse engineering?

11.5.3 LONG-ANSWER TYPE QUESTIONS

1. Describe a potential attack instance when the design house is trusted in the PCB manufacturing process. Illustrate the scenario with an appropriate case study.

2. What would be an attack instance on PCBs manufactured in untrusted design houses? Describe with a relevant case study.

3. What are the possible attacks on PCBs? Explain the taxonomy of attacks with a brief description of each attack-type.

4. Describe a hardware Trojan attack instance on an insecure PCB.

5. How can a Modchip attack be mounted on a PCB? Explain elaborately.

REFERENCES

[1] S. Bhunia, M.S. Hsiao, M. Banga, S. Narasimhan, Hardware Trojan attacks: threat analysis and countermeasures, Proceedings of the IEEE 102 (2014) 1229–1247.

[2] R.S. Chakraborty, S. Narasimhan, S. Bhunia, Hardware Trojan: threats and emerging solutions, in: High Level Design Validation and Test Workshop, 2009. HLDVT 2009. IEEE International, IEEE, pp. 166–171.

[3] Y. Alkabani, F. Koushanfar, Consistency-based characterization for IC Trojan detection, in: Proceedings of the 2009 International Conference on Computer-Aided Design, ACM, pp. 123–127.

[4] H. Salmani, M. Tehranipoor, J. Plusquellic, A layout-aware approach for improving localized switching to detect hardware Trojans in integrated 386 circuits, in: Information Forensics and Security (WIFS), 2010 IEEE International Workshop on, IEEE, pp. 1–6.

[5] S. Ghosh, A. Basak, S. Bhunia, How secure are printed circuit boards against Trojan attacks? IEEE Design & Test 32 (2015) 7–16.

[6] W. Jillek, W. Yung, Embedded components in printed circuit boards: a processing technology review, The International Journal of Advanced Manufacturing Technology 25 (2005) 350–360.

[7] S. Paley, T. Hoque, S. Bhunia, Active protection against PCB physical tampering, in: Quality Electronic Design (ISQED), 2016 17th International Symposium on, IEEE, pp. 356–361.

[8] J. Carlsson, Crosstalk on printed circuit boards, SP Rapport, 1994, 14.

[9] B. Sood, M. Pecht, Controlling moisture in printed circuit boards, in: IPC Apex EXPO Proceedings, 2010.

[10] O. Solsjö, Secure key management in a trusted domain on mobile devices, 2015.

[11] Modchip.net, https://www.mod-chip.net/, 2011. (Accessed 10 September 2018).

[12] D. Whitworth, Gaming industry lose 'billions' to chipped consoles – BBC newsbeat, 2011.

[13] S. Chhabra, B. Rogers, Y. Solihin, SHIELDSTRAP: Making secure processors truly secure, in: IEEE International Conference on Computer Design, 2009.

[14] J. Grand, K.D. Mitnick, R. Russell, Hardware Hacking: Have Fun While Voiding Your Warranty, Syngress, 2004.

COUNTERMEASURES AGAINST HARDWARE ATTACKS

HARDWARE SECURITY PRIMITIVES

12

CONTENTS

Hardware Security. https://doi.org/10.1016/B978-0-12-812477-2.00017-4

12.1 INTRODUCTION

The current-world computer system security issues do not encompass only software and information threats or vulnerabilities of the early 2000s. Rather, hardware-oriented security has become an increasing concern due to growing threat and attack complexity. The advent of novel security threats, such as hardware Trojans, counterfeit electronic products, and various physical attacks have nullified the underlying notion of hardware as the root of trust. Furthermore, low-cost and resource-constrained IoT, mobile, and embedded devices now require secure and reliable hardware platforms more than ever for trustworthy communication, privacy protection, defense against numerous software or hardware threats, and vulnerabilities.

In this regard, hardware security primitives and designs play an important role to ensure trust, integrity, and authenticity of electronic chips and systems. Such primitives can work as the hardware-level building blocks to develop a secure platform. Among common hardware security primitives, physical unclonable functions (PUFs) and true random number generators (TRNGs) are most notable for utilizing device-intrinsic process variations and noise to extract entropy [1–3]. These primitives can be used for generating cryptographic keys and IDs to authenticate devices and systems, to produce session keys, nonce, and many more. These primitives, acting as a hardware alternative to key storage, digital fingerprint, or software-generated bitstreams can provide defense against prevailing adversarial threats, such as spoofing and cloning. In addition, researchers have proposed designs for countermeasures, that can defend against IC counterfeiting, tampering, and reverse engineering, by utilizing a different set of device-intrinsic properties. For example, combating die and IC recycling (CDIR) sensor leverages aging and wear-out mechanisms in common CMOS-devices to offer countermeasures against IC counterfeiting (recycling) [4]. Nevertheless, with the rise of emerging threats and vulnerabilities, and longstanding attacks becoming more practical, designers constantly seek for novel primitives and countermeasures that utilize the device's inherent properties to enhance security.

12.2 PRELIMINARIES

12.2.1 COMMON HARDWARE SECURITY PRIMITIVES

Hardware security primitives, such as PUFs and TRNGs, and countermeasures, including design for anti-counterfeit (DfAC) offer safeguards to various potential threats and vulnerabilities arising at different phases of the IC lifecycle and device operation. PUFs generate device-specific digital output that is tied to the intrinsic properties of the device. Hence, a PUF-generated signature can be considered as a digital fingerprint. This fingerprint is usually produced by accumulating inherent minute process variations from the manufacturing steps. Since such process variations are random and static in nature, the generated fingerprint is ideally unclonable from device-to-device, and unpredictable to the adversary. This digital fingerprint can be used for cryptographic key generation, device authentication, and preventing cloning.

TRNGs, on the other hand, generate random digital bitstreams that do not have any predictability whatsoever. They exploit the random transient variations in the system, such as power supply fluctuations, and device intrinsic noise. The source of entropy [5] of a TRNG is, therefore, ideally different from that of a PUF. The random bit-stream generated by a TRNG can be used as assets such as session keys and nonce.

DfACs, such as a CDIR module, provide certain signatures by monitoring the lifetime of a chip. In most cases, a recycled IC experience ample amount of prior usage before getting back into the supply chain as a counterfeit product. Electrical components, such as CMOS transistors, tend to deviate from their ideal characteristics, for example, speed and power consumptions, due to aging. A CDIR module can, therefore, monitor such characteristics deviations and perceive prior usage, if any.

12.2.2 PERFORMANCE OF A CMOS DEVICE

Even after several decades, CMOS-based devices still dominate the semiconductor industry due to improved lithographic techniques, ease of fabrication, and high yield with respect to manufacturing cost. The road to advanced nodes has produced multiple architectures: from regular planar bulk-CMOS devices to high-k/metal-gate transistors and tri-gate/FinFET transistors. All these devices are traditionally intended to offer high-performance with smaller size, higher speed, lower leakage, and provide better reliability. However, with the technology nodes getting more advanced with smaller feature sizes, the semiconductor industry faces major manufacturing and reliability issues. In particular, CMOS devices are now experiencing greater process variations and more aggressive performance degradation due to aging and runtime variations [6]. Figure 12.1 lists some key physical parameters and runtime/reliability factors that can have drastic negative effects on IC performance and reliability [7]. Nevertheless, many such properties and phenomena play a key role in devising the aforementioned hardware security primitives (as shown in the right-hand columns of Fig. 12.1; discussed further in Section 12.2.3).

- *Process Variations:* CMOS device manufacturing process has numerous sources of systematic and random variations that play a critical role in yield and performance. CMOS front-end of the line

CMOS Bulk, HK+MG and FinFET Device Properties for Security Applications

Phenomena		Electrical Manifestation (Performance)	Security Applications
Process Variations	• Geometric Variation (Patterning – W, L) • Random Dopant Fluctuation (RDF) • Line Edge Roughness (LER) • Oxide Thickness (T_{ox}) Fluctuation • Interface defect and traps (ITC) • Polysilicon/Metal Gate Granularity (MGG)	• Threshold Voltage Deviation (ΔV_{TH}) • Carrier Mobility Degradation ($\Delta \mu_n$) • Drain Current Variation (ΔI_{ON}) • Off-state Leakage Current Variation (ΔI_{Leak}) • Drain Induced Barrier Lowering (DIBL)	PUF — • Arbiter • RO • Leakage Current • Bistable Ring • Hybrid Delay/ Cross-coupled PUF
Aging & Wear-out Mechanisms	• Bias Temperature Instability (NBTI/PBTI) • Hot Carrier Injection (HCI) • Time Dependent Dielectric Breakdown (TDDB) • Electromigration (EM)		TRNG — • Thermal/Power Supply Noise • Clock Jitter • Metastability • Oxide soft-breakdown
Runtime Variations	• Power Supply Noise • Temperature Variation		DfAC — • Recycling – Aging (CDIR) • Cloning – Process Variation

FIGURE 12.1

Potential use of inherent device properties for security applications.

(FEOL) variation sources are most notably patterning (proximity) effects, line-edge roughness (LER), nonuniform n/p-type doping, and gate dielectrics, such as oxide thickness variations, defects, and traps. Variations due to random dopant fluctuations and gate material granularity (poly-si or metal gate) are also becoming significant in advanced nodes [6]. These phenomena directly impact the electrostatic integrity of the channel and affect the strength of the device. Back-end of the line (BEOL) sources, such as metal interconnect and dielectric variations, also have a substantial impact [8]. All such variations holistically cause deviation in device characteristics, making every single transistor slightly different from each other with a shift from the nominal performance. Such manufacturing process variations are undesirable for performance-oriented logic and memory applications, yet unavoidable, and often prominent in the advanced nodes.

• *Runtime/environmental variations:* Similar to manufacturing process variations, various runtime/environmental variations, such as temperature fluctuation and power supply noise, also have a direct impact on electrical characteristics of a transistor. For instance, an increase in the operating temperature decreases both carrier mobility (μ) and threshold voltage (V_{th}) of a traditional transistor, and thus impacts the speed (delay) of the device, since they cause an opposing impact on the drain saturation current (I_{DS}) and leakage current (I_{Leak}). However, technology nodes also play a crucial role in the performance impact. For example, technology nodes from 45 nm and below can show an increase in device speed with temperature, whereas it is the opposite in older technologies [9]. In addition, global and local power supply noise has an adverse impact on performance, since such variations also cause a shift in V_{th} and I_{DS} from the nominal value. Hence, for both cases, a system is less robust and prone to produce erroneous results. However, unlike a permanent shift in performance resulting from the manufacturing process variation or aging, a change in the environmental condition usually causes a temporary shift, given that the experienced variations have not caused a permanent damage or wear out. Therefore, it is compensated once the device returns to its nominal operating state.

- *Aging and wear-out mechanisms:* Aging degradation and wear-out mechanisms, such as bias temperature instability (BTI), hot carrier injection (HCI), electromigration (EM), and time-dependent dielectric breakdown (TDDB), lead to a poor device and circuit performance. The magnitude of such degradation largely depends on the device workload, active bias, inherent random defects, and technology nodes under consideration. BTI and HCI are considered key aging mechanisms that directly impact the speed of CMOS devices. BTI slows down transistors as traps are generated at SiO_2/Si interface, resulting in an increase in threshold voltage magnitude ($|V_{th}|$) over time. Typically negative BTI (NBTI) occurring in PMOS transistors is dominant compared to positive BTI (PBTI) occurring in NMOS transistors beyond 65 nm technology nodes. However, the latter is becoming prominent for high-k metal-gate devices [10]. Additionally, HCI slows down a device by generating charged defects in gate oxide, interfacing to increase V_{th}, and by reducing the mobility of a device. HCI is more prominent in NMOS with smaller feature size. However, HCI-induced degradation can be recovered to a certain limit and is affected by voltage, temperature, and device workload [11]. Both of these mechanisms greatly decrease reliability and, eventually, shorten chip-lifetime with increased failure rate. Although such mechanisms are quite slow and the degradation magnitude is relatively hard to precisely predict, since it is statistical in nature, an accelerated aging (that is, running the chip at a higher voltage and/or temperature than the nominal operating condition) allows us to determine the probable impact on the IC performance and lifetime in most cases. This also helps to deploy any compensating mechanisms.

12.2.3 PERFORMANCE AND RELIABILITY VS. SECURITY

It is evident that the CMOS device performance deviates due to process variation, environmental condition, and aging. Therefore, minimizing process variations and other degradation phenomena is of utmost importance for high-performance circuits. However, one can also see that these variations and degradation mechanisms do not necessarily have adverse impacts on hardware security primitives and applications. In fact, some of these variations and degradation mechanisms can be effectively leveraged for ensuring hardware-based security (see Fig. 12.1). For example, PUFs rely on the manufacturing process variations. An increase in physical variations can potentially improve the PUF outcome quality, although high manufacturing variation is undesirable for high performance and yield. In addition, the detection process of some types of counterfeit electronics can benefit from inherent aging and wear-out mechanisms; the signs of prior use can potentially lead to the detection of recycled chips.

Note that, not every phenomenon is always beneficial to all the security applications either. Let us use the terms – *good*, *bad*, and *ugly* – to qualitatively state the relationship between process variations, reliability degradation, and various hardware-based security mechanisms, as shown in Table 12.1. The first column of Table 12.1 shows conventional and security-based applications and primitives, and respective rows refer to how process variation, temperature, power supply noise, aging, and wear-out mechanisms affect the quality of operation. Here, the good indicates that variation or degradation mechanism is actually desirable and beneficial in relation to a security application or primitive; the bad means that it should be avoided if possible, and the ugly means that it is highly undesirable for a reliable operation. For example, in trivial logic/memory applications, manufacturing process variation is highly undesirable (ugly) to ensure better performance; whereas it is one of the key requirements (that

Table 12.1 Design and technology characteristics vs. security trade-off

Application/primitive	Process variation	Temperature	Power supply noise	Aging (BTI/HCI)	Wear-out (EM)
Logic/memory design	Ugly	Bad	Bad	Bad	Bad
PUF	Good	Bad	Bad	Bad	Bad
TRNG	Good	Bad	Good	Bad	Bad
Recycled IC detection	Ugly	Bad	Bad	Good	Good

is, good) for PUF and TRNG applications. Aging and wear-out mechanisms are bad for both regular logic/memory applications and PUFs. However, they can be leveraged (that is, *good*) for detecting recycled electronics [12].

It is, therefore, vital that one establishes proper correlation status among performance, reliability, and security. To achieve this, rather than building security primitives solely relying on trivial logic/memory application-oriented designs, one should make a balance of performance, reliability, and security to obtain the best trade-off depending on the target application.

12.3 PHYSICAL UNCLONABLE FUNCTION
12.3.1 PUF PRELIMINARIES

As indicated in Section 12.2.1, a PUF generates digital fingerprints using device-intrinsic characteristics. Ideally, it is a cryptographically secure one-way function that generates a digital output (response) for a given input (challenge) without revealing any predictable mapping between the challenge and response [1,2,13]. As the name suggests, a PUF can generate digital output (IDs or keys) by leveraging inherent physical variations from the manufacturing process. Therefore, identical (by design and lithography/mask) integrated circuits manufactured by the same fabrication facility and process can generate different challenge-response pairs (or cryptographic keys), as there always exists small, but nondeterministic, variations in the manufacturing process. Generally, the input or challenges to the PUF excite certain electrical characteristics, such as delay or leakage current, variation to extract maximum entropy.

This is a crucial advancement over the conventional nonvolatile memory-based key-storage mechanisms. In traditional methods, secret keys are stored digitally in a nonvolatile memory (NVM), such as flash memory or electrically erasable programmable read-only memory (EEPROM), which is always vulnerable, based on hardware implementation, key-propagation mechanisms, and physical attacks. The NVM that stores the cryptographic keys can be subjected to tampering, probing, and imaging attacks. Therefore, it must be protected by the physical layer of security, in addition to protocol-level protections. Since a PUF can produce a cryptographic key or digital fingerprint which, in addition, is unique from device to device, it eliminates the requirement to "store" the key in a memory, as it can be generated on demand via input triggers. There is no need to program the secret, and it can generate multiple master keys by changing associated challenge sets. Also, any additional physical attack on the PUF, such as probing, impacts the inherent characteristic and drastically change the PUF's response. Therefore, PUFs offer an attractive volatile and tamper-resistant alternative to conventional cryptographic key-storage techniques [14,15].

12.3.2 PUF CLASSIFICATIONS

Based on the underlying challenge-response pair (CRP)-space, PUFs can be broadly categorized into *weak* and *strong* PUFs. A weak PUF, also known as a *physically obfuscated key* (POK), typically can be interrogated with a very limited number of challenges [16,17]. Therefore, its CRP-space is extremely small, often even only one. Such a PUF can be used for generating cryptographic keys. An SRAM-PUF (to be discussed in Section 12.3.4) is a notable example of this type.

In contrast, a strong PUF can accommodate a very large number of challenges to produce corresponding responses [18]. Ideally, the CRP-space grows exponentially with the length of challenge itself. This allows the PUF to undergo multiple queries and use a new challenge-set every time to avoid any collision or replay attacks. The arbiter-PUF and ring-oscillator PUF (to be discussed in Section 12.3.4) are prominent examples of strong PUFs.

One can also bootstrap a strong PUF to external logic and algorithms for providing secure and controlled access to the PUF via an application programming interface (API). Such a PUF design, known as a controlled-PUF, is very much application-oriented and can offer additional security against spoofing and modeling attacks, where the adversary tries to fool the system using a predictive model-generated response (to be further discussed in Section 12.6.1.1) [14].

12.3.3 PUF QUALITY PROPERTIES

In general, an ideal PUF should only exploit physical properties of a device, such as process variation, to generate the response and not rely on stored data. The unclonability indicates that it cannot be replaced with a software model to replicate the PUF outcome, and must be prohibitively difficult to physically duplicate. To make it unclonable, the design should utilize small and random intrinsic variations, so that the exact response cannot be predicted by the adversary and the challenges undergo a one-way transformation (response). Additionally, the PUF itself should be inexpensive to fabricate for a wide variety of low-cost applications, and be intrinsically attack-resilient, that is, must not generate a deterministic response due to external adversarial control.

Although, most of the PUFs proposed in literature possess trivial properties, the response they produce are not necessarily ideal for targeted applications, for example, key generations and authentication. The most popular quality metrics to evaluate PUF responses include uniqueness, randomness (or uniformity), and reproducibility (or reliability). The qualitative assessment of PUFs is important, as a poor PUF may lead to error in cryptographic applications and authentication protocols, and it may be prone to different modeling and machine learning attacks [15,19].

Uniqueness measures the distinctive challenge-response pair (CRP) generation quality, that is, distinguishability, of a PUF with respect to other instances. This is the very first step of quality assessment for both weak and strong PUFs. A common measurement of uniqueness is the inter-PUF hamming distance (inter-HD), calculated over multiple PUFs, given as [19]

$$HD_{\text{inter}} = \frac{2}{n(n-1)} \sum_{i=1}^{n-1} \sum_{j=i+1}^{n} \frac{HD(R_i, R_j)}{k} \times 100\%, \tag{12.1}$$

where n stands for the total number of PUFs under assessment, k is the response length, and $HD(R_i, R_j)$ is the hamming distance between the response R_i from PUF_i and the response R_j from

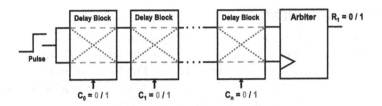

FIGURE 12.2

Standard structure of arbiter PUF.

PUF_j (where $i \neq j$) from the testing pool. An inter-PUF HD of 50% produces the ideal uniqueness, that is, it provides a maximum difference in the response bits between any two PUFs.

Randomness or uniformity stands for the unpredictability of a PUF. Usually, strong PUFs show if there is any measurable trend in the generated response, since an ideal PUF should be free from bias and correlation. In order to assess the randomness of the produced responses from multiple challenges, statistical test suites, such as the NIST test suite [20], DieHARD [21] are commonly used. Additionally, a good diffusive property is expected for strong PUFs, that is, a small change in the input challenge should produce a large variation in the response (also known as the avalanche effect).

Reproducibility or reliability assesses the PUF's quality in terms of its capability to generate same CRPs across different environmental conditions, and over time. This is traditionally measured via intra-PUF hamming distance given as [19]

$$HD_{\text{intra}} = \frac{1}{m} \sum_{y=1}^{m} \frac{HD(R_i, R'_{i,y})}{k} \times 100\%, \tag{12.2}$$

where m stands for the number of samples or run for a PUF, k is the response length from the signature generated by the PUF, and $HD(R_i, R'_{i,y})$ is the hamming distance between the response R_i and the yth sampling $R'_{i,y}$ of the PUF under test. Ideally, a PUF should always maintain the same challenge-response pairs (CRPs) over different operating conditions and/or times resulting into zero-bit error rate (i.e. 0% intra-PUF HD).

12.3.4 COMMON PUF ARCHITECTURES

12.3.4.1 Arbiter PUF

Arbiter-PUF is one of the most notable CMOS logic-based PUF architecture that exploits the randomness of path delay due to uncontrollable process variation [2]. Figure 12.2 shows the generic design of an arbiter-PUF. Each of the building blocks is an individual delay unit with path-switching capability controlled by the challenge bit (denoted by c_i). Given a pulse at the input of a delay stage, it can traverse through two design-wise identical, but different paths (selected by challenge) and reach the final arbiter (or decision-making) component. If the signal in the upper path reaches the arbiter first, it generates "1" (and vice versa). Ideally, in the absence of any manufacturing process variation, the delay through both the paths would be the same and the signal would reach the arbiter at the exact same time. However, there always exists some process variation induced delay difference between these two

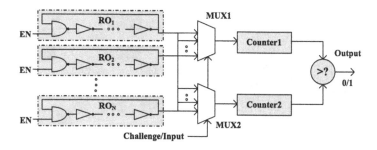

FIGURE 12.3

Conventional RO-PUF.

identical paths, and one of the signals reach the arbiter faster than the other. Since, the paths do not have any systematic or extrinsic delay difference, the shortest/longest path is not deterministic, and only depends on the individual transistor strength and interconnects. As shown in Section 12.2.2, any random deviation in physical or electrical properties would cause this nondeterministic variation. As an increase in the number of delay stages (cascaded one after another in series) exponentially increases possible path-pairs, the arbiter-PUF is capable of generating a large number of CRPs (strong PUF). Another advantage of arbiter PUF is that it takes only one cycle to generate a 1-bit response, although the number of delay stages makes the path (delay) longer.

However, the arbiter PUF has some major drawbacks, one of them being the bias induced at the arbiter itself due to finite delay-difference resolution for the setup, and hold times. Also, this requires symmetric design and routing, which may not be readily available for lightweight and FPGA-applications. Additionally, the arbiter-PUF has been shown to be vulnerable to modeling attack, since it can be represented as a linear delay model.

12.3.4.2 Ring Oscillator (RO) PUF

The schematic of a typical ring-oscillator-based PUF (RO-PUF) is shown in Fig. 12.3. It does not require rigorous design and can be easily implemented in both ASIC and reconfigurable platforms, such as FPGAs [22]. An RO-PUF is generally composed of N identical ring oscillators (ROs), two multiplexers, two counters, and one comparator. When enabled, each of the ROs oscillates at a slightly different frequency from one another due to process variations. A challenge is applied to select one pair of ROs, and the number of oscillations of each of the ROs in the selected pair is counted and compared to generate a "0" or "1", based on which oscillator from the selected RO pair is faster.

Compared to an arbiter PUF, the RO-PUF is larger and slower for generating the same number of response bits. Whereas an arbiter PUF can generate the response bits in one system clock, RO-PUF requires a significant number of counts of the oscillatory signals to obtain a reliable value. The oscillatory switching of the components makes it power-hungry. Since all the components of RO go through significant usage, it suffers from runtime power and temperature variations and aging. This makes the RO-PUF prone to generating erroneous output.

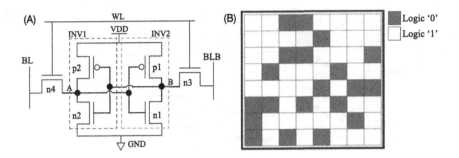

FIGURE 12.4

(A) Typical 6T SRAM cell. (B) Startup fingerprint of an example SRAM array.

12.3.4.3 *SRAM-PUF*

In contrast to custom-designed arbiter- and RO-PUFs, a static random-access memory (SRAM)-based PUF utilizes the widely available SRAM-matrix used in microprocessors, microcontrollers, field-programmable gate arrays (FPGAs) and in standalone chips for embedded systems. Typically, one SRAM bit is implemented by a symmetrically designed 6-transistor cell, as shown in Fig. 12.4A, where either one of the nodes *A* or *B* is pulled high, and the other is pulled low in the stable state once the cell is programmed (written). Due to the feedback provided by the cross-coupled inverter structure, the stable state holds true until the cell is rewritten or the system power is off.

In contrast, during the startup in absence of any "write"/programming command, both the logic nodes tend to pull up to high voltage. However, only one wins via racing condition to reach high voltage (logic 1), and automatically pulls the other node down to low voltage (logic 0). This initialization typically depends on the minute process-induced strength mismatch among the cell transistors (especially between the two pull-up PMOS-transistors), and is completely unpredictable to an external observer. The start-up outcome, being strongly tied to the physical process variation, is static and tends to produce the same outcome for a given cell over multiple power-ups. Therefore, the startup of the SRAM cell can be utilized as a weak PUF for device-intrinsic fingerprint generation [17,23].

It should be noted that the process variation in the SRAM cell may be small enough to be overcome by environmental noise and, therefore, not all cells can produce a reliable response over time and usages. For example, Fig. 12.4B shows the initial startup values of some cells in the SRAM matrix. Among them, only the cells that show the highest reproducibility should be selected to generate the PUF signature. Additionally, advanced SRAM-inclusive commercial off-the-shelf (CoTs) products may not readily provide suitable PUF application due to various initialization and memory-access processes. For example, in some recent Altera and Xilinx FPGA models, RAM blocks are always initialized to certain logic at startup and, therefore, cannot be used to implement the SRAM-PUF based on a random initialization [24].

12.3.4.4 *Butterfly PUF*

The design of Butterfly PUF is inspired by the notion of creating a circuit structure with metastable properties in FPGA matrix [25]. Similar to the SRAM-PUF, the floating state of Butterfly PUF can be exploited to obtain a random state at the startup phase of a pair of cross-coupled latches in the

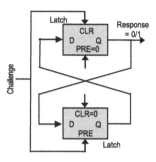

FIGURE 12.5

Typical butterfly PUF schematic.

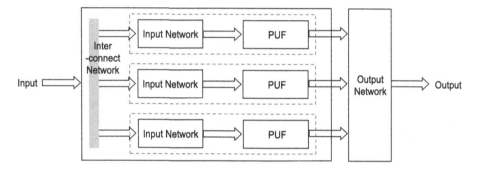

FIGURE 12.6

Generic structure of a lightweight PUF.

FPGA. The latches form a combinational loop that can be excited to an unstable state through a proper signal, that is, challenge as depicted in Fig. 12.5. Although conceived for FPGA implementations, similar implementation can be done utilizing the metastability of any latch or flip-flop-based architecture.

12.3.4.5 Lightweight PUF

Lightweight PUF, as shown in Fig. 12.6 [26], utilizes traditional arbiter-PUF with nontrivial wiring between arbiter stages. Rather than directly feeding the challenges to the PUFs, it creates a networked scheme that breaks down the challenge set into several blocks, and uses them on multiple individual PUFs. The output network then combines all the individual-PUF responses to create a global response, making it more resilient against machine learning attacks [27].

12.3.4.6 Bistable Ring PUF

A bistable ring contains an even number of inverters and can only have two possible stable outcomes. However, due to manufacturing process variation and noise, the bistable ring goes through a set of complex transitions (or metastability) before converging to a stable state.

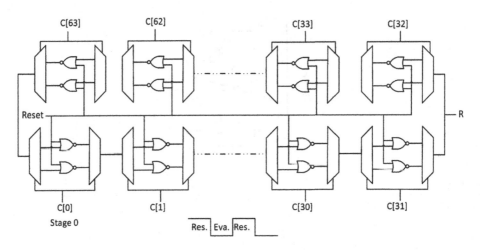

FIGURE 12.7

A 64-stage bistable ring PUF.

As illustrated in Fig. 12.7, a bistable ring PUF can exploit the metastability to generate exponential number of CRPs [28]. Similar to arbiter PUF, it requires a symmetric layout. Nevertheless, this strong PUF offers relatively high resiliency against modeling attacks due to its complex and nonlinear nature, and thereby can be incorporated into emerging PUF applications such as *Virtual Proof of Reality* [29].

12.3.5 PUF APPLICATIONS

12.3.5.1 Secret Key Generation

As mentioned in Section 12.3.1, PUFs can be used to generate secret keys for cryptographic applications. Since weak PUFs have a limited CRP-space, the response from such a PUF can be used as a key, where it does not require to be discarded every time after use. Additionally, a strong PUF can be used to generate a new key every time a cryptographic protocol is under use, for example, to generate a session key in a timely fashion. It should be noted that the "reproducibility" feature of the PUF is extremely crucial for cryptographic applications. Since even a slight mismatch (error) in the generated key due to measurement noise can corrupt the cryptographic application and underlying message, the generated key must be error-free, that is, 0% intra-HD. If not, the PUF (and associated modules) should be bootstrapped with efficient error-correcting code (ECC) memory scheme to provide zero bit flip.

Figure 12.8 shows the cryptographic key generation scheme presented in [22]. The ECC used here gets rid of any unwanted runtime error by initialization and regeneration. Furthermore, the generated key may lack necessary qualities to be treated as an ideal key for certain cryptographic protocols. For example, the key used for RSA needs to satisfy certain mathematical properties, whereas PUF-generated keys are typically arbitrary, due to nondeterministic process variations. Such properties can be achieved by using cryptographic hash algorithms with the PUF responses taken as inputs. Additionally, it helps to prevent any side-channel leakage of the originally generated key. This is especially true for weak PUFs that generates only a single key and, therefore, must be protected against any adversar-

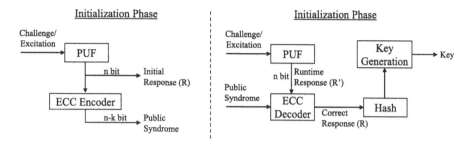

FIGURE 12.8

Cryptographic key generation with PUFs.

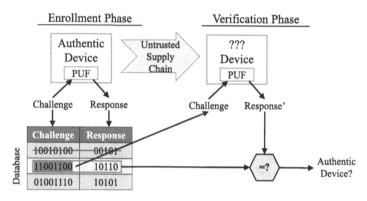

FIGURE 12.9

Strong PUF-based authentication.

ial access. To achieve further mathematical properties for the key (such as in RSA), the hashed output can again be input as a seed to an appropriate key-generation algorithm. Note that none of such steps require storing the key in a nonvolatile memory or leak the key to the outer world, given that a proper secure implementation is undertaken.

12.3.5.2 Device Authentication

Strong PUFs are excellent candidates to provide individual device authentication based on hardware-intrinsic signatures. Figure 12.9 shows a simple PUF-based authentication technique that does not require expensive cryptographic implementations, and can be easily implemented in a resource-constrained platform such as RFID, or in commercial off-the-shelf FPGAs, where cryptographic modules may not be readily available [22].

Since a strong PUF provides a unique and unpredictable output for an individual device, the response can be considered as a device-intrinsic identification signature/fingerprint. This can be used to authenticate (identify) individual devices given that the trusted authenticator already has a recorded copy of the CRPs. A trusted party, therefore, builds the CRP database for an authentic IC by applying random challenges to obtain unpredictable responses. For an in-field authentication operation, the trusted party selects a recorded (but not previously used in the field) challenge and verifies the obtained response with the stored one. To protect against man-in-the-middle and replay attacks, the used CRP is discarded from the future usable CRP pool.

One should also note that practical authentication protocols usually keep an acceptable error margin in matching the stored and in-field responses to allow noise measurement during authentication. However, the PUFs used for authentication should have high a uniqueness to confidently identify different devices (that is, reduces the probability of ID collisions) even in the presence of small errors.

12.3.5.3 Software and IP Licensing

Another application for PUF is for software/IP licensing and certified executions. There have been various proposed schemes for device-bound certified executions [14]. For example, the PUF response can be used as a seed for a public/private key pair, and the seed is used to generate the private key. A certification authority publishes and certifies the public key. So a particular program can be prepared as copy/execution-protected using the PUF response and will not run on any other chip that does not satisfy the keys.

12.3.5.4 Hardware Metering

Researchers have also proposed PUFs for active and passive IC metering. In passive IC metering, the IP rights owner is able to identify and monitor the devices, whereas in active IP metering, the IP owner can actively control, enable/disable, and authenticate a device. This protects the hardware against foundry piracy (overproduction). Alkabani and Koushanfar [30] proposed a finite-state-machine (FSM)-based approach, where the functional specification of the design is modified and tied to the PUF outcome. This modified FSM architecture hides (obfuscates) a state in the large state-space of the FSM. A PUF-generated key puts the design one of the hidden obfuscated states (locked state) and provides a nonfunctional/erroneous outcome. Only an "unlocking key" provided by the IP owner can put the chip into the original functional state.

12.4 TRUE RANDOM NUMBER GENERATOR
12.4.1 TRNG PRELIMINARIES

A TRNG is a hardware primitive widely used in security and cryptographic applications to generate session keys, one-time pads, random seeds, nonces, challenges to PUFs, and so on, and these applications are growing in number with time [3,31,32]. It typically generates a random digital bitstream with high uncertainty, or entropy, where the sequence of producing 0s and 1s are equal, and completely independent to its previous value or any other external control. To generate an output that is truly random, a TRNG must rely on device intrinsic electrical and/or thermal noise that is inherently non-deterministic and uncontrollable.

A typical TRNG consists of an entropy source, entropy extraction or sampling unit and, in most cases, a postprocessing or cryptographic conditioning unit. The entropy source is the focal point of a TRNG, because the quality of the TRNG system highly depends on the raw entropy coming from this entropy source. For a TRNG, such sources are analog in nature, and include random telegraph noise (RTN) found in scaled transistors, power supply noise, radioactive decay, latch metastability, jitter in ring oscillators, and so on [32]. The throughput (speed) and power consumption of the TRNG greatly depend on the physical component (analog or digital) used as a source and the resolution of the exploited noise.

The extraction or sampling unit extracts the entropy from the source into a favorable digital form. However, it should not impact the original physical process that produces the noise. The target of the sampling unit is to achieve maximum entropy under design constraints (such as area and power) and, in many cases, does not focus on the quality of the generated random bitstream.

The postprocessing unit focuses on improving the quality of the extracted bitstream from the sampling units to ensure the true randomness of the output. A good post-processor eliminates any hidden bias of the raw output [33]. Some common postprocessing techniques include Von Neumann Extractor [34] and cryptographic hash functions [35]. In many recent designs, the TRNG may contain additional conditioning blocks that can non-deterministically increase noise and/or makes it robust against runtime environmental variations and active fault and side-channel attacks [36–38].

In contrast to the hardware-based TRNG, a software-based "seemingly" random number generator, commonly known as a pseudo-random number generator (PRNG), relies on algorithms and tends to produce high throughput with lightweight implementations, although the output is statistically deterministic. A PRNG is not effectively secure, because its next state can be predicted from the current state if an adversary gains access to the design and knows the seed. In communication and cryptographic applications, a predictable RNG can expose the sensitive data to the adversary, and it is, in such cases, not "truly random" anymore.

12.4.2 TRNG QUALITY PROPERTIES

Unlike PUF quality metrics, the quality of a TRNG relies mostly on *randomness*. In order to assess the *randomness* of the bits produced by a TRNG, statistical test suites, such as the NIST Test Suite [20] and DieHARD [21], are commonly used and are usually the first (and the easiest) step to analyze the randomness of a TRNG.

One problem with TRNG entropy sources is that although they might be "intuitively random", statistical tests run on the output of the TRNG may show a certain level of bias and predictability, especially under conditions such as environmental and process variations. To combat this, cryptographic hash functions, von Neumann corrector, and stream ciphers are employed to manipulate the raw output of the TRNGs to ensure the uniformity and statistical randomness. Also, additional tuners and processing blocks may be employed to control the TRNG quality and throughput [36].

It should be noted that the operating condition of the TRNG is also a key factor for generating "truly" random numbers, as power supply variation, temperature deviation, clock frequency, added noise, or external signal, etc. can impact the intrinsic entropy source and extracted features. Hence, the *reliability* of the TRNG is also crucial in a sense that the TRNG itself needs maintaining the randomness throughout its operational lifetime and, additionally, show resiliency against attacks tailored with operational condition variation.

12.4.3 COMMON TRNG ARCHITECTURES

Typically, CMOS-based random number generators are designed by comparing two symmetric systems (or devices) that possess some process variation or/and ample amount of random inner noise to serve as an inherent entropy source. Based on the sources of randomness and system architecture, TRNGs can be categorized into: device's inherent noise-based TRNGs, jitter and metastability based TRNGs (that

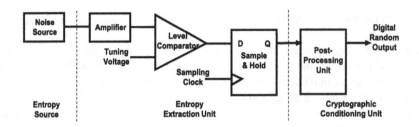

FIGURE 12.10

General schematic of noise-based TRNG.

is, free-running oscillator based TRNGs), chaos TRNGs, and quantum TRNGs [32]. However, not all TRNGs proposed in the literature are entirely CMOS-based, as some may require external optical/laser sources for excitation of the entropy sources. In this section, the discussion is confined to CMOS-based TRNGs.

12.4.3.1 Noise-Based TRNGs

Device-inherent noise is typically random and can be harnessed for generating true random numbers. Common noise sources include TRNG entropy sources (random telegraph noise (RTN)), Zener noise (in semiconductor Zener diodes), Flicker or $1/f$-noise, and Johnson's noise [32]. The basic idea of noise-based TRNG is as follows: the random analog voltage, caused by the noise source, is sampled periodically and compared to a certain pre-defined threshold to produce a "1" or "0" as shown in Fig. 12.10. The threshold can be fine-tuned to produce an ideally equal probability of "1"s and "0"s. However, setting up a proper threshold may be a rigorous process and may need readjustments and fine-tuning, based on run-time conditions.

The earlier version of Intel TRNG was developed leveraging Johnson's noise, where the source of randomness is the random thermal motion of charged carriers [39]. However, a more efficient, faster, and exceptionally simple TRNG was designed in 2011 (see Fig. 12.11) [3]. This TRNG design uses a pair of cross-coupled inverters (or a trimmed RS-type flip-flop), without any analog parts, making it extremely suitable for integrating with the logic chip. Ideally, the design is completely symmetric and both "set" and "reset" inputs are tied together and driven at the same time. Given any random mismatch due to noise, the nodes would be forced to settle to the stable output of either "1" or "0". However, the design is still not entirely free from bias, as any systematic variation would produce a highly biased output. Hence, additional current injecting mechanism and postprocessing techniques, such as raw bit conditioners and PRNGs, are required [3,32].

A major problem with different device-intrinsic noise sources is that not all of them can be appropriately measured, characterized, or controlled during manufacturing phase for proper application. Additionally, with the maturity of the process technology, some noise mechanisms that can be considered as entropy sources get more controlled. Eventually, these are suppressed adequately to not produce a reliable measurement (that is, voltage or current) of the entropy source. Therefore, the extractor unit needs to be quite sophisticated with the capability of strong amplification and sampling for converting the analog noise value to digital bitstream. This introduces further deviations from generated data being "true" random, due to amplifier bandwidth and nonlinear gain limitations. Also, the fast electri-

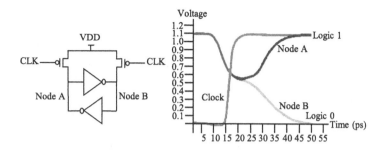

FIGURE 12.11

Intel TRNG. (A) Schematic and, (B) Transient Behavior.

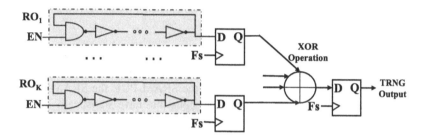

FIGURE 12.12

Ring oscillator-based TRNG.

cal switching of RNG circuitry produce strong electromagnetic interference, creating synchronization among nearby RNGs, causing a drop of overall entropy. Hence, there is a lack of provability of the randomness, since the leveraged noise source cannot be ensured as truly random, because of the effect of extractor unit, and other necessary deterministic postprocessing.

12.4.3.2 Oscillator-Based TRNGs

Another common approach to produce random numbers in the digital domain is to use oscillators and leverage associated jitter and metastability. Odd numbers of back-to-back connected inverters, with a feedback loop, act as a free-running oscillator (FRO), where even without an external input, the oscillator output is capable of driving itself as long as power is on [40]. Figure 12.12 shows a common design of a ring oscillator-TRNG (RO-TRNG). Random electrical noise in the feedback loop causes the frequency and phase of the oscillation to have jitter, that is, the exact time of the signal reaching the extraction point is not deterministic [37]. The entropy is further improved by proper sampling and XORing each FRO output.

One problem with jitter-based TRNG architecture is that the semiconductor industry is constantly working towards the minimization of jitters and noise. Therefore, additional noise-augmenting ring oscillators (NAROs) can be placed near the TRNG in the design to increase power supply noise by exhaustive oscillation [36]. Such NAROs are relatively smaller in length (hence, faster) and can be arbitrarily activated via a linear-feedback shift register (LFSR). Furthermore, in cases when the randomness of output is too weak compared to the load it is driving, the effect of the oscillator sampling may be muffled. For such a scenario, a Schmidt action can be implemented in the input to increase reliability (although the speed is slower). A major concern for this design is that the randomness is not provable. As possible solutions, researchers have proposed different ring oscillator structures, such as Fibonacci ring oscillator and Galois ring oscillator, they can provide variability in the oscillator length (frequency) with different devices (and delay lines) [32].

Additionally, XORing multiple oscillators can produce further entropy in the generated random number, generally with the cost of low throughput. Different postprocessing techniques, such as Von Neumann corrector and cryptographic hash functions can be employed in such cases [41]. Sunar et al. [31] proposed a provable true random number generator with built-in tolerance. Amaki et al. [38] proposed a stochastic behavior modeling-based technique to detect the worst case for deterministic noise, and the oscillator-based TRNG design is noise-tolerant to satisfy the generated random bit-stream quality.

12.4.3.3 Memory-Based TRNGs

One can recall from Section 12.3.4.3 that the power-up states of SRAM blocks are nondeterministic and heavily dependent on the process variation and runtime conditions and noise. This can be used as an entropy source in a TRNG [23]. In contrast to the SRAM-PUF, the SRAM-based TRNG uses the cells with unreliable powerup states, that is, the cells that have statistically equal probabilities to produce "0"/"1" every time the chip powers up. This provides the required entropy that can be extracted by postprocessing to derive the random numbers. However, the throughput and randomness of the SRAM-based TRNG highly depend on the technology and resiliency against runtime variations. Furthermore, it is not always practical to power down and restart the SRAM block every time a new random number is needed.

Metastability-based TRNGs leverage similar technique as they use cross-coupled elements to amplify noise and generate random bits. In a metastability-based TRNG, bits are generated by repeatedly biasing a single cross-coupled element precisely to the point of metastability. The metastability is resolved to a stable logic as determined by the noise.

12.4.4 TRNG APPLICATIONS

Keeping the basic Kerckhoffs' assumption [42] in mind, one can see that the security of a cryptographic system should rely solely on the key, and not on the design of the system (that is, no implementation flaws or side-channel information leakage). This key is often taken from a pool of random numbers. Hence, the quality of numbers generated by a TRNG is extremely important, since it directly determines the security strength of the system. A completely random key can ideally be broken only by brute-force (random guessing) attacks. Any predictability in the key-bits reduces the guessing-space of an adversary, and leads to a weakness in the entire system.

The main application for electronic hardware random number generators is in cryptography, where they are used to generate random cryptographic keys to transmit data securely. They are widely used in Internet encryption protocols, such as secure sockets layer (SSL). For example, Sun Microsystems Crypto Accelerator 6000 [43] contains hardware TRNG to provide the seeds to a FIPS-approved RNG specified in FIPS 186-2 DSARNG, using SHA-1 for generation of cryptographic keys for SSL hardware acceleration (TLS acceleration).

Many other common security protocols require random bits to remain secure and unpredictable by an adversary. True random numbers are widely used in many applications, such as keys and initialization values (IVs) for encryption, Session key generation for conventional encryption, keys for keyed MAC algorithms, private keys for digital signature algorithms, values to be used in entity authentication mechanisms, values to be used in key establishment protocols, PIN and password generation, one time padding, generating nonces to protect against replay attack, and input challenge for strong PUFs.

12.5 DESIGN FOR ANTI-COUNTERFEIT
12.5.1 DfAC PRELIMINARIES

In today's complex electronic component supply chain, it is very challenging to detect and prevent the infiltration of counterfeit chips and FPGAs. As mentioned in Section 12.2.2, a proper exploitation of electrical characteristics can lead to a cheaper, faster, and more successful detection of counterfeit electronics. Since aging and wear-out mechanisms generally make a chip slower over time, one can estimate aging degradation of a circuit under test (CUT) by measuring its speed and comparing it with a reference speed from original unused (golden) chips. However, acquiring such reference (golden) measurements is not always feasible. In addition, manufacturing process variation and defects cause deviation in speed/delay or other electrical measurements, even for golden chips. Hence, the approach requires a large pool of golden data to maintain statistical significance. These issues are more prominent for legacy chips and CoTS [44]. By exploiting such aging issues, researchers have proposed several techniques, such as embedding design for anti-counterfeit (DfAC) structures into the chip, or measuring degradation due to accelerated aging, for recycled IC detection.

12.5.2 DfAC DESIGNS

A combating die and IC recycling (CDIR) scheme takes aging into account to determine whether a chip has gone through a prior use. It is a lightweight and low-cost DfAC sensor with an RO-pair for self-referencing that eliminates the need for golden data [4,45]. The concept behind the RO-CDIR scheme is to put additional circuits or architectures, that is, ring oscillator structures, into new electronic chips in a way that the RO frequency tends to degrade more with aging because the transistors in the RO gets slower with time. The key points here are to employ a very lightweight design that would not practically impact the area, power, and cost requirement of the original chip, and the implemented design should produce readily available data that can reliably predict the aging (if any) or the freshness of the chip; the chip must age rapidly and must not be affected during the testing and validation phase. Also, the impact of process variations and temperature must be minimized, and path delay deviation due to process variations and aging degradation must be satisfactorily separable.

One key point to measure aging-induced delay-degradation is that the RO frequencies are needed to be compared with the golden (fresh) or reference data. The typical RO-CDIR sensor performs a self-referencing scheme to reliably measure delay degradation by comparing the frequencies of two ROs of length, named reference-RO and stressed-RO, respectively (see Fig. 12.13). Reference-RO is designed to age slowly or not age at all, if possible. On the contrary, the stressed-RO is designed to age at a much faster rate. When in operation mode, the stressed-RO's rapid aging reduces its speed

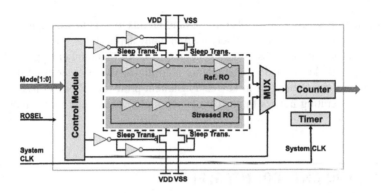

FIGURE 12.13

Combating die recovery (recycling) sensor using stressed and reference RO-pairs.

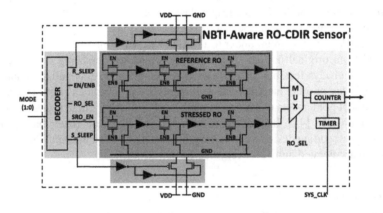

FIGURE 12.14

NBTI-aware RO-CDIR sensor.

(frequency), whereas the reference-RO's speed (frequency) largely remains the same. Thus, a large difference between the RO-frequencies implies that the chip has been used. A close physical placement of the ROs further reduces global and local process variations and environmental variations to give a finer measurement of the usage time. However, a limitation of this approach is that half of the PMOS transistors experience DC NBTI stress, hence experience a limited degradation due to the oscillatory nature of the scheme.

Figure 12.14 shows an NBTI-aware RO-CDIR sensor that exploits NBTI-induced degradation for an improved detection scheme [46]. While in operation mode, it gives maximum NBTI (DC) stress to the stressed-RO by breaking the RO chain and connecting all inverter inputs to the ground, so that they do not get a chance to recover from aging. However, a partial recovery may occur when the chip is completely powered off. The stressed-RO's structure is mimicked by the reference-RO to avoid parametric variations. However, during operation, the reference-RO is kept disconnected from the power and ground line to minimize aging. Since the two ROs have different aging stress, their frequencies continue to deviate over time, and it increases the probability of a more accurate detection.

12.6 **EXISTING CHALLENGES AND ATTACKS**

12.6.1 PUFs

12.6.1.1 Modeling Attacks Against Strong-PUFs

Strong PUFs, by definition, are capable of producing an exponential number of challenge-response pairs (CRPs). However, such a large possible CRP-set makes strong PUFs potentially vulnerable to machine-learning assisted modeling attacks [27]. In general, modeling attacks on strong-PUFs starts with an adversary getting hold of a subset of all CRPs of the PUF under attack. Using this CRP-subset, the adversary tries to derive a numerical model to correctly predict the PUF's responses to additional arbitrary challenges. This further enables the attacker to launch a man-in-the-middle and impersonation attack on the existing PUF-based authentication and key generation protocols. Researchers have launched multiple machine-learning- (ML) technique-based modeling attacks on the traditional arbiter-PUF, an ideal example of strong PUFs, and their successes have led to necessary modifications, resulting in several relatively more attack-resilient compositions of the traditional arbiter-PUF [47].

The basic numerical model of a traditional arbiter-PUF is based on the additive linear delay model. The overall delays of the signals that are propagated through multiple paths of the delay-stages can be expressed as the sum of the delays in the stages and associated interconnects, and the response can be determined by the final delay difference, assuming that the arbiter has ideally zero bias [47]. This simple, yet powerful, model thus leads to creating a two-class classification technique based on linear-delay-based hyperplane, trained with the collected/leaked CRP-subset by the adversary.

Researchers have proposed several techniques to strengthen the modeling-attack resiliency of the traditional arbiter-PUF by introducing nonlinearity into the architecture. One such example is the XOR-arbiter PUF [22], presented in Fig. 12.15. This PUF contains multiple same-length arbiter-PUFs, excited with the same challenge. The output of the individual arbiter-PUFs are XORed in order to produce a final response, and hence provides a high level of nonlinearity.

Nonlinearity of arbiter-PUF can also be increased by introducing feed-forward connections into the delay path, as shown in the simple feed-forward arbiter-PUF structure in Fig. 12.16 [47]. This structure utilizes the "unknown" challenges within the PUF architecture, where the intrinsically generated challenges are fed to the forthcoming delay blocks. Hence, the path switching of the delay stages connected to the "feed-forward loop" depends on the behavior of the previous stages. Such dependency creates a non-distinguishable functional model for the arbiter-PUF. As a result, the feed-forward arbiter PUF shows resiliency against machine-learning attacks that utilize linearly separable or differentiable models. Also, the designer can choose the number of feed-forward loops and connection points as necessary, making the attack model more complicated.

However, both such variant compositions of arbiter-PUF are not absolutely resilient from modeling attacks. Hospodar et al. [48] and Ruhrmair et al. [27] presented exhaustive attack results on different compositions of arbiter-PUFs. It is shown that the traditional arbiter- and xor-arbiter-PUF both can be easily modeled to a very high accuracy (for example, $\sim 99\%$), using popular machine learning

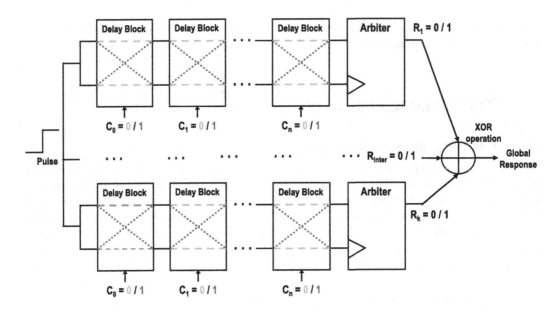

FIGURE 12.15

Schematic of an XOR PUF. It consists of k-chains of n-bit arbiter PUFs. The output of all arbiters are XORed together to generate the final binary response.

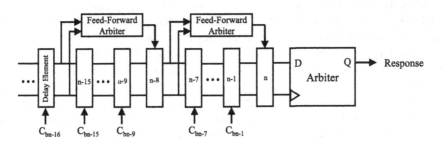

FIGURE 12.16

Structure of feed-forward arbiter PUF, where feed-forward loop size is 8.

techniques, such as logistic regression at the cost of modeling time. Ruhrmair et al. [27] also showed that machine learning techniques that use nonlinear classifications, such as evolution strategies can be used to correctly predict the CRP set of a given feed-forward arbiter PUF to a high accuracy.

12.6.1.2 Environmental and Aging Impacts on PUF

Environmental variations, such as temperature and power supply noise, and aging and wear-out mechanisms, generate unwanted errors in PUF outputs, making it unreliable for cryptographic applications. This is more prominent in RO-PUFs, mostly because of the continuous switching of all those os-

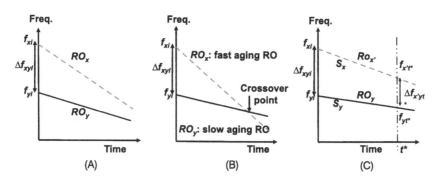

FIGURE 12.17

Bitflip due to frequency degradation in RO-pair. (A) ROs with moderate degradation (stable pair). (B) ROs with high degradation (unstable pair). (C) ROs with negligible degradation (highly stable pair).

cillators. To understand why RO-PUF generates erroneous responses, let us revisit the conventional RO-PUF shown in Fig. 12.3, and consider the frequency profile of a randomly selected RO-pair shown in Fig. 12.17 [49]. For the given RO-pair, if the frequency of RO_x ring oscillator (f_{xi}) is greater than that of RO_y (f_{yi}), then "1" (otherwise "0") is generated as a response (Fig. 12.17A). However, it fails to generate a reliable (that is, the same as before) response if a crossover happens (meaning, $f_{xi} < f_{yi}$ after possible frequency degradation due to environmental variation and aging (Fig. 12.17B). For maintaining maximum reliability, the two frequencies should never cross each other, maintaining a minimum frequency difference (that is, the frequency threshold (Δf_{th})) to compensate counter resolution, if necessary, till the end of operational lifetime t^* (Fig. 12.17C). Other PUF structures also suffer from similar reliability issues.

To produce reliable (error-free) response, bootstrapping efficient error correcting code (ECC) to the PUF can generate reliable output up to a certain margin, despite the presence of noise [50]. However, it relies on helper data that may partially reveal the secret key and potentially compromise the PUF. Most ECC schemes require redundant gates and an additional decode unit. Thus, ECC incurs large area, power, and timing overheads, making it impractical in resource-constrained applications.

NBTI and HCI-aware aging resistant ARO-PUF was proposed by Rahman et al. [49], as shown in Fig. 12.18. It has additional pull-up and pass transistors within the conventional RO-PUF architecture to reduce possible aging degradation. It has two modes of operation. At oscillatory mode (EN = 1), it performs regular PUF operation (Fig. 12.18B). In the nonoscillatory mode (EN = 0) (Fig. 12.18C), it removes DC stress for PMOS transistors, as it ties them to V_{dd} to eliminate NBTI. It also breaks the RO chain and removes AC (oscillatory) stress to eliminate HCI. So, this design successfully minimizes aging degradation, due to NBTI and HCI, by eliminating stress when the PUF is not active.

Yin et al. [51] proposed a temperature-aware cooperative RO-PUF (TAC RO-PUF) scheme to reduce error due to temperature variations. It allows unstable response generation as long as it can be converted into reliable bit by choosing different RO pairs, where temperature variation can cause bit flip. Experimental results indicated an 80% improvement in stable bit-generation capacity. Addition-

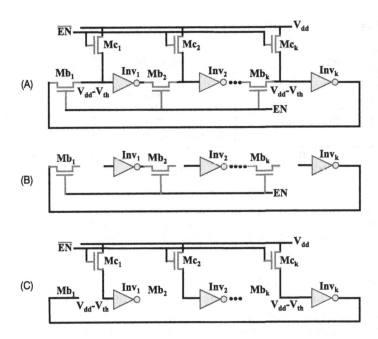

FIGURE 12.18

Operation of the aging-resistant RO (ARO)-PUF: (A) Schematic; (B) Activity in oscillatory mode, and (C) Activity in non-oscillatory mode.

ally, Rahman et al. [52] proposed a reliable pair formation scheme, called RePa, for RO-PUFs to improve robustness against both runtime variation (temperature variation and power supply noise) and aging degradation. It ranks all the ROs based on a predictive aging/voltage-based degradation profile and forms the most-suitable RO-pairs for PUF response generation using a complex algorithm, considering initial frequency differences, speed degradations, and bit-flip probability. This approach has shown to achieve up to 100% reliability, that is, zero error, with $\sim 2.3x$ ROs, eliminating the requirement of a much larger ECC.

12.6.1.3 Cloning SRAM-PUF

Helfmeier et al. [53] have demonstrated the very first physical cloning of the SRAM-PUF. This essentially violates the ideal PUF property of being "unclonable". The physically cloned SRAM-PUF can produce a response that is identical to the original PUF, as shown in Fig. 12.19. It should be noted that this attack is invasive in nature and uses expensive focused ion beam circuit edit (FIB-CE) techniques. This attack first observes the fingerprint of the target SRAM-PUF (see Fig. 12.19A–B) and modifies individual cells of another SRAM-PUF to produce (clone) the exact same signature (see Fig. 12.19C–D). Using the FIB-CE, individual transistors can be modified/removed completely to achieve a deterministic behavior. Also, the individual transistors can be trimmed to alter their dynamic performance and leakage characteristics.

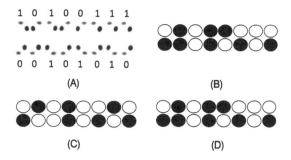

FIGURE 12.19

Physical cloning of the SRAM-PUF: (A) Photonic emission of the target SRAM device; (B) Logic fingerprint of the target device (dark = Logic '0'); (C) Initial fingerprint of the cloned device; (D) Initial fingerprint is modified via FIB CE to match the target device.

12.6.2 TRNGs

A TRNG is affected by limited intrinsic variations, especially, in the older and mature technologies. For such cases, the inherent entropy sources may not be sufficient enough for harvesting true randomness and obtaining maximum throughput. Further, the randomness of TRNGs can become even worse under environmental variations and different aging mechanisms. This opens up a variety of hardware-based attacks on TRNGs. For example, an attacker can vary the device supply voltage (V_{dd}) and temperature beyond the nominal condition, and intentionally bias the output to extract the "predictable" bitstream [36]. A frequency injection attack on RO-based TRNGs can lead to the clock jitter impacting the entropy, and, thereby, can facilitate the guessing of the key, for example from a smart card, with minimal effort [54]. Additionally, electromagnetic attacks can leak this information without physically destroying the chip [55].

Temperature variation poses a more potential threat to SRAM-based TRNGs. Randomness in ICs is, at least partially, coming from physically random thermal noise. For example, the magnitude of thermal noise exploited during powerup state depends on the temperature. A lower temperature reduces the exploitable noise, making the produced bitstream less random, whereas a higher temperatures make the power-up state more random [23].

To achieve more uniformity and statistical randomness in spite of low inherent entropy, researchers have proposed cryptographic hash functions, von Neumann corrector, and stream ciphers to be employed at the TRNG outputs. However, these additional modifications reduce the throughput and increase area and power overhead. Further, vendor agnostic TRNG design for FPGA was proposed by Schellekens et al. [56]. Rahman et al. [36] proposed a technology-independent (TI) TRNG to combat the security issues arising from such various run-time-/environmental-based degradations. It uses a "tunable"-RO architecture to leverage power supply noise along with clock jitter as the entropy source, and can overcome environmental variation and aging-induced bias by controlling jitter, and adjust RO delay by monitoring the run-time condition. A power supply noise enhancement and tuning block, and a self-calibration scheme on bias detection further improve the performance and serve as countermeasures against the hardware-based attack. The TRNG model presented by Robson et al. [57] utilized multiple threshold crossing methods to increase timing jitters.

Device	Manufacturing Variability Sources	Exploitable Features	Reliability Factors
PCM	• Geometric Variation (GST layer thickness and Bottom Electrode Contact Diameter) • Cell Resistance (R_{Cell}) • Write/Read Strength (required min. reset current) • Write current magnitude (I_{Write})	• Cell Variability - Stochastic Resistance Variation per cell • Programming sensitivity - variation in resistance level due to the nature of applied pulses	• Power supply Noise and Temperature Variation • Resistance Drift • Poor Endurance and Retention
Memristor & RRAM	• Variability in dope and undoped region length • Device thickness and Cross-sectional area • Stochasticity in doped and undoped resistance.	• Stochastic switching mechanism and intrinsic variability of devices. • Resistance variability due to applied voltage pulse duration	• Power supply Noise and Temperature Variation • Moderate Endurance and Retention • Read Disturbance
MRAM & STTRAM	• Geometric variation in free layer volume • Spin-torque Switching • Threshold voltage • Thermal Stability • Critical Switching Current	• Read Current variation • Meta-stability of free layer magnetization. • Variation in thermal energy • Back-hopping	• Temperature • External EM field • High Endurance and Retention

FIGURE 12.20

Emerging nanodevice properties for PUF applications.

12.7 PRIMITIVE DESIGNS WITH EMERGING NANODEVICES

Emerging memory devices, such as phase change memory (PCM), memristor, resistive random access memory (RRAM), and spintronic memory devices, such as spin-torque-transfer random access memory (STT-RAM), and magnetic random access memory (MRAM) are gaining popularity for high-capacity and low-power non-volatile storage applications [58]. Apart from being used as a traditional storage space, applications of emerging nano-device as security primitives have also gained much attention, as it can offer authentication and secure operation, reducing area and computational overhead. Researchers have proposed several hardware security primitives, with a majority being PUFs, over the last decade. As shown in Fig. 12.20, these emerging devices contain intrinsic features suitable for PUF applications in a similar fashion to traditional CMOS-based devices [59].

12.7.1 COMPOSITION OF PCM-BASED PUFs

12.7.1.1 Sources of Process-Induced Variability

PCM, one of the emerging NVMs, operates through a reversible transition between the low resistance (crystalline phase) and high-resistance (amorphous phase), which can be controlled through 'set/reset' current pulses with the pre-defined magnitude and pulse duration [60]. The resistance of the PCM cells varies randomly during this programming process, based on the set/reset current pulse. Also, the manufacturing process variation affects the physical dimensions and the strength of PCM cells, consequently inducing stochastic nature in the electrical properties. Cell geometry features (such as GST layer thickness, heater thickness, and bottom electrode contact diameter) and the electrical and thermal conductivities of the GST, and heater material are prominent factors responsible for the process variations [61]. Due to the inherent randomness originating from the cell geometry and other structural and characteristic variations, and the different types of dynamics exhibited by PCM cells, they are well-suited for cryptographic measures, especially for PUF applications.

12.7.1.2 PCM-PUF Designs

The process variation and programming sensitivity of PCM can be exploited to implement PCM-based PUFs. A novel design for generating cryptographic keys via reconfigurable PUF, based on PCM cells, is proposed by Zhang et al. [62]. It uses the variations between PCM cells in an array to generate keys by random cell selection. The PCM-PUF itself is composed of the traditional crossbar architecture, where, for the PUF application, individual PCM cells or a set of cells in the crossbar array can be programmed with a pre-defined pulse, and later read out to produce a unique response. Although all the cells can be programmed with the same pulse (which is analog in nature before any comparative sensing), the generated read-out value will be unique from cell to cell within the same circuit, and also across different circuits, due to the stochastic nature of the PCM cell. Due to the nonvolatile nature of the cell, the same unique response can be regenerated, considering an ideal noise-free scenario. It should be noted that the composition of the PCM-PUF, being a traditional cross-bar architecture, would result in a "weak" PUF, that is, it will have a small number of CRPs, unless the memory access mechanism is designed to perform a random and nonlinear access technique. The produced signature may also require further postprocessing for providing output suitable for cryptographic operations.

Generation of unique signature from PCM crossbar architecture can be further extended by varying the cell-resistance distribution using programming pulse modification [63]. Additionally, the multilevel cell operation of PCM cell has been exploited to generate unique signatures in [64].

12.7.2 COMPOSITION OF MEMRISTOR AND RRAM-BASED PUFS

12.7.2.1 Sources of Process-Induced Variability

Similar to PCM, it is possible to exploit the write mechanism of memristors and RRAMs, and extract random cell behavior influenced by process variations for potential PUF applications. Since these devices have a larger resistance window, one can exploit the uncertainty in the logic state from the undefined region between high and low states. For memristors, such analog resistance variability and associated memory write/read time depends on the cell structure and dimensions, such as device thickness, which can be leveraged as entropy sources due to manufacturing process variation. Additionally, the source of entropy in RRAMs originates from intrinsic features, such as oxide thickness and defect density, and these can very well be exploited for PUF functionalities.

12.7.2.2 Memristor and RRAM-PUF Designs

The effect of process variability in memristor cell operation is exploited in [65] to develop a write-time-based memristive PUF-cell. Here, the time for the write operation is set to the minimum value required to switch the cell from high resistance state to low resistance state. Hence, generating a probability of the output logic being "1" is raised to 50%, and vice-versa. Researchers have also proposed RRAM-based PUFs that utilize the traditional cross-bar memory architecture [66]. This composition improves the accuracy of split references, using dummy cells that eventually reduces the offset by decreasing the transistor size of the split sense amplifier (S/A).

12.7.3 COMPOSITION OF MRAM AND STTRAM-BASED PUFS
12.7.3.1 Sources of Process-Induced Variability
Spintronic devices, such as STT-RAM and MRAM, also offer novel opportunities for hardware security applications as they exhibit device-intrinsic phenomena, such as chaotic magnetization, statistical read/write failures, stochastic retention failure, and back-hopping as depicted in Fig. 12.20 [67]. The chaotic and random dynamics of the free layer of the magnetic tunnel junction (MJT) is exploited by researchers to develop hardware security primitives, for example, PUFs [68,69]. Additionally, the statistical and stochastic nature of read-write failures, back-hopping, and retention times can also be exploited to develop novel spintronic circuit-based PUFs and TRNGs [70]. The compatibility of such spintronic devices with silicon substrate makes them a potential candidate for complementing existing CMOS-based security primitives.

12.7.3.2 MRAM and STT-RAM PUF Designs
Physical variation-dependent MPAM-PUF is proposed by Das et al. [69]. This technique exploits the random tilt generated in the energy barrier of MTJs, due to manufacturing process variations and extracted the randomness to generate PUF responses. As the distribution of tilt angle is Gaussian in nature, the free-layer orientation of the MTJs is inclined to a certain initial value similar to the behavior of the SRAM-PUF. Additional improvements, such as gradual decrement of aspect ratio at a constant volume, and increment of volume at constant ratio, enhance the variation in tilt, and obtain more stable PUF output.

The random initialization of the free layer in STT-RAM is also utilized in designing PUFs [68]. In this technique, the responses are generated during the registration phase by comparing the STT-RAM bits of complimentary rows. Noise and sense amplifier offsets are utilized to produce response bits in the case of comparison bits, which are initialized with similar values. The repeatability of bit generation is ensured by writing the values at MTJs. The write-back is employed to preserve the responses for multiple accesses, and to prevent bit flips due to voltage and temperature variations. However, a downside is that this desing requires post-processing architectures, such as a fuzzy extractor, to maintain and enhance the quality of the PUF output.

12.7.4 PUF COMPOSITION FOR EMERGING APPLICATIONS
In addition to traditional key-based cryptographic applications, researchers have proposed several emerging security applications, such as virtual proofs of reality [29], that utilize the inherent characteristics of the PUF. The idea of virtual proof (VP) is based on the underlying fact that there are possibilities to verify the correctness and authenticity of the digital data obtained from tangible physical system properties or processes between two communicating parties, that is, prover and verifier, located at a distance without using any secret key-based classical mechanisms. As classical keys are

deemed vulnerable to physical- and software/malware-based attack techniques, the avoidance of the keys might lead to safer, cost effective, and compact designs of modern cryptographic hardware. The example of VPs, based on witness objects (WOs), for instance temperature variant ICs, disordered optical scattering media, and quantum systems, can be novel protocols that successfully verify the temperature, relative position of objects, or destruction of specific physical objects.

As for proof-of-concept experimentation, the VPs of temperature, and optical systems for VPs of relative distance, co-locality and destruction are demonstrated in [29]. Several novel variants of PUFs can be exploited in this regard. For example, the temperature proof can be obtained by CMOS-based bistable ring PUF, where the high-temperature sensitivity is advantageously exploited. To verify the VP of distance and destruction claims, one can employ variants of optical PUF.

These virtual proof mechanisms do not necessarily utilize the traditional PUF key-generation concepts, where the CRPs required to maintain some significant properties (for example, CRPs need to be "robust" across all temperature/voltage corners). For instance, the virtual proof of temperature, in fact, utilizes the high error-rate occurring in the CRPs at different temperature corners to obtain temperature-dependent CRPs (or signatures), which allow the verifier or the authenticator to obtain temperature information. For such a specific application, the underlying PUF composition would rather be tailored to be highly impacted by the temperature, as opposed to traditional robust PUFs. Exploiting the active components, such as transistor features, and variations in logic cells, should lead to such PUF designs targeting particular emerging applications.

12.8 HANDS-ON EXPERIMENT: HARDWARE SECURITY PRIMITIVES (PUFs AND TRNGs)

12.8.1 OBJECTIVE

This experiment is designed to give students an exposure to hardware security primitives such as PUFs and TRNGs.

12.8.2 METHOD

The experiment consists of two major parts – first part dealing with the design/analysis of PUFs and the second part with design/analysis of TRNGs. Each part consists of multiple components. All parts of the experiment are designed on the HaHa platform. The first part of the experiment illustrates the design of PUFs. Students will utilize the differences in power-up states in the SRAM to create random binary signatures, which can be used for authentication or cryptographic key generation. They will also map Ring Oscillators (ROs) in the FPGA to create an RO-PUF structure and use it to generate 128-bit keys. Next, the students will vary the operating voltage using a built-in potentiometer in HaHa board to obtain PUF responses at different operating voltages. The second part of the experiment focuses on the TRNG generation, where ROs mapped in the FPGA in the first part are made physically symmetric in order to create high-quality TRNGs.

12.8.3 LEARNING OUTCOME

By performing the specific steps of the experiments, the students will learn ways to exploit the intrinsic manufacturing as well as temporal variations in silicon devices for creating strong security primitives. They will also learn the metrics/processes to analyze various properties of these primitives, such as the level of uniqueness, randomness and robustness as well as hardware overhead of the PUFs and TRNGs.

12.8.4 ADVANCED OPTIONS

Additional exploration on this topic can be done through modification in PUF and TRNG structures to improve their various security properties.

More details about the experiment are available in the supplementary document. Please visit: http://hwsecuritybook.org/.

12.9 EXERCISES
12.9.1 TRUE/FALSE QUESTIONS

1. Weak PUF is ideal for detecting counterfeit ICs via CRP-based authentication schemes.
2. Error Correction Code (ECC) schemes can be used to improve the robustness for both PUF responses and TRNG outputs.
3. A ring oscillator (RO)-PUF is basically a delay-based PUF.
4. A TRNG must rely on random intrinsic or runtime noise.
5. Depending on the startup behavior, the SRAM-array can be used both as a PUF and a TRNG.
6. Runtime variation (such as power supply noise and Vdd fluctuations) is good for PUFs, but unacceptable for TRNGs.
7. DfAC structures, such as CDIR sensors, utilize aging phenomena for detecting prior usages of the IC.
8. Ideally, PUFs should have 50% intra-Hamming distance.
9. Ideally, TRNGs should have 50% intra-Hamming distance.
10. Frequency injection attack on an oscillator-based TRNG reduces the throughput, but entropy remains the same.

12.9.2 LONG-ANSWER TYPE QUESTIONS

1. Briefly discuss the major characteristic differences between PUFs, TRNGs, and DfACs.
2. Briefly discuss the quality metrics used to evaluate PUFs and TRNGs.
3. Explain why RO-PUFs tend to produce more erroneous responses due to runtime noise and aging compared to traditional arbiter-PUFs.
4. Briefly describe what security primitives (strong PUFs, weak PUFs, or TRNGs) are ideal for following applications:
   (a) Chip ID generation.
   (b) Authentication.
   (c) Licensing.

Table 12.2 RO frequency degradation over time

RO Name	Initial Frequency (F_0)	Predicted Frequency After 5 Years ($F_{5\ years}$)
RO1	5.31 MHz	5.27 MHz
RO2	5.30 MHz	5.24 MHz
RO3	5.27 MHz	5.23 MHz
RO4	5.41 MHz	5.35 MHz
RO5	5.35 MHz	5.30 MHz
RO6	5.22 MHz	5.19 MHz
RO7	5.26 MHz	5.22 MHz
RO8	5.39 MHz	5.36 MHz

(d) Cryptographic nonce.

(e) Key-generation for in-situ AES encryption/decryption system.

5. Briefly explain the differences between a TRNG and a PRNG? Which one of them would you consider, if you were only interested in:

(a) High entropy.

(b) High speed.

(c) Low runtime noise.

6. Explain how you can increase the security of the response of a weak PUF (used for key generation) against possible guessing or side-channel attacks. [Hint: One common technique is to use the hashing mechanism.]

7. Briefly explain the major challenges that PUFs and TRNGs suffer.

8. Consider the conventional RO-PUF shown in Fig. 12.3. Assume that it contains eight independent ROs with the initial and predicted free-running frequencies given in Table 12.2. The RO pairs are formed at the very begining of the operation (that is, at time $(t) = 0$) either by choosing randomly or by doing "intelligent" pairing. The given PUF response behavior is

"$True(RO_x \geq RO_y) \Rightarrow Response = 0$".

(a) What is the bit error rate (BER) after 5 years of operation if the RO pairs are formed randomly?

(b) One can perform an "intelligent pairing" by forming the RO pairs with the predicted frequency degradation (due to aging) taken into account. What is the minimum BER after 5 years of operation if the RO pairs are initially formed considering the predicted frequency degradation?

9. Consider the SSL/TLS hardware accelerator (see Section 12.4.4) that is required to generate a 128-bit random key at a speed of 1 Gbps (system clock speed). However, the hardware TRNG inside it produces raw true random bits at a 1000x slower speed. Provide a scheme that can produce random output at a required speed. For simplicity, you can assume the key-bits are generated in parallel.

10. Identify the following security primitives as either PUF or TRNG. Briefly justify your choice.

(a) Figure 12.21A shows that the intra-chip hamming distance = 50% of the output of a security primitive X. That is, for the same primitive/device, the output bits are in average 50% different for the same environmental condition and same input pattern.

(b) Figure 12.21B shows that the inter-chip hamming distance = 50% of the output of multiple security primitives of the same type Y. That is, for a pool of same primitive/device, the output bits are in average 50% different for different instances.

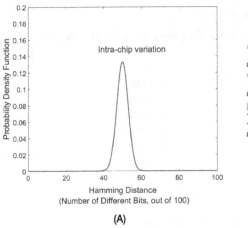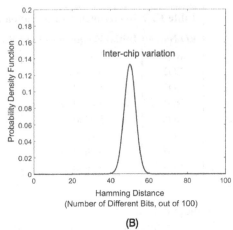

FIGURE 12.21

Hamming Distance for primitive instance X (A) and primitive type Y (B).

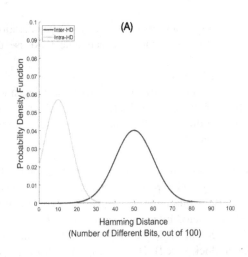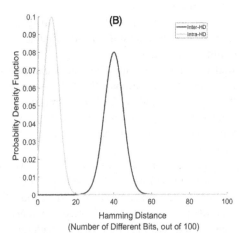

FIGURE 12.22

Inter- and intra-hamming distance for PUF M (A) and PUF N (B).

11. Consider two types of PUFs, namely "M" and "N". Their intra- and inter-hamming distances are presented in Fig. 12.22. Explain which type of the two PUFs serves better for the following applications:
(a) authentication,
(b) key generation.

REFERENCES

[1] R. Pappu, B. Recht, J. Taylor, N. Gershenfeld, Physical one-way functions, Science 297 (2002) 2026–2030.

[2] B. Gassend, D. Clarke, M. Van Dijk, S. Devadas, Silicon physical random functions, in: Proceedings of the 9th ACM Conference on Computer and Communications Security, ACM, pp. 148–160.

[3] G. Taylor, G. Cox, Behind Intel's new random-number generator, IEEE Spectrum 24 (2011).

[4] X. Zhang, M. Tehranipoor, Design of on-chip lightweight sensors for effective detection of recycled ICs, IEEE Transactions on Very Large Scale Integration (VLSI) Systems 22 (2014) 1016–1029.

[5] C.E. Shannon, A mathematical theory of communication, Bell System Technical Journal 27 (1948) 379–423.

[6] K.J. Kuhn, M.D. Giles, D. Becher, P. Kolar, A. Kornfeld, R. Kotlyar, S.T. Ma, A. Maheshwari, S. Mudanai, Process technology variation, IEEE Transactions on Electron Devices 58 (2011) 2197–2208.

[7] F. Rahman, A.P.D. Nath, D. Forte, S. Bhunia, M. Tehranipoor, Nano CMOS logic-based security primitive design, in: Security Opportunities in Nano Devices and Emerging Technologies, CRC Press, 2017, pp. 41–60.

[8] R. Kumar, Interconnect and noise immunity design for the Pentium 4 processor, in: Proceedings of the 40th Annual Design Automation Conference, ACM, pp. 938–943.

[9] R. Kumar, V. Kursun, Reversed temperature-dependent propagation delay characteristics in nanometer CMOS circuits, IEEE Transactions on Circuits and Systems II: Express Briefs 53 (2006) 1078–1082.

[10] S. Zafar, Y. Kim, V. Narayanan, C. Cabral, V. Paruchuri, B. Doris, J. Stathis, A. Callegari, M. Chudzik, A comparative study of NBTI and PBTI (charge trapping) in SiO2/HfO2 stacks with FUSI, TiN, Re Gates, in: VLSI Technology, 2006. Digest of Technical Papers. 2006 Symposium on, IEEE, pp. 23–25.

[11] D. Saha, D. Varghese, S. Mahapatra, On the generation and recovery of hot carrier induced interface traps: a critical examination of the 2D RD model, IEEE Electron Device Letters 27 (2006) 188–190.

[12] F. Rahman, D. Forte, M.M. Tehranipoor, Reliability vs. security: challenges and opportunities for developing reliable and secure integrated circuits, in: Reliability Physics Symposium (IRPS), 2016 IEEE International, IEEE, pp. 4C–6.

[13] C. Herder, M.-D. Yu, F. Koushanfar, S. Devadas, Physical unclonable functions and applications: a tutorial, Proceedings of the IEEE 102 (2014) 1126–1141.

[14] U. Rührmair, S. Devadas, F. Koushanfar, Security based on physical unclonability and disorder, in: Introduction to Hardware Security and Trust, Springer, 2012, pp. 65–102.

[15] C. Böhm, M. Hofer, Physical Unclonable Functions in Theory and Practice, Springer Science & Business Media, 2012.

[16] B.L.P. Gassend, Physical random functions, Ph.D. thesis, Massachusetts Institute of Technology, 2003.

[17] J. Guajardo, S.S. Kumar, G.-J. Schrijen, P. Tuyls, FPGA intrinsic PUFs and their use for IP protection, in: International Workshop on Cryptographic Hardware and Embedded Systems, Springer, pp. 63–80.

[18] U. Rührmair, H. Busch, S. Katzenbeisser, Strong PUFs: models, constructions, and security proofs, in: Towards Hardware-Intrinsic Security, Springer, 2010, pp. 79–96.

[19] A. Maiti, V. Gunreddy, P. Schaumont, A systematic method to evaluate and compare the performance of physical unclonable functions, in: Embedded Systems Design with FPGAs, Springer, 2013, pp. 245–267.

[20] A. Rukhin, J. Soto, J. Nechvatal, M. Smid, E. Barker, A statistical test suite for random and pseudorandom number generators for cryptographic applications, Technical Report, DTIC Document, 2001.

[21] G. Marsaglia, Diehard: a battery of tests of randomness, See http://stat.fsu.edu/geo/diehard.html, 1996.

[22] G.E. Suh, S. Devadas, Physical unclonable functions for device authentication and secret key generation, in: Proceedings of the 44th Annual Design Automation Conference, ACM, pp. 9–14.

[23] D.E. Holcomb, W.P. Burleson, K. Fu, Power-Up SRAM state as an identifying fingerprint and source of true random numbers, IEEE Transactions on Computers 58 (2009) 1198–1210.

[24] A. Wild, T. Güneysu, Enabling SRAM-PUFs on Xilinx FPGAs, in: Field Programmable Logic and Applications (FPL), 2014 24th International Conference on, IEEE, pp. 1–4.

[25] S.S. Kumar, J. Guajardo, R. Maes, G.-J. Schrijen, P. Tuyls, The butterfly PUF protecting IP on every FPGA, in: Hardware-Oriented Security and Trust, 2008. HOST 2008, IEEE International Workshop on, IEEE, pp. 67–70.

[26] M. Majzoobi, F. Koushanfar, M. Potkonjak, Lightweight secure PUFs, in: Computer-Aided Design, 2008. ICCAD 2008. IEEE/ACM International Conference on, IEEE, pp. 670–673.

[27] U. Rührmair, J. Sölter, F. Sehnke, X. Xu, A. Mahmoud, V. Stoyanova, G. Dror, J. Schmidhuber, W. Burleson, S. Devadas, PUF modeling attacks on simulated and silicon data, IEEE Transactions on Information Forensics and Security 8 (2013) 1876–1891.

[28] Q. Chen, G. Csaba, P. Lugli, U. Schlichtmann, U. Rührmair, The bistable ring PUF: a new architecture for strong physical unclonable functions, in: Hardware-Oriented Security and Trust (HOST), 2011 IEEE International Symposium on, IEEE, pp. 134–141.

[29] U. Rührmair, J. Martinez-Hurtado, X. Xu, C. Kraeh, C. Hilgers, D. Kononchuk, J.J. Finley, W.P. Burleson, Virtual proofs of reality and their physical implementation, in: Security and Privacy (SP), 2015 IEEE Symposium on, IEEE, pp. 70–85.

[30] Y. Alkabani, F. Koushanfar, Active hardware metering for intellectual property protection and security, in: USENIX Security, Boston MA, USA, pp. 291–306.

[31] B. Sunar, W.J. Martin, D.R. Stinson, A provably secure true random number generator with built-in tolerance to active attacks, IEEE Transactions on Computers 56 (2007).

[32] M. Stipčević, Ç.K. Koç, True random number generators, in: Open Problems in Mathematics and Computational Science, Springer, 2014, pp. 275–315.

[33] B. Sunar, True random number generators for cryptography, in: Cryptographic Engineering, Springer, 2009, pp. 55–73.

[34] J. Von Neumann, 13. Various techniques used in connection with random digits, Applied Mathematics Series 12 (1951) 3.

[35] B. Preneel, Analysis and design of cryptographic hash functions, Ph.D. thesis, Citeseer, 1993.

[36] M.T. Rahman, K. Xiao, D. Forte, X. Zhang, J. Shi, M. Tehranipoor, TI-TRNG: technology independent true random number generator, in: Proceedings of the 51st Annual Design Automation Conference, ACM, pp. 1–6.

[37] T. Amaki, M. Hashimoto, T. Onoye, An oscillator-based true random number generator with jitter amplifier, in: Circuits and Systems (ISCAS), 2011 IEEE International Symposium on, IEEE, pp. 725–728.

[38] T. Amaki, M. Hashimoto, Y. Mitsuyama, T. Onoye, A worst-case-aware design methodology for noise-tolerant oscillator-based true random number generator with stochastic behavior modeling, IEEE Transactions on Information Forensics and Security 8 (2013) 1331–1342.

[39] B. Jun, P. Kocher, The Intel random number generator, Cryptography Research Inc., 1999, white paper.

[40] N. Stefanou, S.R. Sonkusale, High speed array of oscillator-based truly binary random number generators, in: Circuits and Systems, 2004. ISCAS'04, in: Proceedings of the 2004 International Symposium on, vol. 1, IEEE, pp. I–505.

[41] S.-H. Kwok, Y.-L. Ee, G. Chew, K. Zheng, K. Khoo, C.-H. Tan, A comparison of post-processing techniques for biased random number generators, in: IFIP International Workshop on Information Security Theory and Practices, Springer, pp. 175–190.

[42] L.R. Knudsen, Block Ciphers, in: Encyclopedia of Cryptography and Security, Springer, 2014, pp. 153–157.

[43] Sun crypto accelerator 6000: FIPS 140-2 non-proprietary security policy – Sun Microsystems, http://www.oracle.com/technetwork/topics/security/140sp1050-160928.pdf. (Accessed August 2018).

[44] M.M. Tehranipoor, U. Guin, D. Forte, Counterfeit integrated circuits, in: Counterfeit Integrated Circuits, Springer, 2015, pp. 15–36.

[45] X. Zhang, N. Tuzzio, M. Tehranipoor, Identification of recovered ICs using fingerprints from a light-weight on-chip sensor, in: Proceedings of the 49th Annual Design Automation Conference, ACM, pp. 703–708.

[46] U. Guin, X. Zhang, D. Forte, M. Tehranipoor, Low-cost on-chip structures for combating die and IC recycling, in: Proceedings of the 51st Annual Design Automation Conference, ACM, pp. 1–6.

[47] D. Lim, J.W. Lee, B. Gassend, G.E. Suh, M. Van Dijk, S. Devadas, Extracting secret keys from integrated circuits, IEEE Transactions on Very Large Scale Integration (VLSI) Systems 13 (2005) 1200–1205.

[48] G. Hospodar, R. Maes, I. Verbauwhede, Machine learning attacks on 65nm Arbiter PUFs: accurate modeling poses strict bounds on usability, in: Information Forensics and Security (WIFS), 2012 IEEE International Workshop on, IEEE, pp. 37–42.

[49] M.T. Rahman, F. Rahman, D. Forte, M. Tehranipoor, An aging-resistant RO-PUF for reliable key generation, IEEE Transactions on Emerging Topics in Computing 4 (2016) 335–348.

[50] M.-D.M. Yu, S. Devadas, Secure and robust error correction for physical unclonable functions, IEEE Design & Test of Computers 27 (2010) 48–65.

[51] C.-E. Yin, G. Qu, Temperature-aware cooperative ring oscillator PUF, in: Hardware-Oriented Security and Trust, 2009. HOST'09, IEEE International Workshop on, IEEE, pp. 36–42.

[52] M.T. Rahman, D. Forte, F. Rahman, M. Tehranipoor, A pair selection algorithm for robust RO-PUF against environmental variations and aging, in: Computer Design (ICCD), 2015 33rd IEEE International Conference on, IEEE, pp. 415–418.

[53] C. Helfmeier, C. Boit, D. Nedospasov, J.-P. Seifert, Cloning physically unclonable functions, in: Hardware-Oriented Security and Trust (HOST), 2013 IEEE International Symposium on, IEEE, pp. 1–6.

[54] A.T. Markettos, S.W. Moore, The frequency injection attack on ring-oscillator-based true random number generators, in: Cryptographic Hardware and Embedded Systems-CHES 2009, Springer, 2009, pp. 317–331.

[55] P. Bayon, L. Bossuet, A. Aubert, V. Fischer, F. Poucheret, B. Robisson, P. Maurine, Contactless electromagnetic active attack on ring oscillator based true random number generator, in: International Workshop on Constructive Side-Channel Analysis and Secure Design, Springer, pp. 151–166.

[56] D. Schellekens, B. Preneel, I. Verbauwhede, FPGA vendor agnostic true random number generator, in: Field Programmable Logic and Applications, 2006. FPL'06. International Conference on, IEEE, pp. 1–6.

[57] S. Robson, B. Leung, G. Gong, Truly random number generator based on a ring oscillator utilizing last passage time, IEEE Transactions on Circuits and Systems II: Express Briefs 61 (2014) 937–941.

[58] A. Chen, Emerging nonvolatile memory (NVM) technologies, in: Solid State Device Research Conference (ESSDERC), 2015 45th European, IEEE, pp. 109–113.

[59] F. Rahman, A.P.D. Nath, S. Bhunia, D. Forte, M. Tehranipoor, Composition of physical unclonable functions: from device to architecture, in: Security Opportunities in Nano Devices and Emerging Technologies, CRC Press, 2017, pp. 177–196.

[60] H.-S.P. Wong, S. Raoux, S. Kim, J. Liang, J.P. Reifenberg, B. Rajendran, M. Asheghi, K.E. Goodson, Phase change memory, Proceedings of the IEEE 98 (2010) 2201–2227.

[61] W. Zhang, T. Li, Characterizing and mitigating the impact of process variations on phase change based memory systems, in: Proceedings of the 42nd Annual IEEE/ACM International Symposium on Microarchitecture, ACM, pp. 2–13.

[62] L. Zhang, Z.H. Kong, C.-H. Chang, PCKGen: a phase change memory based cryptographic key generator, in: Circuits and Systems (ISCAS), 2013 IEEE International Symposium on, IEEE, pp. 1444–1447.

[63] L. Zhang, Z.H. Kong, C.-H. Chang, A. Cabrini, G. Torelli, Exploiting process variations and programming sensitivity of phase change memory for reconfigurable physical unclonable functions, IEEE Transactions on Information Forensics and Security 9 (2014) 921–932.

[64] K. Kursawe, A.-R. Sadeghi, D. Schellekens, B. Skoric, P. Tuyls, Reconfigurable physical unclonable functions-enabling technology for tamper-resistant storage, in: Hardware-Oriented Security and Trust, 2009. HOST'09, IEEE International Workshop on, IEEE, pp. 22–29.

[65] G.S. Rose, N. McDonald, L.-K. Yan, B. Wysocki, A write-time based memristive PUF for hardware security applications, in: Proceedings of the International Conference on Computer-Aided Design, IEEE Press, pp. 830–833.

[66] R. Liu, H. Wu, Y. Pang, H. Qian, S. Yu, A highly reliable and tamper-resistant RRAM PUF: design and experimental validation, in: Hardware Oriented Security and Trust (HOST), 2016 IEEE International Symposium on, IEEE, pp. 13–18.

[67] J.S. Meena, S.M. Sze, U. Chand, T.-Y. Tseng, Overview of emerging nonvolatile memory technologies, Nanoscale Research Letters 9 (2014) 526.

[68] L. Zhang, X. Fong, C.-H. Chang, Z.H. Kong, K. Roy, Highly reliable memory-based Physical Unclonable Function using Spin-Transfer Torque MRAM, in: Circuits and Systems (ISCAS), 2014 IEEE International Symposium on, IEEE, pp. 2169–2172.

[69] J. Das, K. Scott, S. Rajaram, D. Burgett, S. Bhanja, MRAM PUF: a novel geometry based magnetic PUF with integrated CMOS, IEEE Transactions on Nanotechnology 14 (2015) 436–443.

[70] S. Ghosh, Spintronics and security: prospects, vulnerabilities, attack models, and preventions, Proceedings of the IEEE 104 (2016) 1864–1893.

SECURITY AND TRUST ASSESSMENT, AND DESIGN FOR SECURITY

13

CONTENTS

Hardware Security. https://doi.org/10.1016/B978-0-12-812477-2.00018-6

13.1 INTRODUCTION

With the emergence of information technology and its critical role in our daily lives, the risk of various cyber attacks is larger than ever before. Many security systems or devices have critical assurance requirements, e.g., high assurance electronic systems – military, aerospace, automotive, transportation, financial, and medical. Their failure may endanger human life and environment, cause serious damage to critical infrastructure, hinder personal privacy, and undermine the viability of the whole business sector. Even the perception that a system is more vulnerable than it really is, hindering, for example, paying with a credit card over the Internet, can significantly impede economic development. The defense against intrusion and unauthorized use of resources with software was given significant attention in the past. Security technologies, including antivirus, firewall, virtualization, cryptographic software, and security protocols, have been developed to make systems more secure.

While the battle between software developers and hackers has raged since the 1980's, the underlying hardware was generally considered safe and secure. However, in the last decade or so, the battlefield has expanded to hardware domain, since—in some aspects—emerging attacks on hardware are shown to be more effective and efficient than traditional software attacks. For example, while the cryptographic algorithms have been improved and have become extremely difficult (if not impossible) to break mathematically, their implementations are often not. It has been demonstrated that the security of cryptosystems, system on chips (SoCs), and microprocessor circuits can be compromised using timing analysis attacks [1], power analysis attacks [2], exploitation of design-for-test (DFT) structures [3] [4], and fault-injection attacks [5]. These attacks can effectively bypass the security mechanisms built in the software level, and put devices or systems at risk. These hardware-based attacks aim to exploit the vulnerabilities, within the hardware design, which are introduced either unintentionally or intentionally during the IC design flow.

Many security vulnerabilities in ICs can be unintentionally created by design mistakes and designers' lack of understanding of security vulnerabilities. Further, today's CAD tools are not equipped with understanding security vulnerabilities in integrated circuits. Therefore, a tool can introduce additional vulnerabilities in the circuit [6,7]. These vulnerabilities can facilitate attacks, such as fault-injection or side-channel-based attacks. Also, these vulnerabilities can cause sensitive information to be leaked through observable points, which are accessible to an attacker or give unauthorized access to an attacker to control, or affect a secure system.

Vulnerabilities can also be intentionally introduced in ICs in form of malicious modifications, generally referred to as hardware Trojans, or backdoors [8]. Due to short time-to-market constraints, design houses are increasingly being dependent on external entities (third parties) to procure IPs. Also, due to the ever-increasing cost of manufacturing ICs, design houses rely on untrusted foundries and assemblies for fabricating, testing, and packaging ICs. These untrusted third-party IP owners or foundries can insert hardware Trojans to create backdoors in the design, through which sensitive information can be leaked and other possible attacks (for example, denial of service and reduction in reliability) can be performed.

It is of paramount importance to identify security vulnerabilities during hardware design and validation process, and address them as early as possible due to the following reasons: 1) there is little or no flexibility in changing or updating post-fabricated integrated circuits; 2) the cost of fixing a vulnerability found at later stages during the design and fabrication processes is significantly higher, following the well-known rule-of-ten (the cost of detecting a faulty IC increases by an order of magnitude as one advances through each stage of design flow). Moreover, if a vulnerability is discovered after manufacturing while the IC is in the field, it may cost a company millions of dollars in lost revenues and replacement costs.

Knowledge of the vulnerabilities and security assessment of a hardware design is not sufficient to protect it. A series of countermeasures/techniques is also required for each vulnerability to prevent adversaries from exploiting it. The development of countermeasures is a challenging task, as they must meet cost, performance, and time-to-market constraints, while ensuring a certain level of protection.

This chapter presents pre-silicon and post-silicon security and trust assessment techniques that can identify potential vulnerabilities in hardware design. Design for security techniques to address the potential vulnerabilities in hardware designs are also discussed.

13.2 SECURITY ASSETS AND ATTACK MODELS

To build a secure integrated circuit, a designer must decide what "assets" to protect, and the possible attacks to be investigated. Further, IC designers must also understand the players (attackers and defenders) and their role in the IC design supply chain. Three fundamental security factors (security assets, potential adversaries, and potential attacks) are associated with security assessment and countermeasures in integrated circuits; they are discussed below.

13.2.1 ASSETS

As defined in [11], an asset is a resource of value, which is worth protecting from the adversary. An asset may be a tangible object, such as a signal in a circuit design, or may be an intangible asset, such as controllability of a signal. Sample assets that must be protected in a SoC are listed below [12] (see Fig. 13.1):

- **On-device key,** namely, private key of an encryption algorithm. These assets are stored on-chip in some form of nonvolatile memory. If these are breached, the confidentiality requirement of the device is compromised.
- **Manufacturer firmware,** low-level program instructions and proprietary firmware. These assets have intellectual property values to the original manufactures. Compromising these assets allows an attacker to counterfeit the device or use pirated firmware on a different device with similar functionality.
- **On-device protected data,** such as user's personal information and meter reading. An attacker can invade someone's privacy by stealing these assets, or can tamper with these assets as in meter reading.
- **Device configuration,** such as, configuration data, determines which resources and services are available to particular users. An attacker may tamper with these assets to gain unauthorized access to these resources.
- **Entropy,** including random numbers generated for cryptographic primitives, for example, initializing vector or cryptographic key generation. Successful attacks on these assets weaken cryptographic strength of a device.

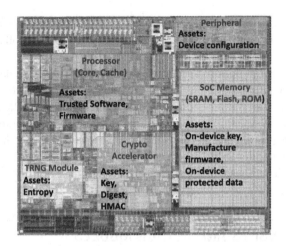

FIGURE 13.1

Example assets in a SoC.

The security assets are known to the hardware designers based on the target specifications of a design. For example, a designer knows the private encryption key used by the cryptomodule and its location in the SoC. Different types of assets and their locations in a SoC are shown in Fig. 13.1.

13.2.2 POTENTIAL ACCESS TO ASSETS

Usually, the aim of an attack is to obtain unauthorized access to assets. Typically, there are four types of such attacks, depending on attackers' abilities: remote attacks, noninvasive physical attacks, semi-invasive physical attacks, and invasive physical attacks.

Remote Attacks: In this case, an attacker has no physical access to the device. The attacker can still perform timing [1] and electromagnetic [13] side-channel attacks to remotely extract private key from devices, such as smartcards or microprocessors used in the cloud system. It has also been demonstrated that an attacker can remotely access the JTAG port and compromise the secret key stored in smartcard of a set-top box [14].

It is also possible to remotely access the scan structure of a chip. For example, in automotive applications, the SoC controlling different critical functions, such as brakes, power-train, and air-bags, goes into "test-mode" every time the car is turned off or on. This key-off/on tests ensure that the critical systems are tested and working correctly before every drive. However, modern cars can be remotely turned on or off, either by trusted parties, such as roadside assistance operators, or by malicious parties, as shown in the recent news [15]. Remotely turning the car on or off allows access to the SoC's test mode, which can be used to obtain information from the on-chip memory or impose unwanted functions.

Remote attacks also include the ones that exploit the weakness of hardware without requiring physical access, such as buffer overflow, integer overflow, heap corruption, format string, and globbing [16].

Noninvasive physical attacks: Basic noninvasive physical attacks consist of using the primary inputs and outputs to take advantage of security weaknesses in the design to obtain sensitive information. Additionally, more advanced attacks use JTAG debug, boundary scan I/O, and DFT structures to monitor and/or control system intermediate states, or snoop bus lines, and system signals [4]. Other noninvasive physical attacks consist of injecting faults to cause an error during the computation of cipher algorithms and exploit the faulty results to extract the asset, for example, private key for AES encryption. Finally, side-channel attacks (SCAs), such as power SCA or EM SCA fall into the category of noninvasive physical attacks. Noninvasive attacks usually require low budget, and do not cause the destruction of the device under attack.

Invasive physical attacks: These attacks are the most sophisticated and expensive attacks and require advanced technical skills and equipment. In a typical invasive physical attack, chemical processes or precision equipments can be used to physically remove micrometer-thin layers of the die of an electronic chip. Microprobes can then be used to read values on data buses, or inject faults into internal nets in the device to activate specific parts, and extract information. Such attacks are usually invasive result in the destruction of the device.

Semi-invasive physical attacks: Semi-invasive attacks fall between noninvasive and invasive physical attacks. These attacks pose a greater threat, because they are more effective than noninvasive attacks, but can be performed at a much lower cost than that of invasive physical attacks. Semi-invasive physical attacks usually require partial depackaging of the chip, or backside thinning to get access to its surface. Unlike invasive attacks, semi-invasive attacks do not require complete removal of the internal layers of the chip. Such attacks include injecting faults to modify SRAM cells content, and changing the state of a CMOS transistor to gain control of a chip's operation, or bypass its protection mechanisms [17].

13.2.3 POTENTIAL ADVERSARY

It is important to understand the potential adversaries who may utilize the security vulnerabilities to perform attacks. This can help designers in comprehending adversaries' capabilities and choosing right countermeasures depending on the targeted adversary and operation. The adversary might be an individual or an organized party who intends to acquire, damage, or disrupt an asset for which he/she does not have permission to access. Considering an integrated circuit design process and entities involved in it, adversaries can be categorized into insiders and outsiders. Figure 13.2 shows the potential adversaries in different stages of a SoC design process.

Insiders: The design and manufacturing of integrated circuits have become more sophisticated and globally distributed at present time. It creates a higher possibility for launching attacks by insiders who understand the details of the design. An insider could be a rogue employee who works for the design house and the system integrator, or could be an untrusted 3PIP or a foundry. Typically, an insider:

- Has direct access to the SoC design, either as an RTL or gate-level netlist, or as a GDSII layout file.
- Has high technical knowledge in the IC design and supply chain.
- Has the capability to make modifications to the design, for example, inserting hardware Trojans [8, 18]. These hardware Trojans can cause denial of service, or create backdoors in the design through which sensitive information can be leaked. Other possible insider attacks include reducing circuit reliability by manipulating circuit parameters and asset leakage.

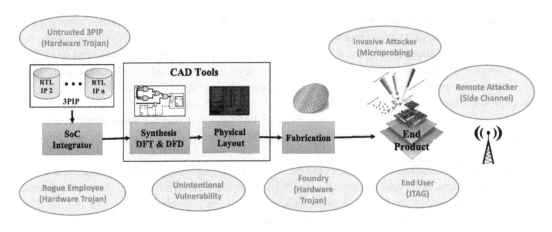

FIGURE 13.2

Potential adversaries in different stages of SoC design process.

Outsiders: This class of attackers is assumed to have access to end products in the market, for example, a packaged IC. Outsider attackers can be divided into three groups based on their capabilities:

- **Remote hacker:** These attackers have no physical access to the device. They must employ remote attacks described in Section 13.2.2, although they may have physical access to a similar device to develop their attack strategy. These attackers generally rely on exploiting software/hardware vulnerabilities, user errors, and design bugs to gain access to assets. Remote hackers include a wide spectrum of attackers, including hobbyist to state-sponsored attackers.
- **End-user:** This group of attackers typically aim to gain free access to contents and services. In this case, the curious end-users may rely on techniques already developed by professional attackers (sometimes available as exploit kit) to carry out their attack. For example, some hobbyists may find a way to jailbreak iPhone or Xbox gaming consoles, and post the procedure on social media, allowing end-users with much less expertise to duplicate the process. Jailbreaking allows users to install jailbreak programs and make companies, such as Apple or Microsoft, lose profits [19].
- **Invasive attacker:** These attackers are security experts and are usually sponsored by nation or industry competitors. Their motives are driven by financial, or political reasons. These groups are capable of executing the more expensive invasive and semiinvasive attacks described in Section 13.2.2.

An insider can introduce or exploit the vulnerabilities in a design more easily compared to an outsider. The main challenge for an outsider to perform an attack is that the internal functionality of the design may not always be known to the attacker. An outsider can reverse engineer the functionality of a chip, but this technique would require extensive resource and time.

The following sections describe the pre-silicon and post-silicon security and trust validation techniques to identify potential vulnerabilities in a hardware design.

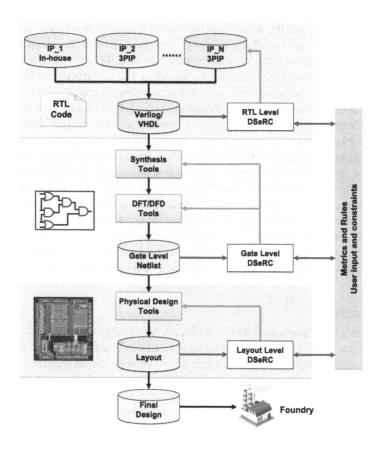

FIGURE 13.3

DSeRC framework.

13.3 PRE-SILICON SECURITY AND TRUST ASSESSMENT FOR SoCs

Different security and trust assessment techniques are employed at the design stage before the chip is fabricated to assess the security and trust issues in a hardware design. This section focuses on the Design Security Rule Check (DSeRC) framework to analyze different vulnerabilities in a hardware design, and consequently assess its security issues at design stage.

13.3.1 DSeRC: DESIGN SECURITY RULE CHECK

In order to identify and evaluate vulnerabilities associated with ICs, DSeRC framework can be integrated into the conventional digital IC design flow, as shown in Fig. 13.3. DSeRC framework reads the design files, constraints, and user input data, and checks for vulnerabilities at all levels of abstraction (RTL, gate-level, and physical layout level). Each of the vulnerabilities is to be tied with a set of rules and metrics, so that each design's security can be quantitatively measured. At RTL abstraction-level, the DSeRC framework assesses the security of IPs, which are either developed in-house or procured from a third party, and provides feedback to design engineers, so that the identified security issues can be addressed. After resolving the security vulnerabilities at RTL, the design is synthesized into gate-level with design-for-test (DFT) and design-for-debug (DFD) structures being inserted. Then, DSeRC framework analyzes the gate-level netlist for security vulnerabilities. The same process is applied to the physical layout design. Through this process, the DSeRC framework allows the designers to identify and address security vulnerabilities at the earliest possible design steps. This significantly improves the security of ICs, and considerably reduces the development time and cost by lowering the time-to-market constraint. Also, the DSeRC framework allows the designers to quantitatively compare different implementations of the same design and, thereby, allows them to optimize performance without compromising the security. However, the DSeRC framework requires some defined inputs from the designer. For example, the security assets need be specified by hardware designers, based on the target specifications of a given design. Note that any technique that performs security assessment for SoCs at any abstraction level falls under the DSeRC concept discussed above.

The DSeRC framework is comprised of three major components: (i) list of vulnerabilities, (ii) metrics and rules to quantitatively assess the vulnerabilities, and (iii) CAD tools for automated security assessment.

13.3.1.1 Vulnerabilities

The vulnerability in a SoC means a weakness, which allows an adversary to exploit and gain access to assets by carrying out an attack. For the development of DSeRC framework, each vulnerability needs to be assigned to one or multiple proper abstraction levels, where it can be identified efficiently. Generally, an IC design goes through specification, RTL design, gate-level design, and, ultimately, physical layout design. DSeRC framework aims at identifying vulnerabilities as early as possible during the design flow, because late evaluation can lead to a long development cycle, and high design cost. Also, vulnerabilities in one stage, if not addressed, may introduce additional vulnerabilities during transition from one level to the next. This section categorizes vulnerabilities based on the abstraction levels (see Table 13.1).

Register-transfer level (RTL): The design specification is first described in a hardware description language (HDL) (for example, Verilog) to create the RTL abstraction of the design. Several attacks performed at the RTL have been discussed in the literature. For example, Fern et al. [20] demonstrated that "Don't-care" assignments in the RTL code can be leveraged as the source of vulnerability to implement hardware Trojans that leak assets. Additionally, in the RTL, hardware Trojans are most likely to be inserted at hard-to-control and hard-to-observe parts of the code [21]. Identifying hard-to-control and hard-to-observe parts of the code can help designers assess the susceptibility of the design to Trojan insertion at the RTL.

In general, vulnerabilities identified at the RTL are comparatively easier to address. However, some vulnerabilities, for instance, the susceptibility of the design to fault-injection or side-channel attacks, are much more challenging, if not impossible, to identify at this level.

Gate-level: The RTL specification is synthesized into gate-level netlist using commercial synthesis tools, such as design compiler. At the gate-level, a design is usually represented by a flattened netlist and, therefore, loses its abstraction. However, more accurate information regarding the design in terms of gates or transistors is available to designers. At gate-level, hard-to-control and hard-to-observe nets can be used to design hard-to-detect hardware Trojans [22]. Also, transition from RTL to gate-level

Table 13.1 Vulnerabilities, metrics, and rules included in DSeRC

	Vulnerability	Metric	Rule	Attack (Attacker)
RTL Level	Dangerous Don't Cares	Identify all 'X' assignments and check if 'X' can propagate to observable nodes	'X' assignments should not be propagated to observable nodes	Hardware Trojan Insertion (Insider)
	Hard-to-control & hard-to-observe signal	Statement hardness and signal observability [21]	Statement hardness (signal observability) should be lower (higher) than a threshold value	Hardware Trojan (Insider)
	Asset leakage	Structure checking and information flow tracking	YES/NO: access assets or observe assets	Asset hacking (End user)
	...	...	...	...
Gate Level	Hard-to-control & hard-to-observe net	Net controllability and observability [22]	Controllability and observability should be higher than a threshold value	Hardware Trojan (Insider)
	Vulnerable Finite State Machine (FSM)	Vulnerability factor of fault-injection (VF_{FI}) & vulnerability factor of Trojan insertion (VF_{Tro}) [7]	VF_{FI} and VF_{Tro} should be zero	Fault-injection, Hardware Trojan (Insider, end user)
	Asset leakage	Confidentiality and integrity assessment [24,25]	YES/NO: access assets or observe assets	Asset hacking (End user)
	Design-for-Test (DFT)	Confidentiality and integrity assessment [24,25]	YES/NO: access assets or observe assets	Asset hacking (End user)
	Design-for-Debug (DFD)	Confidentiality and integrity assessment [24,25]	YES/NO: access assets or observe assets	Asset hacking (End user)
	...	...	...	...
Layout Level	Side-channel signal	Side-channel vulnerability factor (SVF) [26]	The SVF should be lower than a threshold value	Side-channel attack (End user)
	Micro-probing	Exposed area of the security-critical nets which are vulnerable to micro-probing attack [23]	The exposed area should be lower than a threshold value	Micro-probing attack (Professional attacker)
	Injectable Fault/Error	Timing violation vulnerability factor (TVVF) [27]	TVVF higher than a threshold means the implementation is insecure	Timing-based fault-injection attack (End user)
	...	...	...	...

can introduce additional vulnerabilities by the CAD tools. Examples of vulnerabilities introduced by the tools have been discussed in Chapter 6, Section 6.4.2. These vulnerabilities need to be analyzed at the gate-level.

DFT and DFD structures are generally incorporated into the ICs at the gate-level. Therefore, the vulnerabilities introduced by the test and debug structure need to be analyzed at this level.

Layout level: Physical layout design is the last design stage before sending the GDSII design files to fabrication facility, so all the remaining vulnerabilities should be addressed in this level. During the layout design, the placement and routing phase gives information about the spatial arrangements of the cells and metal connections in the circuit. In the layout level, power consumption, electromagnetic emanations, and execution time can be accurately modeled. Therefore, vulnerability analysis of side-channel- and fault-injection-based attacks can be done very accurately at this level. Additionally, some vulnerability analyses, for example, vulnerability to probing attack [23], can only be done at the layout level. However, any analysis done at this level is very time-consuming compared to RTL and gate-level analyses.

13.3.1.2 Metrics and Rules

The vulnerabilities discussed so far are tied with metrics and rules, so that each design's security can be quantitatively measured (see Table 13.1). These rules and metrics of the DSeRC framework can be compared with the well-known design rule check (DRC). In DRC, semiconductor manufacturers convert manufacturing specifications into a series of metrics that enable the designer to quantitatively measure a mask's manufacturability. For the DSeRC framework, each vulnerability needs to be mathematically modeled, and the corresponding rules and metrics must be developed, so that the vulnerability of a design can be quantitatively evaluated. As for the rules, there can be two types; one type is based on quantitative metric, and the other is based on a binary classification (yes/no). A brief description of some of the rules and metrics corresponding to the vulnerabilities are shown in Table 13.1.

Asset leakage: Vulnerabilities associated with asset leakage can be unintentionally created by design-for-test (DFT) and design-for-debug (DFD) structures, CAD tools, and/or by designer's mistakes. These vulnerabilities cause violation of information security policies, that is, confidentiality and integrity policies. Therefore, the metric for identifying these vulnerabilities is confidentiality and integrity assessment. Contreras et al. [24] and Nahiyan et al. [25] presented a framework that validates whether the confidentiality and integrity policies are being upheld in the SoC. The rule for this vulnerability can be stated as follows:

Rule: An asset signal should never propagate to an observe point or be influenced by a control point that is accessible by an attacker.

Vulnerable FSM: The synthesis process of a finite state machine (FSM) can introduce additional security risks in the implemented circuit by inserting additional don't-care states and transitions. An attacker can utilize these don't-care states and transitions to facilitate fault-injection and Trojan attacks. Nahiyan et al. [7] developed two metrics—named vulnerability factor for fault-injection (VF_{FI}) and vulnerability factor for Trojan insertion (VF_{Tro})—to quantitatively analyze how susceptible an FSM is against fault-injection and Trojan attacks, respectively. The higher the values of these two metrics, the more vulnerable the FSM is to fault and Trojan attacks. The rule for this vulnerability can be stated as follows:

Rule: For an FSM design to be secured against fault-injection and Trojan insertion attacks, the values of VF_{FI} and VF_{Tro} should be zero.

Microprobing attack: Microprobing is a type of physical attack that directly probes the signal wires inside the chip in order to extract sensitive information. This attack has raised serious concerns for security-critical applications. Shi et al. [23] developed a layout-driven framework to quantitatively evaluate a post place-and-route design in terms of exposed area of the security-critical nets, which are vulnerable to microprobing attack. The larger the exposed area, the more vulnerable the net is to probing attack. Therefore, the rule for microprobing vulnerability can be stated as follows:

Rule: The exposed area to microprobing should be lower than a threshold value.

Susceptibility to Trojan insertion: Salmani et al. [21] developed a metric named "Statement Hardness" to evaluate the difficulty of executing a statement in the RTL code. Areas in HDL code with large value of Statement Hardness are more vulnerable to Trojan insertion. Therefore, the metric Statement Hardness gives the quantitative measure of a design's susceptibility to Trojan insertion. Next is to define rule(s) to evaluate if the design is secure. For this vulnerability, the rule can be stated as follows:

Rule: For a design to be secured against Trojan-insertion attack, statement hardness of each statement in the design should be lower than SH_{thr}. Here, SH_{thr} is a threshold value that needs to be derived from the area and performance budget.

At the gate-level, a design is vulnerable to Trojan insertion, which can be implemented by adding and deleting gates. To hide the effect of an inserted Trojan, an adversary targets hard-to-detect areas of the gate-level netlist. Hard-to-detect nets are defined as nets which have low transition probability and are not testable through well-known fault-testing techniques (for example, stuck-at, transition delay, path delay, and bridging faults) [22]. Inserting a Trojan in hard-to-detect areas would reduce the probability to trigger the Trojan and, thereby, reduce the probability of being detected during verification and validation testing. Tehranipoor et al. [28] developed metrics to evaluate hard-to-detect areas in the gate-level netlist.

Fault-injection and side-channel attacks: Yuce et al. [27] introduced timing violation vulnerability factor (TVVF) metric to evaluate the vulnerability of a hardware structure to setup-time violation attacks, which are one subset of fault-injection attacks. Huss et al. [29] developed a framework named AMASIVE (adaptable modular autonomous side-channel vulnerability evaluator) to automatically identify side-channel vulnerabilities of a design. Also, a metric named side-channel vulnerability factor (SVF) has been developed to evaluate an IC's vulnerability to power side-channel attacks [26].

Note that the development of these metrics is a challenging task, because ideally the metrics must be independent of attack models and targeted applications, or functionality of a design. For example, an attacker can apply voltage-starving- or clock-glitching-based fault-injection attacks to obtain the private key of AES, or RSA encryption modules. The metric for fault-injection needs to provide a quantitative measure of vulnerability for any design (AES or RSA) against any of such attacks (voltage starving or clock glitching). One strategy would be to first identify the root vulnerabilities that these attacks try to exploit. For this particular example, both voltage starving and clock glitching aim to effect a setup-time violation. The framework must, therefore, evaluate the difficulty of violating setup-time for a given design, for gaining access to the targeted security assets.

13.3.1.3 CAD Tools for Security Validation

The DSeRC framework is intended to be integrated with the conventional IC design flow, so that security evaluation can be made an inherent part of the design process. This requires the development of CAD tools, which can automatically evaluate the security of a design, based on DSeRC rules and metrics. The tools' evaluation times need to be scalable with the design size. Also, the tools should

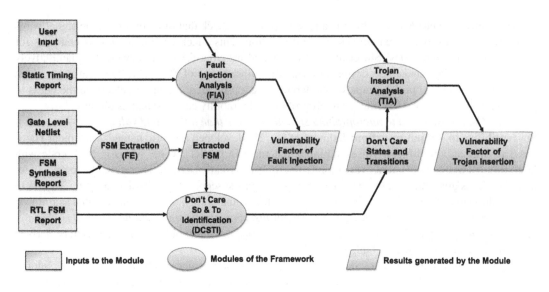

FIGURE 13.4

Overall workflow of the AVFSM framework.

be easy to use, and the outputs generated by the tools need to be understandable by the design engineer. Following is a brief description of some CAD tools, which can be incorporated in the DSeRC framework for security assessment:

CAD tool for analyzing vulnerabilities in FSM: Nahiyan et al. [7] developed a comprehensive framework, called AVFSM, to automatically analyze the vulnerabilities of FSMs against fault-injection and Trojan attacks. AVFSM takes the followings as inputs: (i) gate-level netlist of the design; (ii) FSM synthesis report; and (iii) user given inputs. The framework outputs the list of vulnerabilities found in the given FSM. Here, the user needs to specify which are the protected states and the authorized states. Protected states are those states that can compromise the security of an FSM if these states are either bypassed or accessed from any states apart from the authorized states. Authorized states are those states which are allowed to access a protected state.

The overall workflow of the AVFSM framework is shown in Fig. 13.4. The AVFSM framework is composed of four modules:

- FSM Extraction (FE): To analyze various vulnerabilities in a given FSM, one first needs to extract the state transition graph (STG) from the synthesized gate-level netlist. An automatic-test-pattern-generation-based (ATPG-based) FSM extraction technique can be developed to produce the STG with the don't-care states and transitions from the synthesized netlist. This FSM extraction technique takes the gate-level netlist and the FSM synthesis report as inputs, and automatically generates the STG. The detailed algorithm for this technique can be found in [7].
- Don't-care states and transitions identification (DCSTI): It reports the don't-care states and transitions introduced by the synthesis process of the given FSM. The don't-care states and transitions can create vulnerabilities in the FSM by allowing a protected state to be illegally accessed through

the don't-care states and transitions. These don't-care states, which can access the protected states are defined as Dangerous Don't-Care States (DDCS).

- Fault-injection analysis (FIA): Module FIA uses the vulnerability factor for fault-injection (VF_{FI}) metric to measure the overall vulnerability of the FSM to fault-injection attack. VF_{FI} is defined as follows:

$$VF_{FI} = \{PVT(\%), ASF\} \tag{13.1}$$

The metric VF_{FI} is composed of two parameters {PVT(%), ASF}. PVT(%) indicates the percentage of vulnerable transitions. Vulnerable transition is defined as a set of transitions during which a fault can be injected to gain access to a protected state. ASF provides a probabilistic measure of successful fault-injection attacks during the vulnerable transitions. The detailed algorithm to calculate these metrics is provided in [7]. The greater the values of these two parameters are, the more susceptible the FSM is to fault attacks. A VF_{FI} of (0,0) means that a protected state cannot be accessed by an unauthorized state, and the respective FSM is not vulnerable to fault attacks.

- Trojan-insertion analysis (TIA): Module TIA uses the vulnerability factor for Trojan insertion (VF_{Tro}) metric to evaluate the vulnerability of the FSM to Trojan insertion as follows:

$$VF_{Tro} = \frac{Total\ number\ of\ s'}{Total_{Transition}}, \tag{13.2}$$

where $s' \in DDCS$. When a don't-care state that has direct access to a protected state is introduced, it can create a vulnerability in the FSM by allowing the attacker to utilize this don't-care state to insert a Trojan to facilitate access to the protected state. These states are represented as DDCS. For a secure design, this metric's value should be zero.

Information flow tracking: Contreras et al. [24] and Nahiyan et al. [25] developed an information flow tracking (IFT) framework that detects the violation of confidentiality and integrity policies. This framework is based on modeling an asset (for example, a net carrying a secret) as stuck-at-0 and stuck-at-1 faults, and it leverages the automatic test pattern generation (ATPG) algorithm to detect those faults. A successful detection of faults means that the logical value of the asset-carrying net can be observed through the observe points, or logical value of the asset can be controlled by the control points. In other words, there exists information flow from the asset to observe points, or from control points to the asset. Here, the observe points refer to any primary or pseudo-primary (scan FFs) outputs that can be used to observe internal signals. On the other hand, the control points refer to the primary or pseudoprimary (scan FFs) inputs that can be used to control internal circuit signals.

Figure 13.5 shows the overall flow of the IFT framework and its four main steps: initialize, analysis, propagation, and recursive.

(i) Initialize: This first step takes the name of the asset nets to which IFT will be applied, the gate-level netlist of the design, and the technology library (required for ATPG analysis) as inputs. Then, the framework adds scan capability to all the registers/flip-flops (FFs) in the design to make them controllable and observable. Here, the "What If" analysis feature is used to virtually add and/or remove FFs from scan chain. This feature allows performing partial-scan analysis dynamically, without requiring to re-synthesize the netlist. Also, masks are applied to all FFs, so that asset propagation to each FF can be independently tracked. Applying mask is an important step as it allows controlling fault propagation to one FF at a time.

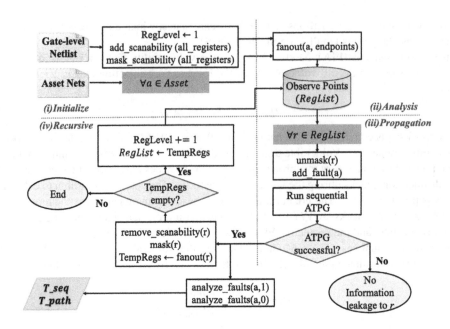

FIGURE 13.5

Information flow tracking (IFT) framework to identify the observe points, where an asset bit propagates to.

(ii) Analysis: This step utilizes fanout analysis to identify which FFs are located in fanout of a particular asset bit. For each asset bit $a \in asset$ (shown in Fig. 13.5), the asset analysis step finds the FFs that are in the fanout cone of a.

(iii) Propagation: This step analyzes the propagation of each asset bit a to each individual FF. To perform a comprehensive analysis of potential points of the asset bit propagation, each FF must be analyzed separately. For each $r \in RegList$ (shown in Fig. 13.5), the applied mask is removed, so the key-bit propagation to r can be tracked. The next step adds the key bit a as the only stuck-at fault in the design, and runs ATPG algorithm in the sequential mode to find paths to propagate $a = 0$, and $a = 1$ to FF r. If both, $a = 0$ and $a = 1$ can be detected from r, then there exists an information flow from a to r and the algorithm marks r as an observe point. The asset-propagation step also stores the propagation path (T_{path}) and the control sequence (T_{seq}) required for the asset-bit propagation for further analysis. Note that, T_{seq} contains the list of input ports and control registers, which controls the information propagation from a to r.

(iv) Recursive: This step leverages the partial-scan technique along with sequential ATPG to find propagation paths through all sequential levels until the output, or the last-level FFs, are reached. Here, the function remove_scanability (shown in Fig. 13.5) makes the ATPG tool treat r as a nonscan FF for simulation purposes, without redoing scan insertion. The FF's output ports Q and QN are used to get a new fanout emerging from r to the next level of registers. To find information flow through multiple levels of registers, the scanability of all identified registers in RegList is removed incrementally, and

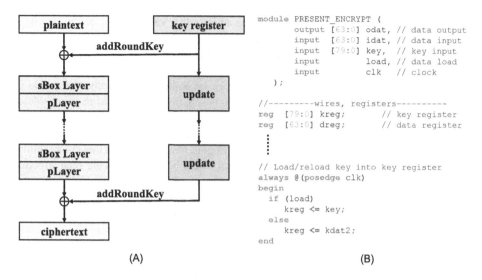

```
module PRESENT_ENCRYPT (
      output [63:0] odat, // data output
      input  [63:0] idat, // data input
      input  [79:0] key,  // key input
      input         load, // data load
      input         clk   // clock
    );

//---------wires, registers----------
reg [79:0] kreg;        // key register
reg [63:0] dreg;        // data register

⋮

// Load/reload key into key register
always @(posedge clk)
begin
  if (load)
    kreg <= key;
  else
    kreg <= kdat2;
end
```

(A)   (B)

FIGURE 13.6

Unintentional vulnerabilities created by design mistakes. (A) Top-level description of PRESENT, (B) Verilog
implementation of PRESENT.

sequential ATPG is used to create propagation paths from asset bit a to subsequent-level registers. This
process continues until the last level of registers.

The output of the IFT framework is a list of observe points (registers/FFs), where the asset bit propagates to, and the propagation path (T_{path}), along with the stimulus vector (T_{seq}) for asset propagation
for each FF, r.

13.3.2 WORKFLOW OF DSeRC FRAMEWORK

This section describes how the rules and metrics are used to identify a vulnerability under DSeRC
framework. Table 13.1 shows the list of vulnerabilities and their corresponding metrics and rules covered by the DSeRC framework. An example of hardware implementation of PRESENT encryption
algorithm is used to illustrate the workflow of DSeRC framework. Figure 13.6A shows the top-level
description of PRESENT encryption algorithm [30]. A segment of its Verilog implementation is shown
in Fig. 13.6B [31]. One can see that the key is directly being assigned to the register, defined as "kreg"
in the module. Although the encryption algorithm itself is secure, a vulnerability is unintentionally
created in its hardware implementation. When this design is implemented, the "kreg" register will be
included in the scan-chain, and an attacker can gain access to key through scan-chain-based attack [4].

The designer first gives the RTL design files and the name of the asset (the "key") as input to DSeRC
framework. DSeRC framework uses the information flow tracking to analyze if the key can be leaked
through any observation points, for example, registers. As for this design, the key can be observed
through the kreg register. Therefore, the framework gives a preemptive warning to the designer that if
the register kreg is included in the DFT structure then, the key can be leaked through scan-chain. It will

be up to the designer to apply a countermeasure to address this vulnerability before moving to next level of abstraction. One possible countermeasure would be to exclude kreg from the scan-chain.

After addressing this vulnerability, the design is synthesized and DFT is inserted. The designer then gives the synthesized gate-level netlist to DSeRC and the framework uses the confidentiality assessment [24,25] technique to analyze if the key can be leaked through any observable point. If the key is secured from leaking, then the DSeRC rule is satisfied and the design is considered to be secured against asset leakage. On the other hand, if the DSeRC framework identifies that the key is still being leaked to scan flip-flops (observable points), then the framework raises a flag and points the scan flip-flops carrying the information about the key. The designer needs to address this vulnerability before moving to physical layout stage. One possible approach would be to apply secure scan structure [4] to counter the vulnerability introduced by the DFT structure.

Note that manually tracking the asset in a SoC to evaluate whether it is being leaked through an observable point is an extremely difficult, if not impossible, task for the designer. DSeRC framework can pinpoint the asset leakage paths, allowing the designers to concentrate the analysis effort on those paths and, therefore, make informed decision.

While DSeRC may be a logical and necessary step in designing secure ICs, it would not necessarily eliminate the need for security subject matter experts. The DSeRC framework is intended to be an automated framework and, therefore, may not take the application of an IC into consideration. For example, the Trojan observability metric reports the difficulty of observing each signal in the design. For Trojan detection, a high observability metric is desired. However, for an encryption module, a high observability metric for the private key poses a serious threat. Therefore, it should be on the designer to interpret the results generated by the DSeRC framework.

13.4 POST-SILICON SECURITY AND TRUST ASSESSMENT FOR ICs

This section presents some of the commonly used post-silicon validation techniques, for example, fuzzing, negative testing, and white-box hacking. These activities inherently depend on human creativity, where tools and infrastructures primarily act as assistants, filling up gaps in human reasoning and providing recommendations.

13.4.1 FUZZING

Fuzzing, or fuzz testing [32], is a testing technique that involves providing invalid, unexpected, or random inputs for hardware or software and monitoring the result for exceptions, such as crashes, failing built-in code assertions, or memory leaks. It was developed as a software testing approach and has since been adapted to hardware/software systems. In the context of security, it is effective for exposing a number of potential attacker entry points, including through buffer or integer overflows, unhandled exceptions, race conditions, access violations, and denial of service. Traditionally, fuzzing uses either random inputs or random mutations of valid inputs. A key attraction to this approach is its high automation compared to other validation technologies, such as penetration testing and formal analysis. Nevertheless, since it relies on randomness, fuzzing may miss security violations that rely on unique corner-case scenarios. To address that deficiency, there has been recent work on "smart" input generation for fuzzing, based on domain-specific knowledge of the target system [33]. Smart fuzzing may provide a greater coverage of security attack entry points, at the cost of more upfront investment in design understanding.

13.4.2 NEGATIVE TESTING

Negative testing looks beyond the functional specification to identify if security objectives are under-specified, or can be subverted. As an example, in case of direct memory attack (DMA), negative testing may extend the deterministic security requirement (that is, abortion of DMA-access for the protected memory ranges) to identify if there are any other paths to the protected memory, in addition to the address translation activated by a DMA access request, and potential input stimulus to activate such paths.

13.4.3 HACKATHONS

Hackathons, also referred to as white-box hacking, fall in the "black magic" end of the security validation spectrum. The idea is for expert hackers to perform goal-oriented attempts at breaking security objectives. This activity depends primarily on human creativity, although some guidelines exist on how to approach them (see discussion on penetration testing in the next section). Because of their cost and the need for high human expertise, such approaches are performed when attacking complex security objectives, typically at hardware/firmware/software interfaces.

13.4.4 PENETRATION TESTING

A penetration test, or intrusion test, is an attack on a system with the intention to find security weakness. It is often performed by expert hackers with deep knowledge of the system architecture, design, and implementation. Roughly, the penetration testing involves iterative applications of the following three phases: attack surface enumeration, vulnerability exploitation, and result analysis.

13.4.4.1 Attack Surface Enumeration

The first task is to identify the features or aspects of the system that are vulnerable to attacks. This is typically a creative process involving a number of activities, including documentation review, network service scanning, and even fuzzing, or random testing.

13.4.4.2 Vulnerability Exploitation

Once the potential attacker entry points are discovered, applicable attacks and exploits are attempted against target areas. This may require research into known vulnerabilities, looking up applicable vulnerability class attacks, engaging in vulnerability research specific to the target, and writing/creating the necessary exploits.

13.4.4.3 Result Analysis

In this phase, the resulting state of the target after a successful attack is compared against security objectives and policy definitions to determine whether the system is indeed compromised. Note that even if a security objective is not directly compromised, a successful attack may identify additional attack surface, which must then be accounted for with further penetration testing.

While there are commonalities between penetration testing and testing for functional validation, there are important differences. In particular, the goal of functional testing is to simulate benign user behavior and (perhaps) accidental failures under normal environmental conditions of design operation, as defined by its specification. On the other hand, the penetration testing goes outside the specification or the limits set by the security objective, and simulates deliberate attacker behavior.

The efficacy of penetration testing critically depends on the ability to identify the attack surface in the first phase previously discussed. Unfortunately, rigorous methodologies for achieving this are lacking. Following are some of the typical activities in current industrial practice to identify attacks and vulnerabilities. They are classified as "easy," "medium," and "hard", depending on the creativity necessary. Note that there are tools to assist the individual in many of the activities below [34,35]. However, determining the relevance of the activity, identifying the degree to which each activity should be explored, and inferring a potential attack from the result of the activity involve significant creativity.

- Easy approaches: These include review of available documentation (for example, specification and architectural materials), known vulnerabilities or misconfigurations of IPs, software, or integration tools, missing patches, and use of obsolete or out-of-date software versions.
- Medium-complexity approaches: These include inferring potential vulnerabilities in the target of interest from information about misconfigurations, vulnerabilities, and attacks in related or analogous products, for example, a competitor product and a previous software version. Other activities of similar complexity involve executing relevant public security tools, or published attack scenarios against the target.
- Hard approaches: These include full security evaluation of any utilized third-party components, integration testing of the whole platform, and identification of vulnerabilities involving communications among multiple IPs, or design components. Finally, the vulnerability research involves identifying new classes of vulnerabilities for the target, which have never been seen before. The latter is particularly relevant for new IPs, or SoC designs for completely new market segments.

13.4.5 FUNCTIONAL VALIDATION OF SECURITY-SENSITIVE DESIGN FEATURES

This is essentially an extension to functional validation but it pertains to design elements involved in critical security feature implementations. An example is the cryptographic engine IP. A critical functional requirement for the cryptographic engine is that it encrypts and decrypts data correctly for all modes. As with any other design block, the cryptographic engine is also a target of functional validation. However, given that it is a critical component of a number of security-critical design features, cryptographic functionality may be crucial enough to justify further validation, beyond the coverage provided by functional validation activities. Consequently, such an IP may undergo more rigorous testing, or even formal analysis. Other such critical IPs may include IPs involved in secure boot, and in-field firmware patching.

13.4.6 VALIDATION OF DETERMINISTIC SECURITY REQUIREMENTS

Deterministic security requirements are validation objectives that can be directly derived from security policies. They include access control restrictions and address translations. Let us consider an access control restriction that specifies a certain range of memory to be protected from DMA access. This may be done to ensure protection against code-injection attacks, or protect a key that is stored in such location. An obvious derived validation objective is to ensure that all DMA calls for access to a protected memory must be aborted. Note that validation of such properties may not be included in the functional validation, since DMA access requests for DMA-protected addresses are unlikely to arise for "normal" test cases, or usage scenarios.

The following sections discuss some countermeasures, which can be adopted at design stage to address the security issues in the hardware design.

13.5 DESIGN FOR SECURITY

This section presents design strategies that make the hardware design inherently resilient to different security issues discussed earlier.

13.5.1 SECURITY ARCHITECTURE

The typical approach for developing a baseline secure architecture depends on the following two steps:

- Use threat modeling to identify potential threats to the current architecture definition.
- Refine the architecture with mitigation strategies covering the threats identified.

The baseline architecture is typically derived from legacy architectures for previous products, adapted to account for the policies defined for the system under exploration. In particular, for each asset, the architect must identify: 1) who can access the asset; 2) what kind of access is permitted by the policies; and 3) at what points in the system execution or product development lifecycle such access requests can be granted or denied. The process can be complex and tedious for several reasons. A SoC design may have a significant number of assets, often in the order of thousands, if not more. Furthermore, not all assets are statically defined; many assets are created at different IPs during the system execution. For example, a fuse or an e-wallet may have a statically defined asset, such as key configuration modes. During system execution, these modes are passed to the cryptographic engine, which generates the cryptographic keys for different IPs, and transmits them through the system network-on-chip (NoC) to the respective IPs. Each participant in this process has sensitive assets (either static or created) during different phases of the system execution. The security architecture must account for any potential access to these assets at any point of execution, possibly under the relevant adversary model.

There has been a significant amount of work toward standardizing architecture to implement access control for different assets. Most of the relevant work has taken the form of developing a trusted execution environment (TEE), viz., a mechanism for guaranteeing isolation between code and sensitive data at different points of the system execution. TEEs, of course, have been a part of computer security for a long time. One of the most common TEE architectures is the trusted platform module (TPM), which is an international standard for a secure cryptoprocessor. It is designed to secure the hardware by integrating cryptographic keys into devices [36]. It covers methods to securely generate cryptographic keys and limit their use, random number generator requirements, and capabilities, such as remote attestation, and sealed storage. In addition to TPM, there has been significant work on architecting other TEEs, both in the industrial platform and in academic research [37,38]. Below, three TEE frameworks specifically developed for SoC designs are presented: Samsung KNOX [39], Intel

Software Guard Extension (SGX) [40], and ARM TrustZone [41]. Note that in spite of differences motivated by the isolation and separation targets, the underlying architectural plans for these TEEs are similar, particularly as it relates to the combination of hardware support (for example, secure operating modes and virtualization), and software mechanisms (such as, context switch agents and integrity check).

13.5.1.1 Samsung KNOX

This architecture is specifically targeted toward smartphones, and provides secure separation features to enable information partition between business and personal content to coexist on the same system. In particular, it permits hot swap between these two content worlds, for example without requiring system restart. The key ingredient of this technology is a separation kernel that implements the information isolation. This architecture permits several system-level services, including the following:

- Trusted boot, that is, preventing unauthorized OS and software from being loaded onto the device at startup.
- Trust-zone-based integrity measurement architecture (TIMA), which continually monitors kernel integrity.
- Security enhancement (SE) for Android, an enforcement mechanism providing protection of system/user data based on confidentiality and integrity requirements through separation.
- KNOX container, which offers a secure environment in which protected business applications can run with guaranteed information separation from the rest of the device.

13.5.1.2 ARM TrustZone

TrustZone technology is a system-wide approach to provide security on high-performance computing platforms. The TrustZone implementation relies on partitioning the SoC's hardware and software resources, so that they exist in two worlds: secure and nonsecure. The hardware supports access control and permissions for the handling of secure/nonsecure applications, and the interaction and communication among them. The software supports secure system calls and interrupts for secure runtime execution in a multitasking environment. These two aspects ensure that no secure world resources can be accessed by the nonsecure world components, except through secure channels, enabling an effective wall-of-security to be built between the two domains. This protection extends to input/output (I/O), connected to the system bus via the TrustZone enabled AMBA3 AXI bus fabric, which also manages memory compartmentalization.

13.5.1.3 Intel SGX

SGX is an architecture for providing a trusted execution environment provided by the underlying hardware to protect sensitive application and user programs or data against potentially malicious, or tampered operating systems. SGX permits applications to initiate secure enclaves or containers, which serve as so-called "islands of trust". It is implemented as a set of new CPU instructions that can be used by applications to set aside such secure enclaves of code and data. This enables 1) applications to preserve the confidentiality and integrity of sensitive data without disrupting the ability of legitimate system software to manage the platform resources; and 2) end users to retain control of their platforms, applications, and services even in the presence of malicious system software.

The TEEs provide a foundation (that is, a mechanism of isolation) for implementing security policies. However, they are a far cry from a standardized approach for implementing policies themselves.

To provide such approaches, it is necessary to 1) develop a language for succinctly and formally expressing security policies; 2) generate a parameterized "skeleton" design that can be easily instantiated to diverse policy implementations; and 3) develop techniques for synthesizing policy implementation from high-level descriptions. Recent academic and industrial research has attempted to address some of these issues. [42] provides a language and synthesis framework for certain security policies. [43] provides a microcontroller-based flexible framework for implementing diverse security policies. There have been optimized architectural support for specific classes of policies, for example, control-flow integrity [44], and Trojan resistance [45].

13.5.2 SECURITY POLICY ENFORCER

This module is responsible for enforcing security policies that are imperative for ensuring security at the hardware level. The readers are referred to Chapter 16 of this book for more details.

13.5.3 SIDE-CHANNEL RESISTANT DESIGN

Different countermeasure techniques have been proposed to counter the power and electromagnetic side-channel attack (details of these attacks have been discussed in Chapter 8). These countermeasure can be broadly categorized as hiding mechanism and masking mechanism. A brief description of these countermeasures are discussed in the following section.

13.5.3.1 Hiding Mechanism

Hiding mechanisms attempt to eliminate the relationship between the leaked information and the secret data, that is, make the leaked information uncorrelated to the secret data. A side-channel attack typically depends on the signal-to-noise ratio (SNR) which is defined as follows:

$$SNR = \frac{var(signal)}{var(noise)}. \tag{13.3}$$

Here, the signal refers to the leaked power signal, which is correlated to the secret data and exploited by the adversaries to perform the side-channel attack. The noise refers to the power signal, which has no correlation to the secret data. The hiding mechanisms decrease the SNR either by increasing the noise or by decreasing the signal to counter the side-channel attack. These mechanisms mainly utilize randomization and equalization techniques to decrease the SNR.

Randomization: These techniques attempt to increase the noise of the circuit to reduce the SNR by constantly changing the execution order, or by generating noise directly [49]. One possible approach for applying randomization is by injecting white noise on the channel (additive white Gaussian noise) [50]. The main idea here is to incorporate noise generation sources in the design, which randomly modifies the current on the power line.

Equalization: These techniques attempt to decrease the leaked power signal, which is correlated to the secret data and reduce the SNR. The main idea here is to make equal power consumption for all operations related to processing secret data. The equalization technique can be realized by a specific type of logic style, which consumes a constant amount of power. Examples of this kind of logic style include dual rail [51] and differential logic [52]. Typically, the output bit transition of a CMOS logic gate depends on the input vectors. For example, a transition from $0 \rightarrow 1$ on the output of an OR gate indicates that either one or two input of the OR gate has a transition from $0 \rightarrow 1$. In other words, the power consumption, which depends on the logic transition of CMOS gates becomes a function of input vectors, and this power consumption is exploited by the adversary for side-channel attack. A solution would be to make the logic circuit consume the same amount of power for every kind of bit transition (i.e. $0 \rightarrow 0$, $0 \rightarrow 1$, $1 \rightarrow 0$, $1 \rightarrow 1$). The dual rail and the differential logic achieve this property by precharging the output in the first half of every clock cycle, and evaluating the correct output value in the second half [49].

13.5.3.2 Masking Mechanism

These mechanisms attempt to randomize the intermediate values (function of the sensitive information) of a cryptographic operation to break the dependencies between these values and the power consumption [50]. Unlike the hiding mechanisms, masking mechanisms are applied at the algorithmic level and can be implemented by standard CMOS logic gates. The main idea here is to conceal each intermediate value by a random mask that is different for every execution. It ensures that the sensitive data is masked with a random value, which eliminates dependencies between the intermediate values and the power consumption [53]. Masking technique can be implemented by Boolean secret sharing technique, which is discussed below.

Let us consider that X and K denote two intermediate values associated with the plaintext and the sub-key of a cryptographic operation. Also, let us consider that another variable Z which is expressed as $Z = X \oplus K$. Z variable is a function of the intermediate value K and any operation on Z variable could leak some information about K. Boolean masking technique attempts to secure the operation of Z by randomly splitting into two shares M_0 and M_1, expressed by the following equation:

$$Z = M_0 \oplus M_1. \tag{13.4}$$

M_1 is referred to as the mask, and M_0 is referred to as the masked variable. M_0 is derived such that $M_0 = Z \oplus M_1$. Any operation on Z leads to the processing of two new shares M_0' and M_1' such that

$$S(Z) = M_0' \oplus M_1', \tag{13.5}$$

where M_1' share is usually generated at random, and M_0' share is derived as $M_0' = S(Z) \oplus M_1'$. The main challenge here is to deduce M_0' from M_0 and M_1 and M_1' without compromising the security of the scheme. When S is linear function, deducing M_0' is relatively an easy task as compared to when S is nonlinear. The detailed derivation of these function is discussed in [53].

13.5.4 PREVENT TROJAN INSERTION

These techniques consist of preventive mechanisms that attempt to thwart hardware Trojan insertion by attackers. The readers are referred to Chapter 5 of this book for more details.

13.6 EXERCISES

13.6.1 TRUE/FALSE QUESTIONS

1. Random number can be an asset.

2. Remote attackers cannot perform attacks exploiting scan structure.
3. Injecting faults to modify SRAM contents is a semi-invasive attack.
4. Side-channel attacks fall into invasive attack category.
5. Vulnerabilities associated with don't-care states are introduced in the RTL stage.
6. Vulnerabilities associated with DFT structure are introduced in the gate-level stage.

13.6.2 LONG-ANSWER TYPE QUESTIONS

1. Describe the "Assets" that can be found in a SoC.
2. How can the entropy asset be exploited?
3. How can a scan-based attack be performed remotely? Show an example.
4. Explain the differences between semi-invasive and invasive attack.
5. Describe the capabilities of an "Insider" attacker. What kind of attacks can an "Insider" perform?
6. How potential vulnerabilities can be introduced by design mistakes? Show an example.
7. How potential vulnerabilities can be introduced by CAD tools? Show an example.
8. Describe the principle of the following tests: (i) Fuzzing, (ii) Negative Testing, (iii) Penetration Testing.
9. How does the "Hiding Mechanisms" protect against side-channel attacks?

REFERENCES

[1] P.C. Kocher, Timing attacks on implementations of Diffie–Hellman, RSA, DSS, and other systems, in: Annual International Cryptology Conference, Springer, pp. 104–113.
[2] P. Kocher, J. Jaffe, B. Jun, Differential power analysis, in: Annual International Cryptology Conference, Springer, pp. 388–397.
[3] D. Hely, M.-L. Flottes, F. Bancel, B. Rouzeyre, N. Berard, M. Renovell, Scan design and secure chip, in: IOLTS, vol. 4, pp. 219–224.
[4] J. Lee, M. Tehranipoor, C. Patel, J. Plusquellic, Securing scan design using lock and key technique, in: Defect and Fault Tolerance in VLSI Systems, 2005. DFT 2005. 20th IEEE International Symposium on, IEEE, pp. 51–62.
[5] E. Biham, A. Shamir, Differential fault analysis of secret key cryptosystems, in: Annual International Cryptology Conference, Springer, pp. 513–525.
[6] C. Dunbar, G. Qu, Designing trusted embedded systems from finite state machines, ACM Transactions on Embedded Computing Systems (TECS) 13 (2014) 153.
[7] A. Nahiyan, K. Xiao, K. Yang, Y. Jin, D. Forte, M. Tehranipoor, AVFSM: a framework for identifying and mitigating vulnerabilities in FSMs, in: Design Automation Conference (DAC), 2016 53rd ACM/EDAC/IEEE, IEEE, pp. 1–6.
[8] M. Tehranipoor, F. Koushanfar, A survey of hardware Trojan taxonomy and detection, IEEE Design & Test of Computers 27 (2010).
[9] K. Xiao, A. Nahiyan, M. Tehranipoor, Security rule checking in IC design, Computer 49 (2016) 54–61.
[10] A. Nahiyan, K. Xiao, D. Forte, M. Tehranipoor, Security rule check, in: Hardware IP Security and Trust, Springer, 2017, pp. 17–36.
[11] ARM Holdings, Building a secure system using trustzone technology, https://developer.arm.com/docs/genc009492/latest/trustzone-software-architecture/the-trustzone-api. (Accessed August 2018), [Online].
[12] E. Peeters, SoC security architecture: current practices and emerging needs, in: Proceedings of the 52nd Annual Design Automation Conference, ACM, p. 144.
[13] T. Korak, T. Plos, Applying remote side-channel analysis attacks on a security-enabled NFC tag, in: Cryptographers' Track at the RSA Conference, Springer, pp. 207–222.
[14] A. Das, J. Da Rolt, S. Ghosh, S. Seys, S. Dupuis, G. Di Natale, M.-L. Flottes, B. Rouzeyre, I. Verbauwhede, Secure JTAG implementation using Schnorr protocol, Journal of Electronic Testing 29 (2013) 193–209.

[15] P. Mishra, S. Bhunia, M. Tehranipoor, Hardware IP Security and Trust, Springer, 2017.

[16] S. Chen, J. Xu, Z. Kalbarczyk, K. Iyer, Security vulnerabilities: from analysis to detection and masking techniques, Proceedings of the IEEE 94 (2006) 407–418.

[17] S.P. Skorobogatov, Semi-invasive attacks: a new approach to hardware security analysis, Ph.D. thesis, University of Cambridge, Computer Laboratory, 2005.

[18] M. Tehranipoor, C. Wang, Introduction to Hardware Security and Trust, Springer Science & Business Media, 2011.

[19] M.A. Harris, K.P. Patten, Mobile device security considerations for small- and medium-sized enterprise business mobility, Information Management & Computer Security 22 (2014) 97–114.

[20] N. Fern, S. Kulkarni, K.-T.T. Cheng, Hardware Trojans hidden in RTL don't cares—automated insertion and prevention methodologies, in: Test Conference (ITC), 2015 IEEE International, IEEE, pp. 1–8.

[21] H. Salmani, M. Tehranipoor, Analyzing circuit vulnerability to hardware Trojan insertion at the behavioral level, in: Defect and Fault Tolerance in VLSI and Nanotechnology Systems (DFT), 2013 IEEE International Symposium on, IEEE, pp. 190–195.

[22] H. Salmani, M. Tehranipoor, R. Karri, On design vulnerability analysis and trust benchmarks development, in: Computer Design (ICCD), 2013 IEEE 31st International Conference on, IEEE, pp. 471–474.

[23] Q. Shi, N. Asadizanjani, D. Forte, M.M. Tehranipoor, A layout-driven framework to assess vulnerability of ICs to microprobing attacks, in: Hardware Oriented Security and Trust (HOST), 2016 IEEE International Symposium on, IEEE, pp. 155–160.

[24] G.K. Contreras, A. Nahiyan, S. Bhunia, D. Forte, M. Tehranipoor, Security vulnerability analysis of design-for-test exploits for asset protection in SoCs, in: Design Automation Conference (ASP-DAC), 2017 22nd Asia and South Pacific, IEEE, pp. 617–622.

[25] A. Nahiyan, M. Sadi, R. Vittal, G. Contreras, D. Forte, M. Tehranipoor, Hardware Trojan detection through information flow security verification, in: Test Conference (ITC), 2017 IEEE International, IEEE, pp. 1–10.

[26] J. Demme, R. Martin, A. Waksman, S. Sethumadhavan, Side-channel vulnerability factor: a metric for measuring information leakage, ACM SIGARCH Computer Architecture News 40 (2012) 106–117.

[27] B. Yuce, N.F. Ghalaty, P. Schaumont, TVVF: estimating the vulnerability of hardware cryptosystems against timing violation attacks, in: Hardware Oriented Security and Trust (HOST), 2015 IEEE International Symposium on, IEEE, pp. 72–77.

[28] M. Tehranipoor, H. Salmani, X. Zhang, Integrated Circuit Authentication: Hardware Trojans and Counterfeit Detection, Springer Science & Business Media, 2013.

[29] S.A. Huss, M. Stöttinger, M. Zohner, AMASIVE: an adaptable and modular autonomous side-channel vulnerability evaluation framework, in: Number Theory and Cryptography, Springer, 2013, pp. 151–165.

[30] A. Bogdanov, L.R. Knudsen, G. Leander, C. Paar, A. Poschmann, M.J. Robshaw, Y. Seurin, C. Vikkelsoe, Present: An ultra-lightweight block cipher, in: International Workshop on Cryptographic Hardware and Embedded Systems, Springer, pp. 450–466.

[31] OpenCores, http://opencores.org. (Accessed August 2018).

[32] A. Takanen, J.D. Demott, C. Miller, Fuzzing for Software Security Testing and Quality Assurance, Artech House, 2008.

[33] S. Bhunia, S. Ray, S. Sur-Kolay, Fundamentals of IP and SoC Security: Design, Verification, and Debug, Springer, 2017.

[34] Microsoft Corporation, Microsoft free security tools—Microsoft baseline security analyzer, https://blogs.microsoft.com/cybertrust/2012/10/22/microsoft-free-security-tools-microsoftbaseline-security-analyzer/. (Accessed August 2018), [Online].

[35] Flexera, http://secunia.com. (Accessed August 2018).

[36] Trusted Computing Group, Trusted platform module specification, http://www.trustedcomputinggroup.org/tpm-main-specification/. (Accessed August 2018), [Online].

[37] A. Vasudevan, E. Owusu, Z. Zhou, J. Newsome, J.M. McCune, Trustworthy execution on mobile devices: what security properties can my mobile platform give me? in: International Conference on Trust and Trustworthy Computing, Springer, pp. 159–178.

[38] J.M. McCune, B.J. Parno, A. Perrig, M.K. Reiter, H. Isozaki, Flicker: an execution infrastructure for TCB minimization, in: ACM SIGOPS Operating Systems Review, vol. 42, ACM, pp. 315–328.

[39] Samsung, Samsung knox, http://www.samsungknox.com. (Accessed August 2018).

[40] Intel, Intel software guard extensions programming reference, https://software.intel.com/sites/default/files/managed/48/88/329298-002.pdf. (Accessed August 2018), [Online].

[41] ARM Holdings, Products Security, https://www.arm.com/products/silicon-ip-security. (Accessed August 2018), [Online].

[42] X. Li, V. Kashyap, J.K. Oberg, M. Tiwari, V.R. Rajarathinam, R. Kastner, T. Sherwood, B. Hardekopf, F.T. Chong, Sapper: a language for hardware-level security policy enforcement, ACM SIGARCH Computer Architecture News 42 (2014) 97–112.

[43] A. Basak, S. Bhunia, S. Ray, A flexible architecture for systematic implementation of SoC security policies, in: Proceedings of the IEEE/ACM International Conference on Computer-Aided Design, IEEE Press, pp. 536–543.

[44] L. Davi, M. Hanreich, D. Paul, A.-R. Sadeghi, P. Koeberl, D. Sullivan, O. Arias, Y. Jin, Hafix: hardware-assisted flow integrity extension, in: Proceedings of the 52nd Annual Design Automation Conference, ACM, p. 74.

[45] L. Changlong, Z. Yiqiang, S. Yafeng, G. Xingbo, A system-on-chip bus architecture for hardware Trojan protection in security chips, in: Electron Devices and Solid-State Circuits (EDSSC), 2011 International Conference of, IEEE, pp. 1–2.

[46] A. Basak, S. Bhunia, S. Ray, Exploiting design-for-debug for flexible SoC security architecture, in: Proceedings of the 53rd Annual Design Automation Conference, ACM, p. 167.

[47] IEEE, IEEE standard test access port and boundary scan architecture, IEEE Standards 11491, 2001.

[48] E. Ashfield, I. Field, P. Harrod, S. Houlihane, W. Orme, S. Woodhouse, Serial Wire Debug and the Coresight Debug and Trace Architecture, ARM Ltd., Cambridge, UK, 2006.

[49] E. Peeters, Side-channel cryptanalysis: a brief survey, in: Advanced DPA Theory and Practice, Springer, 2013, pp. 11–19.

[50] A. Moradi, Masking as a side-channel countermeasure in hardware, ISCISC 2016 Tutorial, 2006.

[51] D. May, H.L. Muller, N.P. Smart, Random register renaming to foil DPA, in: International Workshop on Cryptographic Hardware and Embedded Systems, Springer, pp. 28–38.

[52] F. Macé, F.-X. Standaert, I. Hassoune, J.-D. Legat, J.-J. Quisquater, et al., A dynamic current mode logic to counteract power analysis attacks, in: Proc. 19th International Conference on Design of Circuits and Integrated Systems (DCIS), pp. 186–191.

[53] H. Maghrebi, E. Prouff, S. Guilley, J.-L. Danger, A first-order leak-free masking countermeasure, in: Cryptographers' Track at the RSA Conference, Springer, pp. 156–170.

[54] J.A. Roy, F. Koushanfar, I.L. Markov, Ending piracy of integrated circuits, Computer 43 (2010) 30–38.

[55] R.S. Chakraborty, S. Bhunia, Security against hardware Trojan through a novel application of design obfuscation, in: Proceedings of the 2009 International Conference on Computer-Aided Design, ACM, pp. 113–116.

[56] A. Baumgarten, A. Tyagi, J. Zambreno, Preventing IC piracy using reconfigurable logic barriers, IEEE Design & Test of Computers 27 (2010).

[57] J.B. Wendt, M. Potkonjak, Hardware obfuscation using PUF-based logic, in: Proceedings of the 2014 IEEE/ACM International Conference on Computer-Aided Design, IEEE Press, pp. 270–277.

[58] J. Rajendran, M. Sam, O. Sinanoglu, R. Karri, Security analysis of integrated circuit camouflaging, in: Proceedings of the 2013 ACM SIGSAC Conference on Computer & Communications Security, ACM, pp. 709–720.

[59] R.P. Cocchi, J.P. Baukus, L.W. Chow, B.J. Wang, Circuit camouflage integration for hardware IP protection, in: Proceedings of the 51st Annual Design Automation Conference, ACM, pp. 1–5.

[60] Y. Bi, P.-E. Gaillardon, X.S. Hu, M. Niemier, J.-S. Yuan, Y. Jin, Leveraging emerging technology for hardware security-case study on silicon nanowire FETs and graphene SymFETs, in: Test Symposium (ATS), 2014 IEEE 23rd Asian, IEEE, pp. 342–347.

[61] K. Xiao, M. Tehranipoor, BISA: built-in self-authentication for preventing hardware Trojan insertion, in: Hardware-Oriented Security and Trust (HOST), 2013 IEEE International Symposium on, IEEE, pp. 45–50.

[62] D. McIntyre, F. Wolff, C. Papachristou, S. Bhunia, Trustworthy computing in a multi-core system using distributed scheduling, in: On-Line Testing Symposium (IOLTS), 2010 IEEE 16th International, IEEE, pp. 211–213.

[63] C. Liu, J. Rajendran, C. Yang, R. Karri, Shielding heterogeneous MPSoCs from untrustworthy 3PIPs through security-driven task scheduling, IEEE Transactions on Emerging Topics in Computing 2 (2014) 461–472.

[64] O. Keren, I. Levin, M. Karpovsky, Duplication based one-to-many coding for Trojan HW detection, in: Defect and Fault Tolerance in VLSI Systems (DFT), 2010 IEEE 25th International Symposium on, IEEE, pp. 160–166.

[65] J. Rajendran, H. Zhang, O. Sinanoglu, R. Karri, High-level synthesis for security and trust, in: On-Line Testing Symposium (IOLTS), 2013 IEEE 19th International, IEEE, pp. 232–233.

[66] T. Reece, D.B. Limbrick, W.H. Robinson, Design comparison to identify malicious hardware in external intellectual property, in: Trust, Security and Privacy in Computing and Communications (TrustCom), 2011 IEEE 10th International Conference on, IEEE, pp. 639–646.

[67] Trusted integrated circuits (TIC) program announcement, 2011.

[68] K. Vaidyanathan, B.P. Das, L. Pileggi, Detecting reliability attacks during split fabrication using test-only BEOL stack, in: Proceedings of the 51st Annual Design Automation Conference, ACM, pp. 1–6.

[69] M. Jagasivamani, P. Gadfort, M. Sika, M. Bajura, M. Fritze, Split-fabrication obfuscation: metrics and techniques, in: Hardware-Oriented Security and Trust (HOST), 2014 IEEE International Symposium on, IEEE, pp. 7–12.

[70] B. Hill, R. Karmazin, C.T.O. Otero, J. Tse, R. Manohar, A split-foundry asynchronous FPGA, in: Custom Integrated Circuits Conference (CICC), 2013 IEEE, IEEE, pp. 1–4.

[71] Y. Xie, C. Bao, A. Srivastava, Security-aware design flow for 2.5D IC technology, in: Proceedings of the 5th International Workshop on Trustworthy Embedded Devices, ACM, pp. 31–38.

[72] J. Valamehr, T. Sherwood, R. Kastner, D. Marangoni-Simonsen, T. Huffmire, C. Irvine, T. Levin, A 3-D split manufacturing approach to trustworthy system development, IEEE Transactions on Computer-Aided Design of Integrated Circuits and Systems 32 (2013) 611–615.

[73] K. Vaidyanathan, B.P. Das, E. Sumbul, R. Liu, L. Pileggi, Building trusted ICs using split fabrication, in: 2014 IEEE International Symposium on Hardware-Oriented Security and Trust (HOST), pp. 1–6.

[74] F. Imeson, A. Emtenan, S. Garg, M.V. Tripunitara, Securing computer hardware using 3D integrated circuit (IC) technology and split manufacturing for obfuscation, in: USENIX Security Symposium, pp. 495–510.

[75] K. Xiao, D. Forte, M.M. Tehranipoor, Efficient and secure split manufacturing via obfuscated built-in self-authentication, in: Hardware Oriented Security and Trust (HOST), 2015 IEEE International Symposium on, IEEE, pp. 14–19.

[76] D.B. Roy, S. Bhasin, S. Guilley, J.-L. Danger, D. Mukhopadhyay, From theory to practice of private circuit: a cautionary note, in: Computer Design (ICCD), 2015 33rd IEEE International Conference on, IEEE, pp. 296–303.

HARDWARE OBFUSCATION

14

CONTENTS

14.1 INTRODUCTION

Hardware obfuscation is a method of modifying a design, so that it becomes significantly difficult to reverse engineer, or copy. Figure 14.1 provides high-level view of the hardware obfuscation process, which transforms a design with respect to its functional behavior, and its structural representation. The

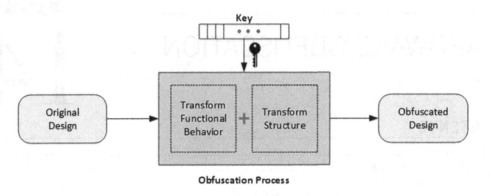

FIGURE 14.1

High level view of the hardware obfuscation process.

transformation process requires a "key", which is used to lock the design. An obfuscated design works in two modes. On application of the correct key, it gets "unlocked", and operates in normal mode, that is, it produces its normal functional behavior. With an incorrect key, it remains "locked"; it works in obfuscated mode, and produces wrong outputs.

Hardware obfuscation is an active field of research. It presents a fundamentally different approach to IP protection than existing ones. Existing approaches include passive solutions, such as patenting, copyrighting, and watermarking, which provide a mechanism to prove and claim ownership of an IP in the court of law, when an IP infringement is suspected. Existing security approaches fail to provide an active protection of an IP against piracy and reverse engineering in untrusted facilities. To address the limitations of existing approaches, over the past decade, hardware obfuscation has been studied as a promising defense mechanism that can ensure security of hardware IPs along the supply chain. In particular, its effectiveness has been studied on the basis of three major threats on hardware IP: (1) reverse engineering, (2) piracy, and (3) malicious modifications (i.e., hardware Trojan attacks, as described in Chapter 5). Although the majority of obfuscation research is aimed at addressing the first two threats, some methods have also been shown to provide protection against Trojan attacks in untrusted foundry. Obfuscation has been investigated for both ASIC and FPGA design flows, and for different levels of abstraction, for example, gate-level and register-transfer level IPs. Similar to encryption, the security model here relies on the secrecy of the key, not the algorithm used for obfuscation.

Hardware obfuscation requires application of a systematic set of transformations intended to provide provably robust protection. Figure 14.2 illustrates the major goals of the design transformation, and how they are achieved. One major goal is preventing black-box usage, which indicates that the transformed IP cannot be used as a "black-box" in a larger design, for instance, in an SoC to provide the desired functionality. This is achieved through the locking mechanism. The locking is accomplished by inserting specialized logic structures or gates controlled by the key that produce incorrect functionality for wrong keys, and vice versa. A strong lock, that is robust against functional or structural analysis attacks, is desired for a strong obfuscation. The second major goal is to conceal the design intent through judicious structural transformation. This is essential for two reasons: (1) it protects the lock itself, since a lock, which can be easily identified, can also be removed easily; and (2) it prevents leakage of design secrets, such as type of

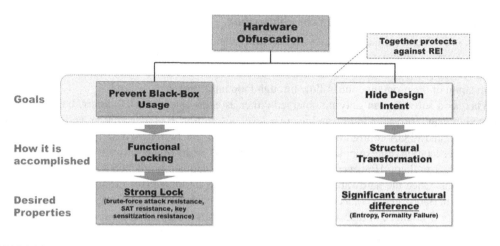

FIGURE 14.2

Main goals of hardware obfuscation and properties to assess the obfuscation.

function realized and, logic style, which may provide important clues about a design to potential adversaries. Even partial extraction of design knowledge can be extremely useful for an adversary. For example, improper obfuscation of an arithmetic logic unit can reveal important features of the design, such as the overflow mechanism or pipeline structure. Hardware for many applications (for instance, digital signal processing, graphics, etc.) have very regular logic structure. Obfuscation for them presents even more difficult challenges with respect to hiding design intent.

14.1.1 PRELIMINARIES

In this section, we present definitions of obfuscation for both software and hardware, and point out the differences between them. We also talk about the advantages of hardware IP obfuscation over encryption.

14.1.1.1 Definition

The term "obfuscation" represents the method of obscuring or covering the actual substance of an information or the functional behavior of a product to protect the inherent intellectual property. In cryptology and software, an obfuscator Z is formally characterized as a "compiler" that reconstructs a program P to an obfuscated form $Z(P)$. $Z(P)$ must have the same functionality as P while being incomprehensible to an attacker aiming to construct P from $Z(P)$.

Obfuscation, in the context of a hardware design, i.e., "hardware obfuscation" is concerned with the protection of hardware IPs. These IPs are reusable block of logic, memory, or analog circuits, which are owned by their developers, and used by themselves, or other SoC design houses. Though the techniques for obfuscating hardware and software differ significantly, the primary goal of obfuscation remains unchanged: protection of IP from bad actors that are capable of piracy, reverse engineering, and malicious modification.

14.1.1.2 *Software Versus Hardware Obfuscation*

Software obfuscation primarily focuses on obscuring the implementation of the algorithm represented as code. Software obfuscation relies on various techniques, ranging from the addition of simple comments, changing symbol names, or the removal of white spaces to more sophisticated methods, such as modification of the program control-flow through loop unrolling [1].

Whereas a software can only be obtained either as code or a compiled binary, hardware can be obtained in many forms, including architecture-level description, RTL description, netlist, layout, fabricated chip, and FPGA configuration bitstream. As long as the hardware description can be found in textual representation (for example, RTL, gate-level netlist), many of the software obfuscation solutions can be applied to them. However, they may not provide adequate protection against aforementioned threat models. Once the hardware design is represented as an image (for instance, GDSII layout) or physical form (fabricated ICs), a completely different approach is required. For instance, the RTL code of a hardware IP could be obfuscated by leveraging some form of keyless software obfuscation method, such as redundant code injection. However, once the design is synthesized, the redundant portion that does not impact the actual functionality of the circuit could get eliminated, due to the inherent optimization goals of the synthesis tool. This would allow an attacker to observe the original functionality in synthesized representations of the hardware.

Electronic system design lifecycle is significantly different compared to its software counterpart. Unlike the software development process, hardware design, manufacturing, and testing process often require access to the hardware design, for example, the entire SoC. It gives opportunity to an adversary in an untrusted design/fabrication/test facility to have complete access to the design, and hence makes all IPs vulnerable to piracy and RE. Finally, for distributing software to evaluators and selling them to end-users, appropriate licensing mechanisms (for instance, node-locked licensing) can be used. However, such licensing approaches for hardware IPs to prevent piracy are difficult to accomplish. We discuss this topic in more detail in the next section.

14.1.2 WHY NOT ENCRYPT HARDWARE IPs?

Encryption provides a secure mechanism for IP delivery where robustness is mathematically provable. One might argue that good encryption algorithms (for example, Advanced Encryption Standard or AES) could be used to securely deliver and use hardware IPs in an untrusted supply chain. Encryption could be applied to protect hardware IPs in certain parts of the supply chain with commensurate support from CAD tools. In particular, it can work effectively to protect IPs in an FPGA design flow, where vendor-specific toolset manages the encryption/decryption process. However, in many stages of the supply chain, where an IP is utilized as a white-box, for example, synthesis and physical design, encryption does not apply. For instance, to be able to create the mask of a design, the actual GDSII file must be provided to the foundry. It could be encrypted during transportation to the untrusted foundry, but before fabrication, the IP must be decrypted, and the foundry would have access to the original (unencrypted) form. The same applies to DFT insertion facility that is responsible for inserting design for test resources (such as scan chain and test points) within a design.

During the functional simulation and FPGA prototyping of a soft IP, the design could come in encrypted form. However, the CAD tool, responsible for simulation and synthesis of the design, must obtain the encryption key. This is because only the decrypted version of the design maintains the functional and structural properties of a design that are required to simulate or synthesize it. Under

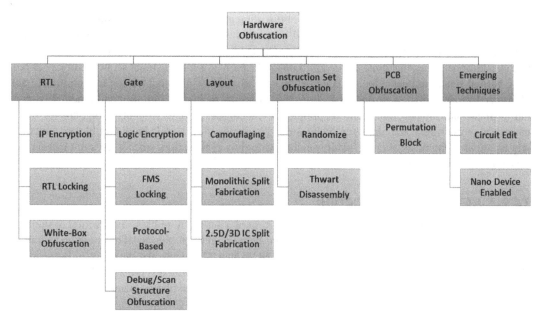

FIGURE 14.3

A taxonomy of hardware obfuscation techniques.

this framework, an IP is protected as long as the CAD tool responsible for key management is not compromised. Hence, due to the requirement of white-box usage of an IP at various untrusted stages in the supply chain, encryption is not considered as a viable solution for hardware IP protection.

14.2 OVERVIEW OF OBFUSCATION TECHNIQUES

Researchers have developed various hardware obfuscation techniques over the past decade. A taxonomy of these techniques is presented in Fig. 14.3, and briefly described below.

14.2.1 RTL OBFUSCATION

Register-transfer level IPs, that is, soft IPs, use high-level constructs to describe an IP using HDL, such as, Verilog or VHDL. Obfuscation of soft IPs typically represent more difficult challenges than their gate-level counterparts. This is because RTL constructs are easier to interpret in terms of the control and data flow, which makes hiding design intent more difficult. IP encryption has been generally used to protect soft IPs. In this method, the entire soft IP can be encrypted by common encryption techniques, such as AES or RSA. Key management is usually handled by the EDA tools (which are assumed to be trusted), and a design house that legally acquires an encrypted IP simply uses it in a design as a black-box.

Apart from encryption, various key-based obfuscation approaches have been studied for protection of soft IPs [2,3]. The RTL code of an IP could be first transformed into a control and data flow graph (CDFG) [2] or state transition graph [3]. The graph could then be modified by inserting "key states", that is, additional states that must be traversed on application of a specific input sequence or key to produce normal functional behavior. On application of a wrong key, it remains stuck in a nonfunctional, obfuscated mode. Soft IPs can also be obfuscated in terms of its intelligibility and readability, similar to traditional software obfuscation approaches. Techniques such as loop unrolling, change in net name, and reordering of statements could be applied to render an RTL code unintelligible, yet functionally identical to the original code [4]. It is called white-box obfuscation, since it does not incorporate functional or structural transformations.

14.2.2 GATE LEVEL OBFUSCATION

A gate-level IP, referred to as firm IP, comes in the form of a netlist. A netlist is a collection of standard logic cells and the nets, which represent connections between cells. A gate-level obfuscation technique requires insertion of extra gates, such as XOR, XNOR, and MUX into the netlist of a design [5,6]. These gates (and their logical output) are controlled by key bits, which serve as additional inputs to the netlist. These key bits can be stored in a tamper-resistant nonvolatile memory inside a chip or be derived from physical unclonable functions (described later in Chapter 12). Correct logic values ("1" or "0") at the key bits ensure intended functional behavior for the netlist. Without the correct values at the key bits, logic gates controlled by them generate wrong logic values at the internal circuit nodes, which lead to faulty outputs for the netlist. The process of controlling selected internal nodes of a circuit by external inputs is very similar to controllable test point insertion [7], which has been traditionally used to improve testability in a design. The internal nodes, which are connected to the key bits are strategically chosen to maximize output corruption (for wrong keys) and to increase structural changes across the netlist. A detailed study of such gate-level obfuscation techniques is presented in Section 14.3.

Another class of gate-level obfuscation techniques focuses on obfuscating the state space for IP protection. These techniques are applicable to gate-level sequential circuits. They transform the state transition function of the underlying finite state machine (FSM) [8]. The transformation serves the following two purposes: a) First, it locks the FSM, such that without application of a specific input sequence that serves as the key, the FSM remains locked, that is, does not produce correct functional behavior; and b) With application of correct key, the state machine is "unlocked", that is, it transitions to normal mode of operation. The locking of the FSM is accomplished by integrating an obfuscation FSM (OFSM) into the original FSM, which creates an FSM that operates into two modes: (1) obfuscation mode, where the state machine transitions through wrong states; and (2) normal mode, where it transitions through correct states. The approach uses the locked states of the FSM to transform the internal nodes of the combinational logic associated with the state machine. It is done in a very similar manner as the gate-level obfuscation techniques described above. Instead of taking the key values from additional key bits, it generates the enabling key values from the state elements. The key values drive "modification cells", as in the gate-level obfuscation, and create faulty internal values in the combinational logic for wrong key.

Sequential obfuscation has also been used to obfuscate the scan-chain of a design. As described earlier, scan-chains are DFT structures inserted into a design to improve its testability. It is important to enable security of scan-chain, such that they cannot be used by unauthorized user to leak secrets on chip, which are accessible through the scan chain [9]. Various obfuscation techniques have been developed to prevent such test infrastructure exploits. For example, researchers have proposed the use of test compression structures that compress the value of several scan flip-flops into a single output, thereby making the observation of individual FF values infeasible. Locking techniques have also been proposed that allow the designer to scramble the responses of the scan-chain (chain of scan FFs), unless a secret key is applied. More details on protection of scan structure is presented in Chapter 9.

14.2.3 LAYOUT LEVEL OBFUSCATION

Layout-level IPs, also known as hard IPs, come in the form of physical layout of a design. It consists of geometrical and spatial information related to a specific fabrication process. Such information is directly used in the fabrication of chips by a foundry. In order to protect the layout from piracy and possible malicious alterations (that is, Trojan implantation) by an untrusted foundry, several split manufacturing techniques have been proposed [10–12]. These individual approaches are applicable to either conventional or emerging (2.5D/3D) IC technologies. Split manufacturing techniques rely on fabricating part of a design—usually the expensive transistor/active layer, and few lower metal layers, called front-end-of-line (FEOL) layers—in an untrusted foundry using advanced processes, and then completing the remaining less expensive fabrications steps—usually, upper level metal layers, called back-end-of-line (BEOL) layers—in a trusted foundry using a less advanced process technology [13]. Since it hides the connectivity information from an untrusted foundry, the approach has inherent benefits in terms of IP protection. However, methods that place the routing resources (such as, interconnects and vias) judiciously, such that security-critical nets are routed in upper level metal layers in trusted foundry, can maximize the obfuscation.

Whereas the split manufacturing concept is attractive for IP protection, attacks have been mounted on published approaches. These attacks utilize proximity data to recover the missing connectivity information. It is based on the assumption that EDA tools use certain parameters, for example, gate distance to minimize wire length [14]. Moreover, the biggest hurdle to split manufacturing is that the design house is still required to maintain a foundry to complete the BEOL, which could be prohibitively expensive depending on the split layer. Further, foundry compatibility and wafer alignment with such monolithic split-fabrication techniques may also hurt IC yield.

Camouflaging: Another class of obfuscation uses configurable cells in strategic locations of a design to disable normal operation, and to hide design intent [15]. These configurable cells can be programmed after fabrication to implement different logic functions. Since an untrusted design/fabrication facility would not know their function, they act as "camouflaged" cells. These cells often have a layout that makes them appear similar to other standard cells (such as NAND, NOR, or XOR) in a library. To an attacker in the foundry, and someone who performs destructive reverse engineering of an IC to extract the design, "camouflaged" cells do not reveal the design from its layout. This technique has been discussed in detail in Section 14.3.2.

2.5D/3D IC obfuscation: Recent advances in 2.5D/3D integration technology can facilitate split manufacturing. One can perform wire-lifting on a layout, so that the lifted wires are fabricated as a separate layer in a trusted facility. Next, the complete IC can be assembled by using through-silicon-via (TSV) bond points in a normal 3D IC design flow [11]. Every gate in the design in the FEOL layers is structurally akin to at least k other gates in the same design (as the BEOL information of the upper tier is missing). This makes it difficult for an attacker (for instance, in an untrusted foundry) to identify the gates, and thus to extract the complete design, or insert malicious changes.

2.5D IC technology could be leveraged further to securely partition a gate-level design, so that two or more partitions of the design can be fabricated at an untrusted foundry, and the interposer layer connecting these partitions can be fabricated at a trusted facility [16]. Unfortunately, split manufacturing based on 2.5D/3D IC technology suffers from the same drawbacks of requiring a separate fabrication facility. Further, these techniques usually demand significant amounts of gate-swapping and wire-rerouting operations for obfuscation, leading to large area and delay overheads.

14.2.4 INSTRUCTION SET OBFUSCATION

Every processor has an underlying instruction set architecture (ISA), which represents the type of commands and data, address space, and operation codes (opcodes) supported by it. The ISA serves as an intermediary between the software and hardware of the computer, and is usually public knowledge. Unfortunately, this also means that the well-known ISA and the vulnerabilities (example, buffer overflow) of a processor used in the system make it vulnerable to remote or even invasive attacks (for instance, via compromise of the memory unit holding the instructions). Identical ISA across million of processors used in IoT, and other systems, helps an attacker in software infection, software IP piracy, and malware propagation (from one computer to another through a network).

To combat the predictability of the ISA, a software code can be obfuscated, such that it runs in only one computer and remains locked in another. One such example is as follows: Each byte of a code can be scrambled using pseudorandom numbers, and during execution, it can be unscrambled to produce the original code [17]. This means that any unauthorized program, which was never scrambled, will be unscrambled to random bits, thereby preventing any targeted malicious behavior. Alternatively, the instructions could be XORed with a secret key as they are transmitted between the processor, and the main memory [18]. Such obfuscation of code either requires support from OS, which securely deobfuscates it before execution, or judicious modification in the processor's hardware that deobfuscates the code at runtime to ensure correct operation.

Instruction set obfuscation can also disrupt the disassembly phase of reverse engineering a machine code, that is, converting the machine code to human-readable form [19]. This can be accomplished by carefully inserting "junk bytes" in the instruction stream of the code. These junk bytes cause an automatic disassembler to either misinterpret the instructions, or the control flow of the program, but do not affect the program's functionality (semantics), as they are unreachable instructions during runtime.

14.2.5 PCB OBFUSCATION

PCB designs are vulnerable to similar security issues as IPs used in SoC. Effective obfuscation of a PCB design can prevent piracy, reverse engineering, or tampering during manufacturing and deployment. A possible solution for PCB design obfuscation is to insert permutation blocks on the board [20]. The permutation block, implemented with a complex programmable logic device (CPLD), or an FPGA, would take a set of critical interconnects (for example, data bus of microcontrollers) and permute them based on a key before they reach their destination. The permutation could be resolved to the correct configuration only when the correct key is applied to the CPLD, or the FPGA that realizes the permutation block.

14.3 HARDWARE OBFUSCATION METHODS

In this section, we discuss some of the well-researched obfuscation methods applied to gate and layout-level hardware designs in detail.

14.3.1 LOGIC LOCKING

Logic locking methods hide the true functionality and the structure of a hardware IP through the insertion of new gates in the combinational logic [6,21,22]. We refer to these gates as "key gates". As discussed earlier, these new gates effectively "lock" the design. Once these gates are inserted, the design is resynthesized and technology-mapped (that is, mapped to the standard cell library for the target technology node). This step optimizes the design in the presence of key gates, and propagates the structural transformation into the design beyond the key gates. In order to make the obfuscated design functional, the exact key must be applied to the obfuscated IP. Wrong key input into those gates would produce wrong output. Hence, an authorized user of the IP must obtain the key for properly using the obfuscated design.

Choice of the locations where key gates are inserted depend on the obfuscation objectives. Many heuristics for key-gate insertion have been studied. In its simplest form, key gates are inserted in random locations into the design [6]. This possibility facilitates the advantage of randomly distributing the key gates and the resultant structural changes across the design. Other heuristics include cone-based key-gate insertion, which tries to account for fan-in and/or fan-out cone of an internal node. A node that has large number of inputs in its logic cone has the advantage of making brute-force, or fault-analysis-based attacks more difficult, as described later in this chapter. On the other hand, a node that has large output cone is likely to cause more output corruptions for a wrong key, than the ones with smaller output cone.

Let us illustrate the logic locking method using an example. Figure 14.4A shows an original design in form of a gate-level netlist, which is obfuscated using three key-gates in Fig. 14.4B. The functional inputs of the original design are *A, B, C,* and *D*. Input lines *K1, K2,* and *K3* are key-inputs, which are connected to key-gates (XOR and XNOR gates). Upon the application of the correct key value ($K1 = 0$, $K2 = 1$, $K3 = 0$), the design will produce correct outputs. If not, it will produce wrong outputs.

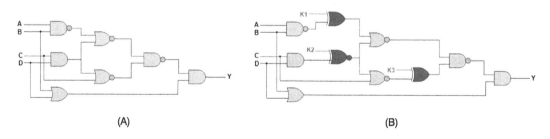

(A) | (B)

FIGURE 14.4

(A) Original circuit; (B) Obfuscated circuit with three key gates (red ones; dark gray in print version).

14.3.1.1 Security Properties and Metrics

A good obfuscation method needs to provide acceptable protection against IP piracy and reverse engineering. It, however, comes at additional design and test/verification cost. Most obfuscation methods incur considerable design overhead in terms of area, power or delay. It is important to enable a designer to perform quantitative analysis of an obfuscation method, so that security vs. design/test cost can be traded-off at the design stage. Next, we present relevant properties of obfuscation and the metrics that provide quantitative measures of security.

(i) **Correctness:** The logic locking techniques should maintain the original and correct functionality, that is, upon the application of the correct key, the design should produce the correct output(s). This property is inherited from conventional encryption techniques.

(ii) **Entropy and Hamming distance:** The technique should be resilient against attacks that guess the correct outputs by observing previous input-output combinations. To hinder these attacks, the entropy of the output response of a design, due to the application of wrong keys, should be increased. In other words, the Hamming distance between the output responses of the design under correct and wrong key should be ideally 50%. This Hamming distance represents the entropy of the output response under a faulty key input [21].

(iii) **Entanglement:** The key-gates of the obfuscated design should be irremovable. Since an attacker (for example, one in an untrusted foundry) is expected to have access to the internal nodes of an obfuscated design, he/she can simply remove the key-gates, and then retrieve the original design.

(iv) **Output corruptibility:** It is desirable to have higher output corruptibility to prevent both black-box usage, and to hide the design intent. First, it is important to ensure wrong outputs for large population of incorrect keys. Second, for each wrong key, it is important to increase the number of outputs that fail to produce correct function. Poor output corruptibility creates vulnerability against "bypass attacks". For example, an obfuscated netlist, which creates wrong output for only one key pattern, can be easily fixed to produce original functionality by checking for the specific pattern, and forcing correct values (that is, "bypassing" the obfuscated logic) at the output for that pattern [23]. An obfuscated design with such "bypassing" can then be used as a black-box. Furthermore, a design with poor corruptibility can be more vulnerable to key sensitizing attack (KSA), or other attacks.

(v) **Resistance against key-guessing attacks:** An attacker could try to guess the correct key value from previously observed input-output pairs. To render the obfuscated design resistant to such key-guessing attacks, key-gates should be placed in such a way that the number of input-output pairs required to obtain the correct key value is increased exponentially with key size.

(vi) **Design overhead:** The logic locking techniques should aim to minimize the area, power, and delay overheads. The security properties listed above should be traded-off with the overheads to meet specific targets for an application.

14.3.1.2 Possible Attacks on Logic Locking

Multiple attacks have been reported against existing logic locking techniques. In these attacks, the main target of an attacker has been discovering the locking key. Note that a "brute-force attack" on obfuscation would be to try all possible key combinations, and observe the output values. The main aim of the attacker in this case becoming aware that the observed outputs match golden functional outputs is determined to be the correct key. In the worst case, an attacker needs to try 2^N possible key values for a key of size N bits. Similar to conventional encryption techniques, difficulty of discovering the key here is an exponential function of the key size. Hence, for a reasonably large key size, for example, 128-bit or larger, discovering the key using brute-force attack becomes computationally infeasible. Note that a wrong key can produce correct functional behavior for some patterns at the original inputs of a circuit. Hence, in order to guarantee that the correct key is found, it is important to verify correct functional behavior for all possible input combinations.

Key sensitizing attacks (KSA) [24]: The value of a key-bit can be obtained by using automatic test pattern generation (ATPG) tool, which comes from different CAD tool vendors (such as Synopsys, Cadence, Mentor), and are widely used by test engineers to generate efficient test patterns for a design. This attack assumes the availability of an unlocked chip or golden functional behavior of an IP. An attacker sensitizes a key-bit without masking or corruption by the other key-bits and/or outputs. By observing the output, it is possible to determine the value of the sensitized key-bits, provided that other key-bits have no interference in the sensitized path. Once an attacker determines an input pattern, which can sensitize a key-bit to an output without interference, he/she can then apply it to the functional IC. At this point, this pattern will be used to sensitize the correct value of the key-bit to an output. By observing the output, an attacker can resolve the key value.

Boolean satisfiability (SAT) attacks [24,25]: The SAT attack is a powerful attack for discovering the correct key from an obfuscated design by modeling it as a Boolean satisfiability problem, and using heuristic based algorithms to solve it. Similar to KSA, it also assumes the availability of the unlocked chip or golden functional outputs. SAT attack minimizes the key search space, and thus—compared to a brute-force attack on finding the key—it significantly reduces the effort required to find the correct key value. SAT attack rules out incorrect key values by using distinguishing input patterns (DIPs). An input value, for which at least two different key values produce different outputs, is called a DIP. In some cases, a single DIP can rule out more than one incorrect key value. The SAT attack randomly chooses the DIPs (or aligns with those dictated by the underlying SAT engine). With large number of incorrect keys being ruled out by a single DIP, very few patterns are needed to find out the correct key.

Let us consider the example circuit in Fig. 14.4B, which is an obfuscated version of the circuit in Fig. 14.4A. We will now discuss the SAT attack on this circuit. For this attack, an attacker needs the obfuscated netlist and a functional IC (or golden functional outputs). The obfuscated netlist can be obtained from different sources (for example, from an untrusted DFT-insertion facility or foundry), and a functional IC can be obtained from open market. During this attack, the first step is to find the input-output pairs from the functional IC. Then, a SAT solver tool randomly chooses the DIPs and attempt to rule out the wrong key values. Figure 14.5 shows the iterative process for ruling out invalid keys.

Figure 14.5 shows the functional outputs for different input patterns. It also shows the outputs for different combinations of input and key values for the circuit in Fig. 14.4. In Fig. 14.5, the eight possible key values for the three bit-keys are denoted as $key0, key1, ...key7$, where $key = \{K1,K2,K3\}$ and $key0 = \{0, 0, 0\}, key1 = \{0, 0, 1\}, ... key7 = \{1, 1, 1\}$, and so on. The outputs for different key values are marked in green (light gray in print version) and red (dark gray in print version) colors. Red and green denote wrong and correct outputs, respectively. In the first iteration, we assume that the DIP is chosen to be 1111. In this iteration, the SAT solver finds $key1$ as a wrong key combination, since the output for this key combination does not match with the functionally correct output. Hence, it removes $key1$ from the list of valid key values. In second iteration, 0011 is chosen as the DIP, and $key5$ is ruled out in the same way as in iteration 1. The SAT solver tool goes through multiple iterations to gradually rule out wrong key values. In this example, after 5 iterations, 5 key values ($key1, key3, key5, key6, key7$) are ruled out, and only 3 key combinations are left from which an attacker can easily find the

Inputs				Output	Output for Different Key Values								Ruled out key(s) in
A	B	C	D	Y	key0(000)	key1(001)	key2(010)	key3(011)	key4(100)	key5(101)	key6(110)	key7(111)	each iteration (i)
0	0	0	0	0	0	0	0	0	0	0	0	0	
0	0	0	1	1	1	1	1	1	1	1	1	1	
0	0	1	0	0	0	0	0	0	0	0	0	0	
0	0	1	1	1	1	1	1	1	1	0	1	1	i=2 >> key5
0	1	0	0	1	1	1	1	1	1	1	0	1	
0	1	0	1	1	1	1	1	1	1	1	0	1	
0	1	1	0	1	1	1	1	1	1	1	1	0	i=3 >> key7
0	1	1	1	1	1	1	1	1	1	0	1	1	
1	0	0	0	0	0	0	0	0	0	0	0	0	
1	0	0	1	1	1	1	1	1	1	1	0	1	i=5 >> key6
1	0	1	0	0	0	0	0	0	0	0	0	0	
1	0	1	1	1	1	1	1	1	1	1	1	1	
1	1	0	0	0	1	1	0	1	1	1	1	1	
1	1	0	1	0	1	1	0	1	1	1	1	1	
1	1	1	0	1	1	1	1	0	1	1	1	1	i=4 >> key3
1	1	1	1	1	1	0	1	1	1	1	1	1	i=1 >> key1

FIGURE 14.5

Elimination of invalid key values under SAT attack to reduce the key search space.

correct key by trying them in the obfuscated netlist. However, if the SAT solver considers 1100 or 1101 as the DIP, all the incorrect key values will be ruled out in just one iteration.

In a practical scenario, SAT solver does not consider each of the key bits. It chooses a part of the key-bits; for instance, in the above example, 2 key-bits will be set to a known value, considering other ones as "don't care". At this point, if the SAT solver finds a DIP, it will just rule out those values of key-bits to be incorrect, and in this way, the correct key search space can be significantly minimized.

Countermeasures to attacks: In order to make the design resistant to key-guessing attacks, key-gates should be inserted in such a way that an attacker cannot propagate the output of a single key-gate [26], that is, the observed output should be a function of multiple key-gates. Key-gates can be inserted judiciously, so that they block each other's sensitization path. This method forms a "clique". With the increase in the size of the clique, the attacker's effort will increase as well.

To achieve resistance against SAT attacks, some cryptographic primitives or SAT-resistant logic circuits, called anti-SAT blocks, can be incorporated into the design. The idea is to prevent a SAT solver from efficiently minimizing the key space, that is, forcing it to go through exponentially large number of iterations. Anti-SAT block is a small circuit, which takes inputs from internal nodes of the original circuit along with some key inputs, and it exponentially increases the key search space. It corresponds to a high level of difficulty for a SAT solver to find the correct key values.

14.3.2 GATE CAMOUFLAGING-BASED OBFUSCATION

Gate camouflaging is an obfuscation technique, which is shown to provide effective countermeasure for RE attacks [15,27–29]. In this technique, a designer incorporates configurable camouflaged gates in selected locations of a design. This is similar in concept to logic locking, except configurable gates are inserted instead of key gates. The camouflaged CMOS logic cells can be configured to perform a variety of logic functions for the same layout. Figure 14.6A shows an example of a cell, where 19 contacts are used in the configurable CMOS cell [15]. If contacts 2, 4, 6, 8, 11, 12, 16, 17 are true, and the rest are dummy, the camouflaged cell operates as a NAND gate. Figure 14.6B shows an obfuscated circuit, where two logic gates have been replaced by configurable CMOS cells $C1$ and $C2$. Although an

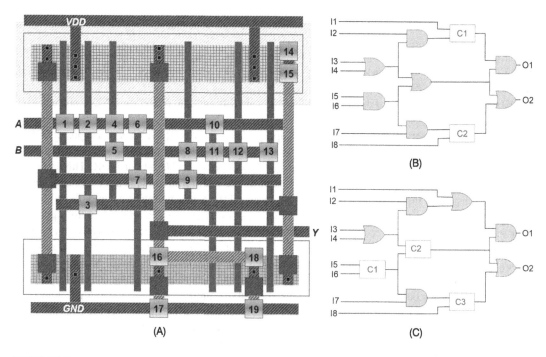

FIGURE 14.6

(A) A configurable CMOS cell with 19 contacts having the functionalities of a NAND, NOR, or XOR gate, where the configuration is made by programming the true and dummy contacts; (B) A circuit with two camouflaged gates $C1$ and $C2$; (C) Improved cell distribution to prevent a VLSI testing-based attack.

attacker may be able to successfully reverse engineer the layout of the circuit, it is difficult to determine the true functionality of the camouflaged logic gate. This, in turn, hides the functionality of the design, and makes the design resistant to both black-box usage and structural reverse engineering.

A possible approach to design configurable CMOS cells is to use true and dummy contacts [27, 28]. A true contact joins the dielectric between two nearby layers, which corresponds to an electrical connection. However, a dummy contact has a gap in between these connections (usually filled by an insulator such as SiO_2), and thus creates a fake connection. When an attacker tries to perform top-down image processing-based RE attack, he/she will not be able to detect whether a contact is true or dummy, since these are not identifiable through existing imaging technologies.

14.3.2.1 Attacks and Countermeasures

To know the exact functionality of the design shown in Fig. 14.6B, an attacker will have to evaluate $3^2 = 9$ possible combinations, since the cells $C1$ and $C2$ can be either XOR, NAND, or NOR gates. Furthermore, in the absence of scan-chain access, the attacker can only apply vectors to the circuit's primary inputs (PIs), and observe the corresponding output, to verify whether any guess is correct or wrong. This makes the attacker's job extremely challenging, as the logical effect of the camouflaged gate might not be directly observable at the primary output. In the example discussed above, we can observe the following:

(i) the output of a camouflaged gate, in response to the input "00", can differentiate XOR from NAND and NOR. This is because input "00" for XOR produces an output of 0, whereas both NAND and NOR produce a 1 output;

(ii) the output in response to the input "01" or "10" can differentiate NAND and NOR, since NAND outputs 1, whereas NOR outputs 0.

Based on these observations, the attacker can apply a test vector "001XXXXX" (X represents don't care values) at the PIs. This justifies the camouflaged gate $C1$'s inputs as "00", and sensitizes $C1$'s output to primary output (PO) $O1$. When $O1$ is 1, $C1$ will either be NAND or NOR. This is known as a VLSI-testing-based attack. In such an attack, finding the entire truth table is not necessary, since a number of sensitizing input-output pairs is enough to reveal the functionality of a camouflaged cell.

To thwart VLSI testing-based attack, selective gate camouflaging can be applied. In this approach, logic gates that interfere with each other are camouflaged, so that they cannot be sensitized, and their output cannot be directly observed [15]. When one gate lies on the path between the other gate and an output, or the outputs of two gates merge into the same gate, interference will occur in between these two gates. Consider the example shown in Fig. 14.6C, where none of the camouflaged gates can be resolved. $C1$'s output cannot be observed from any of the POs without resolving $C2$ and $C3$. Then, $C3$'s inputs are not controllable unless $C1$ is resolved first. Furthermore, both the controllability of inputs and the observability of output of $C2$ depend on the functionality of $C1$. This will force the attacker to employ brute-force, that is, searching all possible functional combinations of these camouflaged gates [15]. For each possible combination, the attacker will have to simulate the design and compare the outputs with those of a correctly operational circuit.

Although enhanced IC camouflaging, based on gate interference, prevents VLSI-test based attacks, it does not ensure security against other possible attacks. For example, a SAT-based formulation may be used by an attacker to determine the true functionality of the camouflaged gates. In this attack, the SAT solver returns camouflaged gate assignments, which complies with the input-output patterns obtained from a functional IC.

14.3.3 FINITE-STATE-MACHINE-BASED (FSM-BASED) HARDWARE OBFUSCATION

Logic locking approaches described earlier target obfuscation of combinational circuits. They do not directly modify the state machine of a sequential design. Whereas logic locking can indirectly impact the next state transition logic of a state machine, state space obfuscation techniques aim at directly modifying both the state machine and the associated combinational logic.

In digital sequential circuits, FSM is an abstract machine which is commonly used to implement the control logic. FSMs have finite number of states, and they transition from one state to another. The transitions between states are triggered by the input(s) to the FSM, and the current state. Often, the states of an FSM is used to drive output control signals. A simple example of an FSM is shown in Fig. 14.7, which shows its state transition diagram and the state table.

14.3.3.1 State Space Obfuscation

To enable state space obfuscation, a designer can modify the state-transition function of an FSM and internal circuit structure in such a way that the circuit operates in normal mode, only upon application of

State Table

Current State	Input	Next State
S0	00	S1
S0	01	S2
S0	10	S3
S0	11	S0
S1	00	S2
S1	01	S2
S1	10	S1
S1	11	S1
S2	00	S1
S2	01	S3
S2	10	S0
S2	11	S2
S3	00	S1
S3	01	S0
S3	10	S3
S3	11	S3

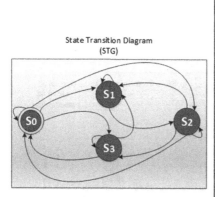

State Transition Diagram (STG)

FIGURE 14.7

An example of FSM and its state-transition table showing all valid transitions.

a predefined enabling sequence of patterns at primary inputs, that is, the "key" [8]. The state-transition function of a sequential circuit could be modified by inserting an additional FSM called obfiscation FSM (OFSM). The inserted FSM could have all, or a subset of the primary inputs of the circuit as its inputs (including the clock and reset signals), and could have multiple outputs. At the start of operations, the OFSM would reset to its initial state, forcing the circuit to be in the obfuscated mode. Depending on the applied input sequence, the OFSM would go through a state-transition sequence, and only on receiving N specific input patterns in sequence would go to a state, which enables the circuit to operate in its normal mode. The initial state, and the states reached by the OFSM before a successful initialization, constitute the "pre-initialization state space" of the FSM. The states reached after the circuit enters its normal mode of operation constitute the "post-initialization state space". Figure 14.8 shows the state diagram of such an FSM, with $P0 \Rightarrow P1 \Rightarrow P2$ being the correct initialization sequence. The input sequence $P0$ through $P2$ would be decided by the IP designer during obfuscation.

The OFSM could be used to control the mode of circuit operation. It could also modify the selected nodes in the design, using its outputs and a modification cell, for example, $M1$ through $M3$ in Fig. 14.8. The modified nodes are selected, such that they can greatly affect the behavior of the modified system if the correct key is not applied. Hence, if a user is unable to apply the correct input sequence (or key) to the FSM, the design will not reach the normal mode, and will traverse through invalid states in the obfuscated mode, producing incorrect functionality.

14.3.3.1.1 Efficiency Metric for State-Space Obfuscation

To quantify the quality of obfuscation, two different metrics can be used. First, the functional difference can be represented using the number of failing vectors for a large number of input patterns. The structural obfuscation efficiency can be represented by the structural difference between the original, and obfuscated design. One approach to measure structural difference is to derive % of failing verifi-

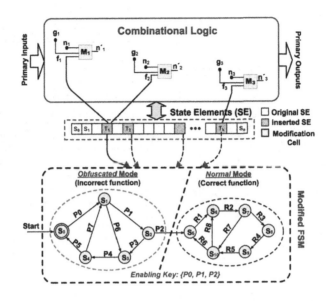

FIGURE 14.8

Functional and structural obfuscation of a state machine by modification of its state-transition function and internal node structures of the combinational part.

cation points when the original and obfuscated netlists are provided to a formal verification tool. The verification tool compares the two design based on a set of verification points, for example, flip-flop (FF) input or primary outputs. The obfuscation efficiency metric provides a way to assess the quality of state space obfuscation at design time, and allows the designer to maximize security under certain area, power, and delay constraints.

14.3.3.1.2 Comparison With Other Obfuscation Methods

While choosing the appropriate obfuscation method for a given IP, several factors need to be considered. The IP class (combinational/sequential), its representation within the design flow (RTL/gate-level), acceptable overhead, and required security benefits are some of the relevant parameters to consider. Figure 14.9 illustrates these features for three major classes of obfuscation. State-space obfuscation can be applied to almost all representations of digital IPs. Furthermore, they increase the reachable state space exponentially by adding few extra FFs, and hence provide an exponential increase in entropy. The area, power, and performance overhead of state-space obfuscation methods have also been shown to be very modest. Attacks on logic locking, for example, SAT attacks, which target key-recovery, are demonstrated on combinational circuits. Their effectiveness for a sequential design is not well-studied. To make SAT attack or KSA successful for sequential design, one needs to either: (1) unroll the sequential design into a combinational one, which involves exponential complexity in terms of number of possible states; or (2) obtain internal outputs of the combinational logic, which are input to the FFs. The later can be obtained by observing the values dumped to a scan-chain in response to an input pattern. However, that is often difficult to obtain due to the fact that many FFs may not

	State-Space Obfuscation	Logic Locking	Camouflaging
Approach	Transforms & locks the state transition function using a key	Adds dummy cells controlled by input key in select locations	Adds programmable cells (that require fuses) to layout
Abstraction Level	RTL, gate-level netlist, & layout	Gate-level netlist, layout	Layout
Manufacturing Type	Conventional and split manufacturing	Conventional & split manufacturing	Primarily targeted to split manufacturing
Overhead	Low (5-10% of area and power, no performance overhead); No new port needed	Moderate to high; adds new input ports for the key	Moderate to high; needs programming logic
Entropy Increase	Exponential	Linear	Linear
Applicability	FPGA & ASIC	FPGA & ASIC	ASIC
Security	❑ Exponential increase in RE difficulty ❑ Strong protection against black-box IP usage ❑ Strong protection against Trojan attack	❑ Known vulnerabilities (against SAT & ATPG attacks) ❑ Questionable protection against Trojan attacks	❑ Known vulnerabilities ❑ Questionable protection against Trojan attacks

FIGURE 14.9

Comparative analysis of sequential and combinational obfuscation.

be part of scan-chain, or the scan access can be prevented by a chip manufacturer after production testing.

On the other hand, logic locking has been shown to be vulnerable against several functional and structural analysis attacks. An effective obfuscation method is the one, which: (1) prevents deriving the key based on functional analysis (for instance, through SAT-based modeling), and (2) prevents structural signatures that make it vulnerable to remove the key gates or other structural changes incorporated to lock the design.

14.4 EMERGING OBFUSCATION APPROACHES

14.4.1 FPGA BITSTREAM OBFUSCATION

The FPGA configuration file, also called bitstream, is a valuable IP, which is susceptible to variety of attacks during system design and deployment. Attacks on bitstream include unauthorized reprogramming, reverse engineering, and piracy. Modern high-end FPGA devices support encrypted bitstreams, where vendor-specific FPGA synthesis tools produce an encrypted bitstream, which is decrypted inside an FPGA device before mapping the design. These FPGAs include on-chip decryption hardware. Encryption of bitstream provides some measure of security against major attacks, including piracy. However, it comes at the cost of on-chip decryption hardware, which requires additional hardware resources and adds to the configuration latency and energy. This is why low-end FPGA devices typically do not support encrypted bitstreams.

Security of the encrypted bitstream relies on the security of the encryption key. In the current business model, when FPGAs are used in a specific product (for example, a network router), all instances of the product uses the same encryption key. An original equipment manufacturer (OEM) often outsources

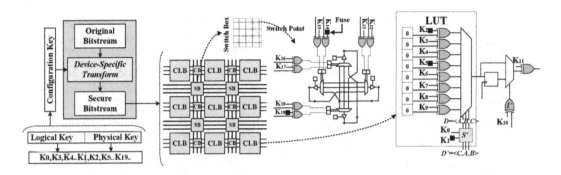

FIGURE 14.10

Overview of the bitstream obfuscation method using diversified FPGA architecture. From left to right: a two part (logical and physical) key is used to perform a device-specific obfuscation of the bitstream that is generated for a particular architecture. The obfuscated bitstream is mapped to appropriate FPGA device. Internal FPGA hardware resources are augmented with logic, which implements the inverse transform to make the bitstream functional. This ensures that bitstreams mapped to unauthorized devices will be nonfunctional. Because the logical key is time-varying, the architecture is changeable over time, and thus prevents known design attacks.

the FPGA programming step to third-party vendors, which need to have access to the encryption key. Besides, for remote upgrade, bitstreams are generally transmitted along with the decryption key. Both practices create significant vulnerability for key leakage, and hence compromises the security of an encrypted bitstream. Mathematically, encryption algorithms are known to be highly secure against brute-force attacks. However, in many cases, attackers can have physical access, and most encryption hardware are susceptible to side-channel attacks, for example, by key extraction through power profile signatures [30].

An adversary can convert an unencrypted bitstream to a netlist [31], thereby enabling IP piracy and malicious modifications, including Trojan insertion. The conversion step may not be necessary for Trojan insertion. Techniques such as unused resource utilization [32], which inserts Trojans in empty spaces in the configuration file, and mapping rule extraction [33], a type of known design attack, can be mounted on a bitstream for malicious modification. Moreover, if the hardware itself is cloned [34], a pirated bitstream could be used in a counterfeit hardware.

FPGA bitstream obfuscation provides a promising solution for bitstream protection against the aforementioned attacks. FPGA architecture could be modified using programmable elements, such that each device would become architecturally different from each other [35]. This changes the association between the FPGA device and bitstream, which is based on a configuration key. In this technique, each bitstream has its unique configuration key, resulting in unique bitstream for each device. A specific bitstream works for each physical FPGA device.

It provides protection against in-field bitstream reprogramming and IP piracy. This could be considered as a security-through-diversity approach to FPGA bitstream security. Furthermore, both physical (static) and logical (time–varying) configuration keys could be incorporated to ensure that attackers cannot use a priori knowledge about one device to mount an attack on another. Examples of architectural changes that allow the application of such configuration key is shown in Fig. 14.10, where the configuration storage (that is, SRAM cells) in the internal FPGA resources (look-up tables, switch boxes) are connected with XOR gates. Hence, even if the bitstream is stored onto these resources in obfuscated form, during operation when the correct configuration key is applied to the XOR gates, desired functionality is achieved.

The device-specific bitstream transformation can be done in the back-end of a vendor's tool flow, for example, after place & route, but before bitstream generation. Based on the configuration key of a particular device, the bitstream would be obfuscated, which would be node-locked onto a particular FPGA device. In addition to the node-locking of the configuration, bitstream obfuscation prevents an attacker from using the same bitstream in other devices, it also increases the difficulty of making an intelligent modification of the bitstream to compromise the system.

The bitstream obfuscation mechanism could also be incorporated in legacy FPGAs without any architectural modification [36]. FPGA dark silicon, that is, unused look-up-table resources (LUT resources), already available in these FPGAs could be used to enable obfuscation of the LUT contents. It helps to drastically reduce the overhead of the obfuscation method. The typical island-style FPGA architecture consists of an array of multi-input, single-output LUTs. Generally, LUTs of size n can be configured to implement any function of n variables, and require 2^n bits of storage for function responses. The nature of FPGA architecture requires that sufficient resources be available to accommodate for the worst-case mapping requirements. For example, some newer FPGAs may support 7 input functions, requiring 128 bits of storage for the LUT content. However, typical designs are more likely to use 5 or fewer inputs, while less frequently utilizing all 7. One can exploit the underutilized or unused LUT resources for the purpose of obfuscation. For example, an unused input of an LUT can be converted into a key input, where a specific value of the key input (0 or 1) would select the original function, whereas the other produces wrong output. For instance, consider a 3-input LUT, which contains 8 content bits, used to implement a 2-input function, $Z = f(X, Y)$. A third input K can be added, in such a way that the function becomes $Z' = f(K, Z)$, where $Z' = Z$, if the correct value of K is applied. Since designs with moderate complexity occupy thousands of LUTs, a large key would be used to obfuscate the whole IP. Thus, an attacker without the key would be unable to use the IP, or modify it intelligently. In this approach, the obfuscated design could be node-locked if a device-specific physical unclonable function generated key is used for obfuscation, making the bitstream functional only when mapped onto a specific FPGA device.

14.5 USE OF OBFUSCATION AGAINST TROJAN ATTACKS

Hardware obfuscation could be leveraged to protect against Trojan attacks. With respect to Trojan attacks, obfuscation can help in two ways: (1) it facilitates Trojan detection through functional, or side-channel, analysis by hiding the design intent, in particular, by hiding the rare events or attractive payloads from an intelligent adversary; and (2) by making the Trojan insertion difficult and possibly invalid in an obfuscated design.

Researchers have studied the role of state space obfuscation as a countermeasure against Trojan attacks [37]. The obfuscation scheme is based on modifying the state transition function of a given circuit by expanding its reachable state space, and enabling it to operate in two distinct modes: the normal mode and the obfuscated mode. Such a modification obfuscates the rareness of the internal circuit nodes, thus making it difficult for an adversary to insert hard-to-detect Trojans. It also decreases the

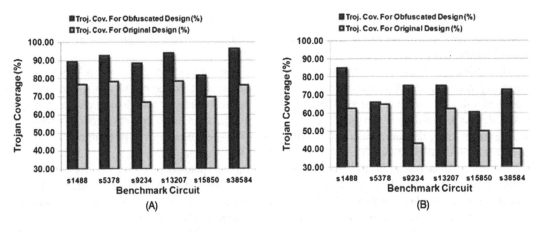

FIGURE 14.11

Improvement of Trojan coverage in several obfuscated ISCAS89 designs (using state space obfuscation) compared to the original design for (A) Trojans with two trigger nodes, and (B) Trojans with four trigger nodes.

potency of some inserted Trojans by making them activate only in the obfuscated mode. The combined effect leads to higher Trojan detectability and higher level of protection against such attack.

To find the rare trigger conditions, an adversary would require accurate estimations of internal node signal probability. One approach to accomplish that is through multiple random initialization of a given circuit to a reachable state, and then applying random input vectors. However, if the starting state in the adversary's simulations is in the obfuscated mode, because of the extreme rareness of the condition that allows the transition from obfuscated to normal mode, the simulations would most likely remain confined in the obfuscated mode. As a result, the signal probability for the circuit nodes calculated by the adversary would deviate significantly from those calculated if the simulations would have taken place with the states in the normal mode. Similar situation would prevent the adversary from finding the poorly observable nodes as potential payloads of a Trojan. Hence, if the adversary designs and inserts a Trojan based on wrong controllability/observability, there is a high probability that the Trojan would be triggered and detected with post-manufacturing logic testing. To increase this probability, the size of the obfuscation state space should be made as large as possible compared to the normal state space, by the addition of n extra state elements. State space obfuscation can provide a large improvement in Trojan coverage for random patterns, as shown in Fig. 14.11.

14.6 HANDS-ON EXPERIMENT: HARDWARE IP OBFUSCATION
14.6.1 OBJECTIVE

This experiment is designed to help the students explore the concepts of hardware obfuscation for IP protection. Using the HaHa platform, the students will learn how to apply various hardware obfuscation techniques to protect a design from unintended usage, for example, piracy and reverse engineering.

The experiment will also give the students the ability to perform attacks on an obfuscated design, with the goal of retrieving the functional behavior, or the structure of the original design.

14.6.2 METHOD

The first part of the experiment illustrates combinational obfuscation of a design, and the second part will focus on the sequential obfuscation. Students have to initially map an example design into the FPGA inside the HaHa platform. Next, they will apply a key-based logic locking mechanism, where the locked design will keep producing invalid outputs until the inserted key value is correct.

14.6.3 LEARNING OUTCOME

By performing the specific steps of the experiments, the students will learn how to apply a hardware obfuscation technique to any given design. They will also gain experience about the challenges with respect to balancing the security and design overheads (for example, area, power, or performance).

14.6.4 ADVANCED OPTIONS

Additional exploration on this topic can be done by applying more sophisticated attacks (such as SAT-based attack) to break the obfuscation and obtain the key, and improving the robustness of the obfuscation process.

More details about the experiment are available in the supplementary document. Please visit: http://hwsecuritybook.org.

14.7 EXERCISES
14.7.1 TRUE/FALSE QUESTIONS

1. Reverse engineering of hardware IP is considered illegal.
2. None of the software obfuscation approaches are applicable to hardware IPs.
3. The design house is untrusted in certain scenarios in an IC supply chain.
4. For maximum output entropy in logic locking, Hamming Distance should be 100%.
5. SAT attack directly finds the key used for obfuscation.
6. The features of design integrated with gate camouflaging can never be reverse engineered.
7. The entire truth table is not needed to attack a design obfuscated by camouflaging.
8. In state space obfuscation, modification cells are added to hide the newly inserted FSM.
9. An attacker cannot reverse engineer the FPGA netlist from the obfuscated bitstream.
10. FPGA-mapped designs are efficiently mapped, keeping almost no unused space in look-up-table memory cells.

14.7.2 SHORT-ANSWER TYPE QUESTIONS

1. In a semiconductor supply chain, what are the security and trust issues in an untrusted design house from the IP vendor's point of view?

2. List all possible security and trust issues in an IC supply chain when the design house sends the design for fabrication to an untrusted facility.
3. Why is encryption not a good enough solution for protecting hardware IP? What are the limitations of such an approach?
4. Briefly discuss SAT attack on logic locking. Also, describe the effect of a distinguishing input pattern (DIP) generated during the SAT attack.
5. What are the programmable resources within the FPGA architecture that could be modified to enable bitstream obfuscation?
6. During state space obfuscation, what would be the minimum clock cycle for applying a 256-bit key for an obfuscated IC with 18 primary inputs? Assume only 16 of the primary inputs can be used for applying the obfuscation key.
7. What is a possible way for the attacker to identify the inserted FSM that applies the obfuscation key in FSM-based obfuscation?
8. Discuss the differences between combinational and sequential obfuscation.

14.7.3 LONG-ANSWER TYPE QUESTIONS

1. Determine the correct key for the logic encrypted circuit below in Fig. 14.12 (in other words, what key makes x = x' and y = y'). Explain your answer.

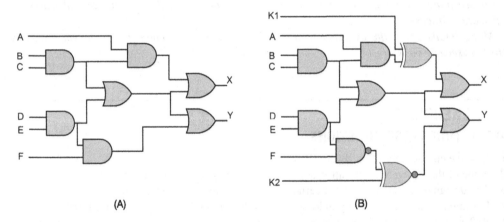

(A)   (B)

FIGURE 14.12

(A) Original design, (B) Obfuscated design.

2. Describe the vulnerabilities in each step of the supply chain of an IC.
3. Briefly describe the possible obfuscation-based solutions for countering hardware IP piracy at each step of the supply chain.
4. For state space obfuscation, describe possible attacks on an obfuscated design to reverse engineer it, considering both functional and structural attacks. Is it SAT attack resistant? Provide reasoning behind your answer.
5. Discuss how a certain hardware obfuscation method could make Trojan insertion difficult. Elaborate with respect to any of the well-known obfuscation methods.

6. Discuss different methods for RTL obfuscation.

7. Describe the two methods of node-locking FPGA bitstream, and compare their main differences.

8. Suppose a 2-input XOR function mapped to a 3-input LUT (Fig. 14.13A) is obfuscated with an additional key K (Fig. 14.13B). What could be the value of the bitstream that renders the XOR function for the correct key, K = 0? If a wrong key is applied, the function is inverted. Write the 8 bits in the following sequence: $Bit_{111} \text{ - - - - - - - } Bit_{000}$

Hint: Look at the obfuscation method described in [36].

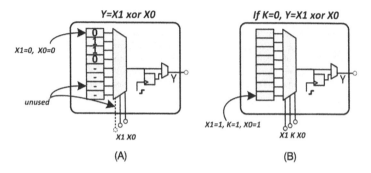

FIGURE 14.13

(A) Lookup table with 2-input function, (B) Obfuscated look-up table expanded to 3-input function.

REFERENCES

[1] C. Collberg, C. Thomborson, D. Low, A taxonomy of obfuscating transformations, Technical Report, Department of Computer Science, The University of Auckland, New Zealand, 1997.

[2] R.S. Chakraborty, S. Bhunia, RTL hardware IP protection using key-based control and data flow obfuscation, in: VLSI Design, 2010. VLSID'10. 23rd International Conference on, IEEE, pp. 405–410.

[3] A.R. Desai, M.S. Hsiao, C. Wang, L. Nazhandali, S. Hall, Interlocking obfuscation for anti-tamper hardware, in: Proceedings of the Eighth Annual Cyber Security and Information Intelligence Research Workshop, ACM, p. 8.

[4] M. Brzozowski, V.N. Yarmolik, Obfuscation as intellectual rights protection in VHDL language, in: Computer Information Systems and Industrial Management Applications, 2007. CISIM'07. 6th International Conference on, IEEE, pp. 337–340.

[5] J.A. Roy, F. Koushanfar, I.L. Markov, Ending piracy of integrated circuits, Computer 43 (2010) 30–38.

[6] J. Rajendran, Y. Pino, O. Sinanoglu, R. Karri, Logic encryption: a fault analysis perspective, in: Proceedings of the Conference on Design, Automation and Test in Europe, EDA Consortium, pp. 953–958.

[7] N.A. Touba, E.J. McCluskey, Test point insertion based on path tracing, in: VLSI Test Symposium, 1996.

[8] R.S. Chakraborty, S. Bhunia, HARPOON: an obfuscation-based SoC design methodology for hardware protection, IEEE Transactions on Computer-Aided Design of Integrated Circuits and Systems 28 (2009) 1493–1502.

[9] B. Yang, K. Wu, R. Karri, Scan based side channel attack on dedicated hardware implementations of data encryption standard, in: Test Conference, 2004. Proceedings. ITC 2004. International, IEEE, pp. 339–344.

[10] K. Vaidyanathan, R. Liu, E. Sumbul, Q. Zhu, F. Franchetti, L. Pileggi, Efficient and secure intellectual property (IP) design with split fabrication, in: Hardware-Oriented Security and Trust (HOST), 2014 IEEE International Symposium on, IEEE, pp. 13–18.

[11] F. Imeson, A. Emtenan, S. Garg, M.V. Tripunitara, Securing computer hardware using 3D integrated circuit (IC) technology and split manufacturing for obfuscation, in: USENIX Security Symposium, pp. 495–510.

[12] U. Rührmair, S. Devadas, F. Koushanfar, Security based on physical unclonability and disorder, in: Introduction to Hardware Security and Trust, Springer, 2012, pp. 65–102.

[13] K. Vaidyanathan, B.P. Das, E. Sumbul, R. Liu, L. Pileggi, Building trusted ICs using split fabrication, in: Hardware-Oriented Security and Trust (HOST), 2014 IEEE International Symposium on, IEEE, pp. 1–6.

[14] J.J. Rajendran, O. Sinanoglu, R. Karri, Is split manufacturing secure?, in: Proceedings of the Conference on Design, Automation and Test in Europe, EDA Consortium, pp. 1259–1264.

[15] J. Rajendran, M. Sam, O. Sinanoglu, R. Karri, Security analysis of integrated circuit camouflaging, in: Proceedings of the 2013 ACM SIGSAC Conference on Computer & Communications Security, ACM, pp. 709–720.

[16] Y. Xie, C. Bao, A. Srivastava, Security-aware design flow for 2.5D IC technology, in: Proceedings of the 5th International Workshop on Trustworthy Embedded Devices, ACM, pp. 31–38.

[17] E.G. Barrantes, D.H. Ackley, T.S. Palmer, D. Stefanovic, D.D. Zovi, Randomized instruction set emulation to disrupt binary code injection attacks, in: Proceedings of the 10th ACM Conference on Computer and Communications Security, ACM, pp. 281–289.

[18] G.S. Kc, A.D. Keromytis, V. Prevelakis, Countering code-injection attacks with instruction-set randomization, in: Proceedings of the 10th ACM Conference on Computer and Communications Security, ACM, pp. 272–280.

[19] C. Linn, S. Debray, Obfuscation of executable code to improve resistance to static disassembly, in: Proceedings of the 10th ACM Conference on Computer and Communications Security, ACM, pp. 290–299.

[20] Z. Guo, M. Tehranipoor, D. Forte, J. Di, Investigation of obfuscation-based anti-reverse engineering for printed circuit boards, in: Proceedings of the 52nd Annual Design Automation Conference, ACM, p. 114.

[21] J. Rajendran, H. Zhang, C. Zhang, G.S. Rose, Y. Pino, O. Sinanoglu, R. Karri, Fault analysis-based logic encryption, IEEE Transactions on Computers 64 (2015) 410–424.

[22] S. Dupuis, P.-S. Ba, G. Di Natale, M.-L. Flottes, B. Rouzeyre, A novel hardware logic encryption technique for thwarting illegal overproduction and hardware Trojans, in: On-Line Testing Symposium (IOLTS), 2014 IEEE 20th International, IEEE, pp. 49–54.

[23] Xiaolin Xu, Bicky Shakya, Mark M. Tehranipoor, Domenic Forte, Novel bypass attack and BDD-based tradeoff analysis against all known logic locking attacks, in: International Conference on Cryptographic Hardware and Embedded Systems, Springer, 2017, pp. 189–210.

[24] P. Subramanyan, S. Ray, S. Malik, Evaluating the security of logic encryption algorithms, in: Hardware Oriented Security and Trust (HOST), 2015 IEEE International Symposium on, IEEE, pp. 137–143.

[25] M. El Massad, S. Garg, M.V. Tripunitara, Integrated circuit (IC) decamouflaging: reverse engineering camouflaged ICs within minutes, in: NDSS.

[26] J. Rajendran, Y. Pino, O. Sinanoglu, R. Karri, Security analysis of logic obfuscation, in: Proceedings of the 49th Annual Design Automation Conference, ACM, pp. 83–89.

[27] L.-w. Chow, J.P. Baukus, C.M. William Jr., Integrated circuits protected against reverse engineering and method for fabricating the same using an apparent metal contact line terminating on field oxide, 2002, US Patent App. 09/768,904.

[28] L.W. Chow, J.P. Baukus, B.J. Wang, R.P. Cocchi, Camouflaging a standard cell based integrated circuit, 2012, US Patent 8,151,235.

[29] R.P. Cocchi, J.P. Baukus, L.W. Chow, B.J. Wang, Circuit camouflage integration for hardware IP protection, in: Proceedings of the 51st Annual Design Automation Conference, ACM, pp. 1–5.

[30] A. Moradi, A. Barenghi, T. Kasper, C. Paar, On the vulnerability of FPGA bitstream encryption against power analysis attacks: extracting keys from Xilinx Virtex-II FPGAs, in: Proceedings of the 18th ACM conference on Computer and Communications Security, ACM, pp. 111–124.

[31] J.-B. Note, É. Rannaud, From the bitstream to the netlist, in: FPGA, vol. 8, p. 264.

[32] R.S. Chakraborty, I. Saha, A. Palchaudhuri, G.K. Naik, Hardware Trojan insertion by direct modification of FPGA configuration bitstream, IEEE Design & Test 30 (2013) 45–54.

[33] P. Swierczynski, M. Fyrbiak, P. Koppe, C. Paar, FPGA Trojans through detecting and weakening of cryptographic primitives, IEEE Transactions on Computer-Aided Design of Integrated Circuits and Systems 34 (2015) 1236–1249.

[34] K. Huang, J.M. Carulli, Y. Makris, Counterfeit electronics: a rising threat in the semiconductor manufacturing industry, in: Test Conference (ITC), 2013 IEEE International, IEEE, pp. 1–4.

[35] R. Karam, T. Hoque, S. Ray, M. Tehranipoor, S. Bhunia, MUTARCH: architectural diversity for FPGA device and IP security, in: Design Automation Conference (ASP-DAC), 2017 22nd Asia and South Pacific, IEEE, pp. 611–616.

[36] R. Karam, T. Hoque, S. Ray, M. Tehranipoor, S. Bhunia, Robust bitstream protection in FPGA-based systems through low-overhead obfuscation, in: ReConFigurable Computing and FPGAs (ReConFig), 2016 International Conference on, IEEE, pp. 1–8.

[37] R.S. Chakraborty, S. Bhunia, Security against hardware Trojan attacks using key-based design obfuscation, Journal of Electronic Testing 27 (2011) 767–785.

PCB AUTHENTICATION AND INTEGRITY VALIDATION

15

CONTENTS

15.1 PCB AUTHENTICATION

A counterfeit PCB typically differs in functionality, performance, or reliability, but is sold as an authentic one. Similar to ICs, PCBs typically rely on a long and globally distributed development cycle that connects multiple untrusted parties. As shown in Fig. 15.1, PCB life cycle may include design houses, manufacturers, board assemblers, testing partners, and system integrators. Due to increasing reliance on various third-party entities, PCBs are vulnerable to counterfeiting attacks. Counterfeiting

Hardware Security. https://doi.org/10.1016/B978-0-12-812477-2.00020-4

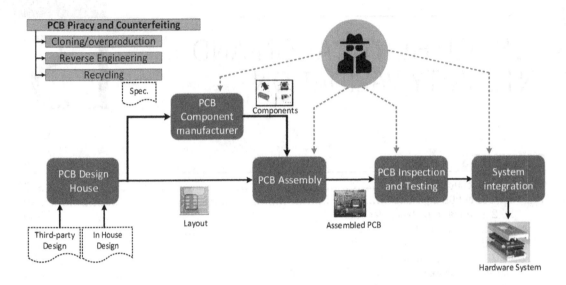

FIGURE 15.1

Typical stages in a PCB supply chain, which are vulnerable to counterfeit PCB insertion by an untrusted party through cloning, overproduction, reverse engineering, or recycling of discarded/used PCBs.

can be done by an untrusted third party, who obtains the layout of the PCB and generates a clone, or overproduces it. Furthermore, PCBs are relatively easier to reverse engineer compared to ICs, which again makes them highly vulnerable to cloning attacks by an adversary, who may not even have the PCB layout and specifications. Hence, counterfeiting of a PCB has become prevalent. Number of effective solutions have been reported to date to defend counterfeiting of ICs. However, existing chip-level integrity validation approaches cannot be readily applied to PCBs.

Counterfeit PCBs can be classified into various major categories. The most common form of counterfeiting is downright cloning of the complete PCB. This could be accomplished by an untrusted entity with access to the original design and specifications. As mentioned earlier, PCBs are mostly manufactured at untrusted fabrication facility. A bad actor in such a facility can clone or overproduce a PCB design. It could also be done by reverse engineering the bill-of-materials (BoM), and layout from a manufactured PCB deployed in the field. Further, discarded faulty PCBs from a PCB foundry or testing facility could be picked up by ghost shift workers in such factories. Those PCBs could be assembled with components, and then sold to customers as real products. Certain PCBs are bought, used, refurbished, and then sold as new, involving multiple parties in the process. The quality of these counterfeit PCBs may be poor, causing early failures, performance degradation, or potential damage, and loss of information to the end-users. This could happen because of the unreliable board material, or poor construction of such boards. The discarded and refurbished PCBs could be referred to as recycled PCB in the classification of counterfeit PCBs. These counterfeit PCBs can potentially have additional undesired functionalities, or malicious circuits, that is, Hardware Trojans [1].

Researchers have studied various PCB-specific parameters to create a unique and authentic board-specific signatures, which could be used for authentication of a PCB. The key idea is to obtain unique identifying signatures after the PCB is manufactured. This is similar to the use of PUF in authentication of an IC through generation of unique fingerprint, as described in Chapter 12. This golden signature would be stored in a database. In the field, whenever the authenticity of a PCB needs to be verified, the signature of the PCB would be generated and compared with the golden reference. If the two signatures differ beyond a pre-determined threshold, the PCB would be marked as counterfeit, or unauthenticated. In this chapter, we present some of these signature-based authentication techniques. Section 15.2 presents different sources of variations that can be leveraged to extract the PCB signature. The methods of extracting signature are discussed in Section 15.3. Section 15.4 presents the metrics used for assessing the quality of the signatures. Finally, in Section 15.5, other potential authentication techniques are discussed.

15.2 SOURCES OF PCB SIGNATURE

Different physical, electrical, and chemical variations are introduced in a PCB by its manufacturing process. Such intrinsic sources of variations could be used for generating the authentication signature for a PCB. In the presence of a robust and unique signature, an authentic PCB could easily be differentiated from its cloned counterpart. Such an ideally, any signature to be used for authentication should have the following characteristics: 1) Random: the signature must be unpredictable; 2) Unclonable: signature of each unit would be unique and cannot be cloned by another; and 3) Robust: the signature should be captured reliably, even under varying environmental conditions (e.g., supply voltage, temperature). If the signature is extremely sensitive to environmental conditions, authentication may fail when such conditions vary. The above-mentioned desirable features would only be present in a signature if the source of variations inherently provide them. The entropy sources used in some of the intrinsic board-level signature generation techniques for PCB authentication are shown in Fig. 15.2 and discussed in the next section. Note that an alternative approach to PCB authentication is based on storing a device-specific unique identification number onto one-time programmable fuses inside a PCB. However, compared to the intrinsic counterpart mentioned above, extrinsic signatures are prone to various forms of invasive attacks, which may access and alter them. Such signatures are also vulnerable to cloning, where an adversary can deliberately assign them onto cloned PCBs.

15.2.1 TRACE IMPEDANCE VARIATION

PCBs typically consist of hundreds to thousands of metal traces distributed across the board (Fig. 15.3A). These metal traces are commonly made of copper (Cu) lines of different thicknesses. These traces are subject to random intrinsic manufacturing process variations, such as a random shift in length or width. Such differences cause variations in DC resistance, AC impedance, and signal propagation delay through these lines. Hence, the variation in trace impedance could be used for the board-level unique signature generation [2].

Two basic trace types of PCB are: (1) microstrip and (2) stripline. On a single layer PCB, the microstrip trace is the dominant type of trace for the underlying pattern of copper wire. However, in a multilayer PCB, both types of traces are used. Thus, different PCBs may have different wire impedance models, considering the copper trace and substrate dielectric. Cross-sections of these trace types are shown in Figs. 15.3B and 15.3C. Impedance (Z_0) of these traces rely on width and thickness of the copper trace, thickness, and dielectric constant of the substrate. During the PCB manufacturing process, the dimensions of the traces would not be perfectly uniform in both width and height, and the dielectric constant of the substrate varies over the area of the PCB. These factors will result in a process-induced variation of the trace impedance. This impedance would vary from board to board and can be measured by a test equipment. Impedances from multiple traces in a board can collectively construct unique signatures from each board, which essentially acts as a PUF, and hence can be used for PCB integrity validation, or authentication.

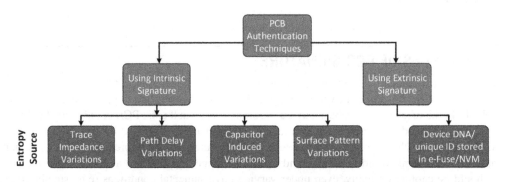

FIGURE 15.2

PCB authentication methods and corresponding entropy sources.

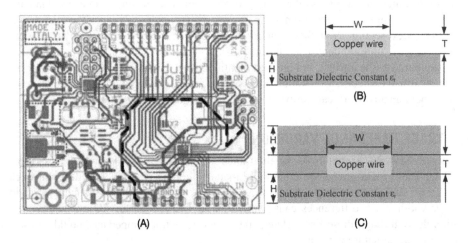

FIGURE 15.3

(A) The layout of the Arduino UNO R3 SMD Edition with a selected trace (highlighted in yellow [black in print version] dash line). Most PCB layouts contain a large number of traces similar to this; (B) Microstrip Trace in a single layer or multilayer PCB; and (C) Stripline Trace in a multilayer PCB.

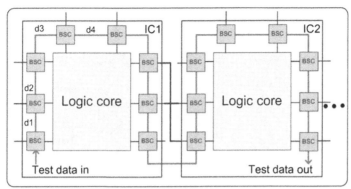

A PCB design

FIGURE 15.4

Boundary scan-paths surrounding the logic core of the ICs within a PCB design. The paths contain several scan cells connected in sequence.

15.2.2 DELAY VARIATION

PCBs can also be authenticated using high-quality delay-based signatures captured through the JTAG test infrastructure [3]. Boundary-scan chain architecture (BSA), inherent in most modern ICs, is a prevalent DFT structure used by the majority of PCBs today. As illustrated in Fig. 15.4, within this scan architecture several boundary-scan cells (BSCs) are connected in a chain. These BSCs are connected to one another in a manner identical to a shift register to form the boundary-scan register. They are used to shift specific test patterns to the logic core of an IC during the PCB testing process. The corresponding response of the IC under test can also be shifted out through the scan-chain. Multiple PCBs fabricated for a given design contain identical routing of the scan-path. However, data passing through identical scan-paths across different boards are still expected to experience a slightly different delay because of subtle variations in the manufacturing process of both the IC and the PCB. By measuring this delay of the BSC paths, a unique signature for authentication can be generated.

15.2.3 CAPACITOR-INDUCED VARIATION

One can include additional traces or components in a PCB, e.g., capacitive units, to deliberately introduce a source of entropy. They can be used to generate unique signatures in the manufactured boards. Such capacitive units could consist of a set of carefully-crafted copper patterns dedicated to maximizing manufacturing process induced variations [4]. Each capacitive unit could be incorporated with dedicated sensing hardware in the PCB. The sensing hardware outputs a signal that contains a specific frequency-value depending on the manufacturing variation of the corresponding capacitive unit. By comparing the frequencies extracted from these individual capacitive areas, a PUF logic can be implemented. To be able to ensure the generation of robust and distinguishable signature, each capacitive unit should contain a specific capacitance that experiences a large enough variation during manufacturing. At the same time, the capacitance should be large enough compared to on-board parasitics for providing noise immunity.

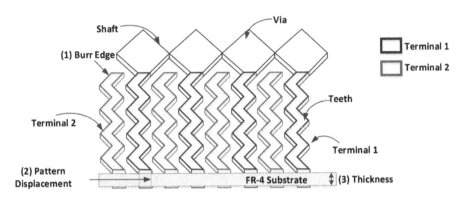

FIGURE 15.5

3-D representation of the two-layer comb-shaped trace pattern fabricated on PCB, acting as the capacitor that provides a source of variation for the signature generation process.

The capacitor unit could be designed in different layers of PCB, with a specific number of terminals, as shown in Fig. 15.5. These terminals may consist of copper traces drawn following a specific pattern that increases the chances of variation during manufacturing [4]. Researchers have tested zigzag copper patterns (Fig. 15.5). Each layer would contain such patterns, and they could be connected with vias on the "shaft". This facilitates a "teeth-like" structure, where every "teeth" is surrounded by teeth of another terminal, creating sideward and vertical electrical field when charged. Furthermore, the capacitor units could be buried in the internal layers of PCB for noise immunity. Process-induced variations in different parameters introduce physical discrepancies in the trace patterns. These discrepancies could change internal electrical fields of capacitors and vary their capacitance values. Some of the manufacturing variations are the following:

- Misalignment of the pattern mask leading to varied shapes of copper patterns (local variation)
- Variation in chemical etching process (local variation)
- Different thickness of the boards (global variation)
- Subtle misalignment/shift within PCB layers (global variation)

Among the aforementioned variations, local variation refers to imperfections that impact individual units locally, whereas global variations indicate a boardwide impact.

15.2.4 SURFACE PATTERN VARIATION

Imperfections in the PCB manufacturing process could result in variations in visual surface patterns of the PCBs. This surface pattern variation can be used to generate the signature for PCB authentication. These visual patterns could be found in various observable components of the PCB, such as interlayer connecting vias, routing and power traces, surface mount devices (SMD), and pads [5]. Figure 15.6 illustrates some of these components in PCB. Interlayer connecting vias that are commonly found in all modern PCBs are basically small-plated holes in the PCB surface. These vias are used for several reasons, but their main purpose is to connect different PCB layers. Their quality has a crucial role in

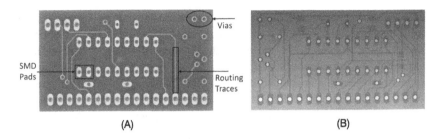

FIGURE 15.6

(A) Image of a PCB surface with vias, routing and power traces, SMD pads; (B) X-ray computer tomography image of the PCB surface [5].

assuring PCB quality. Surface pattern deviation of the vias could be contributed by several factors, including:

- Finishing process of the via surface
- Variation in drilled holes
- Separation between solder mask boundary, and via edges
- Angle present in the via hole (observable in 3D view)

The via surface of a PCB contains several small lines of different size, shape, and orientation. These variations could be observed in the microscopic image of a via. Figure 15.7 shows the patterns present in two vias [5]. Various randomly shaped/sized marks and dots can be observed on the surface, resulting from manufacturing process induced deviations. These random noise-like patterns could be leveraged

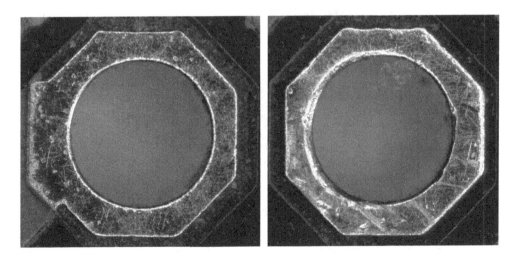

FIGURE 15.7

Randomly shaped/sized marks and dots on the via surface resulting from the manufacturing process [5].

to create a unique identifier for the PCB. Since via alignment is a very challenging task, it is unlikely to have no misalignments in all vias of a PCB during manufacturing. Hence, an abundant source of variation should always be present. Furthermore, the differences among visual surface patterns are absolutely unpredictable and cannot be controlled as well. Via-based surface fingerprints should be robust even under harsh environmental derivations. These via patterns also remain unused in the field and no electronic components are soldered over them. Finally, they provide excellent physical access for capturing surface patterns. Overall, surface vias have the potential to deliver unique and robust signatures for PCB authentication.

15.3 SIGNATURE PROCUREMENT AND AUTHENTICATION METHODS

While IC-level process variations have been extensively leveraged to implement PUFs [6], there has been a dearth of study exploiting board-level variations using such functions. In the absence of an effective signature extraction method, the underlying variation would not be utilized properly. The extracted signature for each PCB could be stored onto a central database during manufacturing, as shown in Fig. 15.8. A third-party facility other than the original manufacturer could also be hired for this enrollment process. In the field, to verify the authenticity of a given PCB, the associated signature extraction method has to be followed. The extracted signature needs to be sent to the central database to verify if that particular PCB is authentic. If the signature is present in the database, the PCB is verified to be authentic. Otherwise the PCB is deemed fake. Below, we discuss the corresponding signature generation and authentication methods developed for each source of variation discussed earlier in Section 15.2.

15.3.1 LEVERAGING PCB IMPEDANCE VARIATION

Automated test fixtures are commonly used in modern PCB production processes. Flying probes are used as the test fixtures that securely connect with test points in a design to provide quality assurances to the manufacturer and the system designer. For capturing the trace-impedance-based signature of a

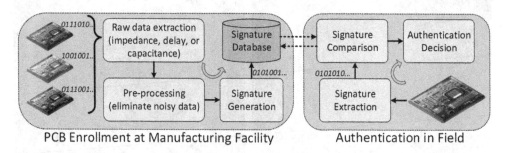

FIGURE 15.8

A generic flow of PCB enrollment and authentication process: during manufacturing, signature from each PCB is captured and stored in a central database. In field, the authenticity of a PCB can be verified by generating its signature and querying the central database.

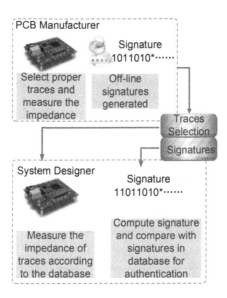

FIGURE 15.9

Overall steps of the trace-impedance-based PCB authentication procedure.

PCB, some of the existing probes could be used, or extra probes could be introduced to automatically measure impedance, and resistance of a set of predefined traces.

The overall approach of the trace-impedance-signature-based authentication method proposed in [2] is divided into two phases as shown in Fig. 15.9. In the first phase, an appropriate set of wire traces are selected by the PCB manufacturers. The impedance of those traces is measured under a stable frequency on all authentic PCBs. Signatures are produced off-line, based on the impedance measurements. The selection of traces and the corresponding signatures are stored in a database. In the second stage, system designers or end-users, who acquire the PCBs from the market need to measure the same selected traces for each PCB, and compute the signature, which is then compared to the signatures stored in the database. A PCB is determined to be counterfeit if the produced signature does not match with the one in the database.

Since PCBs contain hundreds of traces, a practical way to select traces for the signature generation would be to pick the ones that go through multiple vias. Recall from Chapter 4, that a via is a small hole drilled in a circuit board that connects the top layer of copper to the bottom layer. Each board manufacturer has a different process for etching the copper off the substrate, and drilling and plating the vias. These different methods have different intrinsic resistances associated with them. Hence, if the traces for signature generation are selected in an above-mentioned manner, the achievable randomness in signature could be maximized.

15.3.2 AUTHENTICATION USING DELAY VARIATION

Delay-based PCB authentication using JTAG is separated into two stages [3]. The flow is described in Fig. 15.10. In the first stage, a PCB manufacturer configures the JTAG device(s) on a PCB into an

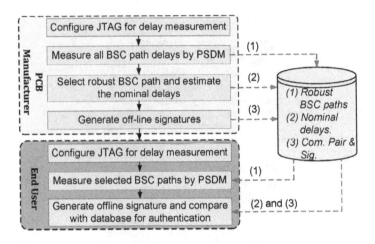

FIGURE 15.10

Major steps in the proposed JTAG-based PCB authentication process.

appropriate state needed to measure the delay of the BSC paths on all authentic PCBs. Some paths have fluctuating delay values when temperature or supply voltage vary. Those paths should not be selected in the signature generation process. Afterward, the signatures are produced off-line. The PCB manufacturer and end-user calculate the signature, based on the nominal delay value. A single bit of signature can be obtained by comparing the delay of two paths. For instance, when comparing path x and y with delay d_x and d_y, we can get a signature bit s as the follows:

$$ s = \begin{cases} 1, & d_x > d_y, \\ 0 & \text{else.} \end{cases} $$

Following this technique, a large string of bits (that is, 256 bits) could be obtained as a complete signature for identifying every PCB. The locations of the BSC paths, the nominal delays, and signatures need to be stored in a central database. In the second stage, an end-user in the field needs to configure the JTAG on a PCB in the same way, and measure the delays of the selected BSC paths. Then, the signature is computed, which is compared with the signatures stored in the database. As before, the PCB is deemed to be counterfeit if the produced signature is not found in the database.

15.3.3 EXPLOITING CAPACITOR-INDUCED VARIATION

In order to generate an identifying signature from variations inherent to board capacitance, several capacitor units could be installed, as shown in Fig. 15.11. The capacitor units connect to measurement circuits through some auxiliary components. Each measurement circuit generates a signal that reflects the variation present in the corresponding capacitor unit through its frequency. The frequencies are typically different among capacitor units due to manufacturing process-induced deviations. Measured frequencies are compared in pairs to generate signature bits. A complete signature would have several bits, each generated from a unique frequency pair. These signature bits are permuted, based on a

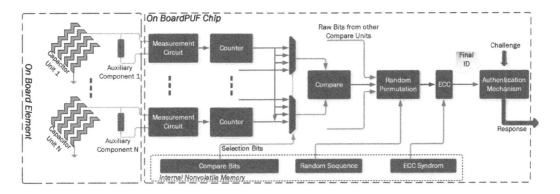

FIGURE 15.11

Extraction process of capacitance-induced variations and corresponding authentication technique using generated signatures.

pre-stored random sequence. The permuted signature represents the initial form of the PCB identity. It is worth noting that fluctuations in environmental and operational conditions may introduce errors in the generated identity, or signature. This initial signature is, therefore, corrected with the support of pre-stored error correction code (ECC), and the final signature is generated.

After manufacturing of the boards, an enrollment process is performed, where signatures for different challenge inputs are collected for each PCB. The challenge basically defines, which capacitor unit frequencies would be compared. Hence, for each PCB, several different challenge-response pairs are present, which is good in terms of security. During the enrollment process, different signatures for different challenges, with their corresponding random sequences could be stored in a database. During authentication in the field, the end-user verifying the board applies a specific challenge, and a signature for that given challenge is generated within the PCB. The correctness of the generated response is cross-checked with the one that was stored in the database during enrollment. If the signature is matched, the PCB would be considered authentic.

15.3.4 USING SURFACE PATTERN VARIATION OF PCB

To generate fingerprints from PCB surface patterns, high-resolution photos of the surface must be captured. Even minor surface details (for example, marks, texture, size, and shape distortion) must be captured in the pictures. Hence, the photos must be taken with high-resolution quality optics. The resolution is expected to be at least double the size of the target features [5].

It starts with the digitization of the PCB surface, using an appropriate imaging technique. The preprocessing step deals with noise present in the analog-to-digital conversion process [5]. The segmentation step deals with detection of signatures, providing regions within the PCB surface image. The next step computes the similarity between the suspect and the golden signature/fingerprint for a particular board. Finally, in the counterfeit detection step, a given test image is recognized as a counterfeit or authentic one. Since most electronic devices are covered with plastic covers, a technique to acquire the image during in-field authentication, without removing the cover, must be available. This could be

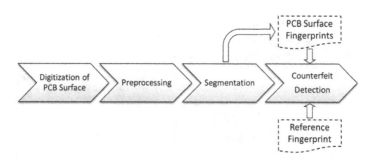

FIGURE 15.12

Various steps of the surface pattern variation based authentication process.

achieved by X-ray computer-tomography-based (CT-based) technique. Current industrial CT hardware can capture even minor details at micro-resolution. Figure 15.6B shows x-ray tomography image of a PCB surface. The subsequent steps for PCB surface authentication are shown in Fig. 15.12. Since the image-capturing process may encounter geometrical distortions, due to surface misalignment, a preprocessing step can be used. This step may involve averaging of several images, and further application of median filtering to reduce noise. It can greatly enhance the quality of the captured photos.

A template-matching scheme is applied to identify target regions within the captured image during the segmentation step. Since the region of interest for capturing the signature must be focused on a sub-region within the board, the segmentation step is crucial. Finally, the segmented region(s) can be used for signature generation in several ways. One way would be to extract quantitative values of several predetermined features from the target regions. If a large number of features are present, a signature could be obtained from that. However, existing methods directly use the isolated segment(s). During authentication, the segmented image of the target PCB is compared with golden one, using similarity measure techniques, such as normalized cross-correlation (NCC), which is commonly used for human fingerprints recognition.

The golden signature (segmented preprocessed surface image) for all authentic PCBs would be captured after the manufacturing process is complete. The captured signature would be stored in a database. During authentication in field, the NCC value of the golden and the target PCB image needs to be calculated. If the similarity is less than a pre-defined threshold, the PCB is considered to be different from the golden one. Hence, it would be detected as a counterfeit PCB.

15.4 SIGNATURE ASSESSMENT METRIC

The most common metric used for assessing the quality of signature-based-PCB-authentication schemes is the hamming distance (HD). HD is the amount of variation present within two signatures. To clearly distinguish between two boards, the HD of their signatures should be ideally 50%. This board-to-board signature variation is called inter-PCB HD. Likewise, the signature of the same board captured at two different time instances should ideally be the same. However, there are often some differences, due to measurement and environmental variations. Hence, the within-the-board or intra-board distance of the signature should be very close to 0%.

Figure 15.13A shows the histogram of intra-PCB HD for several PCB signatures generated from trace impedance variations. It is evident that the distribution is primarily focused near 50% (0.5) HD area. Conversely, the intra-PCB HD is mostly 0%. Hence, the signatures generated from trace impedance appear to be unique and robust. A similar conclusion can be drawn for signatures generated from scan-chain path delays captured via JTAG (Fig. 15.14).

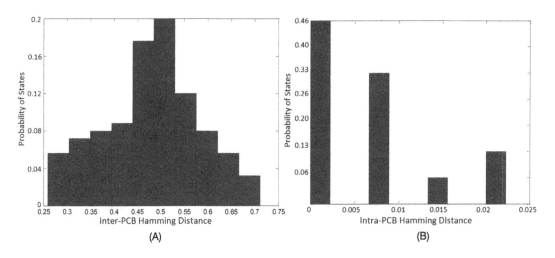

FIGURE 15.13

(A) Inter-PCB HD; and (B) Intra-PCB HD for signatures collected from trace impedance variations.

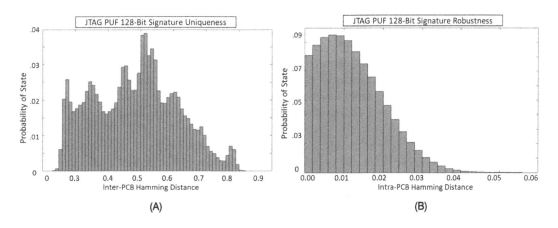

FIGURE 15.14

(A) Inter-PCB HD; and (B) Intra-PCB HD for signatures collected from delay variations.

15.5 EMERGING SOLUTIONS

15.5.1 SYSTEM-LEVEL MUTUAL AUTHENTICATION

A system-level mutual authentication approach can be used to authenticate both the hardware and firmware, as described in [8]. In this method, the hardware is used to authenticate the firmware by verifying the firmware's checksum during power-up. On the other hand, firmware can verify the identity of the hardware, and will not produce correct results, unless it receives a unique hardware fingerprint.

In this framework, a system ID (SID) is first generated after the PCB is assembled, and returned to the system designer. SID is created from the IDs of different chips (CIDs) present in a system, and is the XOR summation of these chip IDs. This ID is unique and resistant to cloning, as it is never exposed to the outside world. Once a system is assembled, each SID for a system is created and stored in a secure database at the trusted system integrator's site for future authentication. To prevent the use of cloned PCB, the firmware for the target hardware is obfuscated in such a way that it can only work upon receiving a correct system ID. Once the systems are manufactured and assembled, they must be shipped to the original system designer to compensate the obfuscated firmware.

When a system is powered-up in the field, it is necessary to construct the SID for proper operation. The in-system processing unit (e.g., processor, digital signal processor, FPGA, or microcontroller) is responsible for creating the SID. There is also a secure protocol for the processor to collect all the encrypted SIDs from the chips. The unique SID provides excellent protection for the hardware. If one of the ICs (including the processor) is replaced with a new one (recycled or low-grade counterpart having a different SID), it will be reflected in the SID. For the compromised system, the SID is never registered in the system integrator's database. The system ID provides an easy way of detecting a non-authentic hardware. However, it cannot prevent an adversary from creating this non-authentic hardware. On the other hand, an adversary cannot reconstruct an original firmware from the obfuscated one. Incorporating these two can prevent an adversary from creating a non-authentic system.

15.5.2 AUTHENTICATION USING RESONANCE FREQUENCY

A novel coil-like structure is proposed in [9] to capture different sources of variations to generate unique signatures for PCBs. Figure 15.15A shows the proposed coil structure. The assumption is that, due to the presence of a high number of notches, the proposed star-coil structure should provide increased resistance (wire resistance), capacitance (due to the comb-shaped multilayer design), and inductance (due to the coil shape) variation compared to typical straight-coil designs. Hence, this method can capture several sources of manufacturing imperfections, including edge rounding, density, and alignment variations.

The star-coil structure could be used for exploiting resonance frequency (RF), which is expected to be unique for each coil. The frequency of the star-coil can be swept from minima to maxima when a voltage is being applied to excite the coil. At a specific frequency, the current through the coil becomes maximum (that is, impedance becomes minimum). This frequency is considered as the resonance frequency. The following equation defines the resonance frequency for an RLC circuit:

$$f_{\text{res}} = \frac{1}{2\pi\sqrt{LC}}.$$

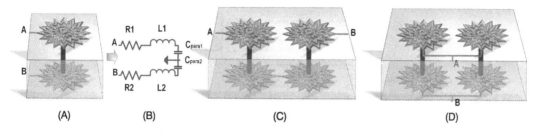

FIGURE 15.15

Star-coil structure: (A) base configuration, (B) equivalent RLC circuit, (C) series connected coils, and (D) parallel coil combination.

In the equation above, f_{res} refers to the resonance frequency in Hz, L is the inductance in Henry, and C refers to the capacitance in Farads. Since there is an inverse relationship between impedance and resonance frequency, a minute change in the impedance translates to a large change in the resonance frequency. Therefore, the value of f_{res} should be different across several boards. The single star-coil design can be extended by using multiple such coils connected together in a serial or parallel fashion (Fig. 15.15C–D). This would incorporate more variations, resulting in a large number of unique signatures.

The previous star-coil-based structure only provides one signature per board. Ideally, a secure and reliable authentication scheme would require a large number of challenge-to-signature pairs. To accommodate this feature, several stages of star-coils could be connected in various possible combinations to form a path through external jumpers. This connection combination could be defined with a challenge input during authentication, and the corresponding signature for each challenge (path configuration) would be unique.

15.6 PCB INTEGRITY VALIDATION

PCBs are an integral part of almost all electronic systems, including the ones that are responsible for performing various security-critical applications. Therefore, these boards are vulnerable to in-field alteration. The alteration can be caused by mounting ICs, soldering wires, rerouting paths to avoid or substitute existing blocks, adding or replacing components, exploiting traces, ports or test interfaces, and by many other ingenious ways. Circumventing digital rights management (DRM) by tampering with the PCB of a gaming console has been the most common example of PCB tampering [10]. Physical alteration to disable built-in restrictions allows the user to play pirated, burnt, or unauthorized versions of a game on the hacked console. One way to prevent such in-field alteration is to actively monitor the integrity of the PCB after deployment. However, there are very few methods available today for PCB integrity validation infield. Below we introduce some of these validation techniques.

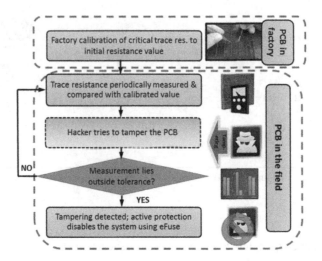

FIGURE 15.16

Block diagram showing the general approach of PCB security through sensing of trace resistance.

15.6.1 TRACE-IMPEDANCE-BASED VALIDATION

Copper traces within the PCB work as the interconnect among the components. In order to make any given component interact with the PCB, the component pins must be connected to some of the PCB traces in a direct or indirect manner. This could cause an observable change in the impedance of the copper trace. Hence, the impedance values of critical traces could be monitored to indicate this additional circuitry within the system.

In order to implement this method, the PCB vendor must collect the ideal trace impedance values for a large number of critical traces before deployment (Fig. 15.16). These impedance values must be stored within a nonvolatile memory, from which the values would be extracted and compared with the real-time measurements periodically—during operation—to ensure the integrity of the critical paths. Even the presence of a solder drop (used to connect wire/pins to the trace) would cause a measurable difference in the affected trace, and the tampering effort would be detected. The system could be equipped with features that disable the PCB as soon as a physical attack is identified.

15.6.2 JTAG-BASED INTEGRITY VALIDATION

JTAG-based PCB authentication method has already been discussed earlier in this chapter. The same idea could be extended for integrity validation purpose. Since the paths connecting the boundary-scan cells could be accessed through JTAG infrastructure, a board-specific signature could be extracted from the delays of these paths. Delay values from a large number of paths could be combined to create a unique signature of the board. Any modification that impacts any of these paths would lead to delay variations. Hence, if the ideal delay values of all scanpaths for a given board are known, that could be used to assess if any trace, pins, or component connected directly or indirectly to the JTAG chain has been tampered. The validation protocol could obtain the ideal values from a tamper-proof nonvolatile memory, or from the cloud at system startup. Similar to the trace-impedance-based validation, the ideal delay values would be compared with the actual delay values of the board in a regular interval during operation. One important requirement of this technique is that the ideal delay values should be updated over a long period of operation, as the delay could change as the device ages.

15.7 HANDS-ON EXPERIMENT: PCB TAMPERING ATTACKS (MODCHIP)
15.7.1 OBJECTIVE

In this experiment, the students will have the opportunity to apply a physical attack, namely a Modchip attack, to a PCB to alter its functionality.

15.7.2 METHOD

Using the HaHa platform, the students will target modifying the behavior of the EEPROM, which stores the secret cryptokey. The first part of the experiment allows students to locate the main modules, observe the connectivity, and identify data/supply ports. Next, the students will incorporate a malicious design modification that forces the EEPROM to provide a forced cryptokey value to the target module.

15.7.3 LEARNING OUTCOME

By performing the specific steps of the experiments, the students will learn how to apply a Modchip attack, and learn how to minimally modify the system under attack to break its security primitives, and to cause the highest impact. They will also experience the challenges with respect to protecting a device against tampering attacks.

15.7.4 ADVANCED OPTIONS

Additional exploration on this topic can be done through the application of a more controllable tampering attack, for example, the ones which allow the attacker to control the key value sent to the modules, and more sophisticated change in the system behavior.

More details about the experiment are available in the supplementary document. Please visit: http://hwsecuritybook.org/.

15.8 EXERCISES
15.8.1 TRUE/FALSE QUESTIONS

1. A PCB cannot be reproduced for cloning purposes unless the attacker steals the original PCB layout from the manufacturer.
2. Most IC authentication techniques can be directly used for PCB authentication.
3. Identical traces within the same board would have identical path delay and impedance.
4. Boundary-scan chain architecture (BSA) can be used for enabling design-for-test (DFT) solutions.

5. Capacitor units implanted for signature generation could be buried into the internal layers of PCB for noise immunity.
6. Misalignment of the PCB layers during manufacturing only causes local variation of parameters (that is, trace impedance).
7. Vias are only used for connecting different layers of a PCB.
8. Though the sources of variation for various signature-based PCB authentication process is different, the signature extraction process is identical.
9. Change in signature due to environmental variations could be tackled by using error-correcting codes.
10. Presence of several unique signatures for a given PCB does not add any value in authentication.

15.8.2 SHORT-ANSWER TYPE QUESTIONS

1. Classify the different types of counterfeit PCBs.
2. What are some of the desirable features of a good signature for PCB authentication?
3. Why do multiple PCBs manufactured from the same design have variations in impedance and delay among identical traces?
4. What is the traditional use of boundary-scan chain architecture (BSA) in an IC or PCB design?
5. What are some of the manufacturing imprecisions that could cause the capacitance of the capacitor units implanted for PCB signature generation to be different?

15.8.3 LONG-ANSWER TYPE QUESTIONS

1. Describe two different possible sources of variation that could be used for PCB authentication.
2. Describe how variation in board capacitance could be leveraged for PCB signature generation and authentication.
3. Discuss the metrics that are commonly used for understanding the quality of signatures for PCB authentication.
4. How could a star-coil trace structure in PCB be used for designing physical unclonable functions? Can you come up with a similar novel structure to extract more variation from PCB? Describe your mechanism in detail.
5. When a PCB is deployed in a harsh environmental condition (for instance, extreme heat), the generated signature from the PCB could vary from its golden reference. What would be your mechanism to tolerate these errors?

REFERENCES

[1] S. Ghosh, A. Basak, S. Bhunia, How Secure are Printed Circuit Boards against Trojan Attacks? IEEE Design & Test 32 (2015) 7–16.
[2] F. Zhang, A. Hennessy, S. Bhunia, Robust Counterfeit PCB Detection Exploiting Intrinsic Trace Impedance Variations, in: VLSI Test Symposium (VTS), 2015 IEEE 33rd, IEEE, pp. 1–6.
[3] A. Hennessy, Y. Zheng, S. Bhunia, JTAG-based Robust PCB Authentication for Protection against Counterfeiting Attacks, in: Design Automation Conference (ASP-DAC), 2016 21st Asia and South Pacific, IEEE, pp. 56–61.
[4] L. Wei, C. Song, Y. Liu, J. Zhang, F. Yuan, Q. Xu, BoardPUF: Physical Unclonable Functions for Printed Circuit Board Authentication, in: Computer-Aided Design (ICCAD), 2015 IEEE/ACM International Conference on, IEEE, pp. 152–158.

[5] T. Iqbal, K.-D. Wolf, PCB Surface Fingerprints based Counterfeit Detection of Electronic Devices, Electronic Imaging 2017 (2017) 144–149.

[6] G.E. Suh, S. Devadas, Physical Unclonable Functions for Fevice Authentication and Secret Key Generation, in: Proceedings of the 44th Annual Design Automation Conference, ACM, pp. 9–14.

[7] HuaLan Technology, PCB clone, http://www.hualantech.com/pcb-clone, 2017. (Accessed 3 December 2017), [Online].

[8] U. Guin, S. Bhunia, D. Forte, M.M. Tehranipoor, SMA: a System-Level Mutual Authentication for Protecting Electronic Hardware and Firmware, IEEE Transactions on Dependable and Secure Computing 14 (2017) 265–278.

[9] V.N. Iyengar Anirudh, S. Ghosh, Authentication of Printed Circuit Boards, in: 42nd International Symposium for Testing and Failure Analysis, ASM International.

[10] S. Paley, T. Hoque, S. Bhunia, Active Protection against PCB Physical Tampering, in: Quality Electronic Design (ISQED), 2016 17th International Symposium on, IEEE, pp. 356–361.

EMERGING TRENDS IN HARDWARE ATTACKS AND PROTECTIONS

SYSTEM LEVEL ATTACKS & COUNTERMEASURES

16

CONTENTS

Hardware Security. https://doi.org/10.1016/B978-0-12-812477-2.00021-6

16.1 INTRODUCTION

In modern computing systems, the hardware and software stack coordinate with each other to implement the system functionality. Whereas the previous chapters have focused on security issues of the hardware itself, they have not covered another important aspect of hardware security that concerns with providing an infrastructure for secure software execution. In particular, the role of hardware in protecting the assets stored in a chip or PCB (as defined earlier in Chapter 1) from malicious software have not been described in detail. Similarly, protection of the data/code of one application from another potentially malicious one, have not been addressed. The hardware needs to support security against software attacks, considering all levels of the software stack, from the operating system to application software. These attacks can be mounted through either functional or side-channel vulnerabilities. In this chapter, we will discuss various scenarios of software-induced attacks on hardware and possible countermeasures.

The software stack in a system runs on a central processing unit (CPU), which is most commonly implemented, nowadays, as an System on Chip (SoC) that integrates a processor IP. These systems increasingly integrate, along with a CPU, FPGAs and GPUs, which act as an accelerator for specific applications. This phenomenon has introduced increasingly complex hardware-hardware and hardware-software interactions, ultimately raising the question, "How do we secure our systems?" In this chapter, we first look into the security issues present in an SoC. Next, we focus on some requirements for designing a secure SoC. But before we move into system-level security issues, we need to understand the architecture of modern SoCs, and how hardware-software interaction takes place inside an SoC. We also need to understand the current practices for SoC security. The remainder of the chapter provides relevant background for SoC security, discusses various vulnerabilities and attack scenarios that can be mounted through hardware-software interactions, and presents various solutions.

16.2 BACKGROUND ON SoC DESIGN

The principal components of a standard, simplified SoC are shown in Fig. 16.1. It integrates IP blocks developed in the SoC design house, or acquired from various IP vendors, using an interconnection fabric to achieve desired functionality. Major IP blocks that are integrated into an SoC include a processor core (that runs the software stack), memory (that serves as the processor cache), crypto module (for functional security measures), the power management, and the communication module (for example, a USB module). The interconnect fabric (also called "fabric") can be realized in one of the following three ways, or any combination of them: (1) a point-to-point connection among the IP blocks; (2) bus-based communication architecture that uses a shared bus with appropriate arbitration logic; (3) a network-on-chip (NoC) architecture, where IPs communicate through specially designed "routers", which are responsible for transferring messages from one point to another. Figure 16.2 illustrates the three major types of communication architecture. In general, performance of the SoC design heavily depends upon the efficiency of its communication architecture.

Usually IP blocks in a SoC are designed with several standardized interfaces and communication protocols to interface with bus-based and NoC architectures. SoC integration process for the IPs with the fabric requires configuring the interfaces of IP blocks, and insertion of glue logic to connect them to the fabric. Standards of on-chip bus architecture were developed to facilitate the SoC integration pro-

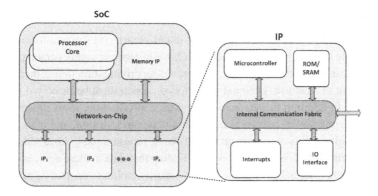

FIGURE 16.1

A modern SoC architecture that consists of multiple IP blocks connected by an interconnect fabric.

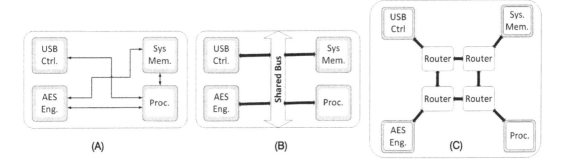

FIGURE 16.2

SoC architecture with (A) Point-to-point interconnect, (B) Shared bus interconnect, (C) Network-on-chip interconnect.

cess. These standards are often specific to the processor architecture, and consistent with the ecosystem produced by an IP vendor. For example, CoreConnect bus architecture from IBM [1] and AMBA from ARM [2] are tied to the corresponding processor, for example, PowerPC and ARM processor, respectively, and the IP ecosystem. Point-to-point architecture are not suitable for large complex SoCs due to lack of standardized IP interface, and integration process. They also suffer from scalability issues with increasing number of IPs.

16.3 SoC SECURITY REQUIREMENTS

In this section, we give an introduction into the security requirements SoC designers need to consider. These requirements are determined based on potential adversaries and attack vectors at different stages of SoC life cycle.

16.3.1 ASSETS IN SoC

SoC assets can be broadly defined as system-critical and security-sensitive information stored in the chips. With computing devices being employed for a large number of highly personalized activities (for example, shopping, banking, fitness tracking, and providing driving directions), these devices have access to a large amount of sensitive, personal information, which must be protected from unauthorized or malicious access. In addition to personalized end-user information, most modern computing systems contain highly confidential collateral from the architecture, design, and manufacturing, such as cryptographic and digital rights management (DRM) keys, programmable fuses, on-chip debug instrumentation, and defeature bits. It is crucial to our well-being that data in these devices are protected from unauthorized access and eventual corruption. Hence, security architecture, that is, mechanism to ensure protection of sensitive assets from malicious, unauthorized access, constitutes a crucial component of modern SoC designs.

16.3.2 ADVERSARIAL MODEL

To ensure that an asset is protected, the designer needs comprehension of the power of the adversary. Effectiveness of virtually all security mechanisms is critically dependent on how realistic the model of the adversary is. Conversely, most security attacks rely on breaking some of the assumptions made regarding constraints on the adversary. The notion of adversary can vary, depending on the asset being considered. For example, in case of protecting DRM keys, the end-user would be an adversary, whereas the content provider (and even the system manufacturer) may be included among adversaries in the context of protecting private information of the end-user. Rather than focusing on a specific class of users as adversaries, it is more convenient to model adversaries corresponding to each asset, and define protection and mitigation strategies with respect to that model. Defining and classifying the potential adversary is a creative process. It needs various considerations, such as whether the adversary has physical access, and which components they can observe, control, modify, or reverse engineer.

16.3.3 DESIGN-FOR-DEBUG IN SoC

As mentioned in Chapter 1, security requirements for SoC often represent a conflict with Design-for-test (DFT) and Design-for-debug (DfD) infrastructure. DfD refers to on-chip hardware for facilitating post-silicon validation of a chip's functional and security properties. A key requirement for post-silicon validation is observability and controllability of internal signals during silicon execution. DfD in modern SoC designs includes facilities to trace critical hardware signals, dump contents of registers and memory arrays, patch microcode and firmware, and to create user-defined triggers and interrupts. To reduce the risk of an adversary from snooping on data flowing through debug infrastructure (for example, from a crypto IP to a processor IP), data should be protected using standard cryptography primitives. In the case of off-chip key generation for the SoC, the key bits must be protected from the potential snooping from other IPs, especially any untrusted IP. This can be achieved by creating a security-aware test and debug infrastructure, which involves commensurate modification to local test/debug cells of an IP that effectively blocks other IPs from observing key bits [3]. Figure 16.3 shows such sample modifications.

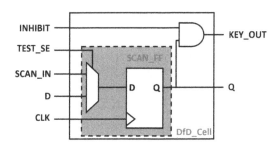

FIGURE 16.3

Modified scan cell to allow for secure key transfer by masking the output with the *INHIBIT* signal [3].

16.3.4 INTRODUCTION TO SoC SECURITY POLICIES

SoC security is driven by the requirement to protect system assets against unauthorized access. Such access control can be defined by confidentiality, integrity, and availability (CIA) requirements [4]. The goal of a security policy is to map the requirements to "actionable" design constraints that can be used by IP implementers, or SoC integrators, to develop protection mechanisms. Next, we present two examples of SoC security policies.

- *Example 1:* During boot time, data transmitted by the cryptoengine cannot be observed by any IP in the SoC other than its intended target.
- *Example 2:* A programmable fuse containing a secure key can be updated during manufacturing, but not after production.

Example 1 is a confidentiality requirement, whereas Example 2 is an integrity constraint. However, the policies provide concrete conditions to be checked by the design for accessing an asset. Furthermore, access to an asset may vary, depending on the state of execution (for example, boot time or normal execution), or position in the development lifecycle. Following are some representative policy classes. They are not exhaustive, but illustrate the diversity of policies employed.

Access control: This is the most common class of policies, and specifies how different agents in an SoC can access an asset at different points of the execution. Here, an "agent" can be a hardware or software component in any IP of the SoC. Examples 1 and 2 above are examples of such policy. Furthermore, access control forms the basis of many other policies, including information flow, integrity, and secure boot.

Information flow: Values of secure assets can sometimes be inferred without direct access, through indirect observation or "snooping" of intermediate computation, or communications of IPs. Information flow policies restrict such indirect inference. An example information-flow policy might be the following:

- *Key obliviousness:* A low-security IP cannot infer the cryptographic keys by snooping only the data from crypto engine on a low-security communication fabric.

Information-flow policies are difficult to analyze. They often require highly sophisticated protection mechanisms and advanced mathematical arguments for correctness, typically involving hardness or complexity results from information security. Consequently, they are employed only on critical assets with very high confidentiality requirements.

Liveness: These policies ensure that the system performs its functionality without "stagnation" throughout its execution. A typical liveness policy is that a request for a resource by an IP is followed by an eventual response, or grant. Deviation from such a policy can result in system deadlock or livelock, consequently compromising system availability requirements.

Time-of-check vs. time-of-use (TOCTOU): This refers to the requirement that any agent accessing a resource requiring authorization is indeed the agent that has been authorized. A critical example of TOCTOU requirement is in firmware update; the policy requires that firmware eventually installed on update is the same firmware that has been authenticated as legitimate by the security, or crypto engine.

Secure boot: Booting a system entails communication of significant security assets, for example, efuse configurations, access control priorities, cryptographic keys, firmware updates, and post-silicon observability information. Consequently, boot imposes stringent security requirements on IPs and communications. Individual policies during boot can be access control, information flow, and TOCTOU requirements. However, it is often convenient to coalesce them into a unified set of boot policies.

Most system-level policies are defined at the risk assessment phase by system architects. However, they continue to be refined along different phases of the architecture, and even during early design and implementation activities, as new knowledge and constraints come to light. For example, during architecture definition of a specific product, one may realize that the key obliviousness policy cannot be implemented as stated for that product, since several IPs need to be connected on the same NoC as the cryptographic engine due to resource constraints. This may lead to a refinement in the policy definition by marking some IPs to be "safe" for observing some of the keys. Policies may also need to be refined or updated in response to changing customer or product needs. Such refinements may make it highly challenging to develop a validation methodology, or even a disciplined security architecture. To exacerbate the issue, security policies are rarely specified in any formal, analyzable form. Some policies are described in natural language in different architecture documents, and many (particularly, refinements identified later in the system lifecycle) remain undocumented.

In addition to the system-level policies, there are "lower-level" policies, for example, communication among IPs is specified by fabric policies. Following are some obvious fabric policies:

Message immutability: If IP A sends a message m to IP B then the message received by B must be exactly message m.

Redirection and masquerade prevention: If A sends a message m to B, then the message must be delivered to B. In particular, it should be impossible for a (potentially rogue) IP C to masquerade as B, or for the message to be redirected to a different IP D in addition to, or instead of, B.

Nonobservability: A private message from A to B must not be accessible to another IP during transit.

The above description does not adequately describe the complexity involved in implementing policies. Consider the SoC configuration shown in Fig. 16.4. Suppose that IP0 needs to send a message to the DRAM. Ordinarily, the message would be routed through Router3, Router0, Router1, and Router2. However, such a route permits message redirection via software. Each router includes a base address register (BAR), which is used to route messages for specific destinations. One of the routers in the proposed path, Router0 is connected to the CPU. The BARs in this router are subject to potential

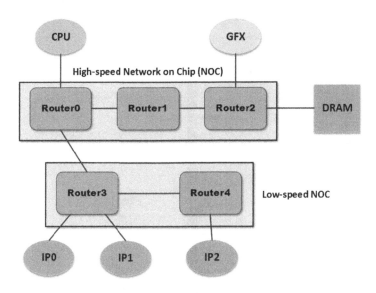

FIGURE 16.4

An illustrative simple SoC configuration. SoC designs include several on-chip fabrics with differing speed and power profiles. For this configuration, there is a high-speed fabric with three routers connected linearly, and a low-speed fabric with two routers also connected linearly.

overwrite by the host operating system, which can redirect a message passing through Router0 to a different destination. Consequently, a secure message cannot be sent through this route unless the host operating system is trusted. Note that understanding the potential of redirection requires knowledge of fabric operation, routers design (for example, the use of BARs), and the capabilities of the software in an adversarial role.

In addition to the above generic policies, SoC designs include asset-specific communication constraints. A potential fabric policy relevant to secure boot is listed below. This policy ensures that a key generated by the fuse controller cannot be sniffed during propagation to the crypto engine for storage.

- **Boot-time key nonobservability:** During the boot process, a key from the fuse controller to the crypto engine cannot be transmitted through a router to which any IP with user-level output interface is connected.

16.4 SECURITY POLICY ENFORCEMENT

This module is responsible for enforcing security policies that are imperative for ensuring security at the hardware level. The following sections discuss a number of security policies and a "Centralized Policy Definition Architecture," which is responsible for enforcing security policies.

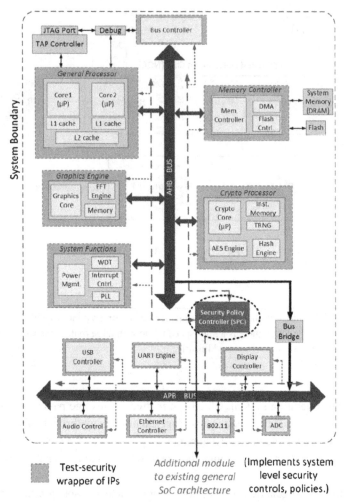

Representative SoC external I/O ports not illustrated

FIGURE 16.5

SoC security architecture based on E-IIPS for efficient implementation of diverse security policies.

16.4.1 A CENTRALIZED POLICY DEFINITION ARCHITECTURE

Current industrial practice in implementing security policies follow a distributed ad-hoc implementation. Such an approach, however, typically comes at high design and verification cost. Recent work [5, 30], has attempted to develop a centralized, flexible architecture called E-IIPS for implementing security policies in a disciplined manner. The idea is to provide an easy-to-integrate, scalable infrastructure IP that serves as a centralized resource for SoC designs to protect against diverse security threats, at minimal design effort and hardware overhead. Figure 16.5 shows the overall architecture of E-IIPS. It includes a microcontroller-based firmware upgradable module called security policy controller (SPC) that realizes system-level security policies of various forms and types using firmware code, following existing security policy languages. The SPC module interfaces with the constituent IP blocks in a SoC using "security wrappers" integrated with the IPs. These security wrappers extends the existing test (for instance, IEEE 1500 boundary scan based wrapper [32]) and debug wrapper (for example, ARM's CoreSight interface [31]) of an IP. These security wrappers detect local events relevant to the implemented policies and enable communication with the centralized SPC module. The result is a flexible architecture and approach for implementing highly complex system-level security policies, including those involving interoperability requirements, and trade-offs with debug, validation, and power management. The architecture is realizable with modest area and power overhead [5]. Furthermore, more recent work has shown that the existing design instrumentations, such as for DfD, could be exploited in implementing the architecture [30]. Of course, the architecture itself is only one component of the policy definition. Several challenges remain, including: 1) defining a language for security policy specification that can be efficiently compiled to SPC microcode; 2) study of bottlenecks related to routing and congestion across communication fabrics in implementing the architecture; and 3) implementing security policies involving potentially malicious IPs (including malicious security wrappers or Trojans in the SPC itself). Nevertheless, the approach shows a promising direction toward systematizing policy implementations. Furthermore, by enclosing the policy definitions to a centralized IP, it enables security validation to focus on a narrow component of the design, thereby potentially reducing validation time.

16.5 SECURE SoC DESIGN PROCESS

Modern-day SoCs are an efficient amalgamation of internal (in-house) and external (third-party) IPs to incorporate numerous functionalities in one single chip. Contemporary SoC design processes involve a systematic progression through several major phases of development lifecycle. Building a secure SoC, however, requires security considerations, and iterative evaluation from very early stages of the product development. Figure 16.6 illustrates how a secure development lifecycle of an SoC can be designed by incorporating security evaluation at every major phase of the design flow. The entire security analysis process of modern-day SoCs can be broadly classified into three crucial phases, that is, early security validation, pre-silicon security validation, and post-silicon security validation. A brief description of each of the phases with associated security analyses is provided below:

16.5.1 EARLY SECURITY VALIDATION

Early security validation includes a set of additional steps integrated with the conventional SoC design flow to ensure secure SoC design from the very beginning. Such validation is performed during the architecture and design stages of the development lifecycle. The first task of early security validation is to review the specification of the SoC, and conduct a security analysis. This process involves identifying the security assets in the system, their ownership, and protection requirements, collectively defined as security policies. The result of this process is typically the generation of a set of documents, often referred to as, product security specification (PSS), which provides the requirements for downstream architecture, design, and validation activities. At this phase, the SoC designers incorporate microarchi-

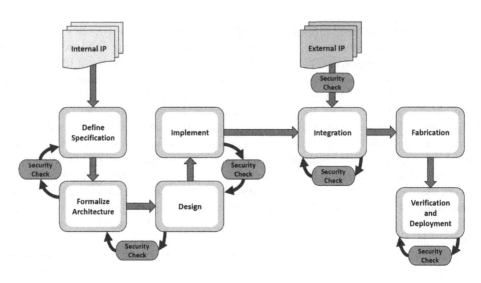

FIGURE 16.6

Secure development lifecycle of System on Chips.

tectural changes that facilitates design-for-security (DFS) and validation. The primary purpose of DFS and validation is to make the SoC immune to vulnerabilities, starting from the rudimentary levels of the microarchitecture to bottom up. The second task is threat modeling and risk mitigation. Development of the threat model includes breaking down of discrete security requirements, and analyzing the risk mitigation techniques. The third task is to review the high level design. This task involves generation of test cases to validate the implementation. The practice of employing good design methods and avoiding potential pitfalls are also vital parts of the SoC security validation process at early stage. A well-defined set of design security rules that can be verified by the autochecking tools facilitates such validation.

16.5.2 PRE-SILICON SECURITY VALIDATION

The pre-silicon security validation is performed at the implementation phase of the SoC development cycle. During this stage, the SoC architects perform static analysis of the design. Static analysis includes manually reviewing the RTL code. However, the process of reviewing the RTL is a one-time task, as the code changes over the design cycle. The designers also employ design automation tools for conducting the static analysis. In addition to static analysis, the SoC designers create targeted test cases, and run simulation to validate the desired output. The inherent problem with targeted testbench is that the verifiability has a very limited scope, and the process is hardly scalable beyond individual IPs. Apart from the simulation-based testing, the designers also employ formal verification tools to get exhaustive coverage. The formal verification tools, however, are challenged by the complexity of

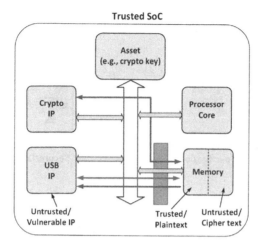

FIGURE 16.7

Illustrative SoC model depicting secure/insecure information flow.

modern SoCs, and fail to scale at system-level verification. Prototyping the SoC platform is often done to increase the speed of testing, and validate early software flows.

16.5.3 POST-SILICON SECURITY VALIDATION

In the SoC platform, the components or IP modules communicate with each other over the interconnect fabric. Testing and validating the interaction among the platform components is crucial, as illegal access of IPs to secure regions can cause security breaches. Such intercomponent analysis is performed during the post-silicon validation of the SoCs. The SoC designers employ debug and validation tools to probe deeper into the silicon. Verification tools are utilized at this phase to check and analyze system-level flows. The tests are performed by tools that can generate scenarios involving multiple concurrent transactions. Secure information-flow checking is an example of such system-level flow analysis, where the security engineers check for possibility of a security-critical signal being propagated to insecure peripherals, or untrusted IPs. The SoC designers also employ advanced hacking techniques to breach the security, including blackbox and white-box fuzzing. Lastly, a comprehensive software testing is done to finalize the post-silicon validation.

16.5.4 CASE SCENARIO: ENSURING A SECURE INFORMATION FLOW

To provide better insights about the criticality and significance of secure information flow, an illustrative example is presented in this section with an illustrative SoC model (shown in Fig. 16.7 [33]). The SoC model is designed with a processor core, a crypto IP, a memory IP as a platform component, a key storage IP for preserving the assets, and a USB IP. The memory addresses are classified into trusted and untrusted regions. The SoC is designed to operate in a manner that IPs with valid crypto ID are given access to the plain text sent to the crypto-engine. The cipher text is stored in the untrusted region

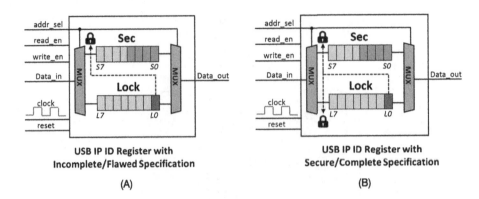

FIGURE 16.8

Microarchitectural illustration of the USB IP ID register (A) Sec and Lock registers with incomplete/flawed security specification, (B) Sec and Lock registers with secure/complete security specification.

of memory, and can be accessed by other IPs for operational purposes. The crypto IP is designed to read the plaintext from the trusted part of the memory, and encrypt the text using the keys stored in the Asset IP. Once the encryption is completed, it stores the cipher text to the untrusted memory region that can be accessed by external entry points, such as the USB IP. A firewall is placed on the memory to prevent the untrusted IPs, for instance, the USB IP, to prevent the leakage of the plain text. The firewalls determine the access privilege of the USB IP by registering its ID. Figure 16.8 [33] depicts the microarchitecture of USB IP ID register located at the firewall. The USB ID register is modeled as a security register with lock bit. The registers of the SoC model are basically flip-flops, triggered on the positive edge of the clock. The ID register, *Sec*, only uses the lower 4 (S[3:0]) bits of data-in, and bit 0 of data-in is used for the lock mechanism. Data-out always reads 8 bits from Read, or Lock. As it works as a secure gateway to access the trusted memory regions, it is crucial to perform thorough security analysis of the registers, and fully comprehend the vulnerabilities that might arise from poor design constraints. The ID of the IPs are generated using the 4 lower significant bits of an 8-bit register named *Sec*. To prevent unauthorized writes on the *Sec* register, another register named *Lock* is added to the design. The LSB of *Lock* is used to enable or disable write operations on the *Sec* register.

A threat model for the illustrative SoC model described above would have several crucial aspects that needs to be considered. For instance, the objective of the threat model is prevention of illegal write operations on the *Sec* register, when the lock bit of the *Lock* register is set to 1. This is a security policy that ensures data integrity property on the Sec register. The asset for this particular threat model is the ID and the *Sec* register. An attack scenario for the given threat model would be, any attempt made by untrusted software to modify the *Sec* register once the lock bit is set. Other properties like confidentiality and availability of *Sec* and *Lock* registers are trivial for this case study.

Once a well-defined threat model is structured, the next task of security analysis is the identification of vulnerabilities. For instance, a closer look at the code snippet shown below will reveals that it is possible to circumvent the data integrity of *Sec* register by exploiting poorly written specifications for accessing the *Sec* register. Consequently, the bad design and incomplete specification can aid the attacker to modify the *Lock* bit to disable the locking mechanism. Hence, the untrusted software becomes capable of modifying the *Sec* register (shown in Fig. 16.8).

RTL Code with incomplete specification:

```
if
  Addr_sel == 0 AND Lock==1
          Write_En_in==0
Else
          Write_En_in == Write_En
```

On the other hand, a complete set of specification for the design under consideration would protect the write operation on the *Sec* register by the lock mechanism. Also, it should be specified that the *Lock* register is self-locking. So, the corrected implementation would be gating the Write-en by the lock mechanism for both the registers (depicted in Fig. 16.8).

RTL Code with complete specification:

```
if
  (Addr_sel == 0 OR Addr_sel == 1) AND Lock==1
          Write_En_in==0
Else
          Write_En_in == Write_En
```

Apart from complete specifications, another critical aspect of designing security features is the definition of right size mitigations. For instance, the security analyst must be able to answer if it is required to design security mechanism for all the registers of the USB IP. If the security features are not adequate, then there is a possibility that some registers of the untrusted IP might contain malicious software. On the other hand, overprotection of the assets can be detrimental to the functional flow of the SoC, and can lead to the obsoleteness of security mechanisms.

16.6 THREAT MODELING

Threat modeling is the activity for optimizing SoC security by identifying objectives and vulnerabilities, and defining countermeasures to prevent, or mitigate the effects of, threats to the system. As noted above, it is a vital part of the security architecture definition. It is also a key part of the security validation, particularly in negative testing and white-box hacking activities. Threat modeling roughly involves the following five steps, which are iterated until completion:

Asset definition. Identify the system assets governing protection. This requires identification of IPs and the point of system execution, where the assets originate. As discussed above, this includes statically defined assets, and those generated during system execution.

Policy specification. For each asset, identify the policies that involve it. Note that a policy may "involve" an asset without specifying direct access control for it. For example, a policy may specify how a secure key $\mathcal{K}$ can be accessed by a specific IP. This in turn may imply how the controller of the fuse, where $\mathcal{K}$ is programmed can communicate with other IPs during boot process for key distribution.

Attack surface identification. For each asset, identify potential adversarial actions that can subvert policies governing the asset. This requires identification, analysis, and documentation of each potential "entry point", that is, any interface that transfers data relevant to the asset to an untrusted region.

The entry point depends on the category of the potential adversary considered in the attack, for example, a covert-channel adversary can make use of nonfunctional design characteristics, such as power consumption or temperature to infer the ongoing computation.

Risk assessment. The potential for an adversary to subvert a security objective does not, in and of itself, warrant mitigation strategies. The risk assessment and analysis are defined in terms of the so-called DREAD paradigm, composed of the following five components: (a) Damage potential; (b) Reproducibility; (c) Exploitability, that is, the skill and resource required by the adversary to perform the attack; (d) Affected systems, for instance, whether the attack can affect a single system or tens or millions; and (e) Discoverability. In addition to the attack itself, one needs to analyze factors, such as the likelihood that the attack can occur on-field, and the motives of the adversary.

Threat mitigation: Once the risk is considered substantial, given the likelihood of the attack, protection mechanisms are defined, and the analysis must be performed again on the modified system.

Implementation example: Consider protecting a system against code injection attacks by malicious or rogue IPs by overwriting code segments through direct memory access (DMA). The assets being considered here are appropriate regions of memory hierarchy (including cache, SRAM, secondary storage), and the governing policy may be to define DMA-protected regions, where DMA access is disallowed. The security architect needs to go through all memory access points in the system execution, identify memory access requests to DMA-protected regions, and set up mechanisms, so that DMA requests to all protected accesses will fail. Once this is done, the enhanced system must be evaluated for additional potential attacks, including attacks that can potentially exploit the newly set-up protection mechanisms themselves. Such checks are performed typically via negative testing, that is, looking beyond what is specified to identify if the underlying security requirements can be subverted. For example, such testing may involve looking for ways to access the DMA-protected memory regions, other than directly performing a DMA access. The process is iterative and highly creative, resulting in a collection of increasingly complex line-up of protection mechanisms, until the mitigation is considered sufficient with respect to the risk assessment.

In the following subsections, we will describe some practical attacks on SoC that exploit either functional or side-channel bugs, and describe possible countermeasures.

16.6.1 SOFTWARE-INDUCED HARDWARE FAULTS

Many attacks performed in recent times have shown faults in hardware can be induced through software leading to security issues. Next, we provide some examples of such attacks.

16.6.1.1 CLKSCREW

CLKSCREW is a prime example of how security-oblivious performance tweaks can lead to major security breaches. This particular fault can be introduced in the hardware directly from software, and can lead to privilege escalation, and even the stealing of encryption keys from the TEE of the device [6]. Dynamic voltage and frequency scaling (DVFS) [7] is a widely used approach to improve energy efficiency of a processor. In this approach, voltage and frequency of a processor are dynamically scaled to save power, and reduce heating effect. There can, however, be bugs in a DVFS system that can allow an attack to happen. But to understand the attack, let us first look at how DVFS is implemented.

DVFS Implementation

Hardware-level support: When a complex SoC is designed, different IPs coming from different vendors may provide widely varying functionality and performance. They also typically have their own voltage and current requirements. For example, the voltage requirement for a processor core is likely to be different from the memory IP, or the communication IP. Hence, in order to properly integrate these components, designers include several voltage regulators [6], and embed them into the power management integrated circuit (PMIC) [8]. Moreover, to regulate different frequencies, a frequency synthesizer is typically integrated into the processor. This frequency synthesizer/phase-locked loop (PLL) circuit can output frequencies within a specified range, with the step function depending on the implementation. For example, in a Nexus 6 device, a standard PLL circuit provides a base frequency of 300 MHz. A high-frequency PLL (HFPLL) is responsible for the dynamic modulation of the output frequency. For fine-tuning, half the signal from the HFPLL is channeled through a frequency divider [6].

Software-level support: PMIC drivers [9,10] are provided by the vendor to control the hardware level regulators. Linux CPUfreq can perform OS-level power management by assessing the requirements of the system, and indirectly instructing the hardware regulators to make changes to the frequencies and voltages of different components. It is important to note that an application software cannot directly regulate the voltage or frequency, but can make changes to certain registers, which are later read by the hardware to perform the actual voltage/frequency scaling [6].

CLKSCREW Fault:

CLKSCREW fault may occur if we "overclock" (i.e., apply higher than rated maximum clock frequency) or undervolt (meaning, apply lower than rated minimum voltage) the system. Let us first describe a few basic concepts before we move on to the fault. In a standard delay flip-flop, a change in the output (Q) happens if the value at the input (D) is switched, and if the flip flop detects a rising clock edge. Typically, between two flip-flops, we have combinational logic. Let us assume T_{clk} is the clock cycle period; T_{FF} is the time for which the input to the flip-flop must be kept stable; T_{setup} is time for which the input signal must be stable before the clock edge appears; T_{max_path} is the delay of the combinational circuit, and K is a constant for the assumed microarchitecture [6]. In Fig. 16.9 we see the above-mentioned variables and their role during the digital circuit operation. Therefore, the condition below must hold to ensure no faults triggers in the circuit.

$$T_{clk} \geq T_{FF} + T_{max\_path} + T_{setup} + K$$

If the constraint above is violated by overclocking, and thus reducing $T_{clk,}$ or by undervolting, and thus increasing the T_{max_path}, then we will be able to introduce a hardware fault [6]. Due to the constraint violation, the output of the second flip-flop fails to switch state because of the input delay, as shown in Fig. 16.10. Note that this fault can be induced into the hardware by a rogue software.

Attack Based on CLKSCREW Fault:

Let us take a practical example of how CLKSCREW fault can leak an encryption key. We have noticed in Chapter 8 that differential fault attack, or DFA [11], can guess the AES keys if we can obtain a pair of ciphertext from a plaintext, such that one of the ciphertexts was a victim of single corrupted computation. DFA can reduce the key search space from 2^{128} (for a 128-bit AES Key) to 2^{12}, if we can introduce a random single-byte data corruption at the 7th AES round, and the corrupted data feeds

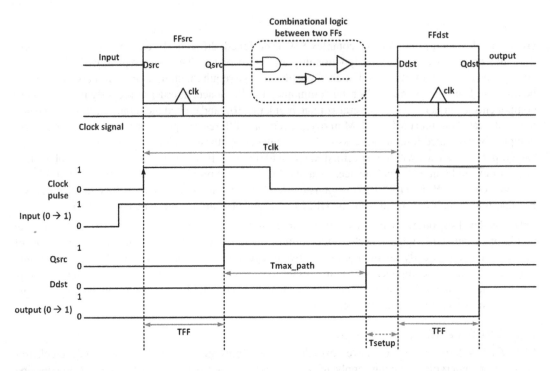

FIGURE 16.9

Different timing variables during the operation of a standard digital circuit [6].

into the next round. Once the search space is reduced to 2^{12}, one can perform brute-force search to find the correct key [6]. The data corruption can be achieved through the CLKSCREW Method. This is an example of a small exploit of the fault from a much bigger possible fault space.

Defense Against CLKSCREW Fault:

One easy countermeasure against such attack is to impose a hard limit to the upper and lower values of voltage and frequency, using extra limit-checking components, or by using e-fuses [6]. This mechanism imposes a constraint on the device during design phase, but to find the true operational limits, we must run intensive electrical testing after the device is manufactured. Process variation during fabrication can also impose extra variance making this solution very hard to uniformly implement across different devices and designs.

16.6.1.2 Rowhammer Attack

Rowhammer is a recently reported system level attack that introduces a bit flip in the DRAM memory and can lead to privilege escalation [12], or other malicious effects. Bitflip errors can be randomly introduced in the memory due to background radiations and neutrons from cosmic ray secondaries [13]. We will discuss remedies in later sections. Researchers have reported reliable solutions to this

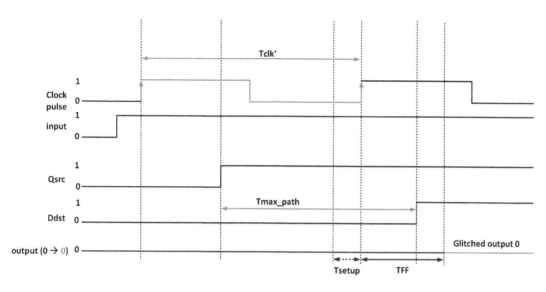

FIGURE 16.10

Glitch introduced in the output of the second flip-flop due to violation of the timing constraint [6].

problem with certain noncritical drawbacks. These solutions—although designed for normal bitflip error correction—works well towards mitigating a Rowhammer attack.

Bit errors that can be controlled to an extent, and are repeatable, impose a real threat to the security of the system. Rowhammer is one such technique that allows an attacker to cause a targeted bitflip in a certain memory location, allowing read access to restricted memory, and can even cause a privilege escalation. Eighty-five percent (85%) of the DDR3 modules tested in [14] were found to be susceptible to Rowhammer attack [15]. Even DDR4 modules can be attacked, using the Rowhammer exploit as pointed out in [16].

Rowhammer Attack Model

As can be seen in Fig. 16.11, we can visualize DRAM [12] as a rectangular block, with each row representing a word of a certain length, and number of rows determining the overall capacity of the DRAM. To access a row or word in the memory we perform the following steps:

1. Allow the Row-buffer access to the selected row. This makes the Row-buffer hold the word from the selected row.
2. Read the information from the row buffer.
3. Disconnect the Row-buffer from the previously selected row, so that the next word can be accessed.

To carry out a Rowhammer attack, an attacker performs the following: [14]

1. Select a target row in DRAM to introduce a bitflip.
2. Rapidly access the adjacent row of the target row to cause the bitflip.
3. Exploit the bitflip to gain access to the system.

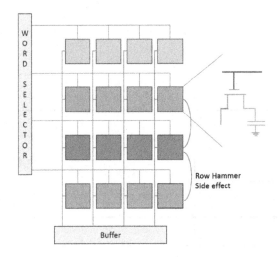

FIGURE 16.11

Standard DRAM structure from high-level perspective. Green (medium gray in print version) rows are being constantly accessed leading to a bitflip in the red (dark gray in print version) row. Note that this figure shows the double-sided hammering. The standard variant of the attack only makes repeated access to one of the adjacent rows of the target row.

For a DDR3 Ram [14], it is observed that 139,000 or more subsequent memory access can exhibit a memory error.

A variant of this attack is shown in Fig. 16.11. This is termed as double-sided hammering and involves high-frequency access to both of the adjacent memory rows of the target row [14]. This version of the attack has a higher chance of success and requires less access frequency than the original.

The following is a sample code [12,14,17] that can lead to a Rowhammer attack.

Rowhammer attack code

```
codeXYZ:
  mov (X), %eax  // read from address X
  mov (Y), %ebx  // read from address Y
  clflush (X)    // flush cache for address X
  clflush (Y)    // flush cache for address Y
  mfence
  jmp CodeXYZ
```

In the code above, the memory locations X and Y are repeatedly accessed to trigger a Rowhammer attack. Every time X and Y are fetched from the main memory, a copy is stored in the cache. Next time the code tries to access X and Y memory locations, the data will be fetched from the cache instead of main memory, provided that dirty bit is not set. This does not allow the attacker to trigger the Rowhammer attack, and that is why the attacker uses clflush() to release the content of the memory locations X and Y from the cache after each fetch, so that every access to X and Y is an access to the main memory

DRAM. On March 9, 2015, [14], Google's Project Zero exposed two working exploits for Rowhammer attack that caused privilege escalation. The first attack was on the Google Native Client (NaCl) [12]. The attacker was able to escape from within a sandbox, and directly execute system calls. In the other attack, page table entries [12] were modified by coupling memory, spraying with Rowhammer disturbance error. Both of these attacks rely on the clflush() call, which in x86-64 architecture cannot be converted into a privileged function. There are also ways [18] to perform a Rowhammer attack without the use of clflush(). The idea is to cause cache misses, so that the same main memory location is repeatedly accessed, triggering the Rowhammer effect. To achieve this effect, a particular memory access pattern is formulated, based on the cache replacement policy used by the target OS [14]. Although this method appears to be unscalable across different OS and cache replacement policies, there are certain adaptive cache eviction policies proposed to address the issue [12]. This particular flavor of Row-hammer attack is called the memory eviction attack.

Cause of Rowhammer Attack

Hammering a specific location of a DRAM memory electrically interferes with neighboring rows. It causes voltage fluctuation, which in turn causes the adjacent row to discharge faster than usual, and if the memory module is unable to refresh the cell in time, we see a bitflip [14]. Increase in DRAM density has led to memory cells holding smaller charges, while also being closely packed together. This fact makes the cells vulnerable to electromagnetic interactions from neighboring cells, which lead to the introduction of memory error.

Countermeasures Against Rowhammer Attack

Error-correction code (ECC): Although not intended as a countermeasure to Rowhammer attack, ECC works relatively well in dealing with this problem [12]. Single-error correction and double-error detection (SECDED) Hamming code [13] is an extremely popular ECC mechanism. Chipkill ECC ensures correction of multiple bit errors, up to full-chip data recovery, and can be used, but with high overhead. Even Non-ECC chips with parity support can prevent a Rowhammer attack by detecting it.

Avoid clflush: A few of the Rowhammer attacks—as discussed above—can be mitigated by modifying systems, such that they do not allow the clflush statement to execute [17].

Shared libraries: Shared libraries being available across processes allow the attacker to perform Rowhammer attack on these codes to escalate privilege. If libraries are not shared among processes with different privilege, then clflush, and memory eviction attack may be prevented [15].

16.6.2 SOFTWARE-INDUCED HARDWARE TROJAN ATTACKS

Recall from Chapter 5 that hardware Trojans are malicious logic in a design that can be triggered under rare circumstances, such as by an external signal, or at certain internal circuit condition, so as to avoid detection. The trigger condition initiates the Trojan functionality, and once triggered, the payload of the Trojan makes some modification in the data stream, or can send out some information from the data stream to the attacker. In this section, we look at hardware Trojans that can be activated by a signal sent from the software layer [21].

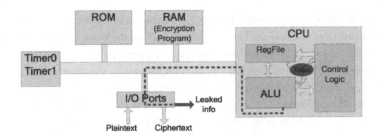

FIGURE 16.12

Example of a software controlled hardware Trojan.

16.6.2.1 Hardware Trojan Trigger on Microprocessor

Hardware Trojans if triggered based on inputs to a processor, or based on its output, can be exploited from the software layer. Figure 16.12 shows a Trojan that is inserted in a CPU, and based on the data stream inside the control logic, ALU and registers, leak information outside the system via the I/O ports [21]. Software exploitable hardware Trojans could be designed to support general attacks with variable payload effects, defined by the malicious software. However, such Trojans are more suitable for general-purpose processors or complex embedded processors that already have hardware supported security features, where various attacks could be performed, based on corrupting the security features through Trojan-induced backdoors [21].

Trojan Trigger Condition

The simplest Trojan is an always-on Trojan, which does not require any trigger condition to start malfunctioning. Though generally easier to implement, it is likely to get detected during post-manufacturing testing, due to the evident side-channel footprint. To avoid this, it has been proposed to make the Trojan trigger condition either controllable externally, by an attacker, or to use rare conditions in the internal circuitry to activate the Trojan [21].

Three aspects of a processor can be leveraged by a Trojan to act as a trigger condition from the software level [21]. They are:

1. Specific sequence of instructions.
2. Specific sequence of data.
3. Combination of both instruction, and data sequence.

This gives the control of the Trojan entirely to the attacker. For a processor running an operating system that supports multiple users, the trigger condition can be made even more complex to avoid accidental discovery by a defense mechanism, or during standard verification.

Trojan Payload

Regarding the Trojan payload, many options have been proposed in the literature, starting from simply inverting the data at some internal node, corrupting memory or primary output, or leaking sensitive information stored inside the hardware [21]. Channels available for leaking information can be realized through output ports, modulation of existing outgoing information, or the carrier frequency, phase, and

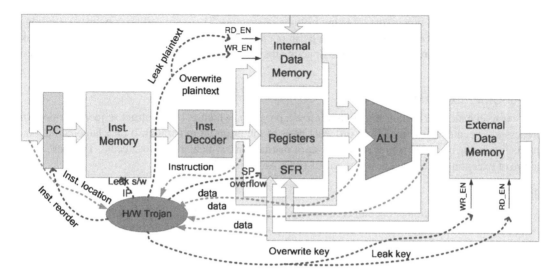

FIGURE 16.13

Possible software induced Trojan triggers.

amplitude to piggyback on existing modes of communication, or side-channels, such as power trace and EM radiation. For example, as shown in Fig. 16.13, a Trojan payload can be constructed to leak secret information during operation through output ports. When an instruction is fetched from the instruction memory to the register, it is also passed onto the LED ports for display. In reality, the information-leakage channel could be temporarily unused ports, or other side channels. A payload causing malfunction can perform an illegal memory write, or modify stack pointers, or change the inputs at the branch predictor.

16.6.3 SOFTWARE-INDUCED SIDE-CHANNEL ATTACK

Given the little effort spent on the cross-layer security during design time, attackers with a good understanding of both hardware and software components of a system can come up with a combined attack that can cripple the system. In this section, we will look at some well-known exploits that can be carried out, due to hardware vulnerability, but with the attack vector originating from the software layer. Although they rely on hardware bugs, these attacks, in most cases, can be remotely performed, and potentially have a huge cascading impact in the computing world and the world economy. The current solutions to these attacks are also discussed, but none are without major drawbacks [12,22,23].

16.6.3.1 Spectre

By exploiting the speculative execution of modern processors, Spectre attack can trick the system into executing instructions that are not supposed to be executed given the current system state [22]. This exploit, coupled with a side-channel attack, can lead to the exposure and theft of critical secret information from a victim system. This particular vulnerability can be exploited in a wide range of

AMD, Intel, and ARM processors affecting billions of systems. There are still no conclusive solutions to this problem and, as of writing, this remains an open field of research. In this section, we shall look into some concepts required to understand Spectre attack, the spectre attack model, and some proposed remedies.

Out-of-Order Execution

In order to enhance performance and parallelize a program, which is by construct sequential, modern processors execute instructions from different parts of the program in parallel. It may happen that one instruction being executed is preceded by a set of instructions, which are yet to execute. This particular nature of executing a code is known as out-of-order execution [22].

Branch Prediction

When a branch instruction is encountered, the processor makes a prediction on the direction in which the program will flow, and starts the speculative execution. The performance improvement due to this scheme is directly dependent on the number of right guesses the processor makes. For making a guess, certain components are implemented in the system. Typically, a predictor comprises of local and global predictors for improved accuracy. To further increase performance, whenever a branch instruction is executed, the corresponding correct jump location is cached in the Branch Target Buffer (BTB), and can be used as a guess for the same branch instruction when it is again executed [24].

Speculative Execution

While performing out-of-order execution, it may happen that the processor arrives at a branch for which the condition is dependent on values that are yet to be computed in preceding instructions. At this stage the processor has two choices, either wait for the preceding instructions to complete and incur a huge performance delay, or speculate [22], and guess the result of the conditional branch. After the guess is made, the current register state is stored as a checkpoint, and subsequent instructions start to execute. Once the previous instructions on which the condition of branch dependent on are finished, the guess made is validated, and if the guess was wrong, the program state is reverted back to a checkpoint, and the execution of the correct path is initiated. Also in case of a wrong guess, all pending instructions are abandoned, so that it does not make any visible effect.

Spectre Exploit on Conditional Branch

The main idea is to use the spectre vulnerability to read unauthorized data during speculative execution, and retrieve the data using a side-channel attack. Let us first look at how to read the unauthorized data. For the code below, let us assume that the code is part of kernel syscall.

Spectre exploit on conditional branch [22]

```
if (i < SizeOfArray1)
    A = Array2[Array1[i] * 256];
```

The attack follows the following steps:

1. **Train the predictor:** At first the conditional statement is accessed using values of i that are truly less than SizeOfArray1. With more such accesses, the chance of the processor to guess i < SizeOfArray1 increases.

2. **Craft i:** Maliciously pick a value for i, such that Array1[i] denotes a secret value 'S' in the memory that should not be accessible by the current process.
3. **Ensure conditions:** It is important to make sure that SizeOfArray1 and Array2 are not in cache, but the secret S is in the cache (which can be difficult to achieve).
4. **Side-channel probe:** While the processor is busy fetching SizeOfArray1 and Array2 from the main memory, the vulnerable data can be probed through side channel.

The first and third steps can be naturally present, or forced by the attacker. To evict SizeOfArray1 and Array2 from the cache, the attacker can dump a huge amount of random data into the cache indirectly by reading them from the memory. The attacker needs to know the cache replacement policy being used by the OS to properly carry out this step. To fetch the value S in the cache, the attacker can invoke a function that uses S. For example, if S is a cryptographic key, the attacker can trick the kernel into using the encryption function, which is easily accomplished. The final side-channel probe can be accomplished by identifying the change in cache configuration, and inferring information about the asset [22].

Side-Channel Probe to Complete the Attack

After the sensitive data is accessed, and is stored in the cache, the attacker has about 200 instruction execution time [22] to read the sensitive data from the cache. There are several ways this final step can be carried out. If the attacker has access to Array2, then the value stored can be easily probed by detecting the cache state change. Another alternative method is to use prime-and-probe [25] attack. In this method the attacker accesses known attack data from the main memory, so that the cache can be filled with those data. Once the cache is filled with known attack data, for any new data to be stored in the cache, some portion of the attacker data is evicted, and that can be traced by the attacker to infer information about the asset.

Evict+Time: A Variation

In this variant of the Spectre exploit [22,25], the attacker first trains the processor to predict wrongly during the speculation. Assume 'i' contains a secret, which is otherwise inaccessible to the process. Now during speculative execution, the attacker can perform the read Array1[i], even if i is out of bound for the Array1. Evict + Time attack assumes that the value of i is initially in the cache, then a portion of the cache is evicted through accessing his or her own memory which maps to the same cache set. If during this eviction the i is also evicted, then the subsequent read Array1[i] instruction will take a longer time to execute. If not, it will be fast, as it remains in the cache. The attacker systematically evicts portions of the cache, and notes the time of execution to infer information about the asset.

```
if (Predicted True but false)
  read Array1[i]
read [j]
```

Spectre Exploit on Branch Target Buffer

The second spectre exploit involves manipulating indirect branches by poisoning the BTB. Indirect calls or branches are common occurrences at the assembly level. They are the result of programming abstractions, such as function pointers and object-oriented class inheritance, both of which resolve to jumps with destination addresses realized at runtime. As you may recall, the BTB maps the address of the source instruction to a destination address. However, the BTB only uses the lower bits of the source instruction. This design choice creates the potential for aliased addresses. Therefore, the attacker can fill the BTB with illegal destinations from source addresses that are aliases of the target branch instruction. Now, when the victim indirect branch is encountered with an uncached destination, the processor will jump to the illegal address provided by the tainted BTB, and begin speculative execution. The attacker must choose addresses of gadget code to be speculatively executed that will access secret memory, and leave evidence to be detected by side-channel attacks.

Spectre Prime: A Variation

A variant of spectre called Spectre Prime [26] uses Prime+Probe threat model. Unlike the normal Spectre, this affects a system with multiple cores. In multiple core systems, there are separate caches associated with each core. If one of the cores makes a change to a particular resource in its cache, then it is necessary that the caches of the other cores reflect the change as well, in order to avoid incoherent reads.

Countermeasures Against Spectre

There are no attractive solution for Spectre attack as of yet, but certain solutions have been proposed. If the processor does not perform speculative execution in a sensitive section of the code, then that can perhaps stop the Spectre attack [22]. Serializing instructions [27] can sometimes perform exactly that and halt some of the attacks for Intel x85 processors, but this is not a complete solution and not applicable for all processors. In addition to disabling, hyperthreading, and forcing a branch prediction state, refreshing at each context switch is another proposed solution, but is probably not possible to implement in current architectures [22,28].

16.6.3.2 Meltdown

Meltdown [23] is a side-channel attack made possible due to out-of-order execution in a majority of the processors we use. Intel microarchitectures released since 2010 are vulnerable to this attack, and more likely than not, processors released even before are also vulnerable. The attack can be carried out in any OS, and is purely a hardware vulnerability. Memory isolation is an important security feature of any modern system, which essentially partitions the memory, and allows access to each partition, based on the privilege level of the process making the memory access request. The Meltdown exploit, however, can completely undermine memory isolation, and lead to the access of kernel-memory by user processes. This allows an attacker to steal critical information stored in kernel memory, such as passwords and encryption keys.

Out-of-Order Execution

The main reason for the success of Meltdown exploit is out-of-order execution [23]. As previously discussed, out-of-order execution is a performance tweak, that allows a processor to predict jump addresses and branch directions, so that it can compute ahead while the real address and branch condition are being evaluated [22]. A more detailed discussion is present in the Spectre Section. Any instruction that is executed out-of-order and vulnerable to potential side-channel attacks is termed as a transient instruction [22].

The Attack Environment

For the Meltdown attack certain assumptions are made on the attack environment [23]. They are as follows:

1. **Target:** The targets of this attack are any personal computers and different virtual machines that are hosted on the cloud [23].
2. **Attacker initial access:** To initiate the attack, the attacker must have full underprivileged access to the personal computer, or the virtual machine [23].
3. **Physical access:** No physical access to the systems is required by the attacker for using Meltdown Exploit [23].
4. **Defenses assumed:** For this attack, the systems can be protected by address space layout randomization (ASLR) and Kernel ASLR. Also, CPU features, such as SMAP, NX, SMEP, and PXN can be present [23]. All these will fail to defend the system against Meltdown.
5. **OS bugs:** The attacker assumes that the operating system has no bugs, and does not rely on the exploitation of any to gain access to secret information, or to attain kernel privilege.

The Attack Model

For carrying out a successful Meltdown attack, the steps are as follows [23]:

1. **Choose target memory:** First the attacker needs to decide, which directly inaccessible memory location contains valuable information that is worth extracting by this exploit [23].
2. **Load:** Load the target memory address into a register [23].
3. **Transient instruction exploit:** A transient instruction originated due to out-of-order execution is used to access a particular line of the cache, based on what is stored in the register [23].
4. **Flush+Reload:** Using Flush+Reload [29] side-channel attack, the attacker can perform a fine-grained version of Evict+Time to infer information about the asset by using the *cache flush* command [23].
5. **Repeat if needed:** These steps can be repeated to dump as much of the kernel memory as required. Theoretically, the attacker can dump the entire physical memory if he or she wishes so [23].

In any modern OS, the kernel memory can be addressed from any user process, but the processor triggers an exception if the user process does not have the permission to access the kernel memory as shown in Fig. 16.14. But due to speculation, while the exception is being processed, instructions are executed beforehand, and cause a leak in the kernel memory. Once the data is leaked, Meltdown exploits the Flush+Reload [29] technique to retrieve the stolen data from the cache [23]. Flush+Reload [29] is similar to Evict+Time [25], and uses cache-manipulation techniques. In the flush phase, the memory portion being monitored is evicted from the cache. In the wait phase of the attack, if the victim access that same memory location, the content comes back to the cache. In the reload phase, the attacker tries to access the same memory location, and if the content is in the cache, then the reload operation will take a much shorter time as compared to when the content is not in the cache. This allows the attacker to know if the right target location of the cache is flushed, and—subsequently—can infer the content of the target memory location [23].

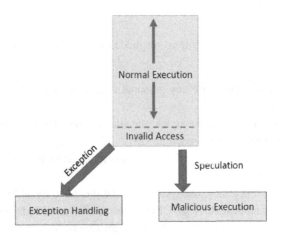

FIGURE 16.14

Meltdown vulnerability [23].

Meltdown Prime: A Variant

This is a multicore variant of the Meltdown exploit and is very similar to Spectre Prime and the original Meltdown itself [23,26]. The exploit preys on the vulnerability of the cache coherence protocols that ensure coherence among multiple cache instances of different cores. The vulnerable cache-line invalidation scheme of these protocols, along with speculation, allows the exploit to go through.

Countermeasures

Completely removing speculation and out-of-order execution is the trivial solution to the problem, but not a practical one, as speculation and out-of-order execution leads to a huge performance gain. This exploit is kind of a race between the attacker trying to retrieve sensitive information, and the processor trying to determine if the speculation was valid or not. The processor, unfortunately, takes a very long time to determine the fate of the speculative executions and it may happen that by the time speculation is validated or invalidated, around 200 instructions are already executed along the predicted path [22, 23]. If the position of the kernel space and user space in the virtual memory space can be hard fixed, then using as few as a 1-bit comparison, the processor can determine if an invalid access is going to take place. This leaves far less room for the attacker to carry out the attack, though, in fact, it may be impossible to entirely solve this class of problems. But it is important to note that these solutions are not applicable for Spectre [22,23].

Comparison Between Spectre and Meltdown

Meltdown can be only exploited currently on specific architectures, but Spectre is pervasive and affects all processors that employ speculative execution. For both Meltdown and Spectre, the attacker must be allowed to execute code in the system as an unprivileged user. Both the exploits use the inherent vulnerability that exists due to speculation and out-of-order execution. Fixing Meltdown at the software level is possible, but with high overhead. As for Spectre, even software solution is not easy to implement. Both of these vulnerabilities can greatly benefit from efficient hardware-based solutions.

16.7 HANDS-ON EXPERIMENT: SoC SECURITY POLICY
16.7.1 OBJECTIVE

This experiment is designed to help students understand components of SoC architecture, common security-critical assets in an SoC, which are accessible to constituent IP blocks, and protection mechanisms based on security policies.

16.7.2 METHOD

First, students will map a given Verilog description of a simple SoC consisting of 4-10 IP blocks, including processor core, memory, cryptomodule, and communication module. The IPs will be connected using a point-to-point interconnect framework. Students will perform functional simulation of the SoC to understand how the IPs work, and interact with each other by way of a SoC to appreciate how a key used by cryptomodule is vulnerable to unauthorized access. Next, students will design a few simple access-control security policies to safeguard the cryptokey against unauthorized access.

16.7.3 LEARNING OUTCOME

Through this experiment, students are expected to be familiar with several important notions in system level security. They are expected to understand the security issues arising from possible CIA violations on on-chip assets, and policy-based solutions to protect these assets. Finally, students can use the experience to achieve better understanding of software attacks that can lead to CIA violations, and how security policy can help to achieve robust protection.

16.7.4 ADVANCED OPTIONS

Additional exploration on this topic can be done through investigation on more complex interconnect fabric, such as bus-based or NoC-based architecture. Students may also consider adding more IP blocks, including IPs that use firmware, and mount firmware-based attacks on security assets.

More details about the experiment are available in the supplementary document. Please visit: http://hwsecuritybook.org.

16.8 EXERCISES
16.8.1 TRUE/FALSE QUESTIONS

1. Meltdown does not rely on speculative execution; it exploits only out-of-order execution.
2. Internet-of-things ecosystem cannot be attacked using any hardware-software exploit because it is too diverse for the attacker.
3. Software Trigged Hardware Trojans can be used to cause denial-of-service (DoS) attack.
4. Preventing the execution of the clflush (cache flush) command can deter all types of Rowhammer attacks.
5. During a Spectre exploit, once the processor starts to perform speculative execution, it gives the attacker theoretically unlimited amount of time to finish the attack.

6. Trusted Execution Environment can prevent DoS attacks.
7. Evict+Time requires knowledge of cache structure to properly trigger cache contention in a system.
8. Security policies no longer need to be defined when using Security Policy Enforcement Architectures.
9. Modifications to DfD are needed to maintain both security and controllability of internal signals.
10. For pre-silicon verification, formal verification can be applied on large designs.

16.8.2 SHORT-ANSWER TYPE QUESTIONS

1. What is the difference between Meltdown and Meltdown Prime?
2. What is the potential overhead if we disable out-of-order execution in an attempt to address the Spectre exploit?
3. In a 32-bit RISC architecture with 5-bit instruction opcode, what is the probability of activating a software-induced hardware Trojan with a trigger condition of 5 ADD instructions in a row?
4. Explain how ECC can sometimes deal with Rowhammer attack.
5. How can overclocking and undervolting lead to a CLKSCREW attack?
6. Which phase of SoC Verification can be used to detect side-channel attacks. Why?
7. Instead of the centralized policy engine described earlier, a designer decides to implement distributed policy enforcement (relevant security policies are described in the corresponding IP instead of a centralized engine). Describe two advantages of a centralized policy engine over a distributed one, and vice versa.
8. Which access control policies, if any, can address software induced hardware Trojans?
9. Describe an encryption method that is ideal for securing data in a DfD structure with cost-effective area overhead, and key management.
10. An attacker uses the same trigger condition from the Trojan in Question 3 Short Answer, to toggle the secure mode flag in a microprocessor with a trusted execution environment (TEE). Assess this Trojan using the DREAD method.

16.8.3 LONG-ANSWER TYPE QUESTIONS

1. Why is the Meltdown bug easier to mitigate than Spectre?
2. Describe the preventive measures that can be taken to address CLKSCREW exploit.
3. How is the Evict+Time variant of Spectre different from the standard version? Explain both methods and compare.
4. For pre-silicon verification, compare and contrast simulation and formal verification.
5. Where are the security loopholes in an IoT ecosystem? Point them out from a very high level perspective.
6. Using Fig. 16.7, what other vulnerabilities can exist in this scenario?
7. Describe the potential overhead of the Security Policy Architecture without access to the DfD infrastructure.
8. Even with thorough security policy implementation and analysis, vulnerabilities like Spectre and Meltdown still surface. Describe the potential drawbacks and complexities that exist in defining system wide security policies throughout the design process.
9. Briefly describe the security policies needed to protect the lock bit in Fig. 16.8. Explain each chosen policy with a violating scenario.

REFERENCES

[1] IBM Microelectronic, Coreconnect bus architecture, IBM White Paper Google Scholar, 1999.

[2] D. Flynn, AMBA: enabling reusable on-chip designs, IEEE Micro 17 (4) (1997) 20–27.

[3] K. Rosenfeld, R. Karri, Security-aware SoC test access mechanisms, in: VLSI Test Symposium (VTS), 2011 IEEE 29th, IEEE, 2011, pp. 100–104.

[4] S.J. Greenwald, Discussion topic: what is the old security paradigm, in: Workshop on New Security Paradigms, 1998, pp. 107–118.

[5] A. Basak, S. Bhunia, S. Ray, A flexible architecture for systematic implementation of SoC security policies, in: Proceedings of the 34th International Conference on Computer-Aided Design, 2015.

[6] A. Tang, S. Sethumadhavan, S. Stolfo, CLKSCREW: exposing the perils of security-oblivious energy management, in: 26th USENIX Security Symposium (USENIX Security 17), USENIX Association, Vancouver, BC, 2017, pp. 1057–1074.

[7] J.L. Hennessy, D.A. Patterson, Computer Architecture: A Quantitative Approach, 5th ed., Morgan Kaufmann Publishers Inc., San Francisco, CA, USA, 2011.

[8] F. Shearer, Power Management in Mobile Devices, Newnes, 2011.

[9] Qualcomm krait pmic frequency driver source code, [Online]. Available: https://android.googlesource.com/kernel/msm/+/android-msm-shamu-3.10-lollipop-mr1/drivers/clk/qcom/clock-krait.c.

[10] Qualcomm krait pmic voltage regulator driver source code, [Online]. Available: https://android.googlesource.com/kernel/msm/+/android-msm-shamu-3.10-lollipop-mr1/arch/arm/mach-msm/krait-regulator.c.

[11] M. Tunstall, D. Mukhopadhyay, S. Ali, Differential fault analysis of the advanced encryption standard using a single fault, in: C.A. Ardagna, J. Zhou (Eds.), Information Security Theory and Practice. Security and Privacy of Mobile Devices in Wireless Communication, Springer Berlin Heidelberg, Berlin, Heidelberg, 2011, pp. 224–233.

[12] M. Seaborn, T. Dullien, Exploiting the DRAM rowhammer bug to gain kernel privileges: how to cause and exploit single bit errors, BlackHat, 2015.

[13] P.K. Lala, A Single Error Correcting and Double Error Detecting Coding Scheme for Computer Memory Systems, in: Proceedings. 18th IEEE International Symposium on Defect and Fault Tolerance in VLSI Systems, 2003.

[14] Y. Kim, R. Daly, J. Kim, C. Fallin, J.H. Lee, D. Lee, C. Wilkerson, K. Lai, O. Mutlu, Flipping bits in memory without accessing them: an experimental study of dram disturbance errors, in: 2014 ACM/IEEE 41st International Symposium on Computer Architecture (ISCA), June 2014, pp. 361–372.

[15] D. Gruss, C. Maurice, S. Mangard, Rowhammer.js: a remote software-induced fault attack in JavaScript, CoRR, arXiv: 1507.06955, 2015, [Online]. Available: http://arxiv.org/abs/1507.06955.

[16] P. Pessl, D. Gruss, C. Maurice, S. Mangard, Reverse engineering Intel DRAM addressing and exploitation, CoRR, arXiv: 1511.08756, 2015, [Online]. Available: http://arxiv.org/abs/1511.08756.

[17] M. Seaborn, T. Dullien, Exploiting the DRAM rowhammer bug to gain kernel privileges, Project Zero team at Google, [Online]. Available: https://googleprojectzero.blogspot.com/2015/03/exploiting-dram-rowhammer-bug-to-gain.html, 2015.

[18] D. Gruss, C. Maurice, Rowhammer.js: a remote software-induced fault attack in JavaScript, GitHub.

[19] Semiconductor industry association (SIA), Global billings report history (3-month moving average) 1976-March 2009, [Online]. Available: http://www.sia-online.org/galleries/statistics/GSR1976-march09.xls, 2008.

[20] R.S. Chakraborty, S. Narasimhan, S. Bhunia, Hardware Trojan: threats and emerging solutions, in: 2009 IEEE International High Level Design Validation and Test Workshop, Nov 2009, pp. 166–171.

[21] X. Wang, T. Mal-Sarkar, A. Krishna, S. Narasimhan, S. Bhunia, Software exploitable hardware Trojans in embedded processor, in: 2012 IEEE International Symposium on Defect and Fault Tolerance in VLSI and Nanotechnology Systems (DFT), Oct 2012, pp. 55–58.

[22] P. Kocher, D. Genkin, D. Gruss, W. Haas, M. Hamburg, M. Lipp, S. Mangard, T. Prescher, M. Schwarz, Y. Yarom, Spectre attacks: exploiting speculative execution, ArXiv e-prints, Jan. 2018.

[23] M. Lipp, M. Schwarz, D. Gruss, T. Prescher, W. Haas, S. Mangard, P. Kocher, D. Genkin, Y. Yarom, M. Hamburg, Meltdown, ArXiv e-prints, Jan. 2018.

[24] S. Lee, M.-W. Shih, P. Gera, T. Kim, H. Kim, M. Peinado, Inferring fine-grained control flow inside SGX enclaves with branch shadowing, in: 26th USENIX Security Symposium (USENIX Security 17), USENIX Association, Vancouver, BC, 2017, pp. 557–574.

[25] D.A. Osvik, A. Shamir, E. Tromer, Cache attacks and countermeasures: the case of AES, in: D. Pointcheval (Ed.), Topics in Cryptology – CT-RSA 2006, CT-RSA 2006, in: Lecture Notes in Computer Science, vol. 3860, Springer, Berlin, Heidelberg, 2006.

[26] C. Trippel, D. Lustig, M. Martonosi, MeltdownPrime and SpectrePrime: automatically-synthesized attacks exploiting invalidation-based coherence protocols, ArXiv e-prints, Feb. 2018.

[27] Intel 64 and IAa-32 architectures software developer manual, vol 3: system programmer's guide, section 8.3, 2016.

[28] Q. Ge, Y. Yarom, G. Heiser, Do hardware cache flushing operations actually meet our expectations?, CoRR, arXiv:1612.04474, 2016, [Online]. Available: http://arxiv.org/abs/1612.04474.

[29] Y. Yarom, K. Falkner, FLUSH+RELOAD: a high resolution, low noise, l3 cache side-channel attack, in: 23rd USENIX Security Symposium (USENIX Security 14), USENIX Association, San Diego, CA, 2014, pp. 719–732.

[30] A. Basak, S. Bhunia, S. Ray, Exploiting design-for-debug for flexible SoC security architecture, in: Proceedings of the 53rd Annual Design Automation Conference, ACM, p. 167.

[31] E. Ashfield, I. Field, P. Harrod, S. Houlihane, W. Orme, S. Woodhouse, Serial Wire Debug and the Coresight Debug and Trace Architecture, ARM Ltd., Cambridge, UK, 2006.

[32] IEEE, IEEE standard test access port and boundary scan architecture, IEEE Standards 11491, 2001.

[33] J. Portillo, E. John, S. Narasimhan, Building trust in 3PIP using asset-based security property verification, in: VLSI Test Symposium (VTS), 2016, pp. 1–6.

THE HARDWARE HACKING (HaHa) PLATFORM FOR HANDS-ON TRAINING

In this Appendix, we provide details of the custom hardware module, HaHa, which is designed by the authors to perform all the hands-on experiments in a single platform. The experiments described in the book are listed in Table A.1. These experiments are designed to provide valuable practical experience on various security issues at the chip and PCB level and countermeasures for some of the major threats. More details about the experiments are available in the supplementary document. Please visit: *http://hwsecuritybook.org*.

Table A.1 Hands-on experiments described in the book

	Experiment	Expected Learning Outcome	Chapter
1	Reverse engineering attacks	*The vulnerability of PCBs to RE and cloning attacks*	4
2	Hardware Trojan attacks	*Different forms of Trojan attacks with varying triggers/payloads, and possible protection mechanisms*	5
3	Power side-channel attacks	*Leakage of the secret key from a crypto module through supply current measurement and analysis of data*	8
4	Fault injection attacks	*Leakage of the secret key from a crypto module through injection of fault*	8
5	JTAG-based attacks in PCB	*Information leakage or functional manipulation of PCB using the JTAG interface*	9
6	Bus snooping attacks	*Information retrieval from a PCB through physical access (probing of metal traces)*	11
7	Design of security primitives: (a) Physical unclonable function, (b) True random number generator	*Design philosophy and quality assessment of major security primitives*	12
8	Hardware obfuscation: (a) combinational locking, (b) finite state machine based obfuscation	*Techniques for functional and structural transformation of a design to prevent RE and evaluation of the techniques*	14
9	PCB tampering attacks (Modchip)	*Physical manipulation of PCB traces to alter their functionality*	15
10	SoC security policy	*SoC security architecture and protection for the assets*	16

The experiments use different features and configurable options provided in the HaHa platform. Students can work on this platform to understand the working principle and structure of a computer system, and ethically "hack" it at different levels. They can examine it to understand various security

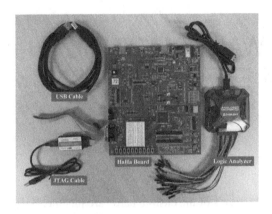

FIGURE A.1

The HaHa kit provides a unique self-contained platform for hardware security training and education. The kit is suitable for online offering of a hardware security lab course, where the students can acquire the kit from various possible sources, and perform all the experiments at home without the need for a physical lab, or special benchtop equipments.

vulnerabilities, mount attacks, and implement countermeasures. Figure A.1 depicts the HaHa board, a JTAG programming cable, a USB connector, an oscilloscope, and logic analyzer (example, Analog Discovery 2 from Digilent Inc.), which together make the HaHa kit self-contained and suitable for performing all these experiments at home without the need for any benchtop equipment, such as an oscilloscope, power supply, or waveform generator. The HaHa board needs to be interfaced with a computer's USB port. Two software modules, as described later in this Appendix, need to be installed on the computer. The HaHa kit provides a unique take-home lab for learning innards of a computer system, different aspects of hardware security issues, and associated countermeasures. Figure A.2 illustrates how these components can be connected with a computer to create the experimental platform.

FIGURE A.2

The experimental setup using the components of the HaHa kit. The HaHa board needs to be connected to a computer through its USB port for most of the experiments.

| HaHa 1.0 | HaHa 1.1 | HaHa 2 | HaHa 2S | HaHa 3.0 | HaHa 3.0 Plus |

FIGURE A.3

Design of the HaHa board has been revised over the years to improve its capability to run diverse hardware security experiments. The figure shows three generations of HaHa board and their relative sizes.

Figure A.3 shows the evolution of HaHa board over several years. It has been updated over three generations to improve students' learning experience and to augment its flexibility to run different hardware security experiments in one platform. The later is not possible with commercially available FPGA or processor development boards, or special-purpose boards, such as the Sakura side-channel attack evaluation board (http://satoh.cs.uec.ac.jp/SAKURA/link.html). These existing boards are suitable for implementing one or few experiments (for example, Trojan attacks or security primitive design in Altera/Xilinx FPGA development boards, or power side-channel attack in Sakura board), but are not amenable for implementing many others.

Students at University of Florida and Case Western Reserve University have got access to the HaHa board for the past five years in their hardware security lab courses. Figure A.4 shows students using different versions of the board to implement different parts of a computing system (for example a smart

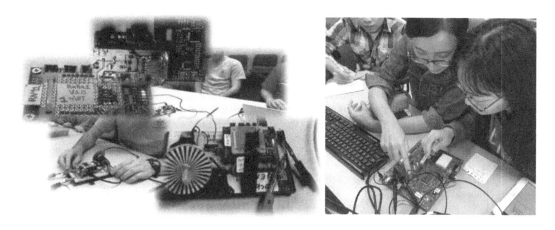

FIGURE A.4

Students in Case Western Reserve University and University of Florida work with different versions of the HaHa kit to implement models of computer systems and perform various hardware security experiments.

fan or pedometer) and then mounting diverse hardware attacks (such as, chip-/PCB-level hardware attacks), and countermeasures. The development of the board has been supported in part by United States National Science Foundation (NSF) through a grant.

The book website provides a companion material with detailed lab instructions for students to perform these experiments, make necessary observations, and write reports. Most of the experiments include advanced options, which are appropriate for students who like to explore further and are interested to perform more complex attacks and implement sophisticated countermeasures. The platform is designed with the flexibility for implementing simple models of various computing systems. Table A.2 lists the key features of the HaHa board. It includes both an FPGA (Altera MAX 10 series FPGA with embedded temperature sensor) and a microcontroller/processor (ARM or Atmel, depending on the model), along with a nonvolatile memory (EEPROM or flash), accelerometer, programmable voltage source, current sensing mechanism, JTAG connection between the FPGA and the microcontroller, instrumentation amplifier to improve signal-to-noise (SNR) ratio for side-channel measurements, and an optional socket for PCB to support experiments, such as Trojan detection and security primitive design, which involve measurements over multiple FPGA chips.

Table A.2 Select list of features of the HaHa board

Number	Feature description	Benefit for security experiments
1	The board includes both FPGA and microcontroller chips	Helps to implement diverse types of a computing systems using either of the components or both
2	FPGA and microcontroller both have embedded flash and are easily programmable via JTAG	Both devices are easy to program; FPGA can act as an accelerator for the microcontroller
3	FPGA and microcontroller communicate with the nonvolatile memory	Helps to build an independent computing system with its own memory to store configuration and input data
4	Bidirectional connection between FPGA and microcontroller	Offers various system configurations with any of them acting as the CPU, for example, microcontroller as CPU and FPGA as an accelerator
5	Connection to all peripherals through both the FPGA and the microcontroller	Offers flexibility to access any peripheral through either FPGA or microcontroller
6	Current/power monitoring for FPGA	Performs side-channel analysis and attack experiments
7	Current/power monitoring for the entire board (only available in the latest version of the HaHa board)	Offers side-channel analysis for the board and PCB authentication
8	Voltage control of FPGA using a potentiometer	Offers robustness analysis capabilities for PUF/TRNG experiments and fault injection attacks with power glitch
9	Voltage control of microcontroller using a potentiometer	Offers robustness analysis capabilities for PUF/TRNG experiments and fault injection attacks in embedded software with power glitch
10	JTAG chain for FPGA and microcontroller	Performs JTAG programming, JTAG Testing, and JTAG attack experiments
11	Two-layer board	Facilitates reverse engineering through visual inspection

(continued on next page)

Table A.2 (*continued*)

Number	Feature description	Benefit for security experiments
12	Simple layout with clearly marked regions	Provides a clear understanding of the board design and configurations, and helps to perform reverse engineering attack
13	Embedded breadboard and user headers	Allows an user to include additional components and small custom circuits in the board
14	Configurable Bluetooth module	Offers Bluetooth connection between boards to build a connected system and Bluetooth attack experiment
15	Embedded temperature sensor in the FPGA	Enables temperature-triggered Trojan attack experiment, PUF/TRNG reliability analysis and side-channel experiments
16	Plenty of configurable headers	Enables physical tampering (Modchip) attack experiment
17	Clock source and PLL inside the FPGA	Fault injection attack using the clock
18	Integration of expansion headers	Offers flexibility to add more components or sister boards to HaHa to expand its functionality
19	Multiple probing points on the buses	Enables bus snooping attack and PCB tampering experiments

Next, we describe the design of the HaHa board (Version 2) in detail and provide the schematic, layout, and bill-of-materials (BoM), so that readers who are interested to create their own HaHa kit, which requires fabrication, assembly, and testing of the custom board, can accomplish the task. Additionally, the whole kit, and its components can be individually purchased from third-party vendors. While current edition of the book includes 10 experiments as listed in Table A.1, the authors intend to add more experiments using the HaHa kit as a companion material in the future, which will be available through the book website. These new experiments are expected to cover system-level security issues and solutions, such as the timing side-channel attack, EM analysis attack, more complex forms of Trojan attacks, and additional security primitives, such as aging sensors for counterfeit IC detection. The authors expect to add these new experiments to the online companion materials within a year from the publication of this book.

A.1 HaHa BOARD

This section describes the features and design characteristics of the HaHa board in detail.

A.1.1 LAYOUT AND COMPONENTS

A photograph of the HaHa board is shown in Fig. A.5, which illustrates the configuration of the board and highlights the locations of all connectors and key components.

The following hardware components are included in the HaHa board:

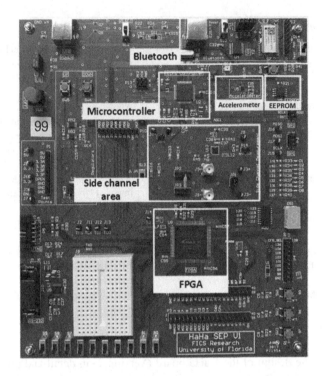

FIGURE A.5

The HaHa board (Version 2) showing the major components.

- Intel Altera MAX 10 FPGA device (with 50,000 logic elements)
- Atmel AVR 8-bit microcontroller
- JTAG header for programming the FPGA and the microcontroller
- SPI (Serial Peripheral Interface) expansion headers
- USB Type B port for programming the microcontroller
- High-performance 3-axis accelerometer
- 1 Mbit serial EEPROM memory
- Bluetooth specification v4.0 compliant Bluetooth network processor
- Adjustable regulator providing variable power source from 1.5V to 3.6V
- Two toggle switches for selecting the power source from the fixed 3.3V or the adjustable source
- 1 Ohm current sensing resistor and instrumentation amplifier
- 3 pushbutton switches
- 10 slide switches
- 8 user LEDs
- 50-MHz and an 8-MHz oscillator for clock sources
- 3 I/O pin expansion headers
- 7 segment display
- Photodiode

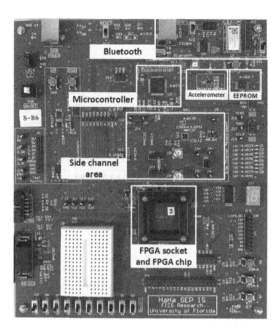

FIGURE A.6

Version of the HaHa board with a socket for the FPGA chip.

An alternative version of the HaHa board (shown in Fig. A.6) is developed with a socket for the FPGA. The socket is for the 144-pin Intel Altera MAX 10 FPGA, and the chip can be inserted or taken off the socket very easily. The socket is surface-mounted on the board with all other components and configurations remaining unchanged. With this version of the board, users can perform certain experiments that require multiple FPGA chips, for example, Trojan detection or the security primitive (PUF/TRNG) design experiments. These experiments often require multiple measurements of some physical parameters (such as, static or dynamic supply current, signal propagation delay) over a number of chips to evaluate the impact of process variations, environmental parameter (such as, power supply noise or temperature) variations, and aging.

A.1.2 BLOCK DIAGRAM OF THE HaHa BOARD

Figure A.7 shows the block diagram of HaHa board. Two major components of the board are the FPGA and the microcontroller. These chips are interconnected with the JTAG chain. They can be programmed and tested using the JTAG interface. Additionally, they are connected through a 9-bit bus. One of the bus lines can be used as the clock. In that case, it becomes an 8-bit bus with a clock.

Figure A.7 also shows the chips' peripheral functions. Multiple serial peripheral interface (SPI) devices can be connected to the microcontroller using the SPI interface. The SPI devices include an accelerometer, a nonvolatile memory (EEPROM or flash), and a Bluetooth module. Two additional

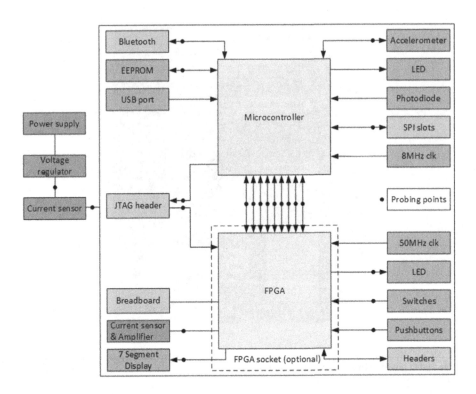

FIGURE A.7

Block diagram of the HaHa board.

SPI slots are provided that allow more chips, or sister boards with SPI interface to be connected to the board.

The FPGA, which comes with more I/O pins than the microcontroller, enables connections to a larger number peripheral devices. These peripheral devices include slide switches, push buttons, LEDs, a 7-segment display, and user expansion headers.

All of the peripherals are accessible by both chips. For example, when the FPGA wants to communicate with the on-board accelerometer, it can use the microcontroller as the medium to talk to the accelerometer. If a user wants to control the microcontroller with a switch, the FPGA can be programmed to work as the medium. Therefore, both chips can talk to any peripheral device on the board, and hence, act as the central processing unit (CPU) of a computing system that can be built on the HaHa board.

The board has well-defined configurable user expansion ports, which make it very flexible to meet a user's needs. It is equipped with three user expansion headers that are connected to the FPGA, two SPI slots that are connected to the SPI interface of the microcontroller, and a breadboard that can be used to mount other chips and implement a user's custom circuit. These headers, slots, and the breadboard use standard components, and are compatible with connectors, wires, and chips that are not included in the HaHa board.

Users can also reconfigure the ways that the chips are connected to each other. There are several accessible pins available to the users for the two main chips. In addition, other peripherals, such as the Bluetooth module, have multiple pins capable of reconfiguration. The users of the board have the freedom to change the way that the components talk to, and work with, each other. Later, we provide some examples to show how the board can be configured to perform different experiments for hardware security education and research.

Two or more HaHa boards can be connected using wire or wireless connection mechanism in various configurations to build a connected system. The headers, probing points, and breadboards make it possible to connect two boards using jumpers and wires. On the other hand, the Bluetooth module enables each HaHa board to communicate and control another. The ability to reconfigure the HaHa boards into a connected system offers a vast number of experimental options for users.

A.1.3 COMPONENTS OF HaHa

In this section, we provide information on each major component of the board.

- Altera 10M50SAE144C8G FPGA
  - 50k logic elements
  - 1638k M9k memory
  - 5888Kb user flash memory
  - 101 user I/O pins
  - 4 PLLs
  - 1 ADC with a temperature sensor
  - Boundary-scan capabilities according to the JTAG standard
- Atmel ATmega16U4-au microcontroller
  - 16KB of in-system self-programmable flash
  - 1.25KB internal SRAM
  - Boundary-scan capabilities according to the JTAG standard
  - USB 2.0 full-speed/low-speed device module
  - SPI serial programmable
- EEPROM
  - 256-byte page
  - Built-in write protection
  - 6 ms max. write cycle time
- JTAG header
  - On-board header for programming both the FPGA and microcontroller
- SPI header
  - On-board header for programming the microcontroller
  - Offers expansion slots for add-on SPI modules
- USB B port
  - On-board USB B port for programming the microcontroller
  - Provide power source for the board
- High-performance 3-axis accelerometer
  - SPI digital output interface
  - 8-bit data output

- Motion detection
- Embedded temperature sensor
- Embedded First-in, first-out (FIFO)
- Bluetooth processor
  - Bluetooth v4.0 compliant
  - SPI based application controller interface
  - AES security co-processor
- Adjustable regulator
  - Provides a flexible power source ranging from 1.5V to 3.6V
  - 64 steps resolution
  - 500 mA current capability
  - Two push-buttons control to increase or decrease the voltage
- 2 slide switches to select between power sources
  - Select from fixed 3.3V and adjustable source
  - When the switch is "OFF", the supply power source is fixed 3.3V
  - When the switch is "ON", the supply power source is the adjustable voltage source (1.5V to 3.6V)
- Current sensing resistor
  - 1 Ohm resistance
  - 0.5% tolerance
  - 20A maximum current
  - Instrumentation amplifier incorporated into the power supply lines across the sense resistors
  - Sense resistor placed between the decoupling capacitors and the supply pins to maintain high-frequency components in dynamic current
- Pushbutton switches
  - 3 pushbutton switches
  - Denouncing switch
- Slide switches
  - 10 slide switches
  - A switch causes logic 0 when in the ON (Left) position and logic 1 when in the OFF (Right) position
- LEDs
  - 8 LEDs connected to the FPGA
  - 1 Red LED connected to the microcontroller
  - The Red LED can be controlled by an 8-bit timer/counter with PWM (Pulse Width Modulator)
- Clock inputs
  - 8-MHz oscillator for the microcontroller
  - 50-MHz oscillator for the FPGA
  - The microcontroller shares its clock through chip interconnection
  - Both the chips have internal clocks
- Two I/O pin expansion headers
  - Connected to the I/O pins of the FPGA
  - Has 40 pins and 20 pins respectively
- 7 segment display

- One 7 segment display connected to the FPGA
- Photodiode
  - One photodiode connected to the ADC (analog-to-digital converter) pin of the microcontroller
  - Peak optical wavelength 890 nm
- Breadboard
  - Double-sided tape with 170 tie-points

A.2 OPERATION INSTRUCTIONS

In this section, we provide instructions on using the HaHa board to perform various experiments.

A.2.1 POWERING UP THE HaHa BOARD

A USB Type A to B cable is included with the HaHa kit. It connects the HaHa board to computer or USB power port. One should perform the following steps to power up the board.

1. Ensure the power ON/OFF switch on the HaHa board is in the OFF position and 4 stands on the 4 corners are properly mounted. Place the board on a stable flat surface; make sure there are no conductive paths underneath the board to ground that may cause an electrical short-circuit.
2. Select the power source for the FPGA and the microcontroller. Turn OFF both selection switches to direct the power source to fixed 3.3V. Turn OFF the reset switch for the microcontroller.
3. Plug in the USB cable's Type-B port into the board and Type-A port into a computer's USB port.
4. Turn on the power ON/OFF switch. A red LED will light up to indicate the power is on.

A.2.2 INSTALL SOFTWARE MODULES IN THE COMPUTER

Altera Quartus software (edition 15 or later) needs to be installed on the computer. The Quartus Lite edition is a free version of the tool available for download from Altera's official website. You also need to install the Atmel Studio (Version 7 or later) on your computer. This software is available for free to download from the official website of Microchip.

A.2.3 CONFIGURING THE ALTERA MAX 10 FPGA

The HaHa kit includes a USB-Blaster Download Cable as shown in Fig. A.8, which can be used to program the Altera MAX 10 FPGA. One side of the USB-Blaster needs to be connected to a computer's USB Port, and the other side needs to be connected to the JTAG 10-pin header on the board.

Secure the 10-pin female connector (Fig. A.9) and the JTAG header on the HaHa board. Connect the marked pin numbers on the HaHa board accordingly. Note: the red wire in the band is for pin 1.

After connecting the USB-Blaster Download Cable into the HaHa board and a computer, locate the 2 chips in the JTAG chain on the board (the FPGA and the microcontroller). In the program window of Altera Quartus (Fig. A.10), "Auto Detect" can be used to detect two devices: the FPGA and the microcontroller. Replace the FPGA with the SOF-file that you made, then you can start programming the FPGA.

FIGURE A.8

Altera USB-Blaster Download Cable.

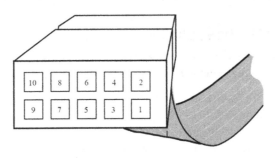

FIGURE A.9

10-pin female connector.

Note: The FPGA will lose all the configurations after it is powered off. Hence, you need to reprogram it when the board is powered-up again.

A.2.4 CONFIGURING THE MICROCONTROLLER THROUGH THE USB PORT

The Atmel AVR microcontroller ATmega16U4-au can be configured in various ways, including JTAG, SPI, and USB. The JTAG and SPI methods require a separate component, namely, the Atmel Debugger, that is not included with the HaHa board.

Note: To obtain more information about programming the AVR microcontroller using different kinds of debuggers, visit the MicroChip/Atmel website.

You can directly program the 16-KB in-system self-programmable flash through the USB port. After powering-up the HaHa board, it should detect the microcontroller in the Atmel Studio. Open the device programming window as shown in Fig. A.11. Secure the microcontroller to verify that it is connecting with the computer. The device signature can be read, and the whole chip can be erased using the interface.

Configure the programmable flash by selecting the HEX-file you generated, and clicking the program button.

Note: The content of the flash will not be erased after the power is OFF. Therefore, you can use the same function multiple times until you reset the chip by turning on the reset switch. Moreover,

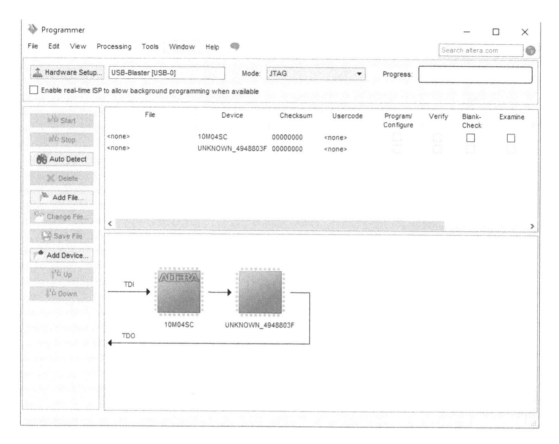

FIGURE A.10

Program window of Altera Quartus, showing that the FPGA and the microcontroller are autodetected.

the program may not run correctly immediately after programming is finished. You need to power the board OFF, and then ON, to make the programmed functions work.

Due to this feature, when you need to program both the microcontroller and the FPGA, always program the microcontroller first, power OFF and ON the board, and then program the FPGA.

A.2.5 CONFIGURING THE VOLTAGE SOURCE

Both then FPGA and the microcontroller need a 3.3V power supply. The HaHa board provides two voltage sources: a fixed 3.3V and an adjustable voltage. The FPGA and the microcontroller have a corresponding slide switch to select the voltage source.

Most often you will need the fixed 3.3V voltage source to obtain the best chip performance. Therefore, please make sure you turn OFF both select switches before you powerup the HaHa board. When you are doing certain experiments that require changing the voltage level, such as the fault injection or

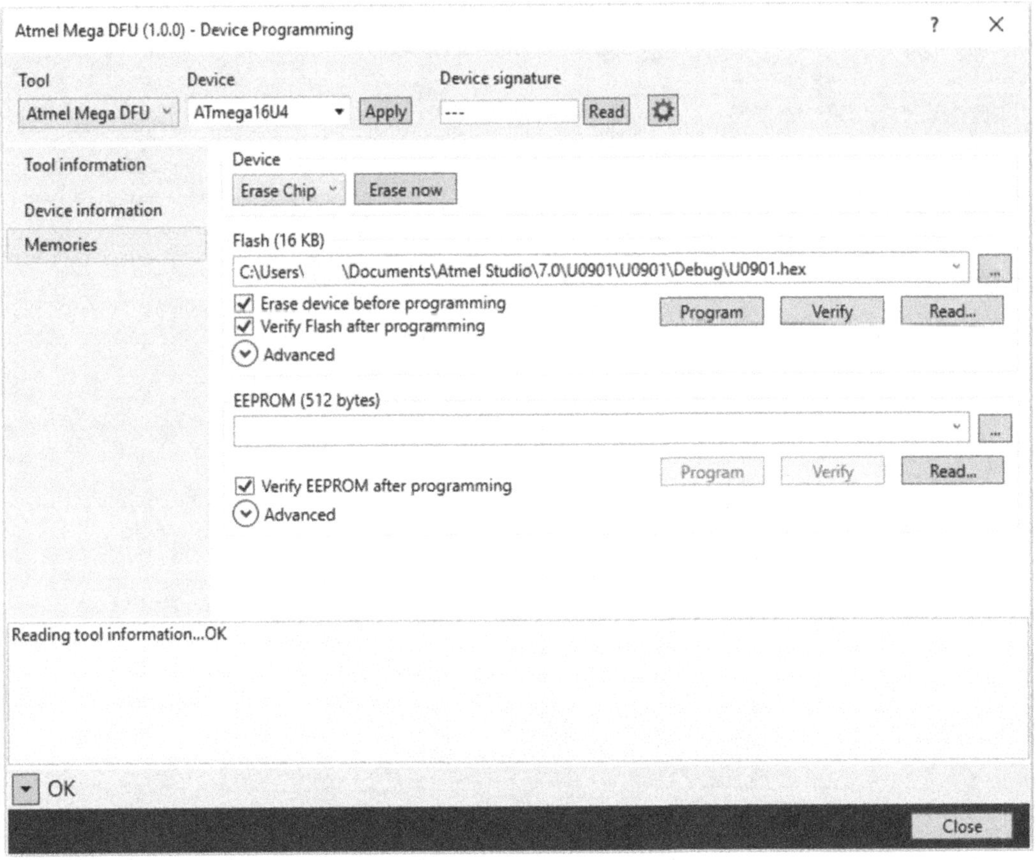

FIGURE A.11

Atmel Studio Device Programming window. It shows that the microcontroller is detected.

the PUF experiment (for reliability assessment of a PUF design), you may need to use the adjustable voltage source. For these experiments, turn on the voltage source selection switch before you powerup the board.

The adjustable voltage has a range from 1.5V to 3.6V. You can control the voltage level by pressing two buttons: SWup and SWdown. There is a total of 64 voltage steps. The regulator can store the voltage value when the power is OFF. It is recommended that every time you finish using the adjustable voltage source, set the voltage back to 3.3V (i.e., the nominal voltage) before you poweroff the board.

A.2.6 CHIP INTERCONNECTIONS

There are, in total, 9 possible interconnections on the board between the two major chips (the FPGA and the microcontroller).

Table A.3 Interconnection between FPGA and microcontroller

Signal Name	Microcontroller Pin No.	FPGA Pin No.	Function
CM0	PD0	29	Data
CM1	PD1	27	Data
CM2	PD2	36	Data
CM3	PD3	25	Data
CM4	PD4	22	Data
CM5	PD5	23	Data
CM6	PD6	21	Data
CM7	PD7	20	Data
CLK_inter	PC7	28	Data or clock

Their pin numbers and functions are listed in Table A.3.

The two chips can communicate through the interconnection fabric to all the devices on the HaHa board. For example, if the microcontroller wants to control the 7-segment display, even though the 7-segment display is not directly connected to it, the FPGA can be configured as an interface connecting the microcontroller and the 7-segment display, so that microcontroller can access it.

A.2.7 USING THE SWITCHES AND LEDs

The HaHa board provides 3 pushbutton switches, 8 slide switches (sliders), and 8 LEDs, all connecting to the FPGA. There is only one LED connected to the microcontroller.

For the 3 pushbutton switches connected to the FPGA, each one provides a low logic level (0 volts) when it is not pressed, and provides a high logic level (3.3 volts) when pressed. Table A.4 lists the corresponding pin numbers on the FPGA.

Table A.4 Pushbutton switch pin number list

Signal Name	FPGA Pin No.	Description
SW1	93	Pushbutton [1]
SW2	96	Pushbutton [2]
SW3	97	Pushbutton [3]

The 8 slide switches on the HaHa board are not debounced and are intended for use as level-sensitive data inputs to a circuit. Each switch is connected directly to a pin on the FPGA. When a switch is ON, it provides a low logic level (0 volts) to the FPGA, and when it is OFF, it provides a high logic level (3.3 volts). Table A.5 lists the pin numbers connected to the switches.

There are 8 user-controllable LEDs on the HaHa board. Each LED is driven directly by a pin on the FPGA; driving its associated pin to high logic level turns the LED on, and driving the pin to low logic level turns the LED off. Table A.6 lists the pin numbers connected to the LEDs.

Table A.5 Slide switches pin number list

Signal Name	FPGA Pin No.	Description
S0	44	Slide Switch [0]
S1	43	Slide Switch [1]
S2	42	Slide Switch [2]
S3	41	Slide Switch [3]
S4	40	Slide Switch [4]
S5	39	Slide Switch [5]
S6	38	Slide Switch [6]
S7	33	Slide Switch [7]
S8	32	Slide Switch [8]
S9	30	Slide Switch [9]

Table A.6 User LED pin number list

Signal Name	FPGA Pin No.	Description
D1	141	LED [1]
D2	140	LED [2]
D3	135	LED [3]
D4	133	LED [4]
D5	132	LED [5]
D6	131	LED [6]
D7	129	LED [7]
D8	127	LED [8]

A.2.8 USING THE 7-SEGMENT DISPLAY

The HaHa board includes one 7-segment display. As indicated in Fig. A.12, the seven segments are connected to different pins on the FPGA. Applying a low logic level to a segment causes it to light up. On the contrary, applying a high logic level turns it off.

Each segment in the display is identified by an index from **a** to **g**, with the corresponding position shown in Fig. A.12. In addition, the decimal point is identified as DP. Table A.7 shows the connections between the FPGA pins to the 7-segment display.

A.2.9 USING THE EXPANSION HEADERS

The HaHa board provides 3 expansion headers. Two of them have 40 pins, and one has 20 pins. There is a total of 52 FPGA input-output (I/O) pins connected to the header pins.

A.2.10 CLOCK CIRCUITRY

The HaHa board includes a 50 MHz clock signal for the FPGA, and an 8 MHz clock signal for the microcontroller.

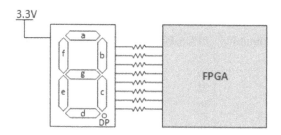

FIGURE A.12

Connections between the 7-segment display and the FPGA.

Table A.7 Pin assignments for the 7-segment display		
Display Index	**Signal Name**	**FPGA Pin No.**
a	D11	123
b	D12	120
c	D13	119
d	D14	118
e	D15	117
f	D16	116
g	D17	111
DP	D18	110

The clock connected to the FPGA is used for clocking the user logic. In addition, the clock input is connected to the phase-locked loops (PLL) clock input pin of the FPGA. The user can use the clock as a source clock for the PLL circuit.

As mentioned in Section A.2.6, there is a chip interconnection that can also be used as the clock source for the FPGA. The I/O pin will output clock signal for the FPGA when the user configures the microcontroller. The reconfiguration will enable the two chips to be synchronized to the same clock.

Various I/O pins on the FPGA can be used as the clock input pin. I/O pins connected to the expansion header can connect to external clock signals, if needed.

Pins that can be used as external clock inputs are listed in Table A.8.

A.2.11 USING SPI DEVICES

There are three SPI devices that can work as an SPI slave, controlled by the microcontroller: an EEP-ROM, an accelerometer, and a Bluetooth processor. There are also two SPI slots on the HaHa board. Users can connect more devices to the microcontroller through the slots.

Note: SPI pin names–MISO, MOSI, SCK and SS′ are the names used by AVRs. Other devices may use a different set of names. Check the datasheet of the particular device you are using to learn the SPI pin names.

The SPI setup: the microcontroller has three simultaneous slaves. Users can select which slave to communicate by asserting the SS′ (Slave Select) pin of the slave devices. The I/O pins used for slave

FPGA Clock Input Pin	FPGA Pin No.	Signal Name	Function Description
CLK0n	25	CM3	Chip interconnection
CLK0p	26	CM2	Chip interconnection
CLK1n	27	CM1	Chip interconnection
CLK1p	28	CLK_inter	Chip interconnection
CLK6n	51	H_A_2	Expansion header pin
CLK6p	52	H_B_3	Expansion header pin
CLK7n	53	H_A_3	Expansion header pin
CLK7p	55	H_B_4	Expansion header pin
CLK2n	88	CLK_50M	50 MHz clock source
CLK2p	89	H_B_17	Expansion header pin
CLK3n	90	H_2B_17	Expansion header pin
CLK3p	91	H_2B_18	Expansion header pin

Table A.8 FPGA clock input pins and their connections

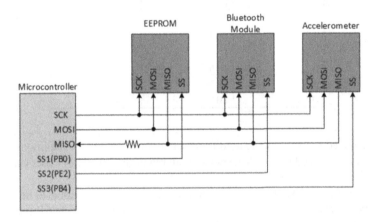

FIGURE A.13

Setup used with SPI interface on the HaHa board.

selection is shown in Fig. A.13. When selecting one of the slaves to communicate, assert the SS' signal of that slave device by setting it Low. In order to avoid conflict, SS' for other devices must be set to High. Note that the microcontroller can only communicate with one SPI device at a time.

When using the SPI devices, please refer to their datasheets. Carefully read and write data from the correct addresses. Note that writing to reserved addresses of an SPI device may cause permanent damage to the device. Some addresses that contain the factory calibration values should not be changed.

Figure A.14 shows the SPI slot pin configurations. A user can incorporate additional SPI devices by connecting corresponding pins to the slot. He/she can also use it as locations to probe signals on the board.

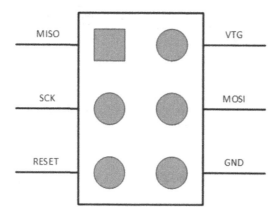

FIGURE A.14

SPI header pin location.

A.2.12 SIDE-CHANNEL MEASUREMENT

There is a dedicated area as shown in Fig. A.15A designed for side-channel (example, power or current) measurement on the board. A precise 1 Ohm current sensing resistor is mounted between the FPGA and the power supply source. By measuring the voltage drop across the resistor, the current which represents the power consumption can be obtained. SubMiniature version A (SMA) connectors are also provided.

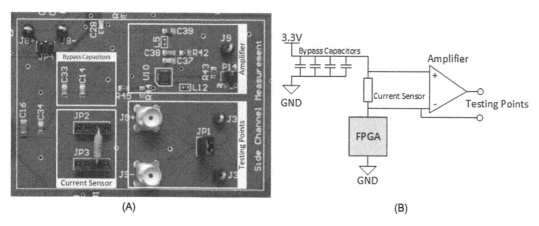

FIGURE A.15

(A) Side-channel measurement area on the HaHa board; (B) The schematic diagram showing two measurement options: with or without amplification.

The side-channel measurement circuit integrates an instrumentation amplifier. It can amplify the voltage difference across the current-sensing resistor by four times. The bandwidth of the part is as high as 2.4 GHz. The voltage drop can be measured either across the sense resistor or across the amplifier. The latter provides an increased SNR, as shown in Fig. A.15B.

A.3 EXAMPLES FOR PROGRAMMING THE FPGA AND THE MICROCONTROLLER

This section provides a number of example circuits and codes, which can be mapped into the FPGA and microcontroller chips, respectively. These circuits/codes are intended to serve as practice runs before the actual experiments are performed. The examples are designed to demonstrate some of the basic features of the board, such as, operation of the output LEDs and input switches. The source codes (Verilog and Assembly code) are provided for each demonstration.

A.3.1 PROGRAMMING THE FPGA

A.3.1.1 A Counter Implemented in the FPGA

Implementing a simple circuit into the FPGA: the module maps a 4-bit up counter into the FPGA, and connects it to 3 inputs and 1 output. One input works as the clock, one resets the output to 0000, and the other input enables counting. The output is a 4-bit binary number representing the value counted. Therefore, 1 clock source, 2 switches, and 4 LEDs will be used. The steps are as follows:

1. Create a new project in Quartus. Select the right device that the HaHa board uses, which is 10M50SAE144C8G, as shown in Fig. A.16.

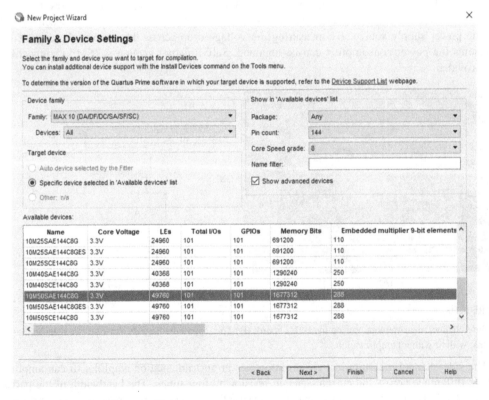

FIGURE A.16

Selecting the device on the HaHa board.

2. Create a new Verilog hardware description language (HDL) file and add it to the project. Create the up counter module in the v-file. The code is given below. The code contains two modules: the up counter module and a sub-module, which is a frequency divider. This example uses a 50 MHz clock source, which is considerably faster than a human eye can observe the counted values. Hence, the frequency divider makes the frequency of count operation much slower. Type in the code, then perform analysis and elaboration of the code.

Verilog Code

```verilog
module up_counter(clk, reset, enable, out);
    input clk; //clock input for the counter: 50MHz
    input reset; //reset the output to be 0000
    input enable; //enable signal
    output reg [3:0] out; //4-bit output
    wire clk_slow; //a divided clock

    always @(posedge clk_slow) begin
        if (reset) out=4'b0000;
        else if (enable) out=out+4'b0001;
    end

    f_divider U0 (.clk(clk),.clkout(clk_slow));//sub module frequency divider instantiated
endmodule

/* Below is the frequency divider submodule that makes the clock frequency slower, so that LED output can be
observed clearly.*/

module f_divider(clk, clkout);
    input clk; //clock input
    output reg clkout; //divided clock output
    reg [25:0] cnt; //26-bit register

    always @(posedge clk) begin
        cnt=cnt+1;
        if (cnt==26'b00111110101111000010000000)
            begin
                clkout=~clkout;
                cnt=26'b0;
            end
    end
endmodule
```

3. Assign signals to the right pins. Open the pin planner window as shown in Fig. A.17. Assign the signals to the right location according to the HaHa user manual.

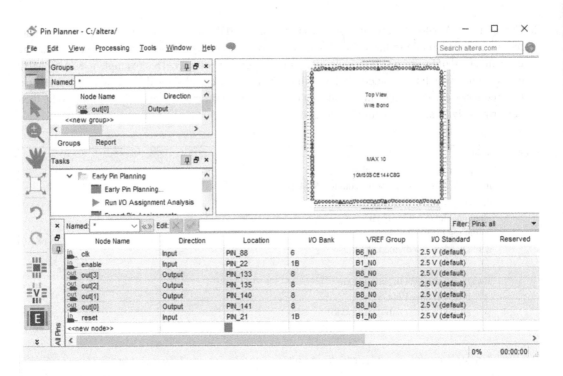

FIGURE A.17

Pin planner window in Quartus.

4. Start compilation. When finished, the SOF-file will be created. This file is a representation of the FPGA bitstream produced by the vendor tool.
5. Open the programmer window. Use the SOF-file to program the FPGA.

A.3.1.2 Arithmetic and Logic Unit

This example shows mapping of a simple arithmetic-logic unit (ALU) into the FPGA. The ALU has two 4-bit inputs **a** and **b**, and one 2-bit function selection input **sel**. The ALU performs various operations according to different input values at the function selection input.

Selection bits	Function (o)
00	a plus b
01	a multiply b (only the least 4 bits)
10	a AND b (bitwise)
11	an OR b (bitwise)

Input ports can be used to provide the operands and selection bits. Switches and buttons on the HaHa board can be used for this purpose. The outputs can be displayed on four LEDs.

Using Verilog HDL, the ALU can be described in several ways, such as using 'case' statement, as shown in the example code below.

Verilog Code

```
module alu(a, b, sel, o);
    input [3:0] a, b;
    input [1:0] sel;
    output reg [3:0] o;

    always @(a or b) begin
        case (sel)
            2'b00: o = a + b;
            2'b01: o = a * b;
            2'b10: o = a & b;
            2'b11: o = a | b;
            default: o = a + b;
        endcase
    end

endmodule
```

After compilation, use pin planner to assign the I/O ports to suitable pins of the FPGA, as shown in Fig. A.18.

Node Name	Direction	Location
in a[3]	Input	PIN_21
in a[2]	Input	PIN_22
in a[1]	Input	PIN_23
in a[0]	Input	PIN_25
in b[3]	Input	PIN_26
in b[2]	Input	PIN_27
in b[1]	Input	PIN_29
in b[0]	Input	PIN_30
out o[3]	Output	PIN_141
out o[2]	Output	PIN_140
out o[1]	Output	PIN_135
out o[0]	Output	PIN_133
in sel[1]	Input	PIN_85
in sel[0]	Input	PIN_86

FIGURE A.18

ALU pin plan.

Verify that the function is implemented correctly by generating the FPGA bitstream file and programming the FPGA.

A.3.1.3 Finite State Machine

A finite-state machine (FSM) or simply a state machine is a mathematical model of computation used to realize sequential logic circuits. It represents an abstract machine that can perform transition through a finite number of states, and is typically used to implement control circuits in a design.

Example: One of the University of Florida parking lots has only one entrance gate and it can accommodate only 10 cars. Only one car can pass through the entrance gate (either exit or enter at a time). Two light sensors, separated by 1 meter, detect whether the car is entering or exiting. A sign to indicate if the parking lot is FULL or FREE is positioned at the entrance.

Verilog Code

```
module parking_lot_controller (clk, rstn, sense0, sense1, sign_full, sign_free);

    // maximum number of cars in the lot at once
    parameter max_cars = 10;

    // sense0 and sense1 are the two light sensors: sense0 is "outside" sensor (closer to outside)
    // and sense1 is "inside" sensor (closer to inside)
    // we assume they are active low, e.g., "on" when the light beam is broken and output is 0

    input clk, rstn, sense0, sense1;
    output sign_full, sign_free;

    integer cars_in_lot;
    reg [3:0] state;

    // we assume that to enter, sense0 is broken first, followed by both sense0 and sense1
    // as they are only 1 meter apart, and finally only sense1.

    assign sign_full = (cars_in_lot >= max_cars)? 1'b1: 1'b0;
    assign sign_free = ~sign_full;

    always @ (posedge clk or negedge rstn) begin
        if (rstn == 1'b0) begin
            cars_in_lot = 0;
            state = 4'b0000;
        end
        else begin
            // this state should
            if (state == 4'b0000) begin
                if (sense0 == 1'b0 && sense1 == 1'b1) begin // incoming cars
                    state = 4'b0001;
                end
                else if (sense0 == 1'b1 && sense1 == 1'b0) begin //exiting cars
                    state = 4'b0100;
                end
                else begin // continue to wait for a car
                    state = 4'b0000;
```

```verilog
            end
    end
    else if (state == 4'b0001) begin // incoming car
        // car is still crossing outside sensor
        if (sense0 == 1'b0 && sense1 == 1'b1) begin
            state = 4'b0001;
        end
        // car has crossed both sensors
        else if (sense0 == 1'b0 && sense1 == 1'b0) begin
            state = 4'b0010;
        end
        // something else happened (e.g. car has just pulled in, but left before entering)
        else begin
            state = 4'b0000; // return to init state without changing count
        end
    end
    else if (state == 4'b0010) begin // car crossed both sensors on its way in
        // car is still crossing threshold
        if (sense0 == 1'b0 && sense1 == 1'b0) begin
            state = 4'b0010;
        end
        // car has finished crossing outside sensor, and is passing inside sensor
        else if (sense0 == 1'b1 && sense1 == 1'b0) begin
            state = 4'b0011;
        end
        // something else happened (e.g. car left without entering)
        else begin
            state = 4'b0000;
        end
    end
    else if (state == 4'b0011) begin // car has finally entered; increment count and go to initial state
        cars_in_lot = cars_in_lot + 1;
        state = 4'b0000;
        $display("Car has entered lot (%2d total).", cars_in_lot);
    end
    else if (state == 4'b0100) begin // exiting car
        // car is still crossing inside sensor
        if (sense0 == 1'b1 && sense1 == 1'b0) begin
            state = 4'b0100;
        end
        // car has crossed both sensors
        else if (sense0 == 1'b0 && sense1 == 1'b0) begin
            state = 4'b1000;
        end
```

```
                    // something else happened (e.g. car has just pulled in, but left before entering)
                    else begin
                         state = 4'b0000; // return to init state without changing count
                    end
               end
               else if (state == 4'b1000) begin
                    // car is still crossing threshold
                    if (sense0 == 1'b0 && sense1 == 1'b0) begin
                         state = 4'b1000;
                    end
                    // car has finished crossing inside sensor, and is passing outside sensor
                    else if (sense0 == 1'b0 && sense1 == 1'b1) begin
                         state = 4'b1100;
                    end
                    // something else happened (e.g. car left without entering)
                    else begin
                         state = 4'b0000;
                    end
               end
               else if (state == 4'b1100) begin // car has finally exited; decrement count and go to initial state
                    cars_in_lot = cars_in_lot - 1;
                    state = 4'b0000;
                    $display ("Car has exited lot (%2d total).", cars_in_lot);
               end
               else begin // otherwise something went wrong - go back to init state
                    state = 4'b0000;
               end
          end
     end
endmodule
```

State Diagram:

Go to Tools → Netlist Viewer → State Machine Viewer to verify if the designed FSM fulfills the specifications.

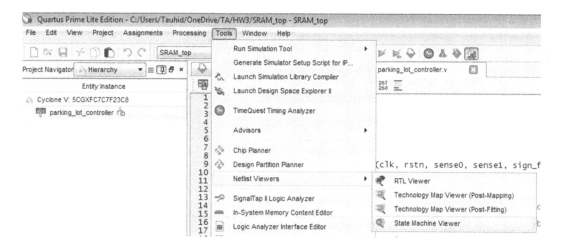

Simulation:

Go to New → University Program VWF → Edit → Insert → Insert Node or Bus → Node Finder → list → Select all → Insert values for the inputs → Simulation.

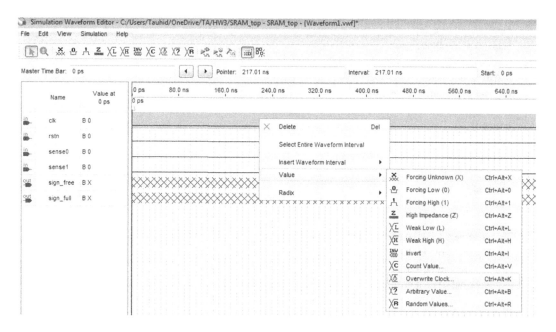

A.3.1.4 Read-Write Operation of an SRAM

The following Verilog code can be used to read (write) data from (to) an SRAM array. This operation reads or writes 8-bit data.

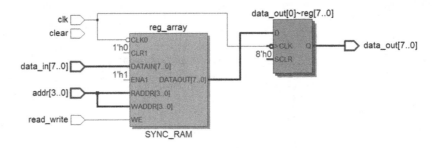

Verilog Code for SRAM read-write operation

```verilog
module SRAM_top(clk, addr, read_write, clear, data_in, data_out);
parameter n = 4;
parameter w = 8;

input clk, read_write, clear;
input [n-1:0] addr;
input [w-1:0] data_in;
output reg [w-1:0] data_out;

// Start module here!
reg [w-1:0] reg_array [2**n-1:0];

integer i;
initial begin
    for( i = 0; i < 2**n; i = i + 1 ) begin
        reg_array[i] <= 0;
    end
end

always @(negedge(clk)) begin
    if( read_write == 1 )
        reg_array[addr] <= data_in;
    data_out = reg_array[addr];
end
endmodule
```

A.3.2 PROGRAMMING THE MICROCONTROLLER

A.3.2.1 *Counter Programmed in the Microcontroller*

This tutorial programs a simple counter into the microcontroller. The function is similar to that of the circuit described in Section A.3.1, except that this time it is carried out in relation to the microcontroller. Since the microcontroller is not connected to many switches, and LEDs, due to its I/O pin limitation, it gets access to the peripherals through the FPGA, which works as an interface between them. The steps are described below:

1. Open the Atmel Studio software and create a new AVR assembler project. Select ATmega16U4, which is the right device.
2. Type in code in the ASM-file.

Assembly Code

```
    .include "m16u4def.inc"
    .org 0
    rjmp main

main:
    ;configure PD0 to PD3 to be output pins and configure PD4 to PD7 to be input pins:
    ldi r16, 0b00001111
    out DDRD, r16

    ldi r17, 0x00 ;reset register r17 to be 0x00

loop:
    sbic PIND, 4 ;skip the next line if enable not asserted
    inc r17 ;increase the value of r17 by 1

    sbrc r17,4 ;skip the next line if value isn't bigger than 00010000
    ldi r17, 0x00 ;clear the counter value
    sbis PIND, 5 ;skip the next line if reset not asserted
    ldi r17, 0x00 ;reset the value to be 0
    out PORTD, r17 ;output the value to the IO ports
    call delay ; slow down so human eyes can see the values clearly
    rjmp loop
;the code below is to delay the program by letting it count
delay:
    ldi r23, 0x00
delay_inc:
    call delay1
    inc r23
    sbrs r23, 7
    rjmp delay_inc
```

```
    ret
delay1:
    ldi r24, 0x00
delay1_inc:
    inc r24
    sbrs r24, 7
    rjmp delay1_inc
    ret
```

3. Build the project. A HEX-file will be created once the project is built.
4. Program the microcontroller with the HEX-file as shown in Fig. A.19.

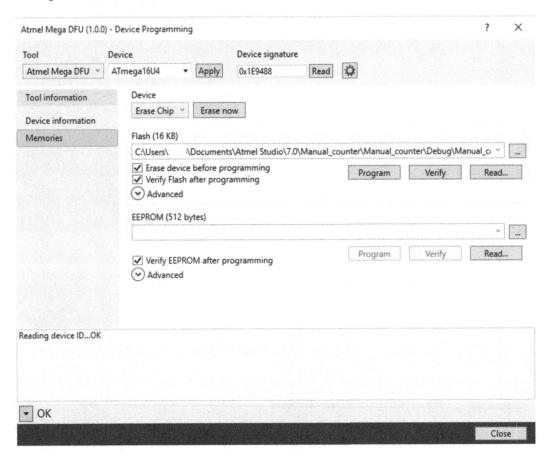

FIGURE A.19

Microcontroller programming window.

5. Power the HaHa board OFF and On. Program the FPGA so that 4 LEDs are directly connected to the microcontroller's I/O pins PD0 to PD3. Two switches are directly connected to the microcontroller's I/O pins PD4 and PD5. This will require repeating the steps in Section A.3.1, but with different code.

A.3.2.2 Light Up a LED Through an I/O Port

The user has to configure the pin first before using an I/O port. Each port pin consists of three register bits: DDxn, PORTxn, and PINxn. The DDxn bit in the DDRx register selects the direction of this pin. If DDxn is written logic one, Pxn is configured as an output pin. If DDxn is written logic zero, Pxn is configured as an input pin.

In the HaHa board, there is a red LED connected to PORTB7. Therefore, configure this port as output using code:

    sbi DDRB, 7

Make the 7th bit of PORTB to be "1" to produce a high level on that port:

    sbi PORTB, 7

Finish the program by entering into an endless loop:

    Loop: rjmp loop

The program code is shown below.

Assembly Code

```
    .include "m16u4def.inc"
    .org 0
    rjmp main

main:
    sbi DDRB, 7
    sbi PORTB, 7

loop:
    rjmp loop
```

A.3.2.3 Make the LED Blink

The LED will blink when the I/O port toggles between 1 and 0. The I/O can output a low level by writing the code:

    cbi PORTB, 7

One cannot see the LED blink if the LED blinks at the frequency of the chip's internal clock. To slow it down, a delay can be inserted.

A delay function can be created by making a working register count in a loop, and the program jumps out of the loop when the register counts to a certain value. The delay function can be written as:

```
delay:
      ldi r23, 0x00
delay_inc:
      inc r23
      sbrs r23, 7
      rjmp delay_inc
      ret
```

In the beginning of the delay function, the value of the working register r23 is initialized to 0x00 by using ldi instruction. Then, its value is increased by one, by using INC instruction. The program will jump back to the label delay INC, until the 7th bit of r23 is set to 1. Here, the function of SBRS is to check the value of the 7th bit of register r23. When the bit value is 1, the following instructions will be skipped. The code of the whole program is given below.

Note: The delay time provided in this program is still not long enough for human eyes to see it clearly. Users can make the delay longer by calling another delay in the delay loop.

Assembly Code

```
     .include "m16u4def.inc"
     .org 0
     rjmp main

main:
     ldi r16, 0xFF
     out DDRB, r16


loop:
     sbi PORTB, 7
     call delay
     cbi PORTB, 7
     call delay
     rjmp loop

delay:
     ldi r17, 0x00
delay_inc:
     inc r17
     sbrs r17, 7
     rjmp delay_inc
     ret
```

A.3.2.4 Read a Value From an SRAM Address and Send It to I/O Ports

There is an embedded SRAM array inside the microcontroller. Users can read a value from an SRAM address and store the value to a working register by inserting the following code:

lds r17, 300; 300 is an SRAM address

Configure all the bits of PORTD to be output port:

ldi r16, 0xFF
out DDRD, r16

Send the value from a working register to the ports by using:

out PORTD, r16

The complete program is as follows:

Assembly Code

```
    .include "m16u4def.inc"
    .org 0
    rjmp main

main:
    ldi r16, 0xFF
    out DDRD, r16

    lds r17, 300
    out PORTD, r17
loop:
    rjmp loop
```

A.3.2.5 Program Controlled by an Input Port

Occasionally, a program might need to read signals from an I/O port, which is configured as an input port. For example, let us consider a scenario, where a program is waiting for a high level, that is, "1" from an input port to start the execution. If the signal coming into the port is always low, "0", then the program will not be executed.

Assembly Code

```
    .include "m16u4def.inc"
    .org 0
    rjmp main

main:
    cbi, DDRC, 7
```

```
loop:
    sbis PINC, 7
    rjmp loop

    ; below is the code, which will be executed when PC7=1
```

A.3.2.6 IO Value to Control an LED

An user can propagate a value from an input port to an output port. For example, let us consider an input port connected to a switch, and an output port connected to a LED. In this case, the switch can control the LED by propagating its value to the LED.

Assembly Code
```
    .include "m16u4def.inc"
    .org 0
    rjmp main

main:
    ;set pc7 as input
    cbi DDRC, 7

    ;set pb7 as input
    sbi DDRB, 7

loop:
    ;do not set pb7 if pc7 is clear
    sbic PINC, 7
    sbi PORTB, 7
    ;do not clear pb7 if pc7 is set
    sbis PINC, 7
    cbi PORTB, 7
rjmp loop
```

A.3.2.7 Simple Programming Example

The instruction set of the microcontroller consists of arithmetic and logic instructions. Arithmetic instructions include ADD, SUB, and MUL. This example will show how to implement a simple function using several working registers. Let us consider a function: $f(x) = 255 - 2x$, if $x < 128$; otherwise $f(x) = 0$.

The required Instructions for the example include MUL, SUB, and a branch. The result will be visible as the output of portD. The code is provided below.

Assembly Code

```
.include "m16u4def.inc"
    .org 0
    rjmp main

main:
    ;set PortD as output
    ldi r16, 0xff
    out DDRD, r16

    ;store x=100 in r18 and store 2 in r19
    ldi r18, 0x64
    ldi r19, 0x02

    ;if x is 128 or bigger, jump to big_option
    sbrc r18, 7
    rjmp big_option

    ;calculate 2*100 and store the result in r18
    mul r18, r19
    mov r18, r0

    ;calculate 255-r18 and store the result in r18
    ldi r19, 0xff
    sub r19, r18
    mov r18, r19

    rjmp loop

big_option:
    ldi r18, 0x00

loop:
    ;output the final result
    out PORTD, r18
    rjmp loop
```

A.4 DESIGN SPECIFICATIONS

This section provides the bill-of-materials (Table A.9), schematic, assembly diagram (Fig. A.20) and layout (Fig. A.21) of the HaHa board (version 2).

Table A.9 Bill-of-materials (BOM)			
Manufacturer	**Manufacturer No**	**Quantity**	**Designator**
Omron Electronics	XM2C-0942-112L	1	J10
CUI	UJ2-BH-1-TH	2	J1, J18
Texas Instruments	THS4302RGTR	1	U10
Microchip	RN4870-V/RM118	1	U7
C&K Components	PTS645SM43SMTR92 LFS	6	SW1, SW2, SW3, SW4, SW5, SW6
C&K Components	OS102011MS2QN1	15	S0, S1, S2, S3, S4, S5, S6, S7, S8, S9, S10, S11, S12, S13, S14
Optek / TT Electronics	OP980	1	D16
TDK Corporation	MPZ1608S101ATAH0	6	L3, L4, L5, L7, L8, L12
Apem	MHPS2283	1	PWR
Microchip	MCP2200-I/SS	1	U4
LVK Series	LVK12R010DER	1	CS1
Lite on	LTST-C194KSKT	1	D14
Lite on	LTST-C190KRKT	6	D5, D6, D7, D8, D9, D12
Lite on	LTST-C190KGKT	5	D1, D2, D3, D4, D13
Lite on	LTL2R3KRD-EM	1	D15
Lite on	LSHD-7501	1	DS1
STMicroelectronics	LIS2DE12TR	1	U5
STMicroelectronics	LF33ABDT-TR	1	U3
Taiyo Yuden	LBC3225T100KR	5	L1, L2, L9, L10, L11
Fairchild Semiconductor	FSV8100V	1	D10
Fox	FOXSDLF/080-20	1	Y1
Panasonic	ERJ-P06D8200V	1	R45
Panasonic	ERJ-6GEYJ560V	5	R17, R37, R38, R39, R40
Panasonic	ERJ-6GEYJ472V	2	R27, R41
Panasonic	ERJ-6GEYJ471V	1	R25
Panasonic	ERJ-6GEYJ470V	5	R24, R33, R34, R35, R36
Panasonic	ERJ-6GEYJ223V	3	R9, R10, R14
Panasonic	ERJ-6GEYJ220V	3	R2, R7, R8
Panasonic	ERJ-6GEYJ103V	9	R3, R4, R6, R15, R22, R29, R30, R31, R32
Panasonic	ERJ-6GEYJ102V	2	R21, R26
Panasonic	ERJ-6GEYJ101V	1	R43
Panasonic	ERJ-6ENF3303V	1	R19
Panasonic	ERJ-6ENF3302V	3	R11, R12, R23
Panasonic	ERJ-6ENF3300V	2	R13, R28
Panasonic	ERJ-6ENF2102V	1	R16
Panasonic	ERJ-6ENF2050V	1	R44

Table A.9 (*continued*)

Manufacturer	Manufacturer No	Quantity	Designator
Panasonic	ERJ-6ENF1200V	1	R1
Panasonic	ERJ-6ENF1002V	1	R18
Panasonic	ERJ-6ENF68R0V	1	R5
Panasonic	ERJ-6ENF30R1V	1	R42
Maxim Integrated	DS1809U-100+	1	PM2
Murata Electronics	CSTCE12M0G55-R0	1	Y2
Kemet	C1206C107M9PACTU	2	C10, C16
Kemet	C0805C470J5GACTU	1	C37
Kemet	C0805C226M9PACTU	1	C39
Kemet	C0805C225K8RACTU	1	C2
Kemet	C0805C200J1GACTU	2	C20, C31
Kemet	C0805C106K8PACTU	4	C19, C26, C34, C35
Kemet	C0805C105K4RACTU	6	C5, C6, C8, C15, C17, C21
Kemet	C0805C104J5RACTU	23	C1, C3, C4, C7, C9, C12, C13, C22, C23, C24, C25, C27, C30, C32, C33, C36, C38, C53, C54, C55, C56, C57, C58
Kemet	C0805C103K5RACTU	3	C11, C14, C29
Kemet	C0805C101J3GACTU	2	C18, C28
Microchip Technology / Atmel	ATmega16U4-au	1	U2
Abracon LLC	ASFL1-50.000MHZ-EC-T	1	Y4
Analog Devices	ADP3334ARMZ-REEL7	1	RG2
Analog Devices	ADM3202ARUZ-REEL7	1	U9
Molex	702471051	1	P5
3M	961240-6404-AR	2	P3, P8
3M	961220-6404-AR	1	P4
3M	961208-6404-AR	1	P11
3M	961206-6404-AR	3	P2, P9, P13
3M	961110-6404-AR	2	P1, P10
3M	961108-6404-AR	1	P12
3M	961102-6404-AR	3	JP1, JP4, P14
3M	929870-01-04-RA	2	JP2, JP3
Keystone Electronics	5006	18	J2, J3, J3+, J3-, J4, J5, J6, J7, J8+, J8-, J9, J11, J12, J13, J14, J15, J16, J17
Bourns	4816P-1-560LF	1	R20
Bel Fuse	0697H1000-02	1	F1
Nexperia	74HC3G14DC-Q100H	1	U1
Microchip	25LC1024-E/SM	1	U6
Intel / Altera	10M50SAE144C8G	1	U8
TE Connectivity	5-1814832-1	2	J9+, J9-
Fairchild Semiconductor	1N4148	1	D11

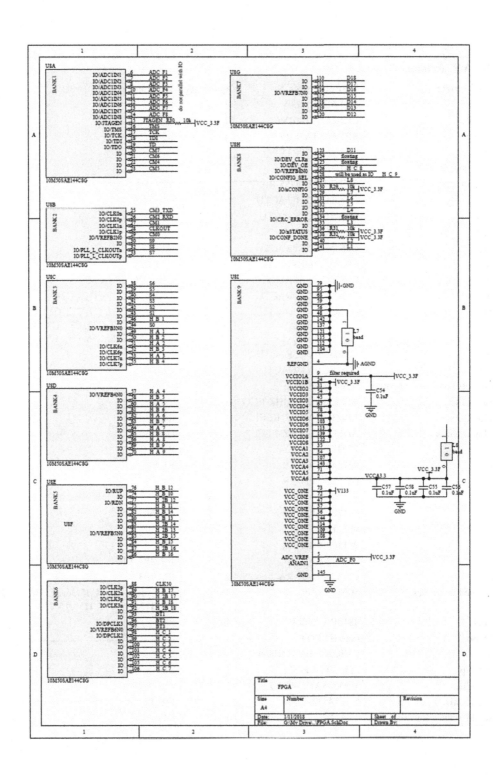

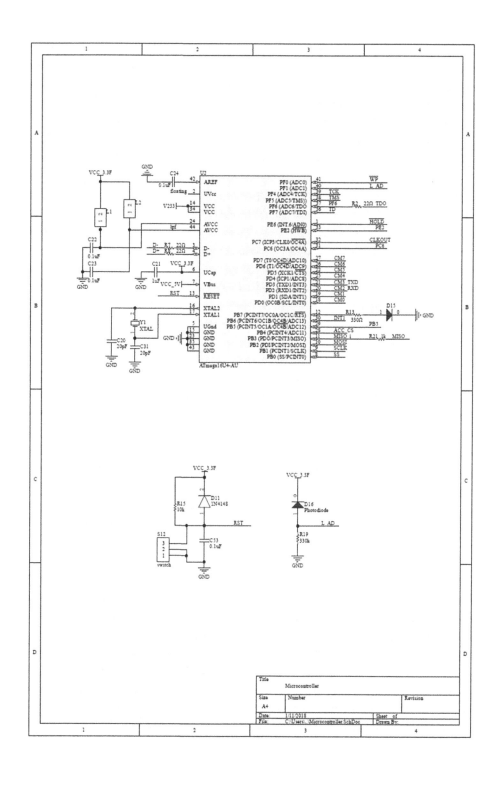

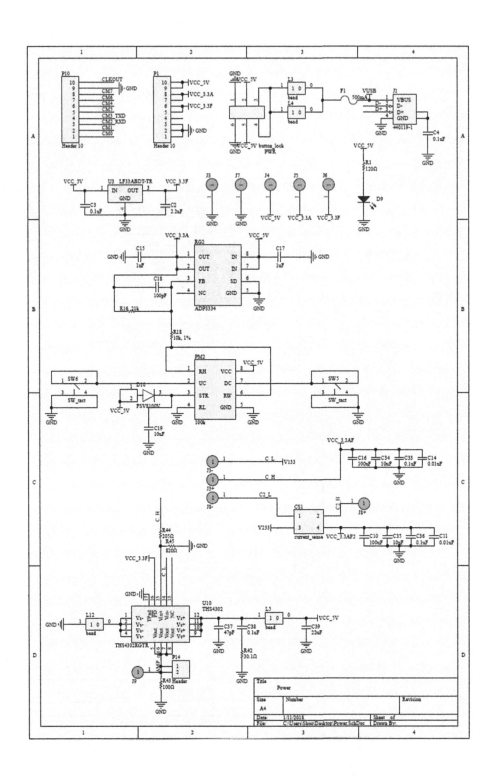

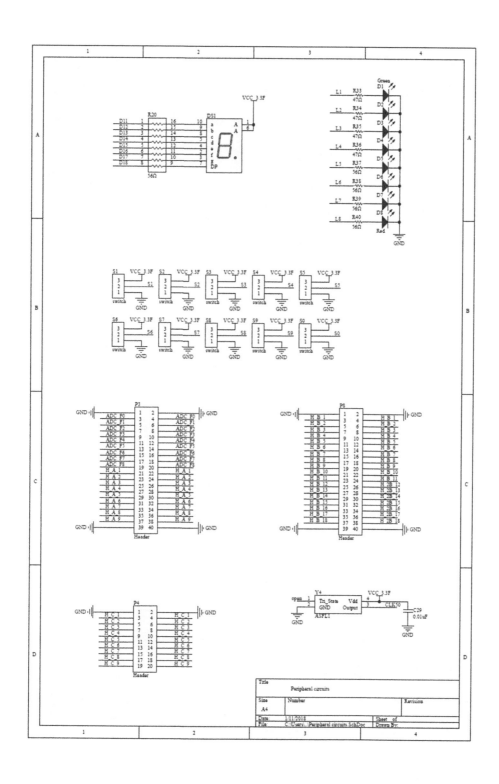

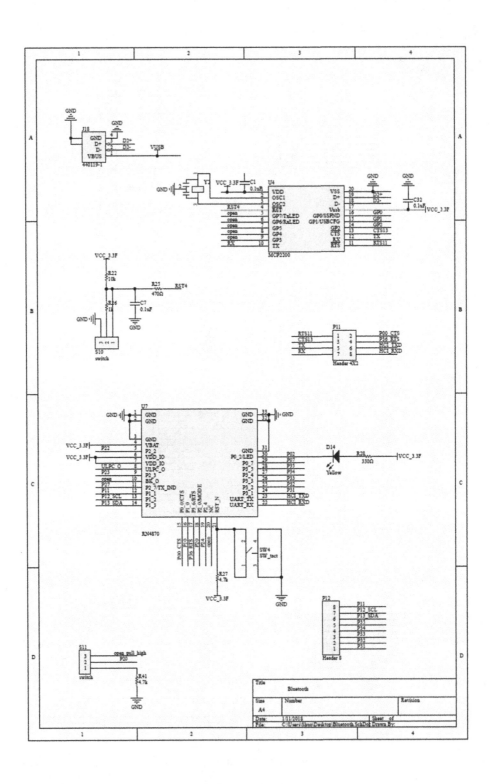

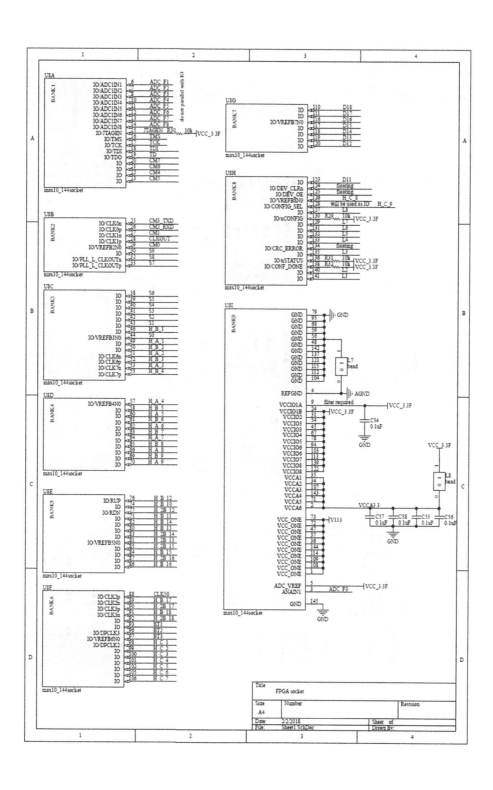

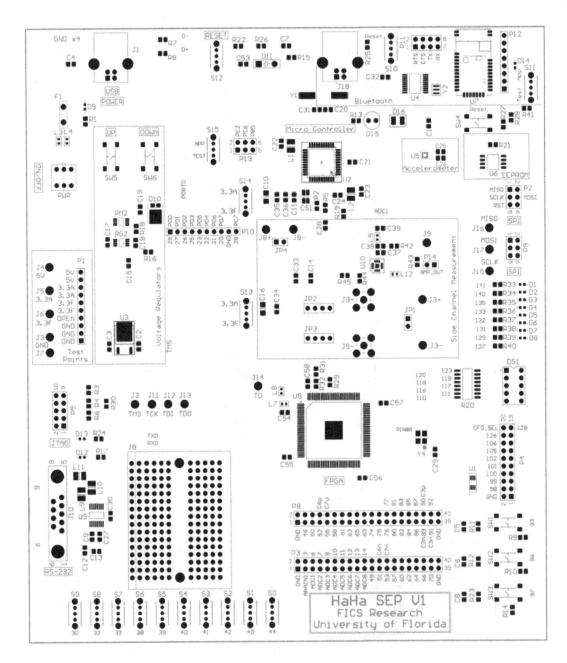

FIGURE A.20

Assembly diagrams of the HaHa board.

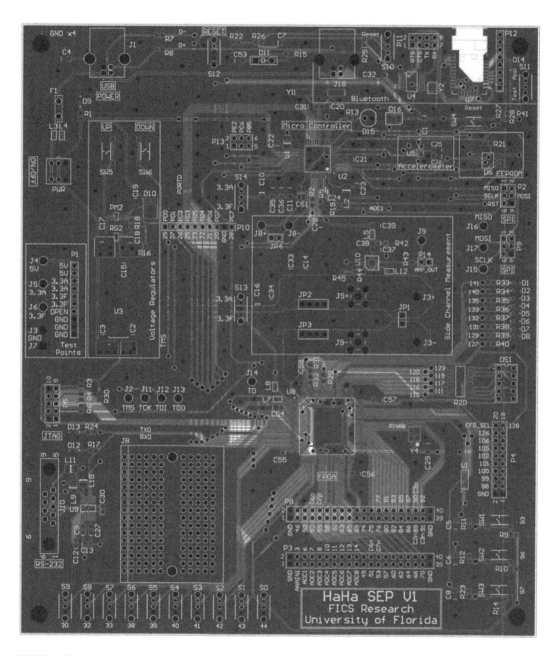

FIGURE A.21

Layout of the HaHa board.

Index

Printed in the United States
By Bookmasters